APPLICATIONS OF MONTE CARLO METHODS IN BIOLOGY, MEDICINE AND OTHER FIELDS OF SCIENCE

Edited by **Charles J. Mode**

Applications of Monte Carlo Methods in Biology, Medicine and Other Fields of Science
Edited by Charles J. Mode

Published by InTech
Janeza Trdine 9, 51000 Rijeka, Croatia

Publishing Process Manager Ana Nikolic

Technical Editor Teodora Smiljanic

Cover Designer InTech Design Team

Additional hard copies can be obtained from orders@intechopen.com

Applications of Monte Carlo Methods in Biology, Medicine and Other Fields of Science
Edited by Charles J. Mode
p. cm.
ISBN 978-953-307-427-6

For EU product safety concerns:
IN TECH d.o.o., Prolaz Marije Krucifikse Kozulić 3, 51000 Rijeka, Croatia,
info@intechopen.com or visit our website at intechopen.com.

Meet the editor

Charles J. Mode received a Ph.D. in Genetics from the University of California, Davis, which also entailed course work at the University of California, Berkeley. While at the University of California, he also studied Mathematics and Theoretical Statistics. During 1956-57 he studied Statistical Genetics while on a postdoctoral fellowship at North Carolina State University and spent the spring semester of 1957 at the University of Florida, Gainsville, teaching a course in Experimental Design to Graduate Students in Agronomy. For the rest of his active career he has served in either Departments of Mathematics or Statistics. In 1970 accepted a position in the Department of Mathematics, Drexel University, Philadelphia, Pennsylvania, where he is now a Professor Emeritus.

Contents

Preface

During the last seven or so decades, Monte Carlo simulation methods have been applied in various fields including business, economics, engineering and virtually every field of the physical and biological sciences such as chemistry, physics, genetics, biological evolution and stochastic models of epidemics of infectious diseases in human and other populations. Monte Carlo methods have also had a profound effect on the development of several branches of mathematical sciences such as statistics and numerical analysis. In statistics the phrase, Markov Chain Monte Carlo Methods, denotes a class of methods for estimating parameters within the Bayesian paradigm, and in numerical analysis a widely accepted method for estimating the value of a multi-dimensional integral is known as Monte Carlo integration. But, Monte Carlo methods are, fundamentally, anchored in pure mathematics and are part of such fields as number theory and abstract algebra which underlie the computer generation of "random" numbers. It is beyond the scope of this brief preface to go into the mathematical details underlying the generation of random numbers, but suffice it to say that an investigator should be aware that the random generator being utilized has passed numerous statistical tests for randomness, even though we know the sequence of "random" numbers have been computed by a purely sequential deterministic procedure that is repeatable. More details of these procedures will be briefly discussed at the end of this preface.

That this volume is an eclectic mix of applications of Monte Carlo methods in many fields of research should not be surprising, because of the ubiquitous use of these methods in many fields of human endeavor. In an attempt to focus attention on a manageable set of applications, the main thrust of this book is to emphasize applications of Monte Carlo simulation methods in biology and medicine. But it became necessary, due to the acceptance of a large number of papers for publication, to also accommodate a few other papers that may contain ideas that are potentially applicable to biology and medicine or of general scientific interest.

Chapter 1 is devoted to a paper by A. Kim on Monte Carlo methods in environmental engineering which center around such issues as expected sacristy of fossil fuels and the designing of new paradigms for environmentally friendly, green, or zero-emission processes to eliminate potential adverse effects on nature from undesired technological by-products. A paper by M. Andrecut on applications of Monte Carlo methods to multi-dimensional switch-like model of stem cell differentiation provides the content of chapter 2 and is of basic interest in biology and medicine due to its focus on gene regulatory systems. Chapter 3 contains a paper by S. Kinase et al. on voxel models and their application to internal dosimetry.

A paper by K. I. Tenekedjiev et al. on applications of Monte Carlo methods in modeling biochemical process makes up the content of chapter 4. Dynamic models of complex metabolic systems are typically multi-parametric and non-linear. The stochastic nature of the data necessitates the use of non-linear regression models and other statistical procedures to estimate the many parameters from data. Chapter 5 contains a paper by Y. Hirano on the application of Monte Carlo methods to problem in bio-medical imagining, and chapter 6 is devoted to a paper by M. A. Al-Harthi on applying Monte Carlo methods in simulating free radical polymerization processes.

The contents of chapter 7 is a paper by F. Bourhaleb et al. on the use of Monte Carlo simulation methods for beam delivery line design in radiation therapy in heavy ion beams. The immune systems of vertebrates are very complex systems that have evolved a set of mechanisms to destroy potential pathogens that individuals may encounter, and chapter 8 is devoted to a paper by F. Castiglione on the Monte Carlo simulation of cytotoxic T lymphocytes repertoire. A paper by K. Chan et al. on the application of Monte Carlo simulation methods in treatment planning for radiation oncology constitutes the content of chapter 9.

The implantation of radioactive particles in organs to treat cancer is a familiar term for many people who have developed cancer. A paper by M. Sadeghi et al. on applying Monte Carlo methods on dosimetric characteristics of brachytherapy sources provides the content of chapter 10. The rapid growth in genetics and molecular biology combined with the development of techniques for genetically engineering small animals has increased interest in vivo imaging of small animals. The contents of chapter 11 are a paper by S. Branco et al. on using Monte Carlo methods in the evaluation of respiratory motion effect in small animals by PET and other images. Raman spectroscopy is a vibrational spectroscopic technique capable of optically probing bio-molecular changes in tissues and is useful in diagnosing cancers in early stages. Chapter 12 contains a paper by Z. Huang on applying Monte Carlo methods to fiber-optic Raman probes with a ball lens for improving Raman measurements in epithelial tissue.

Chapter 13 contains a paper by V. A. Gribkov et al. on the Monte Carlo simulation of powerful neutron interactions with matter. Among the goals of such simulation experiments is the disclosure of hidden explosives and fissile materials, methods for treating cancer and the comparison of real and simulated data. Monte Carlo simulation software may be used for the partial description of particle physics production at high energy such as those arising at the LHC (large hadron collider) in CERN, Switzerland. The content of chapter 14 is a paper by G. Marchesini on such software. Thermoluminescence dosimetries (TLDs) are routinely used for in-vivo dosimetry as well as in other applications in medicine and industry. Chapter 15 is devoted to a paper by S. R. Mahdavi et al. on the Monte Carlo simulation of the response function in scattered radiation applications.

The development of stochastic models accommodating two sexes and population density is an area of theoretical evolutionary genetics of considerable interest. Chapter 16 is devoted to a paper by C. J. Mode et al. on the Monte Carlo implementation of a two sex density dependant branching process, which is very difficult to analyze mathematically due to its complexity but its Monte Carlo implementation is straight forward. This paper also contains a description of embedding a non-linear deterministic model in a stochastic process, which is a departure from the methods that are frequently used for introducing stochasticity into non-linear dynamic systems.

What is usually done in converting a deterministic system into a stochastic process is to start with a deterministic system and then tweak it by adding a linear random term or perhaps entertaining models in which the parameters are random variables. But the approach taken in this paper differs from the customary approach. For, in the beginning there is a stochastic process and a deterministic model is embedded in this process by the use of a statistical estimation procedure centered on estimating the sample functions of the process as functions of time. This embedding approach is also useful in dealing with controversies. In mathematical biology there are at least two schools of thought. One school of thought is that deterministic models are sufficient to describe biological systems and that the introduction of stochastic systems leads to unnecessary complications. But, according to the stochastic school, deterministic systems are inadequate, because they do not accommodate the intrinsic variability that is omnipresent in most biological populations. The formulation set forth in Mode et al. in chapter 16 and elsewhere provides a framework within which the predictions of the embedded deterministic system and a statistically summarized Monte Carlo of the sample functions of the process may be compared. For the case of sexual selection, an example reported in chapter 16 such that, given the same numerical assignments of parameters, the deterministic model predicts that a novel mutant genotype that was favored by sexual selection would predominate in the population in the long run, but in the Monte Carlo sample of the process, this mutant genotype did not appear in the population in large numbers so that the prediction of the two models were not in agreement.

A paper on Monte Carlo modeling of light propagation in neonatal skin by J. A. Delgado Atencio et al. makes up the content of chapter 17. From the historical point of view, this paper is also of interest, because a brief account of the history of a statistical sampling process, which became known as the Monte Carlo method, is contained in this paper. The contents of chapter 18 are a paper by I. Plante and F. A. Cucinotta on the Monte Carlo simulation of ionizing radiation tracks. The contents of this paper have applications in medicine consisting of not only in the detection of cancer but also in its treatment by radiation. Chapter 19 contains a paper by D. Khankin et al. on a Monte Carlo tool for simulating evanescent wave's spectroscopy fiber, which is used in medical applications. Also contained in this paper is a discussion of the software engineering process that leads to correct software to obtain the desired objectives.

Chapter 20 is devoted to a paper with the title "Strain Effects in p-type Devices using Full-Band Monte Carlo Simulations" by V. Aubry-Fortuna et al. Physics is the primary focus of this paper and form the mathematical point of view mention of the Boltzmann transport equation for the distribution function of some stochastic process is of interest. The contents of chapter 21 are a paper by S. Lindset on using Monte Carlo simulation methods in evaluating the case of barrier options under stochastic interest rates. Applications in business are the primary focus of this paper, but the kinds of structures set forth in this paper may also have potential applications in biological evolution in random environments. There is also a potential application of Monte Carlo methods in business. The recklessness of some members of the financial services industry driven by greed has recently led to a world wide recession, which has had a devastating effect on the finances of many innocent people. The international community should undertake a concerted effort to introduce the use of Monte Carlo simulation methods for assessing the potential risks of the securitization of packages of mortgages and other instruments so that in the future the mindless recklessness of some financial mangers can be curbed. Chapter 22, the last chapter of the book, contains a paper by V. Durmaz et al. on a rapidly mixing Monte Carlo method for the simulation of slow molecular processes, which has potential applications for many of the biochemical process that occur in many forms of life.

With the continuing development of computer technologies into the future, which will give rise to platforms with greater memory capacities and faster speeds of execution, the need to generate very long sequences of random numbers in a computer will increase. All algorithms for the computer of generation of random numbers have finite periods so that once the period of a generator is reached the sequence will be repeated. This repetition of a sequence does not conform to the mathematical idea of an infinite sequence of independent and uniformly distributed random numbers of the interval [0.1], which underlie the theoretical basis of Monte Carlo methods. Moreover, at the present time, random number generators implemented in many computers and software packages are sequentially linear-congruential generators that have a rather large but finite period. They also fall short of many of the theoretical properties of uniform random number on the interval [0,1]. A brief introduction to the literature on random number generation may be found in section 2 of the paper by Mode and Gallop (2008), which in cited in the references of chapter 16. From an example presented in this section, if one used random number generator that has been implemented on many computers and software packages, the scientific integrity of a computer experiment that required very long sequences of random number to complete could be seriously compromised.

From such examples, it becomes clear that in the future an investigator or team of investigators should be fully cognizant of the properties of the random generator used in their experiments so as to maximize the scientific integrity of their experiment. In this connection, Mode and Gallop (2008) chose to implement a random number generator such that the random number generated in the somewhat distant past was used to calculate any number in the sequence. An interested reader may consult equation (2.11) in Mode and Gallop (2008) for a precise definition of the generator. It was also shown by other investigators that this generator, which was designed to operate on computers with 32 bit words, had a very long period and that sequence of numbers so generated passed many statistical tests for randomness. Of course, if a computer platform with 64 bit words were used, then it would be necessary to use a generator that was designed for computers with 64 bit words. The literature cited in Mode and Gallop (2008) would be helpful in finding generators designed for computers with 64 bit words.

Another problem that often arises is that of the communication of the results of computer simulation experiment to other members of a community. Quite often the necessary description of the technical substance of an experiment and a description for using the software trump the basis of the mathematical model underlying a Monte Carlo simulation procedure. This problem is, perhaps, more acute in the biological than the physical sciences. Nevertheless, it would be helpful if the author or authors of every paper utilizing Monte Carlo simulation methods would make available a sufficiently detailed description of the mathematical model underlying the simulation procedure so that an investigator or team of investigators could write software in a programming language of their choosing so an interest party could, in principle, duplicate the results of a reported experiment. The use of mathematics in such instances seems to be justified, for from a scientific and technological point of view, mathematics constitutes a language that is essentially international.

Special words of thanks are due Dr. Candace K. Sleeman, who gave much help to the writer in navigating the internet to obtain readable copies of all papers in this book that could be stored on his personal network of desktop computers.

Charles J. Mode
Professor Emeritus
Department of Mathematics
Drexel University
Philadelphia,
USA

1

Bias Monte Carlo Methods in Environmental Engineering

Albert S. Kim
Civil and Environmental Engineering, University of Hawaii at Manoa
USA

1. Introduction

In the 21st century, vital resources for human beings such as food, energy, and water (FEW) are being rapidly depleted. Global water scarcity has already become a serious world-wide problem; "the cheap energy" – fossil fuels – will last only a few decades; and skewed global food distributions are marked by serious obesity in one region and deadly starvation in another. The standard role of environmental engineering now vigorously extends from providing conventional sanitation guidelines to contributing crucial information to environmental policy-making and futurological issues. Unlike other engineering and closely related disciplines (such as chemical engineering, electrical engineering, material science, and computer and information sciences), environmental engineering deals with poorly or incompletely defined problems whose scientific origins are in multiple sub-categories of physics, chemistry, biology and mathematics; and spontaneously gives birth to novelties in interdisciplinary research areas.

In general, medicine is classified into curative and preventive technologies. One can make an analogy of the curative medicine (alleviating pain from diseases) to conventional engineering that tries to improve the quality of human life. Preventive medicine is analogous to the corresponding role of environmental engineering which, in part, is to conserve the natural environment by eliminating or minimizing environmental risks. The term "conservation" is often regarded as passive human responses to return a degraded system to its original state after accidents. Prevention refers to keeping something from unexpected happening or arising. Active engineering responses can include designing new paradigms for environmentally friendly, green, or zero-emission processes to eliminate potential adverse effects on nature from undesired technological by-products.

A question arises to researchers in environmental engineering and science,

"What do we prevent and how, if we do not know what is really happening?"

Perhaps this question may be a senseless one, if one develops new products such as cellular phones, computer chips, or sign-recognition software, because market demands truly control developers' objectives to generate better money-making commercial products. As an environmental engineer, how do we choose *probably* the most urgent and long-term-impact problems; and then clearly define *probably* beneficial outcomes for human beings by solving the uncertain problems? Considering these questions and above issues, don't we have enough reasons to deal with fundamentals of probability and statistics and see how these are used in thermodynamics in order to deeply understand natural and engineered phenomena? *What are the likelihood, chances, and probabilities in nature?*

1.1 Probability

The primary objective of this chapter is to introduce how to use statistical mechanics to deal with engineering problems, specifically with environmental engineering applications. In physics, subjects of conservation laws include mass-energy, (translational and rotational) momentum, electric charge, and (more importantly?) probability, which are kept constant during the time in a closed system. Excluding conversion between mass and energy which rarely happens in practical engineering processes, one can explain energy conservation, indicating total energy as the sum of the kinetic energy and potential energy, which is always the same number. However, one should notice that this relationship stems from Newton's second law and energy is nothing but a constant generated by integrating

$$\boldsymbol{F} = m\boldsymbol{a} = -\nabla V(\boldsymbol{r}) \tag{1}$$

with respect to the object's position $\boldsymbol{r}$ in a conservative field where $\boldsymbol{F}$ is a force acting on an object, m is the object mass, $\boldsymbol{a}$ is the acceleration, and $V(\boldsymbol{r})$ is the potential energy. In one dimension, multiplying v on both sides of Eq. (1) yields

$$mv\frac{dv}{dt} = -\frac{dx}{dt}\frac{dV}{dx} \tag{2}$$

which is integrated as

$$m\int_{v_1}^{v_2} v dv = -\int_{x_1}^{x_2} dV \tag{3}$$

$$\frac{1}{2}mv_2^2 - \frac{1}{2}mv_1^2 = -V(x_2) + V(x_1) \tag{4}$$

assuming that the particle of mass m is at x_1 having velocity v_1 at time $t = t_1$ and moves to x_2 having velocity v_2 at time $t = t_2$. Thus,

$$\frac{1}{2}mv_1^2 + V(x_1) = \frac{1}{2}mv_2^2 + V(x_2) = E = \text{Constant} \tag{5}$$

which implies that the sum of kinetic and potential energies is a constant, denoted as E. Feynman et al. (1963) indicated that

> "It is important to realize that in physics today, we have no knowledge of what energy *is*. We do not have a picture that energy comes in little blobs of a definite amount. It is not that way. However, there are formulas for calculating some numerical quantity, and when we add it all together it gives '28' – always the same number. It is an abstract thing in that it does not tell use the mechanism or the *reasons* for the various formulas."

As noted above, we do not know what energy is exactly but we know that it has a constant character with respect to time. Similar to Feynman's description about energy, probability is assumed to be implicitly understood by readers; and sometimes a more non-technical word, "chance", is alternatively and widely used. If a sales person signed an important contract today, he might ask to himself: What is the chance that I will get a promotion call from my boss next week? A Hawaii politician might be interested in the question: What is my chance of being elected mayor of Honolulu? These chances are hard to estimate because the questioners do not have enough information, and the knowledge is sometimes too uncertain to be quantified.

Without exception, the probability is a fraction, i.e., a dimensionless number between 0 and 1, often measured as percentage. The widely used examples in the study of probability include tossing a coin and rolling a dice, and the following questions are often asked: What is the

Number	1	2	3	4	5	6
Regular	1/6	1/6	1/6	1/6	1/6	1/6
Modified	0/6	1/6	1/6	1/6	2/6	1/6

Table 1. Probability distribution of the regular and modified dice.

probability of heads when tossing a coin?; and, what is the probability getting a 2 when rolling a dice?. The answers to the first and second questions are 1/2 and 1/6, respectively, which almost nobody refutes. But, why? More specifically, why do heads and tails have the same chances of 1/2? Or, why do the six consecutive numbers of a dice have the same probability of 1/6 to be thrown? A simple answer is that we assigned an equal chance to all probable outcomes. If so, again, why do we do that? Perhaps, it is because we do not have any better knowledge than that of the equal distribution. This was called the "principle of incomplete reasons" (PIR). A similar concept, "equipartition principle", can be found in statistical mechanics, i.e, putting exactly 1/3 of the total energy to each direction of homogeneous and isotropic three-dimensional space. Note that homogeneity and isotropy are also our great assumptions.
These are excellent pedagogical examples but truly ideal. What if someone has a damaged coin that is not flat enough, so that we cannot convince ourselves of the equal probabilities of heads and tails? What if someone added four more dots on the surface of the dice with one dot and now it displays 5 (see Figure 1), but we keep throwing the dice without knowing about the significant change in the probability distribution. Then, sample space, technically called "ensemble", was modified, so that the uniform distribution fails to statistically describe the system.

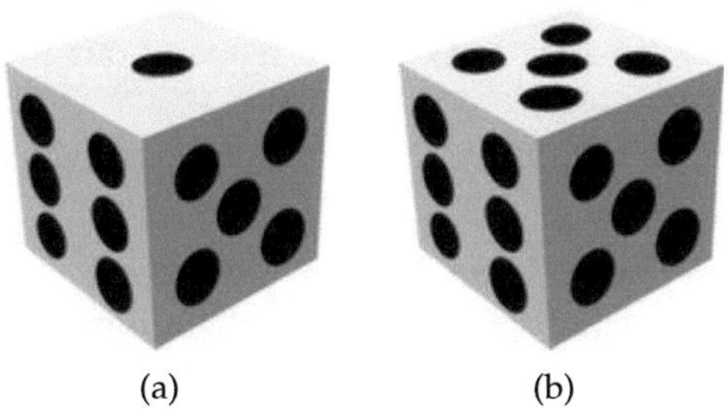

Fig. 1. Dice with (a) 1 to 6 and (b) 1 replaced by 5

Now, heads and tails have different probabilities of occurrence due to the uneven shape; and by tossing the modified dice, the probability of throwing 1 is zero, and that of 5 is 2/6, not 1/6. How do we evaluate the expected values of the two examples after the changes? The dice case would be easier to reconstruct the probability distribution as shown in Table 1. After a large number of tosses, the average outcome, i.e., expectation value, is

$$1 \times \frac{0}{6} + 2 \times \frac{1}{6} + 3 \times \frac{1}{6} + 4 \times \frac{1}{6} + 5 \times \frac{2}{6} + 6 \times \frac{1}{6} = \frac{25}{6} = 4.167$$

Note that we still use the principle of incomplete reasons by assigning equal probability of 1/6 to rolling 2, 3, 4 or 6; and moving the probability 1/6 from 1 to 5. The expectation value of the regular dice is 3.5, which is similar to 4.167. If our number of tosses is not large enough, then the modified probability distribution would not be achieved and the expectation value can be accepted within a reasonable(?) range of tolerance error. In the above case of the modified dice, we implicitly assume that the shape is a regular cubic. When a coin is damaged, i.e., curved and/or stretched, then the uneven probability distribution must be made even and is not easy to build.

We do not have enough information at the micro-mechanics level from which we can definitely say that "The probability of tossing heads on the damaged coin is $\sqrt{2}/2$ and that of tails is $1 - \sqrt{2}/2$." There are many important features in tossing the damaged coin: tosser's specific way of flipping the coin into air, the number of spins before landing, the landing conditions such as falling velocity and bouncing angle, all of which were ignored for the undamaged coin. To average out these specific impacts on the probabilities of throwing heads or tails using the damaged coin, we need to have the number of tossings much more than that of tossing a regular coin. In other words, we cannot equally distribute the probabilities to heads or tails, and we do not know how much the two probabilities are different from 1/2. So, we do a large number of tossing experiments to estimate probabilities of landing on heads and tails, keeping the fact that a sum of the two equal probabilities is always 1, no matter how much the coin was damaged. Note that we used our basic belief of equal probability distribution for tossing the modified dice; and on the other hand, we actually did a number of tossing experiments of the damaged coin to estimate the probability distribution. This is because it is mathematically formidable to calculate probability distribution of the damaged coin; and we still believe the probabilities to throw 2, 3, 4 and 6 of the modified dice are equally 1/6.

1.1.1 Conventional point of view: Frequency

Reif (1965) indicated in his book that the probability of the occurrence of a particular event is defined with respect to a particular ensemble consisting of a very large number of similarly prepared systems; and is given by the fraction of systems in the ensemble which are characterized by the occurrence of the specific event. Therefore, the fraction, called *frequency probability*, is the ratio of a certain occurrence of our interest to the total number of possible occurrences. This surely implies that unless we do a large number of experiments, the measured frequency fraction is not accurate enough. In general, spanning all the possible cases is a formidable task, especially for a complex system.

1.1.2 Bayesian Point of view: Distribution

An alternative approach is the *conditional probability*, which allows one to localize the sampling space and provide a new probability distribution. The probability that both a and b occur is expressed as

$$P(a \cap b) = P(a|b)\,P(b) = P(b|a)\,P(a) \tag{6}$$

indicating that $P(a \cap b)$ is equal to

1. the probability of a occurring, $P(a)$, times the probability of b occurring given a has occurred, $P(b|a)$, and
2. the probability of b occurring, $P(b)$, times the probability of a occurring given b has occurred, $P(a|b)$.

so that $P(a|b)$ is written as

$$P(a|b) = \frac{P(b|a)\,P(a)}{P(b)} \tag{7}$$

The proof for Eq. (6) uses two basic probability relationships: the sum rule and the product rule, i.e.,

$$P(a|b) + P(\tilde{a}|b) = 1 \tag{8}$$

and

$$P(a \cap a'|b) = P(a|b)P(a'|b) \tag{9}$$

respectively. Eq. (8) indicates that, given b has occurred, the sum of probabilities of a occurring, $P(a|b)$, and not a occurring (i.e., $\widetilde{a}$), $P(\widetilde{a}|b)$, is equal to 1. The product rule of Eq. (9) means the probability of occurring a and a' given that b has occurred, $P(a \cap a'|b)$, is equal to the probability of a, given b, $P(a|b)$, multiplied by the probability of a' given b, $P(a'|b)$.

1.1.3 Examples

In this section, well-known examples are selected and solved using the frequency and conditional probabilities. In addition, logical ways of solving the example problems are included. The purpose of this section is to show that the conditional probability method is as powerful as the other two methods.

A. Monty Hall dilemma

Suppose you're on a game show, and you're given the choice of three doors. Behind one door is a car; behind the others, goats. You pick a door, say #1, and the host, who knows what's behind the doors, opens another door, say #3, which has a goat as behind it. He then says to you,

"Do you want to switch to door #2, or stay with door #1?"

Is it to your advantage to change your choice? It is better to stay with door #1 or is it better to switch to door #2 or is the probability of winning the same for either choice?

Fig. 2. The Monty Hall paradox first appeared in 1975 on the American television game show *Let's Make a Deal*, hosted by Mr. Monty Hall (1921 – present). The game show aired on NBC daytime from December 30, 1963, to December 27, 1968, followed by ABC daytime from December 30, 1968, to July 9, 1976, along with two primetime runs. It also aired in syndication from 1971 to 1977, from 1980 to 1981, from 1984 to 1986, and again on NBC briefly from 1990 to 1991. Historical records from Wikipedia (`http://en.wikipedia.org/wiki/Monty_Hall`) and special thanks to Tae Chun for the illustration.

(a) Solution using logical thinking

When you selected door #1, the probability of winning the car is 1/3. No question at all! But there are also two other doors. The host opened door #3, showing a weird-looking goat. This makes the original probability assigned to door #3 equal to zero. Where has it gone since the sum of the probability of all possible events should always be one. You don't think the winning probability on door #1 has changed. Then, there is only one possibility, i.e., the probability of door #3 moved to that of door #2. So, if you switch to door #2, your winning chance will be doubled: from 1/3 to 2/3. So, you are switching now!

(b) Solution using conditional probability

Perhaps the logical solution above might not be clear enough. So let's calculate the conditional probability using Bayes' rule (Bayes and Price, 1763). The game show can be mathematically described as three sets with possible cases:

- S = my Selection = {1, 2 or 3}
- H = Host open = {1, 2 or 3} $\notin S$
- C = Door for car = {1, 2 or 3} $\notin H$

You want to know the probability of winning after switching from door #1 to #2. Without loosing generality, this probability can be written as $P(C_2|S_1 \cap H_3)$, which is the probability that the car is behind door #2 given that you selected door #1 and the host opened door #3 showing a goat (not a car!). By substituting $a = C_2$ and $b = S_1 \cap H_3$ into Eq. (7), one can write in a symmetric form

$$P(C_2|S_1 \cap H_3) = \frac{P(S_1 \cap H_3|C_2)\, P(C_2)}{P(S_1 \cap H_3)} \tag{10}$$

of which each probability can be addressed as follows.

First, $P(C_2)$ is the probability that the car is behind door #2, which is equal to

$$P(C_2) = \frac{1}{3} = P(C_1) = P(C_3) \tag{11}$$

because the probability of finding the car is equally distributed among the three doors. This resembles the energy equipartition principle.

Second, $P(S_1 \cap H_3|C_2)$ is the probability of S_1 and H_3 given C_2 so substituting into Eq. (9) yields

$$P(S_1 \cap H_3|C_2) = P(S_1|C_2)\, P(H_3|C_2) \tag{12}$$

where C_2 confines a sub-domain of probability for S_1 and H_3. Because we do not know which door will reveal the car, our first selection of a door is independent of the probability of the car being behind door #2:

$$P(S_1|C_2) = P(S_1) = \frac{1}{3} \tag{13}$$

However, the host knows that the car is behind door #2 and he also saw that you selected door #1. Therefore, given C_2 (that the host is aware of), the probability that the host opens door #3 is

$$P(H_3|C_2) = 1 \tag{14}$$

so that

$$P(S_1 \cap H_3|C_2) = \frac{1}{3} \times 1 = \frac{1}{3} \tag{15}$$

Third, you need to calculate $P(S_1 \cap H_3)$, the probability that S_1 and H_3 (and vice versa) will happen, which is simply equal to the probability of S_1 multiplied by the probability of H_3, i.e.,

$$P(S_1 \cap H_3) = P(S_1)\, P(H_3) = \frac{1}{3} \cdot \frac{1}{2} = \frac{1}{6} \tag{16}$$

because we select one door out of three and the host opens one out of the two remaining doors.

Finally, the winning probability after switching from door #1 to #2 is calculated as

$$P(C_2|S_1 \cap H_3) = \frac{P(S_1 \cap H_3|C_2)\, P(C_2)}{P(S_1 \cap H_3)} = \frac{\frac{1}{3} \cdot \frac{1}{3}}{\frac{1}{6}} = \frac{2}{3} \tag{17}$$

and the winning probability by staying with door #1 is calculated using the the sum rule:

$$P(C_1|S_1 \cap H_3) = 1 - P(C_3|S_1 \cap H_3) - P(C_2|S_1 \cap H_3) = 1 - 0 - \frac{2}{3} = \frac{1}{3} \tag{18}$$

Note that the probability of the car being behind door #3 after the host opened #3 is zero, i.e., $P(C_3|S_1 \cap H_3) = 0$. This indicates if you stay in door #1, then the probability of winning the car is 1/3, i.e., $P(C_1|S_1 \cap H_3) = 1/3$, but if you switched to door #2, the probability is doubled! *So, always switch your door!* Additional analysis of the conditional probability can be found in section 5.1.

(c) Solution using frequency probability
Let's assume that the car is behind door #1.

1. If you select door #1, the host will open either door #2 or #3. Let's say, door #3. If you switch your door, then you won't get the car.
2. If you select door #2, there is no question at all that the host will open door #3. If you switch from door #2 to #1, then you will win the car.
3. If you select door #3, the host will open door #2. If you switch from door #3 to #1, then you will win the car.

So among the three possible cases above with unconditional switch no matter which door is selected, two cases give car-winning opportunities. Therefore, the probability of winning the car by switching to the other door is 2/3. This solution method seems to be easier than that of the conditional probability above, but building a complete sample space is not always easy.

B. Prisoner's Dilemma

This example is taken from a book written by Mosteller (1965). "Three prisoners, A, B, and C, with apparently equally good records have applied for parole. The parole board has decided to release two of the three, and the prisoners know this but not which two. A warder friend of prisoner A knows who will be released. Prisoner A realizes that it would be unethical to ask the warder if he, A, is to be released, but thinks of asking for the name of *one* prisoner *other than himself* who is to be released. He thinks that before he asks, his chances of release are $\frac{2}{3}$. He thinks that if the warder says "B will be released," his own chances have now gone down to $\frac{1}{2}$, because either A and B or B and C are to be released. And so A decided not to reduce his chances by asking. However, A is mistaken in this calculations. Explain."

(a) Solution using logical thinking
The probability that A will be released is $\frac{2}{3}$ because two out of the three will be released. The decision of the parole board is independent of A's knowledge. Therefore, A still has a 2/3 chance of being released.

(b) Solution using conditional probability

The probability of A being released, given that B will be released, can be expressed as

$$P(A|B) = \frac{P(B|A)P(A)}{P(B)} \tag{19}$$

One calculates $P(A) = 2/3$, $P(B) = 1$, and $P(B|A) = P(B) = 1$ because A does not affect B. Therefore,

$$P(A|B) = \frac{1 \cdot \frac{2}{3}}{1} = \frac{2}{3} \tag{20}$$

indicating that no matter whether A knows about B's fate or not, the probability of A's release is 2/3.

(c) Solution using frequency probability

The possible pairs to be released are AB, BC, and AC, which have equal probability of 2/3. Then, the probabilities of possible cases in the sample space are calculated as

Released	Warder says	Probability
AB	B	1/3
AC	C	1/3
BC	B	1/6
BC	C	1/6

Thus, the probability of A being released is equal to

$$\frac{\text{Probability of } AB \text{ to be released}}{\text{Probability of } AB \text{ to be released + Probability of } BC \text{ to be released}}$$

given that B will be released. Therefore, A's probability of being released is

$$\frac{\frac{1}{3}}{\frac{1}{3} + \frac{1}{6}} = \frac{2}{3} \tag{21}$$

As shown above in the two examples, conditional probability is as powerful as frequency probability and has mathematical elegance. Now we will see how conditional probability is efficiently used in statistical physics when dealing with a large population.

1.2 Thermodynamics and statistical mechanics

1.2.1 Heat and work

Statistical mechanics, as a branch of theoretical physics, studies macroscopic systems from a microscopic or molecular point of view, dealing with systems in equilibrium. It is often referred to as *statistical thermodynamics* as it links (classical) thermodynamics with molecular physics. Thermodynamic laws describe the transport of heat and work in thermodynamic processes.

- The 0th law of thermodynamics: If two thermodynamic systems are each in thermal equilibrium with a third, then they are in thermal equilibrium with each other. In other words, if $A = B$ and $B = C$, then $A = C$.
- The 1st law of thermodynamics: Energy is neither created nor destroyed. Increase in the internal energy E of a system is equal to the heat Q supplied to the system subtracted by the work W done by the system, i.e., $\mathrm{d}E = đQ - đW$. The symbol "đ" indicates that the

differential is inexact. Q and W are path functions, and E is a state function. Specifically in equilibrium, $\mathrm{d}E = T\mathrm{d}S - P\mathrm{d}V$, where the temperature T and pressure P are integral factors of $\mathrm{d}S$ and $\mathrm{d}P$, respectively.

- The 2nd law of thermodynamics: Spontaneous natural processes increase entropy overall. In other words, heat can spontaneously flow from a higher-temperature region to a lower-temperature region, but not the other way around:

$$\Delta S = S_T - S_0 = \int_{T_0}^{T} \frac{dQ}{T} \geq 0 \tag{22}$$

where $\Delta S = 0$ is for the reversible process.

- The 3rd law of the thermodynamics: As the temperature approaches absolute zero, the entropy of a system approaches a constant minimum. Briefly, this postulates that entropy is temperature dependent and results in the formulation of the idea of absolute zero. At $S_0 = 0$, T is defined at 0K.

The heat absorbed by the system from the surroundings during the change from state A to state B is

$$Q = \int_A^B đQ = \int_A^B T\mathrm{d}S \tag{23}$$

where T is the absolute temperature and S is the entropy. The pressure-volume work done by a thermodynamic system on its surroundings that goes from state A and state B is

$$W = \int_A^B đW = \int_A^B P\mathrm{d}V \tag{24}$$

where P is the pressure exerted by the surroundings on the system and $\mathrm{d}V$ is an infinitesimal change in volume. The work Q and heat W have different values for different paths from state A to B so that Q and W are *path functions*. However, the first law of thermodynamics states that the infinitesimal difference between Q and W is independent of the path, i.e.,

$$\mathrm{d}E = đQ - đW \tag{25}$$

where E is a state function and called the internal energy. The second integrals in Eqs. (23) and (24) are valid for *reversible* processes in which there exist integral factors: T for $đQ$ and P for$đW$. Therefore, $\mathrm{d}S$ and $\mathrm{d}V$ are exact differentials: S and V are *state* functions. Thus,

$$\Delta S = \int_A^B \frac{đQ}{T} \geq 0 \tag{26}$$

where the equals sign is for a reversible process. Eq. (26) indicates the second law of thermodynamics. In an irreversible process, the entropy of the system and its surroundings increase; in a reversible process, the entropy of the system and its surroundings remains constant. In other words, the entropy of the system and its surroundings never decreases! The third law of thermodynamics allows us to calculate the absolute entropy of a substance:

$$S - S_0 = \int_0^T \frac{đQ}{T} \tag{27}$$

where $S_0 = 0$ at $T = 0$K. For simple systems, the first law of Eq. (25) can be expressed as

$$\mathrm{d}E = T\mathrm{d}S - P\mathrm{d}V \tag{28}$$

1.2.2 Microstates in phase space

The number of possible cases that N particles exist in m distinct microstates in phase space is

$$W = \frac{N!}{n_1!\, n_2! \cdots n_i! \cdots n_m!} = \frac{N!}{\prod_{i=1}^{m} n_i!} \tag{29}$$

where n_i is the number of particles in state i running from 1 to m so that

$$\sum_{i=1}^{m} n_i = N \tag{30}$$

or

$$\sum_{i=1}^{m} f_i = 1 \tag{31}$$

where frequency f_i is defined as

$$f_i = \frac{n_i}{N} \tag{32}$$

Usually, N and n_i are large numbers, which allow us to use Stirling's formula (Reif, 1965):

$$x! \approx x \ln x - x \tag{33}$$

to obtain

$$\begin{aligned} \frac{1}{N}\ln W &= \frac{1}{N}\ln N! - \frac{1}{N}\ln\left[\prod_i n_i!\right] \\ &\approx \ln N - 1 - \frac{1}{N}\sum_i (n_i \ln n_i - n_i) \\ &= -\sum_i^{m} f_i \ln f_i \end{aligned} \tag{34}$$

The system energy can be expressed as the sum of the product of the energy of state i and the number of particles in the state:

$$\sum_{i=1}^{m} f_i \epsilon_i = E \tag{35}$$

Our goal is to find function f_i that maximizes $(\ln W)/N$ with the two constraints of Eqs. (30) and (35) (Giffin, 2008; 2009). Using Lagrange multipliers, α and β, one can write

$$\frac{1}{N}\ln W = -\sum_i^{m} f_i \ln f_i - \alpha\left(\sum_{i=1}^{m} f_i - 1\right) - \beta\left(\sum_i f_i \epsilon_i - E\right) \tag{36}$$

and maximize $(\ln W)/N$ as

$$\begin{aligned} \Delta\left(\frac{1}{N}\ln W\right) &= -\sum_i \Delta f_i \ln f_i - \sum_i f_i \frac{\Delta f_i}{f_i} - \alpha \sum_i \Delta f_i - \beta \sum_i (\Delta f_i)\, \epsilon_i \\ &= \sum_i \Delta f_i \left(-\ln f_i - 1 - \alpha - \beta \epsilon_i\right) \\ &= 0 \end{aligned} \tag{37}$$

Therefore, f_i is calculated as

$$f_i = e^{-(1+\alpha+\beta\epsilon_i)} \tag{38}$$

Eq. (30) indicates the sum of f_i should be one:

$$1 = \sum_i f_i = e^{-1-\alpha} \sum_i e^{-\beta\epsilon_i} \tag{39}$$

so that

$$e^{-1-\alpha} = \left[\sum_i e^{-\beta\epsilon_i}\right]^{-1} = \frac{1}{Z} \tag{40}$$

where Z is partition function, defined as

$$Z = \sum_i e^{-\beta\epsilon_i} \tag{41}$$

The final form of function f_i is written as

$$f_i = \frac{e^{-\beta\epsilon_i}}{Z} \tag{42}$$

which makes the mean energy E represented in terms of the partition function:

$$E = \sum_i f_i\epsilon_i = \frac{1}{Z}\sum_i \epsilon_i e^{-\beta\epsilon_i} = -\frac{1}{Z}\frac{\partial}{\partial\beta}\left(\sum_i e^{-\beta\epsilon_i}\right) = -\frac{\partial \ln Z}{\partial\beta} \tag{43}$$

1.2.3 Canonical ensemble

In classical thermodynamics, there are seven primary quantities: (1) the number of particles (or molecules) N, (2) the volume V of the system containing the particles, (3) the temperature T, (4) the pressure P due to collisions of particles on box walls, (5) the total energy E, (6) the entropy S measuring the disorderness of the system, and (7) the chemical potential of μ (i.e., molar Gibbs free energy). An ensemble sets three (out of seven) variables to constants and defines a characteristic energy-function (i.e., a thermodynamics function that has a unit of energy) with the three constant variables as arguments. The partition function determines the characteristic energy-function. The other four variables are determined using the energy function and its partial derivatives with respect to the three variables chosen for the ensemble. For example, the canonical ensemble sets N, V, and T as constants and defines the Helmholtz free energy as

$$F = E - TS = -k_B T \ln Z \tag{44}$$

where k_B is the Boltzman constant and Z is the (canonical) partition function:

$$Z(N, V, T) = \frac{1}{N!h^{3N}} \int e^{-H(\mathbf{\Gamma})/k_B T} d\mathbf{\Gamma} \tag{45}$$

where h is Planck's constant, $H(\mathbf{\Gamma})$ is the Hamiltonian, $\mathbf{\Gamma}$ and $\mathrm{d}\mathbf{\Gamma} = \mathrm{d}^N\boldsymbol{r}\mathrm{d}^N\boldsymbol{p}$ represent a specific state and the infinitesimal element, respectively, in the phase space of $3N \times 3N$ dimension. Given a specific Hamiltonian as the sum of kinetic and potential energies of N

particles in a conservative field, i.e.,

$$H = \sum_{i=1}^{N} \left(\frac{\overrightarrow{P_i} \cdot \overrightarrow{P_i}}{2m_i} + V\left(\overrightarrow{r_i}\right) \right) \tag{46}$$

and using the infinitesimal relationship of the Helmholtz free energy

$$dF = \mu dN - PdV - SdT \tag{47}$$

the rest of four variables in the canonical ensemble are calculated as

$$\mu = \left(\frac{\partial F}{\partial N}\right)_{V,T} \tag{48}$$

$$P = -\left(\frac{\partial F}{\partial V}\right)_{N,T} \tag{49}$$

$$S = -\left(\frac{\partial F}{\partial T}\right)_{N,V} \tag{50}$$

$$E = -k_B T \ln Z - TS \tag{51}$$

where subscripts N, V, and T of the partial differentials are kept constant.
On the other hand, one can write mean energy E as an ensemble average of the Hamiltonian:

$$E = \langle H \rangle = \int H \cdot \rho(\Gamma)\, d\Gamma \tag{52}$$

where ρ is the probability density function (PDF) that quantifies the chances of the system having a specific value of the Hamiltonian:

$$\rho = \frac{e^{-\beta H}}{Z} \tag{53}$$

where $\beta = 1/k_B T$. Using the PDF, the second law of thermodynamics can be revisited by calculating

$$\Delta E = \int \Delta H \cdot \rho\, d\Gamma + \int H \cdot \Delta\rho\, d\Gamma \tag{54}$$

Here, the first term of Eq. (54) indicates the average of the Hamiltonian charge, which must be heat provided to the system by the surroundings:

$$\int \Delta H \cdot \rho\, d\Gamma = \delta Q \tag{55}$$

where "δ" has a similar meaning to $đ$, implying an inexact differential of which the associated quantity (e.g., Q) is a path function. The second term of Eq. (54) indicates energy change in part by variation of probability distributions, $\Delta\rho$. As a response to the applied (infinitesimal) heat δQ, the system does some work without noticeable change of the total energy; and their difference is stored as the internal energy change. In a reversible process, this work accompanies an infinitesimal volume expansion keeping the system pressure invariant. As the system is heated by the surroundings, the molecules will have more thermodynamic states because the entropy never decreases. Then, the change in the probability distribution is negative and the second integral term of Eq. (54) is expressed as negative (infinitesimal) work:

$$\int H \cdot \Delta\rho \, d\Gamma = -\delta W \tag{56}$$

By combining Eqs. (54) –(56), we revisited the second law of the thermodynamics from the view point of statistical mechanics, i.e.,

$$\Delta E = \delta Q - \delta W \tag{57}$$

which is equivalent to Eq. (25).

2. Monte Carlo sampling

2.1 Importance sampling

As the first law of thermodynamics describes energy changes as heat is absorbed or subtracted by work done, the average energy of canonical ensemble of subsystems in an equilibrium state is described as its ensemble average (Eq. 52). Constraints embedded in the canonical ensemble are N, V, and T. The other four thermodynamic variables such as E, P, μ, and S are calculated using the definition of ensemble average:

$$\langle \mathcal{A} \rangle = \int \mathcal{A} \cdot \rho(\mathbf{\Gamma}) \, d\mathbf{\Gamma} \tag{58}$$

where $\mathcal{A}$ is an thermodynamic variable of interest. Numerical integration of $\mathcal{A} \cdot \rho(\mathbf{\Gamma})$ in phases space is almost formidable due to the large dimension of $3N \times 3N$. Another approach is to generate a number of samples of $\mathcal{A}$ where $\rho(\mathbf{\Gamma})$ is significant.

For example, if a Hawaii researcher tries to build a PDF of shoppers at Ala Moana Shopping Center[1], then the researcher needs to have a number of assistants who stay for a given time (e.g., 10 minutes) at uniformly distributed stations in the mall areas and count the number of people passing by them. This is a very direct way to build the shopper PDF throughout the mall. If the researcher wants to know the average number of shoppers per 10 minutes, then he/she will multiply the number of shoppers counted at each station to the normalized frequency of shoppers at each station and sum over all the stations. For simplicity, assume that a shopper is not simultaneously double counted by assistants at different stations, and all shoppers are counted. Using this method, construction of a master PDF is a primary, time-consuming step before calculating any statistical quantity of interest. Isn't there any faster method to accurately estimate the mean number of shoppers? Assume the researcher knows, by previous knowledge, the shopper PDF in the mall. Then, the survey stations can be distributed following the shopper PDF. Once each station provides the number of shoppers counted during 10 minutes, then the sum of the numbers of shoppers of all stations can be a good estimation of the mean shopper number during 10 minutes!

Monte Carlo sampling, called importance sampling, follows the same idea. Instead of spanning all the possible cases and measuring a quantity of interest, sampling can be done following a PDF of thermodynamic states. Obviously, this approach to use the PDF for sampling, which should be obtained by sampling, is controversial. The Hawaii researcher can use a dynamic sampling method to reduce the sampling number required to build a trustful PDF. Initially, the survey stations can be distributed with a uniform, random, or mixed manner throughout the mall. A station assigned to Leia[2] is located between a parking lot and

[1] The largest shopping mall in Honolulu, Hawaii, the fifteenth largest shopping mall in the United States, and the largest open-air shopping center in the world

[2] Hawaiian female name, meaning child of heaven

a shopping area. Leia counted the number of people, say s_1 at position $\boldsymbol{x}_1$. She randomly selected a new position $\boldsymbol{x}_2$ (not far away from her original location $\boldsymbol{x}_1$), counted the number of shoppers, say s_2, and found that $s_2 > s_1$. Then, she updated her numbers from s_1 to s_2. Her third position $\boldsymbol{x}_3$ is chosen randomly near $\boldsymbol{x}_2$. At this time, s_3 is less than s_2. Now, she thinks that if she keeps selecting new positions with higher numbers than that at a previous station, the measurement is not correct and statistics will overestimate the total number of people in the mall. In this case, she needs a criterion to accept movement to a station where the number of people counted will be lower.
She decides on a simple protocol as follows:

- If a new position provides more people, then stay at the new position and update the number.
- If the number of shoppers decreases by moving to a new position, she stay at the new position if she tosses heads on a coin.

By doing this, she can measure more frequently where there are more shoppers, but not completely discard data from stations having less shoppers. She can test various criteria to stay at a new position with a lower number of shoppers. If the ratio of the number of shoppers at the new station to that of old, i.e, $N_{\text{new}}/N_{\text{old}}$ is less than 0.5, she returns to the old position, discarding the number counted at the new position. Because the new position is rejected, she counts the number of people at the old position one more time before she randomly selects a new position. Including the random selection of $\boldsymbol{x}_1$, the number of positions used for measurement should be equal to the number of accepted measurements. Some of positions must be used multiple times. After a certain number of measurements, let's say 50, Leia can assemble a series with the number of shoppers, i.e., $\{N_1, N_2, N_3, \ldots, N_i, \ldots, N_{50}\}$. The difference between N_{i+1} and N_i must be large if i is small. Leia can take an average of the number of people using only the later half of the data set, i.e, $i = 26 - 50$. If the researcher has more assistants, he or she can sum the number of shoppers counted by the assistants, divide it by the number of assistants, and calculate the average number of people seen per 10 minutes at the shopping mall.

2.2 Formalism

Monte Carlo simulation is in general an integration process in a large dimensional space. As stated above, the key issue is to reduce the sampling numbers using the importance sampling technique, i.e., sampling more data where the probability density is higher. The sampling frequency distribution should resemble the PDF of the thermodynamic states. Monte Carlo simulation starts at a location in the phase space. The next position is selected to satisfy that a series of accepted locations follow the frequency distribution of the thermodynamic state. Therefore, searching probable states in the phase space is a self-consistent process that supports the PDF.
After integration with respect to N-particle momentum, $\mathrm{d}\boldsymbol{p}^N$, the probability distribution function of a particle configuration state $\boldsymbol{R}\,(=\{\boldsymbol{r}_1, \boldsymbol{r}_2, \cdots, \boldsymbol{r}_i, \cdots, \boldsymbol{r}_N\})$ occurring is

$$\rho(\boldsymbol{R}) = \frac{e^{-\beta V(\boldsymbol{R})}}{Z_R} \tag{59}$$

where

$$Z_R = \int e^{-\beta V(\boldsymbol{R})} \mathrm{d}\boldsymbol{R} \tag{60}$$

Now, we define $W(\boldsymbol{R}'|\boldsymbol{R})$ as the probability to make a transition from state $\boldsymbol{R}$ to $\boldsymbol{R}'$, i.e., the conditional probability of occurring state $\boldsymbol{R}$ given that state $\boldsymbol{R}'$ has occured. Two constraints $W(\boldsymbol{R}'|\boldsymbol{R})$ are:

(a) sum rule

$$\int W(\boldsymbol{R}'|\boldsymbol{R})\mathrm{d}\boldsymbol{R}' = 1 \tag{61}$$

(b) detailed balance

$$W(\boldsymbol{R}'|\boldsymbol{R})\,\rho(\boldsymbol{R}) = W(\boldsymbol{R}|\boldsymbol{R}')\,\rho(\boldsymbol{R}') \tag{62}$$

In Eq. (62), left-hand-side is the probability of state $\boldsymbol{R}$ occurring multiplied by the transition probability to state $\boldsymbol{R}'$ given $\boldsymbol{R}$; and right-hand-side is the probability of state $\boldsymbol{R}'$ occurring multiplied by the transition probability to state $\boldsymbol{R}$ given $\boldsymbol{R}'$. Therefore, each represents the probability of both configuration states $\boldsymbol{R}$ and $\boldsymbol{R}'$ occurring in canonical ensemble, i.e., $P(\boldsymbol{R} \cap \boldsymbol{R}')$.

The transition probability W is described as

$$W(\boldsymbol{R}'|\boldsymbol{R}) = A(\boldsymbol{R}'|\boldsymbol{R})\,T(\boldsymbol{R}'|\boldsymbol{R}) \tag{63}$$

where $A(\boldsymbol{R}'|\boldsymbol{R})$ is the acceptance probability of the move from $\boldsymbol{R}$ to $\boldsymbol{R}'$ and $T(\boldsymbol{R}'|\boldsymbol{R})$ is the selection probability of a new configuration $\boldsymbol{R}'$ given an old $\boldsymbol{R}$, chosen to satisfy

$$\int T(\boldsymbol{R}'|\boldsymbol{R})\mathrm{d}\boldsymbol{R}' = 1 \tag{64}$$

such that $\boldsymbol{R}$ and $\boldsymbol{R}'$ are accessible to each other.

If configuration $\boldsymbol{R}'$ is a higher energy state than $\boldsymbol{R}$, which indicates that a transition from state $\boldsymbol{R}'$ to $\boldsymbol{R}$ is always accepted, i.e.,

$$A(\boldsymbol{R}|\boldsymbol{R}') = 1 \tag{65}$$

Substitution of Eq. (63) into Eq. (62) yields

$$A(\boldsymbol{R}'|\boldsymbol{R}) = \frac{T(\boldsymbol{R}|\boldsymbol{R}')\,\rho(\boldsymbol{R}')}{T(\boldsymbol{R}'|\boldsymbol{R})\,\rho(\boldsymbol{R})} \tag{66}$$

where the form of $T(\boldsymbol{R}'|\boldsymbol{R})$ can be arbitrarily chosen. Now, we define

$$q(\boldsymbol{R}'|\boldsymbol{R}) = \frac{T(\boldsymbol{R}|\boldsymbol{R}')}{T(\boldsymbol{R}'|\boldsymbol{R})} \exp\left(-\beta\left[V(\boldsymbol{R}') - V(\boldsymbol{R})\right]\right) \tag{67}$$

and represent a general form of the acceptance probability:

$$A(\boldsymbol{R}'|\boldsymbol{R}) = \min\left[1, q\left(\boldsymbol{R}'|\boldsymbol{R}\right)\right] \tag{68}$$

If $V(\boldsymbol{R}') < V(\boldsymbol{R})$, $q(\boldsymbol{R}'|\boldsymbol{R}) > 1$ and therefore $A(\boldsymbol{R}'|\boldsymbol{R}) = 1$. Otherwise, $A(\boldsymbol{R}'|\boldsymbol{R}) = q(\boldsymbol{R}'|\boldsymbol{R}) < 1$.

2.3 Metropolis Monte Carlo (MMC)

In principle, it is possible to make simultaneous N-particle moves. However, in practice, a one particle move is preferred because the acceptance probability of the N-particle move is exceedingly small for a reasonable step size. For this reason, we restrict ourselves to the one-particle move at a Monte Carlo step, and simplify Eq. (68) to

$$A(\boldsymbol{r}_i'|\boldsymbol{r}_i) = \min\left[1, q\left(\boldsymbol{r}_i'|\boldsymbol{r}_i\right)\right] \tag{69}$$

which implies that, during the transition of particle i from $\boldsymbol{r}_i$ to $\boldsymbol{r}_i'$, all other particles will stay at their original positions $\boldsymbol{r}_j$ for $j = 1, 2, \cdots, i-1, i+1, \cdots, N$.

To implement the Metropolis solution of the acceptance probability, the selection probability needs to be specified, which is designed to move particle i from $\boldsymbol{r}_i$ into any one of its neighboring position $\boldsymbol{r}_i'$ in a cubic region $\mathscr{R}$ with an equal probability. See Fig. 3 for details. The cube is centered at $\boldsymbol{r}_i$ and has sides of $2\delta r_{\max}$. Then, the random displacement

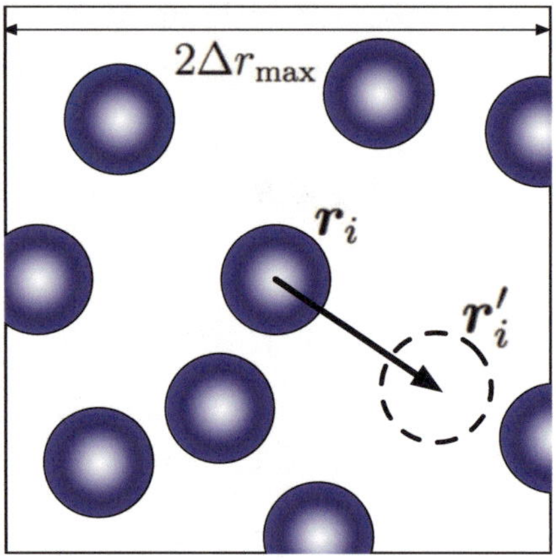

Fig. 3. Trial movement of particle i from position $\boldsymbol{r}_i$ to $\boldsymbol{r}_i'$ that can be any point within the square domain $\mathscr{R}$ of each side $2\Delta r_{\max}$.

$\Delta \boldsymbol{r}_i = \boldsymbol{r}_i' - \boldsymbol{r}_i$ is selected via

$$\Delta x_i = x_i' - x_i = (2\xi_1 - 1.0) \times \Delta r_{\max} \tag{70a}$$
$$\Delta y_i = y_i' - y_i = (2\xi_2 - 1.0) \times \Delta r_{\max} \tag{70b}$$
$$\Delta z_i = z_i' - z_i = (2\xi_3 - 1.0) \times \Delta r_{\max} \tag{70c}$$

where ξ_1, ξ_2, and ξ_3 are independent uniform random numbers between 0 and 1. The value of $\Delta r_{\max}$ must be optimally chosen. If $\Delta r_{\max}$ is too large, then the acceptance probability can be small due to physical overlap between rigid particles and/or the energy difference can be much larger than $k_B T$. The selection probability of $\boldsymbol{r}_i'$ from $\boldsymbol{r}_i$ is then

$$T(\boldsymbol{r}_i'|\boldsymbol{r}_i) = \begin{cases} \tau_0 & \boldsymbol{r}_i' \in \mathscr{R} \\ 0 & \boldsymbol{r}_i' \notin \mathscr{R} \end{cases} \tag{71}$$

where τ_0 is a constant, which can be chosen as $1/\left(2\Delta r_{\max}\right)^3$ or $1/N_{\mathscr{R}}$ where $N_{\mathscr{R}}$ is the finite number of a new position. The numerical value of τ_0 does not influence the evaluation of the acceptance probability because the constant character of τ_0 implies its intrinsic symmetricity with respect to the sequence of $\boldsymbol{r}_i$ and $\boldsymbol{r}_i'$, which provides the final form of

$$q(\boldsymbol{r}_i'|\boldsymbol{r}_i) = \frac{\tau_0\, \rho(\boldsymbol{r}_i')}{\tau_0\, \rho(\boldsymbol{r}_i)} = e^{-\beta[V(\boldsymbol{r}_i') - V(\boldsymbol{r}_i)]} \tag{72}$$

from Eq. (67) and further the acceptance probability of the one-particle move as

$$A(\boldsymbol{r}_i'|\boldsymbol{r}_i) = \min\left[1, q\left(\boldsymbol{r}_i'|\boldsymbol{r}_i\right)\right] \tag{73}$$

as suggested by Metropolis et al. (1953).

2.4 Force Bias Monte Carlo (FBMC)

Pangali et al. (1978) proposed the modified selection probability along the direction of forces. The primary reason is that particle movements in (deterministic) molecular dynamics per time step is usually biased in the direction of the intermolecular forces and torques, whereas the moves sampled according to the standard Metropolis algorithm are chosen randomly in an arbitrary direction. Therefore, if the influence of forces acting on a particle can be included in selecting a new position, then the Monte Carlo can be more accurate, potentially avoiding congestion near a bottleneck in phase space.

Expansion of the potential function $V(\boldsymbol{r}_i)$ around $\boldsymbol{r}_i$ gives for the one-particle move

$$T(\boldsymbol{r}_i'|\boldsymbol{r}_i) = \begin{cases} C^{-1}\exp\left[\beta\lambda \boldsymbol{F}_i(\boldsymbol{r}_i)\cdot\Delta\boldsymbol{r}_i\right] & \boldsymbol{r}_i' \in \mathscr{R} \\ 0 & \boldsymbol{r}_i' \notin \mathscr{R} \end{cases} \tag{74}$$

where λ is an arbitrary parameter and $\boldsymbol{F}_i(\boldsymbol{r}_i) = -\nabla_{\boldsymbol{r}_i}V(\boldsymbol{r}_i)$ is a force vector acting on particle i from all other particles, and C is a normalization constant that depends on λ and $\boldsymbol{F}_i$. The normalization condition of Eq. (64) gives

$$C = \int\int\int_{\boldsymbol{r}-\Delta\boldsymbol{r}_{\max}}^{\boldsymbol{r}+\Delta\boldsymbol{r}_{\max}} \mathrm{d}x'\mathrm{d}y'\mathrm{d}z' \exp\left[\beta\lambda\left\{F_x\cdot(x'-x)+F_y\cdot(y'-y)+F_z\cdot(z'-z)\right\}\right] \tag{75}$$

where the particle index i is omitted since it does not change the final representation of C. The integration with respect to x' calculates

$$\int_{x-\Delta r_{\max}}^{x+\Delta r_{\max}} \mathrm{d}x' \exp\left[\beta\lambda F_x\cdot(x'-x)\right] = \frac{2\sinh\left[\beta\lambda F_x\Delta r_{\max}\right]}{\beta\lambda F_x}$$

and so

$$C = \frac{8\sinh\left[\beta\lambda F_x\Delta r_{\max}\right]\sinh\left[\beta\lambda F_y\Delta r_{\max}\right]\sinh\left[\beta\lambda F_z\Delta r_{\max}\right]}{(\beta\lambda)^3F_xF_yF_z} \tag{76}$$

Note that F_x, F_y, and F_z are force components that particle i experiences at $\boldsymbol{r} = (x, y, z)$. The coefficient C' of the selection probability of $\boldsymbol{r}_i$ from $\boldsymbol{r}_i'$ is accordingly calculated as

$$C' = \frac{8\sinh\left[\beta\lambda F_x'\Delta r_{\max}\right]\sinh\left[\beta\lambda F_y'\Delta r_{\max}\right]\sinh\left[\beta\lambda F_z'\Delta r_{\max}\right]}{(\beta\lambda)^3F_x'F_y'F_z'} \tag{77}$$

with F_x', F_y', and F_z' at $\boldsymbol{r}' = (x', y', z')$. So that

$$\begin{aligned} q(\boldsymbol{r}'|\boldsymbol{r}) &= \frac{T(\boldsymbol{r}|\boldsymbol{r}')\rho(\boldsymbol{r}')}{T(\boldsymbol{r}'|\boldsymbol{r})\rho(\boldsymbol{r})} \\ &= \frac{C'}{C}\exp\left(-\beta\left[V(\boldsymbol{r}')-V(\boldsymbol{r})+\lambda(\boldsymbol{F}+\boldsymbol{F}')\cdot\Delta\boldsymbol{r}\right]\right) \\ &= \exp\left(-\beta\left[\delta V+\lambda(\boldsymbol{F}+\boldsymbol{F}')\cdot\Delta\boldsymbol{r}+\Delta\mathcal{W}_{\mathrm{FB}}\right]\right) \end{aligned} \tag{78}$$

where

$$\Delta V = V(\boldsymbol{r}') - V(\boldsymbol{r}) \tag{79}$$

and

$$\Delta\mathcal{W}_{\mathrm{FB}} = k_BT\ln\left(\frac{C'}{C}\right) \tag{80}$$

If the maximum displacement $\Delta r_{\max}$ is set to be small, then C'/C can be approximated using the Taylor expansion. If we consider terms only in the x-coordinate,

$$\left(\frac{C'}{C}\right)_x = \frac{\sinh[\eta + \Delta\eta]}{\eta + \Delta\eta}\frac{\eta}{\sinh[\eta]} \tag{81}$$

where $\eta = \beta\lambda F_x \Delta r_{\max}$ and $\Delta\eta = \beta\lambda\Delta F_x \Delta r_{\max}$. Using

$$\frac{\sinh t}{t} = 1 + \frac{1}{6}t^2 + \cdots \tag{82}$$

one approximates C'/C as

$$\begin{aligned}\left(\frac{C'}{C}\right)_x &\approx \frac{1 + \frac{1}{6}(\eta + \Delta\eta)^2}{1 + \frac{1}{6}\eta^2} \\ &= \left[1 + \frac{1}{6}(\eta + \Delta\eta)^2\right]\left[1 - \frac{1}{6}\eta^2 + O\left(\eta^4\right)\right] \\ &= 1 + \frac{1}{6}\left[2\eta\Delta\eta + (\Delta\eta)^2\right] + O\left(\eta^4\right) \\ &\approx 1 + \frac{1}{6}\left[2F_x\Delta F_x + \Delta F_x^2\right]\beta^2\lambda^2\Delta r_{\max}^2 \\ &\approx \exp\left(\frac{1}{6}\left[2F_x\Delta F_x + \Delta F_x^2\right]\beta^2\lambda^2\Delta r_{\max}^2\right)\end{aligned} \tag{83}$$

so that in general

$$\Delta\mathcal{W}_{\mathrm{FB}} \approx \frac{1}{6}\left(2\boldsymbol{F}\cdot\Delta\boldsymbol{F} + \Delta\boldsymbol{F}\cdot\Delta\boldsymbol{F}\right)\beta\lambda^2\Delta r_{\max}^2 \tag{84}$$

Finally, a move from $\boldsymbol{r}$ to $\boldsymbol{r}'$ of i particle is accepted with the probability:

$$A(\boldsymbol{r}'|\boldsymbol{r}) = \min\left[1, q\left(\boldsymbol{r}'|\boldsymbol{r}\right)\right] \tag{85}$$

where

$$q(\boldsymbol{r}'|\boldsymbol{r}) = \exp\left(-\beta\left[\delta V + \lambda(2\boldsymbol{F} + \Delta\boldsymbol{F})\cdot\Delta\boldsymbol{r} + \frac{1}{6}\beta\lambda^2\Delta r_{\max}^2\left(2\boldsymbol{F} + \Delta\boldsymbol{F}\right)\cdot\Delta\boldsymbol{F}\right]\right) \tag{86}$$

An alternative representation with $\lambda = 1/2$ is

$$q(\boldsymbol{r}'|\boldsymbol{r}) = \exp\left(-\beta\left[\delta V + \langle\boldsymbol{F}\rangle\cdot\Delta\boldsymbol{r}_{\mathrm{FB}}\right]\right) \tag{87}$$

where $\langle\boldsymbol{F}\rangle$ indicates the average forces between position $\boldsymbol{r}$ and $\boldsymbol{r}'$:

$$\langle\boldsymbol{F}\rangle = \frac{1}{2}\left(\boldsymbol{F} + \boldsymbol{F}'\right) = \boldsymbol{F} + \frac{1}{2}\Delta\boldsymbol{F} \tag{88}$$

and $\Delta\boldsymbol{r}_{\mathrm{FB}}$ is the proposed displacement for a move:

$$\Delta\boldsymbol{r}_{\mathrm{FB}} = \Delta\boldsymbol{r} + \frac{1}{12}\beta\Delta r_{\max}^2\Delta\boldsymbol{F} \tag{89}$$

The first and second terms in the RHS of Eq. (89) are under the influence of random forces (from surrounding solvent molecules) and systematic forces (from other nearby Brownian particles), respectively. Note that $\beta^{-1}|\Delta \boldsymbol{F}|\Delta r_{\max}$ has an energy unit. The simplified representation of the acceptance probability q of Eq. (87) evolves from two conditions: (1) $\lambda = 1/2$, and (2) $\Delta r_{\max}$ is small enough (typically in comparison to particle size) to ensure that $\beta\lambda|\boldsymbol{F}|\Delta r_{\max} \ll 1$. With the same conditions, the "Smart Monte Carlo (SMC)" provides identical representations of Eqs. (87) - (89) developed by Rossky et al. (1978). Northrup and McCammon (1980) have used SMC to investigate protein structure fluctuations.

In the FB algorithm, $\Delta \boldsymbol{r}$ is randomly chosen using a uniform random number generator as indicated in Eq. (70): however, in the SMC algorithm, $\Delta \boldsymbol{r}/\Delta r_{\max}$ is chosen to have zero mean and unit variance; in other words,

$$\langle \Delta \boldsymbol{r} \rangle = 0 \tag{90a}$$

$$\langle \Delta \boldsymbol{r} \cdot \Delta \boldsymbol{r} \rangle = \Delta r_{\max}^2 \tag{90b}$$

and the isotropy indicates

$$\langle \Delta x \rangle = \langle \Delta y \rangle = \langle \Delta z \rangle = 0 \tag{91a}$$

$$\langle (\Delta x)^2 \rangle = \langle (\Delta y)^2 \rangle = \langle (\Delta z)^2 \rangle = \frac{1}{3}\Delta r_{\max}^2 \tag{91b}$$

A Gaussian random number with zero mean and unit variance can be generated using two typical methods.

A. Box and Muller's Algorithm

Box and Muller (1958) Let U_1 and U_2 be independent random variables from the same rectangular density function on the interval $(0, 1)$. Consider the random variables:

$$X_1 = \sqrt{-2\ln U_1}\,\cos 2\pi U_2 \tag{92}$$

$$X_2 = \sqrt{-2\ln U_1}\,\sin 2\pi U_2 \tag{93}$$

Then, $-\infty \le X_1, X_2 \le +\infty$ will be a pair of independent random variables from the same normal distribution with mean zero, and unit variance. Either X_1 or X_2 can be used if only one Gaussian random number is necessary at a time.

B. Summation Algorithm

Allen and Tildesley (1987) This method involves two steps and the generation of 12 uniform random variates:

1. generate 12 uniform random variables, $U_1, \cdots, U_{12}$ in range $(0, 1)$;
2. calculate $X = \sum_{i=1}^{12} U_i - 6$

This method yields number X's which are sampled from an approximately normal distribution (by virtue of the central limit theorem of probability). Clearly, random variates outside the range $(-6, +6)$ will never be generated using this method, but it is adequate for most Monte Carlo purposes, and is quite fast.

2.5 Move Bias Monte Carlo (MBMC)

In natural and engineered systems, molecules and particles are considered as point masses and spherical objects, respectively. However, long polymer chains with finite length are of great importance in chemical engineering processes. Since a polymer can be viewed as a linear connection of many identical monomers, trial movement of a polymer requires constraints such as sequence, bond length, and bond angle of associated monomers.

Mapping the movement of a polymer chain is an interesting problem. de Gennes (1971) developed the reptation model where a polymer chain of n monomers moves like a reptile. When the position of the first monomer is randomly selected and accepted without any overlap between the other monomers, the second monomer moves to the previous position of the first, the third monomer moves to the previous position of the second monomer, and so forth: simply, $\boldsymbol{r}_1^{\text{old}} \rightarrow \boldsymbol{r}_1^{\text{new}}$ and $\boldsymbol{r}_i \rightarrow \boldsymbol{r}_{i-1}$ for $i = 2 - n$. In programming, this is actually equivalent to moving the last monomer to the position of the first monomer and updating the monomer index such that

$$i \rightarrow \text{mod}(i, m) + 1 \tag{94}$$

i.e., $1 \rightarrow 2, 2 \rightarrow 3, ..., i \rightarrow (i+1), (m-1) \rightarrow m$, and $m \rightarrow 1$.
This reptation model is efficient when polymers are in a dense system so that their lateral movements are restricted by volume exclusion. However, when polymer rheology is of interest, one can use an isothermal-isobaric ensemble with a constant number of particles (i.e., monomers in polymer solution), pressure, and temperature. Simulation starts with a sparse distribution of polymers of random shapes in an arbitrarily chosen large volume. Configurations of polymers and system volume change during the NPT simulation to reach an equilibrium state that calculates a mean pressure close to the preset value of the pressure. While the volume shrinks, polymers find energetically nested positions. In this case, an effective sampling in the phase space should include lateral movement of monomers within a polymer in addition to the reptation. To avoid configurational jamming of polymers in a canonical ensemble, one can use parallel tempering which simulates M replicas of the original system of interests at different temperatures and swap a pair of configurations comparing energy between the two subsystems (Earl and Deem, 2005).
A partial polymer can have a new configuration. A terminal section of a chain, let't say m monomers, is annihilated and then regrown one by one. Each of the new m monomers can be created at a random position near the previous one in the sequence. The energy difference between the new and old terminal sections is calculated, and the standard Metropolis Monte Carlo scheme is used to accept or reject the new configuration of the terminal section. This is called configurational bias Monte Carlo (CBMC), originally proposed by Rosenbluth and Rosenbluth (1955) and further developed by Siepmann and Frenkel (1992) and de Pablo et al. (1992). As the force bias MC was designed to simulate water and aqueous solutions (Pangali et al., 1978), it is possible to combine the move bias and force bias Monte Carlo algorithms for an efficient sampling of polymer configurations in phase space.

3. Hybrid Monte Carlo

The term "hybrid" indicates a combination of two different elements. In general, thermodynamic states can be classified into equilibrium and non-equilibrium states, often called "static" and "dynamic", respectively. The true equilibrium state exists in an isolated system through which neither mass nor energy can transfer. Therefore, no thermodynamic quantity in an isolated system changes with respect to time, which is mathematically depicted as $\partial[\,]/\partial t = 0$. In engineering processes, mass and energy continuously enter and leave from an operational unit. When the mass/energy transport rate is kept constant, the system is said to be in a steady state or dynamic equilibrium. Principles and theories of statistical mechanics developed under pure equilibrium are often adopted to explain and analyze engineering processes at the steady state.
Particles found in gaseous and liquid flows are influenced by external force fields and inter-particle interactions. Hydrodynamic drag forces exerted on suspended particles in a fluid medium contribute to convective (or advective) transport of particles in a plethora of natural and engineering processes. Brownian motion (Brown, 1828) of particles involves

a tremendous amount of bombastic collisions of fluid molecules with suspended particles. Relative motion of particles flowing in fluid media generate resistant forces in the opposite direction to the particle's translational motion. To rigorously deal with this phenomena, Newton's second law should be numerically solved for positions and velocities of particles as a function of time. The exerted forces can be classified into conservative and dissipative ones; the former include external and interparticle forces solely depending on particle positions, and the latter on hydrodynamic drag force proportional to particle velocities. Because the Monte Carlo methods described thus far propose efficient ways of sampling in phase space, it should be ensured that the system to be investigated is in a static equilibrium state of conservative force field. Then, isn't there any method to include the dissipative force with the standard Monte Carlo method and phenomenologically simulate steady-state configurations of many particles in a fluid system? The answer is the hybrid Monte Carlo.

Arya and Panagiotopoulos (2004) used a coarse-grained lattice Monte Carlo approach to model surfactants, while the shear is implemented by assigning a "pseudopotential" as included into the MC acceptance criteria. Their model systems consist of cylindrical micelles located between two impermeable walls, and each micelle is depicted as 4 head and 4 tail monomers, i.e., 4H4T lattice surfactants. For the sake of simplicity, they impose attractive potential energy between only two tail monomers associated in the same or different micelles: $\epsilon_{\text{TT}}/k_B T = -2$, and $\epsilon_{\text{TH}} = \epsilon_{\text{HH}} = 0$ where subscripts H and T indicate head and tail, respectively. A fictitious potential energy gradient ∇U_d to the drag force experience by each monomer is given by

$$\nabla U_d = \zeta v_x \tag{95}$$

where v_x is the fluid velocity in the x direction and ζ is a friction coefficient. In a linear shear flow, $v_x = \dot{\gamma} y$ where $\dot{\gamma}$ is the shear rate and y is the coordinate perpendicular to the slit. The pseudo-energy difference term of monomer i moving from (x_1, y_1, z_1) to (x_2, y_2, z_2) is given by

$$\nabla U_{d,i} = -\zeta \dot{\gamma} \langle y \rangle (x_2 - x_1) \tag{96}$$

where $\langle y \rangle = (y_1 + y_2)/2$. The final acceptance criterion for an MC move of an amphiphile (4H4T monomers) is assigned as

$$P_{\text{acc}} = \min \left(1, \exp \left[- \left(\Delta V + \sum_{i=1}^{N=8} \Delta U_{d,i} \right) / k_B T \right] \right) \tag{97}$$

where ΔU is the usual interaction energy contribution, and the shear contribution has been summed over the 8 monomers per amphiphile. Three dimensional lattice MC simulations showed various alignments due to the shear rate and dimensionless temperature (defined as $k_B T/\epsilon_{\text{TT}}$). The shear force breaks micelles perpendicular to the shearing direction into small ones, and these smaller micelles align and grow in the shearing direction. This approach can be considered as a hybrid MC which includes dissipative force as an origin of the pseudo-potential energy.

Kim et al. (2001) already used a similar approach of combining conservative inter-particle potential energy and dissipative hydrodynamic drag force in a hybrid Monte Carlo to study shear-induced micellar deformation. Lennard-Jones (LJ) potentials were assumed for TT and TH pairs with different potential well depths, i.e., ϵ_{TT} and ϵ_{TH}. The HH pair interaction include LJ as well as Coulomb potentials to characterize electrostatic repulsion between two head groups. The shear force exerted on each monomer is calculated as

$$F_{x,j}(y) = 3\pi\mu\sigma_{jj}\dot{\gamma}y_j \tag{98}$$

where j is H or T, σ is diameter, and μ is the solvent viscosity. Shear force is treated as a bias influence in a trail MC move of a tail or head. The standard force bias MC was employed by switching the gradient of the pair potential energy with the hydrodynamic force, and a trial move is accepted following the acceptance probability of Eq. (87). Micellar deformation was investigated as a function of Peclet number (Pe) and rapid transition from spherical to oval shapes was observed near Pe = 1. This indicated that if the move displacement is small enough, then Brownian dynamics, smart MC, and force bias MC are equivalent (Chen and Kim, 2004).

Kim et al. (2001) and Arya and Panagiotopoulos (2004) used similar approaches of including hydrodynamic force in the Metropolis MC. One important aspect which was ignored by both papers was that the microscopic hydrodynamic force is significantly influenced by the number of neighbors and their relative positions. When particles accumulate and form a porous media, drag force increases with respect to the particle volume fraction. Then, Stokes' drag needs to be modified quantitatively. Happel (1958) developed a tangential-stress-free cell model, which maps a uniform distribution of particles to a sphere embedded in a concentric spherical cell. On the surface of the cell, tangential stress was assumed to be zero. Then, the ratio of force exerted on a spherical particle of radius a within a sphere-packed porous media of volume fraction ϕ to that on an isolated sphere is given as

$$\Omega = \frac{F(\phi)}{6\pi\mu a u} = \frac{6 - 9\phi^{1/3} + 9\phi^{5/3} - 6\phi^2}{6 + 4\phi^{5/3}} \tag{99}$$

where u is the superficial velocity. To calculate the force ratio Ω, the local volume fraction near a particle that will move should be calculated. Because the potential energy is assumed to be pairwise, center-to-center distances between a particle and all others need to be calculated. One can make an equivalent cell whose volume is equal to that of the search domain of new position, i.e., $(2\Delta r_{\max})^3$ of Fig. 3, count the number of particles within the cell, and calculate the local volume fraction near the particle that is about to move. This technique was developed to investigate the structure of the cake layer, i.e., boundary layer of rejected particles, on membrane surfaces by Kim and Hoek (2002) and Chen et al. (2005), and a comprehensive review can be found elsewhere (Chen and Kim, 2006).

4. Concluding remarks and perspectives

With more than a half century history (Metropolis et al., 1953), Monte Carlo methods are widely used in science and engineering, focused on the properties and phase equilibria of polymers, colloids, proteins, biological and synthetic membranes, liquid crystals, semiconductors, solid-liquid and liquid-liquid interfaces, nano-materials, and materials for energy production and storage. Use of MC methods in environmental engineering is still in a burgeoning stage. However, because water and air are primary subjects of the discipline, MC simulations of particles in air and water or their interfaces can significantly contribute to a fundamental understanding of natural phenomena. All the MC simulations are, mathematically speaking, numerical integrations of large dimensions. Specific phenomenological modeling does not need to include rigor and formalism of statistical physics. Transition probability leads a system of random initial configuration to an equilibrium state. Efficient simulation requires advanced sampling techniques using biased probability and distributed parallel computing can be readily employed for rapid MC simulations.

In the future, it is expected that rapid and accurate MC algorithms will be generated and that these algorithms are readily applicable to real situations. Specific ensembles and thermodynamic properties will be updated as MC algorithms develop. More unified MC algorithms will be developed for easier use and a multi-scale version will be available. A more efficient sampling method is desired by using bias schemes which follows basic statistical physics as well as carefully mimicking phenomena of interest.

5. Appendix

5.1 Additional analysis of Monty Hall Dilemma

A complex way of calculating $P(S_1 \cap H_3)$ of Eq. (16) is as follows.

$$\begin{aligned} P(S_1 \cap H_3) &= P(S_1 \cap H_3|C_2) + P\left(S_1 \cap H_3|\widetilde{C_2}\right) & (100)\\ &= P(S_1 \cap H_3|C_2) + P(S_1 \cap H_3|C_1 \text{ or } C_3) & (101)\\ &= P(S_1 \cap H_3|C_2) + P(S_1 \cap H_3|C_1) + P(S_1 \cap H_3|C_3) & (102)\\ &= P(S_1 \cap H_3|C_2) + P(S_1 \cap H_3|C_1) & (103)\end{aligned}$$

where $P(S_1 \cap H_3|C_3) = 0$ because if the car is behind door 3, then the host will not open door 3. Further calculations provide

$$\begin{aligned} P(S_1 \cap H_3|C_2) &= P(S_1|C_2)\,P(H_3|C_2)\,P(C_2) & (104)\\ &= P(S_1)\,P(H_3|C_2)\,P(C_2) & (105)\\ &= \frac{1}{3}\cdot 1 \cdot \frac{1}{3} = \frac{1}{9} & (106)\end{aligned}$$

where $P(H_3|C_2) = 1$ because the host has to open door #3 given that the car is behind door #2 after we selected door #1, and

$$\begin{aligned} P(S_1 \cap H_3|C_1) &= P(S_1|C_1)\,P(H_3|C_1)\,P(C_1)\\ &= P(S_1)\,P(H_3|C_1)\,P(C_1)\\ &= \frac{1}{3}\cdot\frac{1}{2}\cdot\frac{1}{3} = \frac{1}{18}\end{aligned}$$

where $P(H_3|C_1) = 1/2$ because the host can open either door #3 or #2 if I selected door #1. Therefore, as expected, we here obtain the identical answer to Eq. (16):

$$P(S_1 \cap H_2) = \frac{1}{9} + \frac{1}{18} = \frac{3}{18} = \frac{1}{6} \quad (107)$$

6. References

M. P. Allen and D. J. Tildesley. *Computer Simulation of Liquids*. Oxford University Press, Oxford, UK, 1987.

G. Arya and A. Z. Panagiotopoulos. Monte carlo study of shear-induced alignment of cylindrical micelles in thin films. *Phys. Rev. E*, 70(3):031501, 2004.

M. Bayes and M. Price. An essay towards solving a problem in the doctrine of chances. *Phil. Trans. Roy. Soc. London*, 53:370–418, 1763.

G. Box and M. Muller. A note on the generation of random normal deviates. *The Annals of Mathematical Statistics*, 29(2):610–611, 1958.

R. Brown. A brief account of microscopical observations. *Phil. J.*, pages 358–371, 1828.

J. C. Chen and A. S. Kim. Brownian dynamics, molecular dynamics, and monte carlo modeling of colloidal systems. *Adv. Colloid Interface Sci.*, 112(1-3):159–173, 2004.

J. C. Chen and A. S. Kim. Monte carlo simulation of colloidal membrane filtration: Principal issues for modeling. *Adv. Colloid Interface Sci.*, 119(1):35–53, 2006.

J. C. Chen, M. Elimelech, and A. S. Kim. Monte carlo simulation of colloidal membrane filtration: Model development with application to characterization of colloid phase transition. *J. Membr. Sci.*, 255(1-2):291–305, 2005.

P. de Gennes. Reptation of a polymer chain in the presence of fixed obstacles. *J. Chem. Phys.*, 55(2):572–579, 1971.

J. de Pablo, M. Laso, and U. Suter. Simulation of polyethylene above and below the melting point. *J. Chem. Phys.*, 96(3):2395–2403, 1992.

D. Earl and M. Deem. Parallel tempering: Theory, applications, and new perspectives. *Phys. Chem. Chem. Phys.*, 7(23):3910–3916, 2005.

R. F. Feynman, R. B. Leighton, and M. Sands. *The Feynman Lectures on Physics*. Addison-Wesley Publishing Company, 1963.

A. Giffin. *Maximum Entropy: The Universal Method for Inference*. PhD thesis, University of Albany, Department of Physics, 2008.

A. Giffin. From physics to economics: An econometric example using maximum relative entropy. *Physica A: Statistical Mechanics and its Applications*, 388(8):1610–1620, 2009.

J. Happel. Viscous flow in multiparticle systems: slow motion of fluids relative to beds of spherical particles. *AIChE J.*, 4(2):197–201, 1958.

A. S. Kim and E. M. V. Hoek. Cake structure in dead-end membrane filtration: Monte carlo simulations. *Environ. Eng. Sci.*, 19(6):373–386, 2002.

A. S. Kim, S. Bhattacharjee, and M. Elimelech. Shear-induced reorganization of deformable molecular assemblages: Monte carlo studies. *Langmuir*, 17(2):552–561, 2001.

N. Metropolis, A. W. Rosenbluth, M. N. Rosenbluth, A. H. Teller, and E. Teller. Equation of state calculations by fast computing machines. *J. Chem. Phys.*, 21(6):1087–1092, 1953.

F. Mosteller. *Fifty Challenging Problems in Probability with Solutions*. Dover Publications, New York, 1965.

S. Northrup and J. McCammon. Simulation methods for protein structure fluctuations. *Biopolymers*, 19(5):1001–1016, 1980.

C. Pangali, M. Rao, and B. J. Berne. On a novel Monte Carlo scheme for simulating water and aqueous solutions. *Chem. Phys. Lett.*, 55(3):413–417, 1978.

F. Reif. *Fundamentals of Statistical and Thermal Physics*. McGraw-Hill, New York, 1965.

M. Rosenbluth and A. Rosenbluth. Monte carlo calculation of the average extension of molecular chains. *J. Chem. Phys.*, 23(2):356–359, 1955.

P. J. Rossky, J. Doll, and H. Friedman. Brownian dynamics as smart Monte Carlo simulation. *J. Chem. Phys.*, 69(10):4628–4633, 1978.

J. Siepmann and D. Frenkel. Configurational bias monte carlo: a new sampling scheme for flexible chains. *Mol. Phys.*, 75(1):59 – 70, 1992.

2

Monte-Carlo Simulation of a Multi-Dimensional Switch-Like Model of Stem Cell Differentiation

M. Andrecut
*Institute for Space Imaging Science,
Department of Physics and Astronomy,
University of Calgary, Alberta, T2N 1N4
Canada*

1. Introduction

The process controlling the diferentiation of stem, or progenitor, cells into one specific functional direction is called lineage specification. An important characteristic of this process is the multi-lineage priming, which requires the simultaneous expression of lineage-specific genes. Prior to commitment to a certain lineage, it has been observed that these genes exhibit intermediate values of their expression levels. Multi-lineage differentiation has been reported for various progenitor cells (Akashi et al., 2003; Graf, 2002; Hu et al., 1997; Kim et al., 2005; Loose & Patient, 2006; Miyamoto et al., 2002; Patient et al., 2007; Swiers et al., 2006), and it has been explained through the bifurcation of a metastable state (Chickarmane et al., 2009; Huang et al., 2007; Roeder & Glauche, 2006). During the differentiation process the dynamics of the core regulatory network follows a bifurcation, where the metastable state, corresponding to the progenitor cell, is destabilized and the system is forced to choose between the possible developmental alternatives. While this approach gives a reasonable interpretation of the cell fate decision process, it fails to explain the multi-lineage priming characteristic. Here, we describe a new multi-dimensional switch-like model that captures both the process of cell fate decision and the phenomenon of multi-lineage priming. We show that in the symmetrical interaction case, the system exhibits a new type of degenerate bifurcation, characterized by a critical hyperplane, containing an infinite number of critical steady states. This critical hyperplane may be interpreted as the support for the multi-lineage priming states of the progenitor. Also, the cell fate decision (the multi-stability and switching behavior) can be explained by a symmetry breaking in the parameter space of this critical hyperplane. These analytical results are confirmed by Monte-Carlo simulations of the corresponding chemical master equations.

2. Stem cell differentiation

The processes describing the interactions in systems like transcriptional regulatory networks are extremely complex. Genes can be turned on or off by the binding of proteins to regulatory sites on the genome (Ozbundak et al., 2002; Ptashne & Gann, 2002). The proteins are known as transcription factors, while the DNA-binding sites are known as promoters. Transcription factors can regulate the production of other transcription factors, or they can regulate their

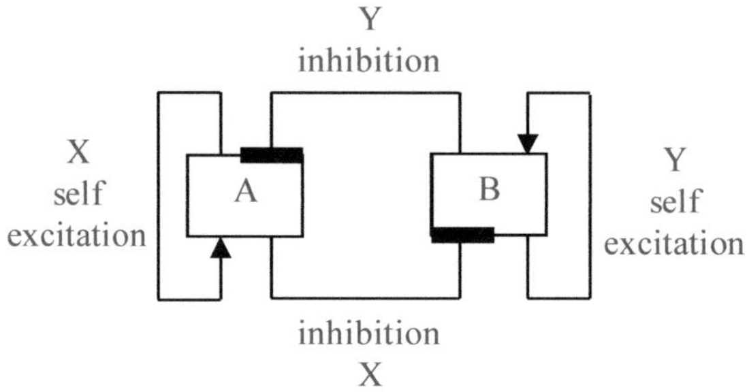

Fig. 1. The architecture of the self-excitation and inhibition mechanisms in the binary cell fate decision circuit.

own production. The transcription process can be described by a sequence of reactions, in which RNA polymerase (R) binds to a gene's promoter leading to the transcription of a complete messenger RNA molecule. The genetic information transcribed into messenger RNA molecules is then translated into proteins by ribosomes. Thus, the general assumption is that the genes can be excited or inhibited by the products of the other genes in the network, generating complex behavior like multi-stability and switching between different steady state attractors. Based on these general assumptions, it has been shown that a simple gene regulatory circuit (Fig. 1) in which two transcription factors, X and Y, inhibit each other, and in the same time activate themselves, can be used as a model of binary cell fate decision in multipotent stem or progenitor cells (Chickarmane et al., 2009; Huang et al., 2007; Roeder & Glauche, 2006). This circuit can generate multistability and explains the symmetric precursor state, in which both factors are present in the cell at equal (low) amounts. This circuit typically produces three stable *attractor* states that correspond to observable cell states. The state 1, with the expression pattern $X \gg Y$, and the state 2, with the opposite pattern $Y \gg X$ represent the cell fates, while the state 3, with a balanced expression $X \simeq Y$ represents the undecided multipotent state. This simple model provides a conceptual framework for understanding cell fate decisions, and it will be used as a starting point in the development of our model.

3. Monte-Carlo simulation approach

The Monte-Carlo simulation approach employed here is based on the well known Gillespie algorithm (Gillespie, 1977), which is a variety of a dynamic Monte Carlo method. The traditional continuous and deterministic description of biochemical rate equations, modeled as a set of coupled ordinary differential equations, relies on bulk reactions that require the interactions of millions of molecules. In contrast, the Gillespie stochastic algorithm simulates every reaction explicitly, and calculates the time evolution of the system by determining the probabilities of each discrete chemical reaction and the resulting changes in the number of each molecular species presented in the system. This algorithm has rigorous theoretical foundations, and gives the exact solution for a system of elementary chemical reactions in the approximation of a well-mixed environment. When simulated, a Gillespie realization represents a random walk that exactly represents the distribution of the chemical master equation. The algorithm is computationally expensive and several modifications have been proposed to speed up computation, including the next reaction method, tau-leaping, as well as hybrid techniques where abundant reactants are modeled with deterministic behavior (Gibson & Bruck, 2000; Rathinam et al., 2003; Slepoy et al., 2008). These adapted techniques

provide a compromise between computational speed and the exactitude of the theory behind the algorithm as it connects to the chemical master equation. Here we use the standard stochastic simulation algorithm, known as the Gillespie's direct method. The rigorous derivation of the algorithm has been given elsewhere and it has been shown to remain "exact" for arbitrary low number of molecules (Gillespie, 1977).
Consider a system composed of N chemical species X_ν $(\nu = 1, ..., N)$, interacting through M reactions R_μ $(\mu = 1, ..., M)$ in the cell volume V. Every chemical reaction R_μ is characterized by its stochastic rate constant k_μ, which depends on the physical properties of the molecules taking part in the reaction. The product $k_\mu dt$ is the probability that one elementary reaction R_μ happens in the next infinitesimal time interval dt. The main steps of the Gillespie algorithm consist of:

(a) calculating the waiting time τ for the next reaction to occur;

(b) determining which reaction μ in the system actually will occur.

These quantities are computed by generating two random numbers according to the following probability density function:

$$P(\tau, \mu) = a_\mu \exp(-a_0 \tau), \tag{1}$$

where

$$a_\mu = m_\mu k_\mu, \tag{2}$$

and

$$a_0 = \sum_{\mu=1}^{M} a_\mu. \tag{3}$$

Here, m_μ is the number of distinct reactant combinations available for the reaction R_μ at the given state of the system. The coefficient a_μ is called the propensity of reaction R_μ. Thus, $P(\tau, \mu)$ is the probability that the next reaction will occur in the infinitesimal time interval dt and that it will be the R_μ reaction. After determination of τ and μ, the numbers of molecules in the system are adjusted according to the reaction R_μ. Also, the time t is advanced to $t + \tau$. The larger the propensity is, the greater is the chance that a given reaction will happen in the next step of the simulation. It is worth noting that there is no constant length for a time-step in the simulation. The length of each time-step is determined independently in every iteration, and takes different values depending on the state of the system.
The implementation of the Gillespie algorithm is straightforward, and one can find excellent descriptions of it in the literature (Adalsteinsson et al., 2004; Kierzek, 2002). Below we give the pseudo-code of the algorithm:

#Gillespie's direct method
1. Set initial numbers of molecules, set time $t \leftarrow 0$;
2. Calculate the propensities, a_μ, for all $\mu = 1, ..., M$;
3. Choose μ with the probability:

$$\Pr(reaction = \mu) = \frac{a_\mu}{\sum_{\mu=1}^{M} a_\mu}; \tag{4}$$

4. Choose τ with the probability:

$$\Pr(time = \tau) = \left(\sum_{\mu=1}^{M} a_\mu\right) \exp\left[-\tau \left(\sum_{\mu=1}^{M} a_\mu\right)\right]; \tag{5}$$

5. Change the number of molecules to reflect execution of reaction μ;
6. Set $t \leftarrow t + \tau$, and go to step 2.

4. 2-Dimensional model

We consider the two gene circuit shown in Figure 1. We will focus on the elementary processes that must occur, such as the promoter binding of the transcription factors X and Y to the promoters, A and B, respectively, and the activation and degradation of transcription factors. Also, we propose a general approach to integrate the two inputs to each gene, which does not depend on the assumption of cooperativity or other explicit modeling. In order to provide a quantitative model of this genetic circuit, we employ a formalism originally developed for the mean-field description of the stochastic interactions in transcriptional regulatory networks (Andrecut & Kauffman, 2006; Andrecut et al., 2008). The promoter binding and unbinding, subsequent self-activation, inhibition, dissociation and the degradation reactions for X, and respectively Y, are:

$$A + R \xrightarrow{k_{AR}} A + R + X \tag{6}$$

$$A + X \xrightarrow{k_{AX}^{+}} AX \tag{7}$$

$$AX \xrightarrow{k_{AX}^{-}} A + X \tag{8}$$

$$AX + R \xrightarrow{k_{X}^{+}} AX + R + X \tag{9}$$

$$A + Y \xrightarrow{k_{AY}^{+}} AY \tag{10}$$

$$AY \xrightarrow{k_{AY}^{-}} A + Y \tag{11}$$

$$X \xrightarrow{k_{X}^{-}} \varnothing \tag{12}$$

$$B + R \xrightarrow{k_{BR}} B + R + Y \tag{13}$$

$$B + Y \xrightarrow{k_{BY}^{+}} BY \tag{14}$$

$$BY \xrightarrow{k_{BY}^{-}} B + Y \tag{15}$$

$$BY + R \xrightarrow{k_{Y}^{+}} BY + R + Y \tag{16}$$

$$B + X \xrightarrow{k_{BX}^{+}} BX \tag{17}$$

$$BX \xrightarrow{k_{BX}^{-}} B + X \tag{18}$$

$$Y \xrightarrow{k_Y^-} \emptyset \tag{19}$$

Here, k_{AX}^+, k_{AX}^-, k_{BY}^+, k_{BY}^-, describe the binding and release rates between the transcription factor and the promoter element, k_{AY}^+, k_{AY}^-, k_{BX}^+, k_{BX}^- correspond to the cross inhibition rates, while k_X^+, k_X^-, k_Y^+, k_Y^- reflect the activation and the degradation rates of the transcription factors. We assume that the role of the first reaction for each transcription factor, Equation 6 and respectively Equation 13, is just to provide a small "basic level of expression" (with the rates k_{AR}, and respectively k_{BR}), in order to avoid their complete extinction. It's effect is equivalent to a positive noise term $\eta_{X,Y}$ in the differential equation describing the dynamics of the transcription factor. Therefore, in the following analysis we will neglect the contribution of this reaction, since it doesn't really have an influence on the "logic functionality" of the circuit. The dynamical behavior (rate of change of active levels of the proteins) of the isolated transcription factors is therefore described by the stochastic differential equations:

$$\frac{d}{dt}[X] = k_X^+[AX] - k_X^-[X] + \eta_X, \tag{20}$$

$$\frac{d}{dt}[Y] = k_Y^+[BY] - k_Y^-[Y] + \eta_Y, \tag{21}$$

where [.] denotes concentration. Assuming that the reversible binding-unbinding processes are in equilibrium, we have:

$$k_{AX}[A][X] = [AX], \tag{22}$$

$$k_{BY}[B][Y] = [BY], \tag{23}$$

$$k_{AY}[A][Y] = [AY], \tag{24}$$

$$k_{BX}[B][X] = [BX], \tag{25}$$

where $k_{AX} = k_{AX}^-/k_{AX}^+$, $k_{BY} = k_{BY}^-/k_{BY}^+$, $k_{AY} = k_{AY}^-/k_{AY}^+$, $k_{BX} = k_{BX}^-/k_{BX}^+$. Also, since the promoters can be in three different states we have:

$$[AX] + [AY] + [A] = [A_0], \tag{26}$$

$$[BY] + [BX] + [B] = [B_0], \tag{27}$$

where $[A_0]$ and $[B_0]$ are the total concentrations of the two promoters. From the above equations, and neglecting the noise terms, we obtain the following system of deterministic differential equations:

$$\frac{d}{dt}x = \alpha x \left(\frac{a_3}{a_1 x + a_2 y + 1} - 1 \right), \tag{28}$$

$$\frac{d}{dt}y = \beta y \left(\frac{b_3}{b_1 x + b_2 y + 1} - 1 \right), \tag{29}$$

where we assumed that: $x = [X]$, $y = [Y]$, $\alpha = k_X^-$, $\beta = k_Y^-$, $a_1 = k_{AX}$, $b_1 = k_{BX}$, $a_2 = k_{AY}$, $b_2 = k_{BY}$, $a_3 = [A_0]k_{AX}k_X^+/k_X^-$, $b_3 = [B_0]k_{BY}k_Y^+/k_Y^-$.
We are interested in the symmetrical case, where $\alpha = \beta$, $a_1 = b_2$, $a_2 = b_1$, $a_3 = b_3$, such that the system becomes:

$$\frac{d}{dt}x = \alpha x \left(\frac{a_3}{a_1 x + a_2 y + 1} - 1 \right), \tag{30}$$

$$\frac{d}{dt}y = \alpha y \left(\frac{a_3}{a_2 x + a_1 y + 1} - 1 \right). \tag{31}$$

The steady states of the above differential system of equations are given by the solutions of the non-linear system:

$$\frac{d}{dt}x = 0 \Leftrightarrow F(x, y, \alpha, \{a\}) = \alpha x \left(\frac{a_3}{a_1 x + a_2 y + 1} - 1 \right) = 0, \tag{32}$$

$$\frac{d}{dt}y = 0 \Leftrightarrow G(x, y, \alpha, \{a\}) = \alpha y \left(\frac{a_3}{a_2 x + a_1 y + 1} - 1 \right) = 0. \tag{33}$$

In this case, one can easily verify that the system has four steady states:

$$(x_0, y_0) = (0, 0), \tag{34}$$

$$(x_1, y_1) = \left(\frac{a_3 - 1}{a_1}, 0 \right), \tag{35}$$

$$(x_2, y_2) = \left(0, \frac{a_3 - 1}{a_1} \right), \tag{36}$$

$$(x_3, y_3) = \frac{1}{a_1 + a_2} \left(a_3 - 1, a_3 - 1 \right), \tag{37}$$

corresponding to the extinction, exclusive and coexistence equilibria. These fixed points are positively defined if $a_3 > 1$.
In order to evaluate the local stability we calculate the eigenvalues, λ and μ, of the Jacobian matrix at these steady states:

$$J(x, y, \alpha, \{a\}) = \begin{bmatrix} \frac{\partial F}{\partial x} & \frac{\partial F}{\partial y} \\ \frac{\partial G}{\partial x} & \frac{\partial G}{\partial y} \end{bmatrix} = \alpha \begin{bmatrix} \frac{a_3(a_2 y+1)}{(a_1 x+a_2 y+1)^2} - 1 & -\frac{a_3 a_2 x}{(a_1 x+a_2 y+1)^2} \\ -\frac{a_3 a_2 y}{(a_2 x+a_1 y+1)^2} & \frac{a_3(a_2 x+1)}{(a_2 x+a_1 y+1)^2} - 1 \end{bmatrix}. \tag{38}$$

The eigenvalues of the Jacobian for the extinction state (x_0, y_0) are:

$$\lambda = \alpha(a_3 - 1) > 0, \tag{39}$$

$$\mu = \alpha(a_3 - 1) > 0. \tag{40}$$

Thus, this steady state is always unstable, since $a_3 > 1$. The eigenvalues for the exclusive steady states, (x_1, y_1) and (x_2, y_2), are:

$$\lambda = -\alpha \frac{a_3 - 1}{a_3}, \tag{41}$$

$$\mu = -\alpha \frac{(a_3 - 1)(a_2 - a_1)}{a_1 + a_2(a_3 - 1)}, \tag{42}$$

and respectively:

$$\lambda = -\alpha \frac{(a_3 - 1)(a_2 - a_1)}{a_1 + a_2(a_3 - 1)}, \tag{43}$$

$$\mu = -\alpha \frac{a_3 - 1}{a_3}. \tag{44}$$

Therefore, the exclusive equilibria are stable if $a_2 > a_1$, and unstable if $a_2 < a_1$. In contrast, the eigenvalues for the coexistence equilibrium (x_3, y_3) are:

$$\lambda = -\alpha \frac{(a_3 - 1)(a_1 + a_2)}{a_3(a_1 + a_2)}, \tag{45}$$

$$\mu = -\alpha \frac{(a_3 - 1)(a_1 - a_2)}{a_3(a_1 + a_2)}. \tag{46}$$

Since $\lambda < 0$, this steady state is stable if $\mu < 0$, and it looses stability if $\mu > 0$. One can easily see that the stability condition, $\mu < 0$, is equivalent to $a_2 < a_1$. Thus, a change in the ratio $\rho = a_1/a_2$, triggers a bifurcation from one stable steady state (x_3, y_3), when $\rho < 1$, to two stable steady states (x_1, y_1) and (x_2, y_2), when $\rho > 1$.

In Fig. 2 and Fig. 3 we give the results of the Monte-Carlo simulations. The initial concentrations and the main reaction constants are set as: $R = 100$, $A_0 = B_0 = 1$, $X_0 = Y_0 = 0$, $k_X^- = k_Y^- = 0.01$, $k_A = k_B = 0.01$, $k_X^+ = k_Y^+ = 0.01$, $k_{AX}^+ = k_{BY}^+ = 1$, $k_{AY}^+ = k_{BX}^+ = 1$. Fig. 2 gives the trajectories $x(t) = X(t)/R$ and $y(t) = Y(t)/R$ for $\rho < 1$, when there is one noisy attractor, corresponding to the coexistence equilibrium, (x_3, y_3) (Fig. 2(a)), and for $\rho > 1$, when there are two noisy attractors, corresponding to the exclusive equilibria, (x_1, y_1) and (x_2, y_2) (Fig. 2(b)). Also, in Fig. 3 we have represented graphically the probability density distribution, $P(x, y)$, of the transcription factors (obtained by averaging over $M = 10^4$ trajectories with $T = 10^7$ reactions events). One can see that for $\rho < 1$, the system has only one noisy attractor, corresponding to the stable fixed point (x_3, y_3) (Fig. 3(a), $a_1 = 1$, $a_2 = 2$), while for $\rho > 1$, the system exhibits two noisy attractors corresponding to the stable fixed points (x_1, y_1), and respectively (x_2, y_2) (Fig. 3(b), $a_1 = 2$, $a_2 = 1$). We should note that the absolute values of the rate constants do not play a critical role in the simulation, as long as their ratios satisfy the bifurcation constraints.

An important case of the above analysis corresponds to the critical bifurcation parameter $\rho = 1$. In this case the system has the form:

$$\frac{d}{dt}x = \alpha x \Phi(x, y, \{a\}), \tag{47}$$

$$\frac{d}{dt}y = \alpha y \Phi(x, y, \{a\}), \tag{48}$$

where

$$\Phi(x, y, \{a\}) = \frac{a_3}{a_1(x + y) + 1} - 1. \tag{49}$$

One can easily verify that in this case, the exclusive and coexistence equilibria disappear, and the system has an infinite number of steady states $\Omega = \{(x, y) \in \mathbb{R}^2 | \Phi(x, y, \{a\}) = 0\}$, which are practically equivalent to the positive segment of the linear equation: $x + y = (a_3 - 1)/a_1$. These steady states have the following eigenvalues:

$$\lambda = 0, \tag{50}$$

$$\mu = -(a_3 - 1)/a_3 < 0. \tag{51}$$

Therefore, the steady states Ω are stable, and the system undergoes a degenerate bifurcation (see Appendix). This situation is presented in Fig. 2(c) and Fig. 3(c), for $a_1 = a_2 = 1$. One can see that the stochastic system is "undecided", exploring every point of the critical line with non-zero probability. The line is attracting, except along itself, that is, there is no "longitudinal" force on this line. Therefore every state on it is indifferently stable. Thus, the critical line becomes an ergodic attractor.

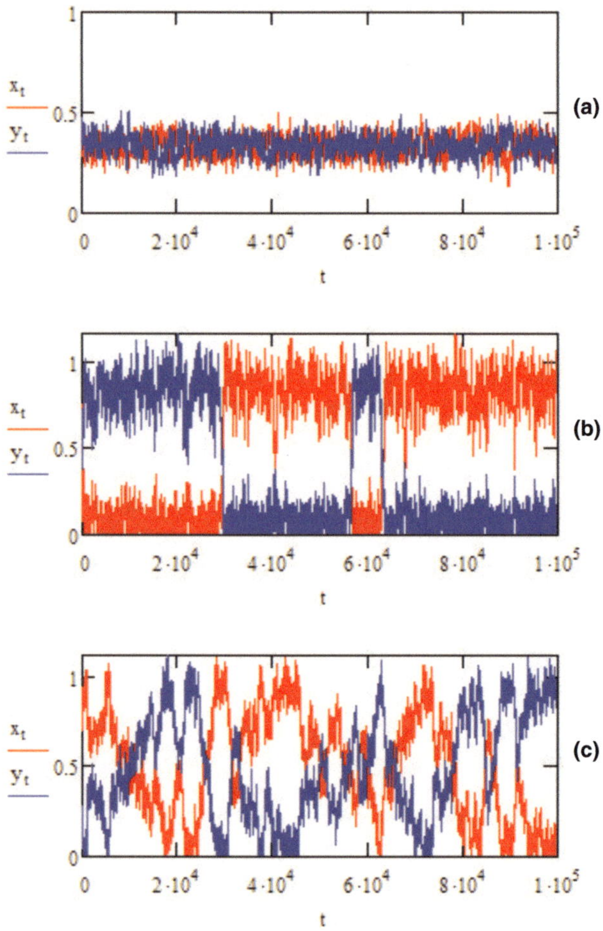

Fig. 2. Monte-Carlo simulation of the 2-dimensional circuit: (a) $\rho < 1$, one attractor ($k^-_{AX} = k^-_{BY} = 0.5$ and $k^-_{AY} = k^-_{BX} = 1$); (b) $\rho > 1$, two attractors ($k^-_{AX} = k^-_{BY} = 1$ and $k^-_{AY} = k^-_{BX} = 0.5$); (c) $\rho = 1$, the critical case of the degenerate bifurcation ($k^-_{AX} = k^-_{BY} = k^-_{AY} = k^-_{BX} = 1$).

5. *N*-Dimensional model

We consider a $N-$gene circuit, where we denote by X_n the transcription factors and by A_n the promoters, $n = 1, ..., N$. For each gene we assume the following set of equations:

$$A_n + R \xrightarrow{k_n} A_n + R + X_n \tag{52}$$

$$A_n + X_m \xrightarrow{k^+_{nm}} A_n X_m \tag{53}$$

$$A_n X_m \xrightarrow{k^-_{nm}} A_n + X_m \tag{54}$$

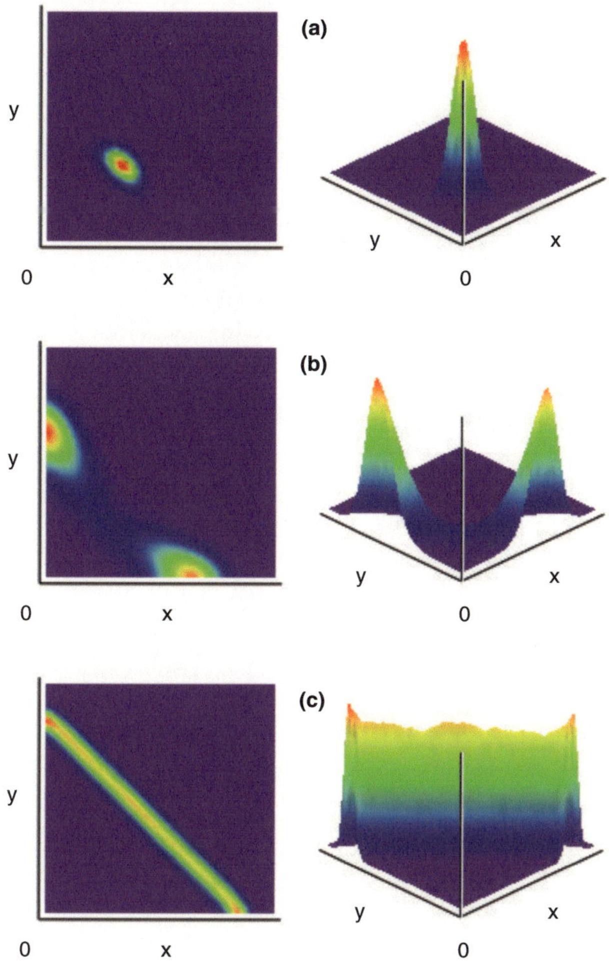

Fig. 3. The probability density distribution, $P(x, y)$, of the stochastic trajectory of the 2-dimensional circuit: (a) $\rho < 1$, one attractor; (b) $\rho > 1$, two attractors; (c) $\rho = 1$, the critical case of the degenerate bifurcation.

$$A_n X_n + R \xrightarrow{k_n^+} A_n X_n + R + X_n \tag{55}$$

$$X_n \xrightarrow{k_n^-} \varnothing \tag{56}$$

Thus, the promoter A_n can bind to any of the N transcription factors. Therefore, the dynamical behavior of the transcription factors is described by the following system of stochastic differential equations:

$$\frac{d}{dt}[X_n] = k_n^+ [A_n X_n] - k_n^- [X_n] + \eta_{X_n}, \quad n = 1, ..., N, \tag{57}$$

where η_{X_n} is the noise term corresponding to the first reaction (52). Assuming that the reversible binding-unbinding processes are in equilibrium, we have:

$$k_{nm}[A_n][X_m] = [A_nX_m], \quad n,m = 1,...,N, \tag{58}$$

where $k_{nm} = k^-_{nm}/k^+_{nm}$. Also, since the promoters can be in $N+1$ different states we have:

$$\sum_{m=1}^{N} [A_nX_m] + [A_n] = [A^0_n], \quad n = 1,...,M. \tag{59}$$

where $[A^0_n]$ are the total concentrations of the promoters. From the above equations, and neglecting the noise terms, we obtain the following system of deterministic differential equations:

$$\frac{d}{dt}x_n = \alpha_n x_n \left(\frac{\beta_n k_{nn}}{\sum_{m=1}^{N} k_{nm}x_m + 1} - 1 \right), \quad n = 1,...,N. \tag{60}$$

where we assumed that: $x = [X_n]$, $\alpha_n = k^-_n$, $\beta_n = [A^0_n]k^+_n/k^-_n$.
Let us consider now the symmetric case:

$$\frac{d}{dt}x_n = F_n(x_1,...,x_N,\alpha,\beta,\kappa,\gamma) = \alpha x_n \left(\frac{\beta\kappa}{\kappa x_n + \gamma \sum_{m\neq n} x_m + 1} - 1 \right), \quad n = 1,...,N, \tag{61}$$

where $\kappa = k_{nn}$ and $\gamma = k_{nm}$ for $m \neq n = 1,...,N$. The steady states corresponds to the solutions of the nonlinear system:

$$\frac{d}{dt}x_n = 0 \Leftrightarrow F_n(x_1,...,x_N,\alpha,\beta,\kappa,\gamma) = 0, \quad n = 1,...,N. \tag{62}$$

There are $N+2$ steady states:

$$\left(x_1^{(0)},...,x_N^{(0)}\right) = (0,...,0), \tag{63}$$

$$\left(x_1^{(i)},...,x_n^{(i)},...,x_N^{(i)}\right) = \left(0,...,\frac{\beta\kappa - 1}{\kappa},...0\right), \quad i = 1,...,N, \tag{64}$$

$$\left(x_1^{(N+1)},...,x_N^{(N+1)}\right) = \left(\frac{\beta\kappa - 1}{\kappa + (N-1)\gamma},...,\frac{\beta\kappa - 1}{\kappa + (N-1)\gamma}\right). \tag{65}$$

Again, these states correspond to extinction, $N-$exclusive and coexisting equilibria, and they are positively defined if $\beta\kappa > 1$. The stability of these states can be analyzed using the eigenvalues of the Jacobian matrix:

$$J(x_1,...,x_N,\alpha,\beta,\kappa,\gamma) = \left[\frac{\partial}{\partial x_i}F_n(x_1,...,x_N,\alpha,\beta,\kappa,\gamma)\right]_{n,i=1,...,N}, \tag{66}$$

where

$$\frac{\partial}{\partial x_i}F_n = \begin{cases} \frac{\alpha\beta\kappa\left(\gamma\sum_{m\neq n} x_m + 1\right)}{\left(\kappa x_n + \gamma\sum_{m\neq n} x_m + 1\right)^2} - \alpha \; if \; n = i \\ -\frac{\alpha\beta\kappa\gamma x_n}{\left(\kappa x_n + \gamma\sum_{m\neq n} x_m + 1\right)^2} \quad if \; n \neq i \end{cases}. \tag{67}$$

The eigenvalues of the extinction state are:

$$\lambda_n = \alpha\left(\beta\kappa - 1\right), \quad n = 1,...,N, \tag{68}$$

which means that this steady state is always unstable, since $\beta\kappa > 1$. For the exclusive equilibria the eigenvalues are:

$$\lambda_n = \begin{cases} -\frac{\alpha(\beta\kappa-1)}{\beta\kappa} & if\ n = i \\ -\frac{\alpha(\beta\kappa-1)(\gamma-\kappa)}{\gamma(\beta\kappa-1)+\kappa} & if\ n \neq i \end{cases}, \quad n = 1, ..., N. \tag{69}$$

Therefore, these states become stable if $\gamma > \kappa$, and unstable if $\gamma < \kappa$. In the case of coexisting equilibrium the Jacobian is given by:

$$\frac{\partial}{\partial x_i} F_n = \begin{cases} \frac{\alpha(1-\beta\kappa)}{\beta[\kappa+(N-1)\gamma]} & if\ n = i \\ -\frac{\alpha\gamma(\beta\kappa-1)}{\beta k[\kappa+(N-1)\gamma]} & if\ n \neq i \end{cases}, \tag{70}$$

and it has the following eigenvalues:

$$\lambda_n = \begin{cases} -\frac{\alpha(\beta\kappa-1)}{\beta\kappa} & if\ n = i \\ -\frac{\alpha(\beta\kappa-1)(\kappa-\gamma)}{\beta k[\kappa+(N-1)\gamma]} & if\ n \neq i \end{cases}, \quad n = 1, ..., N. \tag{71}$$

Thus, this state becomes stable if $\gamma < \kappa$, and unstable if $\gamma > \kappa$.
In the critical case, $\kappa = \gamma$, the steady state equations are degenerated and we have again an infinite number of steady states, all of them satisfying the critical hyperplane equation:

$$\sum_{n=1}^{N} x_n = \frac{\beta\kappa - 1}{\kappa}. \tag{72}$$

In this critical case the Jacobian takes the simplified form:

$$\frac{\partial}{\partial x_i} F_n = -\frac{\alpha}{\beta} x_n, \tag{73}$$

and it has the following eigenvalues:

$$\lambda_n = \begin{cases} -\frac{\alpha(\beta\kappa-1)}{\beta\kappa} & if\ n = i \\ 0 & if\ n \neq i \end{cases}, \quad n = 1, ..., N. \tag{74}$$

Thus, one eigenvalue is always negative, since $\beta\kappa > 1$, and the other $N - 1$ eigenvalues are zero. Therefore, the hyperplane containing the infinite number of steady states is attractive and marginally stable.
In Fig. 4 we give the simulation results for a circuit consisting of three genes, $N = 3$. The initial concentrations are set as $R = 150$, $A_1 = A_2 = A_3 = 1$, $X_1 = X_2 = X_3 = 0$. The rate constants are the same as for the 2-dimensional circuit. Fig. 4 gives the trajectories $x_n(t)$ for $\gamma < \kappa$, when there is one noisy attractor, corresponding to the coexistence equilibrium, $(x_1^{(3)}, x_2^{(3)}, x_3^{(3)})$ (Fig. 4(a)), and for $\gamma > \kappa$, when there are three noisy attractors, corresponding to the exclusive equilibria, $(x_1^{(1)}, x_2^{(1)}, x_3^{(1)}) = \left(\frac{\beta\kappa-1}{\kappa}, 0, 0\right)$, $(x_1^{(2)}, x_2^{(2)}, x_3^{(2)}) = \left(0, \frac{\beta\kappa-1}{\kappa}, 0\right)$ and $(x_1^{(3)}, x_2^{(3)}, x_3^{(3)}) = \left(0, 0, \frac{\beta\kappa-1}{\kappa}\right)$ (Fig. 4(b)), and in the degenerate case when the plane $x_1 + x_2 + x_3 = \frac{\beta\kappa-1}{\kappa}$ is the ergodic attractor (Fig. 4(c)).

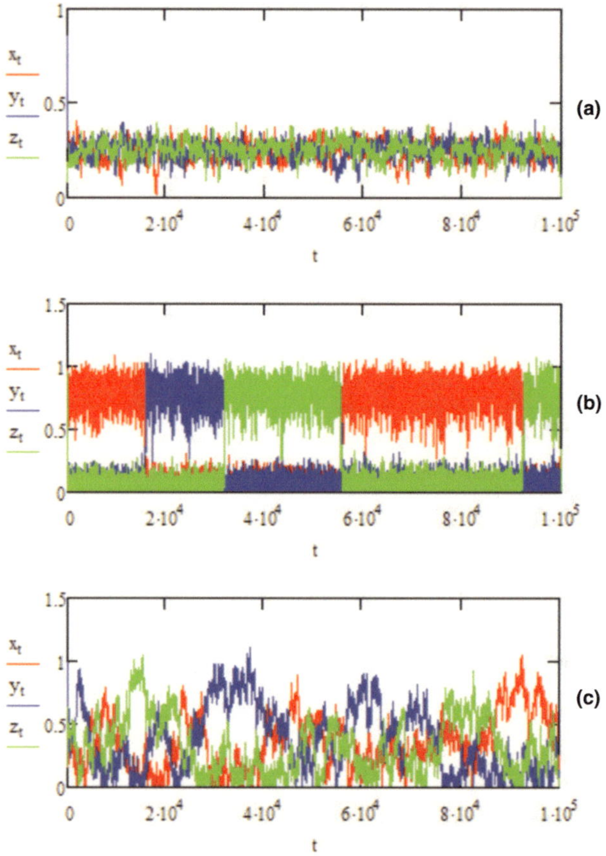

Fig. 4. Monte-Carlo simulation of the 3-dimensional circuit: (a) $\gamma < \kappa$, one attractor; (b) $\gamma > \kappa$, three attractors; (c) $\gamma = \kappa$, the critical case of the degenerate bifurcation.

6. Conclusion

We have presented a new multi-dimensional switch-like model that captures both the process of cell fate decision and the phenomenon of multi-lineage priming. The previous attempts to model the coexistence of three discrete stable states are based on a complicated molecular interaction mechanisms, requiring cooperativity or additional transcription factors (Chickarmane et al., 2009; Huang et al., 2007; Roeder & Glauche, 2006). Here, we have shown that very elementary cross-inhibition between two genes and independent autoactivation can give rise to multistability without cooperativity. It is important to note the obvious fact that the real molecular mechanisms that govern the dynamics of this gene regulatory circuit are by orders of magnitudes more complex, involving perhaps thousands of steps not accounted for in the presented model. However, this simplified description is still able to capture to qualitative cell fate decision behavior, specifically, the existence of an indeterminate multi-potent progenitor state with equal levels of transcription factors, and the generation of stable attractor states with asymmetric expression patterns. Also, we have shown that in the symmetrical interaction case, the system exhibits a new type of degenerate bifurcation, characterized by a critical hyperplane containing an infinite number of critical steady states.

This degeneration of the central attractor state captures the intrinsic heterogeneity of the undecided multipotent state allowing individual cells to a range of states, and may be interpreted as the support for the multi-lineage priming states of the progenitor. Also, the cell fate decision (the multi-stability and switching behavior) can be explained by a symmetry breaking in the parameter space of this critical hyperplane. It is important to note here that the critical hyperplane is also ergodic. Thus, in the critical regime, any stochastic trajectory of the system will be attracted to the critical hyperplane. Also, in this case, the dynamics will become confined to this region, such that the system will visit all the points of the critical hyperplane with non-zero probability (the priming phenomenon). However, any perturbation of this critical hyperplane will force the system to collapse in one of its non-trivial stable steady states (the cell fate decision process).

7. Appendix: Degenerate steady state bifurcation

We consider a 2-dimensional system of stochastic differential equations (SDE), of the following generic form:

$$(S)\ \begin{cases} \dot{x} = \alpha(\bar{x} - x)\Phi(x,y,\{\gamma\})f(x,y,\{a\}) + \eta_x \\ \dot{y} = \beta(\bar{y} - y)\Phi(x,y,\{\gamma\})g(x,y,\{b\}) + \eta_y \end{cases}, \tag{75}$$

where $\Phi, f, g : \mathbb{R}^2 \rightarrow \mathbb{R}$, $x, y, \bar{x}, \bar{y}, \alpha, \beta, \{\gamma\}, \{a\}, \{b\} \in \mathbb{R}$, and η_x, η_y correspond to additive noise terms. Also, we denote by $\Omega = \{(x,y) \in \mathbb{R}^2 | \Phi(x,y,\{\gamma\}) = 0\}$ the set of solutions of the equation $\Phi = 0$, and we assume that: $f(x,y,\{a\}) \neq 0$ and $g(x,y,\{b\}) \neq 0$, for any $(x,y) \in \mathbb{R}^2$.
Theorem 1: The SDE system (S) exhibits a degenerate bifurcation, $(\bar{x},\bar{y}) \rightarrow \widetilde{\Omega} \subset \Omega$, from one steady state $(\bar{x},\bar{y})$ to a subset of steady states $\widetilde{\Omega} \subset \Omega$, if:

$$\max\{-\alpha\Phi(\bar{x},\bar{y},\{\gamma\})f(\bar{x},\bar{y},\{a\}), -\beta\Phi(\bar{x},\bar{y},\{\gamma\})g(\bar{x},\bar{y},\{b\}\} > 0, \tag{76}$$

and

$$\nabla_v\Phi(x,y,\{\gamma\}) = \langle v, \nabla\Phi(x,y,\{\gamma\})\rangle < 0, \tag{77}$$

for any $(x,y) \in \widetilde{\Omega}$ and

$$v = [\alpha(\bar{x} - x)f(x,y,\{a\}), \beta(\bar{y} - y)g(x,y,\{b\})]^T. \tag{78}$$

Proof: A first steady state of the system (S) is $(\bar{x},\bar{y})$. Also the system has an infinite number of steady states Ω, corresponding to the solutions of the equation $\Phi(x,y,\{\gamma\}) = 0$. The stability of the steady states can be analyzed using the eigenvalues, λ_0 and λ_1, of the Jacobian matrix J, which are given by the solutions of the equation $|J - \lambda I| = 0$, where I is the identity matrix. In general, the eigenvalues are complex numbers, and the distance between the solution of the system and thesteady state changes at an exponential rate, given by the real part of the eigenvalue. For simplicity the following discussion is restricted to real eigenvalues, though steady states with complex eigenvalues have similar properties based on the value of the real part of the eigenvalue. A negative eigenvalue implies that the solution approaches the steady state along the corresponding eigenvector, while a positive eigenvalue implies that the solution moves away from the steady state along the eigenvector. In a 2-dimensional system there are three possible cases. A stable steady state has two negative eigenvalues, and hence attracts all the solutions in a surrounding region. An unstable steady state has two positive eigenvalues and all the solutions in its neighborhood move away from it. A saddle point has one negative and one positive eigenvalue. Now let us analyze the stability of the steady states of the system. The eigenvalues of the Jacobian for $(\bar{x}, \bar{y})$ are:

$$\begin{cases} \lambda_0 = -\alpha f(\bar{x}, \bar{y}, \{a\})\Phi(\bar{x}, \bar{y}, \{\gamma\}) \\ \lambda_1 = -\beta g(\bar{x}, \bar{y}, \{b\})\Phi(\bar{x}, \bar{y}, \{\gamma\}) \end{cases}. \tag{79}$$

Thus, this steady state is stable if $\lambda_0, \lambda_1 < 0$, and it looses stability if $\lambda_0 > 0$ or $\lambda_1 > 0$, which is equivalent to the condition imposed by the Equation 76. The other steady states $(x, y) \in \Omega$, have the following eigenvalues:

$$\begin{cases} \lambda_0 = 0 \\ \lambda_1 = \alpha(\bar{x} - x) f \frac{\partial \Phi}{\partial x} + \beta(\bar{y} - y) g \frac{\partial \Phi}{\partial y} \end{cases}, \tag{80}$$

and they are degenerated, since they have at least one zero eigenvalue. Also, these degenerate steady states become stable for $\lambda_1 < 0$. Since $\lambda_1 = \langle v, \nabla \Phi \rangle = \nabla_v \Phi$, this stability condition is equivalent to the condition imposed by the Equation 77, which requires that the derivative of Φ in direction v must be negative. The directional derivative of a manifold Φ along a vector v at a given point (x, y), intuitively represents the instantaneous rate of change of the manifold, moving through (x, y), in the direction of v. One can easily verify that in this case, v is the eigenvector of the Jacobian corresponding to the eigenvalue λ_1, that is we have: $Jv = \lambda_1 v$. Thus, any change in the parameters $\{\gamma\}$, such that the stable steady state $(\bar{x}, \bar{y})$ becomes unstable, and the steady states $\widetilde{\Omega} = \{(x, y) \in \Omega | \nabla_v \Phi(x, y, \{\gamma\}) < 0\}$ become stable, results in a degenerate bifurcation of the dynamics of the stochastic system (S).
A similar property can be formulated for stochastic discrete maps (SDM) of the following generic form:

$$(M) \begin{cases} x_{t+1} = (x_t - \bar{x})[1 - \alpha \Phi(x_t, y_t, \{\gamma\}) f(x_t, y_t, \{a\})] + \bar{x} + \eta_x \\ y_{t+1} = (y_t - \bar{y})[1 - \beta \Phi(x_t, y_t, \{\gamma\}) g(x_t, y_t, \{b\})] + \bar{y} + \eta_y \end{cases}, \tag{81}$$

where $\Phi, f, g : \mathbb{R}^2 \to \mathbb{R}$, $x_t, y_t, \bar{x}, \bar{y}, \alpha, \beta, \{\gamma\}, \{a\}, \{b\} \in \mathbb{R}$, and η_x, η_y correspond to additive noise terms. We denote by $\Omega = \{(x, y) \in \mathbb{R}^2 | \Phi(x, y, \{\gamma\}) = 0\}$ the set of solutions of the equation $\Phi = 0$. Also, we assume that: $f(x, y, \{a\}) \neq 0$ and $g(x, y, \{b\}) \neq 0$, for any $(x, y) \in \mathbb{R}^2$.
Theorem 2: The SDM system (M) exhibits a degenerate steady state bifurcation, $(\bar{x}, \bar{y}) \to \widetilde{\Omega} \subset \Omega$, from one steady state $(\bar{x}, \bar{y})$ to a subset of steady states $\widetilde{\Omega} \subset \Omega$, if:

$$\max\{|1 - \alpha \Phi(\bar{x}, \bar{y}, \{\gamma\}) f(\bar{x}, \bar{y}, \{a\})|, |1 - \beta \Phi(\bar{x}, \bar{y}, \{\gamma\}) g(\bar{x}, \bar{y}, \{b\})|\} > 1, \tag{82}$$

and

$$|1 - \nabla_v \Phi(x, y, \{\gamma\})| < 1, \tag{83}$$

for any $(x, y) \in \widetilde{\Omega}$ and

$$v = [\alpha(x - \bar{x}) f(x, y, \{a\}), \beta(y - \bar{y}) g(x, y, \{b\})]^T. \tag{84}$$

Proof: The steady states of the map (P) are $(\bar{x}, \bar{y})$, and the set Ω, corresponding to the solutions of the equation $\Phi(x, y, \{\gamma\}) = 0$. As before, the eigenvalues, λ_0 and λ_1, are given by the equation $|J - \lambda I| = 0$, where J is the Jacobian of the discrete map (P). In the case of discrete maps, a stable steady state is characterized by $|\lambda_0| < 1$ and $|\lambda_1| < 1$, while an unstable steady state is characterized by $|\lambda_0| > 1$ or $|\lambda_1| > 1$. The eigenvalues of the Jacobian for $(\bar{x}, \bar{y})$ are:

$$\begin{cases} \lambda_0 = 1 - \alpha\Phi(\bar{x}, \bar{y}, \{\gamma\})f(\bar{x}, \bar{y}, \{a\}) \\ \lambda_1 = 1 - \beta\Phi(\bar{x}, \bar{y}, \{\gamma\})g(\bar{x}, \bar{y}, \{b\}) \end{cases} . \tag{85}$$

Thus, this steady state is stable if $|\lambda_0| < 1$ and $|\lambda_1| < 1$, and it becomes unstable if $|\lambda_0| > 1$ or $|\lambda_1| > 1$, which is equivalent to the condition imposed by the Equation 82. The other steady states Ω, have the following eigenvalues:

$$\begin{cases} \lambda_0 = 1 \\ \lambda_1 = 1 - \alpha(x - \bar{x})f\frac{\partial\Phi}{\partial x} - \beta(y - \bar{y})g\frac{\partial\Phi}{\partial y} \end{cases} , \tag{86}$$

and they are degenerated, since they have at least one eigenvalue equal to one. These degenerate steady states become stable for $|\lambda_1| < 1$, which is equivalent to the condition imposed by the Equation 83. Also, one can verify that v is the eigenvector of the Jacobian, corresponding to the eigenvalue λ_1. Thus, any change in the parameters $\{\gamma\}$, such that the stable steady state $(\bar{x}, \bar{y})$ becomes unstable, and the steady states $\widetilde{\Omega} = \{(x, y) \in \Omega |\, |1 - \nabla_v\Phi(x, y, \{\gamma\})| < 1\}$ become stable, results in a degenerate bifurcation of the dynamics of the stochastic discrete map (M).

8. References

Adalsteinsson, D., McMillen, D. & Elston, T. C. (2004). Biochemical network stochastic simulator (BioNetS): software for stochastic modeling of biochemical networks. *BMC Bioinformatics*: 5, 1471-2105.

Akashi, K., He, X., Chen, J., Iwasaki, H., Niu, C., Steenhard, B., Zhang, J., Haug, J. & Li, L. (2003). Transcriptional accessibility for genes of multiple tissues and hematopoietic lineages is hierarchically controlled during early hematopoiesis. *Blood*: 101, 383-389

Andrecut, M. & Kauffman, S.A. (2006). Mean-field model of genetic regulatory networks. *New Journal of Physics*: 8, 148.

Andrecut, M., Cloud, D. & Kauffman, S. A. (2008). Monte Carlo simulation of a simple gene network yields new evolutionary insights. *Journal of Theoretical Biology*: 250(3), 468-474.

Chickarmane, V., Enver, T. & Peterson, C. (2009). Computational modeling of the hematopoietic erythroid-myeloid switch reveals insights into cooperativity, priming, and irreversibility. *Plos Computational Biology*: 5(1), e1000268.

Cross, M. A. & Enver, T. (1997). The lineage commitment of hematopoietic progenitor cells. *Current Opinion in Genetics & Development*: 7, 609-613.

Gibson, M. A. & Bruck, J. (2000). Efficient Exact Stochastic Simulation of Chemical Systems with Many Species and Many Channels. *Journal of Physical Chemistry*: A 104, 1876-1889.

Gillespie, D.T. (1977). Exact stochastic simulation of coupled chemical reactions. *Journal of Physical Chemistry*: 81, 2340-2361.

Graf, T. (2002). Differentiation plasticity of hematopoietic cells. *Blood*: 99, 3089-3101.

Hu, M., Krause, D., Greaves, M., Sharkis, S., Dexter, M., Heyworth, C. & Enver, T. (1997). Multilineage gene expression precedes commitment in the hematopoietic system. *Genes & Development*: 11, 774-785.

Huang, S., Guo, T-P, May, G. & Enver, T. (2007). Bifurcation dynamics in lineagecommitment in bipotent progenitor cells. *Developmental Biology*: 305, 695-713.
Kim, C.F., Jackson, E.L., Woolfenden, A.E., Lawrence, S., Babar, I., Vogel, S., Crowley, D., Bronson, R.T. & Jacks, T. (2005). Identification of bronchioalveolar stem cells in normal lung and lung cancer. *Cell*: 121, 823-835.
Kierzek, A. (2002). STOCKS: STOChastic kinetic simulations of biochemical systems with Gillespie algorithm. *Bioinformatics*: 18, 470-481.
Loose, M. & Patient, R. (2006). Global genetic regulatory networks controlling hematopoietic cell fates. *Current Opinion in Hematology*: 13, 229-236.
Miyamoto, T., Iwasaki, H., Reizis, B., Ye, M., Graf, T., Weissman, I. L. & Akashi, K. (2002). Myeloid or lymphoid promiscuity as a critical step in hematopoietic lineage commitment. *Developmental Cell*: 3, 137-147.
Ozbundak, E. M., Thattai, M., Kurtser, I., Grossman, A. D. & van Oudenaarden, A. (2002). Regulation of noise in the expression of a single gene. *Nature Genetics*: 31, 69-73.
Patient, R., Swiers, G. & Loose, M. (2007). Transcriptional networks regulating hematopoietic cell fate decisions. *Current Opinion in Hematology*: 14, 307-314.
Ptashne, M. & Gann, A. (2002). *Genes and signals*. Cold Spring Harbor Laboratory Press, New York.
Rathinam, M., Petzold, L. R., Cao, Y. & Gillespie, D. T. (2003). Stiffness in stochastic chemically reacting systems: The implicit tau-leaping method. *Journal of Chemical Physics*: 119 (24), 12784-12794.
Roeder, I. & Glauche, I. (2006). Towards an understanding of lineage specification in hematopoietic stem cells: a mathematical model for the interaction of transcription factors GATA-1 and PU.1. *Journal of Theoretical Biology*: 241, 852-865.
Slepoy, A., Thompson, A. P. & Plimpton, S. J. (2008). A constant-time kinetic Monte Carlo algorithm for simulation of large biochemical reaction networks. *Journal of Chemical Physics*: 128 (20), 205101.
Swiers, G., Patient, R. & Loose, M. (2006). Genetic regulatory networks programming hematopoietic stem cells and erythroid lineage specification. *Developmental Biology*: 294, 525-540.

Application of Monte Carlo Simulation and Voxel Models to Internal Dosimetry

Sakae Kinase, Akram Mohammadi and Masa Takahashi
Japan Atomic Energy Agency
Japan

1. Introduction

There has been a considerable accumulation of usage of voxel models for internal radiation dosimetry (Xu & Eckerman, 2009 ; Zaidi & Tsui, 2009). The human voxel models of the Reference Male and Reference Female have been introduced and used to evaluate the energy deposition in organs resulting from internal radiation exposures by the International Commission on Radiological Protection (ICRP) (ICRP, 2009). Inter-comparisons on Monte Carlo modeling for *in vivo* measurements of radionuclides in knee and torso voxel models were undertaken to upgrade dosimetry programmes in EU (Gomez-Ros, *et al.*, 2008; Gualdrini & Ferrari 2008). At the Japan Atomic Energy Agency (JAEA), several studies have been conducted on the use of voxel models for internal dosimetry (Kinase, *et al.*, 2003; 2004; 2007a; 2007b; 2008a; 2008b; 2009a; 2009b; Mohammadi & Kinase; Takahashi, *et al.*). Specific absorbed fractions (SAFs) and S values have been evaluated for preclinical assessments of radiopharmaceuticals using human voxel models and a mouse voxel model. Computational calibration of *in vivo* measurement system has been also made using Japanese and Caucasian voxel models, the knee and torso voxel models. In addition, for radiation protection of the environment, absorbed fractions (AFs) have been evaluated using a frog voxel model. Each study has been made by using Monte Carlo simulations. These data by Monte Carlo simulations and voxel models could adequately reproduce those by measurements. Voxel models are significant tools for internal dosimetry since the models are anatomically realistic.

2. Voxel models

The voxel models are based on actual image data obtained from computed tomography, magnetic resonance imaging and cryosections. Hence, the shape of the voxel models is more realistic than for the stylized models such as the Medical Internal Radiation Dose (MIRD) mathematical model (Cristy & Eckerman, 1987). The voxels of tissue are grouped together to form appropriate organ volumes. Every voxel belongs to organ/tissue which is assigned a unique identification number and appropriate attenuation properties which are assumed to be uniform in all voxels within the organ/tissue.

Several voxel models have been used for internal dosimetry at JAEA: the Japanese adult male human "Otoko"(Saito, *et al.*, 2001), the Japanese adult female human "Onago"(Saito, *et al.*, 2008), the Caucasian adult male human "MAX06"(Kramer, *et al.*, 2006), the Caucasian adult female human "FAX06"(Kramer, *et al.*, 2006), ICRP/ICRU reference adult male human "RCP-AM"(ICRP, 2009, Hadid, *et al.*, 2010), the male mouse "Digimouse"(Dogdas, *et al.*, 2007), and the frog (Kinase, 2008b; 2009b). The frog voxel model, shown in Figure 1, was developed for radiation protection of the environment. The GSF child female human "Child"(Veit, *et al.*, 1989)and the MIRD-type voxel models were used for validation of Monte Carlo simulations. In addition, the knee and torso voxel models were used in the inter-comparisons on Monte Carlo modeling for *in vivo* measurements of radionuclides. Table 1 shows the characteristics of the voxel models used at JAEA.

Fig. 1. Image of the frog voxel model.

Name	Image	Organization
Otoko	CT	JAEA
Onago	CT	JAEA
MAX06	CT	Federal University of Pernambuco
FAX06	CT	Federal University of Pernambuco
RCP-AM	CT	ICRP/ICRU
Digimouse	Micro-CT and color cryosection	University of Southern California
frog	Cryosection	JAEA
Child	CT	Helmholtz Zentrum München
MIRD-type	Combinatorial geometry	JAEA
knee	CT	EURADOS/CIEMAT
Livermore torso	CT	EURADOS/IRSN

Table 1. Voxel models with their characteristic.

3. Monte Carlo codes

Two Electron Gamma Shower (EGS) version 4 (Nelson, *et al.*, 1985) user codes were developed for internal dosimetry: the UCSAF (Kinase, *et al.* 2003) and UCWBC codes (Kinase, *et al.* 2007b) . Although the EGS4 code is very popular as a general purpose package for Monte Carlo simulation of the coupled transport of electrons and photons in an arbitrary geometry for particles with energies above a few keV up to several TeV, users have to write complicated geometries such as voxel models in an extended FORTRAN language known as Mortran. It is hard for users to write the geometries accurately. Hence, the UCSAF and UCWBC codes have been developed as packages of subroutines plus model data, and prevents users from writing geometries in Mortran. The UCSAF code is used for evaluations of organ doses from internal radiation exposures, particularly SAF evaluations. The UCWBC code allows accurate *in vivo* measurements of radionuclides in human body. In the UCWBC code, specifications of modeling are also made using the combinatorial geometry (CG) method. Rayleigh scattering, Doppler broadening in Compton scattering, linearly polarized photon scattering and electron impact ionization are included by means of options. The cross–section data for photons are taken from PHOTX (RSIC,1989), and the data for electrons and positrons are taken from ICRU report 37 (ICRU, 1984). The paremeter reduced electron-step transport algorithm (PRESTA) is used to improve the electron transport in the low-energy region.

4. AFs, SAFs, S values and calibration factors

4.1 Absorbed fractions (AFs) and specific absorbed fractions (SAFs)

The absorbed fraction (AF) is the fraction of the energy emitted by source organ that is absorbed in target organ. The AF is a key quantity for evaluating internal organ doses. AFs in organisms from internal sources are evaluated for the protection of the environment.

From the viewpoint of kidney toxicity, self-irradiation AFs for photons and electrons in the kidneys were evaluated for the Otoko, Onago, MAX06, FAX06, RCP-AM, Digimouse and frog voxel models using the UCSAF code. The self-irradiation AFs were calculated by using the energy emitted from the kidneys and energy deposited within the kidneys. Table 2 compares the masses of the kidneys of the voxel models. The sources of photons and electrons were assumed to be monoenergetic in the energy range 10 keV to 4 MeV, uniformly distributed in the kidneys of the voxel models. Photon and electron histories were run at numbers sufficient to reduce statistical uncertainties below 5 %. The transport of photons and electrons had been followed until their energies fell below energy cutoffs of 1 keV for photons and 10 keV for electrons.

To examine suborgan dosimetry for the kidneys, self-irradiation AFs were evaluated for photons and electrons in the kidneys of the RCP-AM voxel model. Since the RCP-AM voxel model has a multiregion model of the kidney that consists of cortex, medulla and pelvis, it allow evaluations of regional kidney doses not previously conducted by the current single-region models. The sources of photons and electrons were assumed to be monoenergetic in the energy range 10 keV to 10 MeV, uniformly distributed in the kidneys of the RCP-AM voxel models.

In addition, to evaluate the interspecies scaling of organ doses from mouse to human, the self-irradiation AFs in the kidneys of the Digimouse voxel model were compared with those of the Otoko voxel model. Interspecies scaling of organ doses is of scientific and practical interest in the evaluation of new radiopharmaceuticals. The interspecies scaling factors were obtained from the ratio of the self-irradiation AFs for the Otoko voxel model to those for the Digimouse voxel model. In the MIRD Pamphlet No. 11, it is noted that the self-irradiation dose from photons with energies above 100 keV appears to be proportional to -2/3 power of the organ mass. Hence, the interspecies scaling factors for photons were corrected by the cube root of the organ masses. The interspecies scaling factors for photons and electrons can be expressed in equations in the form

$$(\text{Scaling factor})_{\text{Photon}} = \frac{AF_{\text{human}}}{AF_{\text{mouse}}\left(\dfrac{m_{\text{human}}}{m_{\text{mouse}}}\right)^{\frac{1}{3}}} \quad (1)$$

and

$$(\text{Scaling factor})_{\text{Electron}} = \frac{AF_{\text{human}}}{AF_{\text{mouse}}}, \quad (2)$$

where m is the organ mass.
Self-irradiation specific absorbed fractions (SAFs) for the kidneys in the Child and MIRD-type voxel models were evaluated for validation of Monte Carlo simulations. The self-irradiation SAF was derived as the AF in the kidneys per unit mass of the kidneys.

Name	Kidneys (kg)
Otoko	2.7×10^{-1}
Onago	2.6×10^{-1}
MAX06	3.1×10^{-1}
FAX06	2.8×10^{-1}
RCP-AM	3.1×10^{-1}
left, cortex	1.1×10^{-1}
left, medulla	3.8×10^{-2}
left, pelvis	7.6×10^{-3}
right, cortex	1.1×10^{-1}
right, medulla	3.9×10^{-2}
right, pelvis	7.9×10^{-3}
Digimouse	5.1×10^{-4}
frog	2.2×10^{-4}

Table 2. The kidney masses for the voxel models.

4.2 S values

S value ($\mu Gy/MBq\cdot s$) is mean absorbed dose to a target organ per unit cumulated activity in the source organ. S values are essential for absorbed dose evaluations in the MIRD system.

Nuclides	E_{max} (MeV)	E_{mean} (MeV)
^{18}F	0.634	0.250
^{90}Y	2.281	0.934

Table 3. Maximum E_{max} and mean E_{mean} energies of the beta-rays for ^{18}F and ^{90}Y.

Self-irradiation S values to the kidneys from uniformly distributed beta-ray emitters within the kidneys were evaluated for the Otoko, Onago, MAX06, FAX06, RCP-AM, Digimouse and frog voxel models. The beta-ray emitters were ^{18}F and ^{90}Y of potential interest in the kidney dosimetry. Table 3 shows the maximum and mean energies for ^{18}F and ^{90}Y. To evaluate the self-irradiation S values, the total energies deposited in the kidneys per source particles were calculated using the UCSAF code.

4.3 *In vivo* measurements

Whole-body counters are commonly used in radiation protection to identify unintended intakes of radioactive material and assess the radiation exposure to the individual. Calibration methods of whole-body counters using Monte Carlo simulations and voxel models are of considerable practical significance in order to obtain calibration data such as counting efficiencies applicable to a given subject.

Counting efficiencies of a whole-body counter installed at JAEA were evaluated for the Otoko and MAX06 voxel models by the UCWBC code. Figure 2 shows the geometry of the simulation model of the JAEA whole-body counter and MAX06 voxel model. The model was accurately constructed to represent the actual whole-body counter, which has three p-type closed-ended coaxial high purity germanium (HPGe) semiconductor detectors. The crystal of the detector is 73.2 mm in diameter and 85.8 mm in length. The apparent dead layer thickness on the outer surface of the Ge semi-conductor crystal is 0.9 mm. The peak efficiency, relative to that of a 76.2 mm diameter×76.2 mm thick NaI(Tl) crystal, is 80 %, measured for 1,332 keV photons from a source of ^{60}Co at 250 mm. The whole-body counter has a shielding that consists of a room with 2,500 (height) ×2,000 (width) ×2,500 (length) mm^3 internal dimensions and a 200 mm thick wall of steel. The inner side of the room is lined with 3 mm of lead, 1mm of copper and faced plastic wall. The counting efficiencies were evaluated by dividing the number of photons that deposited all initial energy in the detectors, by the number of simulated histories. The photon sources were assumed to be isotropic, and to be homogeneously distributed within the voxel models.

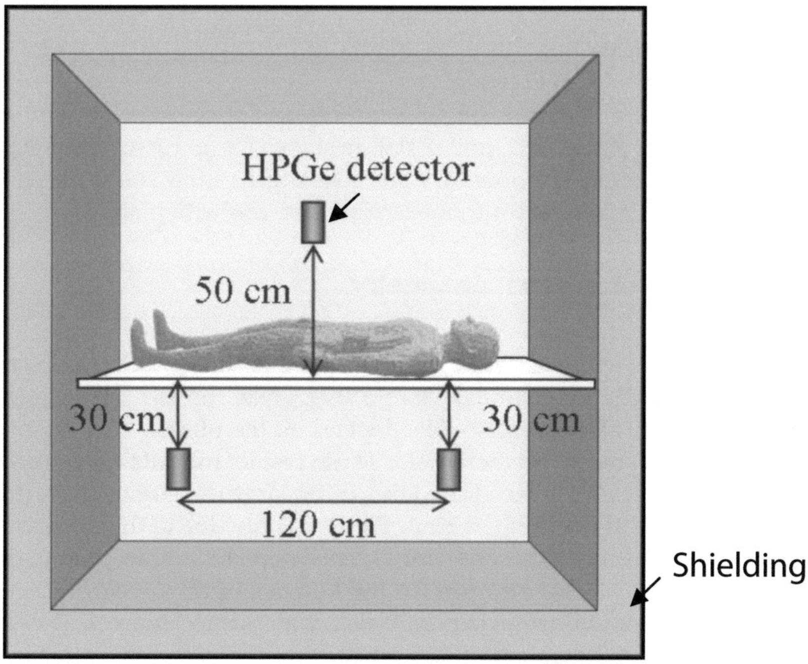

Fig. 2. Geometric model of the whole-body counter and the MAX06 voxel model.

In addition, counting efficiencies of the whole-body counter were evaluated for heterogeneous distributions of radionuclides, ^{137}Cs in the MAX06 voxel model. The radionuclide distributions were derived from the biokinetic models provided by the ICRP. The biokinetic models include transfer of the intake radionuclides from inhalation to excretion. Radioactivities differing with time in compartments that indicate separated organs are expressed as first-order kinetics. A single intake of ^{137}Cs by inhalation was assumed. The absorption types for the respiratory tract organs were assumed to be type F for ^{137}Cs. The Activity Median Aerodynamic Diameter (AMAD) was 5 µm. To assess the influence of radionuclide distributions within the MAX06 voxel model on whole-body counting, the counting efficiencies for heterogenous distributions were compared with those for homogenous distributions.

4.4 Inter-comparison on *in vivo* measurements

In recent years, two inter-comparisons on *in vivo* measurements have been conducted in EU. The "International comparison on Monte Carlo modeling for *in vivo* measurement of Americium in a knee phantom" was organized within the EU Coordinated Action CONRAD (Coordinated Network for Radiation Dosimetry) as a joint initiative of EURADOS working groups 6 and 7. The "International comparison on Monte Carlo modelling for *in vivo* measurement of Enriched Uranium in the lungs of a Livermore phantom" has been carried out as an EURADOS working groups 6 and 7 joint collaboration.

Response function of a detection system consisting of a pair of Low Energy (LE) Ge semi-conductor detectors was evaluated for ^{241}Am in the knee voxel model by the UCWBC code. A ^{241}Am source was assumed to be homogeneously distributed in the bone of the knee voxel model. Each LE Ge detector contains a germanium crystal 70mm in diameter and 25mm in thickness. An entrance window made of carbon fibre and epoxy resin of thickness 0.6mm is separated from the Ge crystal by a 5mm vacuum gap. The response function was folded with Gaussian distributions, since the effects of fluctuation in the signal of the detector are not considered in the UCWBC code.

Response functions of the four LE Ge semi-conductor detector system were evaluated for enriched uranium (^{234}U, ^{235}U and ^{238}U) in lungs of a torso voxel model, namely the Livermore voxel model. Two tasks were challenged: lung counting simulations with the torso voxel model without extra-thoracic plate and one with plate.

5. Applications for internal dosimetry

5.1 AFs

Figure 3 shows the self-irradiation AFs for photons in the kidneys of the Otoko, Onago, MAX06, FAX06, RCP-AM, Digimouse and frog voxel models in the energy range from 10 keV to 4 MeV. The self-irradiation AFs depend on the photon energy and decrease with an increase in photon energy on the whole. These results indicate that the self-irradiation AFs for the Digimouse and frog voxel models exhibit large deviations from those for the human voxel models in the high-energy region. This is mainly due to the different shape and size of the kidneys. The self-irradiation AFs for kidneys depend on the organ mass.

The self-irradiation AFs for electrons in the kidneys of the Otoko, Onago, MAX06, FAX06, RCP-AM, Digimouse and frog voxel models are shown in Figure 4. These finding leads to a conclusion that the self-irradiation AFs for the voxel models are almost unity in the electron energy range from 10 keV to 100 keV and that the self-irradiation AFs for the Digimouse and frog voxel models are inconsistent with those for the human voxel models in the higher energy region. The apparent inconsistency is attributed to the different size of the kidneys. The electrons with energy 4 MeV (csda range 2.0 g/cm^2) are not always absorbed within the kidneys of the Digimouse and frog voxel models.

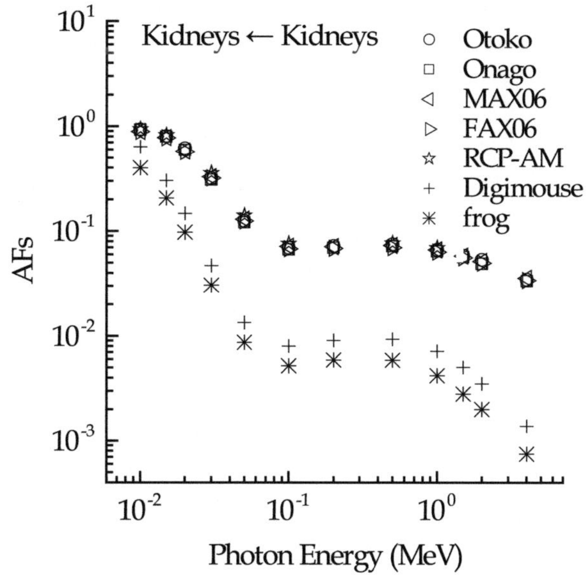

Fig. 3. Self-irradiation AFs for the >Kidneys in the Otoko, Onago, MAX06, FAX06, RCP-AM, Digimouse and frog voxel models in the photon energy 10keV-4MeV.

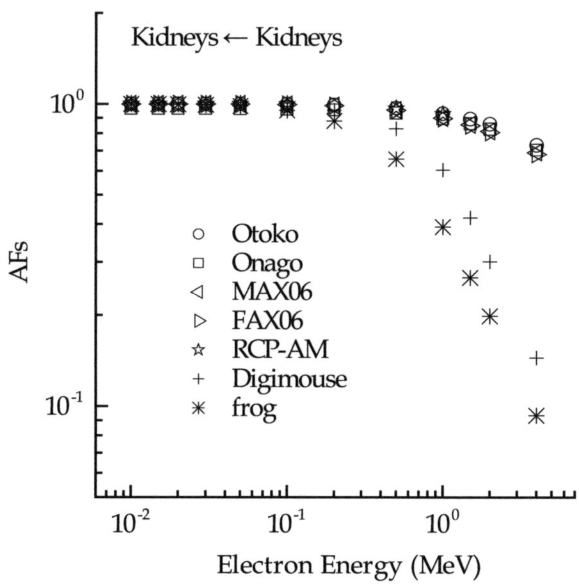

Fig. 4. Self-irradiation AFs in the Kidneys for the Otoko, Onago, MAX06, FAX06, RCP-AM, Digimouse and frog voxel models in the electron energy 10keV-4MeV.

The self-irradiation AFs in the regional kidney of the RCP-AM voxel model are listed in Tables 4 and 5. The self-irradiation AFs for photons decrease with an increase in energy. The self-irradiation AFs for electrons remain unchanged up to around 1 MeV, above which they decrease abruptly. This result is consistent with the self-irradiation AFs in the whole kidneys. The self-irradiation AFs for electrons up to around 1 MeV are in accord with the ratio of the mass of the regional kidney to the mass of the whole kidneys. The self-irradiation AFs for photons and electrons in the left kidney are lower than those in the right kidney. As mentioned in the previous studies, this is due to the different size of each kidney.

Energy (MeV)	left, cortex	left, medulla	left, pelvis	right, cortex	right, medulla	right, pelvis
0.01	3.2×10^{-1}	1.2×10^{-1}	2.4×10^{-2}	3.3×10^{-1}	1.3×10^{-1}	2.5×10^{-2}
0.015	2.7×10^{-1}	1.1×10^{-1}	2.3×10^{-2}	2.8×10^{-1}	1.2×10^{-1}	2.4×10^{-2}
0.03	1.1×10^{-1}	5.1×10^{-2}	1.1×10^{-2}	1.2×10^{-1}	5.3×10^{-2}	1.1×10^{-2}
0.05	4.4×10^{-2}	2.0×10^{-2}	4.0×10^{-3}	4.7×10^{-2}	2.1×10^{-2}	4.4×10^{-3}
0.06	3.4×10^{-2}	1.5×10^{-2}	3.1×10^{-3}	3.6×10^{-2}	1.6×10^{-2}	3.4×10^{-3}
0.08	2.6×10^{-2}	1.2×10^{-2}	2.4×10^{-3}	2.8×10^{-2}	1.2×10^{-2}	2.6×10^{-3}
0.1	2.4×10^{-2}	1.1×10^{-2}	2.2×10^{-3}	2.6×10^{-2}	1.1×10^{-2}	2.4×10^{-3}
0.3	2.4×10^{-2}	1.1×10^{-2}	2.2×10^{-3}	2.6×10^{-2}	1.1×10^{-2}	2.4×10^{-3}
0.5	2.4×10^{-2}	1.1×10^{-2}	2.2×10^{-3}	2.6×10^{-2}	1.1×10^{-2}	2.4×10^{-3}
0.8	2.3×10^{-2}	1.0×10^{-2}	2.1×10^{-3}	2.4×10^{-2}	1.1×10^{-2}	2.3×10^{-3}
1	2.2×10^{-2}	9.8×10^{-3}	2.0×10^{-3}	2.3×10^{-2}	1.0×10^{-2}	2.2×10^{-3}
3	1.4×10^{-2}	6.3×10^{-3}	1.3×10^{-3}	1.5×10^{-2}	6.7×10^{-3}	1.4×10^{-3}
6	8.8×10^{-3}	4.0×10^{-3}	8.3×10^{-4}	9.6×10^{-3}	4.2×10^{-3}	9.1×10^{-4}
8	7.1×10^{-3}	3.1×10^{-3}	6.5×10^{-4}	7.7×10^{-3}	3.3×10^{-3}	7.1×10^{-4}
10	6.0×10^{-3}	2.6×10^{-3}	5.3×10^{-4}	6.5×10^{-3}	2.7×10^{-3}	5.8×10^{-4}

Table 4. Self-irradiation AFs for photons in the kidneys of the RCP-AM voxel models.

Energy (MeV)	left, cortex	left, medulla	left, pelvis	right, cortex	right, medulla	right, pelvis
0.01	3.5×10^{-1}	1.2×10^{-1}	2.5×10^{-2}	3.5×10^{-1}	1.3×10^{-1}	2.5×10^{-2}
0.015	3.5×10^{-1}	1.2×10^{-1}	2.5×10^{-2}	3.5×10^{-1}	1.3×10^{-1}	2.5×10^{-2}
0.03	3.5×10^{-1}	1.2×10^{-1}	2.5×10^{-2}	3.5×10^{-1}	1.3×10^{-1}	2.5×10^{-2}
0.05	3.5×10^{-1}	1.2×10^{-1}	2.5×10^{-2}	3.5×10^{-1}	1.3×10^{-1}	2.5×10^{-2}
0.06	3.4×10^{-1}	1.2×10^{-1}	2.5×10^{-2}	3.5×10^{-1}	1.3×10^{-1}	2.5×10^{-2}
0.08	3.4×10^{-1}	1.2×10^{-1}	2.5×10^{-2}	3.5×10^{-1}	1.3×10^{-1}	2.5×10^{-2}
0.1	3.4×10^{-1}	1.2×10^{-1}	2.5×10^{-2}	3.5×10^{-1}	1.3×10^{-1}	2.5×10^{-2}
0.3	3.4×10^{-1}	1.2×10^{-1}	2.5×10^{-2}	3.5×10^{-1}	1.3×10^{-1}	2.5×10^{-2}
0.5	3.3×10^{-1}	1.2×10^{-1}	2.4×10^{-2}	3.4×10^{-1}	1.3×10^{-1}	2.5×10^{-2}
0.8	3.2×10^{-1}	1.2×10^{-1}	2.4×10^{-2}	3.3×10^{-1}	1.3×10^{-1}	2.5×10^{-2}
1	3.1×10^{-1}	1.2×10^{-1}	2.4×10^{-2}	3.2×10^{-1}	1.3×10^{-1}	2.5×10^{-2}
3	2.5×10^{-1}	1.1×10^{-1}	2.2×10^{-2}	2.6×10^{-1}	1.2×10^{-1}	2.4×10^{-2}
6	1.9×10^{-1}	9.2×10^{-2}	1.9×10^{-2}	2.0×10^{-1}	9.7×10^{-2}	2.1×10^{-2}
8	1.6×10^{-1}	7.7×10^{-2}	1.6×10^{-2}	1.7×10^{-1}	8.1×10^{-2}	1.7×10^{-2}
10	1.4×10^{-1}	6.4×10^{-2}	1.3×10^{-2}	1.5×10^{-1}	6.8×10^{-2}	1.5×10^{-2}

Table 5. Self-irradiation AFs for electrons in the kidneys of the RCP-AM voxel models.

The interspecies scaling factors of self-irradiation doses for the kidneys from the Digimouse voxel model to the Otoko voxel model are plotted against radiation energy in Figure 5. The interspecies scaling factors, which decrease with an increase in organ mass, show energy dependence. The photon scaling factors are close to unity in the energy range from 50 keV to 500 keV. The electron scaling factors are also close to unity in the energy range from 10 keV to 200 keV. The important finding is that the scaling factor for the photon self-irradiation AF, which is corrected by the cube root of the organ mass, shows the similar trend as a function of energy with the scaling factor for the electron self-irradiation AF.

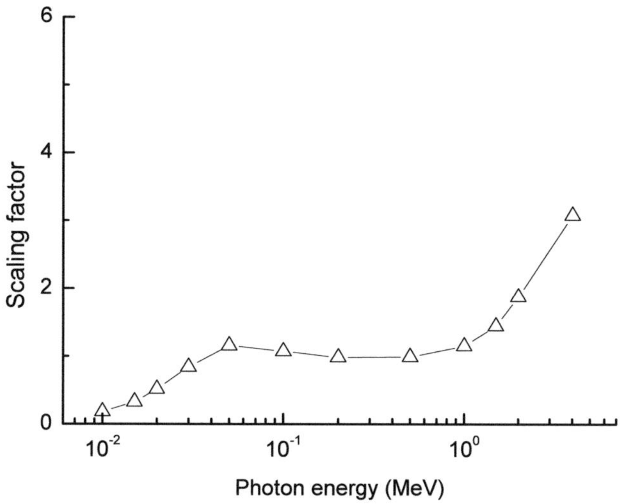

(a) Photon

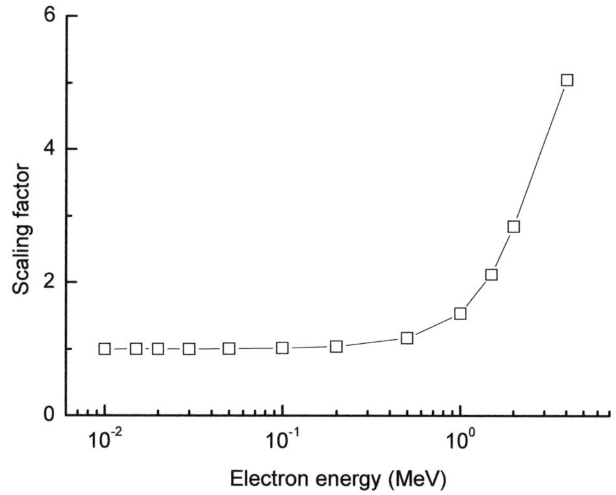

(b) Electron

Fig. 5. Interspecies scaling factors of self-irradiation doses for the kidneys from the Digimouse voxel model to the Otoko voxel model in the energy 10keV-4MeV. (a) Photon, (b) Electron.

5.2 SAFs

The self-irradiation SAFs in the Child voxel model were evaluated by the UCSAF code considering energy deposition due to secondary electrons. Table 6 shows the results in comparison with the SAFs obtained at GSF, in which the kerma approximation -SAFs calculated by considering the energy to be deposited at the point of photon interaction- has been used. The SAFs by the UCSAF code under kerma approximation agree with the GSF data. The statistical uncertainty for the SAF at the worst case was 4.0 %. Consequently, the above results substantiated that the UCSAF code can be used to calculate SAFs. The SAF considering secondary electrons induced by photons is about 0.75 times that by the kerma approximation for photon energy 4 MeV. The discrepancy is due to different energy deposition within the volume of interest due to the removal of energy by the secondary electrons within the kidneys. It may be deduced that SAFs for target tissues that are also the source evaluated by the kerma approximation are appropriate in the photon energy of 10 keV to 1 MeV and not in the photon energy of several MeV.

Self-irradiation SAFs for the kidneys in the MIRD-type voxel models are also shown in Table 6. The SAFs by the UCSAF code are in good agreement with those evaluated in ORNL. The SAFs by the UCSAF code exhibits slightly deviations from the ORNL data in the photon energy above 1 MeV. It is attributable to the treatment of secondary electrons.

Energy (MeV)	Child			MIRD	
	Electron transport	Kerma	GSF Kerma	Electron transport	ORNL Kerma
0.01	4.9	4.9		3.1	3.1
0.015	4.1	4.1		2.7	2.6
0.02	3.1	3.1	3.2	2.0	2.0
0.03	1.6	1.6	1.7	1.1	9.9×10^{-1}
0.05	5.9×10^{-1}	5.9×10^{-1}	6.3×10^{-1}	4.1×10^{-1}	4.0×10^{-1}
0.1	3.3×10^{-1}	3.3×10^{-1}	3.4×10^{-1}	2.3×10^{-1}	2.3×10^{-1}
0.2	3.4×10^{-1}	3.4×10^{-1}	3.4×10^{-1}	2.4×10^{-1}	2.4×10^{-1}
0.5	3.5×10^{-1}	3.6×10^{-1}	3.6×10^{-1}	2.5×10^{-1}	2.5×10^{-1}
1	3.2×10^{-1}	3.3×10^{-1}	3.3×10^{-1}	2.2×10^{-1}	2.3×10^{-1}
1.5	2.8×10^{-1}	3.0×10^{-1}	3.0×10^{-1}	2.0×10^{-1}	2.1×10^{-1}
2	2.5×10^{-1}	2.8×10^{-1}	2.8×10^{-1}	1.7×10^{-1}	2.0×10^{-1}
4	1.7×10^{-1}	2.2×10^{-1}	2.5×10^{-1}	1.2×10^{-1}	1.6×10^{-1}

Table 6. Comparison of self-irradiation SAFs in the kidneys of the Child/MIRD-type voxel models between those evaluated by the UCSAF code and those evaluated in GSF/ORNL.

5.3 S values

Figure 6 shows the self-irradiation S values for the kidneys of the Otoko, Onago, MAX06, FAX06, RCP-AM, Digimouse and frog voxel models, for ^{18}F and ^{90}Y. It can be seen that the self-irradiation S values for the small voxel models are much larger than those for the large voxel models.

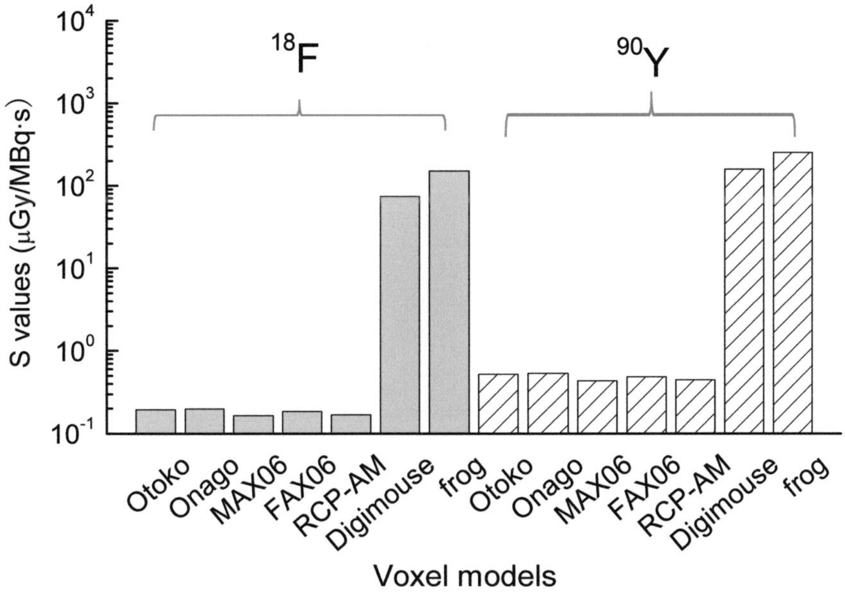

Fig. 6. Self-irradiation S values for ^{18}F and ^{90}Y in the kidneys of the Otoko, Onago, MAX06, FAX06, RCP-AM, Digimouse and frog voxel models.

5.4 Counting efficiencies of a whole-body counter

Figure 7 shows the counting efficiencies of the JAEA whole-body counter for the Otoko and MAX06 voxel models. The counting efficiencies for the Otoko voxel model are slightly larger than those for the MAX06 voxel model over the whole energy range. This is due to geometric differences between the two models.

Table 7 shows the fractions of activity in the organ to total residual amounts in body at 0.5, 3, 10 and 365 days after single intake of ^{137}Cs. The activity of the whole body was defined as sums of those in the blood and total body compartments. At 0.5 days, nasal passage becomes a major source organ because of the entrance compartment for the inhaled material.

Organ	Time after intake (day)			
	0.5	3	10	365
Whole body	68	96	100	100
Nasal passage	32	4		

Table 7. Fractions (%) of ^{137}Cs in organs to total residual amounts.

Figure 8 shows the counting efficiencies for 662 keV photons from ^{137}Cs in the MAX06 voxel model. From the figure, it can be stated that the counting efficiency decreases by 20 % compared with that for the homogenous distribution at 0.5 days after an intake. However, the counting efficiencies do not depend on elapsed times following several days of intake since ^{137}Cs are distributed throughout all organs and tissues of the whole body at 3 days after single intake.

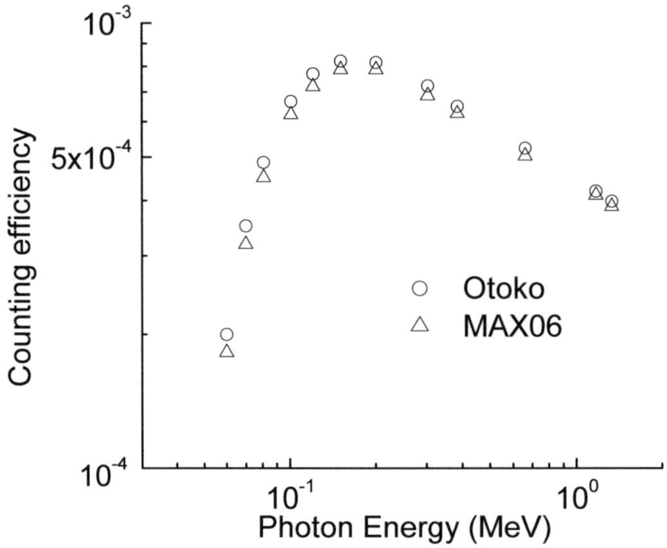

Fig. 7. Comparison of the counting efficiencies for the Otoko voxel model and those for the MAX06 voxel model.

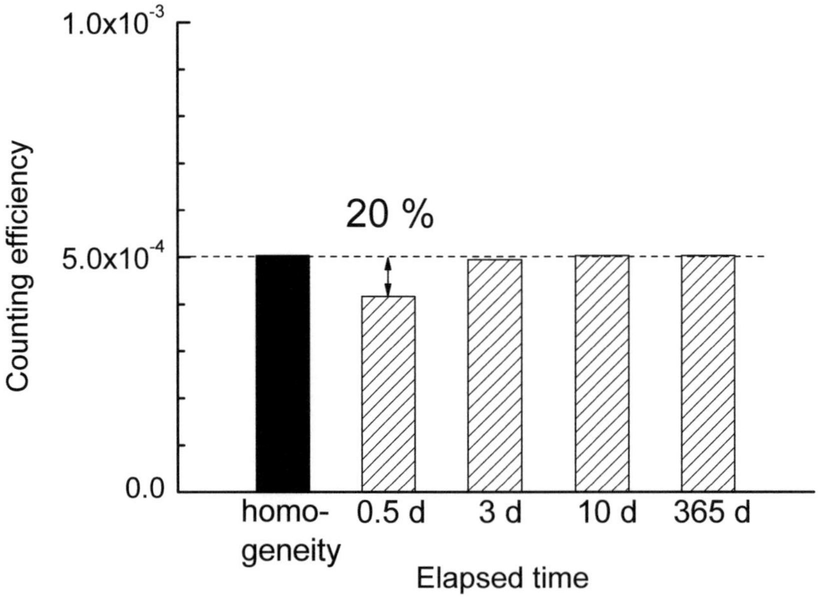

Fig. 8. Counting efficiencies for ^{137}Cs with homogeneous and heterogeneous distributions in the MAX06 voxel model at the elapsed times of 0.5, 3, 10 and 365 days after an intake.

5.5 Inter-comparison

Figure 9 shows calculated and measured response functions of the LE Ge semiconductor detectors for ^{241}Am source in the knee voxel model. These results are consistent with the measurements. It was found that the calculated results represent all important interactions that take place within the LE Ge semiconductor detectors. The response function between the Compton edges (11.3 keV) and the back-scatter peaks (48.2 keV) and X-ray escape peaks (Ge : 11 keV) is reproduced by the calculations. The slight deviation of the calculation from the mesurement in Figure 9 are considered to be due to having no regard for the directional dependence of peak positions in the calculations. From the figures, it can be stated that the calibration data by the UCWBC codes can adequately reproduce those by measurements.

Figure 10 shows calculated response functions of the LE Ge semiconductor detectors for uranium source in the torso voxel model. There is significant difference in the response functions for torso voxel model between with and without plate. The difference is attributed to the attenuations of photons from the lungs in the plate. The response function is reproduced by the calculations.

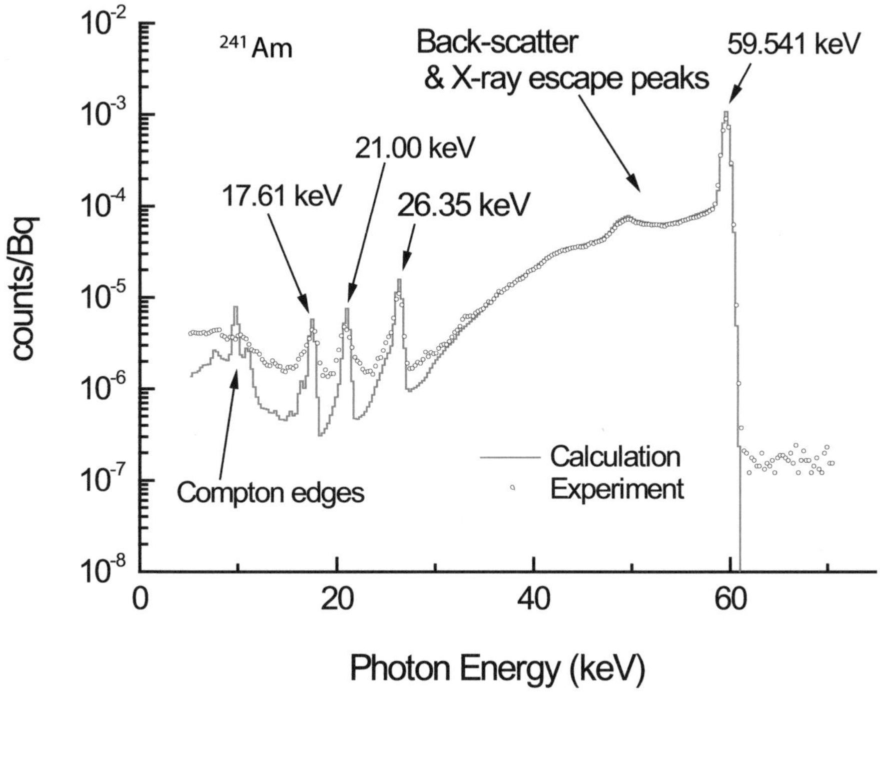

Fig. 9. Comparison of the measured and calculated response functions for the knee voxel model.

6. Conclusion

Monte Carlo simulations and voxel models were found to be significant tools for internal dosimetry. In particular, voxel models were confirmed to be useful for internal organ dose evaluations since they are anatomically realistic. This fact indicates that several studies on correction of the *in vivo* measurement efficiency for the variability of human subjects and interspecies scaling of organ doses will succeed.

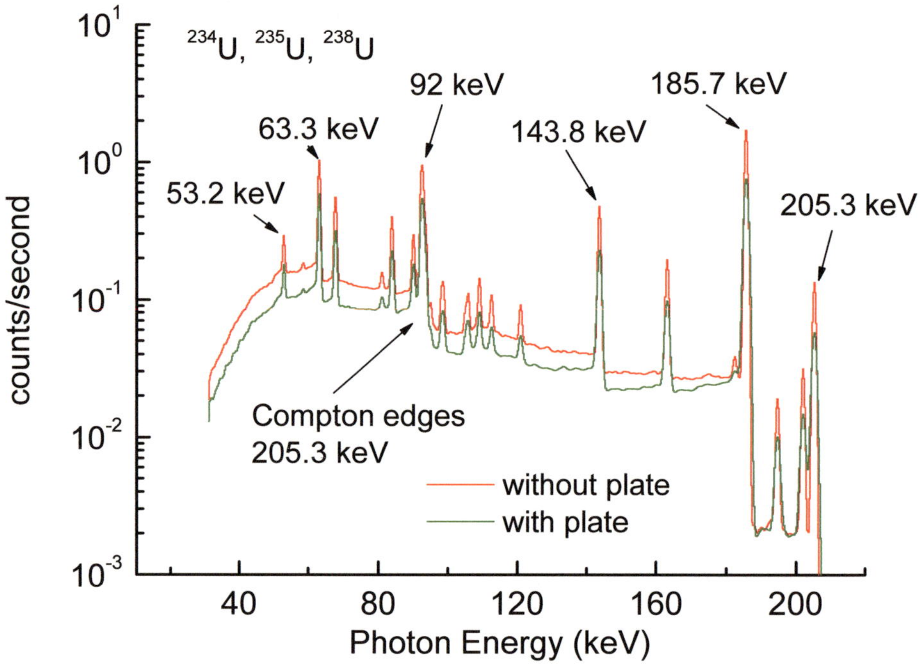

Fig. 10. Response functions of the LE Ge semiconductor detectors for uranium source in the Livermore torso voxel model.

7. References

Cristy, M. & Eckerman, K. (1987). Specific absorbed fractions of energy at various ages from internal photon sources, ORNL/TM-8381 (Oak Ridge, TN :Oak Ridge National Laboratory).

Dogdas, B., Stout, D., Chatziioannou, A. F., *et al.* (2007). Digimouse: a 3D whole body mouse atlas from CT and cryosection data. *Phys. Med. Biol.* 52, 577-587.

Gomez-Ros, J. M., de Carlan, L., Franck, D., *et al.* (2008). Monte Calro modelling of Germanium detectors for the measurement of low energy photons in internal dosimetry: results of an international comparison, *Radiat. Meas.* 43, 510-515.

Gualdrini, G. & Ferrari, P. (2008). *Proceedings of the International workshop on uncertainty assessment in computational dosimetry,* ISBN 978-3-9805741-9-8, Bologna, October 2007, EURADOS.

Hadid, L., Desbree, A., Schlattl, H. *et al.* (2010). Application of the ICRP/ICRU reference computational phantoms to internal dosimetry: calculation of specific absorbed fractions of energy for photons and electrons, *Phys. Med. Biol.*, 55, 3631-3641.

ICRP (2009a). Adult reference computational phantoms, ICRP Publication 110.

ICRP (2009b). Environmental protection: the concept and use of reference animals and plants, ICRP Publication 108.

ICRU (1984). Stopping powers for electrons and positrons. ICRU Report 37.

Kinase, S., Zankl, M., Kuwabara, J., *et al.* (2003). Evaluation of specific absorbed fractions in voxel phantoms using Monte Carlo simulation *Radiat. Prot. Dosim.*, 105, 557-563.

Kinase, S., Zankl, M., Funabiki, J., *et al.* (2004). Evaluation of S values for beta-ray emitters within the urinary bladder, *J. Nucl. Sci. Technol. Suppl.*4, 125, 136-139.

Kinase, S. & Saito, K. (2007a). Evaluation of self-dose S values for positron emitters in voxel phantoms, *Radiat. Prot. Dosim.*, 127, 197-200.

Kinase, S., Takagi, S., Noguchi, H., *et al.* (2007b). Application of voxel phantoms and Monte Carlo method to whole-body counter calibration, *Radiat. Prot. Dosim.*, 125, 189-193.

Kinase, S., Takahashi, M. & Saito, K. (2008a). Evaluation of self-absorbed doses for the kidneys of a voxel mouse, *J. Nucl. Sci. Technol. Suppl.*5, 268-270.

Kinase, S. (2008b). Voxel-based frog phantom for internal dose evaluation, *J. Nucl. Sci. Technol.* 45, 1049-1052.

Kinase, S., Matsuhashi, S. & Saito, K. (2009a). Inter-species scaling of self-organ doses from a voxel mouse to voxel humans, *Nucl. Technol.*, 168, 154-157.

Kinase, S. (2009b). Monte Carlo simulations of photon absorbed fractions in a frog voxel phantom, *Proc. IEEE* 97, 2086-2097.

Kramer, R., Khoury, H. J., Vieira, J. W., *et al.* (2006). MAX06 and FAX06: update of two adult human phantoms for radiation protection dosimetry, *Phys. Med. Biol.*, 51, 3331-3346.

Mohammadi, A. & Kinase, S. Monte Carlo simulation of photon specific absorbed fractions in a mouse voxel phantom, *Prog. Nucl. Sci. Technol.* (in press).

Nelson, W. R., Hirayama, H., Rogers, D. W. O. (1985). The EGS4 code system, *SLAC-265*.

RSIC (1989). DLC-136/PHOTX Photon interaction cross section library (contributed by National institute of standards and technology)

Saito, K., Wittmann, A., Koga, S., *et al.* (2001). Construction of a computed tomographic phantom for a Japanese male adult and dose calculation System, *Radiat. Environ. Biophys.* 40, 69-76.

Saito, K., Koga, S., Ida, Y., *et al.* (2008). Construction of a voxel phantom based on CT data for a Japanese female adult and its use for calculation of organ doses from external electrons. *Jpn. J. Health Phys.*, 43, 122-130.

Takahashi, M., Kinase, S. & Kramer, R. Evaluation of counting efficiencies of whole-body counter using Monte Carlo simulation with voxel phantoms. *Radiat. Prot. Dosim.* (in press).

Veit, R., Zankl, M., Petoussi, N., *et al.* (1989). Tomographic anthropomorphic models: part 1, GSF-Bericht 3/89 Neuherberg, Germany.

Xu, X. G. & Eckerman, K. F. (2009). *Handbook of Anatomical Models for Radiation Dosimetry,* CRC Press, ISBN 978-1-4200-5979-3, New York.

Zaidi, H. & Tsui, B. M. W. (2009)., Review of computational anthropomorphic anatomical and physiological models, *Proc. IEEE* 97, 1938-1953.

4

Applications of Monte Carlo Simulation in Modelling of Biochemical Processes

Kiril Ivanov Tenekedjiev[1], Natalia Danailova Nikolova[1] and Krasimir Kolev[2]
[1]*N. Y. Vaptsarov Naval Academy, Varna*
[2]*Semmelweis University – Budapest*
[1]*Bulgaria*
[2]*Hungary*

1. Introduction

The biochemical models describing complex and dynamic metabolic systems are typically multi-parametric and non-linear, thus the identification of their parameters requires non-linear regression analysis of the experimental data. The stochastic nature of the experimental samples poses the necessity to estimate not only the values fitting best to the model, but also the distribution of the parameters, and to test statistical hypotheses about the values of these parameters. In such situations the application of analytical models for parameter distributions is totally inappropriate because their assumptions are not applicable for intrinsically non-linear regressions. That is why, Monte Carlo simulations are a powerful tool to model biochemical processes. The classification of Monte Carlo approaches is not unified, so here we comply with the interpretation given in (Press et al., 1992), where the general Monte Carlo approach is to construct parallel virtual worlds, in which the experimental estimates will play the role of true parameters, if the way in which the true parameters generate a sample is known. Bootstrap is a modification of Monte Carlo, which uses very few premises imposed on the data, and does not need to know the mechanism by which the true parameters generate experimental samples. Instead, resampling with replacement from the experimental sample is used to construct synthetic samples.

As far as confidence intervals (CI) are concerned, literature offers multiple types, but each of them belongs to one of the two main groups: root (Politis, 1998) and percentile intervals (Efron & Tibshirani, 1993). The difference in the philosophy of those two CI types is substantial for the biochemical interpretation of results. The difference here is explained with the difference between classical statistics (where the parameters are fixed unknown quantities) and Bayesian statistics (where the parameters are random variables with unknown distributions), and also with the philosophical differences between objectivity and subjectivity of scientific research. The main conclusion is that root confidence intervals are confidence intervals of the investigated parameters, whereas percentile confidence intervals refer to the estimates of the investigated parameters.

Address for correspondence: K. Kolev, Semmelweis University, Department of Medical Biochemistry, 1094 Budapest, Tűzoltó u. 37-47

Our first application of Monte Carlo and Bootstrap simulation procedures is with a simulation platform for training students in medical biochemistry (Tenekedjiev & Kolev, 2002). In this system, students search for estimates and confidence intervals of parameters of a given biochemical system for different enzyme-substrate pairs. The platform applies Monte Carlo simulation on two stages. Initially, a Monte Carlo procedure is applied to emulate a biochemical experimental measurement setting along with given enzyme kinetic reactions as realistically as possible. The system is in position to simulate continuous enzyme assay (used for adjustment of the "experimental" conditions) and end-point enzyme assay "measurements" (suitable for parameter identification). We use an ordinary differential equation (ODE) as basis of the generation of pseudo-experimental data. The pseudo-real nature of the generated data is ensured by the random incorporation of three types of errors for each repetition of the experiments. The Briggs-Haldane steady-state model is fitted to the pseudo-measured and end-point assay data obtained by the system. The kinetic parameters can be calculated by χ^2-minimization. The task is simplified by the existence of a good initial guess from a linearized Lineweaver-Burk model. The two-dimensional root confidence regions of the parameters can be calculated by either Monte Carlo or Bootstrap, following similar procedures. The best point estimate is identified using trimmed mean over the flipped parameters taking only the values from the identified root confidence region.

In the majority of biochemical reactions, parameters are unknown in very wide intervals, and may have different numerical order. Finding the root confidence regions (intervals) includes parameter flipping, which often generates results with an incorrect sign. That is why, in a second example (Tanka-Salamon et al., 2008) we propose a multiplicative modification for the estimation of root confidence regions and the best estimate of the parameters, which ensures that all estimates will have a physical meaning. The main assumption is that the ratio between the true parameter value and the optimal parameter value derived from the true data sample has the same distribution as the ratio between the optimal parameter value derived from the true data sample, and the optimal synthetic parameter value derived from the synthetic data sample. The assumption is equivalent to performing classical Bootstrap over the logarithms of the estimated parameters. This method is applied in a real experimental set-up for the estimation of root confidence regions of kinetic constants and root best estimates in amidolytic activity of plasmin under the influence of three fatty acids. By doing so, the inhibition effect of the three fatty acids can be proven and quantified. The measured data have the form of continuous reaction progress curves with several replicas. The product concentrations are predicted by three different models with increasing complexity. We model the instability of the inhibited enzyme and represent the resulting continuous assay model with concomitant inactivation of the enzyme as a system of two stiff ODE. From there, we derive the closed form of the progress curve. The four-dimensional root confidence regions are acquired by Monte Carlo simulation in every data point in each of the progress curves using an analytical model of the measured standard deviation, similarly to the first example.

2. Monte Carlo and Bootstrap confidence regions of parameters

Statistical simulation methods are a powerful tool in the analysis of complex systems. The most popular among them is Monte Carlo. The numerical techniques that stand behind this method are based on statistical simulation, i.e. on any method that uses random number sequences to conduct a simulation. The essence of the method is that it provides integral measures of uncertainty of the simulated system based on the known uncertainties of its parts (Hertz & Thomas, 1983). The integral measures are calculated on the basis of a large number of system instances in different pseudo-realities, each defined by a specific set of randomly generated states of its parts. The Monte Carlo approach is successfully employed in finding estimates of parameters that define the behavior of different stochastic systems. The flexibility, the very few premises imposed on the data and the application in hypothesis tests and statistical parameter assessment are what makes simulation techniques widely accepted.

Following the interpretation of (Press et al., 1992), one can assume that there is an experiment that intends to assess a certain set of M parameters that define the behavior of a measurable stochastic system. The true values $\vec{a}_{true}$ of those parameters are unknown to the observer, but they are statistically realized in a set of real measurements D_0 available to the observer (called a learning sample), which incorporates some random error. Then the experimenter can assess the parameters of a given model so that the discrepancy between the modeled and the measured data is minimized (e.g. using χ^2-minimization or some other method) and a set of real parameters $\vec{a}_0$ is formed. Due to the random character of the sample generating process, repetitions of the experimental measurement would generate many other possible measurement sets - D_1, D_2, D_3, ... - with identical structure as D_0. Those in turn would generate sets of real parameters respectively $\vec{a}_1, \vec{a}_2, \vec{a}_3$, ... that slightly differ from each other. So the estimate $\vec{a}_0$ is just an instance of the M-dimensional random variable $\vec{a}$.

The task is to find the distribution of the deviation of the real parameters from the true ones, when just D_0 is available. This random variable is called a *root* (Beran, 1986; DiGiccio & Romano, 1988). As long as $\vec{a}_{true}$ is not known, the general approach is to create a fictitious world, where the true parameters are substituted with the real ones. The main assumption is that the root in the real world has the same distribution as in the fictitious world.

If we know the process that generates data under a given set of parameters $\vec{a}_0$, then we can simulate synthetic data sets D_1^S, D_2^S, ..., D_Q^S. with the same structure as the learning sample. The Bootstrap method (Efron & Tibshirani, 1993) applies to cases where the process that generates the data and/or the nature of the measurement error are unknown, and the learning sample D_0 is formed out of N independent and identically distributed (*iid*) measurements. The Bootstrap generates synthetic samples D_1^S, D_2^S, ..., D_Q^S with the same structure as D_0 by drawing with replacement from D_0. In (Press et al., 1992) this type of Bootstrap is called *quick-and-dirty Monte Carlo*. There is another Bootstrap version, called *exact Bootstrap*, which forms all synthetic samples that can be generated by drawing with replacement from D_0. However, this method is rather impractical in a real problem so we shall not stress it here.

The parameters $\vec{a}_1^S$, $\vec{a}_2^S$, ..., $\vec{a}_Q^S$ can be identified from the synthetic samples in exactly the same way as $\vec{a}_0$ was identified from D_0, which in turn would generate instances $\vec{r}_q^f = \vec{a}_q^S - \vec{a}_0$ (q=1, 2, ..., Q) of the root $\vec{r}^f$ in the fictitious world. If sufficiently large number of such instances Q is created, then it is possible to construct the empirical distribution of the root $\vec{r}^f$ in the fictitious world, which according to the main assumption coincides with the distribution of the root $\vec{r}^{true} = \vec{a} - \vec{a}_{true}$.

The ultimate step in the simulation is to assess confidence intervals or confidence regions of the investigated M-dimensional parameter. There are different methods to assess one-dimensional CIs (e.g. percentile-t, bootstrap-t, bias-correction, simple bootstrap interval, etc.; see (Davison & Hinkley, 1997; MacKinnon & Smith, 1998)), yet for multi-dimensional CIs practically there are only two methods - root and percentile methods. The distinction of those two stems from the different approaches to probabilities in general.

If the frequentist definition of probabilities is adopted (Von Mises, 1946), then the likelihood inference has to be applied in parameter identification (Berger & Wolpert, 1988). Here the parameters $\vec{a}_{true}$ are considered unknown, but deterministic values. In that sense, the estimate $\vec{a}_0$ is the only value, which is random, so its confidence region can be calculated. Since the distribution of $\vec{r}^f$ and $\vec{r}^{true}$ coincide, then the following is true for the random variable $\vec{a}$: $\vec{a} = \vec{a}_{true} + \vec{r}^{true} = \vec{a}_{true} + \vec{r}^f$. Then, the instances $\vec{a}_q$ of $\vec{a}$ may be generated by replacing $\vec{a}_{true}$ with $\vec{a}_0$ as the only available estimate: $\vec{a}_i = \vec{a}_0 + \vec{r}_q^f = \vec{a}_0 + \vec{a}_q^S - \vec{a}_0 = \vec{a}_q^S$. The so-called *percentile confidence interval (or region)* is identified from the instances of the synthetic parameters $\vec{a}_q^S$ and it is in fact the confidence region of the estimate.

If the subjective definition of probabilities is adopted (Jeffrey, 2004), then Bayesian statistics can be used in the parameter identification (Berry, 1996). Here the parameters $\vec{a}_{true}$ are considered to be random variables, whose distribution can be assessed, and its confidence region may be calculated. Since the distributions of $\vec{r}^f$ and $\vec{r}^{true}$ coincide, then the following is true for the random variable $\vec{a}$: $\vec{a}_{true} = \vec{a} - \vec{r}^{true} = \vec{a} - \vec{r}^f$. Then, the instances $\vec{a}_{true,q}$ of $\vec{a}_{true}$ may be generated by replacing $\vec{a}$ with $\vec{a}_0$ as the only available estimate: $\vec{a}_{true,q} = \vec{a}_0 - \vec{r}_q^f = \vec{a}_0 - \left(\vec{a}_q^S - \vec{a}_0\right) = 2\vec{a}_0 - \vec{a}_q^S$. The so-called *root confidence interval (or region)* is identified from the instances of the flipped (around the real parameters) synthetic parameters $\vec{a}_q^{S,f} = 2\vec{a}_0 - \vec{a}_q^S$ and it is in fact the confidence region of the true parameter. Furthermore, using this approach it is possible to find a point estimate $\vec{a}_{best}$ of $\vec{a}_{true}$ that is better than $\vec{a}_0$. One possibility is to find $\vec{a}_{best}$ as the mean value of the flipped synthetic parameters $\vec{a}_q^{S,f}$. Since the method is sensitive to errors (Davidson & MacKinnon, 1999), it is better to use trimmed mean value (Hanke & Reitsch, 1991). Regardless of the type of mean value, the resulting point estimate $\vec{a}_{best}$ is unbiased unlike $\vec{a}_0$.

3. Generation and processing of data in enzyme kinetics

Metabolomics (Strohman, 2002) deals with the evaluation of the dynamic metabolic networks and links the genetic information to the phenotype through adequate metabolic control analysis. It is a prerequisite in the understanding of the cellular phenotype and its pathological alterations. For that purpose, one not only requires the technical developments that allow stringent monitoring of the metabolic fluctuations induced *in vivo* by biological signals and environmental changes, but also powerful mathematical models capable of treating dynamic metabolic systems in their variability. The principles of metabolomics are well known in biochemistry (Newsholme & Leech, 1984; Voet & Voet, 1995), but the training of biomedical and clinical researchers is still insufficient to exploit the opportunities provided by the up-to-date computer-intensive statistical procedures applicable in the field of enzyme kinetics. For that purpose, our earlier work (Tenekedjiev & Kolev, 2002) introduces a computer-simulated experimental setting, in which the user (a graduate medical student, who is familiar with the basic ideas in enzyme kinetics and the structure of metabolic pathways) acquires skills in adjusting experimental conditions to conform model assumptions, in identification of kinetic parameters and determination of their confidence intervals, in application of these parameters for metabolic predictions in context-dependent *in vivo* situations. In the proposed system, students search for estimates and confidence intervals of the parameters k_p and $K_M = \frac{k_{-1} + k_p}{k_1}$ of an enzyme-catalyzed reaction

$$E + S \underset{k_{-1}}{\overset{k_1}{\rightleftarrows}} ES \xrightarrow{k_p} E + P \tag{3.1}$$

for different enzyme-substrate pairs, where the substrate degrades into product under the influence of the enzyme. The enzyme and substrate bind reversibly to form enzyme-substrate complex, which in turn irreversibly transforms into product.
The proposed system applies Monte Carlo simulations at two levels.

3.1 Simulation of the experimental equipment data generation

Initially, the system uses Monte Carlo simulations to emulate enzyme kinetic reactions as close as possible to the real lab setting. The user can perform continuous enzyme assay and end-point assay "measurements".
The continuous enzyme assay simulates an expensive experiment, where the product concentration is measured at equally spaced time intervals (sampling time), and the mean reaction rate is calculated for different conditions. Here it is not envisaged to make repetitions and perform identification of the parameters. The user sets up the enzyme-substrate pair, the designed concentrations of the total enzyme E_t^{des} (the free enzyme concentration plus the enzyme-substrate complex concentration) and the initial substrate S_0^{des}, the temperature T, the pH, the overall experimental time t_{over} and the sampling time Δt (see Fig. 3.1). As a result, the user gets the time course of the pseudo-measured product $P_{mes}(i.\ \Delta t)$, for i=1, 2, ..., $t_{over}/\ \Delta t$. The time course of the substrate, the product, the free enzyme and the enzyme-substrate complex are recalculated from P_{mes} (see Fig. 3.2). These results form a single replica of the process.

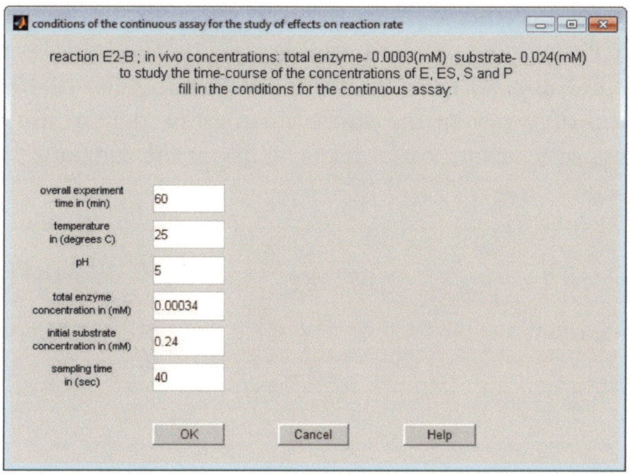

Fig. 3.1. Setting up the designed concentrations of the total enzyme E_t^{des} and the initial substrate S_0^{des}, the temperature T, the acidity pH, the overall experimental time t_{over} and the sampling time Δt for a given enzyme-substrate pair

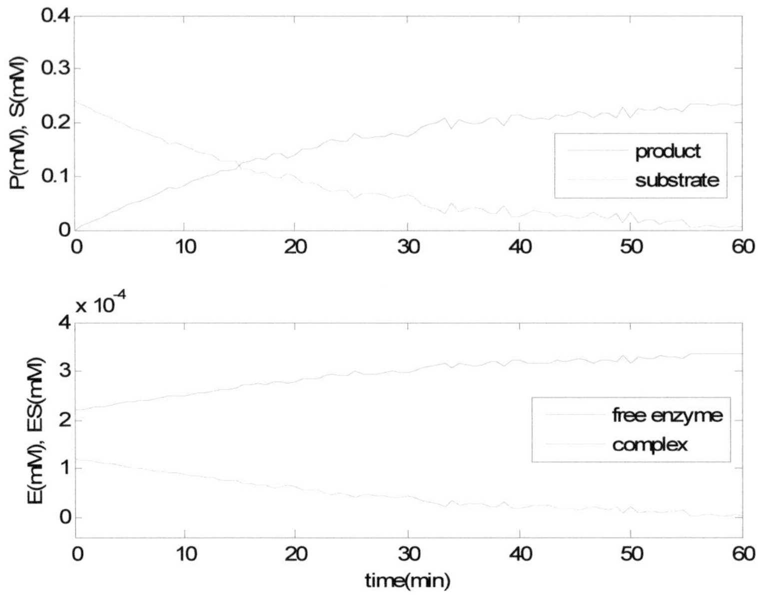

Fig. 3.2. Time course of the substrate, the product, the free enzyme and the enzyme-substrate complex from the setting in Fig. 3.1

For each replica we adopted the Briggs-Haldane steady-state approach (Segel, 1993) to model the transformation of the substrate into product in the biochemical system (3.1) using the ODE:

$$\frac{dP^{true}}{dt} = \frac{k_{p,app}(t,T,pH).E_t^{true}.\left(S_0^{true} - P^{true}\right)}{K_{M,app}(pH) + S_0^{true} - P^{true}}, \tag{3.2}$$

In (3.2), the true concentration of the product P^{true} is a function of the time t; E_t^{true} is the true concentration of the total enzyme; S_0^{true} is the true concentration of the substrate; $k_{p,app}$ and $K_{M,app}$ are the apparent constants k_p and K_M in this replica. The initial condition of (3.2) is that the true concentration of the product is zero at the beginning: $P^{true}(0)=0$.
To model the biological diversity of the substrate-enzyme pair in the real experiment, $k_{p,app}$ and $K_{M,app}$ are instances of random variables. The apparent constant $K_{M,app}$ depends also on pH, whereas $k_{p,app}$ depends on pH, T, and t:

$$K_{M,app} = K_M.\frac{\left(1 + \frac{1}{10^{pH}.Ke_1} + 10^{pH}.Ke_2\right).\left(1 + \frac{1}{10^{pH}.Ka_1} + 10^{pH}.Ka_2\right)}{1 + \frac{1}{10^{pH}.Kes_1} + 10^{pH}.Kes_2}.R_m \tag{3.3}$$

$$k_{p,app} = \frac{10^{A_1 - \frac{A_2}{T+273.16}}}{1 + \frac{1}{10^{pH}.Kes_1} + 10^{pH}.Kes_2}.10^{-Bt}.R_p \tag{3.4}$$

$$\text{where, } B=\begin{cases} A_3.(T-T_d)^g.R_B & \text{if } T>T_d \\ 0 & \text{if } T\le T_d \end{cases} \tag{3.5}$$

In (3.3), (3.4) and (3.5), R_p, R_m and R_B are instances of a positive continuous uniformly distributed random variable on the interval [1- Δ_{par} ; 1+ Δ_{par}], where Δ_{par} <1 is given. The constants T_d, A_1, A_2, A_3, g, Ke_1, Ke_2, Kes_1, Kes_2, Ka_1, Ka_2 are known typical constants for each enzyme-substrate pair, with the following meaning: T_d - the temperature over which the enzyme degradation begins (in degrees C); A_1 - the logscale factor of the apparent k_p constants at t=0 (in 1/min); A_2 - the heat acceleration factor of the apparent k_p constants at t=0 (in 1/min); A_3 - the scale factor of the temporal enzyme degradation constant B; g - the power in the temporal enzyme degradation constant B; Ke_1 - the pK value for the first H+ dissociation constant of the free enzyme; Ke_2 - pK value for the second H+ dissociation constant of the free enzyme; Kes_1 - the pK value for the first H+ dissociation constant of the enzyme-substrate complex; Kes_2 - the pK value for the second H+ dissociation constant of the enzyme-substrate complex; Ka_1 - the pK value of the first acidic dissociation group in the diprotic substrate; Ka_2 - the pK value of the second acidic dissociation group in the diprotic substrate.

To model the imperfection of the setup in the real experiment, S_0^{true} and E_t^{true} are instances of random variables, which slightly deviate from the designed S_0^{des} and E_t^{des} :

$$E_t^{true}=E_t^{des}.R_E \tag{3.6}$$

$$S_0^{true}=S_0^{des}.R_S \tag{3.7}$$

In (3.6) and (3.7), R_E and R_S are instances of positive continuous normally distributed random variables with unit mean values and standard deviations respectively $c.E_t^{des}+d$, and $c.S_0^{des}+d$, where c and d are given.

To model the measurement error in the real experiment, each of the pseudo-measured values of product concentration $P^{mes}(i.\ \Delta t)$, for i=1, 2, ..., $t^{over}/\ \Delta t$ is an instance of a random variable, which slightly deviates from the true product concentration $P^{true}(i.\ \Delta t)$, for i=1, 2, ..., $t^{over}/\ \Delta t$ that results from integrating the ODE (3.2) from 0 to t^{over}:

$$P^{mes}(i.\ \Delta t)= P^{true}(i.\ \Delta t).R_{P,i}, \text{ for } i=1, 2, \ldots, t^{over}/\ \Delta t \tag{3.8}$$

In (3.8), $R_{P,i}$ are instances of positive continuous normally distributed random variables with unit mean values and standard deviations $b.(P^{true}(i.\ \Delta t))^a$, where a and b are given.

After finding P^{mes} it is possible to find the measured time course of the substrate, of the enzyme-substrate complex, and of the free enzyme:

$$\begin{aligned} S^{mes}(i.\Delta t) &= S_0^{true}-P^{mes}(i.\Delta t) \\ ES^{mes}(i.\Delta t) &= \frac{E_t^{true}.S^{mes}(i.\Delta t)}{K_{M,app}+S^{mes}(i.\Delta t)}, \text{ for } i=1, 2, \ldots, t^{over}/\ \Delta t \\ E^{mes}(i.\Delta t) &= E_t^{true}-ES^{mes}(i.\Delta t) \end{aligned} \tag{3.9}$$

The quantities in (3.8) and (3.9) are shown on Fig. 3.2. The measured velocity of the process can be approximated with the formula:

$$V_{mes} = P_{mes}(t_{over})/t_{over} \tag{3.10}$$

The purpose of the end-point assay experiment is to teach the user how to manually setup "optimal" experimental conditions. First of all, the steady-state assumptions have to be checked (that the concentration of the enzyme-substrate complex should stay approximately the same). For example, Fig. 3.2 shows that this condition is not met under the selected experimental conditions. An experiment that meets the requirements of the steady-state is shown on Fig. 3.3. Students can visually check the validity of the empirical "criteria" for the steady-state model (the degraded substrate should be up to 10% of the initial one, and the total enzyme concentration should be far less than the concentration of the initial substrate plus the constant $K_{M,app}$), which otherwise should be proven with complex mathematical procedures (Segel, 1988). The influence of temperature, of acidity, of the substrate and enzyme concentrations, and the overall time of the experiment can be estimated by constructing the velocity graphics of the reaction as a function of the investigated condition. For example, Fig. 3.4 shows the influence of temperature on the product formation. The first graphics shows a continuous monitoring of the product generation in the course of the enzyme-catalysed reaction at various temperatures. The continuous assay illustrates also the intrinsic errors of the sampling procedure, which impose the necessity for repeated sampling. The second graph shows the end-point enzyme activity assay for various sampling time. The data are cross-section of the continuous assay. for 1- and 10-min incubation. Comparison of the two curves illustrates the apparent nature of the "optimal" temperature caused by the time-dependence of the heat denaturation.

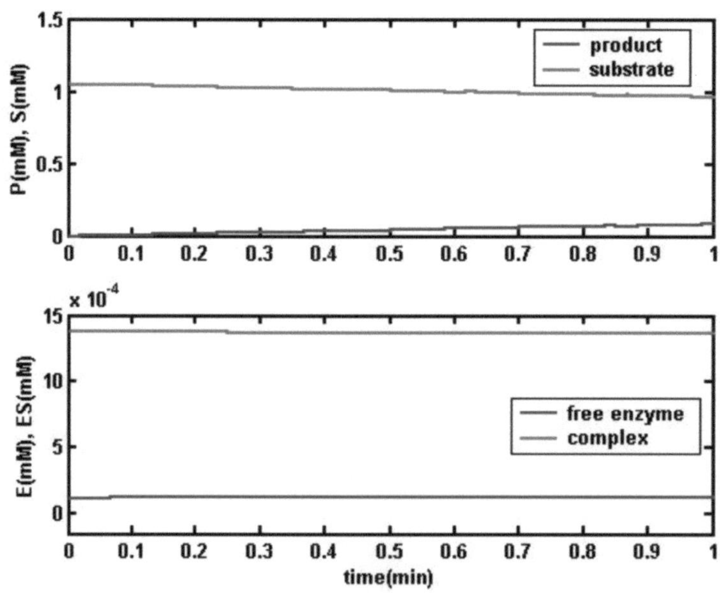

Fig. 3.3. Adjustment of the steady-state experimental conditions

As a whole, the instrumental model for a continuous-time assay is used as a manual Monte Carlo system to find suitable experimental conditions, appropriate for the end-point assay experiment, where the values of the kinetic constants and their confidence regions are identified. The end-point assay simulates a cheap experiment, where the user sets up T, pH,

t^{over}, E_t^{des}, J predetermined initial substrate concentrations $S_{0,1}^{des}, S_{0,2}^{des}, \ldots, S_{0,J}^{des}$, and the number K of replicas for any substrate concentration. The product concentration is measured K times just at time t^{over} for each $S_{0,j}^{des}$ "(for j=1, 2, ..., J).

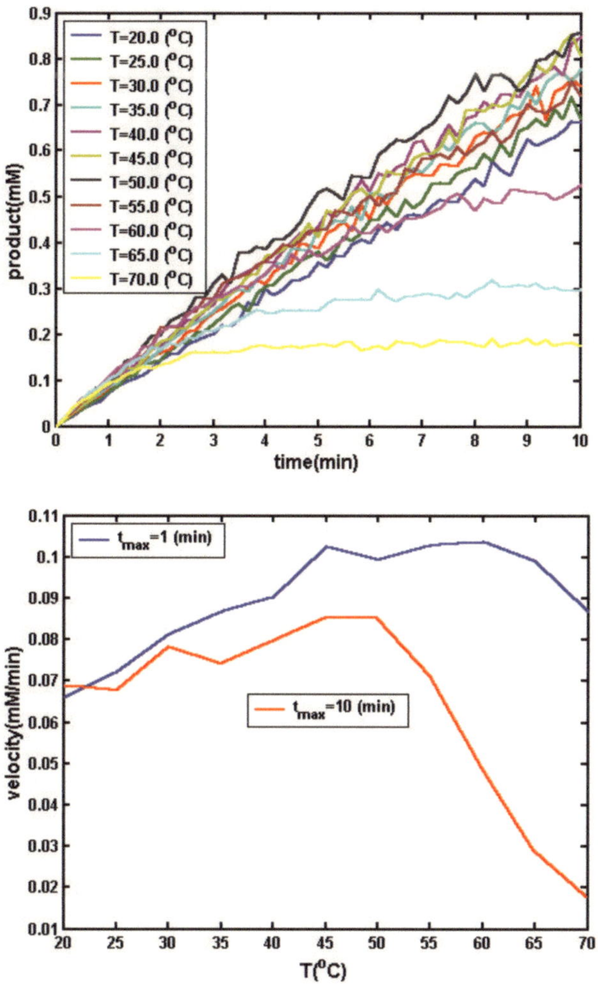

Fig. 3.4. General conditions for optimal enzyme action

3.2 Kinetic parameter identification with Monte Carlo or Bootstrap simulation

Each replica is simulated in the same way as in the continuous-time assay, but the learning sample D_0 only consists of the product concentrations at time t^{over}: $D_0 = \left\{ P_{j,k}^{mes} \,|\, j = 1,2,\ldots,J;\, k = 1,2,\ldots,K \right\}$, where $P_{j,k}^{mes}$ is the k-th measurement of the product concentration P^{mes} at substrate concentration $S_{0,j}^{des}$. As long as all the designed experimental conditions are identical for $P_{j,k}^{mes}$ (k=1, 2, ..., K), they can be referred as a process. Let $P_j^{mes,mean}$ and $P_j^{mes,std}$ are the mean value and the standard deviation for the end-point product concentration of the jth process, calculated by the K instances $P_{j,k}^{mes}$ (k=1, 2, …, K). A non-linear regression model of the standard deviation of the measured final product concentration is created as a function of the mean value of the measured final product concentration:

$$P_j^{mod,std} = P_j^{mes,mean}.10^{a_1.\lg\left(P_j^{mes,mean}\right)+a_2} \text{, for } j=1, 2, \ldots, J \tag{3.11}$$

The constants a_1 and a_2 are determined with χ^2-minimization of:

$$\chi^2(a_1,a_2) = \sum_{j=1}^{J}\left(\lg\left(P_j^{mes,std}\right) - (a_1+1).\lg\left(P_j^{mes,mean}\right) - a_2\right)^2 \tag{3.12}$$

The final product concentrations are predicted by a model different from (3.2), which takes the form of J number of ODEs, which can be solved separately:

$$\frac{dP_j^{mod}}{dt} = \frac{k_p.E_t^{des}.\left(S_{0,j}^{des} - P_j^{mod}\right)}{K_M + S_{0,j}^{des} - P_j^{mod}} \text{, for } j=1, 2, \ldots, J \tag{3.13}$$

The initial conditions of (3.13) are $P_j^{mod}(0) = 0$. In (3.13), k_p and K_M are the kinetic constants. After integrating the ODE (3.13) from time 0 to t_{over}, the value at t_{over} would depend on the values of k_p and K_M. At the same time, $P_j^{mes,mean}$ and $P_j^{mod,std}$ would only depend on the sample D_0. Then the optimal parameters $k_{p,0}$ and $K_{M,0}$ can be found with χ^2-minimization of

$$\chi^2\left(k_p,K_M,D_0\right) = \sum_{j=1}^{J}\left(\frac{P_j^{mod}\left(t_{over},k_p,K_M\right) - P_j^{mes,mean}\left(D_0\right)}{P_j^{mod,std}\left(D_0\right)}\right)^2 \tag{3.14}$$

$$\vec{a}_0 = \left(k_{p,0},K_{M,0}\right) = \arg\left(\min_{k_p,K_m}\chi^2\left(k_p,K_M,D_0\right)\right) \tag{3.15}$$

Solving (3.15) is simplified by the presence of a good initial guess from a linearized model of Lineweaver-Burk (Lineweaver & Burk, 1934).

The two-dimensional confidence region of k_p and K_M is again calculated by Monte Carlo or Bootstrap simulation. The synthetic samples in the Monte Carlo simulation D_q^S (q=1,2,…, Q) are formed so that for the j-th process, the final product concentrations are generated as K number of instances of a normally distributed random variable with mean value $P_j^{mes,mean}$ and standard deviation $P_j^{mod,std}$. The synthetic samples in the Bootstrap simulation D_q^S (q=1,2,…, Q) are formed so that for the j-th process, the final product concentrations are generated by K drawing with replacement from the set $\left\{P_{j,1}^{mes}, P_{j,2}^{mes}, \ldots, P_{j,K}^{mes}\right\}$. Whatever the method for generating D_q^S,

$$\vec{a}_q^S = \left(k_{p,q}^S,K_{M,q}^S\right) = \arg\left(\min_{k_{p,q},K_{p,q}}\chi^2\left(k_p,K_M,D_q^S\right)\right) \tag{3.16}$$

In order to find the root confidence interval, the resulting parameters are flipped in accordance with the discussion in section 2:

$$\vec{a}_q^{S,f} = 2\vec{a}_0 - \vec{a}_q^S = \left(2.k_{p,0} - k_{p,q}^S, 2.K_{M,0} - K_{m,q}^S\right) = \left(k_{p,q}^{S,f}, K_{M,q}^{S,f}\right) \tag{3.17}$$

Let $\chi_q^{2,S} = \chi^2\left(k_{p,q}^{S,f}, K_{M,q}^{S,f}, D_0\right)$ be the discrepancy measure (3.14), calculated over the original sample with the flipped synthetic parameters. Let's renumerate the acquired discrepancy measures $\chi_q^{2,S}$ in ascending order so that $\chi_1^{2,S} \le \chi_2^{2,S} \le \ldots \le \chi_Q^{2,S}$. Then the first Q^*p sorted vectors belong to the two-dimensional (2-D) confidence region with probability p. These vectors are called inside simulated points, and the rest are the outside simulated points. The area of the inside simulated points determines the root confidence region and its borders have constant χ^2 discrepancy measure. The projections of the confidence region on the K_M and k_p axes are the 2-D confidence intervals (Fig. 3.5.). The best point estimate of the parameters is calculated as trimmed mean of $\vec{a}_q^{S,f}$ using just the inside simulated points. The percentile confidence region can be calculated likewise, but instead of the flipped synthetic parameters, one should use just the synthetic parameters.

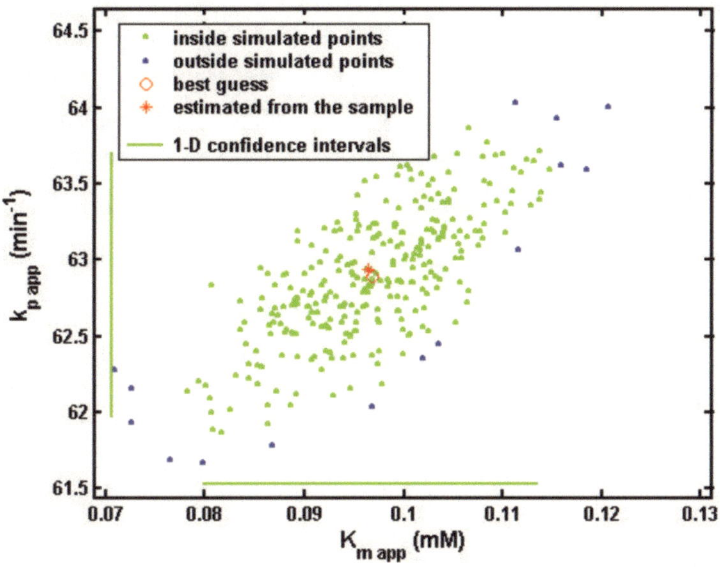

Fig. 3.5. Confidence area of the model parameters based on a Monte Carlo simulation procedure.

The described simulation system has been employed for over 8 years to train medical students in interpretation of the stochastic nature of experimentally estimated model-parameters at the Department of Medical Biochemistry of the Semmelweis University in Budapest (Hungary). After this training, students (and the users in general) are able to perceive the imperative requirements for multiple sampling replicas in experimentation, to interpret the stochastic nature of experimentally estimated model-parameters, as well as to gain insights into the application of in vitro determined kinetic parameters for the modeling of in vivo metabolic events.

4. Influence of fatty acids on the amidolytic activity of plasmin

The dissolution of intravascular thrombi is performed through the hydrolytic degradation of their fibrin matrix catalyzed by the serine protease plasmin (Kolev et al., 2005). Arterial thrombi enclose millimolar concentrations of phospholipids (Varadi et al., 2004) and free fatty acids (Rabai et al., 2007). These lipid constituents of thrombi are reported to modulate the fibrinolytic process (Varadi et al., 2004, Rabai et al., 2007; Hazari et al., 1992; Hazari et al., 1994; Huet et al., 2004). The paper (Tanka-Salamon et al., 2008) investigates the effects of the three most abundant fatty acids in the structure of platelet membranes - arachidonic acid, stearic acid and oleic acid representing respectively 22.0, 19.5 and 18.8 % of the total fatty acid content of platelet phosphoglycerolipids (Rabai et al., 2007).

Plasmin (E_t=20 nM) was incubated with sodium salts of fatty acids for 15 min at 37 °C. Then 180 μl of this mixture was added to 20 μl Spectrozyme-PL (H-D-norleucyl-hexahydrotyrosyl-lysine-p-nitroanilide, American Diagnostica, Stamford, CT) at 7 different concentrations in the range 0.05 - 6 mM yielding final concentration S_{0j} (j=1,2,...,7) in the volume of the reaction mixtures. The light absorbance at 405 nm (A_{405}), which reflects the release of p-nitraniline, was measured continuously at t_i (i=1,2,...,60) time points in the course of 10 min at 37 °C, 4 parallel measurements were done for each S_{0j}. The main problem in the initial data processing is the proper assessment of the baseline absorbance and the delay time of the measurement, which affect profoundly the absolute values of the pNA product. An original algorithm was employed to convert the measured absorbance into product concentration $P_{i,j,k}^{mes}$ (the notation indicates the product concentration at time t_i for the k-th replica with $S_{0,j}$) which form the learning sample D_0: $D_0 = \left\{ P_{i,j,k}^{mes} \middle| i = 1,2,\ldots,60;\ j = 1,2,\ldots,7;\ k = 1,2,3,4 \right\}$. As long as all the designed experimental conditions are identical for $P_{i,j,k}^{mes}$ (k=1, 2, 3, 4), they can be referred as a process. Let $P_{i,j}^{mes,mean}$ and $P_{i,j}^{mes,std}$ are the mean value and the standard deviation for the product concentration of the jth process at time t_i, calculated by four instances $P_{i,j,k}^{mes}$ (k=1, 2, 3, 4). A non-linear regression model of the standard deviation of the measured product concentration for each process is created as a function of the mean value of the measured product concentration:

$$P_{i,j}^{mod,std} = b_j.\left(P_{i,j}^{mes,mean}\right)^{a_j}, \text{ for } j=1, 2, \ldots, 7 \tag{4.1}$$

The constants a_j and b_j are determined with χ^2-minimization of:

$$\chi_j^2\left(a_j, b_j\right) = \sum_{j=1}^{7}\sum_{i=1}^{60}\left(\lg\left(P_{i,j}^{mes,std}\right) - a_j.\lg\left(P_{i,j}^{mes,mean}\right) - \lg\left(b_j\right)\right)^2 \tag{4.2}$$

The product concentrations are predicted by three different models with increasing complexity. In the simplest case (*Model I*) the scheme $E + S \underset{k_{-1}}{\overset{k_1}{\rightleftarrows}} ES \xrightarrow{k_2} E + P$ is assumed, where E is plasmin, S is Spectrozyme-PL, P is p-nitroaniline, k_1, k_2 and k_{-1} are the respective reaction rate constants. With the quasi-steady-state assumption the differential rate equation for this scheme is

$$\frac{dP_j^{mod}}{dt}=\frac{k_p.E_{t0}.\left(S_{0,j}-P_j^{mod}\right)}{K_M+S_{0,j}-P_j^{mod}},\ \text{for } j=1,2,\ \dots,7 \tag{4.3}$$

where E_{t0} and S_0 are the initial concentrations of plasmin and its substrate, $K_M=\frac{k_{-1}+k_2}{k_1}$ is the Michaelis constant, whereas k_p=k_2 is the catalytic constant (Cornish-Bowden, 2004). The integration of (4.3) under initial condition $P_j^{mod}(0)=0$ for j=1,2, …, 7 gives

$$t=\frac{1}{k_p.E_{t0}}P_j^{mod}+\frac{K_M}{k_p.E_{t0}}\ln\frac{S_{0,j}}{S_{0,j}-P_j^{mod}} \tag{4.4}$$

The time t in (4.4) is a strictly increasing function of P_j^{mod} for any combination of K_M and k_p and therefore it has an inverse function $P_j^{mod}=P_j^{mod}(t,K_M,k_p,S_{0,j},E_{t0})$, which can be numerically estimated for all measured time points t_i by a look-up table procedure and the results can be denoted as $P_{i,j}^{mod}$, i=1,2,…, 60; j=1,2,…, 7.

Because in the course of certain experiments the reaction rate declined faster than predicted by *Model I*, the more general scheme $E+S\underset{k_{-1}}{\overset{k_1}{\rightleftarrows}}ES\xrightarrow{k_2}EP\underset{k_{-3}}{\overset{k_3}{\rightleftarrows}}E+P$ was also tested (*Model II*), which accounts for the accumulation of the product and its complex with the enzyme. Assuming steady-state for both *ES* and *EP* complexes the differential rate-equation is

$$\frac{dP_j^{mod}}{dt}=\frac{k_p.E_{t0}.(S_{0,j}-P_j^{mod})}{K_M.(1+K_i.P_j^{mod})+S_{0,j}-P_j^{mod}} \tag{4.5}$$

where $K_M=\frac{(k_{-1}+k_2).k_3}{k_1(k_2+k_3)}$ is the Michaelis constant, $k_p=\frac{k_2.k_3}{k_2+k_3}$ is the catalytic constant, and $K_i=\frac{k_{-3}}{k_3}$ is the equilibrium association constant for the product. Although the Michaelis constant and the catalytic constant derived for *Model I* and *Model II* have different algebraic form, their meaning within the context of the specific catalytic mechanism is identical; the K_M is the substrate concentration at which the initial reaction rate is half of the maximal rate possible for given enzyme concentration, whereas k_p has the properties of a first-order rate constant defining the capacity of the enzyme-substrate complex to form product (Cornish-Bowden, 2004). Integrating (4.5) under initial condition $P_j^{mod}(0)=0$ for j=1,2, …, 7 gives

$$t=\frac{1-K_M.K_i}{k_p.E_{t0}}P_j^{mod}+\frac{K_M(1+S_{0,j}.K_i)}{k_p.E_{t0}}\ln\frac{S_{0,j}}{S_{0,j}-P_j^{mod}} \tag{4.6}$$

The time t in (4.6) is a strictly increasing function of P_j^{mod} for any combination of K_M, k_p and K_i and therefore it has an inverse function $P_j^{mod}=P_j^{mod}(t,K_M,k_p,K_i,S_{0,j},E_{t0})$, which can be numerically estimated for all measured time points t_i by a look-up table procedure and the results can be denoted as $P_{i,j}^{mod}$, i=1,2,…, 60; j=1,2,…, 7.

Because in certain cases the product inhibition could not model the progress curve of the reaction satisfactorily, the instability of the enzyme in the assay system was also considered according to the scheme suggested in (Duggleby, 1995; Duggleby, 2001) (*Model III*):

$$\begin{array}{ccccc} E+S \underset{k_{-1}}{\overset{k_1}{\rightleftarrows}} & ES \xrightarrow{k_2} & EP & \underset{k_{-3}}{\overset{k_3}{\rightleftarrows}} E+P \\ \downarrow J_1 & \downarrow J_2 & \downarrow J_3 & \\ E' & E'S & E'P & \end{array}$$

in which E' indicates the inactive form of the enzyme, J_1, J_2 and J_3 are the rate constants for inactivation of the respective forms of the enzyme (J_1 and J_2 are decay rate constants of the enzyme-substrate complex; J_3 is the decay rate constant of the enzyme product complex). In independent measurements with fatty acids we showed that the inactivation of free plasmin for the duration of the amidolytic assay was negligible (data not shown) and consequently the differential equation for the changes in enzyme concentration was derived only for the scheme with J_2 and J_3 (i.e. J_1=0) yielding seven separately solvable systems of two ODEs:

$$\left.\begin{aligned} \frac{dP_j^{mod}}{dt} &= \frac{k_p.E_{t,j}.(S_{0,j}-P_j^{mod})}{K_M.(1+K_i.P_j^{mod})+S_{0,j}-P_j^{mod}} \\ \frac{dE_{t,j}}{dt} &= -\frac{J_2.E_{t,j}(S_{0,j}-P_j^{mod})/K_M + J_3.E_{t,j}.K_i.P_j^{mod}}{1+K_i.P_j^{mod}+(S_{0,j}-P_j^{mod})/K_M} \end{aligned}\right\} \text{for } j=1,2,\ldots,7 \qquad (4.7)$$

The initial conditions of (4.7) are $P_j^{mod}(0)=0$, $E_{t,j}(0)=E_{t0}$. In (4.7), k_p and K_M have the same meaning as in *Model II*. The integration of ODE systems (4.7) from time 0 to t_{60} was done by quasi-constant step size implementation in terms of backward differences of the Klopfenstein-Shampine family of Numerical Differentiation Formulas of orders 1-5 and the initial steps were determined so that the solution would stay in its domain ($0 \le P_j^{mod} \le S_{0,j}$, $0 \le E_{t,j} \le E_{t0}$) during the whole integration (Shampine et al., 2003). The values of the product concentrations at time points t_i for *Model III* can be found from the first component of the solution: $P_{i,j}^{mod} = P_j^{mod}\left(t_i, K_M, k_p, K_i, J_2, J_3, S_{0,j}, E_{t0}\right)$ for i=1, 2, …, 60 and for j=1,2,…, 7.

Since *Model I* and *Model II* are special cases of *Model III* for given values of J_2, J_3 and K_i, then further discussion only refers to *Model III*.

As in section 3, P_j^{mod} depends only on the kinetic parameters K_M, k_p, K_i, J_2, J_3; $P_{i,j}^{mes,mean}$ and $P_{i,j}^{mod,std}$ would only depend on the sample D_0. Then the optimal parameters $k_{p,0}$, $K_{M,0}$, $K_{i,0}, J_{2,0}, J_{3,0}$ can be found with χ^2-minimization of

$$\chi^2\left(k_p, K_M, K_i, J_2, J_3, D_0\right) = \sum_{j=1}^{J}\sum_{i=1}^{60}\left(\frac{P_{i,j}^{mod}\left(k_p, K_M, K_i, J_2, J_3\right) - P_{i,j}^{mes,mean}\left(D_0\right)}{P_{i,j}^{mod,std}\left(D_0\right)}\right)^2 \qquad (4.8)$$

$$\vec{a}_0 = \left(k_{p,0}, K_{M,0}, K_{i,0}, J_{2,0}, J_{3,0}\right) = \arg\left(\min_{k_p, K_M, K_i, J_2, J_3} \chi^2\left(k_p, K_M, K_i, J_2, J_3, D_0\right)\right) \quad (4.9)$$

The minimization (4.9) was performed using the Nelder-Mead simplex direct search method (Lagarias et al., 1998). Since the optimization assigns values of less than 10^{-12} (sec^{-1}) to J_2, from now on only J_3 shall be considered.

The four-dimensional confidence region of k_p, K_M, K_i, and J_3 is calculated by Monte Carlo simulation. The synthetic samples D_q^S (q=1,2,..., Q) are formed so that for the i-th time point of the j-th process, the product concentrations are generated as four instances of a normally distributed random variable with mean value $P_{i,j}^{mes,mean}$ and standard deviation $P_{i,j}^{mod,std}$. Then

$$\vec{a}_q^S = \left(k_{p,q}^S, K_{M,q}^S, K_{i,q}^S, J_{3,q}^S\right) = \arg\left(\min_{k_p, K_M, K_i, J_3} \chi^2\left(k_p, K_M, K_i, J_3, D_q^S\right)\right) \quad (4.10)$$

Let's find the root confidence region of the parameters. That requires flipping the parameters as in (3.17). However, the resulting values may have no physical meaning (could be negative) unlike the case in section 3, because here we operate with real measurements, and there is no appropriate initial guess for the optimization. This situation is a rule rather than an exception in biochemical analysis, where parameters are supposed to be strictly positive. Therefore, one possible solution to find the root confidence region in such cases is to use a modification of the classical Monte Carlo procedure, called *multiplicative Monte Carlo*. The main assumption here, in accordance with section 1, is that the ratio between the true parameter value and the optimal parameter value derived from the true data sample $\frac{\vec{a}_{true}}{\vec{a}}$ has the same distribution as the ratio between the optimal parameter value derived from the true data sample, and the optimal synthetic parameter value derived from the synthetic data sample $\frac{\vec{a}_0}{\vec{a}_q^S}$. The assumption is equivalent to performing classical Bootstrap over the logarithms of the estimated parameters. Then, the flipped parameters are derived as follows:

$$\vec{a}_q^{S,f} = \frac{2\vec{a}_0}{\vec{a}_q^S} = \left(\frac{2.k_{p,0}}{k_{p,q}^S}, \frac{2.K_{M,0}}{K_{M,q}^S}, \frac{2.K_{i,0}}{K_{i,q}^S}, \frac{2.J_{3,0}}{J_{3,q}^S}\right) = \left(k_{p,q}^{S,f}, K_{M,q}^{S,f}, K_{i,q}^{S,f}, J_{3,q}^{S,f}\right) \quad (4.11)$$

Then the root confidence region is derived in the same way as in section 3. Let $\chi_q^{2,S} = \chi^2\left(k_{p,q}^{S,f}, K_{M,q}^{S,f}, K_{i,q}^{S,f}, J_{3,q}^{S,f}, D_0\right)$ be the discrepancy measure (4.8), calculated over the original sample with the flipped synthetic parameters. The discrepancy measures $\chi_q^{2,S}$ are renumerated in ascending order so that $\chi_1^{2,S} \le \chi_2^{2,S} \le \ldots \le \chi_Q^{2,S}$. The inside and outside simulated points are identified as in section 3. Again, the area of the inside simulated points determines the root confidence region. The best point estimate of the parameters is calculated as trimmed geometrical mean of $\vec{a}_q^{S,f}$ using just the inside simulated points. Since it is impossible to plot the 4D confidence regions, they are visualized in pairs (e.g. Fig. 4.1 shows the confidence region of K_M and k_p, and of K_i and J_3). The kinetic parameters of plasmin in the presence of the three fatty acids at different concentrations are given in Table 4.1. It also gives the 2D confidence intervals (2D) and best estimates, whereas the multi-dimensional confidence regions are given on Fig. 4.2.

Concentration of added fatty acid (μM)	K_M (μM)		k_p (sec^{-1})		K_i (μM^{-1})		J_3 (sec^{-1})	
	BE	CI	BE	CI	BE	CI	BE	CI
None	5.89	5.43-6.38	5.81	5.70-5.93	NA	NA	NA	NA
Oleate								
10	12.58	11.68-13.41	4.54	4.48-4.60	NA	NA	NA	NA
25	20.09	18.76-21.26	3.65	3.56-3.73	NA	NA	NA	NA
45	27.49	26.43-28.57	2.63	2.58-2.68	NA	NA	NA	NA
65	131.09	115.33-146.13	2.75	2.57-2.95	NA	NA	NA	NA
Arachidonate								
10	23.71	22.91-24.58	6.10	6.06-6.15	NA	NA	NA	NA
25	42.65	38.28-47.66	3.57	3.43-3.71	NA	NA	NA	NA
45	57.51	55.24-59.60	3.68	3.62-3.73	NA	NA	NA	NA
65	59.85	56.76-62.73	2.40	2.35-2.44	NA	NA	NA	NA
Stearate								
65	8.17	7.35-9.10	7.03	6.93-7.12	0.025	0.011-0.053	0.026	0.018-0.038
115	11.33	9.42-13.41	7.48	7.37-7.61	0.012	0.008-0.402	0.056	0.001-0.158
175	23.37	20.98-26.88	12.39	11.92-12.73	0.007	0.005-0.009	0.062	0.052-0.069
230	72.96	69.86-75.86	14.77	13.94-23.85	0.002	0.001-0.003	0.074	0.001-0.356

Table 4.1. Kinetic parameters of plasmin in the presence of fatty acids. Numerical values of the best estimates (BE) and their 95% confidence intervals (CI).

The described study implemented a novel numerical procedure based on Monte Carlo to give a quantitative characterization of the modulation of plasmin activity by the presence of three fatty acids. All three fatty acids caused a 10–20-fold increase in the Michaelis constant of plasmin. Based on the ratio of the catalytic and Michaelis constants, all three fatty acids acted as inhibitors of plasmin with various degrees of potency - oleate and arachidonate can be defined as mixed-type inhibitors of plasmin, whereas stearate has a rather unusual effect; the increase in the Michaelis constant is coupled to higher values of the catalytic constant. At saturating concentrations of the substrate this effect is seen as apparent activation of plasmin in the amidolytic assay. Our findings illustrate the general possibility for a modulator to change the kinetic parameters of an enzyme in an independent and controversial manner, so that the overall catalytic outcome may vary with the concentration of the substrate. In physiological context the reported results indicate that acting as mixed-type inhibitors, unsaturated fatty acids stabilize fibrin against plasmin, whereas through its discordant effects on the catalytic and Michaelis constants stearate may destabilize clots in the process of their formation.

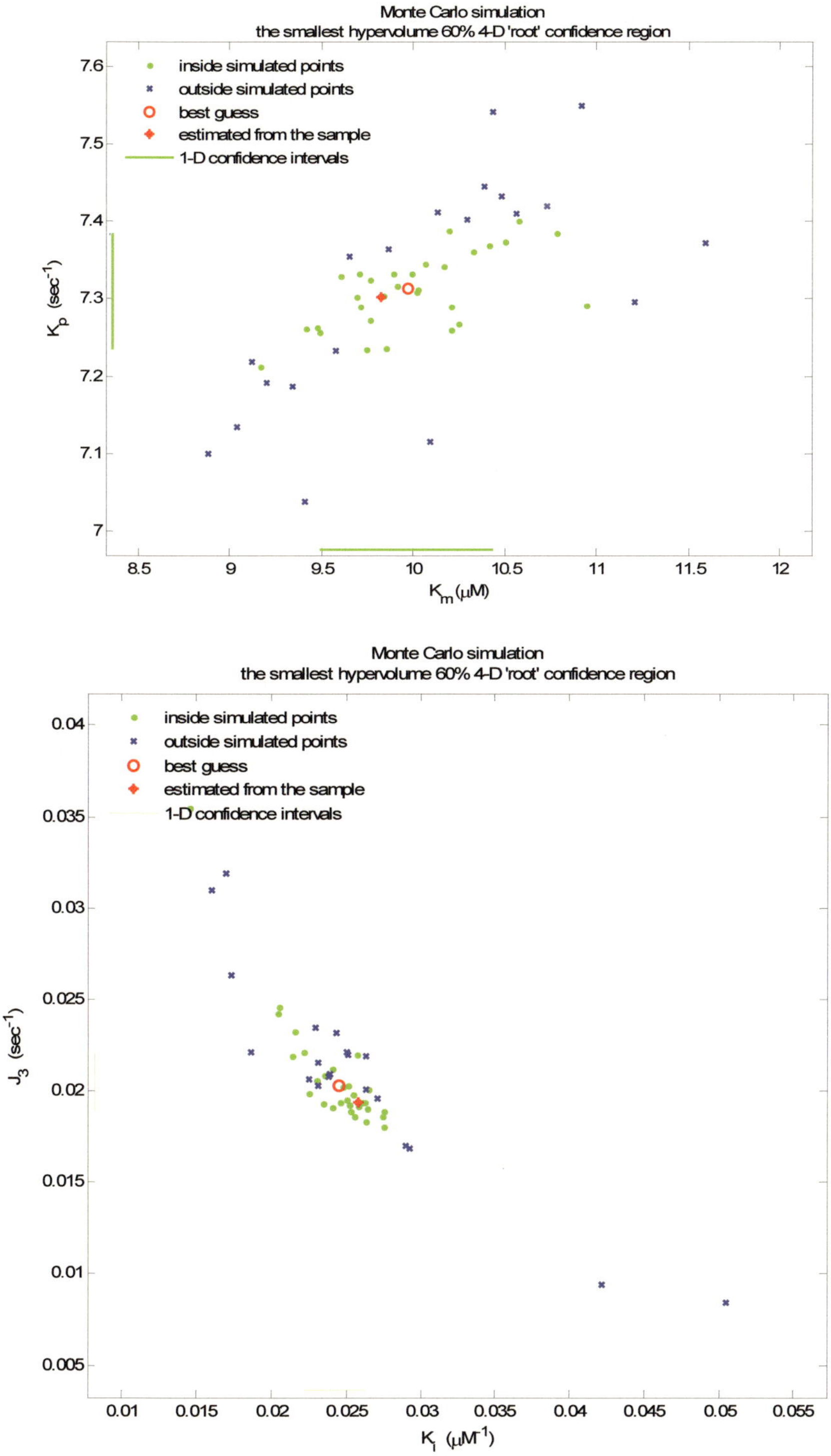

Fig. 4.1. Confidence regions of K_M and k_p (in the first plot) and of K_i and J_3 (in the second plot)

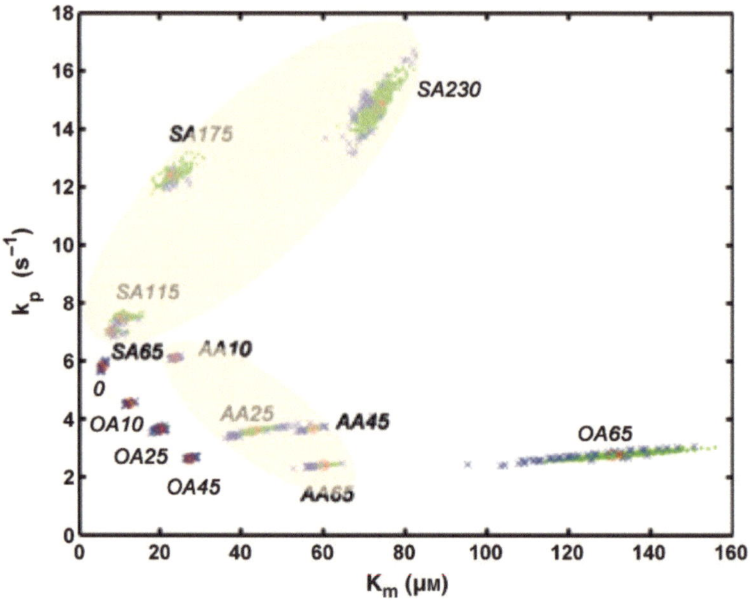

Fig. 4.2. Kinetic parameters of plasmin in the presence of fatty acids (oleate *OA*, arachidonate *AA*, and stearate *SA*), and their multi-dimensional confidence regions

The investigated biochemical problem was a suitable setup to demonstrate the multiplicative Monte Carlo, which provides a reasonable physical meaning of resulting parameters. Its advantages over the classical methods in tasks, where strictly positive parameter values are required, makes it a necessary tool in most biological and biochemical parameter identification studies.

5. Conclusions

The application of Monte Carlo and Bootstrap techniques in a multi-dimensional setup is principally similar to the one-dimensional case. However, instead of CI, we need to find confidence regions that contain certain percentage of the entire probability distribution. As demonstrated, only root and percentile confidence regions are of interest in the multi-dimensional case. The use of either of them stems from the two different approaches to probabilities, so researchers should first clarify their viewpoint to probabilities in general before choosing the type of confidence regions to exploit. Working with root confidence intervals (regions) requires parameter flipping, which in some cases may generate results with an inappropriate sign. This is particularly true for biochemical (biological) processes, where parameters are supposed to be positive most of the cases. Therefore we presented the multiplicative Monte Carlo as a procedure that ensures the physical meaning of parameters.

Since Monte Carlo and Bootstrap are computer intensive methods, all calculation and visualization procedures, discussed and demonstrated here were executed with MATLAB R2009a. Whenever we used root confidence intervals, we also provided a best point estimate, which as a rule is better than the sample estimate. Generally, the mean of the flipped parameters can serve for a best estimate, but having in mind the sensitivity to errors (extreme values, outliers in the sample, etc.) it is recommended to use trimmed means. Regardless of the way to calculate this best estimate though, it will always be unbiased unlike the sample estimate.

The recent expansion of technological tools in biomedical research poses the requirement for appropriate modeling of the processes under investigation. The described examples from our work underscore the applicability of Monte Carlo simulations in biochemical models of variable complexity providing a robust tool to estimate the reliability of estimated parameters.

6. Acknowledgements

This work was supported by grants from the Wellcome Trust [083174] and OTKA [K83023].

7. References

Beran, R. (1986). Discussion to Wu, C.F.J.: Jackknife, Bootstrap and other resampling methods in regression analysis. Ann. Statist., Vol. 14, 1295-1298

Berger, J. & Wolpert, R. L. (1988). *The Likelihood Principle: A Review, Generalizations, and Statistical Implications*, Second Edition, IMS, Hayward, CA

Berry, D. A. (1996). *Statistics: A Bayesian Perspective*, Duxbury Press, CA, USA

Cornish-Bowden, A. (2004). *Fundamentals of Enzyme Kinetics*, Third Edition, Portland Press, London

Davison, A. C. & Hinkley, D. V. (1997). *Bootstrap Methods and Their Application,* Cambridge University Press, Cambridge, NY, USA

Davidson, R. & MacKinnon J. G. (1999). The size distortion of bootstrap tests. *Econometric Theory*, Vol. 15, 361–376

DiCiccio, T. & Romano, J. (1988). A review of bootstrap confidence intervals (with discussion). *J. Roy. Statist. Soc., Ser. B*, Vol. 50, 338-370

Duggleby, R.G. (1995). Analysis of enzyme progress curves by nonlinear regression, *Methods Enzymol*, Vol. 249, 61-90

Duggleby, R.G. (2001). Quantitative analysis of the time courses of enzyme-catalyzed reactions, *Methods*, 24(2), 168–174.

Efron, B. & Tibshirani, R.J. (1993). *An Introduction to the Bootstrap*, Chapman and Hall, NY, USA

Hanke, J. E. & Reitsch A. G. (1991). *Understanding Business Statistics*. Irwin, USA

Higazi A.A.R.; Finci-Yeheskel, Z.; Samara, A.A.R.. Aziza, R. & Mayer, M. (1992). Stimulation of plasmin activity by oleic acid, *Biochem J*, Vol. 282, 863-866.

Higazi, A.A.R.; Aziza, R.; Samara, A.A.R. & Mayer, M. (1994). Regulation of fibrinolysis by non-esterified fatty acids, *Biochem J*, Vol. 330, 251-255.

Hertz, D. & Thomas, H. (1983). *Risk Analysis and its Applications*. John Wiley, NY, USA

Huet, E.; Cauchard, J.H.; Berton, A.; Robinet, A.; Decarme, M.; Hornebeck, W. & Bellon, G. (2004). Inhibition of plasmin-mediated prostromelysin-1 activation by interaction of long chain unsaturated fatty acids with kringle 5, *Biochem Pharmacol*, Vol. 67, 643-654.

Jeffrey, R. (2004). *Subjective Probability – The Real Thing*. Cambridge University Press, Cambridge, UK

Kolev, K.; Longstaff, C. & Machovich, R. (2005). Fibrinolysis at the fluid-solid interface of thrombi, *Curr Medic Chem Cardiovasc Hematol Agents*, Vol. 3, 341-355

Lagarias, J.; Reeds, J.; Wright, M. & Wright, P. (1998). Convergence properties of the Nelder-Mead simplex method in low dimensions, *SIAM J Optimiz*, Vol. 9, 112-147

Lineweaver, H. & Burk, D. (1934). The determination of enzyme dissociation constants, *J A Chem Soc*, Vol. 56: 658–666

MacKinnon, J. G. & Smith, A.A. Jr. (1998). Approximate bias correction in econometrics, *Journal of Econometrics*, Vol. 85 205–230.

Newsholme, E.A. & Leech A.R. (1984). *Biochemistry for the medical sciences*. John Wiley & Sons, Inc., Chichester.

Politis, D.N. (1998). Computer-intensive methods in statistical analysis, *IEEE Signal Proc Mag*, Vol. 15, 39–55

Press, W. H.; Teukolski, S. A.; Vetterling, W. T. & Flannery, B. P. (1992). *Numerical Recipes - The Art of Scientific Computing*. Cambridge University Press, NY, USA.

Rábai, G.; Váradi, B.; Longstaff, C.; Sótonyi, P.; Kristóf, V.; Timár, F.; Machovich, R. & Kolev, K. (2007). Fibrinolysis in a lipid environment: modulation through release of free fatty acids, *J Thromb Haemost*, Vol. 5, 1265-1273

Segel, L.A. (1988). On the validity of the steady state assumption of enzyme kinetics, *Bull. Math. Biol.*, Vol. 50, 579-593

Segel, I.H. (1993). *Enzyme kinetics*. John Wiley & Sons, Inc., NY, USA, pp. 25-29

Shampine, L.F.; Gladwell, I. & Thompson, S. (2003). *Solving ODEs with Matlab*. Cambridge University Press, Cambridge.

Strohman, R. (2002). Maneuvering in the complex path from genotype to phenotype, *Science*, Vol. 296, 701-703

Tanka-Salamon, A.; Tenekedjiev, K.; Machovich, R. & Kolev, K. (2008). Suppressed catalytic efficiency of plasmin in the presence of long-chain fatty acids: identification of kinetic parameters from continuous enzymatic assay with monte carlo simulation, *FEBS Journal*, Vol. 275 1274-1282

Tenekedjiev, K. & Kolev, K. (2002). Introduction to interpretation of stochastic parameters: computer-intensive procedures for evaluation of data in enzyme kinetics, *Biochemistry and Molecular Biology Education*, Vol. 30, 414-418

Váradi, B.; Kolev, K.; Tenekedjiev, K.; Mészáros, G.; Kovalszky, I.; Longstaff, C. & Machovich, R. (2004). Phospholipid-barrier to fibrinolysis: role for the anionic polar head charge and the gel-phase crystalline structure, *J Biol Chem*, Vol. 279, 39863-39871

Voet, D. & Voet, J.G. (1995). *Biochemistry*. Second Edition, John Wiley & Sons, Inc., NY, USA.

Von Mises, R. (1946). *Notes on the Mathematical Theory of Probability and Statistics*. Harvard University Press, USA.

5

Applications to Development of PET/SPECT System by Use of Geant4

Yoshiyuki Hirano
Department of Bio-medical Imaging
National Cerebral and Cardiovascular Center Research Institute
Japan

1. Introduction

In this chapter, two applications of Monte Carlo method in medicine are described. The first application is development of a Single Photon Emission Computed Tomography (SPECT), in which the intrinsic spatial and energy resolutions were estimated by simulating scintillation lights. The adequacy of the simulation was verified by comparisons of experimental results from a high-resolution SPECT. In addition, we proposed a method related to improving the spatial resolution relative to the conventional method, (the Anger method). The usefulness of the method and the performance were estimated by the simulation. The second application is an evaluation of a quantification technique for Positron Emission Tomography (PET). In cardiac PET using the isotope O-15, scatter events originating from outside the field of view (FOV), especially from the liver, influence the quantification of myocardial blood flow. We evaluated this influence by simulating trajectories of gamma rays. In section 1, we briefly describe Monte Carlo simulation tools in medicine and principle of PET/SPECT imaging. In sections 2 and 3, respectively, we describe applications to SPECT and PET.

1.1 Monte Carlo simulation in medicine

Monte Carlo simulation is widely used in development of medical equipments. In development of PET and SPECT, Monte Carlo simulation is a useful tool for understanding the trajectories of gamma rays emitted from radiopharmaceuticals. We employed a Monte Carlo simulation library, Geant4 (Allison J et al., 2006) written in C++. Geant4, a toolkit for the simulation of the passage of particles through matter, was developed by the Geant4 collaboration as a successor to Geant3. The application includes high energy physics, nuclear and accelerator physics. It is also used in medical and space science. GATE (Strul D et al., 2003) is another Monte Carlo software package developed by the international OpenGATE collaboration; it is dedicated to the numerical simulations in medical imaging, and it currently supports PET, SPECT and Computed Tomography (CT). GATE is designed as an user-friendly script of Geant4. Thus, interactions of particles with matters used in GATE are the equivalent of those in Geant4. The relation between GATE and Geant4 is similar to the relation between shell and kernel in Unix/Linux system. The use of GATE is authorized and widespread in PET/SPECT study; however, in this study we worked with Geant4 directly.

1.2 PET/SPECT

PET/SPECT helps elucidate pathologic conditions, and is used in both clinical and research contexts. The applications include oncology, neurology, cardiology and psychiatry. Both PET and SPECT modalities can take images of the distribution of pharmaceuticals labeled with radioisotopes by detecting emitted gamma rays. Thus, in contrast to CT and Magnetic Resonance Imaging (MRI), PET/SPECT provides not morphological images but rather functional images of the pharmaceuticals. Because of their shorter half-lives, it is more difficult to use PET isotopes [F-18 (110 min), O-15 (122 sec), C-11 (20 min), and N-13 (10 min)] than SPECT isotopes [Tl-201 (3 day), I-123 (13 h), and Tc99m (6 h)]. Due to their shorter half-lives, a facility that employs PET must have a cyclotron to produce PET isotopes. This requirement prevents a more rapid increase in clinical use of PET. Meanwhile, SPECT isotopes can be delivered by radiopharmaceutical supply companies. However, PET has better spatial resolution than SPECT as well as better sensitivity. In addition, PET is excellent for quantification. With PET, it is possible to obtain quantitative images with high accuracy, which is important for enhanced sensitivity and specificity in diagnosis. Quantitative images consist of a distribution of absolute values of cerebral and myocardial blood flow; Standard Uptake Value (SUV), an index used in cancer diagnosis; receptor occupancy rate; etc. Techniques of quantification have been under development, and the Monte Carlo method also has played an important role in the development.

The processes to create images in PET/SPECT are described briefly as follows, and shown in Fig. 1. In a PET system, detectors are arranged surrounding a subject. The radiopharmaceutical radiates a positron, and two annihilation gamma rays are emitted with back-to-back angular distribution. The detectors catch the two gamma rays simultaneously (coincidence counting). The line joining two detection points is called the Line of Response (LOR); the LOR tells us the isotope exists somewhere along the line. In a SPECT system, a gamma-ray detector with a collimator made of lead moves around a subject. The LOR is determined by the incoming direction. Next, projection images are created every few degrees. In a SPECT system, we need projection images ranging from 0–360 degrees. In contrast, a PET system requires projections ranging from 0–180 degrees. A two-dimensional map of projection data against degrees is called "sinogram". Finally, image reconstruction algorithm converts the sinogram into an image of pharmaceuticals distribution. Filtered Back Projection (FBP) and Ordered Subset Expectation Maximization (OSEM) are among the basic methods used in PET/SPECT image reconstructions.

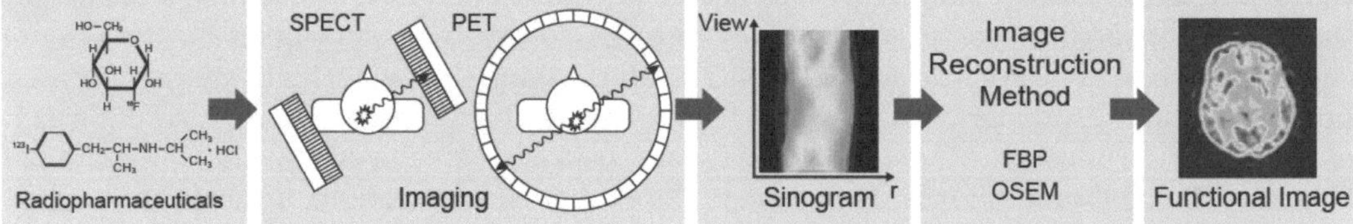

Fig. 1. The procedures for creating functional images in PET/SPECT. Dosed radiopharmaceuticals (tracer) emit annihilation gamma rays, and these are coincidentally detected by scintillators arranged in a circular pattern (PET). In SPECT, tracers radiate single gamma rays, which are collimated and detected by rotating detectors. A set of projections at several degrees, called sinogram, is used for image reconstruction.

2. Application to simulation of scintillation lights in SPECT

2.1 Introduction

A SPECT system mainly consists of gamma-ray detectors, the rotating mechanisms and a data acquisition system. Gamma-ray detectors for clinical SPECT are based on scintillators, a number of photo multiplier tubes (PMT) and a collimator. The scintillators are conventional detectors of nuclear radiation; when gamma rays or other particles interact with scintillators, optical photons are generated at the point of interaction. A particle is detected by sensing the scintillation photons. The interaction points are identified by the distribution of scintillation photons on the PMTs. PMTs linearly convert photons into electric charge. The amount of obtained scintillation photons corresponds to the energy deposited by particles in the scintillator. The mean position of PMTs weighted by the number of detected photons is assumed to be the location of interacting points; this frequently used method is called the Anger method. In an actual system, electric resistances are attached to each PMT; the total resistance at both ends is used as the weighting factor. The intrinsic spatial resolution of the Anger method depends on the number of observed scintillation photons and their distribution on the PMTs. The distinct distribution results in better spatial resolution. In order to estimate spatial resolution in SPECT, we should simulate the action of optical photons in a scintillator. We employed Monte Carlo simulation to simulate scintillation photons, and estimated the spatial resolution. Once the simulation is validated, it will be a strong and reliable tool to estimate the performance of a detector. First, in order to determine the adequacy of the simulation, we compared spatial and energy resolutions derived from the simulation with those of an experiment obtained by a high-resolution SPECT, which we are currently developing. In addition, in order to improve spatial resolution, we proposed an alternative to the Anger method. The details of the method and the performance estimation by the simulation are described.

2.2 High-resolution SPECT for the human brain

We have been developing a high-resolution and quantitative SPECT for human brain, the concept described in (Zeniya T et al., 2009). The system includes two types of detectors. The first of these (large FOV detector) views the whole human brain with a parallel collimator, and the second (small FOV detector) views a specified local region with extremely high resolution (~1 mm). To achieve high resolution in SPECT, adoption of a pin-hole collimator is a common method. However, when the FOV (field of view) is smaller than the subject, as during imaging using a pin-hole collimator, quantification is not assured and is often overestimated. The main problem is due to truncations. To compensate for the overestimation, a reconstruction method has developed (Zeniya T et al., 2007) based on a theory proposed by (Kudo H et al., 2008). In this method, a reconstructed image without truncations, obtained by the large FOV detector, is used as an initial image for reconstruction by the small FOV detector. We already have completed the large FOV detector; the small FOV detector is still under development. The large FOV detector consists of a NaI(Tl) scintillator (147 mm *l* x 252 mm *h* x 6.4 mm *w*) and 15 flat panel-type multi-anode PMTs (H8500 Hamamatsu). An H8500 has 8 × 8 anodes with 5.8 mm^2. The 15 PMTs are arranged in a 5 × 3 matrix. In other words, photo-detectors with 5.8 mm^2 are located in a 40 × 24 matrix. Fifteen PMTs are coupled with the scintillator using optical grease (BC630). The scintillator is covered with a white diffuse reflector to prevent leakage of scintillation photons. The connection side of the PMTs is attached using an optical window. NaI(Tl) must be housed because the material is deliquescent. An electric resistance array used for the Anger method is connected with each anode. The energy spectrum is computed from the total charge of PMTs. The interaction points are calculated using the output of all anodes.

2.3 Experimental performance evaluation

2.3.1 Experimental set up

To measure spatial and energy resolutions and their position dependence within the detector, we designed a special collimator. The collimator has 170 holes of 1.5 mm diameter, and holes arranged in a 17 × 10 grid pattern at 15 mm intervals. The collimator is made of lead of 10 mm thickness, and is mounted on the scintillator. Above the each hole, point sources of Tc-99m, which is frequently used in clinical SPECT are placed. Tc-99m mainly emits a single gamma-ray of 140 keV.

2.3.2 Analysis

The analytical methods used to calculate spatial and energy resolutions are as follows: (i) Select the events from the 140 keV photopeak. The events in a 3-sigma region, as determined by fitting a Gauss function, are extracted. (ii) Using the selected events, interaction points are calculated by the Anger method. (iii) The planar image is projected in the x and y directions. (iv) The spatial resolutions in the x and y directions are derived by fitting a function expressed as follows:

$$f(x) = \int g(x) \cdot h(z-x) dx = \frac{1}{2a}\left\{ erf\left(\frac{a+b-x}{\sqrt{2}\sigma}\right) - erf\left(\frac{b-x}{\sqrt{2}\sigma}\right)\right\},$$

$f(x)$ is a convolution of a uniform function and a Gauss function. The uniform function represents a collimator hole, and the Gauss function expresses blurring. a is the diameter of a hole, and b is the position of a hole edge. The spatial resolution, Full Width Half Maximum (FWHM), expressed in mm, is computed as 2.35 × σ, where σ is the standard deviation of the Gauss function. (v) Finally, energy resolution at each hole is calculated. The events within a 3-sigma range in position, determined in step (iv), are used to generate the energy spectrum. These energy resolutions (FWHM %) are derived from fitting of a Gauss function.

2.3.3 Results

The planar image of 170 point sources is shown in Fig. 2. Around the center of the detector, equal intervals were obtained, but at the edge of the detector, intervals between neighbors shrink, resulting in worse spatial resolution. The mean spatial resolutions in the x and y direction were, respectively, 3.5 ± 0.3 mm and 3.1 ± 0.3 mm; resolutions at the edge were not used for calculation of the mean values. The best resolutions in the x and y direction were 3.0 mm and 2.7 mm, respectively. These values were obtained at the center. Meanwhile, mean energy resolution was 10.3 ± 0.2%, and the best value was 9.9%. We did not observe a distinct position dependence of the energy resolution.

2.4 Simulation of scintillation lights

2.4.1 Geometrical configuration of the simulation

We used Geant4 (version 9.2) to simulate scintillation photons, and estimated the spatial and energy resolutions of the large FOV detector. Geant4 takes into account not only

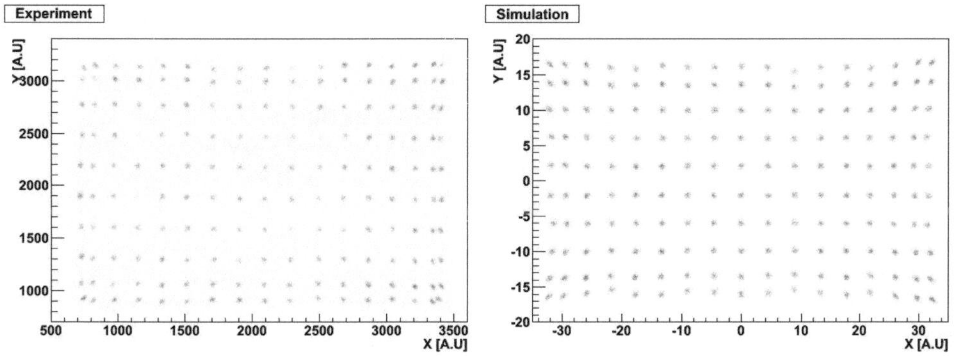

Fig. 2. Planar images of the experiment (left) and the simulation (right). Both results show equal intervals around the center, but shrinkage at the edges.

electromagnetic interactions but also optical photon processes. In this simulation, electromagnetic processes include Compton scattering, Rayleigh scattering, photo-electric effect, ionization, and bremsstrahlung. The first three processes involve gamma rays, and the rest involve electrons. Optical photon processes include absorption, Rayleigh scattering, and boundary processes (refraction/reflection). The details of the optical photon processes are described in next section. Simulation of scintillation photons is difficult; it takes long time due to the large number of optical photons in an event. If a gamma ray interacts with a NaI(Tl) scintillator, 38000 scintillation photons/MeV are generated, all of which must be traced. Moreover, there are many uncertainties (e.g., optical properties of materials). The quantum efficiency of the photo-detector, emission spectrum of the scintillator, and the amount of scintillation photons per unit of energy all must be specified. Strictly speaking, these data have a wavelength dependence. Geant4 does not include these optical properties; hence, in order to conduct an accurate simulation, we must provide them. When estimating the spatial and energy resolutions, it is critical to obtain the distribution of the scintillation lights on the PMTs. We assembled optical property data from brochures and vendor site as much as possible, and fed these values to Geant4.

The simulation processes are as follows: (i) The geometrical configuration shown in Fig. 3 depicts a NaI(Tl) scintillator and 15 PMTs (H8500). Optical window, optical grease, and PMT window are also included between the scintillator and the PMTs. Both the optical and PMT windows are made of borosilicate glass, of thickness 3 mm and 1.5 mm, respectively. The thickness of the optical grease was set as 1 mm. (i) A gamma-ray beam enters the scintillator vertically from above the 170 holes. The source distribution is circular, with a diameter of 1.5 mm. (ii) The gamma ray interacts with the scintillator and deposits its energy. (iii) Scintillation photons are emitted isotropically. The quantity of scintillation photons corresponds to the energy deposited. (iv) The scintillation photons propagate in the scintillator and other materials until they reach the anodes or are absorbed. (v) Some of the scintillation photons reach an anode. The detection of the photon is calculated according to the quantum efficiency and collection efficiency of the H8500. The anodes are assumed to be a perfect absorber. (vi) The interaction point is calculated using the photon distribution on the anodes. Fluctuations of electrical resistance values and anode gains are considered in this simulation. The resistance error and anode gain fluctuation are assigned values of 1% and 17%, respectively, of the number of observed photons. The anode gain fluctuation is derived from the uniformity map of the H8500 (HAMAMATSU, 2007). The given transmittances of NaI(Tl) and borosilicate glass are shown in Fig. 4 (right). A dead space, which surrounds the anodes, is assumed as a perfect absorber. The refractive indexes of NaI(Tl), borosilicate glass, and optical grease are 1.85, in Fig. 4 (right), and 1.45 (Saint-Gobain, 2005-10), respectively. The emission spectrum of NaI(Tl), together with the quantum efficiency, are shown in Fig. 4 (left). The collection efficiency of the H8500 is assigned a value of 60%. In the case of NaI(Tl), 38000 photons/MeV are produced in each interaction. The reflectivity of the white diffusive reflector is 0.95 (Saint-Gobain, 2004-8). Gamma rays from 3000 events enter the scintillator at 170 holes. The experimental analysis, mentioned in the previous section, is applied to the result of the simulation. This simulation was performed on a personal computer (Linux operating system installed on a 2.4 GHz Intel Core 2 Quad with 2 GB of memory). The computing time for 3000 events was ~4000 sec without parallel computation.

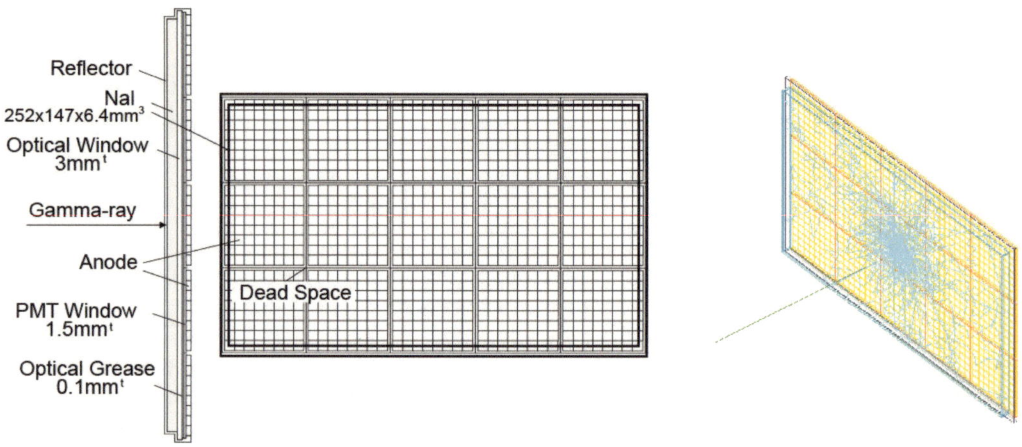

Fig. 3. Simulation geometry of the large FOV detector based on a NaI(Tl) scintillator and position sensitive PMSs (H8500) (left). The optical window, optical grease, and PMT window are included. The scintillator is covered with white diffusive reflector, except on the side connected to the PMTs. The right figure shows a visualization of the simulation. A gamma ray enters the center of the detector. Scintillation photons are emitted isotropically at interaction points.

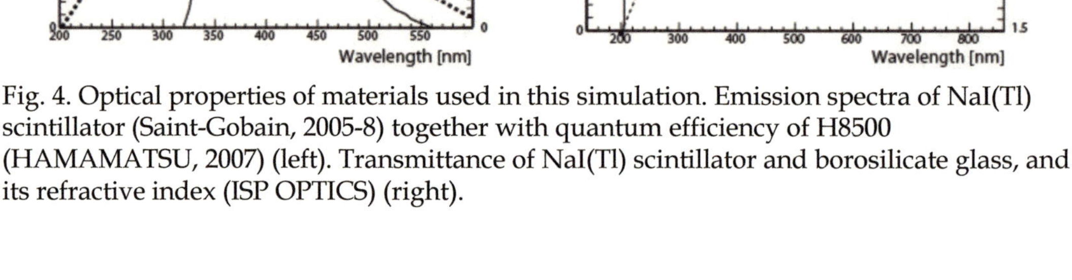

Fig. 4. Optical properties of materials used in this simulation. Emission spectra of NaI(Tl) scintillator (Saint-Gobain, 2005-8) together with quantum efficiency of H8500 (HAMAMATSU, 2007) (left). Transmittance of NaI(Tl) scintillator and borosilicate glass, and its refractive index (ISP OPTICS) (right).

2.4.2 Optical photon process in Geant4

Geant4 can handle optical processes that include G4OpAbsorption, G4OpBoundaryProcess, G4OpRayleigh, and G4OpWLS (wavelength shift). Absorption, Rayleigh scattering and wavelength shift (if registered) are competing processes in the propagation of optical photons. The absorption depends on absorption length, which must be input by the user. If not given, the material is assumed to be perfectly transparent. The cross-section of the Rayleigh scatter also must be input; however, if the material name is specified as "Water", the cross-section is calculated automatically. To include a wavelength shift process, absorption length and emission spectrum of a wave length shifter are required. A time profile of the emission can be input by the users. At a boundary between different materials, G4OpBoundaryProcess is called. Geant4 has two surface types: dielectric_metal (dielectric–metal interface, in which reflection or absorption is applied), and dielectric_dielectric (dielectric–dielectric interface, in which reflection or refraction or absorption is applied); three types of surface model: GLISUR (original Geant3 model), unified (Levin C. M et al., 1996), and LUT (look-up table model available in version 9.3 and more); and six types of surface finish: polished (smooth perfectly polished surface),

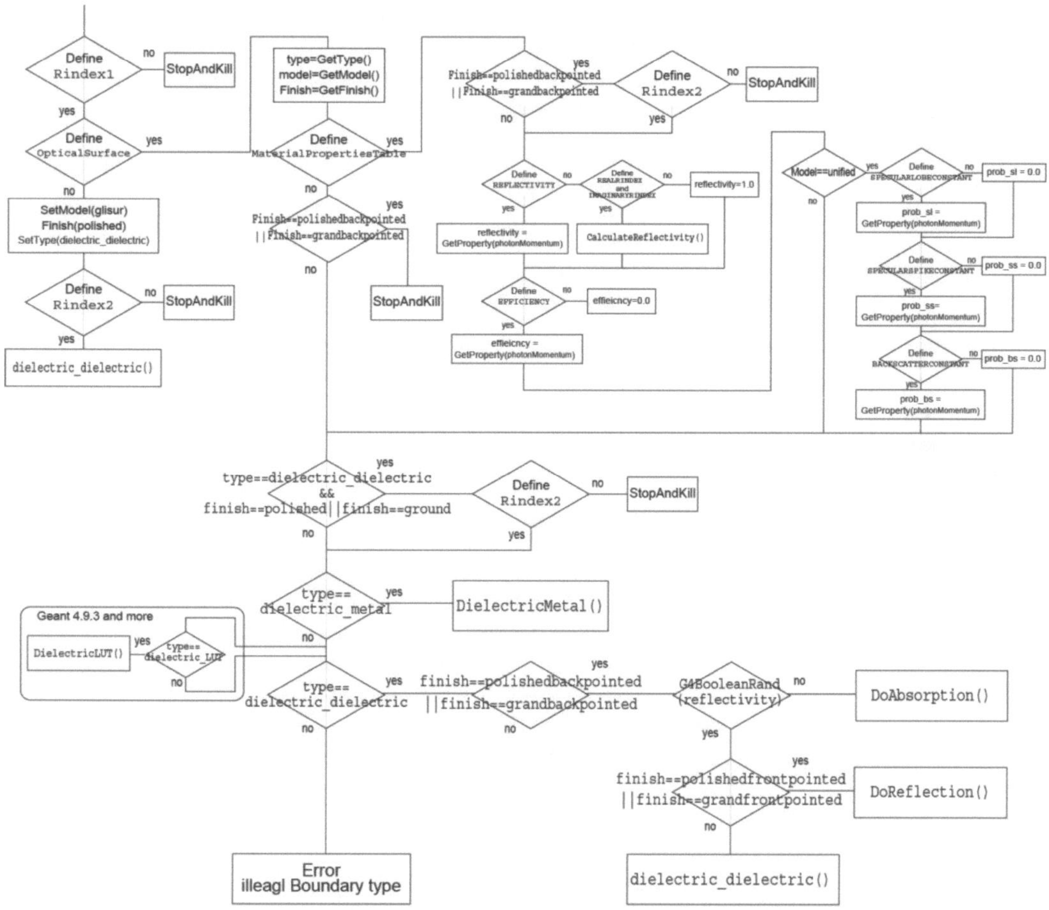

Fig. 5. Flow chart to decide the action of a photon at a boundary. In Geant4.9.3, type of dielectric_LUT is available. In the type, measured angular distributions are used.

polishedbackpainted (smooth top-layer front paint), polishedbackpainted (same as polished but with a back-point), ground (rough surface), grandfrontpainted (rough top-layer front point), and groundbackpainted (same as ground but with a back-point). The unified model, which considers microfacets of the surface, contains four types of reflections: Lambertian reflection, lobe reflection, spike reflection, and back-scattering. The degree of angular fluctuation is parameterized. Depending on these parameters, action at a boundary is determined as refraction, reflection or absorption. Relation between surface parameters and photon behavior at a boundary is somewhat complex. A flow chart illustrating decisions about this relationship is shown in Fig. 5. In this simulation, the surface parameters of the white diffuse reflector are set as follows: unified model, backfrontpointed, and delectric–dicelectric. The parameter of the rough surface is set as 1.0. In this case, a photon is reflected as diffuse reflection.

2.4.3 Results

The planar image of the simulation is shown in Fig. 2, together with the experimental results. The simulation showed the same tendency as in the experiment (equal interval at the center, shrinkage at the edge). The mean spatial resolutions (FWHM) in the x and y directions were 3.3 ± 0.2 mm and 3.0 ± 0.2 mm, respectively, The best resolutions were 2.8 mm and 2.6 mm, respectively, in the x and y directions. The mean energy resolution (FHWM) was 9.1%, and the best resolution was 8.5%. An energy spectrum of the center is shown in Fig. 6 alongside the spectrum obtained by experiment. The comparisons of the resolutions are listed in Table 1.

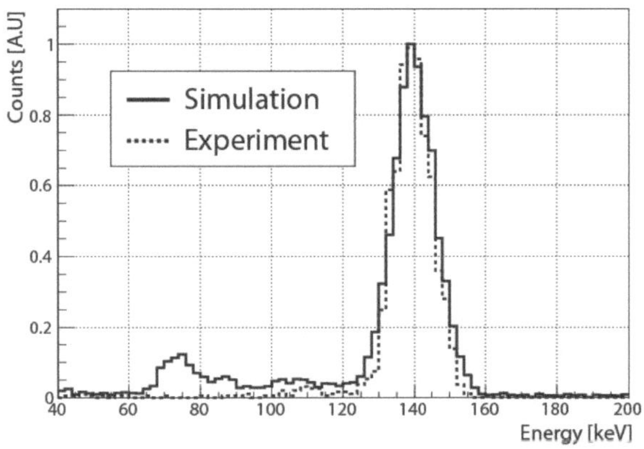

Fig. 6. Energy spectra from experiment and simulation, obtained at 5th row and 6th column. Experimental and simulation resolutions are 10.1% and 9.2%, respectively.

Resolution (FWHM)	Experiment Mean ± S.D (Best)	Simulation Mean ± S.D (Best)
Spatial (X-dir) [mm]	3.5±0.3 (3.0)	3.3±0.2 (2.8)
Spatial (Y-dir) [mm]	3.1±0.3 (2.7)	3.0±0.2 (2.6)
Energy [%]	10.3±0.2 (9.9)	9.1±0.3 (8.5)

Table 1. Comparison of spatial and energy resolutions between simulation and experiment. The mean values are calculated without edge resolutions. The parenthetical values are the best resolutions, obtained at the center.

2.4.4 Discussion

The spatial resolutions of the simulation are consistent with those of the experiment (within 10%). The accuracy seems to be sufficient to estimate resolutions and design new detectors. The simulation also has good agreement with experiment with regard to energy resolution. The energy spectrum is formed from the quantity of obtained photons. The energy resolution of simulations is usually generated using an adjustment parameter decided by an experiment. In this work, however, the energy resolution is calculated without such a parameter, depending on the number of photons. The difference between spatial resolutions in the x and y directions was obtained in both results. We obtained 3.5 mm and 3.1 mm in x and y-directions, respectively, in the experiment. This difference is due to the difference in the number of anodes. Propagation of fluctuation of anode output in the x direction is larger than that of the propagation in the y direction. If a detector has the same number of anode in the x and y directions, the spatial resolutions are comparable, as shown by another simulation (not described in this chapter). Available clinical SPECTs commonly have ~4 mm spatial resolution (FWHM) with a smaller number of PMTs (or anodes). It seems using many anodes does not make much contribution to the improvement of spatial resolution. The large error propagation of anode output deteriorates resolutions.

A simulation is useful for the design of a detector. It is easy to change the thickness or type of scintillator, photo-detector, or other parameters in the simulation. Moreover, the simulation is able to identify the main absorber and the main causes of deterioration of resolutions. As the demonstration, we replaced optical grease with air, whose refractive index is ~1.0. The variations in the absorption fraction of materials relative to total generated photons and number of total internal reflections are listed in Table 2. Because of the disjunction of refractive index at a boundary, the number of total internal reflection increases. The increase in total reflections creates a longer path length for photons in the scintillator, resulting in absorption by the scintillator. About 80 % of total generated photons reached at PMT anodes, and 20 % of reached photons were obtained.

	Boundary of optical grease	Boundary of Air
Detection	12 %	10 %
PMT Anode	73 %	62 %
PMT Window	0.20 %	0.12 %
PMT Dead Space	5.6 %	6.3 %
Reflector	6.9 %	16 %
NaI scintillator	0.91 %	1.84 %
Optical Window	0.73 %	1.2 %
Optical Grease	~0 %	~0 %
Total internal reflection	1	14.7

Table 2. Absorption fraction of materials (%). Detection means a photon reaches at an anode and obtained according to quantum efficiency and collection efficiency. If not obtain, a photon absorbed by a anode (PMT Anode). Number of total internal reflections is normalized against that of optical grease.

The simulation results are always overestimated. Our simulation still does not consider other uncertainties, e.g., fluctuation of the number of electrons in the multiplying process of a PMT, etc. In addition, there are unknown optical properties such as the absorption length of the optical grease (in this study, however, the absorption can be treated as negligible because the grease layer is thin) and almost the properties does not have wavelength dependence. We need a dataset of optical properties of materials, especially those used in scintillation detectors. In order to conduct accurate simulations, it seems better to consider other uncertainties as much as possible. Although some optical properties are neglected, this simulation already has sufficient reproducibility.

2.5 Simulation approach to improve spatial resolution

2.5.1 Methods

We aim at spatial resolution of ~2 mm in the large FOV detector to make a difference from clinical SPECTs. However, we obtained a resolution of ~3.5 mm, which is worse than expected. Therefore, we proposed an alternative to the Anger method to improve the spatial resolution. The method is simple. Previously, photon distributions on anodes were measured at every known position in the detector. In this work, we calculated the distribution of gamma rays on a grid pattern with 1 mm intervals. Each distribution is obtained from average of incident 300 gamma rays. The number of total distributions is 37296 (252×148). One quarter was simulated, and the rest were derived from symmetrical properties. The set of distributions is used as reference data. Every time scintillation photons are radiated, the distribution is compared with the reference dataset. The position of most similar distribution, determined by the least square algorithm, is identified as the point of interaction. In an actual experiment, a reference dataset can be accumulated by scanning collimated gamma rays. We evaluated the usefulness of the method. The result of the simulation in the validation study is reusable for this evaluation.

2.5.2 Results

Examples of reference data are shown in Fig. 7. Fig. 7 shows photon distributions in the case that gamma rays enter at the center (left) or at the edge (right). The planar image and projection in the *y* direction are shown in Fig. 8. In contrast to the Anger method, constant intervals were obtained among grid points. At the edge, however, a point divided into two.

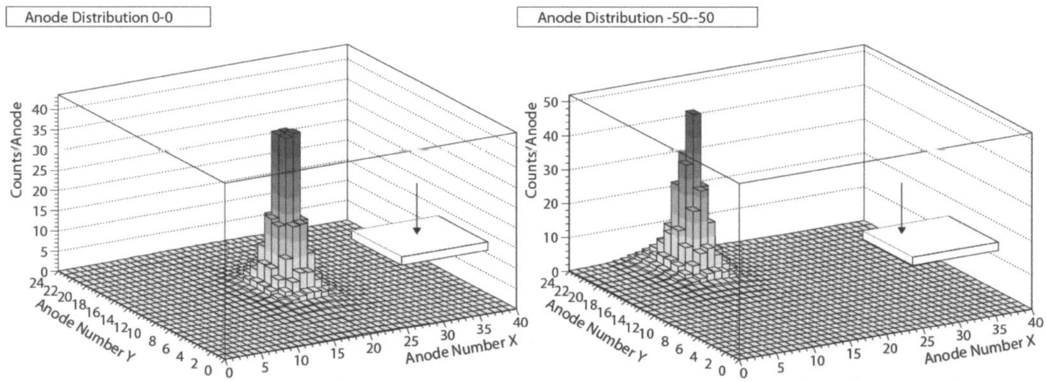

Fig. 7. Examples of photon distribution on the anodes of 15 H8500s. The left figure shows the distribution in the case that gamma rays enter from the center; the right figure shows the case in which the gamma rays enter from (–50 mm,–50 mm) relative to the center. We calculated photon distributions, which are obtained from the known positions of gamma-ray sources. The set of distributions was used as reference data to decide interaction points.

The mean spatial resolutions, without the edge resolutions, were 1.8 ± 0.8 mm and 1.8 ± 0.8 mm in the x and y directions, respectively. The mean energy resolution is 10 ± 5%. An obvious position dependence of the energy resolution was not obtained using this method.

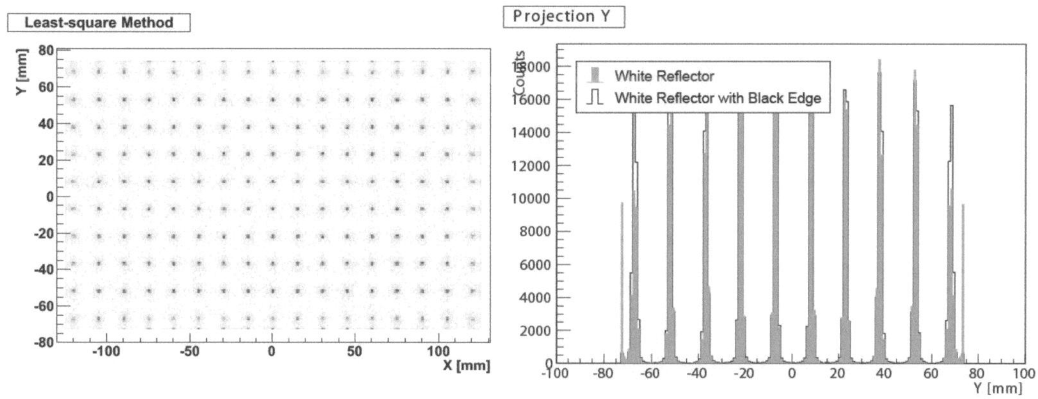

Fig. 8. Planar image obtained by the proposed method using the least-square algorithm. (left), and the projections to the y direction (right). The gray filled histogram is the projection with a white diffusive reflector; the white filled histogram is a projection with a black edge reflector. Misidentifications, especially at the edge, were improved by using the black edge white reflector.

2.5.3 Discussion

The proposed method indicated improvement of spatial resolution from 3.5 mm to 1.8 mm in the x direction. The large FOV detector has the potential for high resolution, ~2 mm. One advantage of this method is that the unit of the planar image is actual length (mm); this is different from the Anger method, in which the unit is arbitrary. We do not need to calibrate position.

At the edge, many misidentifications are seen due to small difference of reference dataset at the edge. To prevent misidentification, it is useful to employ a diffuse reflector with black edge (the side of the scintillator is coated with absorbent material). The projection with the black edge reflector is shown in Fig. 8, together with the original reflector. The false identifications were corrected at the edge. Meanwhile, the energy resolutions at the edge became worse due to a reduction in the number of photons by absorption.

To implement this method, it is essential to install an analog to digital converter (ADC) for each anode. This conversion may take a great deal of time and decrease the cost-effectiveness. However, it is worthwhile to try this method, because once all anode outputs are converted, we can try other methods. A neural network would be one promising method; another would be to employ a modified Anger method using restricted anodes that are peripheral to the largest output anode. We are developing a full digital system for the method. Furthermore, if the reference data is compiled using only simulations with high accuracy, the technique has the potential to discriminate the depth of interactions. It sometimes happens that a gamma ray is scattered before absorbed in the scintillator. In this case, there are multiple sources of scintillation photons, and these events impair spatial resolution. It is difficult to discriminate events with multiple scintillation sources from events with single scintillation source. Chi-square, defined by $\chi^2 = \frac{1}{ndf}\sum_i \frac{(obj_i - ref_i)^2}{error_i^2}$, may help to make the distinction; here, *i*, *obj*, *ref*, *error* *ndf* mean index of anode, anode output, anode output of reference data, error of anode output, and number of degrees of freedom, respectively. A large chi-square indicates an event with multiple scintillation sources. Higher-energy gamma rays, such as 511 keV, tend to be such a event. In a SPECT system, however, because of the low energy of gamma-rays (in the range of several hundred keV), these occurrences are rare, and can safely be ignored.

2.6 Conclusion

Our simulation is in good agreement with the experiment that determined the intrinsic spatial and energy resolutions of the large FOV detector. The proposed method, using ADCs for all anodes, is promising. We expect that this will improve spatial resolution from ~3.5 mm to ~1.8 mm; it also has prospects for use in other identification methods.

The simulation including action of scintillation lights will be helpful for a design of a new SPECT by estimation of the spatial resolution. However, we still used insufficient data regarding optical properties in this work. We hope that data regarding the properties of scintillators and materials are in public.

3. Application to a quantification technique in PET

3.1 Introduction

Quantification in PET is important for improvement in diagnosis. Here, quantification refers to the absolute pixel value in PET images. Examples of quantitative values in PET include SUV, cerebral and myocardial blood flow, cerebral metabolic rate of oxygen, oxygen extraction fraction in ischemia check. An accurate quantification can prevent erroneous diagnosis and provide high-quality data for multi-center studies. However, there are some factors that hamper quantification; these include random events (accidental events) and scatter events. Random events are accidental coincidental counts that originate from two different sources. The scatter events also reflect coincidence counting, but in these cases one or both gamma rays have been scattered. Gamma rays lose their energy by Compton scattering, and it is easy to discriminate the events by selecting the 511 keV photopeak. However, because of the poor energy resolution of detectors, it is impossible to remove all scatter events. These events result in inaccurate LORs and disturb both image quality and quantification. The random events can be corrected by a delayed coincidence technique. The scatter events are also compensated by some kinds of correction theories. However, when significant activity exists outside the FOV (typical PETs have 15–25 cm FOV), verification of scatter corrections in 3D acquisition mode has not yet been thoroughly investigated. Measurements of myocardium blood flow represent an illustrative example. The liver, located outside the FOV, has larger activity than that of the heart, which is within the FOV. The uncorrected scatter events originating from outside the FOV may reduce the accuracy of quantification. One of the advantages of simulations is that they allow an understanding of processes that are difficult or impossible to know in experiments. Scatter events are also difficult to identify in experiments. We conducted a simulation (Geant4 version 9.2) of scatters with a numerical human model, and investigated the effects of scatter events on quantification in cardiac PET using O-15 water.

3.2 PET configuration in the simulation

We reproduced a realistic configuration of a PET (ECAT ACCEL, Siemens) (Herzog H et al., 2004), which is installed in our facility. The PET is based on LSO scintillators consisting of a 2.5 × 2.5 × 6 mm^3 rectangular solid. The detector consists of 9216 scintillators, which are circularly arranged. One ring consists of 384 scintillators, and 24 rings can be arranged in the axial direction. The diameter of the ring is 824 mm, and the aperture plane of the gantry is 562 mm. The FOV is 162 mm. To simplify, in this simulation, the detector is shaped as a ring with the following dimensions: 824 mm diameter, 162 mm width, and 6.5 mm thickness. The structures contain not only scintillators but also PMTs, front shield, septa, bed, body of equipment, etc., shown in Fig. 9. These are included, because such structures slightly increase scatter events originating from activity outside the FOV. The adequacy of this simulation has been evaluated by comparison of the scatter fraction. Scatter fraction is the ratio between total coincident events and scatter events, measured by using a special phantom (scatter phantom); and the measurement method is described in the NEMA standard (NEMA NU 2-2007). The experimental scatter fraction was 45.0%, and that of the simulation is 45.9%. The simulation reproduced the experiment with high accuracy.

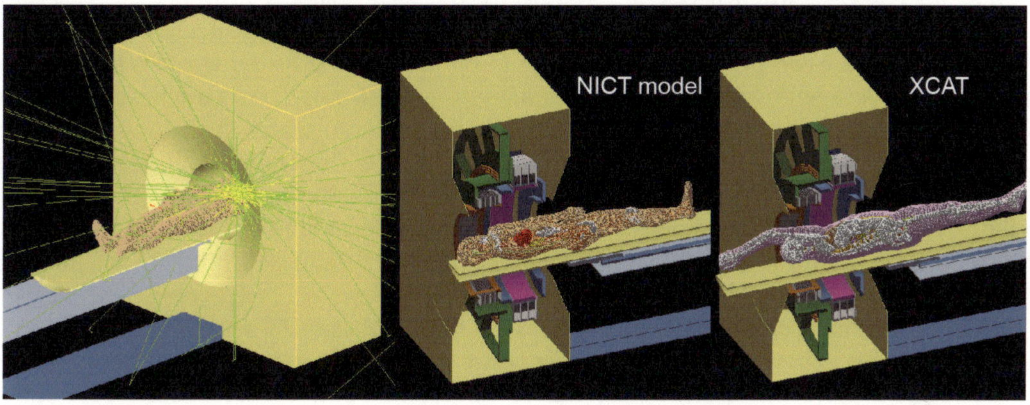

Fig. 9. Geometrical configuration of the simulation in PET. For realistic simulation, we reproduced a PET using the numerical human model generated by NICT (left). The line shows gamma rays. The center and right figures, respectively, show laminagrams of the PET containing the NICT model and XCAT,.

3.3 Simulation with numerical human model

For a realistic simulation, we employed a numerical human model (Nagaoka T et al., 2004) developed by National Institute of Information and Communications Technology (NICT) in Japan. The model is based on MRI images of Japanese people with average height and weight: 173 cm and 65 kg for male; 160 cm and 50 kg for female. The models consist of 320 × 160 × 866 voxels for male, or 320 × 160 × 804 voxels for female; voxels are 2 mm^3. Fifty-one organs or tissues can be identified, and ID numbers are given to each voxel. In addition, models of a child, a pregnant female and an arbitrary pose have been developed. There is another available numerical human model, the 4D NURBS-based Cardiac-Torso (XCAT*) phantom (Segars WP et al., 2003). The organs are constructed using non-uniform rational b-splines, or NURBS surfaces based on the three-dimensional Visible Human CT dataset. XCAT is able to calculate cardiac and respiratory motions. It is powerful tool for evaluating motion effects, and is widely used in nuclear medicine imaging research. The geometrical configuration with NICT model and XCAT are shown in Fig. 9. To simulate interactions of gamma rays with the human body, we need attenuation coefficients for each tissue. We calculated the attenuation coefficients using compositions and density of the tissues found in a web site of Life Sciences Division at Oak Ridge National Laboratory (ORNL), "Description of the mathematical phantoms" and (Akkurt H et al., 2007). Compositions and densities of soft tissue, skeleton, lung, adipose, and glandular tissue are available from "Description of the mathematical phantoms"; compositions of bone, muscle, skin, brain, eyes, thyroid, upper face, larynx, trachea, gastrointestinal tract, testes, ovaries, uterus, urinary bladder, spleen, heart, pancreas, liver, kidney, breast, and blood are available from (Akkurt H et al., 2007). We assigned tissue data listed above to 51 types of tissues. In this work, we used the male NICT model and its 8 voxels are collected up to 1voxel (4 mm cubic) to reduce the computing time.

3.4 Estimation of scatter in cardiac PET

In cardiac PET to measure myocardium blood flow, O-15 water, Rb-82, and N-13-NH_3 are used as tracers. O-15 water is one of the most ideal tracers, because it immediately diffuses into tissues and washes out into veins. That behavior makes it easy to calculate myocardium blood flow with a 2-compartment model (Iida H et al., 1992). Activated water is injected and spreads into the whole body, in which the activity of each organ varies with time. At the first phase, the heart has a large activity, and the tracer accumulates in the liver at the late phase. The time activity curve of the heart, liver and lung is shown in Fig. 10, obtained with a clinical examination. The horizontal axis shows time in seconds; the vertical axis shows activity per organ. In PET images, we can obtain a pixel value as activity per volume (Bq/cc). The activities per organ are derived from experimental data (Bq/cc) × volume of heart (406 cc), liver (3296 cc), and lung (1150 cc), using the NICT model, under the assumption that each organ has uniform activity. In one phase (100 sec in Fig. 10), the liver has 1.5 times the activity of the heart. This phase seems to significantly influence activity outside the FOV. We simulated trajectories of annihilation gamma rays. In this PET study, the scintillation lights are not tracked. Positions of interaction between gamma rays and the scintillator are saved to create a sinogram using the ECAT format for 3D acquisition mode. The image is reconstructed by FBP with the scatter correction algorithm installed in the ECAT image reconstruction system. The image size is a 128 × 128 matrix (47 slices). The scatter correction is single scatter simulation (SSS) (Ollinger JM, 1996). To obtain a quantitative image, an attenuation map for the correction of absorptions is required. In this simulation, the attenuation map is calculated analytically. We created three types of image. The first one is an image reconstructed with scatter correction (normal image). The second one is an image using a sinogram without scatter events, which can be discriminated in the simulation (true image). The third one is an image using only scatter events (scatter image). The last two images are reconstructed without the scatter correction. We can obtain only a normal image in an actual PET study. According to the time activity curve, sinograms of the heart, liver and lung are combined in proportion to their activity at each time, and reconstructed into three types of image. Twenty set of images are created. If scatter events are corrected accurately, the normal image should be same as the true image. By means of comparison between the normal and true images, we evaluated adequacy of the scatter correction. Two billion events were performed in each organ. These computations took ~420 h to complete with a personal computer (Linux operating system installed on a 2.4 GHz Intel Core 2 Quad with 2 GB of memory). However, we can reduce the computing time down to ~20 h using 5 computers with comparable specifications. Twenty processes are able to run in parallel.

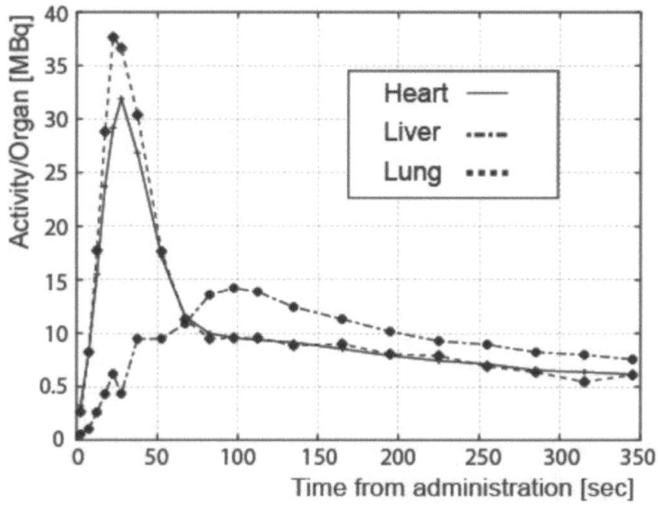

Fig. 10. Time activity curves of the heart, liver and lung. The vertical axis represents the activity of a organ. The horizontal axis represents the time after the administration of O-15 water. For one phase (~100 sec) the liver (located outside the FOV) has 1.5 times more activity than the heart.

3.5 Results

The sets of images of slice 14 (the apex and liver are seen) at 20, 45, 75 120, 210 and 300 sec after the injection are shown in Fig. 12. We placed ROIs (region of interests) on the tissues (anterior, posterior, septal, lateral, and apex) in the normal and true images. The difference between the two ROI values for the apex is shown in Fig. 11. Myocardial blood flows (MBF), which are calculated with time series of ROI values, are listed in Table 3. MBFs of the normal image are normalized by experimental values. The ROI values of normal images overestimate that of the true image due to the insufficient scatter correction. However, myocardium blood flows remained unchanged.

MBF(mL/min/g)	Normal Image	True Image
Apex	1.09	1.11
Anterior	0.81	0.80
Lateral	1.03	1.03
Posterior	0.80	0.79
Septal	0.75	0.73

Table 3. Myocardial blood flow (MBF) calculated using the normal image and true image. The MBFs of normal image are normalized by these of an experimental value. We obtained equivalent vales derived from the normal and true image.

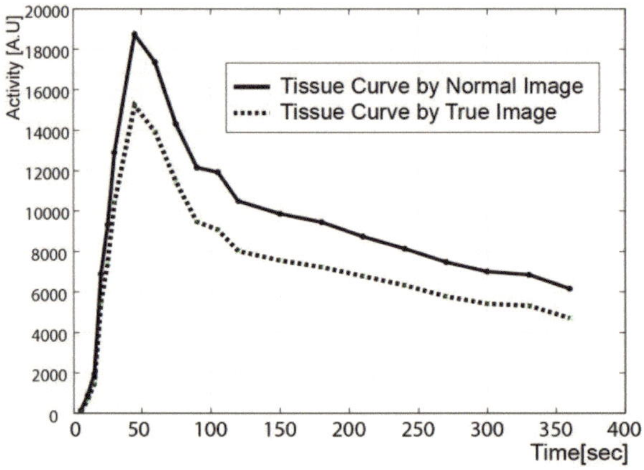

Fig. 11. Time activity curve of a tissue (apex). The solid line is derived from the normal image. The dotted line is derived from the true image. Due to the uncorrected scatters, the normal image is overestimated. At the wash-out phase (~50 sec and after) the both curves have almost the same reduction rate.

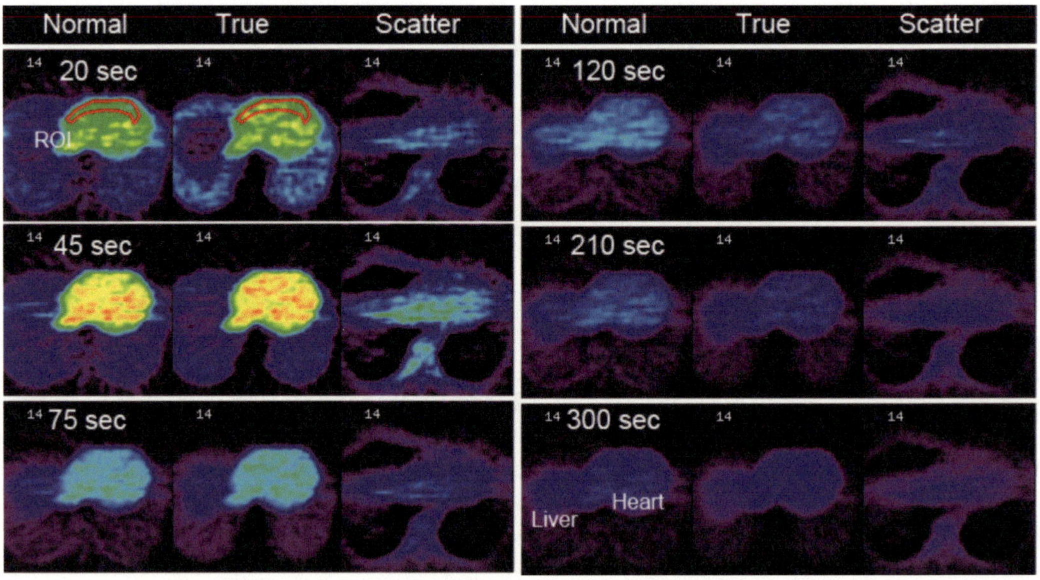

Fig. 12. Reconstructed images of the normal, true, and scatter images at 20, 45, 75, 120, 210, and 300 sec from the injection. At the wash-out phase, scatter distributions are uniform and almost the same in the heart region.

3.6 Discussion

In this simulation, large activity outside the FOV influences quantification of an image. The scatters are not compensated accurately; consequently, ROI values tend to overestimate true values. This result indicates that some quantitative physiological parameters measured by PET may be overestimated. However, physiological parameters do not always depend on absolute ROI values. Quantitative myocardial blood flows determined by O-15 seem to epitomize this case. Because the blood flows are calculated by the tissue wash-out rate,

which is equivalent both in normal images and true images. As shown in Fig. 11, uncorrected scatters make a constant contribution to the ROI values in the heart region at the wash-out phase, and this leaves myocardial blood flow unchanged.
By means of this method, we can evaluate other scatter corrections using other PET configurations. Recently, PET/CT has become a major modality, replacing single PET; in this modality, a CT is installed next to PET detector. The influence of structures of the CT on quantification should be investigated. Our simulation with a realistic geometrical configuration can clarify the influence. In addition, it is useful for estimation of random events. To remove random events originating from activity outside the FOV, it will be essential to improve image quality and reduce measurement dead time. We can design optimized the shielding system by using this simulation.

3.7 Conclusion

We simulated scatter events in cardiac PET using an O-15 tracer. In this work, three types of images (normal image, true image, and scatter image) were created using a sinogram obtained with this simulation and the reconstruction method with scatter correction installed in ECAT system. By comparing between the normal image and true image, we obtained that the scatter correction is not sufficient due to the existence of significant activity outside the FOV. However, even in this case, myocardial blood flow (calculated by tracer wash-out rate) stayed unchanged.

4. Conclusion of this chapter

In this chapter, applications of Monte Carlo method to PET and SPECT studies were mentioned. In both SPECT and PET studies, the spatial and energy resolutions of SPECT by simulating scintillation photons (and scatter events in PET) reproduced the results of experiments. Monte Carlo simulations can be used as a reliable tool in the development of medical equipments.

5. Acknowledgment

The author thanks Professor Hidehiro Iida for many helpful discussions, and Dr. Tustomu Zeniya and Dr. Kazuhiro Koshino for their kind assistance. The author also thanks aid Assistant Professor Hiroshi Watabe for his teaching of operation of the PET. The work on the development of a high-resolution SPECT described in early part of this chapter was supported by part of the Newly Adopted Projects of Regional R&D Programs for FY2008 from the Kansai Bureau of Economy, Trade and Industry, Health Labour Sciences Research Grant; DDS from the Ministry of Health, Labour and Welfare (MHLW); and the Budget for Nuclear Research of the Ministry of Education, Culture, Sports, Science and Technology (MEXT); all funding agencies are in Japan. The work for simulation study in PET was funded by a Grant-in-Aid for Young Scientists (B), also in Japan.

6. References

Akkurt H, & Echerman FK. (2007). Development of PIMAL: Mathematical Phantom With Moving Arms and Legs. *ORNL/TM-2007/14*

Allison J. et al,. (2006). Geant4 developments and applications, *IEEE Transactions on NuclearScience*, Vol.53, No1, pp.270-278, 0018-9499

HAMAMATSU. (2007). H8500 SERESE, October 2010 http://jp.hamamatsu.com/ resources/ products/etd/pdf/H8500C_H8500D_TPMH1308E01.pdf

Herzog H, Tellmann L, Hocke C, Pietrzyk U, Casey ME, & Kuwrt T. (2004). NEMA NU2-2001 guided performance evaluation of four Siemens ECAT PET scanners. *IEEE Transactions on Nuclear Science*, Vol.51, No.5, pp.2662-2669, 0018-9499

Iida H, Christopher GR, Ranil de S, Luis IA, Peter MB, Adriaan AL, & Terry J. (1992). Use of the left ventricular time-activity curve as a noninvasive input function in dynamic oxygen-15-water positron emission tomography. *J Nucl Med,* Vol.33, No.9, pp1669-1677

ISP OPTICS. BK7 Schott Glass, October 2010 http://www.ispoptics.com/PDFs/PDFCatalog/Page14.pdf

Kudo H, Courdurier M, Noo F, & Defrise M. (2008). Tiny a prior knowledge solves the interior problem in computed tomography. *Phys. Med. Biol.*, Vol. 53, No.9, pp.2207-2231

Levin A, & Moisan C. (1996). A More Physical Approach to Model the Surface Treatment of Scintillation Counters and its Implementation into DETECT. *TRIUMF Preprint TRI,* pp.96-64

Nagaoka T, Watanabe S, Sakurai K, Kunieda E, Watanabe S, Taki M, & Yamanaka Y. (2004). Development of Realistic High-Resolution Whole-Body Voxel Models of Japanese Adult Male and Female of Average Height and Weight, and Application of Models to Radio-Frequency Electromagnetic-Field Dosmietry. *Physics in Medicine and Biology,* Vol,49, No.49, pp1-15

NEMA NU 2-2007. Performance Measurement of Positron Emission Tomographs National Electrical Manufactures Association

Ollinger JM. (1996). Model-based scatter correction for fully 3D PET. *Phys. Med. Biol.* Vol. 41, No. 1, pp.153-176

ORNL. Description of the mathematical phantoms, October 2010 http://ordose.ornl.gov/resources/Mird.pdf

Saint-Gobain. (2004-8). Scintillation Products, October 2010 http://www.detectors.saint-gobain.com/uploadedFiles/SGdetectors/Documents/Brochures/Arrays-Brochure.pdf

Saint-Gobain. (2005-10). Detector Assembly Materials, October 2010 http://www.detectors.saint-gobain.com/uploadedFiles/SGdetectors/Documents/Product_Data_Sheets/SGC_Detector_Assembly_Materials_Data_Sheet.pdf

Saint-Gobain. (2005-8). NaI(Tl) Scintillation Material, October 2010 http://www.detectors.saint-gobain.com/uploadedFiles/SGdetectors/Documents/Product_Data_Sheets/NaI%28Tl%29-Data-Sheet.pdf

Segars WP, Tsui BMW, Frey EC, & Fishman EK. (2003). Extension of the 4D NCAT phantom to dynamic x-ray CT simulation. *Nuclear Science Symposium Conference Record, 2003 IEEE,* pp.3195-3199, 1082-3654

Strul D, Santin G, Lazaro D, Breton V, & Morel C. GATE (Geant4 Application for Tomographic Emission): a PET/SPECT general-purpose simulation platform. (2003). *Nucl. Phys. B (Proc. Suppl.),* Vol.125, pp.75-79

Zeniya T, Watabe H, Inomata T, Iida H, Sohlberg A, & Kudo H. (2007). 3DOSEM reconstruction from truncated data in pinhole SPECT. *2007 IEEE Nuclear Science Symposium Conference Record*, Vol. 6, pp.4205-4207, 1082-3654

Zeniya T, Hirano Y, Sakimoto T, Ishida K, Watabe H, Teramoto N, Kudo H, Minato K, Hatazawa J, & Iida H. (2009). Conceptual Design of High Resolution and a Quantitative SPECT system for imaging a selected small ROI of human brain. *2009 IEEE Nuclear Science Symposium Conference Record*, pp. 3484-3486, 1082-3654

6

Applying Dynamic Monte Carlo Simulation for Living Free Radical Polymerization Processes: Emphasis on Atom Transfer Radical Polymerization (ATRP)

Mamdouh A. Al-Harthi
Chemical Engineering Department, King Fahd University of Petroleum & Minerals, Dhahran 31261, Saudi Arabia

1. Introduction

Modeling is the applications of methods to analyze complex, real-world problems in order to make predictions about what might happen with various actions. When it is too difficult, time consuming, costly or dangerous experiments, the modeler resort to computer simulations, or having a computer program imitate reality, in order to study situations and make decisions. Mathematical modeling is being used extensively in the field of polymer reaction engineering to ascertain various parameters. The use of mathematical modeling reduces the need for costly and time consuming experimentation. Mathematical models have been useful tools to enhance the understanding of polymerization processes and have been essential for process design, parameter estimation, sensitivity analysis, process simulation and optimization. Moreover, they are also useful for education and training purposes. [1-4] For example, several models have been proposed to simulate free-radical homopolymerization. The majority of these models predicting only averages molecular properties, but not complete distributions.

Various modeling techniques have been used in the field of polymer engineering depending on the suitability and on the targeted parameters. The most commonly used techniques are namely: 1) Instantaneous distributions, 2) Population balances with the method of moments, and 3) Monte Carlo method. The three methods have their own advantages and disadvantages. For examples, the method of moments cannot predict the molecular weight distribution (MWD) while the instantaneous distribution and Monte Carlo method can easily predict the MWD. In the case of copolymerizations, Monte Carlo technique is capable of predicting both average results and the full distribution. The focal point of this chapter would be on the Monte Carlo method since this technique can give full understanding about the polymerization processes. The modeler of the Mote Carlo simulation have full understanding of the molecular behavior in the reactor and use its programming skills to translate this understanding into valuable results.

Monte Carlo simulation is a probabilistic model involving an element of chance. Monte Carlo method provides approximate solutions to a variety of mathematical problems by performing statistical sampling experiments on a computer. Dynamic Monte Carlo (DMC) is a method for modeling the dynamic behaviors of molecules by comparing the rates of individual steps with random numbers. Unlike the Metropolis Monte Carlo method, which has been employed to study systems at equilibrium, the DMC method is used to investigate non-equilibrium systems such as a reaction, diffusion, and so-forth.

The synthesis and design of polymers with well-defined chain structures is a topic of high interest in academia and industry. Controlled radical polymerization (CRP) is fast becoming an important tool for producing polymers with customized microstructures.[1-2] The most well-established mechanisms of CRP are: (1) atom transfer radical polymerization (ATRP),[3,4] (2) nitroxide-mediated polymerization (NMP),[5,6] and (3) reversible addition-fragmentation chain transfer (RAFT).[7,8] Although the application of CRP processes is still limited to academia, they are promising techniques for the industrial production of specialty polymers. At this stage of CRP research, it is imperative to develop reliable mathematical models in order to better understand and improve CRP processes.

Since 1995, significant effort has been made towards the development, understanding, and application of ATRP to a wide range of monomers. In addition to its ability to control polymer micro-structural details, ATRP is very useful towards different reaction conditions.[9-11] ATRP can also copolymerize a variety of vinyl monomers to form random, gradient, block, and graft copolymers.[12-14] Among these previous chain architectures, gradient copolymers have received considerable interest because they form a new class of materials that have intermediate properties between random and block copolymers.[11]

Several research groups have developed mathematical models for ATRP. The method of moments has been used to study the effect of reactant concentration and rate constants on polymer properties,[15,16] and also used to study the effect of diffusion-controlled reactions using the free volume theory.[17,18] Mathematical models using the concept of pseudo-kinetic rate constants and the method of moments have also been developed to describe ATRP.[19,20]

Even though the method of moments can predict average molecular weights (M_n, M_w, and M_z, for instance) and the polydispersity index (PDI), it cannot predict the complete molecular weight distribution (MWD) and it is well-known that the final properties of the polymer are not only a function of the average properties, but depend on distributions of molecular structural properties such as MWD, copolymer composition distribution (CCD), and sequence length distribution (SLD). The commercial software package PREDICI can be used to model polymerization processes and predict several polymer microstructural distributions, but it is only available to licensed users, while Monte Carlo simulation is an equally powerful technique that is relatively easy to implement, as demonstrated in this paper. PREDICI has been used to study the kinetics of ATRP, and to model chain end functionality.[21-24]

Several publications show the use of Monte Carlo models for different polymerization processes [25-30]. The focus of this chapter will be on ATRP in batch and semi batch reactors. Several case studies are presented to show the ability of DMC in predicting the full distributions.

2. Model description

We have followed Gillespie's algorithm for dynamic Monte Carlo simulation.[31] First, a control volume (V) that contains the reactant molecules is defined at time zero. The reaction system is considered homogenous and several reactions can take place in the control volume. The experimental rates of these reactions are transformed into stochastic rates based on the number of molecules of each reactant present in the control volume at a given reaction time. In the case of copolymerization, the number of monomer molecules, X_A and X_B, in the control volume at a given time is equal to their molar concentrations, $[M_A]$ and $[M_B]$, multiplied by Avogadro's number (N) and the size of the control volume:

$$X_A = [M_A]NV \tag{1}$$

$$X_B = [M_B]NV \tag{2}$$

Similarly, the number of initiator and catalyst molecules, X_i and X_C, are calculated as follows:

$$X_i = [I]NV \tag{3}$$

$$X_C = [C]NV \tag{4}$$

where $[I]$ and $[C]$ are the concentrations of initiator and catalyst, respectively.
The experimental rate constants are transformed into stochastic rate constants with the following equations:

$$k^{MC} = k^{\exp} \text{ for first order reactions} \tag{5}$$

$$k^{MC} = \frac{k^{\exp}}{VN} \text{ for bimolecular reactions between different species} \tag{6}$$

$$k^{MC} = \frac{2k^{\exp}}{VN} \text{ for bimolecular reactions between similar species} \tag{7}$$

This transformation involves the number of independent combinations of molecules participating in each reaction inside the control volume, as explained by Gillespie.[31]
The probability of any reaction (P_v) taking place at a given time can be calculated with the equation

$$P_v = \frac{R_v}{\sum_{v=1}^{N} R_v} \tag{8}$$

where R_v is the reaction rate of the vth reaction and N is the total number of reactions in the polymerization mechanism. The following relation is used to determine which reaction type will take place at a given polymerization time

$$\sum_{v=1}^{\mu-1} P_v < r_1 < \sum_{v=1}^{\mu} P_v \tag{9}$$

where μ is the number of the selected reaction type and r_1 is a random number uniformly distributed between [0,1]. Another random number is generated to determine the time interval (τ) between two consecutive reactions. The time step is related to the inverse of total stochastic rates and the natural logarithmic of r_2 according to the equation:[31]

$$\tau = \frac{1}{\sum_{v=1}^{N} R_v} \ln\left(\frac{1}{r_2}\right) \tag{10}$$

The mechanism of ATRP proceeds in the same manner as conventional free radical polymerization: initiation, propagation, termination, and transfer reactions. In addition to this, it also includes an equilibrium reaction between active and dormant chains. This equilibrium reaction is in favor of the dormant chains and hence reduces the frequency of polymer radical termination or transfer reactions, thus imparting the living character of ATRP. Alkyl halides are frequently used as initiators in ATRP, and complexes between the metal halide and a ligand act as a catalyst. The mechanism for the copolymerization of comonomers A and B by ATRP is described in Equations (11) to (32).

Initiation

$$I + C \xrightarrow{k_a} PR + CX \tag{11}$$

$$PR + CX \xrightarrow{k_d} I + C \tag{12}$$

$$PR + M_A \xrightarrow{k_{iAA}} R_{1,A} \tag{13}$$

$$PR + M_B \xrightarrow{k_{iBB}} R_{1,B} \tag{14}$$

Equilibrium and propagation

$$D_{r,A} + C \xrightarrow{k_{a,A}} R_{r,A} \bullet + CX \tag{15}$$

$$D_{r,B} + C \xrightarrow{k_{a,B}} R_{r,B} \bullet + CX \tag{16}$$

$$R_{r,A} \bullet + M_A \xrightarrow{k_{p,AA}} R_{r+1,A} \bullet \tag{17}$$

$$R_{r,B} \bullet + M_B \xrightarrow{k_{p,BB}} R_{r+1,B} \bullet \tag{18}$$

$$R_{r,A} \bullet + M_B \xrightarrow{k_{p,AB}} R_{r+1,B} \bullet \tag{19}$$

$$R_{r,B} \bullet + M_A \xrightarrow{k_{p,BA}} R_{r+1,A} \bullet \tag{20}$$

$$R_{r,A} \bullet + CX \xrightarrow{k_{d,A}} D_{r,A} + C \tag{21}$$

$$R_{r,B} \bullet + CX \xrightarrow{k_{d,B}} D_{r,B} + C \tag{22}$$

Transfer to monomer

$$R_{r,A}\bullet + M_A \xrightarrow{k_{tr,AA}} P_r + R\bullet \quad (23)$$

$$R_{r,A}\bullet + M_B \xrightarrow{k_{tr,AB}} P_r + R\bullet \quad (24)$$

$$R_{r,B}\bullet + M_B \xrightarrow{k_{tr,BB}} P_r + R\bullet \quad (25)$$

$$R_{r,B}\bullet + M_A \xrightarrow{k_{tr,BA}} P_r + R\bullet \quad (26)$$

Termination by combination

$$R_{r,A}\bullet + R_{m,A}\bullet \xrightarrow{k_{tc,AA}} P_{r+m} \quad (27)$$

$$R_{r,A}\bullet + R_{m,B}\bullet \xrightarrow{k_{tc,AB}} P_{r+m} \quad (28)$$

$$R_{r,B}\bullet + R_{m,B}\bullet \xrightarrow{k_{tc,BB}} P_{r+m} \quad (29)$$

Termination by disproportionation

$$R_{r,A}\bullet + R_{m,A}\bullet \xrightarrow{k_{td,AA}} P_r + P_m \quad (30)$$

$$R_{r,A}\bullet + R_{m,B}\bullet \xrightarrow{k_{td,AB}} P_r + P_m \quad (31)$$

$$R_{r,B}\bullet + R_{m,B}\bullet \xrightarrow{k_{td,BB}} P_r + P_m \quad (32)$$

In Equations (11) to (32), C and CX are the catalyst in its low and high valence states, M_A and M_B are the comonomers, $R_{r,A}\bullet$ and $R_{r,B}\bullet$ are polymer radicals terminated in monomer A and B, P_r is a dead polymer chain, D_r is a dormant polymer chain, k_i is the initiation rate constant, k_a is the activation rate constant, k_d is the deactivation rate constant, k_p is the propagation rate constant, k_{tc} is the rate constant of termination by combination, k_{td} is the rate constant of termination by disproportionation, k_{tr} is the transfer rate constant, and the subscripts r and $m$indicate the number of monomer molecules in the chain. The subscript A denotes that the chain ends with monomer A and the subscript B has an equivalent meaning.

3. Polymerization rate constants

The cross termination rate constants ($k_{t,AB}$ and $k_{t,BA}$) were calculated using the following correlation:[32]

$$\varphi_t = k_{t,AB} / [2(k_{t,AA}k_{t,BB})^{1/2}] \quad (33)$$

The cross propagation rate constants ($k_{p,AB}$ and $k_{p,BA}$) were found from the reactivity ratios r_A and r_B and the values of $k_{p,AA}$ and $k_{p\,BB}$:

$$r_A = \frac{k_{p,AA}}{k_{p,AB}} \quad , \quad r_B = \frac{k_{p,BB}}{k_{p,BA}} \tag{34}$$

The reactivity ratios in free radical copolymerization are function of the type of the propagating species and the type of the monomer units and, generally, they do not depend on the reaction medium. Similar to the reaction rate constants, the reactivity ratios in ATRP are same as in conventional free radical copolymerization. Tables 1 and 2 list the numerical values of the kinetic rate constants and reactivity ratios used in our simulations. The rate constants were kept constant during the simulations, that is, we neglected diffusion effects.

Parameter	**Value**	**Reference**
k_{pAA}	$4.266\times10^{7}\exp(-7769/RT)$ (L/mol s)	33
k_{pBB}	$4.92\times10^{5}\exp(-4353/RT)$ (L/mol s)	34
r_A	0.52	35
r_B	0.46	35
k_{tcAA}	$(k_{p11})^{2}\times1.1\times10^{-5}\exp(12452.2/RT)$ (L/mol s)	36
k_{tdBB}	$9.80\times10^{7}\exp(-701/RT)$ (L/mol s)	34
k_{tdAA}	0	37
k_{tcBB}	0	37
$k_{tr}A$	$(k_{p11})\times2.198\times10^{-1}\exp(-2820/T)$ (L/mol s)	32
$k_{tr}B$	$(k_{p22})\times((9.48\times10^{3}\times\exp(-13880/(RT)))/60)$ (L/mol s)	32
k_aA	0.45 (L/mol s)	43
k_dA	1.15×10^{7} (L/mol s)	43
k_aB	0.055 (L/mol s)	43
k_dB	8×10^{7} (L/mol s)	43
Initial Catalyst Concentration	0.087 mol/L	
Initial Initiator Concentration	0.087 mol/L	
Total Monomer Concentration	8.7 mol/L	
MW_A	104.14 (g/mol)	
MW_B	100.13 (g/mol)	

Table 1. Kinetic rate constants and physical properties for styrene (1) -methyl methacrylate (2) copolymerization.

Parameter	Value	Reference
k_{pAA}	$1.05\times10^{8}\exp(-3663/RT)$ (L/mol s)	38
k_{pBB}	$4.92\times10^{5}\exp(-4353/RT)$ (L/mol s)	33
r_A	0.14	40
r_B	1.3	40
k_{tcAA}	$3.30\times10^{12}\exp(-5400/RT)$ (L/mol s)	41
k_{tdBB}	$9.80\times10^{7}\exp(-701/RT)$ (L/mol s)	34
k_{tdAA}	0	37
k_{tcBB}	0	37
$k_{tr}A$	$4.62\times10^{4}\times\exp(-5837/RT)$ (L/mol s)	32
$k_{tr}B$	$(k_{p22})\times(9.48\times10^{3}\times\exp(-13880/(RT)/60)$ (L/mol s)	32
k_aA	0.1 (L/mol s)	43
k_dA	1×10^{8} (L/mol s)	43
k_aB	0.5 (L/mol s)	43
k_dB	1×10^{7} (L/mol s)	43
Initial Catalyst Concentration	0.087 mol/L	
Initial Initiator Concentration	0.087 mol/L	
Total Monomer Concentration	8.7 mol/L	
MW_A	53.15 (g/mol)	
MW_B	100.13 (g/mol)	

Table 2. Kinetic rate constants and physical properties for the acrylonitrile (1) - methyl methacrylate (2) copolymerization.

4. Results and discussions

The DMC model was applied to describe the copolymerization of styrene/methyl methacrylate, and of acrylonitrile/methyl methacrylate. These comonomer combinations were chosen because they have significantly different reactivity ratios, which will lead to the production of copolymers with distinct CCDs and SLDs. Reaction rate constants were kept constant during the simulations, that is, we neglected diffusion effects.

During living polymerization, the polymer average chain length increases linearly with monomer conversion, the polydispersity index approaches unity and, as a result, the molecular weight distribution is narrow, as shown in Figures 2.a to 2.c.

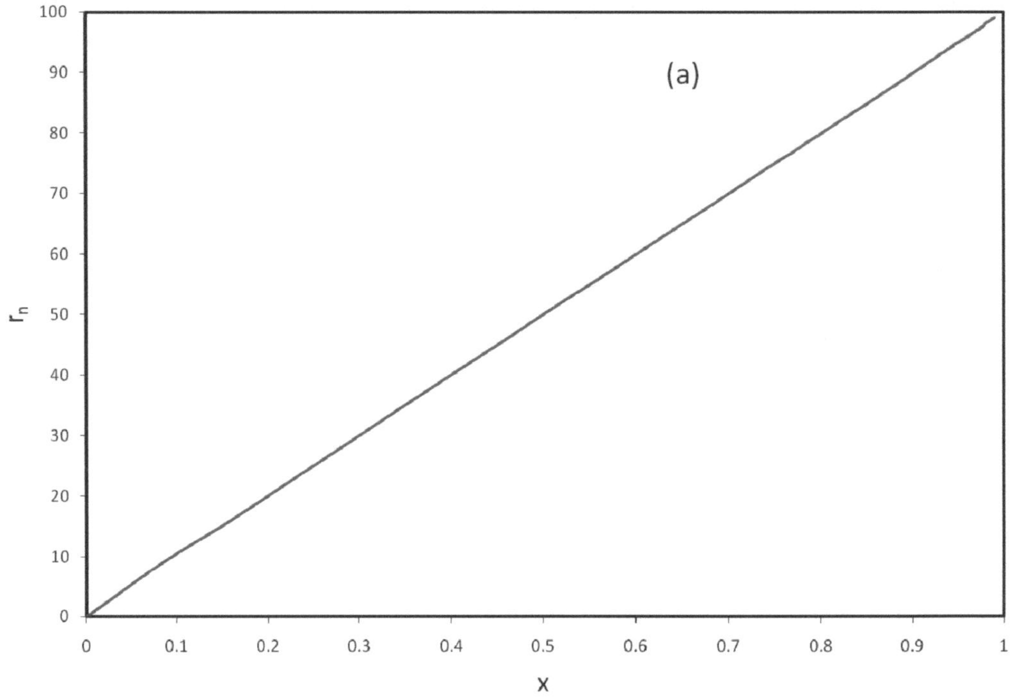
(a)
r_n
0
10
20
30
40
50
60
70
80
90
100
0
0.1
0.2
0.3
0.4
0.5
0.6
0.7
0.8
0.9
1
x

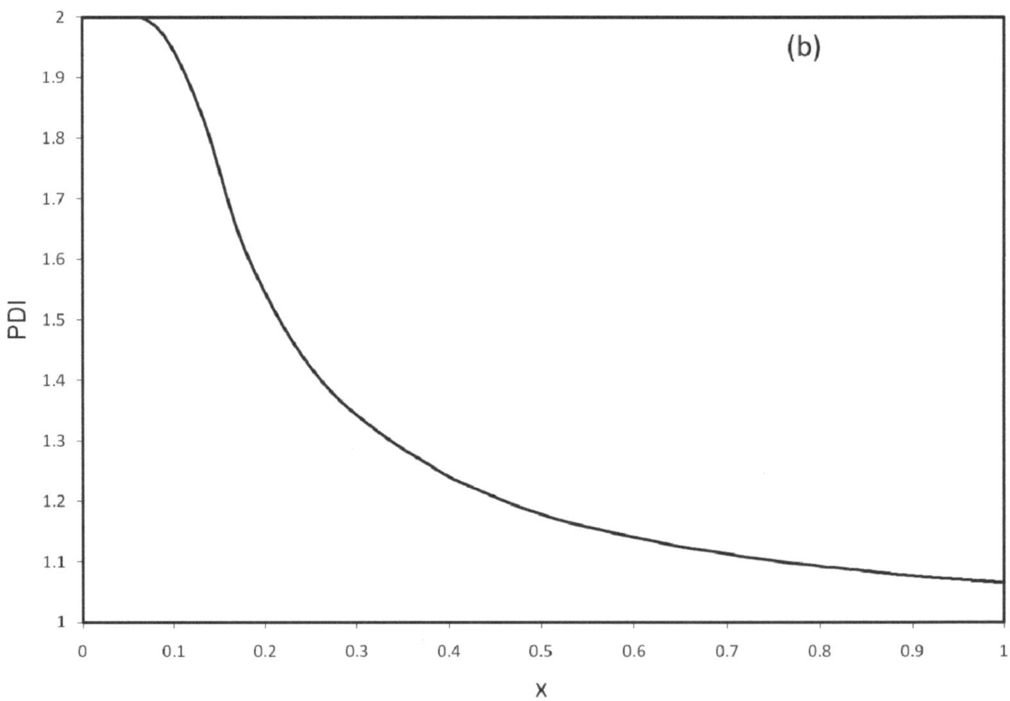
(b)
PDI
1
1.1
1.2
1.3
1.4
1.5
1.6
1.7
1.8
1.9
2
0
0.1
0.2
0.3
0.4
0.5
0.6
0.7
0.8
0.9
1
x

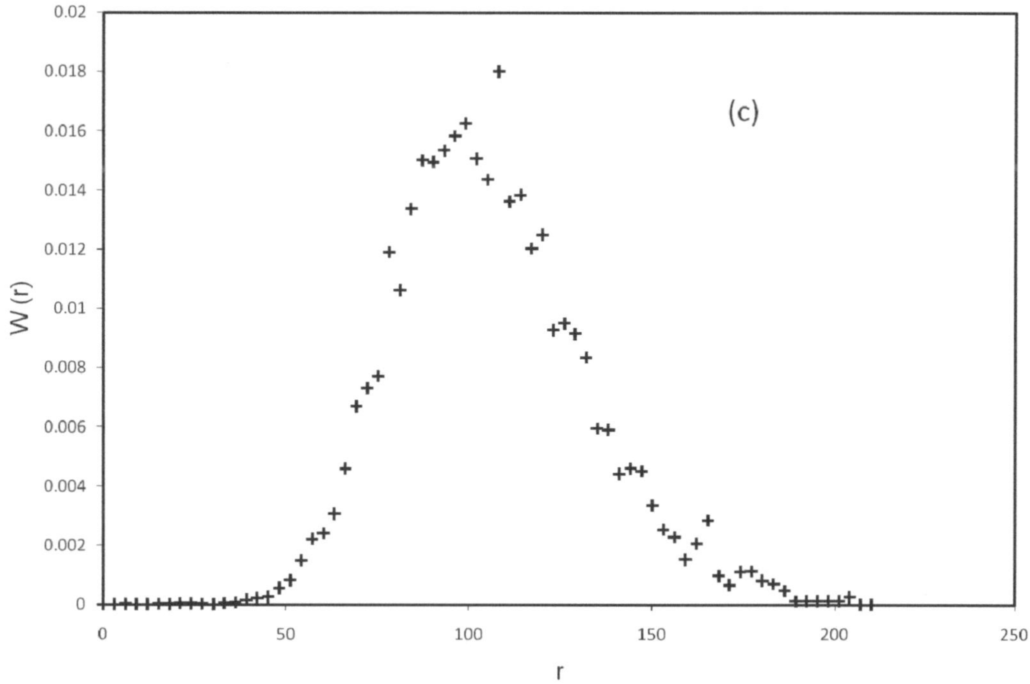

Fig. 2. Monte Carlo simulation results for the copolymerization of styrene and methyl methacrylate : (a) number average chain length (r_n) as a function of conversion (x), (b) PDI as a function of conversion, and (c) chain length distribution when conversion is $x = 0.99$. The initial comonomer molar fractions in the reactor were $f_{0,St} = 0.5$, $f_{0,MMA} = 0.5$.

Figure 3 shows the cumulative molar fraction of methyl methacrylate (MMA) in poly (acrylonitrile-co-methyl methacrylate) (AN-MMA) and poly(styrene-co-methyl methacrylate) (St-MMA). We can clearly see that in the St-MMA copolymer, the cumulative molar fraction of MMA remains almost constant throughout the polymerization. However, for the AN-MMA copolymer, the MMA molar fraction decreases from 0.5 to 0.3.

Figure 4 shows the instantaneous molar fraction of MMA in AN-MMA and St-MMA copolymers. The instantaneous molar fraction of MMA in these copolymers differs significantly because of the difference in the reactivity ratios of the comonomer pairs. Because styrene and methyl methacrylate have very close reactivity ratios (0.53 and 0.46) the molar fraction of MMA does not change significantly with conversion. On the other hand, the molar fraction of MMA in AN-MMA copolymers decreases with conversion because the reactivity ratios (0.14 and 1.3) of the two comonomers are very different. Figure 4 shows that no more MMA is incorporated in the chains after a total monomer conversion of approximately 0.8. A similar trend is observed when the molar fraction of MMA is plotted as a function of the number average chain length. The comonomer composition drift in this case leads to the formation of a gradient copolymer with a terminal block composed of only acrylonitrile units.

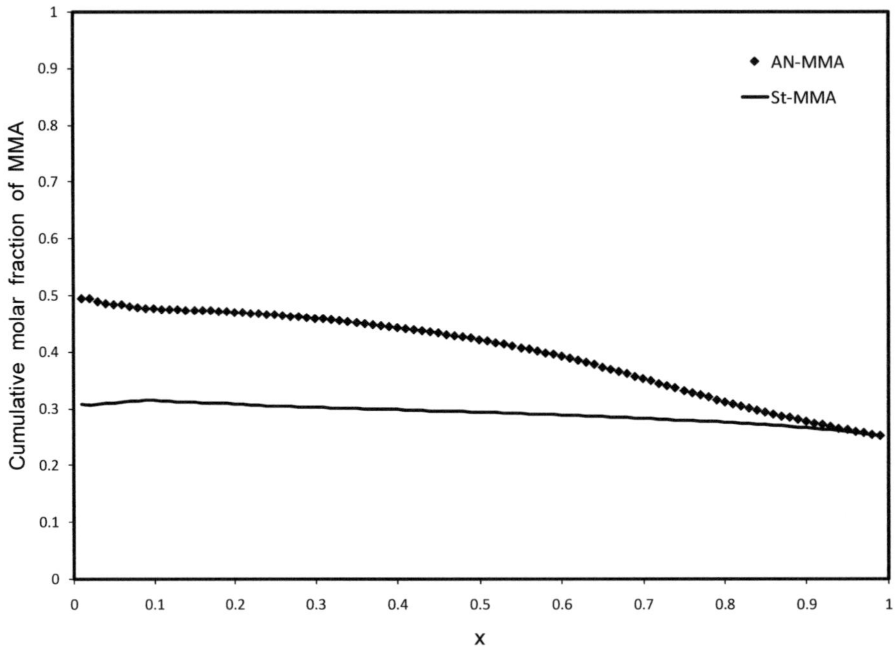

Fig. 3. Cumulative molar fraction of MMA in AN-MMA and St-MMA copolymers as a function of total comonomer conversion. The initial comonomer molar fractions in the reactor were $f_{0,MMA} = 0.25$ and $f_{0,AN} = 0.75$ or $f_{0,St} = 0.75$.

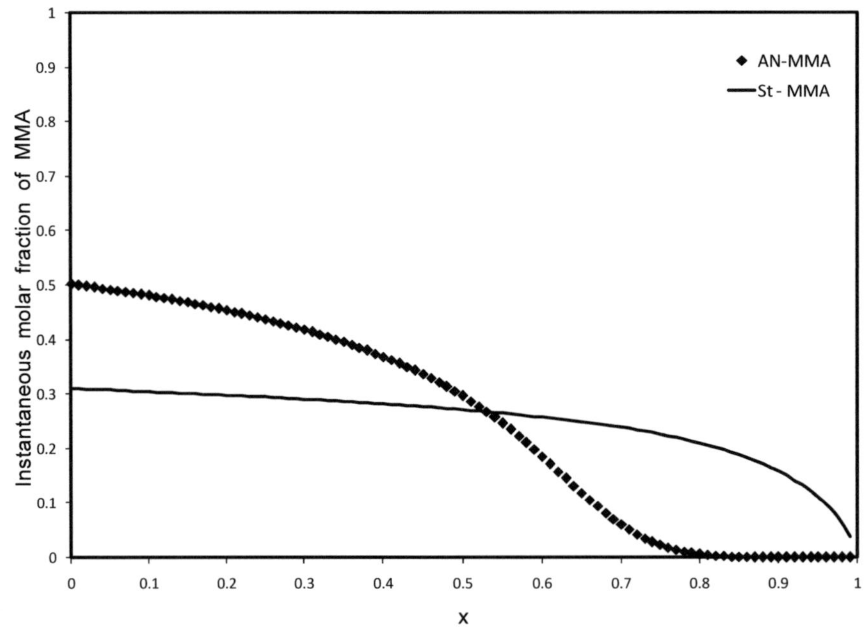

Fig. 4. Instantaneous molar fraction of MMA in AN-MMA and St-MMA copolymers as a function of total comonomer conversion. The initial monomer molar fractions in the reactor were $f_{0,MMA} = 0.25$ and $f_{0,AN} = 0.75$ or $f_{0,St} = 0.75$.

In batch copolymerization using controlled/living polymerization, a gradient copolymer is only produced if comonomer composition drift is significant, i.e when the difference between the reactivity ratios of the comonomers is large and/or the initial comonomer concentrations are very different.

The DMC model also was used to describe the copolymerization of styrene and methylmethacrylate (St-MMA) or acrylonitrile and methylmethacrylate (AN-MMA) in a semibatch reactor. We compared the effect of using different initial comonomer concentrations and of slowly adding styrene, acrylonitrile or methyl methacrylate into the reactor as a side stream during the polymerization. We assumed that the autoclave reactor was isothermal and well-mixed.

Figure 5 compares the polydispersity index (PDI) of AN-MMA copolymers made in semi-batch and batch reactors. Two different initial comonomer molar ratios (AN: MMA = 25:75 and 50:50) were simulated. For the semi-batch simulations, the acrylonitrile concentration was kept constant by slowly feeding the comonomer to the reactor as the polymerization proceeded. Both the batch and semi-batch reactors made copolymers with PDIs that followed the same trend: the PDI was initially high and then approached a value of approximately 1.1, as commonly observed in ATRP processes.

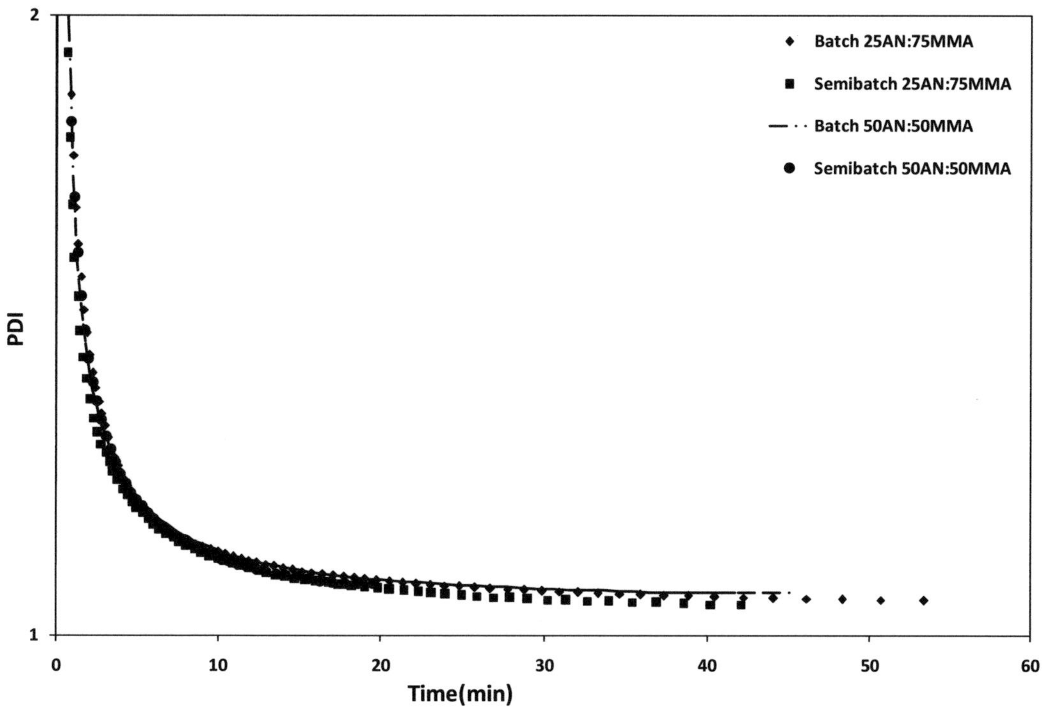

Fig. 5. PDI as a function of time for the copolymerization of AN and MMA in batch and semibatch reactors. The AN concentration was kept constant during the simulation of the semibatch reactor.

Figure 6 shows the instantaneous and cumulative molar fraction of AN in the copolymer as a function of polymerization time respectively. Figure 6.a shows gradient copolymers are

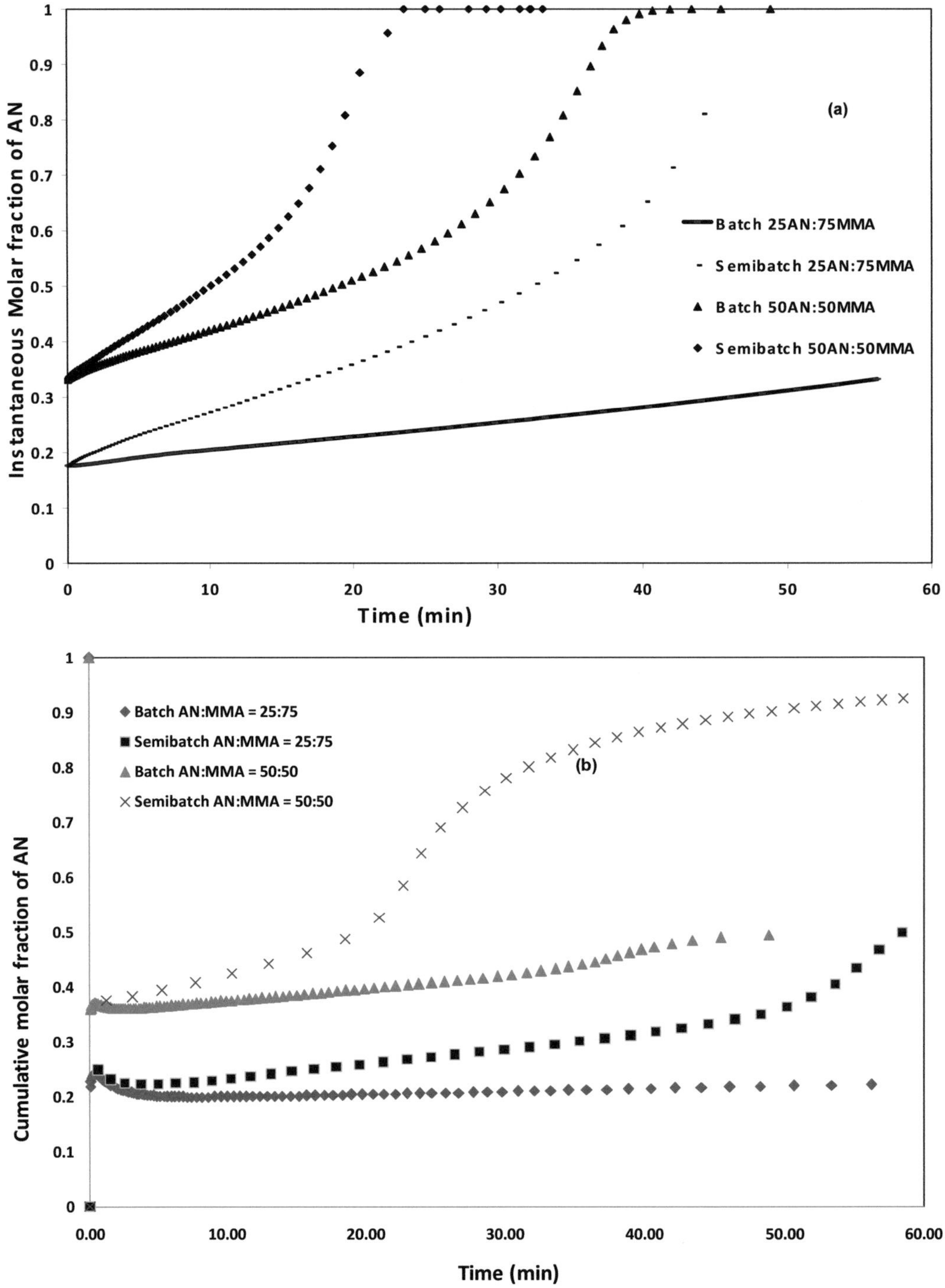

Fig. 6. (a) Instantaneous molar fraction of AN in AN-MMA copolymers as a function of polymerization time in batch and semibatch reactors. (b) Cumulative molar fraction of AN-MMA copolymers as a function of polymerization time in batch and semibatch reactors.

not made in the batch reactor when AN:MMA molar ratio is 25:75, but when AN:MMA is changed to 50:50, gradient copolymers will be produced for longer polymerization times. On the other hand, gradient copolymers are formed in the semi-batch reactor for both initial AN:MMA molar ratios at a shorter polymerization time.

Figure 6.b shows the cumulative molar fraction of acrylonitrile in the copolymer as a function of polymerization time. It clearly indicates the formation of gradient copolymers in a semi-batch reactor. Both initial molar concentrations show the formation of gradient copolymers. The AN:MMA molar ratio of 25:75 does not produce a gradient but when AN:MMA is changed to 50:50, gradient copolymers are formed. A longer AN block is formed while using a semi-batch than batch reactors as described in Figure 6. Thus, better gradient copolymers can be produced using semi-batch reactors.

Figures 7.a and 7.b compare the chain length distribution (CLD) of AN-MMA copolymers made in batch and semi-batch reactors for the two initial comonomer ratios. For an AN:MMA molar ratio of 25:75, the CLD of the copolymer made in the batch reactor is shifted to lower molecular weights. However, when AN:MMA is changed to 50:50, an opposite behavior is observed and the CLD of the copolymer made in the batch reactor is shifted to lower values. In the latter case, the semi-batch reactor can be used to produce a copolymer with higher molecular weight average without increasing the PDI. This is due to the higher propagation constant associated with AN. Hence, when AN content is increased, the rate of propagation is also increased thereby producing copolymer with higher molecular weight.

Figure 8 compares the CCDs of AN-MMA copolymers made in batch and semi-batch reactors. It is apparent that, the CCDs of copolymers made in the batch reactor are narrower than those made in the semi-batch reactor. In addition, the copolymers made in the semi-batch reactor will always have a higher molar fraction or acrylonitrile, as expected.

The comonomer sequence distribution is characterized by its diads, triads, tetrads, and higher sequences, generally measured by NMR spectroscopy. Our DMC simulation program can also predict these sequences. Figures 9 to 14 show model predictions for diads and triads of styrene/MMA copolymers as a function of time when styrene is fed continuously to the reactor. Long polymerization times are needed to make gradient copolymers when MMA is fed to the reactor. Therefore, it is more convenient to produce gradient polymer when styrene is fed as the side stream. This could be attributed to the reactivity ratio of styrene which is slightly higher than MMA. Figures 9 to 14 clearly show that styrene diads and triads increase with increasing time for all initial monomer concentrations. The batch results of the present system did not show any formation of gradient polymers at all concentrations used while the semi-batch results predict the formation of gradient polymers for all the concentrations. Figures 9 to 14 were simulated at a maximum polymerization time of 100 minutes to better understand the formation of various diads and triads at a shorter timescale. As evident a clear increase in AN-AN blocks is found for all concentration except 25-75, but an increase in the timescale would result in the formation of gradient. The MMA-MMA blocks decreases for all concentration. Considering the homotriads, the AN-AN-AN blocks increases for all concentration within the timescale of 100 minutes. While a sharp decrease in the MMA-MMA-MMA triblocks are found for all concentration. Increase in the fraction of block copolymers are also found in our study. Clearly all the concentration form gradient polymers while a St:MMA molar ratio of 50:50 forms better gradient at the least polymerization time. Hence showing semibatch process could be very well utilized for making gradient polymers with styrene as the sidestream.

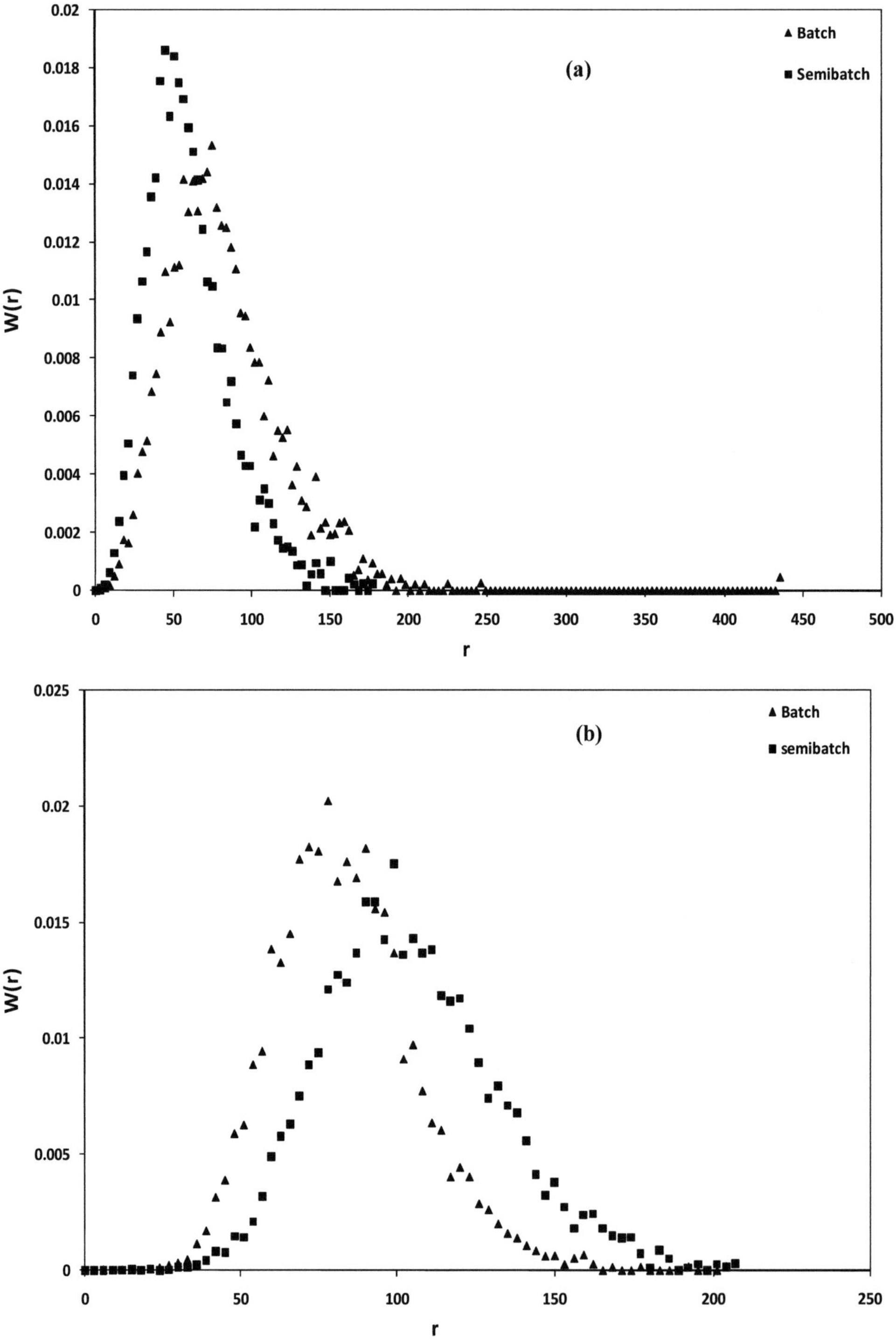

Fig. 7. Chain length distribution of AN-MMA copolymers made in batch and semibatch reactors. (a) AN:MMA = 25/75 (b) AN:MMA = 50/50. Polymerization time = 50 min.

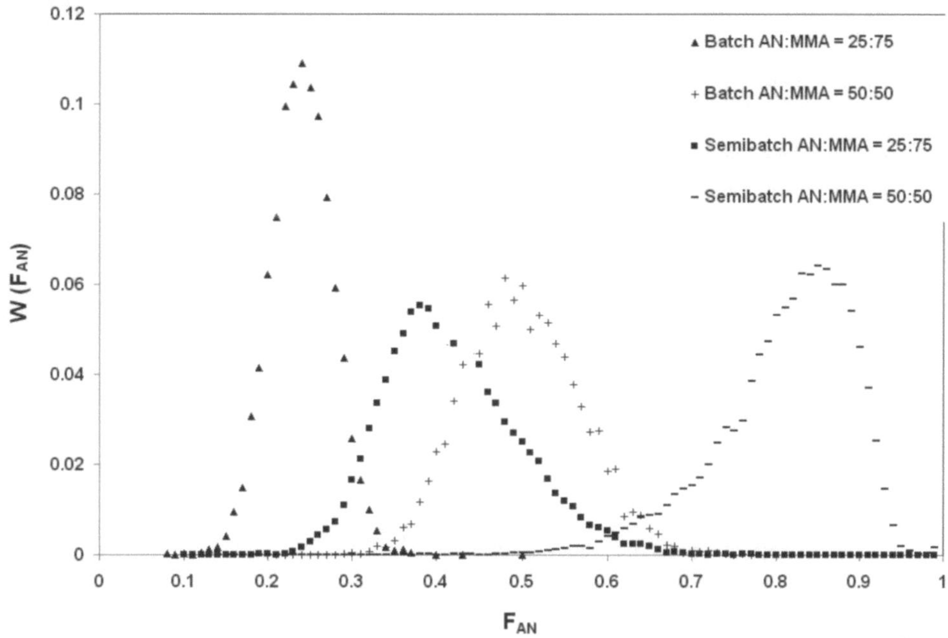

Fig. 8. Chemical composition distributions of AN-MMA copolymers made in batch and semibatch reactors . Polymerization time = 30 min.

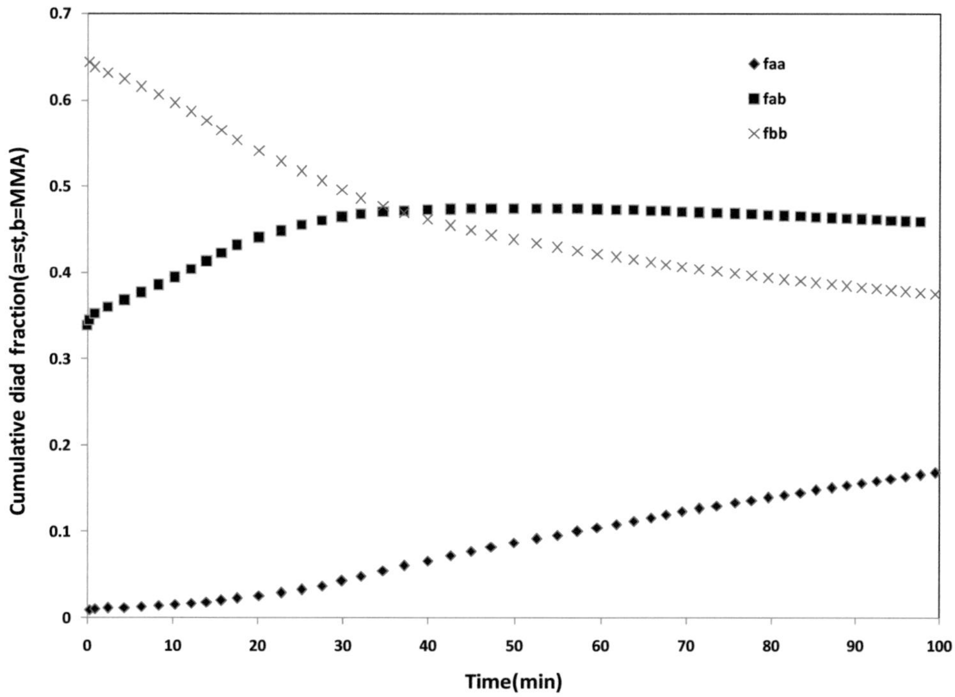

Fig. 9. Cumulative diad fraction as a function of total comonomer conversion for St-MMA system. The initial comonomer molar fractions are $f_{0,MMA} = 0.90$ and $f_{0,St} = 0.10$.

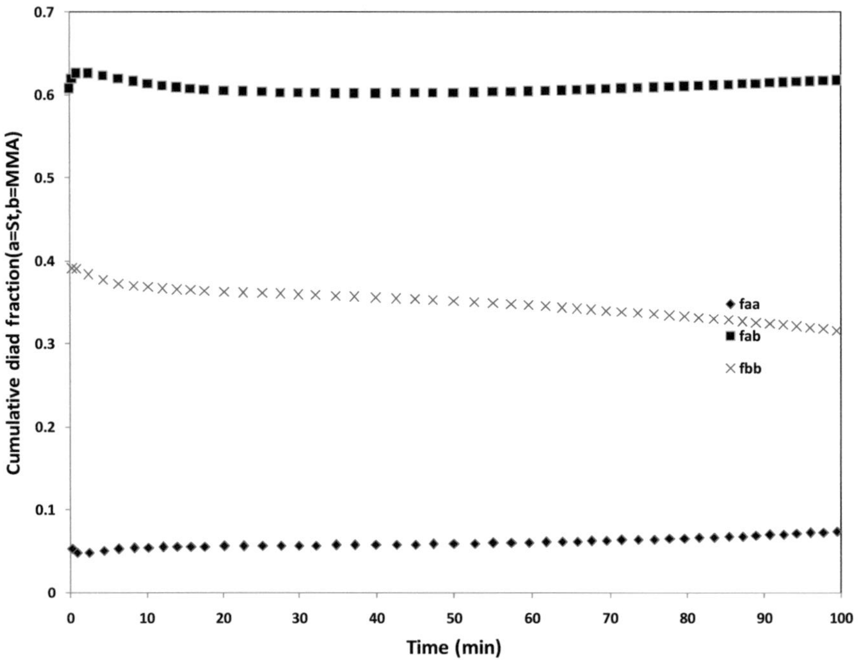

Fig. 10. Cumulative fraction of homodiads as a function of total comonomer conversion for St-MMA system. The initial comonomer molar fractions are $f_{0,MMA} = 0.75$ and $f_{0,St} = 0.25$.

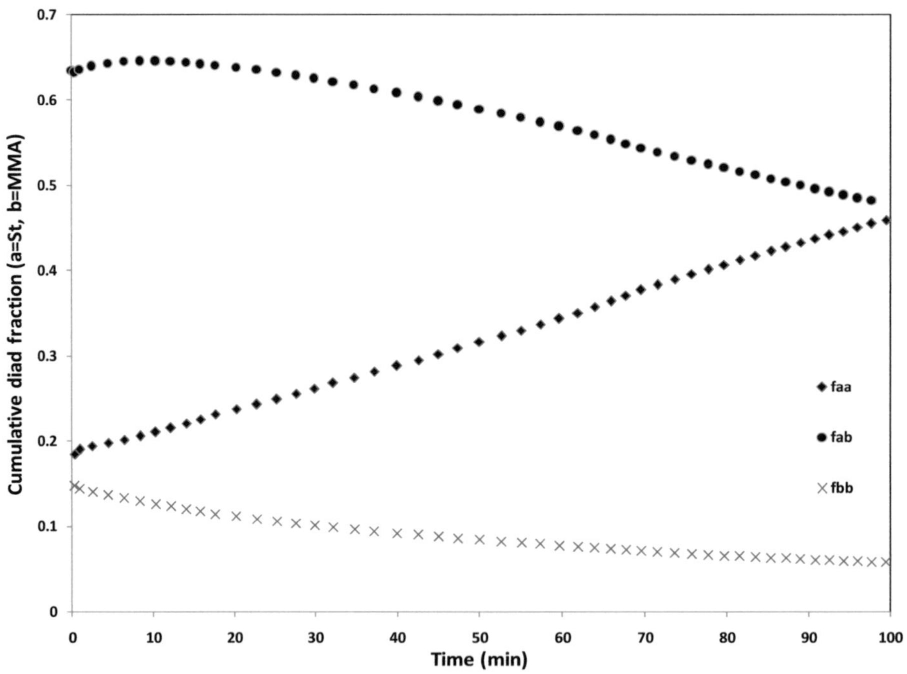

Fig. 11. Cumulative diad fraction as a function of total comonomer conversion for St-MMA system. The initial comonomer molar fractions are $f_{0,MMA} = 0.50$ and $f_{0,St} = 0.50$.

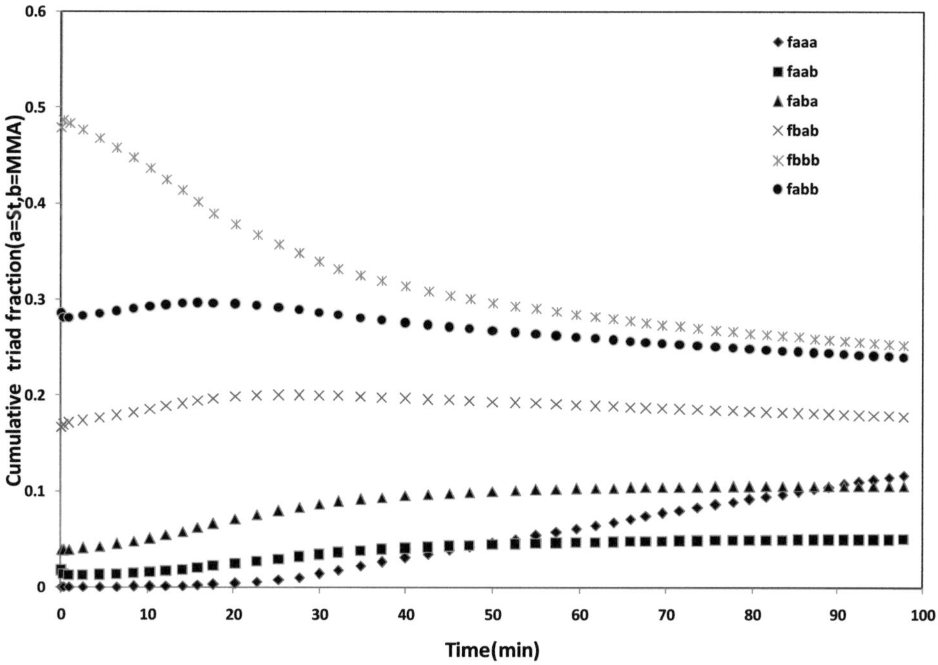

Fig. 12. Cumulative triad fraction as a function of total comonomer conversion for St-MMA system. The initial comonomer molar fractions are $f_{0,MMA}$ = 0.90 and $f_{0,St}$ = 0.10.

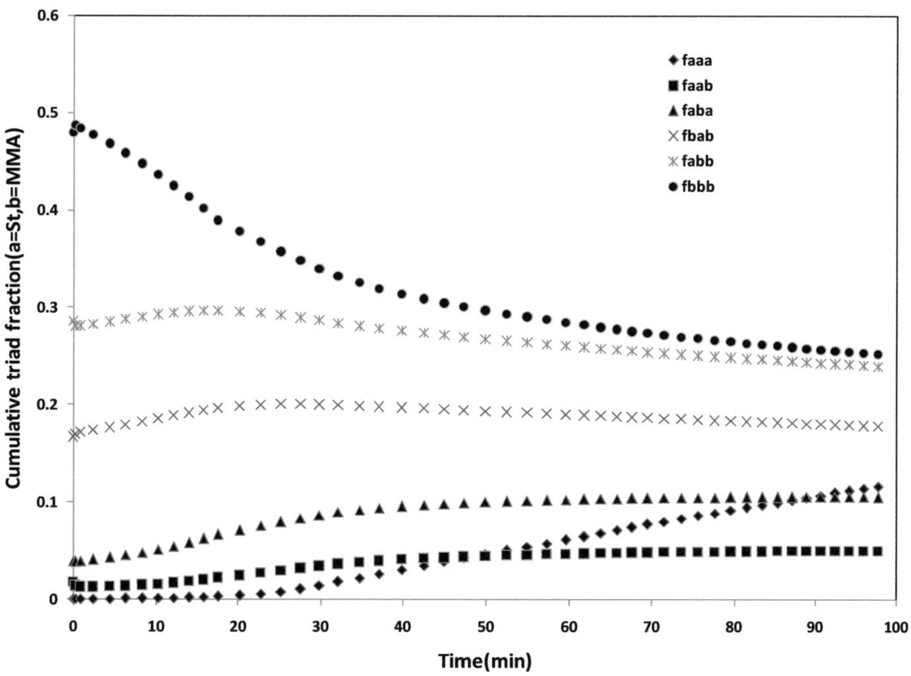

Fig. 13. Cumulative triad fraction as a function of total comonomer conversion for St-MMA system. The initial comonomer molar fractions are $f_{0,MMA}$ = 0.75 and $f_{0,St}$ = 0.25.

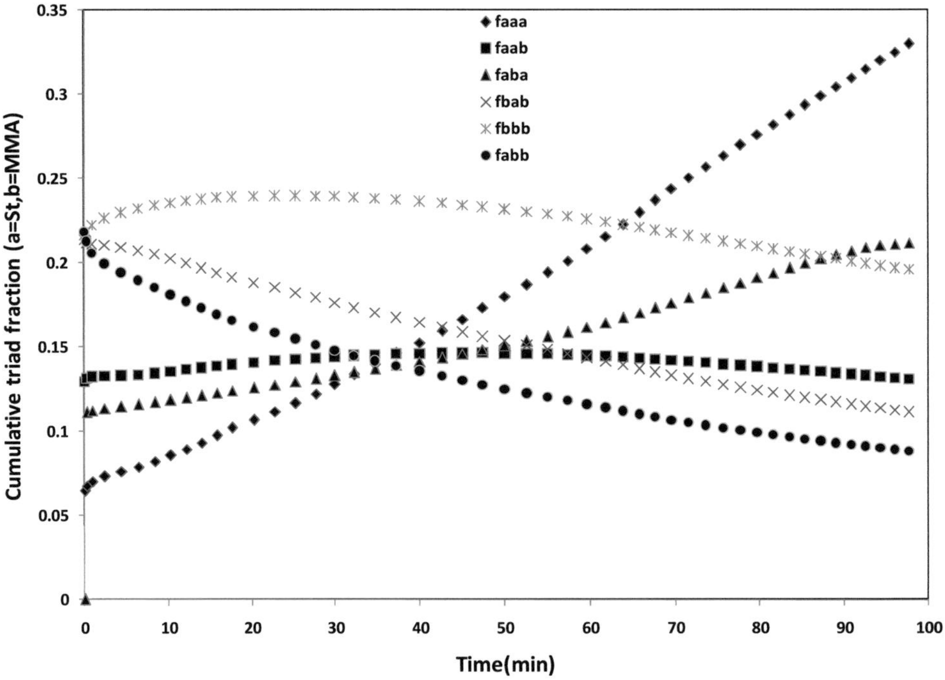

Fig. 14. Cumulative triad fraction as a function of total comonomer conversion for St-MMA system. The initial comonomer molar fractions are $f_{0,MMA} = 0.50$ and $f_{0,St} = 0.50$.

5. Conclusion

DMC model was developed for the simulation of atom transfer radical copolymerization using Monte Carlo simulation. The model can predict average molecular weight, polydispersity index, MWD, CCD, SLD and copolymer composition as a function of polymerization time in semi-batch reactors. Two case studies (styrene-co-methyl methacrylate and acrylonitrile-co-methyl methacrylate) were chosen to demonstrate the effect of semi-batch method and monomer feed composition.

The simulations show that the instantaneous molar fraction of methyl methacrylate does not change significantly for poly(styrene-*co*-methyl methacrylate) copolymers made in a batch reactor starting with different comonomer molar ratios as methyl methacrylate and styrene have close reactivity ratios (0.53 and 0.46) and, therefore, produce nearly random copolymer chains. On the other hand, the instantaneous molar fraction of methyl methacrylate in poly(acrylonitrile-*co*-methyl methacrylate) decreases with conversion and reaches zero around 80% of the total monomer conversion. There is a clear difference in the reactivity ratios (0.14 and 1.3) for this system. Composition drift, in this case, leads to the formation of gradient copolymer chains. The simulation for the varying monomer feed composition showed that the chance of forming gradient acrylonitrile-methyl methacrylate copolymers increases when the initial molar fraction of acrylonitrile is much higher than that of methyl methacrylate.

The simulation clearly showed the impact of using semi-batch for the formation of gradient copolymers. The system utilizing styrene as semi-batch showed that increasing the styrene content formed a gradient while increasing MMA content also formed gradient at the expense of high polymerization time but produced a narrow molecular distribution. The AN-MMA system followed the same trend. Gradient was formed in shorter polymerization time while employing AN as the sidestream. Even though batch process also produced gradient polymers, the semi-batch process utilized lesser polymerization time and lesser concentration of AN than its batch counterpart. The vital fact is the production of gradient polymers with great control enhancing the use of semi-batch technology. The model also showed its capability to produce tailor-made gradient polymers.

6. References

[1] Matyjaszewski K. Prog Polym Sci 2005; 30:858.
[2] Davis KA, Matyaszewski K. Adv Polym Sci 2002; 159:2.
[3] Matyjaszewski K, Xia J. Chem Rev 2001; 101:2921.
[4] Kamigaito M, Ando T, Sawamoto M. Chem Rev 2001; 101:3689.
[5] Benoit D, Chaplinski V, Braslau R, Hawker CJ. J Am Chem Soc 1999; 121: 3904.
[6] Rodlert M, Harth E, Rees I, Hawker CJ. J Polym Sci Polym Chem Ed 2000; 38:4749.
[7] Chiefari J, Chong YK, Ercole F, Krstina J, Jeffery J, Le TPT, Mayadunne RTA, Meijs GF, Moad CL, Moad G, Rizzardo E, Thang SH. Macromolecules 1998; 31: 5559.
[8] Moad G, Chiefari J, Chong YK, Krstina J, Mayadunne RTA, Postma A, Rizzardo E, Thang SH. Polym Int 2000;49: 993.
[9] Matyjaszewski K. J Macromol Sci Pure Appl Chem 1997; A34:1785.
[10] Matyjaszewski K, Xia J. Handbook of radical polymerization. New York: Wiley; 2002. p. 523.
[11] Matyjaszewski K, Ziegler MJ, Arehart SV, Gresztra D, Pakula T. J Phys Org Chem 2000; 13:775.
[12] Arehart, SV, Greszta D, Matyjaszewski K. Polym Prepr Am Chem Soc Div Polym Chem 1997; 38:705.
[13] Chen G, Wu Z, Wu J, Li Z, Li F. Macromolecules 2000;33:232.
[14] Uegaki H, Kotani Y, Kamigaito M, Sawamoto M. Macromolecules 1998; 31:6756.
[15] Al-Harthi M, Soares JBP, Simon LC. Macromol Theory Simul 2006; 15: 198.
[16] Zhu S. Macromol Theory Simul 1999; 8:29.
[17] Delgadillo-Velazquez O, Vivaldo-Lima E, Quintero-Ortega IA, Zhu S. AIChE J 2002;48:2597.
[18] Al-Harthi M, Soares JBP, Simon LC. Macromol Chem Phys 2006; 207:469.
[19] Al-Harthi M, Soares JBP, Simon LC. Macromol React Eng 2007; 1:468.
[20] Zhang M, Ray WH. J Appl Polym Sci 2002; 86:1630.
[21] Szablan Z, Toy AA, Terrenoire A, Davis TP, Stenzel MH, Muller AHE, Barner-Kowollik C. J Polym Sci Polym Chem 2006;44:3692.
[22] Shipp DA, Matyjaszewski K. Macromolecules 2000; 33:1553.
[23] Lutz J, Matyjaszewski K. Macromol Chem Phys 2002; 203:1385.
[24] Fu Y, Mirzaei A, Cunningham MF, Hutchinson RA. Macromol React Eng 2007;1:425.
[25] Tobita H. Macromol Theory Simul 2003; 12:32.
[26] Lu J, Zhang H, Yang Y. Makro Chemie Theory Simul 1993; 2:747.
[27] He J, Zhang H, Chen J, Yang Y. Macromolecules 1997; 30:8010.
[28] Al-Harthi M, Soares JBP, Simon LC. Macromol React Eng 2007; 1:95.

[29] Al-Harthi M, Soares JBP, Simon LC. Macromol Symp Polym React Eng 2006; 243:83.
[30] Al-Harthi M, Soares JBP, Simon LC. Macromol Mat Eng 2006;291:993.
[31] Gillespie DT. J Phys Chem 1977; 81:2340.
[32] Keramopoulos, A. ; Kiparissides, C. ; Macromolecules 2002, *35,* 4155.
[33] Buback, Gilbert, M.; Hutchinson, R.; Klumperman, R.; Kuchata, B.; Manders, F.; O'Driscoll, B.; Russell, K.; Schweer, G. J. Macromol. Chem. Phys. 1995, *196,* 3267.
[34] Achilias, D. S.; Kiparissides, C. Macromolecules 1992, *25,* 3739.
[35] Suzuki, H.; Mathot, V. B. Macromolecules 1989, *22,* 1380.
[36] Hui, A. W. ; Hamielec, A. E. J. Appl. Polym. Sci. 1976, *16,* 749.
[37] Keramopoulos, A. ; Kiparissides, C. Macromolecules 2002, *35,* 4155.
[38] Yaraskavitch, I. M.; Brash, J. L.; Hamielec, A. E. Polymer 1987, *28,* 489
[39] Matyjaszewski, K.; Ziegler, M. J.; Arehart, S. V. J. Phys. Org. Chem. 2000, *13,* 775.
[40] Brandrub, J.; Immergut, E.; Grulke, E. Eds. Polymer Handbook, 4th ed.; Wiley: New York, 1999.
[41] Pittman-Bejger, T. P. Real-Time Control and Optimization of Batch Free-Radical Copolymerization Reactors. Ph.D. Thesis, University of Minnesota, 1982.
[42] Al-Harthi, M.; Abbasi, S. H.; Soares, J. B. P., Chemical Engineering Science, submitted.
[43] Al-Harthi, M.; Soares, J. B. P.; Simon, L. C. Macromol. React. Eng. 2007, 1, 468.

7

Monte Carlo Simulations for Beam Delivery Line Design in Radiation Therapy with Heavy Ion Beams

Faiza Bourhaleb[1], Andrea Attili[2] and Germano Russo[3]
[1]*I-SEE, Internet Simulation Evaluation Envision , I-SEE Company (Academic Spin off of the University of Turin)Via Pietro Giuria 1, 10125, Turin*
[2]*Istituto Nazionale di Fisica Nucleare, INFN, Turin Section, Via Pietro Giuria 1, 10125, Turin*
[3]*University Of Turin, Department of experimental physics, Via Pietro Giuria 1, 10125, Turin*
Italy

1. Introduction

Hadrontherapy is an advanced technique in the field of radiation therapy. It guarantees a high efficiency in conforming a high level of dose to the tumor volume due to the Bragg peak characteristic. Monte Carlo simulations of the Beam Delivery Line (BDL) as well as the treated volume provide all the necessary information on the physical processes. The use of Monte Carlo numerical techniques allows tracking the single particle in different tissues and materials. It permits the evaluation of the dose delivered to the treated volume and the prediction the quality of the irradiation.
The information generated by those simulations can be used for the evaluation of the biological effect on cell survival. The radiobiological equivalent dose can be evaluated using combining Monte Carlo particle tracking with specific radiobiological models, like the Local Effect Model (LEM)(Elsasser and Scholz, 2007).
Monte Carlo simulations for the beam delivery line and for the treated volume provide all the necessary information on the physical processes and related dosimetry and provide a useful tools for the design of passive elements of a BDL. We have described the full BDL of the National Center of Oncologic Hadrontherapy (CNAO) in a Monte Carlo simulation. We estimate the impact of the passive elements of the BDL on the energy distribution on the treated volume.
The simulation is based on the package GEANT4 to estimate the actual distribution in the treated volume of particles and fragments and the corresponding energies. The treated volume is simulated defining different tissues. The evaluation of biological effects was studied using a code based on the LEM. The computational effort was performed using the distributed INFN Grid computing resources.

1.1 Dose delivery techniques

In the field of hadrontherapy two main kinds of beams are used: proton and carbon ion beams.

There are two main techniques for dose delivery used in the field of hadron therapy. The first technique is the passive scattering technique which is largely used for both proton therapy and carbon ion therapy. With this technique the beam is spread by placing scattering material into the path of the incoming particles.

A combination of collimators and compensators conforms the dose to the target volume. To spread out the Bragg peak, a set of range modulator wheels or ridge filters are added in the beam path in the BDL (Figure 1). The passive technique is commonly used with cyclotrons and requires an important effort in the definition of the modulating devices along the beam delivery line to reach a 3D-conformal dose distribution.

In the active scanning techniques, magnets deflect and steer the ion beams. With the guidance of the control system, the scanning magnet steer the single mono-energetic beam to paint voxel by voxel the target volume, in successive layers. The depth of penetration of the Bragg peak is adjusted by varying the initial kinetic energy of the beam (Figure 1). With syncrotons we are able to generate a range of energies which can reach steps of 0.5 mm precision in the particle range.

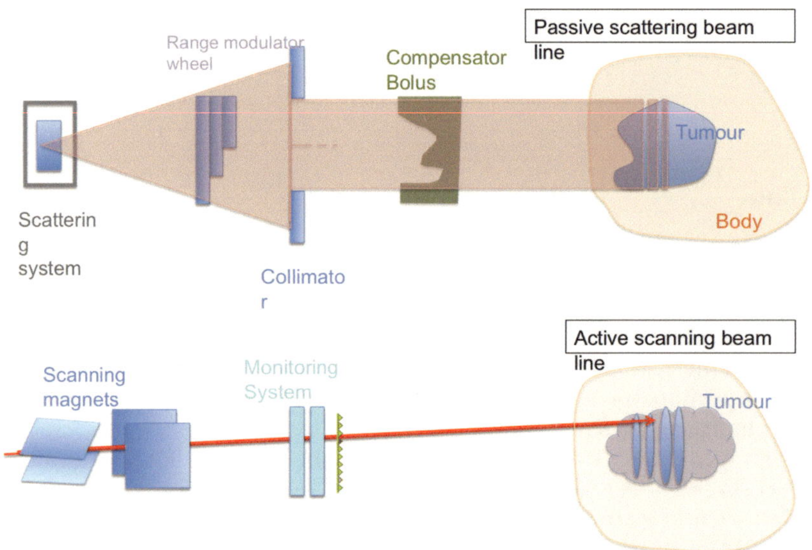

Fig. 1. Passive scattering and active scanning beam delivery systems.

Proton and carbon ion beams have a very sharp Bragg peak. For proton beams of energies smaller than 100 MeV, with a gaussian fit around the region of the maximum of the Bragg peak, we can measure a sigma smaller than 1 mm, while for carbon ion beams, the sigma measured in the same way is smaller than 1mm for energies up to 360 MeV.

In order to use proton and carbon ion beams in hadrontherapy and to achieve an acceptable homogeneity of the Spread Out Bragg Peak (SOBP), the peaks need to be broaden at least few millimeters by means of a properly designed *ripple filter*. The use of a ripple filter is mandatory in particular in conjunction with active scanning techniques for dose delivery, where it helps to reduce the numbers of energy switches necessary to obtain a smooth SOBP, leading also to shorter overall irradiation times.

In this work we studied the design and the simulation of ripple filters used on the BDL for the CNAO. We present a two steps study: the first one is dedicated to proton beams and the second one is for carbon ion beams. Radiobiological effects for ion beams are also evaluated, since they modulate the shape of the radiobiological equivalent dose distribution around the Bragg peak accordingly to the specific ripple filter used.

2. Method and Materials: Beam Delivery Line for active scanning delivery technique

The final decision in the choice of the right design of the BDL elements depends on the impact of those passive elements on the energy distribution in the treated volume. A full BDL is simulated and modeled to estimate the actual distribution in the treated volume of particles and fragments and the corresponding energies and the total scattering of the original beam at the treatment volume.

The BDL is composed by a double online monitoring system (Box1 and Box2), a range shifter and the ripple filters. The monitoring system consists of an emsemble of pixel and strip chambers. We put the ripple filter as the last static device before the patient at 50 cm with respect the isocenter (see Figure 2).

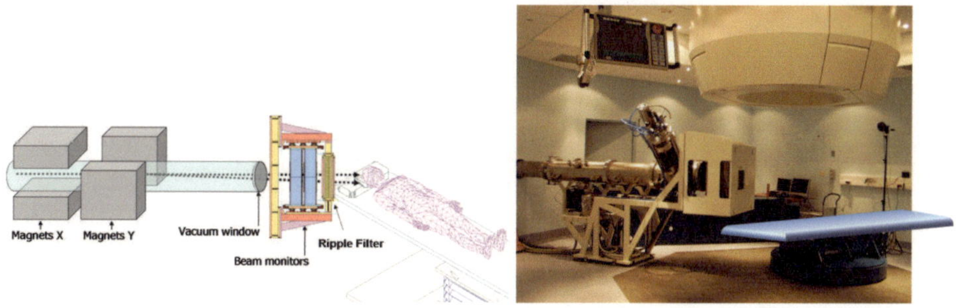

(a) (b)

Fig. 2. Beam delivery system including the scanning magnets , monitoring system and the ripple filter.

The Monte Carlo simulation is implemented with GEANT4 (GEANT4, release september 2010) and it is linked to Root interface (Root, cern Package) which provides an online follow-up of the events generated during the simulation along the beam path. The goal of the implemented simulations is the study the effect of the monitoring system and of the ripple filter on the therapeutic beams. We simulated both proton and carbon ion beams and we check for both beams the 3-dimensional deposited dose distribution.

2.1 Monte Carlo with GEANT4

The physics of the therapeutic carbon ion beams transport was simulated with the GEANT4 Monte Carlo simulation toolkit version 9.3 with patch 01.

GEANT4 is a flexible object oriented code, designed originally for high-energy physics applications but now it is extended to low energies used in heavy ion therapy. For this study, the GEANT4 physics for the electromagnetic processes is activated using the setting of 'Option3' recommended by the electromagnetic working groups of Geant4 collaboration. This setting is designed for applications requiring higher accuracy of electrons, hadrons and ion tracking without magnetic field. To set up the hadronic interaction we used the following hadronic models: 'G4HadronQElasticPhysics' for hadronic elastic model, 'G4HadronInelasticQBBC' for hadronic inelastic models for proton and neutrons and 'G4IonBinaryCascadePhysics' for hadronic inelastic models for ions.

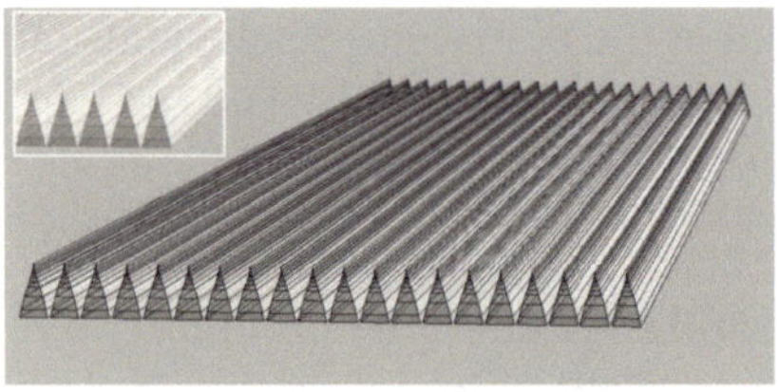

(a) Sigmoidal ripple filter

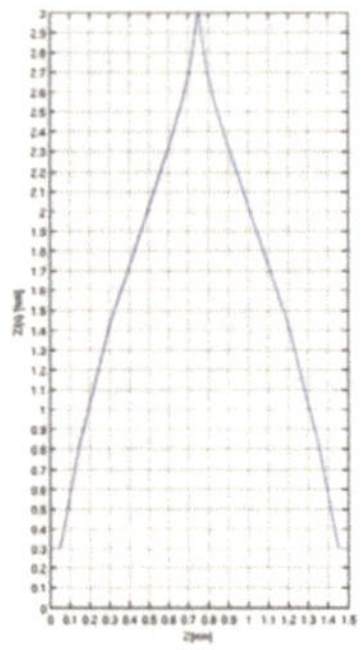

(b) Bidimensional section of the sigmoidal ripple filter

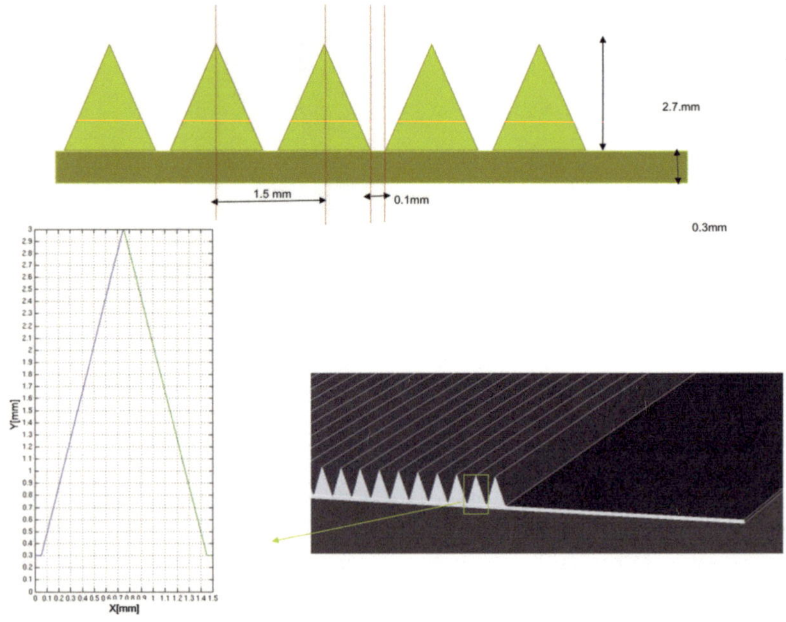

(c) Triangular Ripple filter

Fig. 3. Sections of ripple filters as described by (Weber and Kraft, 1999) of 3 mm (Type B) and the new triangiular one (type A)and as designed and described in the Monte carlo simulation with Geant4 (see also (Bourhaleb et al, 2008)).

2.2 Design of a ripple filter

We simulated the beam delivery line supporting both proton and carbon ion beams using different energies of the beams. We compared the effect of different kind of ripple filters and their advantages.

The effects of different kind of ripple filters are studied in different possible configurations. We designed two different shapes of ripple filters of almost the same dimension. The first one (type A) has a simplified section (triangular section) and a thin base of plexiglass (PMMA) of

20 mm × 200 mm × 0.3 cm and a total thickness respectively of 2 mm and 3 mm (see Figure 3). The second shape (type B) has a sigmoidal section as described by (Weber and Kraft, 1999), as we can see in Figures 3. The sigmoidal shape of the type (B) filter satisfy the requisite to produce filtered Bragg peaks with a gaussian shape that permits a better uniformity when they are added up in a SOBP.
In our study we used PMMA plates of $1.19 g/cm^3$ density. The momentum spread for both protons and carbon ions was fixed at $\Delta p/p = 0.05\%$.
The shape of the Bragg peak resulting from the passage of the ion beam through the beam delivery line is strongly depending on the scattering and the straggling processes that affect the final spatial distribution of the beam energy loss. In fact, as we will see in details in the following section, proton beams, that have higher straggling effects than carbon ions, are deflected and broadened easily and are less sensitive to the shape of the ripple filter. Conversely, carbon ion beams needs more accuracy in the design and the mechanical production of the adequate ripple filter.

2.3 Pre-simulation analytical studies

The full Monte Carlo simulation of the passive elements and the water phantom requires a fairly amount of CPU time, and the iteration over different shapes and dimensions of the ripple filter is a lengthy procedure. To shorten this time and get an approximated solution we studied an algorithm to solve analytically the problem based on a *linear filter approach*. By convolving the shape of the non-filtered Bragg curves with a longitudinal *filter transfer function* one can estimate the energy deposition depth dose curves as modified by the ripple filter

$$D = f * D_0, \qquad (1)$$

where f is the transfer function associated to the specific ripple filter, D is the dose distribution in the volume of interest, which includes the effect of the ripple filter, and D_0 is the dose distribution without the ripple filter.
The transfer function was derived from the profiles of the ripple filters while the non-filtered Bragg curves D_0 were obtained from a Monte Carlo simulation of the full beam line and water phantom but without filter.
With this technique, which has been briefly introduced, one can quickly estimate the effects of the different filter shapes for any given set of proton beam energies. Applying the method to the two types of filters, type A and type B, (an example is reported in Figure 4), we can observe that the profiles of the filtered peaks are very similar and that the differences are less than 3% at the maximum dose.
In the next sections we discuss the impact of the ripple filters on the longitudinal and trasversal energy deposition curves obtained with a full simulation for both proton and carbon ion beams.

2.4 Effect of ripple filters on the Bragg peak

2.4.1 Proton beams

In this study we considered two type (A) filters with a maximal thickness of 2 mm and 3 mm respectively (see Figure 5(a)). For different configurations we compared the longitudinal Bragg peak width (sigma) and the dose uniformity at the SOBP.
The kinetic energies used in proton-therapy with active scanning covers the range between 70 and 250 MeV (see Figure 5(b)). As expected the present study shows that the effects of the ripple filter is more critical for low kinetic energies. At 70 MeV the sigma of the maximum of dose deposition curve along the beam direction is almost doubled by the insertion of the

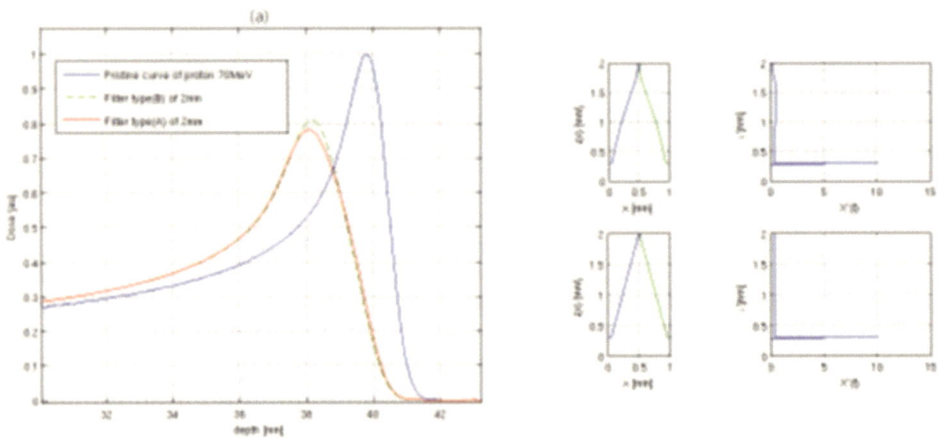

Fig. 4. Comparison of the Bragg curves using the sigmoidal shaped ripple filer and the triangular one with proton beam at 70 MeV.

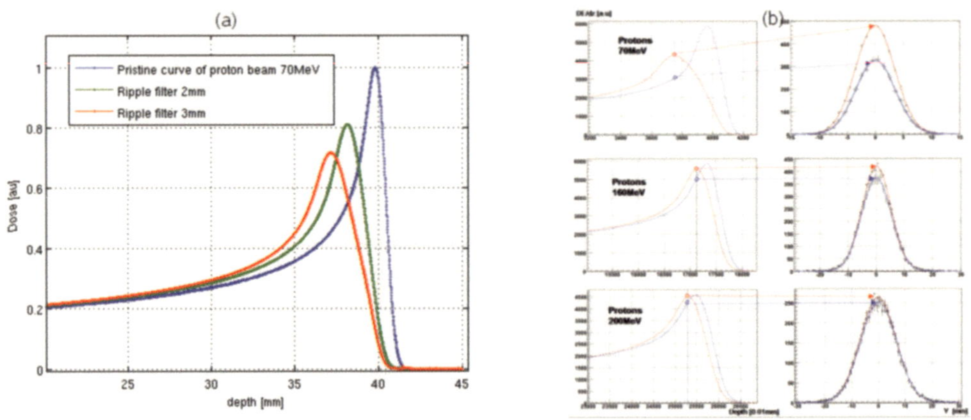

Fig. 5. Comparison of the Bragg curves using triangular ripple filters of 2mm and 3mm thickness with proton beam at different energies.

ripple filter, whilst the difference between 2 and 3 mm thick filter is of the order of 10%. For beam energies greater than 100 MeV the insertion of the ripple filter gives a marginal increase of the sigma (< 10%), which has already a value of several millimeters. The Bragg peak sigma values are reported for three different energies in Table 1. In the same table there are reported the widths for the 2 and 3 mm thick type (A) filters respectively. Even at low energies, the impact on the width of the peaks due to the two ripple filters is negligible (< 10%). However at 70 MeV the shape of Bragg peak falloff (see Figure 5,a) is quite affected by the filter, even if the width does not change by more than 10 %.

In Figure 5,b the longitudinal and transverse energy deposition curves are shown at three beam energies (70, 160, and 200 MeV) for a 2 mm thick type(A) filter and without filter. The energy deposition curves in the transverse plane with respect to the beam direction refer to the longitudinal position of the Bragg peak for the filtered case.

	70 MeV	160 MeV	200 MeV
No ripple filter	0.8	3	4.3
Ripple filter of 3 mm	1.9	3.3	4.4
Ripple filter of 2 mm	1.6	3.0	4.3

Table 1. Sigma values in [mm] from gaussian fits performed on a $\pm 1\sigma$ range around the Bragg peak

2.4.2 Carbon ion beams

It is well known that for carbon ion beams the Bragg peak is narrower than for the proton beams. Similar consideration applies also to the transverse plane. In this case it can be necessary to enlarge the Bragg peak width by using a configuration of two ripple filters used simultaneously (see comparison of peak shapes at Figure 11).

Furthermore, while for protons the effect of a deviation of the ripple filter shape from the ideal one tends to be washed out by the relatively large straggling, the carbon ion Bragg curve is far more sensitive to the shape of the ripple filter.

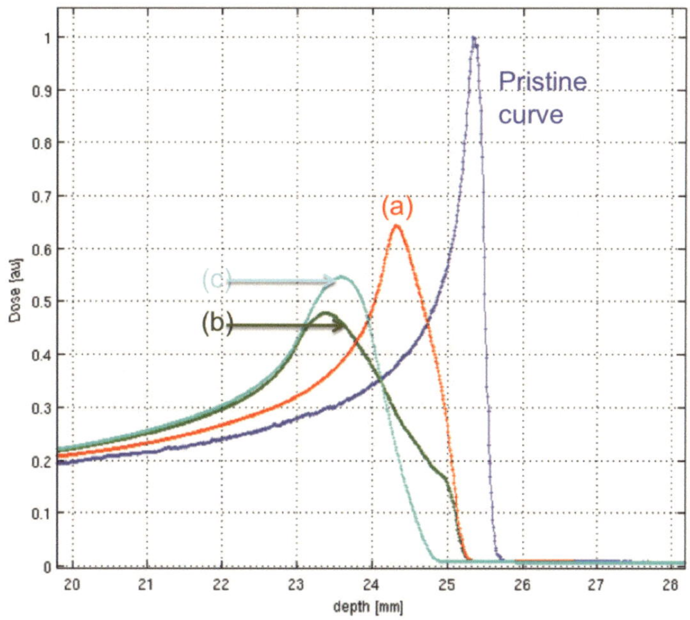

Fig. 6. a) Single triangular ripple filter (2 mm). b) Single triangular ripple filter (3 mm). c) Final design of the *double ripple filters* (2 mm + 2 mm) for carbon ion beams.

The carbon beams energies clinically used and simulated in this study range from 100 MeV/u up to 400 MeV/u. We simulated a *double filter*, with the first filter placed just after the exit window and the second ripple filter at 30 cm from the first, placed at the end of the monitoring system, right before the water tank. The two filters simulated are both of type (A) with 2 mm maximum thickness. For comparison we investigated the single ripple filter setup (2 and 3 mm) with a beam with kinetic energy of 100 MeV/u.

In Table 2) we see the effects of the simple and double filtering on the beam and the accuracy (normalized χ^2) of the gaussian fit performed on a $\pm 1\sigma$ range around the Bragg peak.

	100 MeV/u	270 MeV/u	360 MeV/u
σ (No ripple filter)	0.2	0.7	1.1
σ (One ripple filter of 2 mm)	1.1	1.4	1.6
χ^2 (One ripple filter of 2 mm)	185	35	19
σ (Two ripple filters of 2 mm)	1.6	1.9	2.1
χ^2 (Two ripple filters of 2 mm)	26	2.6	1.0

Table 2. Sigma value in [mm] from gaussian fits performed on a $\pm 1\sigma$ range around the Carbon ion Bragg peak and the corresponding value of the normalized χ^2 of the fit.

From the normalized χ^2 of the fit the similarity of the longitudinal dose deposition shape to a gaussian curve improves as the beam energy increase, but a good fit is obtained only with a double filter. Thus, for a carbon ion beam we conclude that the configuration with double filtering results in a shape which is closer to a gaussian curve with respect to the single filter. With a separate simulation, we probed the single type (B) filter and we found results very similar to the double filtering with type (A). This observation substantiates the original hint that the filter shape, for carbon ions, has a enormous impact on the resulting Bragg curve.
The results of the simulations were also compared with the experimental data taken at *Laboratory Nazionali del Sud* (LSN) in Catania, Italy, where carbon ion beam accelerated with a cyclotron at 62 MeV/u are used with different ripple filter configurations. The simulations are in complete agreement with the experimental data, as it ca be seen in Figure 7.

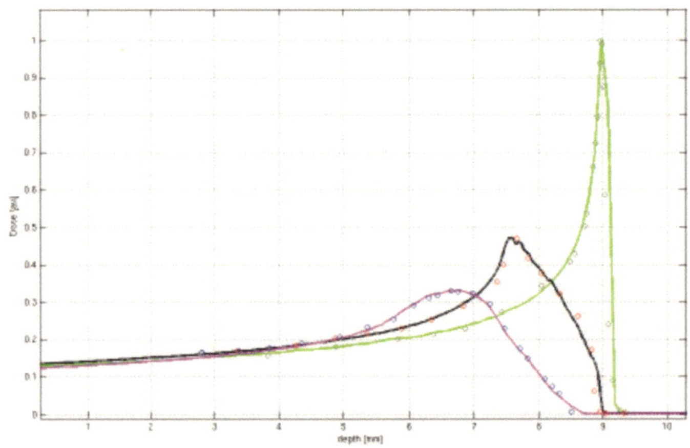

Fig. 7. Experimental measurements of carbon ion beam of 62MeV/u at Laboratori Nazionali del Sud (LNS) at the carbon ion beam line with and without ripple filters and compared to simulated curves.

2.5 Radiobiological effect

An investigation on the impact of the BDL elements for such configurations on particles yields and LET distribution in the treated volume is also performed. This knowledge is important, in particular in the case of carbon ion beams, to estimate the impact on the relative biological effectiveness (RBE) and the biological equivalent dose distribution (i.e. the dose weighted with the knowledge of the RBE) of the passive elements of the beam delivery line. In the case of carbon ions, the RBE usually presents variationin the irradiation fieldm, $1 < RBE < 5$, and

consequently the shape of the biological equivalent dose at Bragg peak is different from the corresponding physical dose. Hence, the evaluation of the transfer functions characterizing each of the element should involve a rigorous estimation of the biological effects.
With the Monte Carlo simulation we get the actual distribution in the treated volume of particles and fragments and the corresponding energies. The evaluation of biological effects was studied using a self developed code based on the LEM. The LEM provides a method to evaluate cell survivals starting from the knowledge of the track dose profiles and from the photon dose response curve. The model is based on the calculation of local biological effects, it thus preserves the details of track structure without averaging of the ionization density over cellular dimensions.
In this study we show a possible procedure to disentangle of the effects of the actual set-up of the beam line, from the information stored in the radiobiological look-up tables used in a treatment planning system (TPS). In principle, new simulations are mandatory for any change in the set-up, for example, the introduction of new ripple filters in the beam line. However, this needs a long computational effort, in particular for the evaluation of the biological effects. This method permits to avoid the re-calculation of the whole radiobiological database and the relative look-up tables when we have a change in the beam line set-up. In this way the TPS can be easily adapted to different beam line setup.

2.5.1 Linear-quadratic filter approach for the biological effects

The idea is to approximate the beam line setup in a way similar to the linear filter approach described in a previous section. In general, in the linear filter approximation we assume that the output of the beam line is sufficiently similar to the *pencil-beam*, i.e. a very narrow monoenergetic beam evaluated without any element in the beam line, and that the form can be reproduced from the latter via a linear operation. The proper transfer function of the beam line can be obtained experimentally with the deconvolution of the measured dose distribution in a water phantom, D, and the distribution, D_0, of the simulated monoenergetic pencil beams in the same phantom, inverting the convolution operation $D = f * D_0$.
In the case of the equivalent biological dose, we assume a Linear Quadratic (LQ) formalism for the description of the cell survival as a function of the physical dose. In order to obtain the actual biological parameters α and β from the pencil-beam ones, α_0 and β_0, is possible to consider the convolution integral as a superposition of several infinitesimal pencil-beams and use the same kind of approach used for the evaluation of the biological effects for mixed-fields irradiations. In this approach the effective LQ parameters are evaluated as:

$$\bar{\alpha} = \frac{\sum \alpha_i}{\sum D_i} \quad (2)$$

$$\bar{\beta} = \frac{(\sum \sqrt{\beta_i} D_i)^2}{(\sum D_i)^2}, \quad (3)$$

that, applied to the linear filter formalism brings to a linear-quadratic convolution:

$$D = f * D_0 \quad (4)$$

$$\alpha = f * [\alpha_0 D_0]/D, \quad (5)$$

$$\beta = (f * [\sqrt{\beta^0} D^0]/D)^2, \quad (6)$$

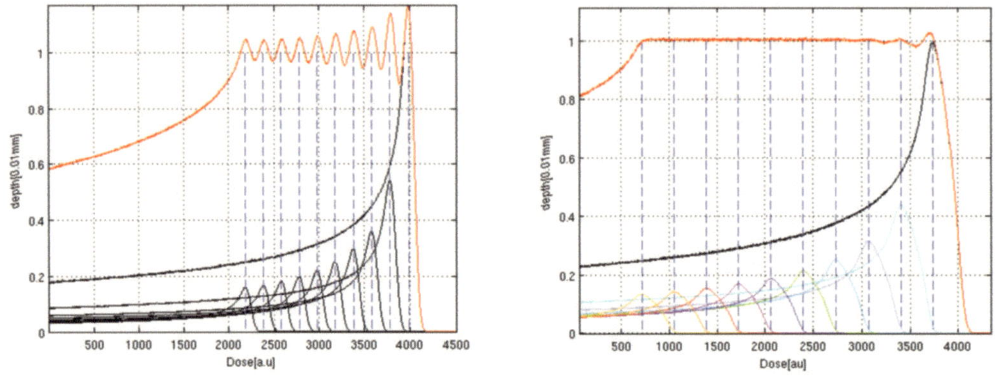

Fig. 8. Spread out of the Bragg peak for proton beam of 70 MeV respectively without ripple filter and with ripple filter type(A) of 3 mm.

Where α_0 and β_0 are LQ parameters evaluated for the pencil-beam set-up while α and β correspond to the beam line set-up. Note that all the linear parameters are not constant but vary within the volume of interest as well as D and D_0.

2.5.2 Monte Carlo physical and biological simulations

In order to verify the linear-quadratic filter method, a set of carbon ions pencil-beams, as well as beams evaluated through a full beam delivery line are simulated. The used beam line is the beam line of the CNAO. The treated volume is simulated defining different material associated to the tissues in the head and neck region. The evaluation of biological effects was obtained using Monte Carlo simulations based on LEM (applied to Chinese Hamster Ovary (CHO) cells).

The LEM code use the particle tracks generated with GEANT4 Montecarlo simulation as an imput to evaluate the local effects in the cell nucleus. The microscopic resolution used in the simulations (of the order of the μm) for the creation of the radio biological data is very time consuming. Thus, the computational effort was performed using the distributed INFN Grid computing resources.

3. Results

3.1 SOBP calculation and dose uniformity

To evaluate the SOBP dose uniformity we overlap several curves as obtained with the simulation of a specific energy to mimic the dose delivery technique. Each curve has been displaced by a given amount with respect to the adjacent one and the dose delivered has been adjusted to obtain a flat average dose deposition. A sketch of the procedure using 10 different positions fixing the step between Bragg peaks as a function of the kinetic energy is depicted in Figure 8.

With this technique we compared the dose uniformity on the SOBP with and without ripple filters. The study was done with the ripple filter type (A) of 3 mm. For 70 MeV protons with the ripple filter and using a step of 3.36 mm the peak-to-peak dose uniformity is found to be $\pm 1\%$ error (see Figure 8). Without ripple filter the deviation increases to $\pm 15\%$ even if the step has been drastically reduced to 2 mm. Similar results for carbon ions of 100 MeV/u are reported also in Figure 9. In this figure we compare the SOBP profile for three different cases: a) no ripple filter and 0.5 mm steps; b) 2 mm type (A) filter and 1 mm steps; c) double

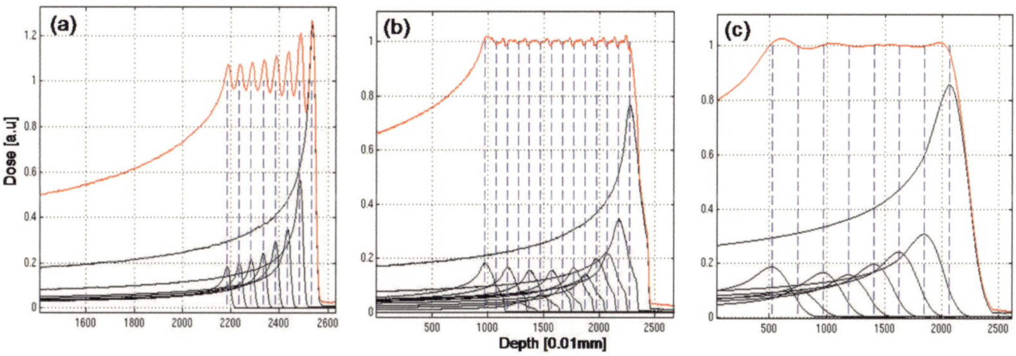

Fig. 9. Spread out Bragg peak of carbon ion beam of 100 MeV/u with: (a) pristine Bragg curve using 8 spots at 0.5 mm step, (b) Bragg curve after passing through one ripple filter type (A) of 2 mm, using 14 single spots at 1 mm step, and (c) Bragg curve after passing through two ripple filters type(A) distant 30 cm, using 8 single spots with step of 2.2 mm.

2 mm type (A) filter and 2.2 mm steps. One can clearly appreciate the improvement of the uniformity going from a) to c) even if the steps are increased from 0.5 mm to 2.2 mm.
The situation is less critic when the beam energy is above 100 MeV. In fact at 160 MeV, using the ripple filter we have a dose uniformity within $\pm 2\%$ and $\pm 3.5\%$ without filter for a scanning step of 6 mm both. For beam energy of 200 MeV the dose uniformity is not depending any more on the use of the ripple filter: we evaluated a peak-to-peak dose uniformity of $\pm 2\%$ with or without filter for scanning steps ranging from 3 mm to 7.6 mm.
To enhance the impact of the filtering on the widening of the Bragg peak we simulated a setup with an aligned double filter. We compared the effect of different longitudinal positions and different way of coupling two type (A) ripple filters of 2 mm to optimize the conditions of the double filtering.
As shown before, the impact of the filter on proton beams is marginal above 100 MeV, thus we checked the effect of the double filter only at 70 MeV. In Figure 10 we compare the Bragg peaks obtained with the configuration without filters to other configurations: type (A) 2 mm thick single filter, and two same type double filter configurations. In one case the filters are 2 cm apart close to the patient and in another case one filter of the pair is placed right after the exit window and the second in front of the patient (30 cm apart).
With a double filter the shape of the resulting Bragg peak is more regular and is a better approximation of a gaussian than the single filtered peak. We deduce that one way to enlarge the Bragg peak preserving the gaussian shape of the peak with a ripple filter of type (A) is to use a double filtering where the first filter should be at the exit windows of the beam and the second one as far as possible from the first. This configuration corresponds to the convolution of two linear transfer functions giving as a result a non-linear transfer function.
The final design of the double ripple filter used in the CNAO beam line is reported in Figure 11. The simulated SOBP is reported in Figure 12.

3.2 Total Scattering effect

During the commissioning phase the full characterization of the beam line and the calculation of the total lateral scattering effect of the passive elemnts, for both proton beam and carbon ion beams, is mandatory. We performed also this kind of study for the commissioning of the CNAO beam line. The results are reported in Figure 13.

htbp

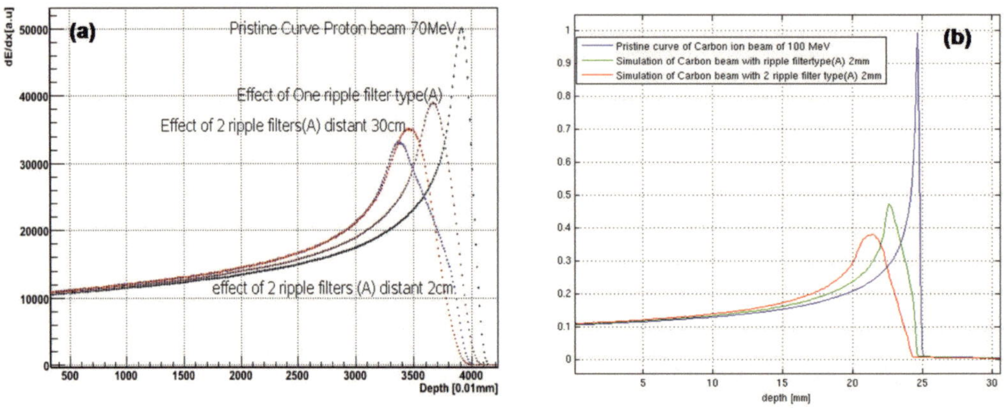

Fig. 10. a) Geant4 simulations of energy losses as functions of depth for different setting of ripple filters in the proton beam path before the water tank; b) Comparisons between depth-dose curve simulated with respectively one and two ripple filters for carbon ion beam of 100 MeV/u.

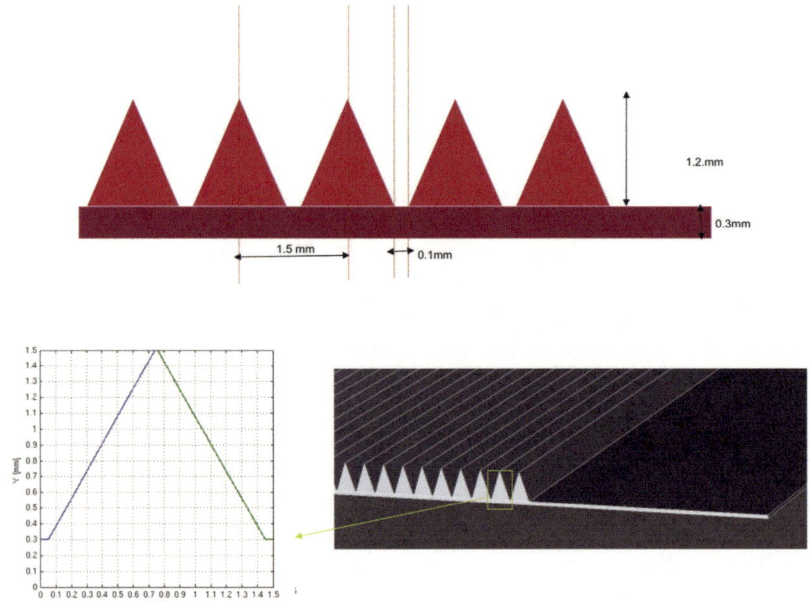

Fig. 11. Final design of the couple of ripple filters for carbon ion beams.

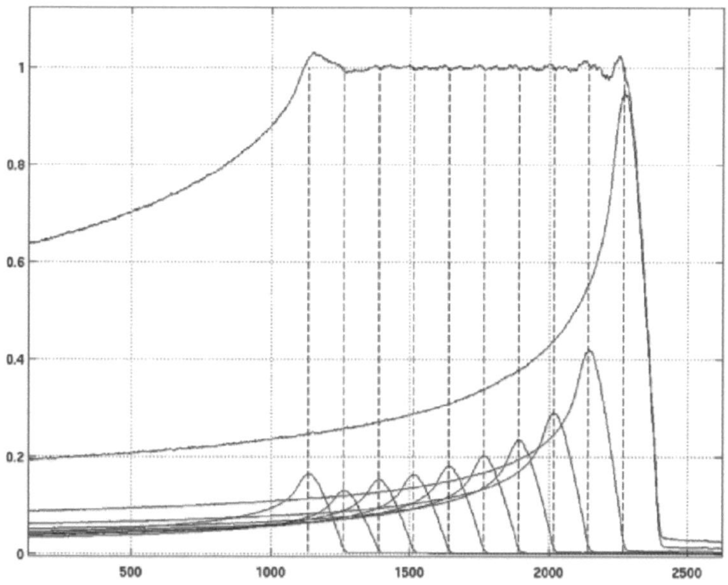

Fig. 12. SOBP corresponding to the final design of the couple of ripple filters for carbon ion beams.

3.3 Radiobiological aspects

3.3.1 Shape of biological equivalent dose using a ripple filter

In order to verify the linear-quadratic filter method, we first studied the case of a simple beam line set-up where only one ripple-filter is inserted. The characterization of the ripple filter is obtained from the knowledge of the transfer function f that can be experimentally and also analytically determined. The result of this comparison is reported in Figure 14, where the α and β curves as a function of depth in the volume, evaluated via full Montecarlo simulations (GEANT4 + LEM), are compared with those produced with the linear-quadratic filter approach. The figure shows a very good agreement of the two methods.
We completed our analysis simulating also the complete full CNAO BDL. We verified the method through the comparison of the radiobiological MC simulations and results using the linear filter approach. The resulting evaluated profiles of the physical and biologiacl equivalent dose are reported in Figure 15.

3.3.2 Ripple filters for radiobiological measurement

Radiobiological equivalent dose is strongly depending on the accuracy of the electromagnetic and hadronic processes modeled in the simulation Monte Carlo package. For the Study of the effect of ripple filter on the shape of the Bragg peak also is important the accuracy of the radiobiological model and its parameters is more important and it has a direct impact on the final shape of dose distribution around the Bragg peak.
The radiobiological cell survival measurements at the Bragg peak have the problem of uncertainties in the positioning of cell samples in the peak region. This due to the very sharp shape of the maximum of energy deposition for carbon ion beams (the guausian fit at the peak is less than 0.1mm sigma). We designed for this specific purpose a special ripple filter

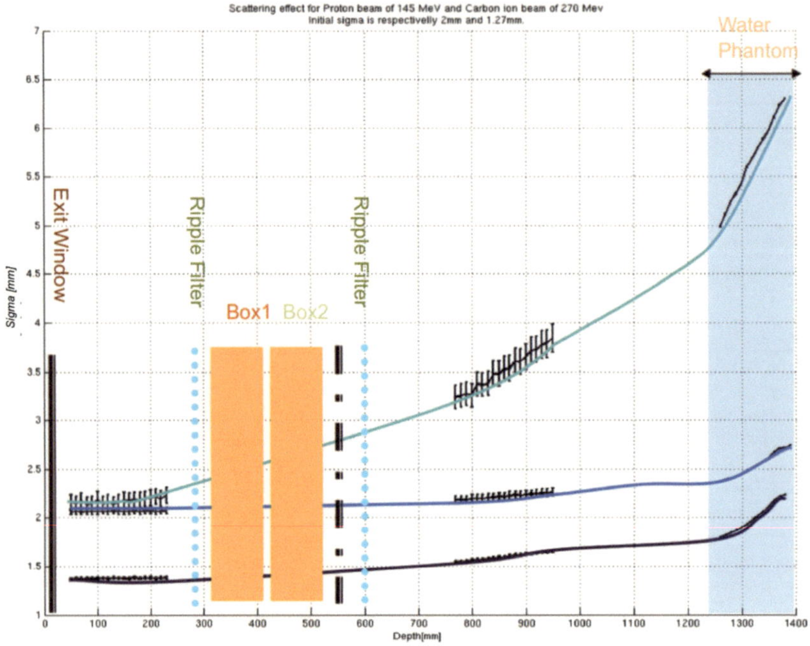

Fig. 13. Scattering effect along the beam delivery for carbon ion beam of 270 MeV/u and proton beam of 145 MeV.

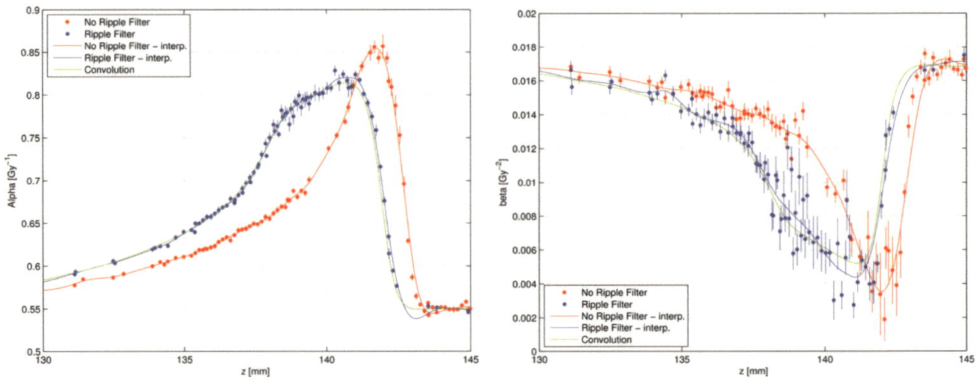

(a) Alpha values

(b) Beta values

Fig. 14. Effect of the ripple filter on the parameters α and β characterizing the biological equivalent dose for a carbon ion beam of 270 MeV/u.

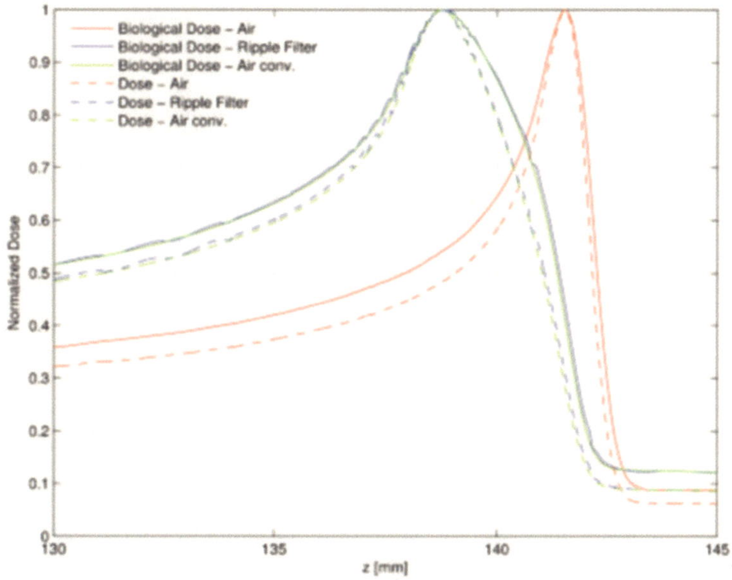

Fig. 15. . The shape of the physical dose at Bragg peak is different from the corresponding biological dose. Though the transfer functions characterizing each of the element should involve a rigorous evaluation of the biological effects.

in order to producea small broadening of the peak region to allow a more reliable positioning of cells samples. The modelization and estimation of the effects of the used ripple filter on the radiobiological response is mandatory in order to have a meaningful analysis of the radiobiological experimental data.
We used a Monte Carlo simulation with GEANT4 already benchmarked for a carbon ion beam of 62 MeV (see Figure 7). The beam line is principally composed of the following elements:the exit window, teh monitoring system, a first ripple filter and s second ripple filter. Actually instead of a detailed monitoring system (MS) we used an 'equivalent MS' in terms of water equivalent thickness. The two ripple filters are designed in such away that the Bragg peak have a guassian shape of about 0.4 mm. We built two ripple filter of 0.75 mm thickness each, and with a triangular shape (see Figure 16).

4. Conclusion

Monte Carlo simulations are a powerful tool helping in the optimization of resources during the design phase of the BDL, particularly in the field of advanced radiation therapy technique, where the accuracy of the dosimetric analyses is a crucial step for an accurate delivery of the treatment to the patient. Furthermore it is a powerful means to estimate the radiobiological effect of heavy ion beams when crossing different elements of the BDL.
The aim of this work is creating a flexible tool for full characterization of the beam delivery line including the biological impact. This characterization can be used in the TPS for modeling the possible effects of the passive elements in the beam line and to design new elements of the beam line. A step in this characterization consists in defining the transfer function and the linear filters related to the beam line elements.
Usually the passive elements on the beam line are optimized only for physical dose profiles. However, it is necessary to consider the biological effect and their impact on the dose

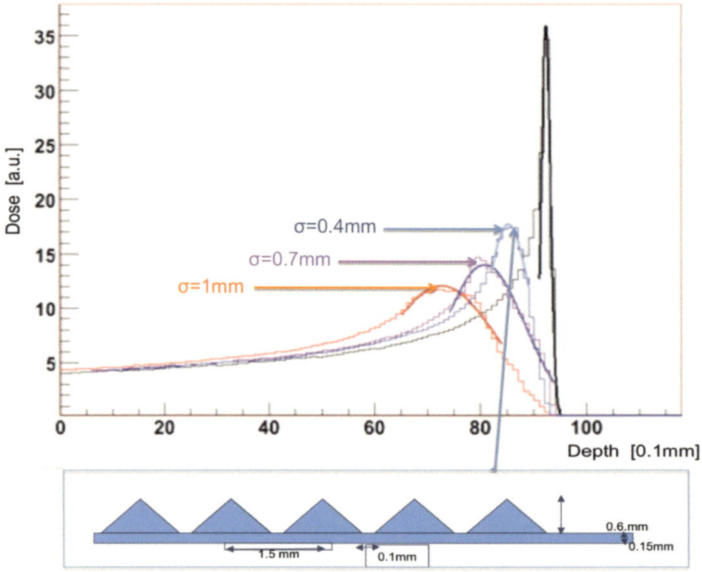

Fig. 16. Design of ripple filters for radiobioilogical measurments with carbon ion beams.

distribution, especially in the Bragg peak region for a correct estimation of the peak spread. A full characterization of the beam delivery line considering the biological impact provides a flexible tool in the treatment planning system for modeling the possible effects.

We estimate the impact on the relative biological effectiveness (RBE) and the biological dose distribution of the passive elements of the beam delivery line. The shape of the physical dose at Bragg peak is different from the corresponding biological dose. Though the transfer functions characterizing each of the element should involve a rigorous evaluation of the biological effects and to evaluate the correct shape of the effective dose.

In particular a biological linear-quadratic transfer function can be a flexible tool in a TPS, for a complete modeling of the biological effect, and in the design and the analysis of radiobiological measurements of cell survival around the Bragg peak region.

5. References

Bourhaleb F. et al. Monte Carlo simulations of ripple filters designed for proton and carbon ion beams in hadrontherapy with active scanning technique. 2008 J. Phys. Conf. Ser. 2008; 102; 012002

Elsasser T. and Scholz M. Cluster effects within the local effect model. Rad Res 2007;167:319-329

Geant4 a simulation toolkit, http: //geant4.web.cern.ch

Root Cern Data Analysis root http: //root.cern.ch

Takada, Y.; Kobayashi, Y.; Yasuoka,K; Terunuma,T. A miniature ripple filter for filtering a ripple found in the distal part of a proton SOBP. Nuclear Instruments and Methods in Physics Research A 524 (2004)

Weber, U. and Kraft, G. Design and construction of a ripple filter for a smoothed depth dose distribution in conformal particle therapy. PMB volume 44 number 11, 2765

8

A Monte Carlo Simulation for the Construction of Cytotoxic T Lymphocytes Repertoire

Filippo Castiglione
Istituto per le Applicazioni del Calcolo "M. Picone" (IAC)
Consiglio Nazionale delle Ricerche (CNR)
Italy

1. Introduction

The immune system of vertebrate living beings is a very complicated system that has evolved a set of mechanisms to get rid of potential pathogens he get in contact with. These mechanisms are so finely tuned that we don't even realize how much work our immune defenses are carrying out each moment to keep us disease free. Unfortunately, as one can figure, the whole system is not error free.

For example, autoimmune diseases arise when at least one of the mechanisms meant to preserve *tolerance of self* breaks. The immune self tolerance is the process by which the immune system refrain from attaching the host own body. This is normally the norm but given the huge complexity of the interdependencies among immune components (cells, molecules, organs, signals, etc.), and also given that the immune defenses are not static but rather dynamic and ever changing during our lifetime, it should not be surprising to learn of the different autoimmune diseases known to date.

Tolerance is the evolutionary result of a multi-layer system whose goal is to weed out self-reactive cells. Of these mechanisms, lymphocytes T education in the thymus organ represents the very first one.

In this article we describe a Monte Carlo method to simulate the maturation of key immune cells. Before describing the algorithm we give a brief introduction of how the immune system works.

The goal of the present work is purely methodological. In fact, while we focus on the specific aspect of the examination phase of the T lymphocytes maturation, we use immuno-informatics data and methods to perform computer simulation of the whole process without taking into account, for example, the anatomical structure of the thymus organ where the process of lymphocytes education takes place. Moreover, for reasons that will be mentioned later, we will specifically deal with $CD8^+$ T-cells (i.e., CTLs) selection rather than on $CD4^+$ T-cells (T helpers).

1.1 About the immune system

The immune system is the sum of a number of functions exerted at different spatial scales, from the micro of molecules to the macro of tissues and organs. White blood cells like the lymphocytes and the phagocytic/dendritic cells are the most important. Their action is to seek out and destroy disease-causing organisms or substances (generically called antigens) like bacteria or virus and to mount a response in terms of production of antibodies or antigen-specific cells. These are the two types of immune response, respectively humoral and cytotoxic. Moreover, talking about immunity we have to distinguish between the innate immunity and the acquired immunity. The first consists of the basic protection mechanisms like the skin/mucosa barriers and the phagocytic *aspecific* activity of certain kinds of cells. The second type of immunity, the adaptive, is the most recent in evolutionary terms, and it is what confers the immune system its adaptability to new invaders which are in turn the result of natural selection pressures.

While the cellular components of the innate immunity recognize structures shared by different classes of microbes, which is as to say that its recognition ability is *hard wired* into the membrane receptors, the adaptive immunity consists of a multitude of *clones* bearing different cell receptors and therefore able to recognize different antigens. The adaptability of this system comes from the fact that the immune response elicited by a pathogen is *specific*: only those clones able to recognize the antigen will start to proliferate, creating an army of cells with tailored weapons against that specific antigen.

A crucial step in the recognition of the antigen by the lymphocytes is its *presentation* by certain types of cells called *antigen presenting cells*. These cells capture the antigen, digest it, and then show, on their membrane surface, bits and pieces of the antigen attached to a molecules called *major histocompatibility complex* (MHC). The lymphocytes through their receptors, can only see the antigen when attached to the MHC.

An important feature of the immune system is its ability to remember already encountered pathogens. Memory resides in antigen-specific cells that live much longer than normal, conferring the system the ability to mount a more effective and swift responses the second time it is threaten by the same pathogen. Memory is the reasons why vaccines can confer long-lasting protection against infections.

1.2 The diversity of lymphocytes receptors

Without going into detail on the mechanisms of generation of receptor diversity (combinatorial and junctional diversification), we note that somatic recombination may result in potentially more than 10^{15} receptors with different specificities. Given this potential diversity, it is estimated that only 10^7 are actually expressed receptors; i.e., different clones circulating in our body every day.

This enormous diversity of receptors occurs during the maturation process of lymphocytes. This process starts from bone marrow stem cells and includes three phases: the proliferation of immature cells, expression of the antigen receptor genes and selection of lymphocytes that express an antigen receptor *useful*. Lymphocytes that are present in the immune system are those who have passed the ripening process. The maturation of T lymphocytes occurs in the thymus and during this phase are the receptors that will recognize any foreign antigens to the body. Since the process of gene recombination is random, thymus deletes those cells whose receptors have high specificity to proteins of the host, while those who are selected will be able to recognize the MHC molecules of the host. This is crucial because the TCR must also recognize residues on the MHC molecule in order to make the recognition of an antigen. A similar process occurs for B cells in bone marrow but mature and not need to recognize MHC molecules.

1.3 Immune effector mechanisms

There are two types of cell-mediated reactions deputies to remove different types of intracellular microbes: the first $CD4^+$ T cells activate macrophages so that they destroy

the microbes contained in their vesicles, the other $CD8^+$ lymphocytes that kill cells micro-organisms in their cytoplasm, eliminating the reservoir of infection. The humoral immunity is mediated by antibodies and instead represents the arm of acquired immunity deputy to neutralize extracellular microbes. Antibodies are molecules of the family of immunoglobulin. Organism are produced five different classes of Ig that are differentiated by their heavy chain constant region determines the effector function.
A B lymphocytes activated by antigen recognition may differentiate into a plasma cell or a cell that produces antibodies. These have the same specific receptor that recognized the antigen but are able to act remotely as soluble. The antibodies act by using the antigen binding region to bind to microbes and toxins by blocking the pathological effects, while using the constant portion of the heavy chain to activate different effector mechanisms that cause the deletion. Effective action can only be made when several antibodies recognize an antigen and bind to it.

1.4 The components of the immune system

Lymphocytes are cells with receptors specific for the antigen and are the central component of acquired immunity. Very similar, the lymphocytes are very heterogeneous in terms of functional and phenotypic.
B lymphocytes: are the only cells that produce antibodies and mediate humoral immunity. Express on their surface antibody molecules that serve as receptors for antigen recognition and to start the activation process. Soluble antigens or bound onto the surface of bacteria or other cells can bind to these receptors, initiating the humoral response.
T Lymphocytes: mediate cellular immunity. Their receptor recognizes antigen peptides only fragments linked to protein molecules specialized in presenting antigen (MHC I or MHC II). The most important T-cells are: or T helper (CD4 + or): Their TCR recognizes peptides bound to MHC class II. Their function is to help B cells produce antibodies and phagocytes to destroy microbes incorporated by cytokine release.
Cytotoxic T lymphocytes (CTL or CD8 + or): Their TCR recognizes peptides bound to MHC class I. Their function is to kill cells infected by intracellular microbes.
Dendritic cells: Although in principle are cells of innate immunity, play their most important function in presenting antigens to compartment specific immunity. Dendritic cells capture antigens that penetrate through the epithelium and transport them to draining lymph nodes. Lymph nodes expose their membrane fragments of microbial protein antigens to activate T lymphocytes with the specific receptor.
The various cells cooperate to protect the body from infections and illness. They can communicate through chemical mediators to orchestrate the response; they circulate throughout the body in the lymphatic and blood system to patrol every single organ. Lymphocytes are equipped with a transmembrane molecule called receptor that are used to bind to antigens. This binding event is the first step in recognizing anything dangerous. It is therefore clear that mother nature has constructed these membrane receptor very carefully. In fact, if the lymphocytes recognize a *self* molecule, soon the immune system would start to destroy it. A self molecule is so called because it belongs to our own body cells, therefore being the target of an immune attack causes inflammation and damage and leads to autoimmune disorders.
The causes of autoimmune diseases are unknown, although it appears that in many cases there is an inherited predisposition to develop them. In a few types of autoimmune disease (such as rheumatic fever), a bacteria or virus triggers an immune response, and the antibodies

or T-cells attack normal cells because they have some part of their structure that resembles a part of the structure of the infecting microorganism.
The membrane receptors of lymphocytes are randomly arranged so, potentially, they can bind to any molecule. How is then tolerance achieved?
One mechanism is to scrutinize the immature lymphocytes for potentially autoreactive ones and eliminating them before they go into circulation. For lymphocytes T helpers and cytotoxic T cells, this step is performed in the organ from which these cells take their name; the thymus. Thymus education represents the very first method to limit autoreactivity.

1.5 The thymus organ

The functioning of the thymus is far from being fully understood. What is surely known is that bone marrow-derived T lymphocytes that do not yet express co-receptor (called double negative DN or $CD4^-CD8^-$), enter the thymus, migrate to the thymic cortex (the outer region) and proliferate. Most of them also begin to express both CD4 and CD8 co-receptors (double positive DP, or $CD4^+CD8^+$) together with the T-cell receptor molecule (TCR) and its associated accessory proteins (the CDR3 protein complex). At this stage the immature lymphocytes express high levels of Fas antigen which can trigger death when ligated and produces very little Bcl-2, a cellular protein that protects against apoptosis. This means that they are very sensitive to signals that can trigger death by apoptosis. These apoptotic signals will come from antigen presenting cells (APCs). In particular, in the thymic cortex they interact with cortical thymic epithelial cells and maturate in single positive (SP) cells ($CD4^+CD8^-$ or $CD4^-CD8^+$). Then they migrate to the medulla and undergo a series of interaction with thymic dendritic cells and medullary thymic dendritic cells. This "walk" inside the thymus lasts for about 2 weeks. Those lucky thymocytes who survive the selection leave the organ to patrol the body in the search for potential pathogenic agents (Murphy et al., 2008).
The interactions with APCs, who act as "examiners", is meant to score the cells according to the ability to recognize the major histocompatbility complex (MHC) molecules (this is called *MHC restriction*), and also to the inability to bind peptides that belong to "self" (this is the *tolerance induction*). These two requirements are important to guarantee that a matured T lymphocyte is fully functional and, at the same time that, should he be able to recognize self molecules, he will not leave the thymus to cause damage.
APCs score T-cells through their T-cell receptor, a membrane protein whose extra cellular domain is able to bind the MHC-peptide complexes. In contrast to B cells, T-cells cannot recognize a pathogen on its own since they need to be presented in the context of an MHC-peptide complex. For most T-cells, the TCR is a heterodimer, composed of an α and a β chain. There is another $\delta\gamma$ based TCR which is seldom encountered. The TCR belongs to the immunoglobulin superfamily and have one N-terminal immunoglobulin variable (V) domain, one constant (C) domain, a transmembrane domain and a short cytoplasmic C terminal segment. The variable region on the TCR is potentially unique for each T-cell, and is composed of three parts on both the α and β chains, called complementary determining regions (CDRs). CDR3 is thought to be the main molecule interacting with the antigen, while CDR2 would be interacting with the MHC molecule. It is important to note that TCRs originate from a limited number of genes (65 V genes, 27 D genes, 6 J genes), but despite this, the immune system is able to engender a great number of receptors (Goldsby et al., 2000; Murphy et al., 2008).
The generation of the TCR is similar to the one of immunoglobulins (BCR) in B cells. The α chain is generated by VJ recombination while the β chain relies on V(D)J recombination. The gene segments are then randomly joined together to produce the final TCR. The CDR3 region

corresponds to the junction of the V and J segment on the α chain and the V D and J β chain, explaining its high variability and its role in antigen binding thereof.
The TCR selection in a primary organ like the thymus is called *central tolerance induction* and is the first mechanism to assure that most auto-reactive cells are eliminated. Fortunately is not the only one. In fact, since this mechanism is not hundred percent efficient, the immune system is equipped with other mechanisms that constitute the *peripheral tolerance* and induce cell death in auto-reactive lymphocytes. If this does not happen, then autoimmune diseases arise.
Understanding the complex machinery of how thymic selection imparts MHC-self-peptide complex restriction and at the same time a high degree of self tolerance on the T-cell repertoire is a very challenging task and a lot of aspects remains unclear (Klein et al., 2009).

1.6 A short review of mathematical models of T-cell development

Few mathematical models have been used to study specific issues of T-cell development. Most of these models are based on ordinary differential equations. For example, one of the first mathematical model to study thymocyte subset dynamics was introduced in (Mehr et al., 1995). In this model the equations define time evolution of thymocyte subsets, including DN, DP, CD4SP, and CD8SP cells. The model predict that negative selection likely operates at the DP stage or later. Moreover the model revealed that the CD4SP over CD8SP cell ratio fits the "instructive" theory of thymic lineage commitment (Germain, 2002; von Boehmer & Kisielow, 1993). In (Mehr et al., 1997) the idea that thymocytopoiesis may be subject to feedback regulation by mature lymphocytes is proposed and experimental data was analyzed using mathematical models. Another equation-based model was used to to compare the intrathymic development of bone marrow precursors, derived either from young or old donors (Mehr et al., 1993). In Mehr et al. (1998) the phenomenon of *MHC-linked syngeneic developmental preference* was analyzed by a mathematical model. In another study, the authors focused on the naïve T-cell compartment defined by the presence of T-cell receptors excision circles formed during T-cell receptor gene rearrangement (Hazenberg et al., 2000).
In contrast to the above mentioned studies, the model introduced in (Efroni et al., 2005) takes into account the spatial information in thymocyte development, by using agent-based modeling. This modeling paradigm is ideal for uniquely identify cellular characteristics, like for example, receptor expression, to distinguish the different stages of the cell cycle in specific anatomical compartments (Efroni et al., 2007; 2003). Another example of a discrete spatial model can be found in (Souza-e Silva et al., 2009). In this study a cellular automaton was constructed to describe thymocyte migration and development in the thymic microenvironment.
The model presented in the present article takes yet another approach. We simulate MHC restriction and tolerance induction by a stochastic model that includes bioinformatics methods to assess the affinity between a cell receptor and an MHC molecule bound to a self peptide. This study follows the lines of Morpurgo *et al.* ((Morpurgo et al., 1995)) but diverges from it in that the molecules represented (i.e., TCRs, MHCs and self peptides) are not strings of zeros and ones (i.e., binary strings) but rather strings of letters representing the twenty amino acids. Moreover, most importantly, the function used to compute the affinity among these molecules is provided by data-driven machine learning bioinformatics methods.
In immunology what is of outmost importance is to "predict" whose part of the antigenic molecule will constitute an immunogenic epitope. Broadly speaking there are two ways of doing it. The first is to simulate the chemical-physical interactions between peptides and

MHC molecules (e.g., NAMD, NAnoscale Molecular Dynamics or ABF, Adaptive Biasing Force software (Darve & Pohorille, 2001)), that takes hours to simulate a single peptide-MHC interaction what in reality lasts fractions of a second. The second possibility is to resort to bioinfomatics approaches that use machine learning and statistical methods to extract and generalize information from available experimental data of MHC-peptide sequences (for a review see e.g., (Lundegaard et al., 2007)). These methods take a fraction of a second to run on common workstations hence, from this point of view, are preferable to the first one.

Immunoinformatics is a new discipline emerging from the growing knowledge gathered for decades in experimental immunology and immunogenomics (Korber et al., 2006; Petrovsky & Brusic, 2002). Being both an experimental and theoretical field, it is foreseen that immunomics will play an important role for the future of immunology (Petrovsky & Brusic, 2006).

The goal of the present work is to use machine learning techniques for molecular-level predictions of major histocompatibility complex-peptide binding interactions (Lund et al., 2004; Nielsen et al., 2007; 2004), and a more general protein-protein potential estimation (Miyazawa & Jernigan, 1999) to perform Monte Carlo simulation of the selection of thymocytes in the thymus.

MHC class I binding predictions methods based on machine learning have increased their accuracy over the years, thus leading to reliable predictions. The same level of predicting power has not yet been reached by class II prediction methods (Lin, Ray, Tongchusak, Reinherz & Brusic, 2008; Lin, Zhang, Tongchusak, Reinherz & Brusic, 2008). This is thought to be partly due to the structure of the MHC molecules, which binding pockets are open in class II, thus allowing peptides of different length to bind to the groove. In contrast, class I molecules restrict the size of the peptides they bind to to 8-12 amino-acids (Yewdell et al., 2003; 1999), with an average length of 9 amino-acids. Therefore for convenience we restrict the attention to the education of $CD8^+$ T-cells rather than on CD4 T-cells (Lund et al., 2005).

2. The construction of the T-lymphocytes repertoire: a Monte Carlo method

The thymus organ is modeled as a simple *two-stage* filter. In the first stage, APCs give a survival signal to immature T-cell if a binding to the MHC-peptide complex occurs but "weakly", i.e., no binding will drive the cell to apoptosis; in the second stage the survival signal is given if the affinity to MHC-peptides presented by APCs is not "too high", i.e., high avidity for self peptides drives the cell to apoptosis (see left panel of figure 1).

In real life, bone marrow-derived T-cells entering the thymus initially home in the *thymus cortex* where they start to proliferate. Shortly after, rearrangement of the gene segments that encode the α and β chain of the T-cell receptor begins. Somatic rearrangement makes the TCRs highly diverse (about 10^8 (Arstila et al., 1999)).

All we need to account in the simulation is this huge variety. We do it by assigning random amino acid string receptors to each lymphocyte. Since the complementarity-determining region (CDR) of TCRs is what interacts directly with antigenic peptides bound to grooves of MHC molecules, the amino acid string we define for each T-cell is meant to represent not the whole TCR but rather its CDR.

The choice for the length of this string, thus the size of the repertoire, is not an easy one. Studies of various T-cell subsets from humans in physiological and pathological conditions have found an average length between 6 and 60 bases with a high variability in the different groups but only for the CDR3 suggesting that the whole CDR is much longer (Nishio et al., 2004). However not all arrangements of the genes gives a functional TCR and therefore for the

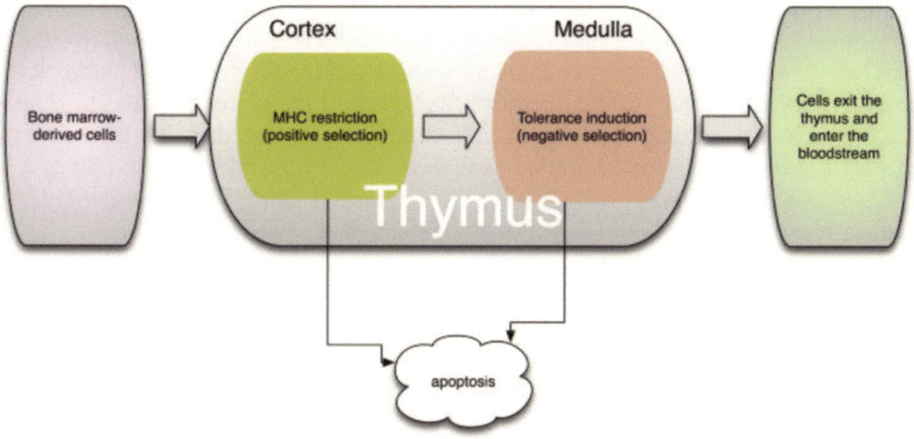

Fig. 1. The two-layer filter realized by the thymus to eliminate auto-reactive T lymphocytes. T-cells develop *self tolerance* during negative selection, whereas they are "discarded" as useless during positive selection.

sake of simplicity we decide to use only 8+12=20 letter to represent respectively the CDR of the α and of the β region of the T-cell receptor.
Self antigens are molecules, products of the organism own cells and as such tolerated by the parent immune system. We represent self molecules as amino acid strings. The question is how long. As we mentioned earlier, the prediction of class I MHC peptides is more accurate than those of class II (Lund et al., 2005). The reason for this is that in contrast to class II MHC that has the ends of the groove open, those of class I MHC are closed so a protein fragment to fit in properly must be about nine amino acid in length. In other words, class I-type epitopes are linear sequences of 8 to 11 amino acids that are processed from any protein of the pathogen. However each MHC class I molecule (whose total number surpasses the thousands of alleles to date (Nielsen et al., 2007)), is characterized by a specific binding motif that is possible to "decode". For the vast majority, the motif length is nine amino acids long, therefore by restricting our study to CTL's tolerance induction, we can define "self" any string of nine amino acids.
To be presented by the APCs, the peptide has to attach to the MHC molecule and therefore we need a method to predict peptide binding to class I MHC.

2.1 Identifying peptides for class I MHC

Methods for class I T-cell epitope prediction rely mainly on machine learning techniques (Lund et al., 2004; Nielsen et al., 2004). In particular neural networks seems to perform well. For example the authors in (Nielsen et al., 2003) show that neural networks trained to predict binding versus non-binding peptides, are superior to other methods (Lin, Ray, Tongchusak, Reinherz & Brusic, 2008; Lin, Zhang, Tongchusak, Reinherz & Brusic, 2008). Furthermore, quantitative neural networks allow the straightforward application of a *query by committee* (QBC) principle, in which particularly information-rich peptides can be identified and subsequently tested experimentally. Moreover, iterative training based on QBC-selected peptides considerably increases the sensitivity of the prediction without compromising its efficiency (Buus et al., 2003).

The Monte Carlo method described herein does not make a direct use of neural network but rather employs a derived *Position Specific Scoring Matrix* (PSSM)-based method. In practice, for each MHC allele we use the *binding motif matrices* generated from the neural network methods as described in (Nielsen et al., 2007). In short, first the neural network is used to rank a set of 10^6 randomly selected natural peptides from the human genome, then the top one percent of the peptides are flagged as binders and used to generate a binding motif, that is a 9 by 20 matrix. These matrices (one for each MHC) are calculated using sequence weights, and are corrected for low counts (Altschul et al., 1997; Nielsen et al., 2004).
Binding motifs matrices are made of *propensities* calculated as $2\log_2(p/q)$, where p is the probability of finding a given amino acid at a given position, and q is the probability of finding that amino acid in any protein in general. These propensities are computed for each of the nine positions on a potential epitope, and give the propensity for each of the 20 amino acids.
Furthermore, we set an allele-specific threshold $\Theta_\mathbf{H}$ as the average score of the low-scoring binders in the top one percent of the binders (see (Nielsen et al., 2003; Yewdell et al., 1999) for details).
Finally, having the PSSM and its corresponding threshold $\Theta_\mathbf{H}$, we can discriminate binders and non binders by calculating the score and comparing it with $\Theta_\mathbf{H}$. More formally, let Ω be the set of amino acid symbols Ω and $\mathbf{p} = [a_1, a_2, \dots, a_{l(\mathbf{a})}]$, represent a contiguous stretch of amino acids, with $l(\mathbf{p})$ the length of the sequence and $a_i \in \Omega$ the ith amino acid in the sequence. For a given 9-mer $\mathbf{p} = [a_1, a_2, \dots, a_9]$, the sum of the values at each position in the scoring matrix $\mathbf{H} = \{\mathbf{h}_{a_i,i}\}_{i=1,\dots,9,a_i\in\Omega}$, of a particular MHC gives the propensity to bind that MHC, i.e.,

$$\mathbf{p} \text{ is a peptide} \iff \sum_{i=1}^{9} \mathbf{h}_{a_i,i} \geq \Theta_\mathbf{H}. \qquad (1)$$

Therefore of all possible 9-mers only those for which $\sum_{i=1}^{9} \mathbf{h}_{a_i,i} \geq \Theta_\mathbf{H}$, where $\Theta_\mathbf{H}$ is the allele-specific threshold, are considered epitopes that can be presented by antigen processing cells.
The second thing we need is to have a way to assess whether a TCR interacts with a given MHC-peptide complex or not.

2.2 Interaction with antigen presenting cells

To date, there is no general method that can be used to predict if, for example, a TCR will interact with any given MHC-peptide complex. For this reason we resorted to the Miyazawa-Jernigan residue-residue potential (Miyazawa & Jernigan, 1996) to score the strength of the interaction. The work performed by Miyazawa and Jernigan on protein energy potentials (Miyazawa & Jernigan, 2000) provides us with a method for assessing the chances of direct interactions among proteins in the simulation. The protein-protein potential concept was derived from the analysis of 3D structures in which the relative position of amino acids were determined. The contact potential matrix estimated by Miyazawa and Jernigan reflects the entropy between two residues; a low entropy means that the pair of residues has low energy and therefore that interaction is possible.
For $CD8^+$ T-cell recognition, the procedure to compute the binding score requires the definition of class I MHC specific *contact matrices*. These matrices can be computed by looking at known protein 3D structures found in the Protein Data Bank (PDB, `www.pdb.org`). In the end, we decided to adopt just one MHC contact matrix for *all* class I alleles. The reason for this is twofold: i) we did not find too much differences among contact matrices of different alleles and ii) the one we decide to use has been calculated from the best resolution data (i.e., 1.4 Å).

This contact matrix (that we call **C**) was calculated taking residues that i) are within a distance of 5 Å and, ii) show contacts between the MHC-epitope complex and the two chains (heavy and light) of a bound TCR.
The distance of 5 Å was selected because most crystal structures with experimentally verified B cell epitopes show that the residues on the antibody in contact with an epitope lie within a 5 Å radius. Again the reason for looking at B cell epitopes is twofold: firstly TCRs and immunoglobulins are not that different, and secondly, there are a lot more antigen Ig structures than MHC-pep-TCR structures.
We extend the use of this value to the minimum distance needed between residues for molecular interaction. By using the solved structures, it is possible to determine which residue on a TCR binds to the MHC or to the peptide. The contact matrix derived for class I binding that we use in the simulation is shown in the right panel of figure 1.
Similarly, one determines the residues that are generally in contact with the TCR. These are what we call MHC *pseudo-sequences* (indicated with `MHC`). Again, the contact residues are defined as being within 5.0 Å of the peptide in any of a representative set of HLA-A and -B structures with 9-mer peptides and TCRs (Nielsen et al., 2007).
The contact potential defined between a TCR and an MHC-peptide complex is thus based on the Miyazawa-Jernigan score as follows. Let $\{\mathbf{M}_{a,b}\}_{a,b\in\Omega}$, be the matrix in (Miyazawa & Jernigan, 2000), $\mathbf{x} = [x_1, \ldots, x_{l(\mathbf{x})}]$ a TCR, $\mathbf{y} = [y_1, \ldots, y_{l(\mathbf{y})}]$ a MHC-peptide complex composed by the pseudo sequence of the MHC and the peptide molecules, and **C** the contact matrix. We first compute the binding affinity between **x** and **y** as

$$\hat{M}(\mathbf{x}, \mathbf{y}) = \sum_{j=1}^{l(\mathbf{x})} \sum_{k=1}^{l(\mathbf{y})} (\mathbf{M}_{x_j, y_k} \cdot \mathbf{C}_{j,k}).$$

Then, since we need to define a probability, this value is normalized and further compared to a threshold value

$$M(\mathbf{x}, \mathbf{y}) = \begin{cases} \frac{\hat{M}(\mathbf{x},\mathbf{y}) - \mu_{\hat{M}}}{k \cdot \sigma_{\hat{M}}} & \text{if } (\hat{M}(\mathbf{x}, \mathbf{y}) - \mu_{\hat{M}})/(k \cdot \sigma_{\hat{M}}) \geq P_{95}, \\ 0 & \text{otherwise} \end{cases} \tag{2}$$

where $\mu_{\hat{M}}$ and $\sigma_{\hat{M}}$ are respectively the average and the standard deviation that have been previously estimated, k is a free parameter chosen to have $M(\mathbf{x}, \mathbf{y}) \leq 1$, and P_{95} is, the 95th percentile rank of the estimated distribution. Finally, we use the binding affinity $M(\mathbf{x}, \mathbf{y})$ of eq(2) as the probability of the binding between **x** and **y**.

2.3 Positive selection of TCRs

Given $\mathtt{n_{mhc}}$ major histocompatibility complex molecules, we calculate the probability to pass the positive selection of a cell bearing a random TCR as follows

$$\Pr^{+} = 1 - \prod_{j=1}^{\mathtt{n_{mhc}}} (1 - M(\mathtt{TCR}, \mathtt{MHC_j}\star)), \tag{3}$$

where $M(\cdot, \cdot)$ is the Miyazawa-Jernigan contact potential in eq(2), and $\mathtt{MHC}\star$ indicates that only residues of the TCR in contact with the MHC are taken into account (the wildcard $\star$ means that no matter what the peptide is, we give more weight to the MHC rather than to the peptide by summing a low constant value for each residue).

2.4 Negative selection of TCRs

If the cell survives the previous step with probability given by equation 3, then it can be negatively selected with probability

$$\mathrm{Pr}^{-} = \Big[\prod_{j=1}^{\mathtt{n_{mhc}}}\prod_{k=1}^{\mathtt{n_{self}}}(1 - M(\mathtt{TCR},\mathtt{MHC_j\,self_k}))\Big]^{\mathtt{E}} \quad (4)$$

where the $\mathtt{MHC_j self_k}$ is a string composed by the pseudo sequence $\mathtt{MHC}_j$ and the chosen peptide $\mathtt{self}_k$. The parameter $\mathtt{E}$ represents the efficiency in the selection process: higher efficiency means better filtering, that is, less self-reactive cells will slip out the thymus. From the point of view of the calculation of the survival rate of the immature cells entering the thymus, the negative selection is treated as if the thymus were composed by $\mathtt{E}$ sub-layers simulating as many encounters with each thymic cell receptor specificity because of the crowded nature of the thymus.

Equation 4 gives the probability that the TCR does not matches any of the self molecules with any of the MHCs.

Finally, we allow the T-cell to leave the thymus and to reach a secondary organ as a mature thymocyte with a probability given by the product of the probability of being positively selected and the probability of being negatively selected,

$$\mathrm{Pr}(\text{TCR is selected}) = \mathrm{Pr}^{+} \cdot \mathrm{Pr}^{-}.$$

The whole algorithm is summarized as pseudo-code in figure 2.

3. The outcome

Figure 3 shows the Logo plots of the TRC sets that have been filtered in during the thymus selection, that is, those bear by cells leaving the thymus as operational CTLs. The height of the letters reflects the Shannon information at individual positions.

In figure 3 it can be observed that there are specific preferential positions for some amino acids (i.e., smaller entropy of amino acid distributions in Logo plots). The analysis of these positions reveals a smaller entropy (i.e., higher bars) which is consistent with the contact matrix shown in the right panel of figure 1; the more contact positions on the TCR, the less the degrees of freedom.

Interestingly, positions 13 and 19 have respectively no interaction (position 13) or just one interaction (position 19) with the peptide (see right panel of figure 1). This means that negative selection does not influence the amino acid distributions for these positions in figure 3, resulting in similar conservation rates. In contrast, position 16 strongly interacts with both MHC (4 contacts) and peptide (3 contacts) so that it provides a strong constraint on the corresponding TCR residues, resulting in a smaller bar of the Logo plot because of a lack of match. Summarizing, the positive selection step sets a strong constraint to TCR sequences whereas the effect of negative selection provides one more constraint to the sequences at position 16.

Once we have selected the TCRs, $\mathtt{tcr}_1, \ldots, \mathtt{tcr}_N$ by executing the algorithm described in figure 2, we can compute the average auto-reactivity as the average of the probability to recognize at least one self peptide attached to one MHC molecule: $\alpha = \frac{1}{N}\sum_i^N(1 - \mathtt{Pr}^{-})$. This value depends on the parameters chosen; for example it depends on $\mathtt{E}$ and on the $\mathtt{MHC}_1, \ldots, \mathtt{MHC}_{n_{mhc}}$. It also depends on the self molecules $\mathtt{self}_1, \ldots, \mathtt{self}_{\mathtt{n_{self}}}$. However, for $\mathtt{n_{self}}$ large enough, the actual amino acid strings are less important their number $\mathtt{n_{self}}$ itself. This

```
input(E, N, n_mhc);                                  input parameters
for (i = 1; i≤ n_mhc; i++) {
        read(H_i);                                   read the MHC specific matrix
        read(MHC_i);                                 read the MHC pseudo sequence
        read(Θ_{H_i});                               read the MHC specific threshold
}
input(n_self);                                       input the number of self molecules
i == 1;
while i ≤ n_self {                                   randomly choose n_self 9-mers
      p_i = random();                                pick randomly a self peptide
      if ( ∃k : binds(H_k, p_i) == true) {           if it binds at least one MHC molecule than accept it
         Self ← p_i;                                 p_i will be shown as self
         i++;
      }
}
i=1;
while i ≤ N {                                        select TCRs
      TCR_i = random();                              generate a random amino acid string for TCR
      Pr+ = compute(TCR_i);                          compute Pr+ as in equation 3
      Pr- = compute(TCR_i);                          compute Pr- as in equation 4
      if (rand(0,1)<Pr+ · Pr-){
         Selected ← TCR_i;                           TCR passes the thymus selection
         i++;
      fi
}
output(Selected = TCR_1, . . . , TCR_N);             TCRs that leave the thymus
```

Fig. 2. We randomly select $\mathtt{n_{self}}$ 9-mers that bind at least one of the $\mathtt{n_{mhc}}$ MHC molecules. Then we generate a random TCR and calculate the probability of being positively selected and those of being negatively selected. We iterate until we stochastically have N TCRs.

dependence is shown in figure 4. As expected, increasing the thymic efficiency E the average self reactivity α decreases. On the other hand for large values of E, α is less influenced by the number of self peptides $\mathtt{n_{self}}$.

The number of self peptides $\mathtt{n_{self}}$ therefore does not dramatically influence α but it does determine the probability for a T-cell to pass the selection instead. In other words it is related to the fraction of cells that leave the thymus. It has been estimated that each day of a young person 60×10^6 immature cells are tested but only 1 to 3% exit the thymus (Goldsby et al., 2000; Murphy et al., 2008). Figure 5 shows the ratio between the number of cells exiting the thymus ("out") and those entering the thymus ("in") against the number of self peptides $\mathtt{n_{self}}$. The figure shows that we can get reasonable out/in ratios with a number of self peptides between 100 and 200. Each point is the average of hundreds of independent runs with a randomly chosen set of self peptides. Note however that in general this curve depends on other parameters (E) and therefore is not too indicative of the real number $\mathtt{n_{self}}$ of self peptides.

An interesting question that has been already investigated long time ago with a computational model ((Celada & Seiden, 1992)) is to calculate the "optimal" number of MHC molecules. We performed similar experiments varying the number of MHC molecules and computing

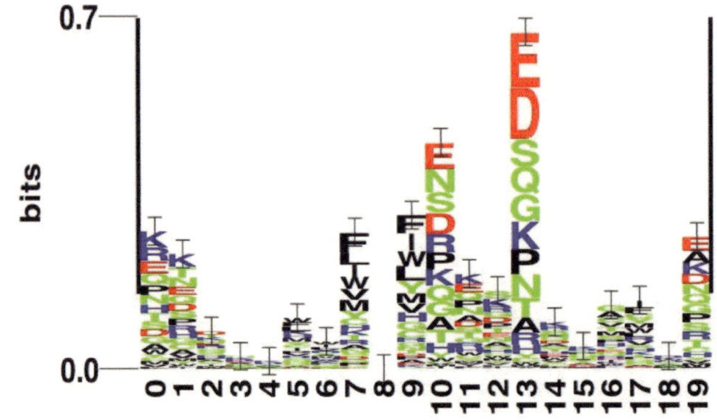

Fig. 3. Logo plots of the TRC sets that leave the thymus as operational CTLs TCRs. The height of the letters reflects the Shannon information at individual positions. Parameters $\mathtt{n_{self}} = 100$ and $\mathtt{E} = 10$. The MHC set is A*0201, A*6841, B*5304, B*5309. The Logo plots have been calculated using a small sample (i.e., 100) of the population of TCRs passing the selection.

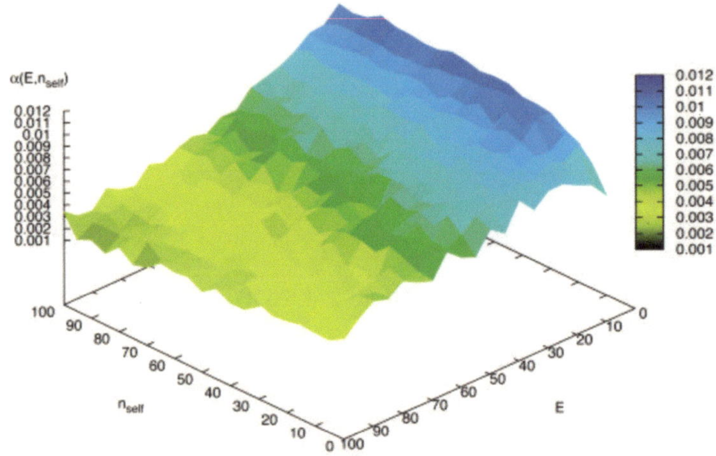

Fig. 4. Auto-reactivity rate $\alpha(\mathtt{E}, \mathtt{n_{self}})$ of the selected cells (those leaving the thymus) with respect to E and $\mathtt{n_{self}}$. Higher E corresponds to less average auto-reactivity. The influence of $\mathtt{n_{self}}$ is only marginal. The MHC alleles used are those reported in the caption of figure 3.

the average self reactivity $\alpha(\mathtt{n_{mhc}})$ of the selected TCRs. What we found is interesting though incorrect. In fact, the minimum of the self reactivity is attained for $\mathtt{n_{mhc}} = 8$ which is close to the real value of 6 alleles (figure 6). The overall curve is however in line with the ambivalent role of the MHCs: on the one hand, more MHCs foster the presentation of self peptides and, on the other hand, it limits the T-cell repertoire in the negative selection. An optimal number is therefore expected as the combination of the two opposed effects.

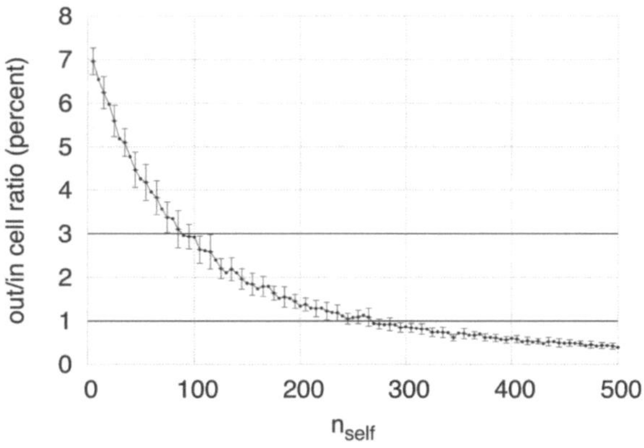

Fig. 5. The ratio between the number of cells entering the thymus ("in") and those leaving the thymus ("out") plotted against the number of self peptides n_{self}. Parameter $E = 10$. MHC-related parameters as in caption of figure 3. Parameters E=60, n_{self}=100.

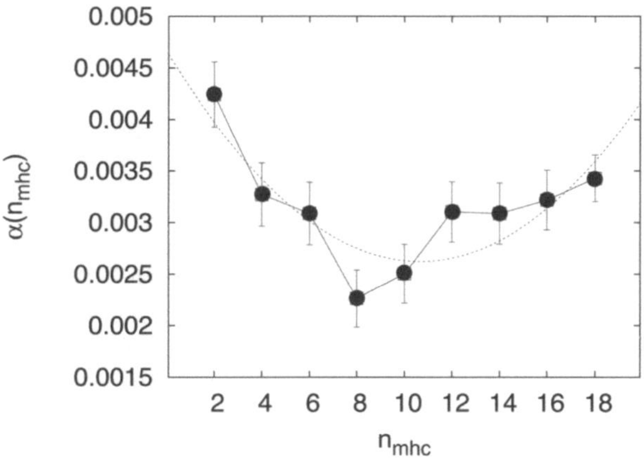

Fig. 6. This plot shows the average self-reactivity as a function of n_{mhc}. Parameters E=60, n_{self}=100.

4. Conclusions

We have described a Monte Carlo simulation of the thymus where CTLs are selected on the basis of the affinity of their TCRs to MHC molecules and self peptides. We have used data-driven prediction tools to identify suitable self peptides for a specific MHC set of molecules. Furthermore, we have defined a general protein-protein binding potential on the basis of the work of Miyazawa and Jernigan on protein energy potentials (Miyazawa & Jernigan, 2000) that provides a method for assessing the chances of direct interactions among proteins.

Finally, the binding affinity between the TCR and the MHC-peptide complex is computed by taking into account a MHC class I specific contact matrix. This matrix was derived by finding

residues in contact between the α and β chains of the TCR and the HLA-A2 heavy chain of an MHC molecule in a high resolution 3D structure (access number 1OGA for Protein Data Bank).
By running a large number of simulations we have estimated the average auto-reactivity rate for a wide range of the parameters and found that auto-reactive cells are able to leave the thymus but their number and their overall ability to recognize self peptides decreases with E, a parameter that indicates the "time" spent in the thymus. However this rate is only slightly affected by the number of self peptide presented n_{self}.
Other simulation performed changing the number of MHC alleles n_{mhc} resulted in a minimum of average self-reactivity for $n_{mhc} = 8$ which is wrong but not too distant from reality.
Take together, these results show that the simulation performs reasonably well. This is encouraging given the number of working assumptions that we had to make at this stage.
This study follows the lines of Morpurgo *et al.* ((Morpurgo et al., 1995)) but diverges from it in that the molecules represented are not binary strings but rather sequences of amino acids and, most importantly, the function used to compute the affinity among these molecules is provided by data-driven machine learning bioinformatics methods. We have already adopted this approach in a previous (Rapin et al., 2010); we believe that, although preliminary and somehow approximate at this stage, it provides a promising way to incorporate immuno-informatics resources (both data and methods) to systemic level stochastic simulations of immunological processes.

5. References

Altschul, S. F., Madden, T. L., Schäffer, A. A., Zhang, J., Zhang, Z., Miller, W. & Lipman, D. J. (1997). Gapped BLAST and PSI-BLAST: a new generation of protein database search programs, *Nucleic Acids Res* **25**(17): 3389–402.

Arstila, T., Casrouge, A., Baron, V., Even, J., Kanellopoulos, J. & Kourilsky, P. (1999). A direct estimate of the human t cell receptor diversity, *Science* 286(5441): 958–961.

Buus, S., Lauemoller, S. L., Worning, P., Kesmir, C., Frimurer, T., Corbet, S., Fomsgaard, A., Hilden, J., Holm, A. & Brunak, S. (2003). Sensitive quantitative predictions of peptide-MHC binding by a 'Query by Committee' artificial neural network approach, *Tissue Antigens* 62(5): 378–384.

Celada, F. & Seiden, P. E. (1992). A computer model of cellular interactions in the immune system., *Immunol Today* 13(2): 56–62.

Darve, E. & Pohorille, A. (2001). Calculating free energies using average force, *J Chem Phys* 115: 9169–9183.

Efroni, S., Harel, D. & Cohen, I. (2005). Reactive animation: Realistic modeling of complex dynamic systems, *Computer* 38: 38–47.

Efroni, S., Harel, D. & Cohen, I. (2007). Emergent dynamics of thymocyte development and lineage determination, *PLoS Computational Biology* 3: 127–135.

Efroni, S., Harel, D. & Cohen, I. R. (2003). Toward rigorous comprehension of biological complexity: modeling, execution, and visualization of thymic t-cell maturation., *Genome Res* 13(11): 2485–2497.

Germain, R. (2002). T-cell development and the cd4-cd8 lineage decision, *Nat Rev Immunology* 2: 309–322.

Goldsby, R., Kindt, T. & Osborne, B. (2000). Kuby immunology, iv ed.

Hazenberg, M., Otto, S., Stuart, J., Verschuren, M., Borleffs, J., Boucher, C., Coutinho, R., Lange, J., de Wit, T., Tsegaye, A., van Dongen, J., Hamann, D., de Boer, R. & Miedema, F.

(2000). Increased cell division but not thymic dysfunction rapidly affects the t- cell receptor excision circle content of the naive t cell population in hiv-1 infection, *Nat Medicine* 6: 1036–1042.

Klein, L., Hinterberger, M., Wirnsberger, G. & Kyewski, B. (2009). Antigen presentation in the thymus for positive selection and central tolerance induction, *Nat Rev Immunol* 9: 833–844.

Korber, B., LaBute, M. & Yusim, K. (2006). Immunoinformatics comes of age, *PLoS Comp Biol* 2(6): 484–492.

Lin, H. H., Ray, S., Tongchusak, S., Reinherz, E. L. & Brusic, V. (2008). Evaluation of MHC class I peptide binding prediction servers: applications for vaccine research, *BMC Immunol* 9: 8.

Lin, H. H., Zhang, G. L., Tongchusak, S., Reinherz, E. L. & Brusic, V. (2008). Evaluation of MHC-II peptide binding prediction servers: applications for vaccine research, *BMC Bioinformatics* 9 Suppl 12: S22.

Lund, O., Kesmir, C., Nielsen, M., Lundegaard, C. & Brunak, S. (2005). *Immunological Bioinformatics*, MIT Press, Cambridge, Mass.

Lund, O., Nielsen, M., Kesmir, C., Petersen, A. G., Lundegaard, C., Worning, P., Sylvester-Hvid, C., Lamberth, K., Roder, G., Justesen, S., Buus, S. & Brunak, S. (2004). Definition of supertypes for HLA molecules using clustering of specificity matrices., *Immunogenetics* 55(12): 797–810.

Lundegaard, C., Lund, O., Kesmir, C., Brunak, S. & Nielsen, M. (2007). Modeling the adaptive immune system: predictions and simulations., *Bioinformatics* 23(24): 3265–3275.

Mehr, R., Abel, L., Ubezio, P., Globerson, A. & Agur, Z. (1993). A mathematical model of the effect of aging on bone marrow cells colonizing the thymus, *Mechanisms of Aging and Development* 67: 159–172.

Mehr, R., Globerson, A. & Perelson, A. (1995). Modeling positive and negative selection and differentiation processes in the thymus, *J Theor Biol* 175: 103–126.

Mehr, R., Perelson, A., Fridkis-Hareli, M. & Globerson, A. (1997). Regulatory feedback pathways in the thymus, *Immunol Today* 18: 581–585.

Mehr, R., Perelson, A., Sharp, A., Segel, L. & Globerson, A. (1998). Mhc-linked syngeneic developmental preference in thymic lobes colonized with bone marrow cells: A mathematical model, *Dev. Immunol* 5: 303–318.

Miyazawa, S. & Jernigan, R. L. (1996). Residue-residue potentials with a favorable contact pair term and an unfavorable high packing density term, for simulation and threading., *J Mol Biol* 256(3): 623–644.

Miyazawa, S. & Jernigan, R. L. (1999). An empirical energy potential with a reference state for protein fold and sequence recognition., *Proteins* 36(3): 357–369.

Miyazawa, S. & Jernigan, R. L. (2000). Identifying sequence-structure pairs undetected by sequence alignments, *Protein Eng.* 13(7): 459–475.
URL: *http://peds.oxfordjournals.org/cgi/content/abstract/13/7/459*

Morpurgo, D., Serenthà, R., Seiden, P. E. & Celada, F. (1995). Modelling thymic functions in a cellular automaton., *Int Immunol* 7(4): 505–516.

Murphy, K., Travers, P., Janeway, C. & Mark, W. (2008). *Janeway's Immunology*, Garland Science, Taylor and Francis, New York.

Nielsen, M., Lundegaard, C., Blicher, T., Lamberth, K., Harndahl, M., Justesen, S., Roder, G., Peters, B., Sette, A., Lund, O. & Buus, S. (2007). NetMHCpan, a method for quantitative predictions of peptide binding to any HLA-A and -B locus protein of known sequence., *PLoS ONE* 2(8): e796.

Nielsen, M., Lundegaard, C., Worning, P., Hvid, C. S., Lamberth, K., Buus, S., Brunak, S. & Lund, O. (2004). Improved prediction of MHC class I and class II epitopes using a novel Gibbs sampling approach., *Bioinformatics* 20(9): 1388–1397.

Nielsen, M., Lundegaard, C., Worning, P., Lauemoller, S., Lamberth, K., Buus, S., Brunak, S. & Lund, O. (2003). Reliable prediction of T-cell epitopes using neural networks with novel sequence representations, *Protein Sci* 12(5): 2007–2017.

Nishio, J., Suzuki, M., Nanki, T., Miyasaka, N. & Kohsaka, H. (2004). Development of tcrb cdr3 length repertoire of human t lymphocytes, *Int Immunol* 16(3): 423–431.

Petrovsky, N. & Brusic, V. (2002). Computational immunology: The coming of age, *Immunol Cell Biol* 80: 248–254.

Petrovsky, N. & Brusic, V. (2006). Bioinformatics for study of autoimmunity, *Autoimmunity* 39: 635–643.

Rapin, N., Lund, O., Bernaschi, M. & Castiglione, F. (2010). Computational immunology meets bioinformatics: the use of prediction tools for molecular binding in the simulation of the immune system, *PLoS ONE* 5(4): e9862. doi:10.1371/journal.pone.0009862.

Souza-e Silva, H., Savino, W., Feijóo, R. & Vasconcelos, A. (2009). A cellular automata-based mathematical model for thymocyte development, *PLoS ONE* 4(12): e8233. doi:10.1371/journal.pone.0008233.

von Boehmer, H. & Kisielow, P. (1993). Lymphocyte lineage commitment: Instruction versus selection, *Cell* 73: 207–208.

Yewdell, J., Reits, E. & Neefjes, J. (2003). Making sense of mass destruction: quantitating mhc class i antigen presentation, *Nat Rev Immunol* 3(12): 952–961.

Yewdell, W, J. & Bennink, J. R. (1999). Immunodominance in major histocompatibility complex class I-restricted T lymphocyte responses., *Annu Rev Immunol* 17: 51–88.

9

Application of Monte Carlo Simulation in Treatment Planning for Radiation Oncology

Kin Chan, Soo Min Heng and Robert Smee
Radiation Oncology Department, Prince of Wales Hospital
Australia

1. Introduction

In radiotherapy, the dose delivered to patients needs to be determined before the treatment. Therefore, it is necessary to have an accurate method for predicting the dose distribution. In the past, planning computers calculate radiation dose using data obtained by measurement in a water phantom. This will lead to about 3% to 10% error in the situations where inhomogeneity and lateral electron disequilibrium occur, especially in small field sizes (Jones AO & Das IJ, 2005). For these situations, Monte Carlo Simulation (MCS) has been proposed to give the most accurate solution. The first available MCS code for treatment planning was developed as part of the OMEGA project, which started in the early 90s by the National Research Council of Canada and the University of Wisconsin in Madison. The MCS code used was called EGS4 and it modelled the transport of photons and electrons. For radiotherapy, the BEAM system (which was based on EGS4) was used for modelling of radiotherapy sources. These days, EGS4 and BEAM have been replaced by EGSnrc and BEAMnrc.
MCS models the transport of photon and electron by recording the interactions of each particle until it reaches the preset threshold energy. Therefore, MCS requires an extensive use of computer power. In the early 90s when the processing speed of computers was slow, one simulation would require several days before a result was available. The time required was impractical for clinical purposes. As an alternative, the Convolution algorithm was developed for treatment planning. It calculates the dose delivered to a volume by convolving the interaction sites with the dose deposition kernel derived from the output spectrum of the linear accelerator. The dose deposition kernel is pre-calculated by MCS. Convolution algorithm has improved dose calculation accuracy but it still has limitation compared to real MCS. For example, convolution algorithm uses density scaling to correct for tissue inhomogeneity. This method breaks down in situation where there is a high atomic number material present, e.g. a steel prosthesis. Nowadays, the speed of the computers has increased and parallel processing is more popular. Therefore, it is now feasible to use MCS for treatment planning. Computer Medical System (CMS) has launched a commercial product called Monaco which uses a fast computer and variance reduction techniques to speed up the MCS calculation for radiotherapy treatment planning.
MCS can also be used as a quality assurance (QA) tool for other MCS treatment planning systems. It is possible to do so because each MCS utilises a different coding and variance reduction technique therefore each calculation is considered independent.
All the work in this chapter is accomplished with a free Monte Carlo Software called MCBEAM which is developed by Fox Chase Cancer Care Centre. MCBEAM originates from

BEAM code with some modifications - it provides an interface with RTOG (Radiation Therapy Oncology Group) protocol so that parameters such as monitor units, field size etc can be imported from the treatment planning system (TPS). MCBEAM implements the multiple source model, as shown in figure 1, as an alternative to the traditional phase space file method. The Multiple source model suggests that a photon beam generated by a linac can be broken down into multiple smaller photon sources that are generated under the flattening filter at different magnitude (shown as arrows in figure 1). The magnitude of each individual source is adjusted so that the sum of all sources matches the data obtained by actual measurement. In order to model the beam correctly, the presence of the jaws (x, y and/or multi-leaf collimator) have to be entered correctly into the model. The details of the multiple source method can be found in the reference (Fippel M et al., 2003). The advantages of the multiple source model over the phase space file method are summarised as follow:

1. Smaller file size. The phase space file size is around a few giga-bytes depending on the number of particles stored. The multiple source file size is only a few kilo-bytes.
2. The multiple source model can simulate unlimited number of particles until it reaches the limit set by EGS4 while the phase space file method must recycle the particles, which might affect the accuracy of the result.
3. The multiple source model does not depend on the dimension of each component in the linear accelerator. This makes the machine modelling process easier.

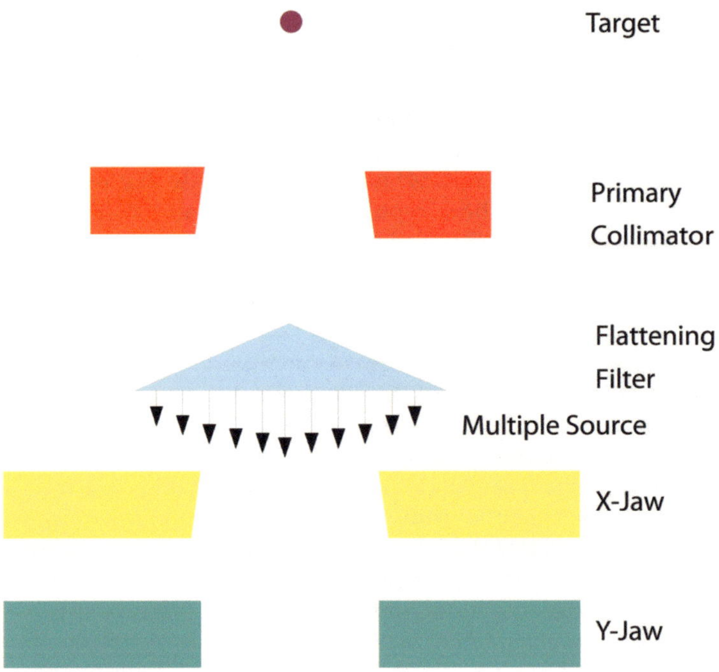

Fig. 1. Diagram of multiple source model

The MCBEAM implements variance reduction techniques to speed up the simulation. These variance reduction techniques can be turned on or off by the user. The techniques used in this work are the photon interaction forcing technique and the electron track repeating technique (Ma CM et al., 2004). From the experience of our department, a treatment plan simulation can be completed within 4 hours.

2. Verification of Monte Carlo Simulation with ion chamber measurement

Some articles have proven that MCS works well under the situation of electron disequilibrium (Ellen W et al., 2008), therefore the MCS results are compared with measurements in a full scatter condition. i.e. in a water phantom, using a field size that is large enough to provide electronic equilibrium to the detector. In our case, the smallest field size measured is 1cm x 1cm. The Scanditronix CC04 and CC01 ion chambers were used in this work.

2.1 Comparison of Percentage Depth Dose (PDD) with Monte Carlo Simulation and ion chamber measurements

Figure 2 shows the PDD comparison results for ion chamber measurements and MCS for field sizes from 1cmx1cm to 10cmx10cm. The differences between measured data and MCS data

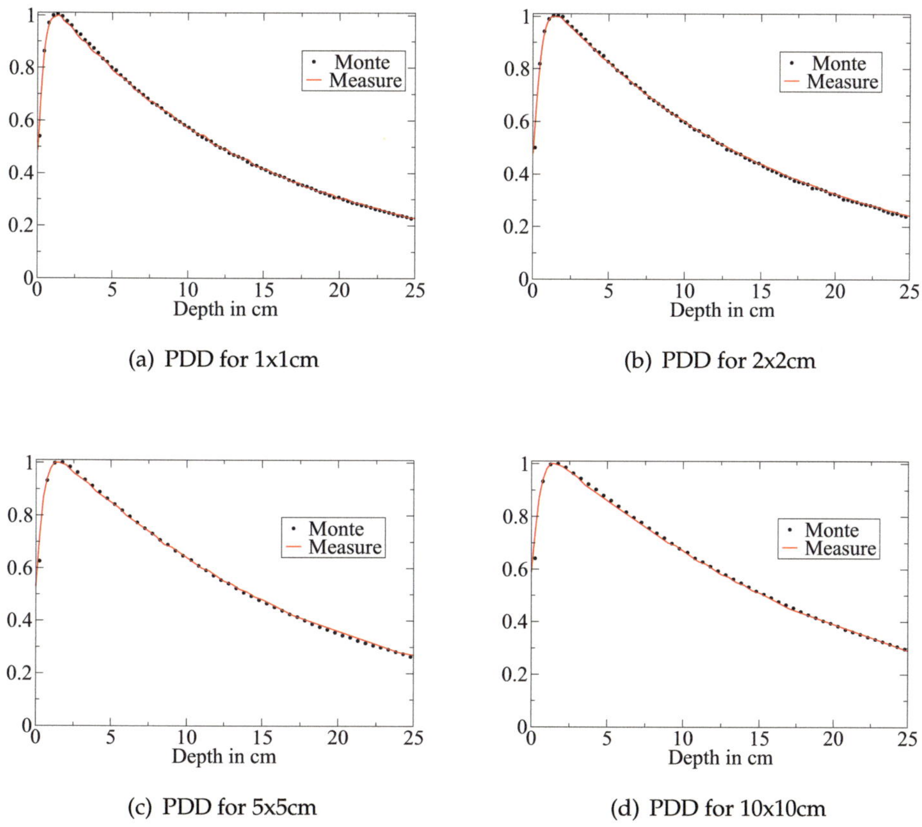

(a) PDD for 1x1cm

(b) PDD for 2x2cm

(c) PDD for 5x5cm

(d) PDD for 10x10cm

Fig. 2. PDDs comparison for field sizes from 1x1cm to 10x10cm

from depth 1.5cm to 25cm are less than 2%. In order to make a fair comparison between ion chamber and MCS, the voxel size used in MCS was set to be comparable to the sensitive volume of the ion chamber. This is particularly important especially around the penumbra region due to the volume averaging effect of the ion chamber.

2.2 Comparison of profiles between Monte Carlo Simulation and ion chamber measurements

Figure 3 shows the results for profile comparisons between monte carlo simulations and ion chamber measurements. From Figure 3a to 3d, the results match to within 2% in the low dose gradient region of the profiles (within 80% of the field width) and match to within 1mm in the penumbra region (90% to 10% at the edge). The MCS is shown to accurately predict the round off in the shoulder region for small field sizes, e.g. for 2x2cm and 1x1 cm. The profiles are compared at 3 depths, dmax (1.5cm for 6MV beam), 10cm and 20cm. They are labelled as dmax, d10 and d20 in figure 3. The measured data and the MCS results were labelled as "Mea" and "Monte" respectively. At the time of writing, only the 6MV photon of a Siemens Oncor linear accelerator has been modelled. Future works will involve modelling other photon energies.

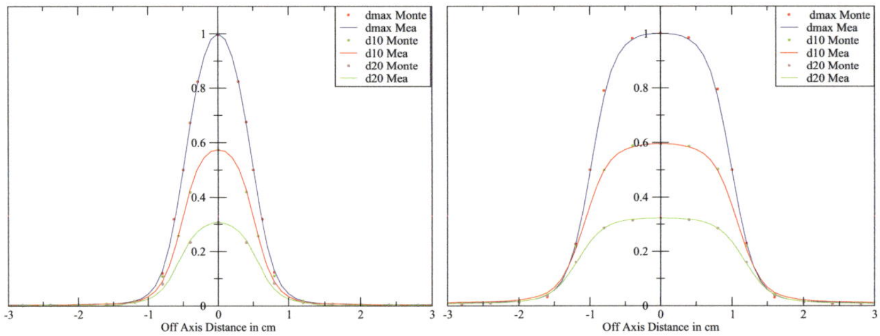

(a) Profiles for 1x1cm (b) Profiles for 2x2cm

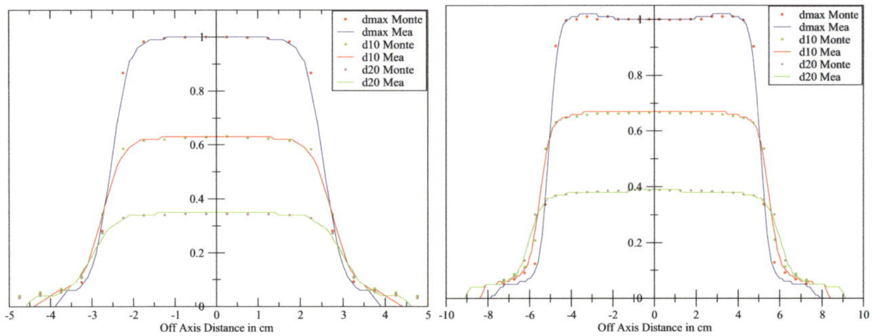

(c) Profiles for 5x5cm (d) Profiles for 10x10cm

Fig. 3. PDDs comparison from field size 1x1cm to 10x10cm

2.3 Comparison of output factors between Monte Carlo Simulation and ion chamber measurements

Output factor is defined as the ratio of a reading taken for a selected field size at dmax to the reading taken for the reference field size (usually 10x10cm) at dmax. Therefore, MCS has to be performed for both field sizes at dmax, and the output factor is calculated by taking the ratio of the two as shown in equation 1.

$$Output\ factor\ (FS) = \frac{Result(FS)}{Result(Ref)} \tag{1}$$

Result(FS): Monte Carlo Simulation result for Field Size selected
Result(Ref): Monte Carlo Simulation result for Reference Field Size (10x10cm)

All parameters, except for the field size, have to be kept constant for both simulations. Table 1 shows the results for a Siemens Oncor machine. The measured data agreed with MCS to within 1% for all field size up to 30cmx30cm except for field size of 2cmx2cm which is 1.13%.

Field size,cm	MCS	Measurement	Difference,%
2x2	0.869	0.859	-1.13
3x3	0.904	0.906	0.22
5x5	0.935	0.932	-0.32
10x10	1.000	1.000	0.00
15x15	1.036	1.034	-0.2
20x20	1.050	1.055	0.44
25x25	1.064	1.070	0.53
30x30	1.0815	1.079	-0.24

Table 1. Output factors comparison between monte carlo simulation and measurements

Table 2 shows the results for an elongated fields. This is known as the collimator exchange effect. The collimator exchange effect is caused by the different positions of X- and Y-jaw within the linear accelerator with respect to the flattening filter. The dose contribution from the jaws are therefore different for a A x B field and a B x A field. The magnitude of the collimator exchange effect can be shown in the case of an elongate field. From table 2, it can be shown that the output for 4x40cm and 40x4cm are 0.976 and 0.958 respectively. Some TPS are not able to model the collimator exchange effect and therefore will result in an error of 1.8% in this situation. Table 2 shows that the MCS are able to predict the dose to an accuracy of within 1% for an elongated field.

Field size,cm	MCS	Measurement	Difference,%
4x40	0.976	0.976	-0.04
40x4	0.956	0.958	0.18
30x10	1.027	1.024	-0.27
10x30	1.039	1.034	-0.46

Table 2. Elongated output factors comparison between monte carlo simulation and measurements

3. Compare Monte Carlo Simulation with planning computer

Figure 4 shows the work flow of comparing dose calculation from MCS and the TPS. Firstly, the medical images(such as CT, MRI etc) are transferred into the TPS. A treatment plan will be computed according to the Radiation Oncologist's prescription. After that, the parameters of the treatment plan are sent to MCS via RTOG format. Using the same plan parameters, MCS independently calculates the dose and compares it to the original plan generated by the TPS. If the dose calculated by both MCS and TPS agree, then the treatment commences. Figure 5 shows the DVH comparison for an IMRT patient with Paranasal sinus carcinoma in 2006. The CMS XiO planning system was used and the dose calculation was performed using the Superposition algorithm. Other than the DVH, the isodoes was also compared. Figure 6

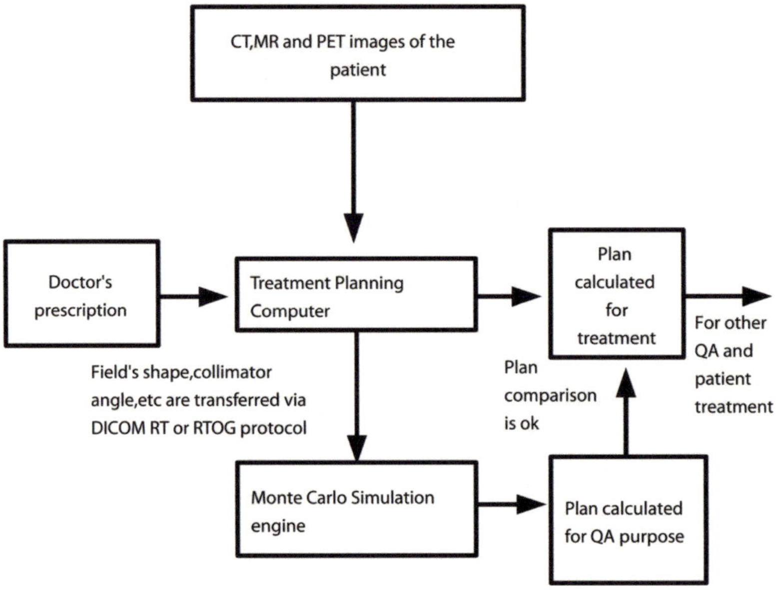

Fig. 4. System diagram for plan comparison between MCS and TPS

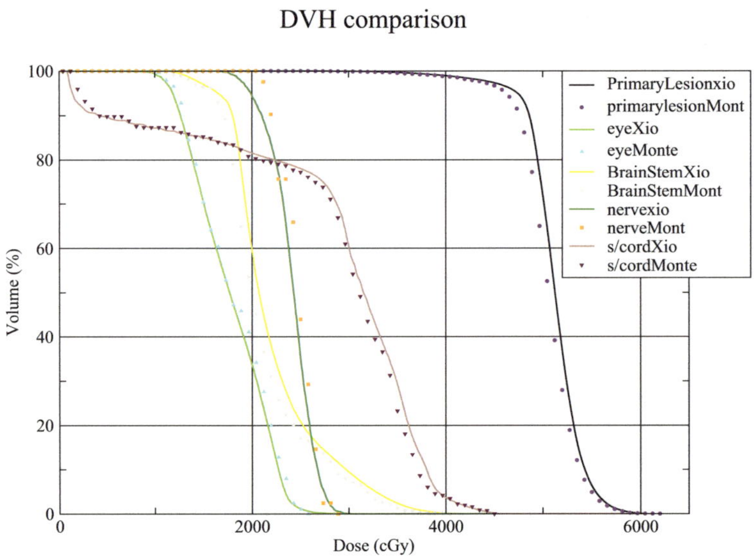

Fig. 5. DVH comparison between MCS and XiO

a, b and c show the isodose comparison for a plan calculated by XiO in the coronal,sagittal and transverse planes. The left column shows isodoses calculated from XiO while the right column shows isodoses calculated from MCS.

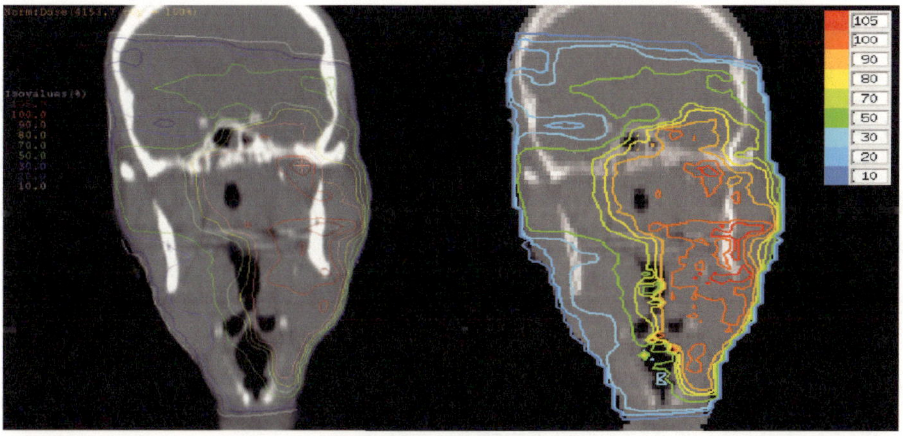

(a) coronal plane

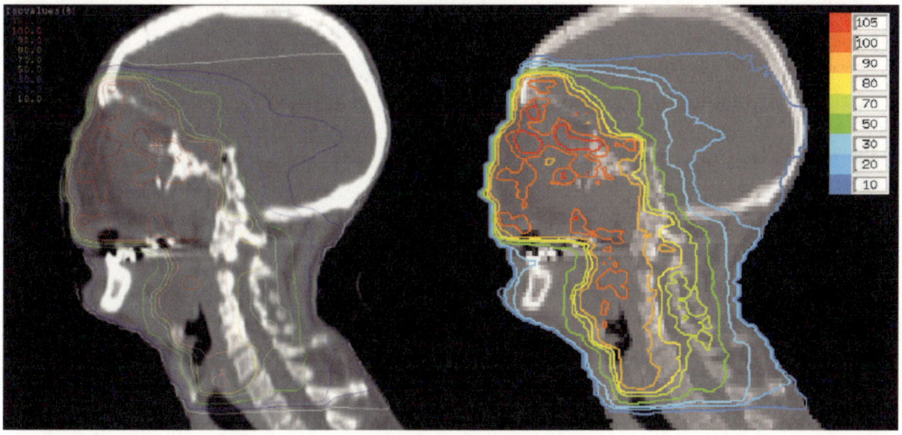

(b) saggital plane

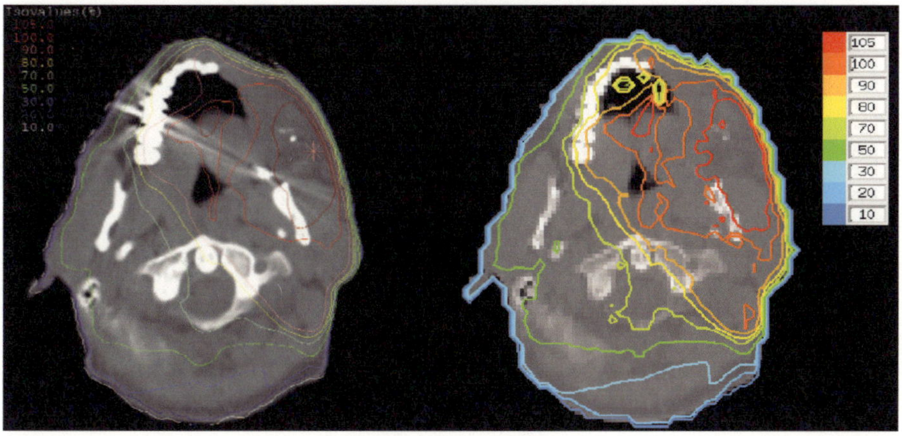

(c) transverse plane

Fig. 6. Isodoses comparison between monte carlo simulation and XiO TPS

4. Acknowledgement

I would like to thank Charlie Ma and Jason Li at the Fox Chase Cancer Centre, Philaphadia, USA for providing the MCBEAM code for this work and Dean Inwood at the Prince of Wales Hosptial, Sydney, Australia for creating the figures 6 used in this chapter.

5. References

Jones AO, & Das IJ. (2005). Comparison of inhomogeneity correction algorithms in small photon fields *Med Phys*, Vol. 32, pp. 766-276.

Ma C-M, Li JS, Pawlicki T, Jiang SB, Deng J, Lee MC, Koumrian T, Luxton M, rain S (2002). Monte Carlo dose calculation tool for radiotherapy treatment planing. *Med Phys*, Vol 25, pp. 1671-1689.

Wang L, Chui CS, Lovelock M (1998). A patient-specific Monte Carlo dose-calculation method for photon beams. *Med Phys*, Vol. 25 pp. 867-878.

Ma CM, Mok E, Kapur A, Pawlicki T, Findley D, Brain S, Forster K, Boyer AL (1999). Clinical implementation of a Monte Carlo treatment planning system *Med Phys*, Vol 26, pp.2133-2143.

FippelM, Kawrakow I, Friedrich K (2003). A virtual photon energy fluence model for Monte Carlo dose calculatin. *Med Phys*, Vol.30 pp.301-311.

Seco J, Evans PM. (2006). Assessing the effect of electron density in photon dose calculations.. *Med Phys*, Vol. 33 pp.540-552.

Schell MC, Bora FC, Larson DA, et al. (1995). AAPM Report No. 54: Stereotactic Radiosurgery. AAPM Task Group 42 *Melville, American Institute of Physics*

Mayles P, Nahum AE, Rosenwald J-C. (2007)Hand book of Radiotherapy Physics. *Oxford, Taylor & Francis* pp. 565-566.

CM Ma, J Li, T Pawlicki, S Jiang Jun Deng. (2004). MCSIM Users Manual. Report No: FCCC-RADPHYS-0201. *Department of Radiation Oncology, Fox Chase Cancer Centre, Philadelphia,PA 19111.*

Ellen E. Wilcox, George M. Daskalov. (2008). Accuracy of dose measurements and calculations within and beyond heterogeneous tissues for 6 MV photon fields smaller then 4cm produced by Cyberknife. *Med Phys*, Vol 25 pp.2259-2266.

10

Dosimetric Characteristics of the Brachytherapy Sources Based on Monte Carlo Method

Mahdi Sadeghi[1], Pooneh Saidi[2] and Claudio Tenreiro[3]
[1]*Agricultural, Medical and Industrial School, P.O. Box 31485-498, Karaj,*
[2]*Engineering Faculty, Research and Science Campus, Islamic Azad University, Tehran,*
[3]*Department of Energy Science, SungKyunKwan University, 300 Cheoncheon-dong, Suwon,*
[1,2]*Iran*
[3]*Korea*

1. Introduction

The term of brachytherapy, also known as "internal radiotherapy, sealed source radiotherapy, curietherapy or endocurietherapy" is from Greek work brachy means short distance and therapy (treatment) and also known as internal radiotherapy or sealed source radiotherapy. Brachytherapy is a special form of radiotherapy where a radioactive source is carefully placed on or inside the area to be treated. Brachytherapy sources are usually encapsulated; they can be used within the body cavities close to the tumor, placed in a lumen of organs, implanted in to the tumor or placed over the tissue to be treated. The main purpose in radiation therapy is controlling disease and reducing side effects. For a good clinical result one must assure the dose concentrate in the tumor mass and surrounding volume which is at risk of the tumor micro-extensions, while minimizing radiation received by the normal tissue. This can be verified by experimental measurement which is the base of Brachytherapy dosimetry. Due to the high dose gradient near the source and low signal to noise ratio at great distances, experimental dosimetry in Brachytherapy is very complicated or even in small distances is impossible. Also the dose variation with angle in 4π geometry of the source must be considered, since routine experimental measurement does not represent this. One of the widely used techniques for solving this problem is Monte Carlo simulation of radiation transport. The calculation of dose distributions at small distances and also validation of experimental measurement can be done by one of the powerful codes such as MCNP, BEAM, EGSnrc, PENELOPE, GEANT4, and ETRAN/ITS. One of the important parameters in the calculation process is validation of the Monte Carlo calculations with measurement results.

This chapter starts with an introduction lecture about brachytherapy history and a short review of the different models for sealed Brachytherapy sources. A brief discuss of brachytherapy dosimetry with computer and measurement is provided. In 1995 the American Association of Physicists in Medicine (AAPM) Task Group No. 43 published a protocol including new formalism for brachytherapy dose calculation and updated in 2004 as TG-43U1. The concept of AAPM recommendation and TG 43 formalism are introduced. Application of Monte Carlo in simulation, guideline for Monte Carlo dosimetry, calculation methodology, requirement for simulation and validation of calculation are then outlined. A short overview of other application of Monte Carlo in brachytherapy such as eye plaque and applicator design, evaluation of treatment planning system calculation is described. Finally an example of Monte Carlo calculations for dosimetric parameters of ^{103}Pd brachytherapy seed in three geometric models based on different location of beads inside the capsule is provided.

2. History

The use of radioactive sources for treatment of cancerous tumours started shortly after the discovery of radium (^{226}Ra) in 1898 by Madame Curie. This was followed in 1901 by Pierre Curie's self exposure experiment. Brachytherapy developed largely through the use of sealed radium and radon sources, but, quantities and forms of radioactivity useful for brachytherapy were not available until 1940s, when civilian applications of nuclear reactors were encouraged. In 1950s Radium-226 tubes with 1 mm Pt filtration remained the dominant intracavitary source through the late 1960s. Due to the revolutionary of all radiotherapy developments like beam therapy and need of experience to position the brachytherapy sources with sufficient accuracy and radiation exposure hazards for personnel, the role of brachytherapy was not secure in that era. However, over the past three decades, there has been renewed interest in the use of brachytherapy for a number of reasons. The discovery of man-made radioisotopes and remote afterloading techniques has reduced radiation exposure hazards. Newer imaging techniques (CT scan, magnetic resonance imaging, ultrasound) and computerized treatment planning has helped to achieve good clinical outcomes. The advantages of brachytherapy to surgery are treatment simplicity, minimum damage to the surrounding normal tissues and the reduction of side effects for patient after treatment. The advantages of brachytherapy to tele-therapy are its ability in radiation localization on tumor tissue, minimizing radiation to the surrounding normal tissues and rapid dose reduction in normal tissues surrounding the tumor (Ataeinia et al., 2009).

226Ra sealed in platinum tubes or needles, was the first radionuclide used in brachytherapy treatments. Radium has the advantage of a very long half-life (1620 years), but it also has the disadvantage of producing the alpha-emitting gaseous daughter product radon. ^{222}Rn, the daughter product of ^{226}Ra has a half-life of 3.83 days, in a gas form was extracted and sealed within a gold seed, was later used for permanent implants. (Baltas et al., 2007). By the early 1950s, both ^{226}Ra and ^{222}Rn have been replaced by newly developed isotopes and brachytherapy had become a well-established and mature modality (Williamson, 2006). In 1950s when produced of other nuclides became available, radium and radon replaced with other new produced radionuclides and they are no longer used. Most common brachytherapy sources emit photons; however, in a few specialized situations such as Craniopharyngiomas which are pediatric tumors, accounting for about 6% of all intracranial tumors in children, β emitting sources are used (Sadeghi et al., 2009a). Brachytherapy photon emitter sources are available in various forms (needles, tubes, seeds, wires, pellets) but are generally sealed to provide shielding against the undesired α and β radiation emitted from the sources and also to prevent leakage. These sources are used in various types of brachytherapy implant. Sources can be place in to the body cavities near to the tumours (intracavitary), trains of sources are loaded within the lumen of organs (interaluminal), sources are implanted within the tumours (interstitial), or a single source is placed into small or large arteries (intravascular). The dose is then delivered continuously, either over a short period of time (temporary implants) or over the lifetime of the source to a complete decay (permanent implants) (Mayles et al., 2007).

3. Sources used in brachytherapy

Depending on the dose rate of the sources at the dose specification point, brachytherapy treatment classified in three categories: high dose rate sources (HDR) >12 Gy/h, high energy photon emitters s like ^{137}Cs, ^{60}Co, ^{192}Ir, ^{198}Au are used, medium dose rate (MDR) 2-12 Gy/h, is not common use; and low dose rate sources (LDR), less than 2 Gy/h with low energy photon emitters such as ^{125}I and ^{103}Pd (Bethesda, 1985). A brachytherapy source is characterized by the rate at which its strength decays (half-life), by how much radioactivity can be obtained for a given mass of the radioactive source (specific activity), by the energies and types of the radiation particles that are emitted from the source (energy spectrum). These physical brachytherapy source characteristics will guide the clinical utilization. Currently the sources used in brachytherapy categorized in high and low energy sources:

i. Cesium-137: ^{137}Cs, a fission by-product, is a popular radium substitute because of its 30-year half-life. It emits β-rays and 0.662 MeV γ-photons. ^{137}Cs intracavitary tubes are mostly used for intracavitary treatment of gynaecological malignancies. The radioactive material is distributed in insoluble glass micro-spheres. The active source material is then sealed in stainless steel encapsulation cylinders.

ii. Cobalt-60: ^{60}Co is produced from thermal neutrons captured by ^{59}Co. it emits 0.318 MeV β-rays, 1.17 MeV and 1.33 MeV γ-photons and has a half-life of 5.27 years. Cobalt sources are encapsulated with 0.1 to 0.2 mm platinum to filter the β-particles.

iii. Iridium-192: ^{192}Ir with a half-life of 73.8 days is the most widely used source for temporary interstitial implants. It emits γ-photons with energies ranging from 9 to 884.5 keV. ^{192}Ir is used in the form of a wire containing an iridium–platinum radioactive core in a sheath of platinum; and also available in seed format (0.5-mm diameter by 3 mm long) with an active core cylinder contained in stainless steel or platinum encapsulation. The seeds are encapsulated in a 0.8-mm-diameter nylon ribbon and can used in wire format.

iv. Gold-198: ^{198}Au is produced by reactor irradiation of pure gold. Insoluble ^{198}Au emits β-rays and 412 keV γ-photons; and decays with half-life of 2.7 days. Sources are available for use in intracavitary treatment of the oesophagus in seeds, grains and wires format. Gold-198 seeds are 2.5 mm long and 0.8 mm in outer diameter, and have 0.15-mm-thick platinum encapsulation.

And low energy sources:

v. Iodine-125: ^{125}I emits γ-rays and X-rays with energies below 0.0355 MeV and have a half-life of 59.7 days. ^{125}I sources are packed in a cylindrical encapsulation of titanium shell of 4.5 mm in length and 0.8 mm in diameter, and used mostly for permanent implant treatments of cancers of the prostate, lung, sarcomas, as well as the temporary implant treatment of ocular melanoma when loaded in an eye plaque.

vi. Palladium-103: ^{103}Pd is an alternative to ^{125}I for permanent implants. ^{103}Pd has lower energy emissions, 20 keV, which allow for a rapid decrease in dose with distance, and also, the short half- life, 17 days, results in higher dose rates and also greater biological effect than ^{125}I. This radionuclide is available in seed format, encapsulated in titanium tube.

Some physical characteristics of these common brachytherapy sources are summrized in Table 1. (Ling et al., 1995; Nath et al., 2005; Antipas et al., 2001; Wuu & Zaider, 1998).

Isotope	Average photon energy (MeV)	Half-life	Half value layer in lead (mm)	Form of use
^{137}Cs	0.662	30 a	6.5	Tube - needle - pellet- seed
^{60}Co	1.250	5.26 a	11	Tube- needle- pellet
^{192}Ir	0.397	73.8 a	3	Wire - seed
^{198}Au	0.412	2.7 d	2.5	Seed
^{125}I	0.028	60 d	0.02	Seed
^{103}Pd	0.021	17 d	0.01	Seed

Table 1. Some Characteristics of Isotopes Used In Brachytherapy

4. Dose distributions around the sources

Dosimetry, as used in brachytherapy, means the methodology of calculating the dose rate value at an interest point from a source in a given medium. It is important that the physicist know the theoretical basic of dose calculation, manually or using a computer algorithm, around the source in adjacent healthy and critical organs. In modern brachytherapy all available sources have a cylindrical geometry, and are fabricated in core and encapsulation form that can assume a cylindrical symmetry of the dose distribution to their longitudinal axis. The base of brachytherapy dosimetry is experimental measurements and any other theoretical calculations must be validated against measured values. But due to the high dose gradient near the source and low signal to noise ratio at great distances, experimental dosimetry in Brachytherapy is very complicated and in small distances has had a higher degree of uncertainty. Calculation the dose in any points and angles is available by theoretical methods. To improve calculation accuracy it is desirable to make use of Monte Carlo method, which is a computational tool that samples from known probability distributions to determine the average behaviour of a system, it is used in medical physics, particularly in brachytherapy to improve our understanding of all processes associated with radiation emission and transport by using random numbers. So Monte Carlo becomes a powerful tool in medical physics applications (Rogers, 2006; Baltas et al., 2007; Calatayud et al., 2009).

In the Monte Carlo calculations the real source geometry and material is considered; to facilitate the calculations the American Association of Physicists in Medicine (AAPM) Task Group No.43, in 1995 published a protocol (TG-43) introducing a new formalism for dose calculation that the different component of the dose calculation be divided into geometry, attenuation, scattering and anisotropy. This approach is used in modern treatment planning systems and suitable for commissioning. After that in 2004 the AAPM Low-energy Interstitial Brachytherapy Dosimetry subcommittee (LIBD) published an update version of the TG-43 protocol for calculation of dose rate distributions around photon-emitting brachytherapy sources (TG-43U1) (Nath et al., 1995; Rivard et al., 2004).

5. The TG-43 formalism

The proposed formula for two-dimensional dose rate is:

$$\dot{D}(r,\theta) = S_K \Lambda \frac{G(r,\theta)}{G(r_0,\theta_0)} g(r) F(r,\theta) \tag{1}$$

Where $\dot{D}(r,\theta)$ is the dose rate in water at the distance r in cm from a line source and θ denotes the polar angle specifying the point of interest as shown in Figure 1, S_K is the air - kerma strength has unit of $U = cGy\ cm^2\ h^{-1}$, Λ is the dose rate constant expressed in $cGy\ h^{2-1}\ U^{-1}$; $\frac{G(r,\theta)}{G(r_0,\theta_0)}$ is the geometry factor; r_0, θ_0 are the reference position, $r_0 = 1\ cm$ and $\theta_0 = 90^0$, $g(r)$ is the radial dose function; and $F(r,\theta)$ is the anisotropy function.

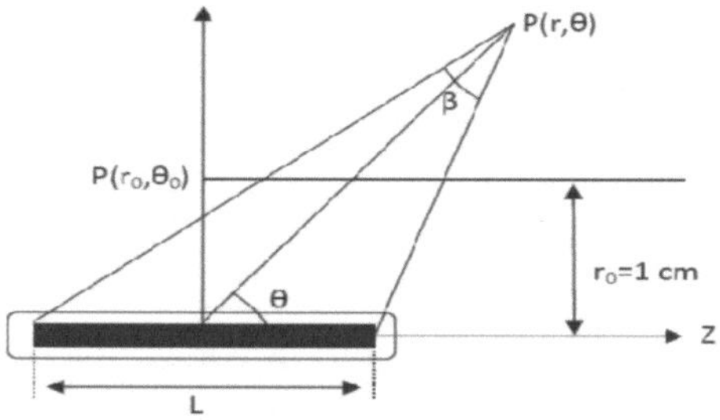

Fig. 1. Coordinate system used for brachytherapy dosimetry calculations.

5.1 Brachytherapy source strength

Source-strength designation has gone through several changes over the years. The earliest quantity (mass of radium) was commonly referred to by the unit, milligram radium and still is used in some cases. For sealed sources, especially those of low energy, the encapsulation reduces the air kerma and dose rates below those which would be produced by the bare source. Thus the strength is generally given as apparent activity, which is less than the encapsulated activity. Apparent activity is the activity of a hypothetical point source of the same radionuclide which would produce the same air kerma rate, at the same large distance, as that measured on the transverse axis of a sealed source. The design of the source capsule also influences the dose distribution around the source. It is quite possible for two sources of the same radionuclide and same apparent activity to have different dose distributions. (Nath et al., 1997).

5.2 Air-kerma strength, S_K

Air-kerma strength is the product of air-kerma rate in free space at the measured distance from the source centre along the perpendicular bisector, *r*, multiplied by the square of this distance, r^2:

$$S_K = \dot{K}_\delta(r) r^2 \tag{2}$$

Distance *r* must be chosen large enough, relative to the linear dimension of the source, to find independent air kerma strength of distance.

$\dot{K}_\delta(r)$ is the air kerma rate in vacuo and for the photons of energy greater than a certain cut-off value of δ which is typically 5 keV for low-energy photon emitting sources . This value is dependent on the assumption that photons with energies up to this cut-off value are not tissue penetrating. The qualification "in vacuo" means that the measurements should be corrected for photon attenuation and scattering in air and any other medium interposed between the source and detector.

5.3 Dose-rate constant, Λ

The dose rate constant, Λ, is defined as the dose rate in water at the reference point, $\dot{D}(r_0, \theta_0)$, namely at a distance of r_0=1 cm on the transverse axis (θ=90^0), per unit air kerma strength, S_K, as seen in Equation (3):

$$\Lambda = \frac{\dot{D}(r_0,\theta_0)}{S_K} \tag{3}$$

The dose rate constant depends on both the radionuclide and source model, and is influenced by both the source design (radioactive distribution and encapsulation) and also the methodology used to determine S_K.

5.4 Geometry function, $G_X(r,\theta)$

The geometry function, $G_X(r,\theta)$, takes into account the effect of the distribution of radioactive material inside the capsule on the dose distribution and is a function of both r and θ. physically it provides an effective inverse square-law and neglects scattering and attenuation of emitting photons around the source (Karaiskos et al., 2000). The subscript "X" is to indicate a point-source, "P" or line-source, "L", geometry function. The values of the geometry function can then be calculated as follow:

$$G_P(r,\theta) = r^{-2} \quad \text{For the point-source}$$

$$G_L(r,\theta) = \begin{Bmatrix} \frac{\beta}{Lr\sin\theta} \\ (r^2 - \frac{L^2}{4})^{-1} \end{Bmatrix} \quad \begin{matrix} if\ \theta \neq 0^o \\ if\ \theta = 0^o \end{matrix} \quad \text{For the line-source} \tag{4}$$

$$\beta = \tan^{-1}(\frac{r\sin\theta}{r\cos\theta - L/2}) - (\frac{r\sin\theta}{r\cos\theta + L/2})$$

Where β is the angle in radians, subtended by $P(r,\theta)$ and two ends of active length of the source. In the case where radioactive material is distributed over a cylindrical volume, the active length, L, will be the length of the cylinder (Fig.1). For brachytherapy sources containing multiple radioactive pellets, L is given by:

$$L_{eff} = \Delta S \times N \tag{5}$$

Where N is the number of discrete pellets contained in the source, and ΔS is the center to center distance of the pellets. The active length should be less than the length of source capsule. In the case where it is greater, the effective length of the seed is considered the distance between proximal and distal aspects of the activity distribution.

5.5 Radial dose function, $g_X(r)$

The radial dose function describes the effect of tissue attenuation on photons emitted from a brachytherapy source and accounts for the dose fall-off along the source transverse axis due to the photon scattering and attenuation. Equation (6) is defined the $g_X(r)$ as:

$$g_X(r) = \frac{\dot{D}(r,\theta_0)}{\dot{D}(r_0,\theta_0)} \frac{G_X(r_0,\theta_0)}{G_X(r,\theta_0)}, \quad X = P \; or \; L \; (Point \; or \; line \; source) \tag{6}$$

5.6 2D anisotropy function, $F(r,\theta)$

The 2D anisotropy function describes the variation of dose in the longitudinal plane of the seed. Variations are due to the distribution of radioactivity within the seed, self-absorption and oblique filtration of the radiation in the encapsulating material. F(r, θ) Is obtained by the following formula:

$$F(r,\theta) = \frac{\dot{D}(r,\theta)}{\dot{D}(r,\theta_0)} \frac{G_L(r,\theta_0)}{G_L(r,\theta)} \tag{7}$$

6. The use of Monte Carlo to obtain the dosimetric parameter

The most important role of Monte Carlo in brachytherapy is to obtain the dosimetric parameters of the sources with high spatial resolution. As mentioned above, "dosimetry" refers to estimation of absorbed dose by means of experimental or fundamental theoretical techniques about single brachytherapy sources. Due to the high dose gradient near the brachytherapy sources at short distances in water or water-equivalent phantoms, near-field dosimetry of brachytherapy sources is very complicated. To avoid dosimeter averaging effects, very high resolution (les than 0.5 mm) dosimeters are required (Chiu-Tsao et al., 2007; Williamson 1991); also low energy-response of some detectors; and lake of reproducibility, increase the uncertainty in experimental dosimetry.
Monte Carlo simulation is the theoretical method for calculation of dosimetric parameters. Monte Carlo simulation easily can obtain dosimetric parameters at small distances and all angles without any limitation and complication. For low energy photon emitters such as ^{125}I and ^{103}Pd, photoelectric absorption contributes a larger proportion of the dose to tissue than for higher energies. Therefore, small variations in tissue atomic number result in significant effects on dose. These effects can also be calculated precisely by Monte Carlo simulation by replacing the different phantom materials in different geometries (Dale et al., 1985; Prasad 1985; Huang 1990).
According to TG-43U1 recommendation, the main guideline items that should be considered in MC simulation for accurate calculations are as follow:

1. The information of source dimension, composition of encapsulation and internal components and their geometry must be specified clearly; typically these data obtained by manufacturer's report and Monte Carlo allows complete flexible description of the real geometry of the sources.
2. Simulation should be performed in a 30 cm water phantom for low energy photon-emitters like ^{125}I and ^{103}Pd, and 40 cm water phantom for high energy photon-emitters such as ^{137}Cs and ^{192}Ir, to consider all the scattering effects of the surrounding medium.
3. To extract the absorbed dose distribution from the particle transport simulation, one has to define a so-called tally or scoring function. The size and position of scoring voxels

(detectors) should define in a way to decrease the uncertainty; usually Monte Carlo uses voxels at radial distances up to 10 cm, for low energy sources and to 15 cm for high energy sources, away from the source at different polar angles. The voxel sizes are an important issue in simulation. To minimize the systematic error, the voxel sizes should be small as low as possible.

4. Enough histories should be calculated to ensure that the statistical uncertainties are in confidence range.
5. The statistical uncertainty should be ≤2% (for r < 5 cm) and ≤1% in S_K with k=1.
6. Due to the lake of old cross-section libraries for low energy photons, modern and new cross-section libraries should be used in Monte Carlo simulation.
7. Mechanical movement of the internal component of the seeds should be considered in the simulation. Because the location of the sources can vary with seed orientations and can affect on dosimetric parameters.

To calculate the dosimetric parameters, two simulations are needed: one with the source model in the medium which is usually water phantom, to obtain the dose at interest points; second simulation by modelling in vacuum to obtain the air kerma strength and geometry function. For low energy photon emitters such as ^{125}I and ^{103}Pd, the source is modelled in a centre of a 30 cm spherical water phantom, large enough to consider effects of the surrounding medium. For HDR sources like ^{137}Cs and^{192}Ir, the photon energies are higher than those emitted by ^{125}I and ^{103}Pd, therefore a 40 cm diameter spherical phantom is considered for modelling (Rivard, 2007; Perez-Calatayud et al., 2004; Melhus and Rivard, 2006). Generally for low energy photon emitters, S_K is calculated in several air-filled detectors at distances ranging from 5 to 150 cm in the transverse plane in free air geometry, which is found to be independent of distance. Due to the low energy of the photons from the low energy sources, it is assumed in the Monte Carlo calculations all electrons generated by the photon collisions are absorbed locally and the electronic equilibrium exists, so dose is equal to kerma at all points of interest [Hosseini et al., 2009 & Sadeghi et al., 2008b].

It should be noted that for high energy sources, electronic equilibrium, and consequently, water kerma dose approximation, may be safely assumed only at distances greater than 1 mm from the sources (Wang & Li 2000, Baltas 2001).

Geometry function just provides the inverse square low correction depending only on the shape of the active core and not on the encapsulation or radionuclide. Thus the medium inside and around the source has been considered as vacuum in order to disregarded the absorption and scattering in the seed and the surrounding media. The geometry function value is given by Equation (4). For calculating geometry function, the mass densities of all materials within the entire computational geometry should be set equal to zero so there were no interaction and particles streamed through the seed phantom geometry and it is common to approximate the active source material distribution within a brachytherapy source by an idealized geometry such as a line. (Levitt et al. 2006, Rivard 2001).

To obtain radial dose function values, Monte Carlo method is the best choice. Due to the complication of experimental measurement at small distances, dose rates are estimated down to the smallest distances and experimental values are only consider for validation of the Monte Carlo simulation results. By applying the Equation (6) radial dose function, which is the radial dependence of the dose rate value at the reference polar angle, θ=90°, is obtained and equal to unity at distance 1 cm. Dose rates can be estimated by linear interpolation from data tabulated at discrete points. The tabulated values are fit to polynomial which is proposed in TG-43U1.

$$g_X(r) = a_0 + a_1 r + a_2 r^2 + a_3 r^3 + a_4 r^4 + a_5 r^5 \tag{8}$$

Parameters a_0 to a_5 should be calculated by fifth order polynomial fit to the tabulated $g_X(r)$ data within ±2%. Commonly radial distance range for low energy sources is from 0.5 to 7.0 cm and for high energy sources is up to 15.0 cm. Depending on the source encapsulation design, in some cases calculation at distance as low as 0.1 cm could be also needed.
The values of the anisotropy function, defined by Equation (7), can be derived from Monte Carlo calculated at different radial distances from r= 0.25 to 7.0 cm for low energy sources and up to 15.0 cm for high energy sources, and different polar angles from θ=0° to 90° for symmetric sources about the transverse plane and from θ=0° to 180° for source design that are asymmetric about the transverse plane. According to Equation (7), the anisotropy function value at any radial distance on transfer plan, is always 1.0. Its value off the transfer plan decreases as: r increases, encapsulation thickness increases, θ approaches 0° or 180° and energy of photon decreases (Bethesda et al., 1985).

7. Validation of Monte Carlo modelling

As the Monte Carlo method has its own uncertainties, the preferred general approach is to use other determination method, and compare the results. According to TG-43U1 recommendation and other research publications, it has been accepted as a standard method that validation of Monte Carlo calculations via independent studies is required. To verify the Monte Carlo calculations, the experimental data sets should be compared with calculated data. For the experimental dosimetry in brachytherapy it is necessary to introduce a dosimeter in the radiation field of a source which should provide a measurable reading and present an adequate sensitivity with small sensitive volume to avoid dose volume averaging. The dosimetric system that provides optimum compromise between these prerequisites is TL dosimetry TLDs are currently considered as the dosimeter of choice for experimental dosimetry in the entire energy range of brachytherapy sources and TLD dosimetry is an accepted approach to validate the Monte Carlo simulation. Because the value of dosimetric parameters strongly depends on source material, seed model, encapsulation thickness and geometry, the experimental measurement should be done for the same seed which is modeled in Monte Carlo simulation. The steep dose gradient around low energy radio-nuclides such as ^{125}I and ^{103}Pd causes significantly dosimetric uncertainty. So the validation should be done for the larger distances, for example 1-5 cm then all other data especially for small distances, can get from Monte Carlo results. For other sources with higher energy like ^{137}Cs and ^{192}Ir, the dependence of dosimetric parameters of source geometry and material is low and measured value can obtain from similar source design. If the Monte Carlo and experimental datasets are compatibles within the acceptable uncertainties, a set of consensus value of dosimetric parameters would be established. The consensus data were defined as the ideal candidate dataset having the highest resolution, covering the largest distance range, and having the highest degree of smoothness. The consensus dose rate constant value should be obtained by the averaged experimental and Monte Carlo Λ values:

$${}_{\text{CON}}\Lambda = [\,{}_{\text{EXP}}\Lambda + {}_{\text{MC}}\Lambda]/2. \tag{9}$$

Or it should be selected as being representative of the collection of values available in the literature.

The consensus values for anisotropy function and radial dose function for most source models are mostly selected from Monte Carlo results that spanned the required range of radial distances and angles and had sufficiently fine spacing to make the interpolation between points accurate. Also Monte Carlo study considers the beta particles and electrons emitted by the source.

8. Other application of Monte Carlo

The Monte Carlo dose calculations are mostly used to obtain the dosimetric parameters around the brachytherapy sources to use in treatment planning systems. Calculated data provide the specific dose distributions based upon the actual locations of the sources in and around the patient; and also as a benchmarking tool for treatment planning systems (Williamson et al., 1999; Anagnostopoulos et al. 2003). The main goal of clinical treatment planning is to find the best way to maximize the tumor dose and minimize the dose to the healthy tissue. Most current commercial treatment planning systems implemented the TG-43 formalism and the recommended dosimetry parameters in their systems to determine the dose distributions. Monte Carlo calculations can obtain the approximations in the calculations done by the treatment planning system. For low-energy sources, a major problem is characterizing tissue heterogeneities, requires estimation of the photoelectric cross section as well as tissue density these can have significant errors near inhomogeneities in the patient. Monte Carlo dose calculations can account for tissue-composition heterogeneities (Chibani and Williamson, 2005; Devic et al. 2000). Monte Carlo dose calculations, when carefully validated against measurements, provide the highest level of accuracy for dose calculation in treatment planning, in situations where measurements are difficult or even impossible. Monte Carlo also can use for study and design of applicators. Intracavitary brachytherapy is mostly used for cancers of the cervix, uterine and vagina.

Several rigid applicators have been used for intracavitary brachytherapy but it requires careful design of the applicators and precise placement of the sources with respect to the tumor volume and surrounding organs. The most clinical complication of intracavity brachytherapy in this case results from the high dose delivered to the critical surrounding organs such as bladder and rectum. Because the common types of source for treatment of gynecology are high energy sources, ^{137}Cs and ^{192}Ir. Monte Carlo simulation can play an important role to keep the dose to these critical organs as low as possible by obtain the dose rate in interest points.

Another use of Monte Carlo in brachytherapy is its application in design of eye plaque. Radioactive eye plaque therapy is incorporating the use of radioactive seeds in a widely used technique for the treatment of ocular tumors. Monte Carlo simulation is performed to fully model the brachytherapy seeds loaded in the eye plaque to obtain the dose distribution in critical ocular structure and central axis of plaque. Brachytherapy seeds are placed in slots within a polymer carrier, Monte Carlo is possible to obtain the attenuation effect of the plaque backing, most often made of gold or stainless steel, and polymer carrier (Acrylic or Silastic) on dose distribution. Physical characteristics of photons emitted by different seed models (position, energy, location, and direction) are strongly dependent on seed construction, especially since brachytherapy sources are often constructed of high atomic number materials. In some cases, due to the presence of seed carrier inside the plaque the emitted photons from sources attenuate, thus more S_K per seed is needed to deliver the prescription dose to the tumor volume, that can be obtained by Monte Carlo simulation. For example Granero et al., 2004 calculated the dose rate around the eye plaque loaded with ^{125}I sources in Acrylic insert and they found Acrylic insert has no attenuation effect on dose rate and the presence of acrylic insert can be negligible in the calculations. In other Mont Carlo simulations Chiu-Tsao et al., 1993, obtained 10% dose reduction at 1cm for Silastic insert; Thomson et al., 2008 reported 17% dose reduction for ^{103}Pd seed at distance of 1 cm in eye plaque due to presence of Silastic insert; and also calculated results by (Melhus & Rivard, 2008) demonstrated approximately 22.6%±0.5%, 13.0%±0.3%, and 10.8%±0.3% more S_K in each ^{103}Pd, ^{125}I, and ^{131}Cs seed contained in a eye plaque, respectively was required to deliver the same dose to the apex of tumor.

According to the Monte Carlo calculated data, size, shape and location of the eye tumor, standard eye plaque should design. Iodine-125 is currently the most commonly used source for radioactive eye plaque therapy. Few centers use palladium-103, and available reports indicate that because of its low energy emissions 20 keV which allow for a rapid decrease in dose with distance; and also, the short half-life, 17 days, result in higher dose rates and favorable dose distribution (Finger et al., 1999; Hall et al. 1991; Finger et al., 1991; Sadeghi & Hosseini, 2010). Generally for the Monte Carlo simulation, the eye plaque is centered in a 15 cm radius water phantom to provide adequate photon backscatter and large enough to consider all the scattering effects of the surrounding medium. The Monte Carlo simulations provide the dose in a voxel per history. The dose rate is calculated by dividing this number by the air kerma strength per history for the relevant seed type and multiplying by the number of seeds and the air kerma strength per seed:

$$\dot{d}(x,y,z) = {}_{SP}\dot{d}(x,y,z)\left[{}_{source}S_K\left(\frac{S_K}{A}\right)^{-1}K\right].n \tag{10}$$

Where $\dot{d}(x,y,z)$ is the dose rate at the position x,y,z to deliver the prescription dose; ${}_{SP}\dot{d}(x,y,z)$ is the dose rate per starting particle at position x,y,z; ${}_{source}S_K$ is the $S_K(U)$ per source needed to deliver $\dot{d}(x,y,z)$; $\frac{S_K}{A}$ is the ratio of the $S_K(U)$ and activity A(mCi) for a given source; K is the photons emitted per unit activity and n is the number of sources. Finally the total dose is calculated by integration $\dot{d}(x,y,z)$ over the prescribed treatment time. According to American Brachytherapy Society recommendation for uveal melanoma the prescription treatment time is 3 to 7 consecutive days to deliver a total prescription dose. The prescription dose depends on the prescription point, method of dose prescription and dosimetry calculation assumption but following the Collaborative Ocular Melanoma Study (COMS) group dosimetry calculation assumption, is 85 Gray to the tumor apex (Nag et al., 2003; Baltimore 1995; Melia et al., 2001; Granero et al., 2010). In fact Monte Carlo Calculated dose rate for the eye plaque at interested point in the eye region has helped design of eye plaque as a valuable brachytherapy dosimetry tool.

9. Example of Monte Carlo calculations for dosimetric parameters of ^{103}Pd brachytherapy seed

This example presents Monte Carlo (MC) simulation results for the dosimetry parameters of the IR-^{103}Pd seed (Saidi et al., 2010).

Dose distributions in this example were simulated with the MCNP5 Monte Carlo (MC) radiation transport code published by Los Alamos National Laboratory (mcnp-green.lanl.gov/index.html., 2008) and the MCPLIB04 photon cross-section library is based on the ENDF/B-VI data (BNL.NCS-17541, 8th ed., 2000). In the calculations, the titanium characteristic X-ray production were suppressed with δ=5 keV (δ is the energy cutoff) (Nath et al., 1995). The spherical water phantom was modeled with a 30 cm diameter with an atomic ratio of 2:1 for H:O and ρ=0.998 g/cm3. The seed source placed in the center of the phantom for the calculation of all dosimetric parameters at radial distances of r= 0.25, 0.5, 0.75, 1, 2, 3, 4, 5 and 7 cm, away from the source and at polar angles relative to the seed longitudinal axis from 0° to 180° with 10° increment. To validate the Monte Carlo simulation, results were compared by experimental values (Raisali et al., 2008). The simulations were performed up to 1.1×10^9 histories. With this number of histories, statistical uncertainty for the source along the longitudinal axis at $r \leq 5$ cm is lower than 1.3%, at 7 cm is 4.5% and at other angles it is between 0.04% and 0.1%. In air, with 1.5×10^8 histories, statistical uncertainty is 0.1%.

Figure 2(a), shows a schematic diagram of the IR-^{103}Pd seed. The seed contains five resin beads, which are packed inside a titanium cylinder of 4.8 mm length, 0.7 and 0.8 mm internal and external diameter respectively, and with an effective length of 3 mm. ^{103}Pd radioactive material is absorbed uniformly in the resin bead volume. As the beads are free to move within the titanium capsule, their location can vary with seed orientations. Saidi et al. (2010), simulated three geometric models of the seed, ideal, vertical and diagonal, as shown in Figure 2(a), (b) and (c) respectively.

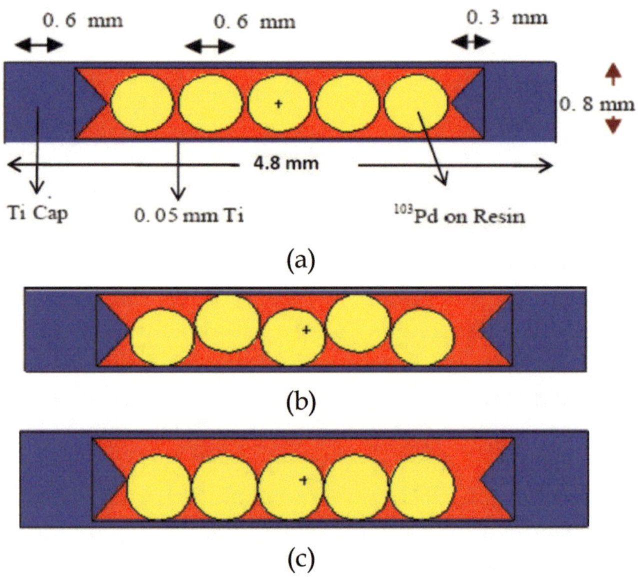

Fig. 2. Schematic diagram of the IR-^{103}Pd seed in Monte Carlo calculation for various seed orientations: (a) Ideal orientation, (b) vertical orientation, and (c) diagonal orientation (^{103}Pd absorbed in resin).

The dose rate constant for the ^{103}Pd seed was calculated by using the Equation (3). Due to the low energy of the photons from ^{103}Pd, it was assumed in the Monte Carlo calculations all electrons generated by the photon collisions are absorbed locally, so dose is equal to kerma at all points of interest (Sadeghi et al., 2008b). The air-kerma rate of the IR-^{103}Pd seed in this example was estimated by calculating the dose in 1 mm-thick air-filled rings in a vacuum.

The rings were bounded by 86° and 94° conics and defined with a radial increment of 5 cm to 150 cm along the transverse axis of the source and also the MCNP F6 tally, was used for calculate the dose distribution around the seed in each of the three orientations consider in this work.

Source type	Method	Medium	Λ (cGy h^{-1} U^{-1})	Reference
IR-^{103}Pd	Monte Carlo (vertical)	Liquid water	0.695±0.021	Saidi et al. (2010)
IR-^{103}Pd	Monte Carlo (ideal)	Liquid water	0.716±0.021	Saidi et al. (2010)
IR-^{103}Pd	Monte Carlo (ideal)	Liquid water	0.706±0.001	Raisali et al. (2008)
New ^{103}Pd	Monte Carlo (vertical)	Liquid water	0.673±0.001	Rivard et al. (2004b)
New ^{103}Pd	Monte Carlo (vertical)	Liquid water	0.675±0.020	Saidi et al. (2010)
MED3633	TLD dosimetry	Solid water	0.688±0.05	Wallac & Fan (1999)
	Monte Carlo	Liquid water	0.677±0.02	Li et al. (2000)
Theragenics 200	TLD dosimetry	Solid water	0.650±0.08	Nath et al. (2000)
	Monte Carlo	Liquid water	0.686±0.03	William (2000)

Table 2. Monte Carlo calculated dose rate constant, Λ, of the IR-^{103}Pd seed and new ^{103}Pd source and comparison with the measured and calculated values of model MED3633 and Theragenics200.

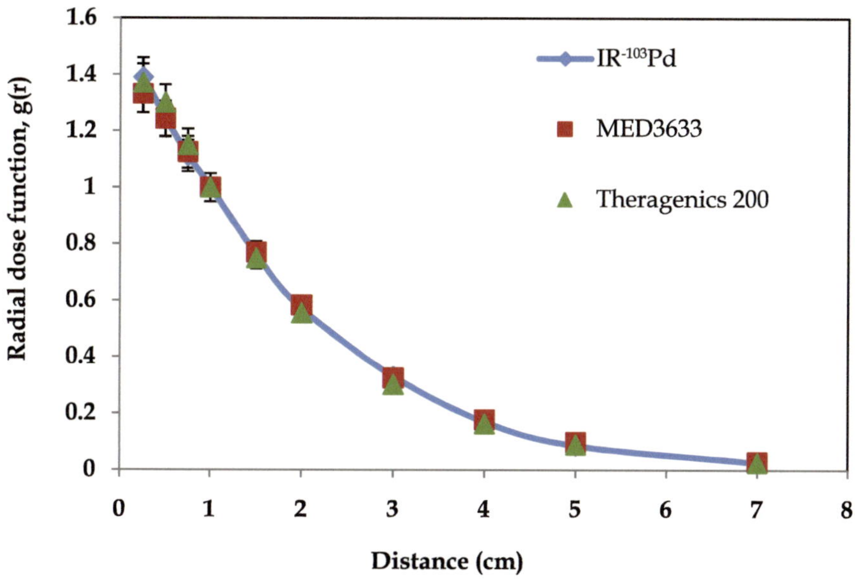

Fig. 3. Comparison of the Monte Carlo calculation radial dose function of IR-^{103}pd (Saidi et al., 2010) seed with the MED3633 and Theragenics model 200 sources (Rivard et al., 2004a).

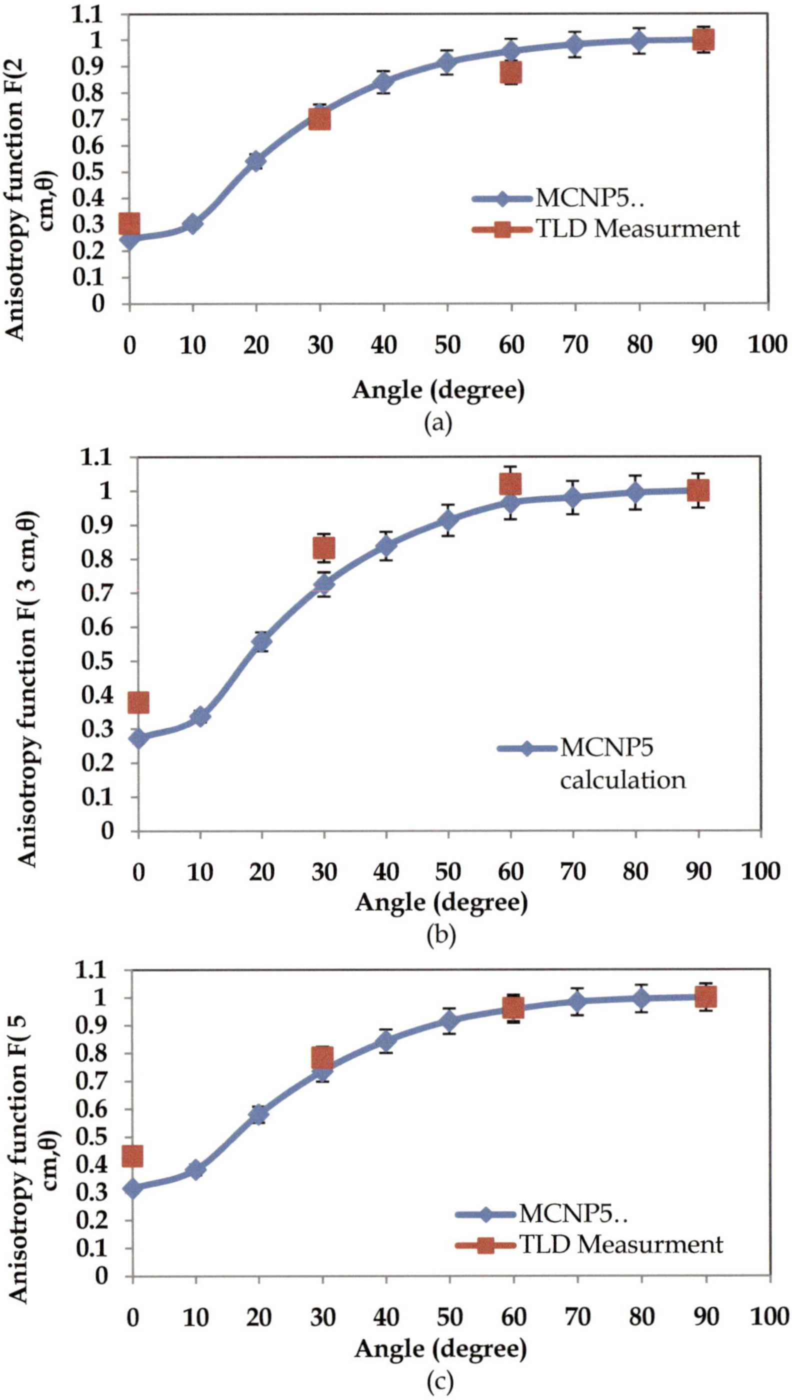

Fig. 4. Comparison between measured (Raisali et al., 2008) and calculated results (Saidi et al., 2010) for IR-^{103}Pd seed anisotropy functions at selected radial distances of (a) 2 cm, (b) 3 cm, (c) 5 cm.

(a) $r^2G(r,\theta)/G(r_0,\theta_0)$ for ideal seed orientation.

r (cm)	0°	10°	20°	30°	40°	50°	60°	70°	80°	90°
0.25	1.529	1.487	1.382	1.260	1.149	1.059	0.992	0.947	0.921	0.912
0.50	1.100	1.098	1.086	1.067	1.046	1.025	1.006	0.992	0.983	0.980
0.75	1.046	1.045	1.041	1.033	1.024	1.015	1.007	1.000	0.996	0.994
1.00	1.025	1.028	1.026	1.021	1.017	1.012	1.007	1.003	1.000	1.000
1.50	1.014	1.016	1.015	1.014	1.011	1.009	1.007	1.005	1.004	1.003
2.00	1.009	1.011	1.011	1.010	1.009	1.008	1.007	1.005	1.005	1.005
3.00	1.001	1.008	1.008	1.008	1.008	1.008	1.007	1.006	1.006	1.006
4.00	1.000	1.008	1.008	1.008	1.007	1.007	1.007	1.006	1.006	1.006
5.00	1.000	1.007	1.007	1.007	1.007	1.007	1.007	1.007	1.006	1.007
7.00	0.998	1.007	1.007	1.007	1.007	1.007	1.007	1.007	1.006	1.006

(b) $r^2G(r,\theta)/G(r_0,\theta_0)$ for ideal orientation calculated by Raisali et al. (2008)

r (cm)	0°	10°	20°	30°	40°	50°	60°	70°	80°	90°
0.25	1.514	1.484	1.383	1.259	1.148	1.058	0.991	0.947	0.920	0.911
0.50	1.102	1.098	1.086	1.066	1.046	1.025	1.006	0.993	0.983	0.981
0.75	1.068	1.044	1.040	1.033	1.024	1.015	1.007	1.000	0.996	0.994
1.00	1.031	1.028	1.025	1.022	1.017	1.012	1.008	1.003	1.001	1.000
1.50	1.006	1.015	1.014	1.013	1.011	1.009	1.007	1.005	1.004	1.002
2.00	1.002	1.011	1.009	1.010	1.009	1.008	1.007	1.005	1.006	1.005
3.00	0.996	1.008	1.008	1.009	1.007	1.007	1.007	1.007	1.006	1.005
4.00	1.002	1.008	1.008	1.008	1.007	1.006	1.007	1.007	1.006	1.005
5.00	0.997	1.007	1.007	1.007	1.006	1.006	1.006	1.007	1.006	1.007
7.00	0.995	1.008	1.007	1.006	1.006	1.007	1.007	1.007	1.006	1.006

(c) $r^2G(r,\theta)/G(r_0,\theta_0)$ for vertical seed orientation.

r (cm)	0°	10°	20°	30°	40°	50°	60°	70°	80°	90°	100°	110°	120°	130°	140°	150°	160°	170°	180°
0.25	1.510	1.436	1.275	1.121	0.944	1.529	1.287	1.225	1.086	0.911	0.919	0.930	0.990	1.057	1.102	1.258	1.380	1.452	1.519
0.50	1.915	1.908	1.791	1.650	1.482	1.379	1.230	1.129	1.056	0.980	0.981	0.987	1.006	1.022	1.039	1.067	1.084	1.101	1.088
0.75	1.476	1.460	1.449	1.377	1.317	1.236	1.167	1.106	1.046	0.994	0.994	1.005	1.005	1.015	1.022	1.034	1.039	1.043	1.044
1.00	1.287	1.324	1.297	1.261	1.226	1.177	1.136	1.075	1.035	1.000	0.998	1.002	1.007	1.010	1.018	1.020	1.025	1.034	1.001
1.50	1.164	1.195	1.186	1.169	1.145	1.141	1.091	1.060	1.029	1.003	1.002	1.005	1.007	1.008	1.014	1.012	1.014	1.021	0.987
2.00	1.114	1.147	1.136	1.121	1.107	1.086	1.058	1.045	1.023	1.005	1.003	1.006	1.007	1.008	1.012	1.009	1.009	1.017	0.986
3.00	1.064	1.098	1.082	1.080	1.077	1.114	1.048	1.035	1.019	1.006	1.004	1.006	1.007	1.007	1.011	1.007	1.009	1.014	0.981
4.00	1.039	1.076	1.065	1.061	1.058	1.048	1.065	1.027	1.018	1.006	1.004	1.007	1.007	1.007	1.011	1.006	1.007	1.013	0.979
5.00	1.026	1.063	1.051	1.047	1.052	1.034	1.029	1.026	1.009	1.006	1.004	1.007	1.007	1.008	1.011	1.006	1.006	1.013	0.978
7.00	1.036	1.046	1.045	1.042	1.034	1.027	1.024	1.027	1.010	1.010	1.004	1.011	1.005	1.005	1.011	1.011	1.011	1.011	1.002

(d) $r^2G(r,\theta)/G(r_0,\theta_0)$ for diagonal seed orientation.

r (cm)	0°	10°	20°	30°	40°	50°	60°	70°	80°	90°	100°	110°	120°	130°	140°	150°	160°	170°	180°
0.25	1.588	1.449	1.324	1.209	1.121	1.027	0.985	0.001	0.909	0.911	0.920	0.929	0.987	1.042	1.097	1.248	1.277	1.435	1.507
0.50	1.020	1.051	1.054	1.046	1.021	1.005	0.994	0.990	0.990	0.980	0.983	0.986	1.004	1.020	1.036	1.062	1.076	1.095	1.073
0.75	0.992	1.001	1.010	1.010	1.000	0.998	0.997	0.994	0.994	1.384	1.388	1.391	1.413	1.432	1.451	1.481	1.498	1.522	1.492
1.00	1.026	0.993	0.993	0.996	0.993	0.996	0.998	0.995	1.000	1.000	1.001	1.002	1.006	1.011	1.016	1.018	1.023	1.031	1.012
1.50	1.012	0.982	0.982	0.984	0.987	0.993	0.998	0.999	1.001	1.004	1.004	1.004	1.006	1.009	1.013	1.011	1.015	1.020	1.002
2.00	0.996	0.977	0.979	0.982	0.984	0.990	0.996	1.002	1.001	1.005	1.005	1.006	1.006	1.009	1.012	1.008	1.012	1.017	0.992
3.00	0.989	0.975	0.977	0.986	0.985	0.992	0.999	1.003	1.002	1.006	1.006	1.007	1.006	1.009	1.011	1.006	1.012	1.014	0.987
4.00	0.998	0.975	0.978	0.989	0.989	0.995	1.002	1.003	1.003	1.007	1.007	1.007	1.007	1.009	1.011	1.006	1.012	1.014	0.983
5.00	1.005	0.985	0.979	0.990	0.992	1.001	1.007	1.007	1.004	1.007	1.007	1.007	1.007	1.009	1.011	1.005	1.007	1.013	0.982
7.00	1.003	0.985	0.978	0.990	0.992	1.001	1.007	1.007	1.004	1.225	1.225	1.225	1.225	1.231	1.231	1.219	1.225	1.237	1.175

Table 3. Monte Carlo calculated $r^2G(r,\theta)/G(r_0,\theta_0)$ for the IR-^{103}Pd seed (Saidi et al., 2010) in (a) ideal orientation , (b) ideal orientation calculated by Raisali et al. (2008), (c) vertical orientation, (d) diagonal orientation.

Also in this example authors benchmarked their MCNP simulation with the new ^{103}Pd source (Rivard et al., 2004b) to demonstrate the accuracy of their simulation. For the three seed orientations, the values of Λ in three orientations, ranged from 0.716 to 0.753 cGyU-1h-1, with the geometry uncertainty of 1.5% for this seed. According to TG43U1, a standard uncertainty of 3% for all Monte Carlo studies seems reasonable. Authors claimed that the difference between the calculated values of dose rate constant by the Raisali et al., (2008) value, derives from the use of different methods to calculate the air-kerma strength, S_K. Raisali et al. calculated S_K only in one air-filled detector placed at a distance of one meter in the transverse plane of the seed. Also use of two different versions of MCNP code, MCNP4C & MCNP5 with two different cross section libraries and two different simulation geometries cause such a difference in the obtained values. Table 2 shows the calculated dose rate constant for the IR-^{103}Pd seed (Saidi et al., 2010), new ^{103}Pd source (Rivard et al., 2004b) and the calculated and measured values of Λ, for NASI model MED3633 and Theragenics model 200 sources (Rivard et al., 2004b).

The Monte Carlo calculated values of geometry function in this example for three orientations are shown in Table 3(a), (c) and (d). They used the form, $r^2G(r,\theta)$, instead of $G(r,\theta)$, for easier calculations and then normalized to $G(1cm, \pi/2)$ for convenience to compare with other published data (Rivard, 2001; King et al., 2001). The results were compared with Raisali et al., (2008) data.

The calculated line and point source radial dose function for the ideal orientation of the IR-^{103}Pd seed in Perspex and water in this example and those determined from calculated and measurement by (Raisali et al., 2008) are presented in Table 4. Figure 3 shows a comparison of the radial dose function of IR-^{103}Pd seed with MED3633 and Theragenics model 200 sources.

As TG43-U1 recommendation, $g_L(r)$ for ideal orientation in water was fit to a fifth order polynomial function (Equation 8):

Where a_0 = 1.534, a_1 = -5.933×10^{-1}, a_2 = 2.731×10^{-2}, a_3 = 2.362×10^{-2}, a_4 = -4.778×10^{-3} and a_5 = 2.783×10^{-4} define $R^2 = 9.998\times10^{-1}$.

r (cm)	$g_L(r)$ (Perspex)			$g_L(r)$ (Water)		$g_P(r)$ (Water)
	MCNP5 Saidi et al. (2010)	TLD Raisali et al. (2008)	MCNP4C Raisali et al. (2008)	MCNP5 Saidi et al. (2010)	MCNP4C Raisali et al. (2008)	MCNP5 Saidi et al. (2010)
0.25	1.532	-	1.168	1.390	1.339	1.092
0.5	1.242	1.15	1.134	1.242	1.239	1.229
0.75	1.077	-	1.070	1.112	1.119	1.114
1	1.000	1.00	1.000	1.000	1.000	1.000
1.5	0.711	0.82	0.849	0.763	0.783	0.773
2	0.668	0.78	0.706	0.573	0.602	0.573
3	0.393	0.51	0.473	0.331	0.348	0.334
4	0.169	0.31	0.306	0.165	0.198	0.166
5	0.085	0.20	0.195	0.089	0.111	0.090
7	0.025	-	-	0.027	0.035	0.027

Table 4. Monte Carlo calculations for radial dose function, $g_L(r)$ and $g_P(r)$ for line and point source geometry for IR-^{103}Pd seed with an effective length of 0.3 mm, in comparison with TLD measurements of Raisali et al., (2008) in Perspex and also calculated in water.

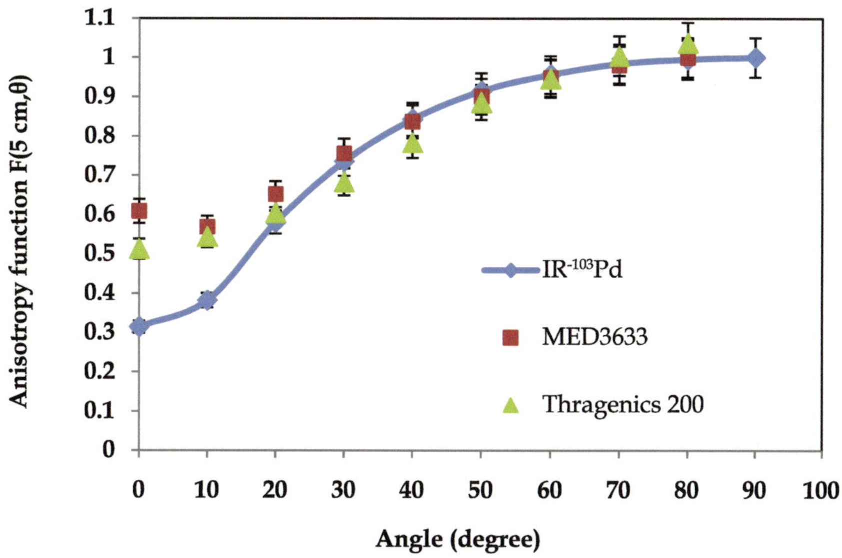

Fig. 5. Comparison of the Monte Carlo calculation anisotropy function of IR-^{103}Pd seed (Saidi et al., 2010) with the MED3633 and Theragenics model 200 sources (Rivard et al., 2004a) at the distance of 5 cm.

The anisotropy function, $F(r,\theta)$, of the IR-^{103}Pd seed was calculated in Perspex phantom at radial distances of r = 0.25, 0.5, 0.75, 1, 1.5, 2, 3, 4, 5and 7 cm relative to the seed center and polar angle, θ ranging from 0° to 90° for ideal orientation and 0° to 180° for vertical and diagonal orientations in 10° increment with respect to the seed long axis. Saidi et al.'s (2010) results are shown in Table 5 and in compared with the measured data by Raisali et al., (2010), for ideal orientation. The data are shown graphically at distances of 2, 3 and 5 cm in Figure 4. Figure 5 shows a comparison of the anisotropy function at r = 5 cm of the IR-^{103}Pd with MED3633 and Theragenics model 200 sources.

10. Acknowledgements

"Research supported by WCU program through NRF Korea funded by MEST (R31-2008-000-10029-0)"

(a) 2D anisotropy function, $F(r,\theta)$ in ideal seed orientation

r (cm)	0°	10°	20°	30°	40°	50°	60°	70°	80°	90°	Φ_{an}(r)
0.25	0.025	0.076	0.656	0.833	0.906	0.950	0.975	0.991	0.998	1.000	1.023
0.50	0.106	0.162	0.505	0.738	0.864	0.926	0.962	0.985	0.996	1.000	0.910
0.75	0.150	0.206	0.505	0.720	0.851	0.921	0.959	0.984	0.996	1.000	0.892
1.00	0.158	0.221	0.482	0.674	0.794	0.862	0.901	0.924	0.936	1.000	0.838
1.50	0.206	0.276	0.529	0.717	0.841	0.915	0.956	0.982	0.995	1.000	0.861
2.00	0.243	0.303	0.541	0.720	0.840	0.914	0.956	0.982	0.995	1.000	0.884
3.00	0.272	0.338	0.557	0.726	0.839	0.914	0.955	0.980	0.994	1.000	0.885
4.00	0.298	0.362	0.571	0.731	0.842	0.912	0.955	0.981	0.995	1.000	0.887
5.00	0.314	0.382	0.581	0.735	0.843	0.915	0.956	0.984	0.995	1.000	0.889
7.00	0.377	0.417	0.610	0.747	0.848	0.916	0.951	0.979	1.000	1.000	0.894

(b) 2D anisotropy function, $F(r,\theta)$ in vertical seed orientation

r (cm)	0°	10°	20°	30°	40°	50°	60°	70°	80°	90°	100°	110°	120°	130°	140°	150°	160°	170°	180°
0.250	0.039	0.487	0.671	0.862	0.966	0.928	0.993	0.989	0.996	1.000	0.807	0.802	0.783	0.778	0.739	0.658	0.459	0.326	0.024
0.500	0.157	0.380	0.528	0.771	0.900	0.953	0.967	0.988	0.979	1.000	0.801	0.814	0.787	0.759	0.731	0.605	0.394	0.283	0.112
0.750	0.217	0.425	0.303	0.748	0.865	0.887	0.917	0.979	0.999	1.000	0.828	0.814	0.756	0.723	0.709	0.598	0.231	0.321	0.180
1.000	0.173	0.354	0.455	0.608	0.732	0.790	0.777	0.801	0.810	1.000	0.809	0.803	0.774	0.782	0.716	0.587	0.422	0.325	0.184
1.500	0.271	0.468	0.639	0.757	0.898	0.931	0.962	0.987	0.993	1.000	0.993	0.990	0.957	0.935	0.883	0.730	0.597	0.437	0.274
2.000	0.308	0.492	0.630	0.762	0.893	0.983	0.962	0.989	0.994	1.000	0.957	0.990	0.957	1.033	0.883	0.735	0.593	0.462	0.307
3.000	0.359	0.523	0.603	0.769	0.898	0.933	0.961	0.989	0.998	1.000	0.997	0.989	0.956	0.927	0.882	0.743	0.568	0.493	0.352
4.000	0.384	0.549	0.704	0.784	0.902	0.931	0.963	0.995	0.999	1.000	0.998	0.990	0.958	0.917	0.883	0.752	0.666	0.514	0.370
5.000	0.422	0.567	0.674	0.782	0.913	0.907	0.961	0.996	0.998	1.000	0.997	0.987	0.955	1.000	0.883	0.756	0.638	0.531	0.398
7.000	0.398	0.408	0.597	0.739	0.873	0.919	0.949	0.996	0.999	1.000	0.998	0.979	0.999	0.900	0.848	0.993	0.999	0.997	0.427

(c) 2D anisotropy function, $F(r,\theta)$ in diagonal seed orientation

r (cm)	0°	10°	20°	30°	40°	50°	60°	70°	80°	90°	100°	110°	120°	130°	140°	150°	160°	170°	180°
0.250	0.026	0.075	0.630	0.801	0.887	0.924	0.970	0.985	0.988	1.000	1.000	1.000	1.000	0.997	0.995	0.995	1.033	0.974	0.974
0.500	0.098	0.170	0.492	0.725	0.846	0.909	0.953	0.985	1.005	1.000	1.000	1.000	1.000	0.997	0.995	0.995	0.986	0.974	0.974
0.750	0.139	0.220	0.490	0.706	0.833	0.906	0.950	0.982	1.002	1.000	1.000	1.000	1.000	0.997	0.995	0.995	0.986	0.974	0.974
1.000	0.223	0.342	0.659	0.927	1.095	1.198	1.260	1.294	1.321	1.000	1.409	1.409	1.409	1.405	1.401	1.401	1.388	1.372	1.372
1.500	0.206	0.292	0.513	0.699	0.822	0.902	0.949	0.978	0.995	1.000	1.000	1.000	1.000	0.997	0.995	0.995	0.985	0.974	0.974
2.000	0.240	0.312	0.525	0.701	0.821	0.900	0.948	0.981	0.993	1.000	1.000	1.000	1.000	0.997	0.995	0.995	0.985	0.974	0.974
3.000	0.270	0.353	0.541	0.709	0.822	0.905	0.950	0.979	0.992	1.000	1.000	1.000	1.000	0.997	0.995	0.995	0.982	0.974	0.974
4.000	0.296	0.383	0.555	0.716	0.829	0.906	0.955	0.981	0.994	1.000	1.000	1.000	1.000	0.997	0.995	0.995	0.982	0.974	0.974
5.000	0.317	0.410	0.566	0.725	0.832	0.911	0.958	0.986	0.995	1.000	1.000	1.000	1.000	0.997	0.995	0.995	0.986	0.974	0.974
7.000	0.380	0.448	0.594	0.736	0.837	0.913	0.953	0.981	1.000	1.000	1.000	1.000	1.000	0.995	0.986	0.987	0.885	0.867	0.876

Table 5. 2D anisotropy functions for the IR-^{103}Pd seed calculated by Monte Carlo method (Saidi et al., 2010) for the (a) ideal orientation, (b) vertical orientation, (c) diagonal orientation.

11. References

Anagnostopoulos, G.; Baltas, D.: Karaiskos, P.; Pantelis, E.; Papagiannis, P. & Sakelliou, L. (2003). An analytical dosimetry model as a step towards accounting for inhomogeneities and bounded geometries in ^{192}Ir brachytherapy treatment planning. *Phys. Med. Biol.*, 48, 11, (May 2003), 1625-1634, ISSN: 1361-6560.

Antipas, V.; Dale, R.G. & Coles, I.P. (2001). A theoretical investigation into the role of tumour radiosensitivity, clonogen repopulation, tumour shrinkage and radionuclide RBE in permanent brachytherapy implants of ^{125}I and ^{103}Pd. *Phys Med Biol.* 46, 10, (September 2001), 2557–2569, ISSN: 1361-6560.

Ataeinia, V.; Raisali, Gh.; Sadeghi, M. (2009). Determination of dosimetry parameters of ADVANTAGETM 103Pd brachytherapy seed using MCNP4C computer code. *NUKLEONIKA*. 54, 3, (May 2009), 181–187, ISSN: 0029-5922.

Baltas, D.; Karaiskos, P.; Papagiannis, P.; Sakelliou, L.; Loeffler, E. & Zamboglou, N. (2001). Beta versus gamma dosimetry close to Ir-192 brachytherapy sources, *Med. Phys.* 28, 9, (June 2001), 1875-1882, ISSN: 0094-2405.

Baltas, D.; Sakelliou, L. & Zamboglou, N. (2007). *The Physics of Modern Brachytherapy for Oncology*. Taylor & Francis, ISBN-13: 978-0-7503-0708-6, London-New York.

Baltimor, M.D. (1995). Collaborative Ocular Melanoma Medium Tumor Trial, Manual of procedure. COMS Coordinating centre.

Chibani, O.; Williamson, J.F. & Todor, D. (2005). Dosimetric effects of seed anisotropy and interseed attenuation for ^{103}Pd and ^{125}I prostate implants. *Med. Phys.* 32, 8, (July 2005), 2557–2566, ISSN: 0094-2405.

Chiu-Tsao, S.; Anderson, L.L.; O'Brien, K.; Stabile, L. & Liu, J.C. (1993). Dosimetry for ^{125}I seed (model 6711) in eye plaque. *Med. Phys.* 20, 2, (November 1992), 383-389, ISSN: 0094-2405.

Chiu-Tsao, S.T.; Schaart, D.R. & Nath, R. (2007). Dose calculation formalism and consensus dosimetry parameters for intravascular brachytherapy dosimetry:

Recommendations of the AAPM Therapy Physics Committee Task Group No. 149. *Med Phys.* 34, 11, (October 2007), 4126-4157, ISSN: 0094-2405.

Cross section Evaluation Working Group, ENDF/B-VI Summary documentation (ENDF-201), Brookhaven National Laboratory Report No. *BNL.NCS-17541, 8th ed.*, 2000. National Nuclear Data Centre.

Dale, R.G. (1982). A Monte Carlo derivation of parameters for use in the tissue dosimetry of medium and low energy nuclides. *Br. J. Radiol.* 55, 658, (October 1982), 748–757, ISSN: 1748-880X.

Devic, S.; Monroe, J.I.; Mutic, S.; Whiting, B. & Williamson, J.F. (2000). Dual Energy CT Tissue Quantitation for Monte-Carlo Based Treatment Planning for Brachytherapy 1-MO E309-01 (Chicago, IL: *IEEE Engineering Medicine and Biology Society*).

Finger, P.T.; Moshfeghi, D.M. & Ho, T.K. (1991). Palladium-103 ophthalmic plaque radiotherapy. *Arch Ophthalmol.* 109, 11, (July 1991), 1610-1613, ISSN: 0003-9950.

Finger, P.T.; Berson, A. & Szechter, A. (1999). Palladium-103 plaque radiotherapy for choroidal melanoma: results of a 7year study. *Ophthalmology.* 106, 3, (March 1999), 606-613, ISSN: 1549-4713.

Gearheart, D.; Drogin, A.; Sowards, K.; Meigooni, A.S. & Ibbott, G.S. (2000). Dosimetric characteristics of a new ^{125}I brachytherapy source. *Med. Phys.* 27, 10, (October 2000), 2278-2285, ISSN: 0094-2405.

Granero, D.; Perez-Calatayud, J.; Ballester, F. & Casal, E. (2004). Dosimetric study of the 15 mm Ropes eye plaque. *Med.Phys.* 31, 12, (December 2004), 3330-3336, ISSN: 0094-2405.

Hall, E.J. & Brenner, D.J. (1991). The dose rate effect revisited: radiobiological considerations of importance in radiotherapy. *Int J Radiat Oncol Biol Phys.* 21, 6, (November 1991), 1403-1414, ISSN: 0360-3016.

Hosseini, S.H.; Sadeghi, M. & Ataeinia, V. (2009). Dosimetric comparison of four new design ^{103}Pd brachytherapy sources: Optimal design using silver and copper rod cores, *Med. Phys.* 36, 7, (July 2009), 3080-3085, ISSN: 0094-2405.

Huang, D.Y.C.; Schell, M.C.; Weaver, K.A. & Ling, C.C. (1990). Dose distribution of ^{125}I sources in different tissues. *Med. Phys.* 17, 5, (September 1990), 826–832, ISSN: 0094-2405.

ICRU, International Commission on Radiation Units and Measurements, (1985). Dose and volume specification for reporting intracavitary therapy in gynecology, *ICRU Report 38.*

Karaiskos, P.; Sakeliou, L.; Sandilos, P. & Vlachos, L. (2000). Limitations of the point and line source approximations for the determination of geometry factors around brachytherapy sources. *Med. Phys.* 27, 1, (January, 2000), 124–128, ISSN: 0094-2405.

King, P.P.; Anderson, R.S. & Mills, M.D. (2001). Geometry function of a linear brachytherapy source. *J. Appl. Clin. Med. Phys.* 2, 2, (April 2001), 69–72, ISSN: 1526-9914.

Levitt, S.H.; Purdy, J.A.; Perez, Vijayakumar, C.A.S. (2006). *Technical Basis of Radiation Therapy.* Practical Clinical Applications. Springer, ISBN-10 3-540-21338-4 Berlin Heidelberg New York.

Li, Z.; Palta, J.R. & Fan, J.J. (2000). Monte Carlo calculations and experimental measurements of dosimetry parameters of a new ^{103}Pd source. *Med. Phys.* 27, 5, (May 2000), 1108-1112, ISSN: 0094-2405.

Ling, C.C.; Li, W.X. & Anderson, L.L. (1995). The relative biological effectiveness of I-125 and Pd-103. *Int J Radiat Oncol Biol Phys.* 32, 2, (May 1995), 373–378, ISSN: 0360-3016.

Mayles, Ph.; Nahum, A.E. & Rosenwald, J.C. (2007). *Hand book of radiotherapy physics: theory and practice.* Taylor & Francis, ISBN-13: 978-0-7503-0860-1, New York London.

Melhus, C.S. & Rivard, M.J. (2006). Approaches to calculating AAPM TG-43 brachytherapy dosimetry parameters for 137Cs, ^{125}I, ^{192}Ir, ^{103}Pd and ^{169} Yb sources. *Med. Phys.* 33, 6, (June 2006), 1729-1737, ISSN: 0094-2405.
Melhus, C.S. & Rivard, M.J. (2008). COMS eye plaque brachytherapy dosimetry simulations for ^{103}Pd, ^{125}I, and ^{131}Cs. *Med. Phys.* 35, 7, (July 2008), 3364-3371, ISSN: 0094-2405.
Melia, B.M.; Abramson, D.H.; Albert, D.M.;, Boldt, H.C.; Earle, J.D.; Hanson, W.F.; Montague, P.; Moy, CS.; Schachat, A.P.; Simpson, E.R.; Straatsma, B.R.; Vine, A.K.; Weingeist, T.A. & Collaborative Ocular Melanoma Study Group. (2001). Collaborative Ocular Melanoma Study (COMS) randomized trial of I-125 brachytherapy for medium choroidal melanoma. I. Visual acuity after 3 years. COMS report no. 16. *Ophthalmology.* 108, 2, (February 2001), 348-366, ISSN: 0003-9950.
Monte Carlo Team, MCNP-A General Monte Carlo N-Particle Transport Code-Version 5, Los Alamos National Laboratory, http://mcnp-green.lanl.gov/index.html, (last reviewed 29-Jan-2004).
Nag, S.; Quivey, J.; Earle, J.; Followill, D.; James Fontanesi J.; Finger, P.T.; F.A.C.S. & American Brachytherapy Society. (2003). The American Brachytherapy Society recommendations for brachytherapy of uveal melanomas. *Int J Radiat Oncol Biol Phys.* 56, 2, (June 2003), 544-555, ISSN: 0360-3016.
Nath, R.; Anderson, L.L.; Luxton, G.; Weaver, K.A.; Williamson, J.F. & Meigooni, A.S. (1995). Dosimetry of interstitial brachytherapy sources: Recommendations of the AAPM Radiation Therapy Committee Task Group No. 43. *Med. Phys.* 22, 2, (February 1995), 209–234, ISSN: 0094-2405.
Nath, R.; Anderson, L.L.; Meli, J.A.; Olch, A.J.; Stitt, J.A. & Williamson, J.F. (1997). Code of practice for brachytherapy physics: Report of the AAPM Radiation Therapy Committee Task Group No. 56. *Med Phys.* 24, 10, (October 1997), 1557–1998, ISSN: 0094-2405.
Nath, R.; Bongiorni, P.; Chen, Z.; Gragnano, J. & Rockwell, S. (2005). Relative biological effectiveness of ^{103}Pd and ^{125}I photons for continuous low-dose-rate irradiation of Chinese hamster cells. *Radiat Res.* 163, 5, (May 2005), 501–509.
Nath, R.; Yue, N.; Shahnazi, K. & Bongiorni, P.J. (2000). Measurement of dose-rate constant for ^{103}Pd seeds with air kerma strength calibration based upon a primary national standard. *Med. Phys.* 27, 4, (April 2000), 655-658, ISSN: 0094-2405.
Perez-Catalayud, J.; Granero, D. & Ballester, F. (2004). Phantom size in brachytherapy source dosimetric studies. *Med. Phys.* 31, 7, (July 2004), 2075-2081, ISSN: 0094-2405.
Perez-Calatayud, J.; Granero, D.; Ballester, F. (2009). *Monte Carlo Application in Brachytherapy Dosimetry*, In: *Riotherapy and Brachytherapy*, Lemoigne, Y. & Caner, A. (Ed.), 239-250, Springer, ISBN: 978-90-481-3096-2, France.
Prasad, S.C. & Bassano, D.A. (1985). Lung density effect on ^{125}I distribution. *Med. Phys.* 12, 1, (January 1985), 99–100, ISSN: 0094-2405.
Raisali, Gh.; Sadeghi, M.; Ataenia, V.; Shahvar, A. & Ghonchehnazi, M. (2008). Determination of Dosimetric Parameters of the Second Model of Pd-103 Seed Manufactured at Agricultural, Medical and Industrial Research School. *Iranian J. Med. Phys.* 5, 1, (July 2008), 9-20. (Persian)
Rivard, M.J. (2001). Monte Carlo calculation of AAPM Task Group Report No.43 dosimetry parameters for the MED3631-A/M ^{125}I source. *Med. Phys.* 28, 4, (April 2001), 629-637. ISSN: 0094-2405.
Rivard, M.J.; Coursey, B.M.; DeWerd, L.A.; Hanson, W.F.; Huq, M.S.; Ibbott, G.S.; Mitch, M.G.; Nath, R. & Williamson, J.F. (2004a). "Update of AAPM Task Group No. 43 Report: A revised AAPM protocol for brachytherapy dose calculations. *Med. Phys.* 31, 3, (March 2004), 633-674, ISSN: 0094-2405.

Rivard, M.J.; Melhus, C.S. & Kirk, B.L. (2004b). Brachytherapy dosimetry parameters calculated for a new ^{103}Pd source. *Med. Phys.* 31, 9, (September 2004), 2466-2470, ISSN: 0094-2405.

Rivard, M.J. (2007). Brachytherapy dosimetry parameters calculated for a ^{137}Cs. *Med. Phys.* 34, 2, (February 2007) 754-762, ISSN: 0094-2405.

Rogers D. W. O. (2006). Fifty years of Monte Carlo simulations for medical physics. *Phys. Med. Biol.* 51, 13, (June 2006), R287–R301.

Sadeghi, M.; Raisali, Gh.; Hosseini, S.H.; Shahvar, A. (2008a), Monte Carlo calculations and experimental measurements of dosimetric parameters of the IRA−^{103}Pd brachytherapy source. *Med. Phys.* 35, 4, (April 2008), 1288-1294, ISSN: 0094-2405.

Sadeghi, M.; Hosseini, S.H.; Raisali, Gh. (2008b). Experimental measurements and Monte Carlo calculations of dosimetric parameters of the IRA1-^{103}Pd brachytherapy source. *Appl. Radiat. Isot.* 66, 10, (October 2008), 1431–1437, ISSN: 0969-8043.

Sadeghi, M.; Karimi, E.; Hosseini, S.H. (2009a). Dosimetric comparison of ^{90}Y, ^{32}P, and ^{186}Re radiocolloids in craniopharyngioma treatments. *Med. Phys.* 36, 11, (November 2009), 5022-5026. ISSN: 0094-2405.

Sadeghi, M.; Hosseini, S.H. (2010). Study of the IsoAid ADVANTAGETM ^{125}I brachytherapy source dosimetric parameters using Monte Carlo simulation. *Appl. Radiat. Isot.* 68, 1, (January 2010), 211-213, ISSN: 0969-8043.

Saidi, P. M. Sadeghi, M, Shirazi, A. & Tenreiro, C. (2010). Monte Carlo calculation of dosimetry parameters for the IR08-^{103}Pd brachytherapy source. *Med. Phys.* 37, 6, (June 2010), 2509-2515. ISSN: 0094-2405.

Thomson, R.M.; Taylor, R.E.P. & Rogers, D.W.O. (2008). Monte Carlo dosimetry for ^{125}I and ^{103}Pd eye plaque brachytherapy. *Med.Phys.* 35, 12, (December 2008), 5530-5543, ISSN: 0094-2405.

Thomson, R.M. & Rogers D.W.O. (2010) Monte Carlo dosimetry for ^{125}I and ^{103}Pd eye plaque brachytherapy with various seed model. *Med. Phys.* 37, 1, (January 2010), 368-376, ISSN: 0094-2405.

Wallace, R.E. & Fan, J.J. (1999). Dosimetric characterization of a new design 103palladium brachytherapy source. *Med. Phys.* 26, 11, (November 1999) 2465-2470, ISSN: 0094-2405.

Wang, R. & Li, X.A. (2000).A Monte Carlo calculation of dosimetric parameters of ^{90}Sr/^{90}Y and ^{192}Ir SS sources for intravascular brachytherapy. *Med. Phys.* 27, 11, (November 1999), 2528, 2000. ISSN: 0094-2405.

Willliamson, J.F. (1991). Comparison of measured and calculated dose rates in water near I-125 and Ir-192 seeds. *Med. Phys.* 18, 4, (July 1991), 776-786, ISSN: 0094-2405.

Williamson, J.F.; Coursey, B.M.; DeWerd, L.A.; Hanson, W.F.; Nath, R.; Rivard, M.J. & Ibbott, G. (1999). On the use of apparent activity (A_{app}) for treatment planning of ^{125}I and ^{103}Pd interstitial sources: Recommendations of the American Association of Physicists in Medicine Radiation Therapy Committee Subcommittee on Low-Energy Brachytherapy Source Dosimetry, *Med. Phys.* 26,12, (December 1999), 2529 - 2530, ISSN: 0094-2405.

Williamson, J.F. (2000). Monte Carlo modelling of the transverse-axis dose distribution of the model 200 ^{103}Pd interstitial brachytherapy source. *Med. Phys.* 27, 4, (April 2000), 643-654. ISSN: 0094-2405.

Williamson, J.F. (2006). Brachytherapy technology and physics practice since 1950: a half-century of progress. *Phys. Med. Biol.* 51, 13, (June 2006), R303–R325, ISSN: 1361-6560.

Wuu, C.S. & Zaider, M. (1998). A calculation of the relative biological effectiveness of ^{125}I and ^{103}Pd brachytherapy sources using the concept of proximity function. *Med Phys.* 25, 11, (November 1998), 2186–2189. ISSN: 0094-2405.

11

Evaluation of the Respiratory Motion Effect in Small Animal PET Images with GATE Monte Carlo Simulations

Susana Branco[1], Pedro Almeida[1] and Sébastien Jan[2]
[1]*Instituto de Biofísica e Engenharia Biomédica Faculdade de Ciências da Universidade de Lisboa*
[2]*Service Hospitalier Frédéric Joliot Commissariat à l'Énergie Atomique*
[1]*Portugal*
[2]*France*

1. Introduction

The rapid growth in genetics and molecular biology combined with the development of techniques for genetically engineering small animals has led to increased interest in *in vivo* small animal imaging (Cherry & Gambhir, 2001; Riemann et al., 2008; Rowland & R., 2008). Small animal imaging has been applied frequently to the imaging of small animals (mice and rats), which are ubiquitous in modeling human diseases and testing treatments. The use of PET in small animals allows the use of subjects as their own control, reducing the interanimal variability. This allows performing longitudinal studies on the same animal and improves the accuracy of biological models (Cherry, 2004). However, small animal PET still suffers from several limitations. The amounts of radiotracers needed, limited scanner sensitivity, image resolution and image quantification issues, all could clearly benefit from additional research (Chatziioannou, 2002; Tai & Laforest, 2005).
Because nuclear medicine imaging deals with radioactive decay, the emission of radiation energy through photons and particles alongside with the detection of these quanta and particles in different materials make Monte Carlo method an important simulation tool in both nuclear medicine research and clinical practice. In order to optimize the quantitative use of PET in clinical practice, data- and image-processing methods are also a field of intense interest and development. The evaluation of such methods often relies on the use of simulated data and images since these offer control of the ground truth. Monte Carlo simulations are widely used for PET simulation since they take into account all the random processes involved in PET imaging, from the emission of the positron to the detection of the photons by the detectors. Simulation techniques have become an importance and indispensable complement to a wide range of problems that could not be addressed by experimental or analytical approaches (Rogers, 2006).
Monte Carlo methods are numerical calculation methods based on random variable sampling. This approach has been used to solve mathematical problems since 1770 and has been named "Monte Carlo" by Von Neumann because of the similarity of statistical simulations to games of chance, represented by the most well known center for gambling:

the Monte Carlo district in the Monaco principality. The general idea of Monte Carlo analysis is to create a model, which is as similar as possible to the real physical system of interest, and to create interactions within that system based on known probabilities of occurrence, with random sampling of the Probability Density Functions (PDFs). As the number of individual events (called histories) increase, the quality of the reported average behavior of the system improves, meaning that the statistical uncertainty decreases. Virtually, any complex system can in principle be modeled: if the distribution of events that occur in a system is know from experience, a PDF can be generated and sampled randomly to simulate the real system. A detailed description of the general principles and applications of the Monte Carlo method can be found elsewhere: (Andreo, 1991; Zaidi, 1999; Ljungberg, 1998, 2004; Zaidi & Sgouros, 2002; Zaidi, 2006).

The simulation of PET imaging using Monte Carlo allows the optimization of system design for new scanners, the study of factors affecting image quality, the validation of correction methodologies for effects such as scatter, attenuation and partial volume, for improved image quantification, as well as the development and testing of new image reconstruction algorithms. Another major advantage of simulations in nuclear medicine imaging is that they allow studying parameters that are not measurable in practice. The fraction of photons that are scattered in a phantom and their contribution to the image are examples of such parameters, and they can only be measured indirectly for a very limited number of geometries. In addition, in a computer model it is possible to turn off certain effects, such as photon attenuation and scattering in the phantom, which means that ideal images, which include camera-specific parameters, can be created and used as reference images. In combination with patient-like phantoms, the Monte Carlo method can be used to produce simulated images very close to those acquired from real measurements. In this context, Monte Carlo simulations are becoming an essential tool for assisting this research and some specific Monte Carlo simulation packages have been evaluated for nuclear medicine applications (Andreo & Ljungberg, 1998; Buvat & Castiglioni, 2002; Buvat et al., 2005; Buvat & Lazaro, 2006). Recently, the Geant4 Application for Tomographic Emission (GATE) platform has been developed (Jan et al., 2004a; GATE, 2010) and validated for the simulation of the microPET® FOCUS 220 system (Jan et al., 2005).

An important aspect of simulation is the possibility of having a realistic model (phantom) of the subject's anatomy and physiological functions from which imaging data can be generated using accurate models of the imaging process (Ljungberg, 2004; Zaidi, 2006; Zubal, 1998; Poston et al., 2002; Peter et al., 2000). Conceptually, the purpose of a physical or computerized phantom is to represent an organ or body region of interest, to allow modeling the biodistribution of a particular radiotracer and the chemical composition of the scattering medium, which absorbs and scatters the emitted radiation in a manner similar to biological tissues. In other terms, a phantom is a mathematical model designed to represent an organ or tissue of the body, an organ system, or the whole-body.

The widespread interest in molecular imaging spurred the development of more realistic 3D to 5D computational models based on the actual anatomy and physiology of individual humans and small animals. The advantage in using such phantoms in simulation studies is that the exact anatomy and physiological functions are known, thus providing a gold standard or truth in order to evaluate and improve imaging devices, data acquisition techniques, and imaging processing and reconstruction methods. Moreover, computer phantoms can be altered in order to model different anatomies and pathological situations. A review of the fundamental and technical challenges of designing computational models of the human anatomy can be found in (Zaidi & Xu, 2007; Zaidi & Tsui, 2009). These reviews summarize the latest efforts and future directions in the development of computational anthropomorphic models for application in radiological sciences.

Based on state-of-the-art computer graphics techniques, the 4D Mouse Whole Body (MOBY) phantoms provide a realistic model of the mouse anatomy and physiology for imaging studies (Segars et al., 2004). The phantom, when combined with accurate models for the imaging process, is capable of providing realistic imaging data from subjects with various anatomies and motions (cardiac and respiratory) in health and disease. With this ability, the phantom has enormous potential to help studying the effects of anatomical, physiological, physical, and instrumentation factors on small animal imaging and to research new instrumentation, image acquisition strategies, image processing and reconstruction methods as well as image visualization and interpretation techniques.

It is known that the localization and detection of thoracic and abdominal lesions in PET imaging is often perturbed due to the displacement of the organs during normal breathing. The respiratory motion compromise image quality and quantification in PET, and affect clinical diagnosis. Motion can actually introduce large biases, for instance tracer uptake underestimation greater than 50% in lung lesion. Moreover, respiratory motion can induce resolution degradation (blurring effect) for PET imaging. Contrast loss of small lesions in PET images due to the above motion blurring effect can adversely affect the lesion detection sensitivity for PET imaging of lung or liver cancers. The degree of motion blurring and contrast loss depends on the lesion size and location.

In order to contribute for the full understanding of this problem, the GATE Monte Carlo platform was used to model the microPET® FOCUS 220 system and the MOBY phantom to produce realistic simulated mouse scans. GATE is a well-validated and very versatile application for Monte Carlo simulations in emission tomography that can be used for highly realistic simulations. MOBY was developed to provide a realistic and flexible model of the mouse anatomy and physiology to be used in molecular imaging research.

2. Material and methods

2.1 The GATE platform

GATE is a Monte Carlo simulator (object-oriented simulation platform) based on Geant4 libraries (a generic Monte Carlo code), providing a scripting interface with a number of advantages for the simulation of Single Photon Emission Computed Tomography (SPECT) and PET systems, including the description of source decay phenomena, moving detector components and time management (Jan et al., 2004a). Since the code is based on Geant4, it profits from the validation of the underlying physics components including testing from a very large scientific community. At the same time, the scripting interface provides a convenient platform for most of the users to create their own simulation of emission tomography experiments and complicated emission tomography system designs.

The use of GATE facilitates the description of the different components necessary for the accurate modeling of a PET system, starting from the geometry configuration, up to the creation of a processing chain for the detected events. Analytical phantoms can also be defined through the use of these basic structures, while voxelized sources can be equally employed in order to represent realistic patient imaging conditions. The physics processes are based on Geant4 libraries including the modeling of radioactive source decays and particles interactions for standard and low energies. Users may also interactively select which gamma-ray interactions should be considered (photoelectric effect, Compton and Rayleigh scattering, and gamma-ray conversion), and may specify the energy cuts applied to the production of secondary gamma-rays and electrons. In addition, Geant4 material libraries in combination with user defined material tables are used to cover all of the object compositions necessary for the modeling of a system. A number of modules are available for modeling the detection process, going from the detection of the gamma-rays by the scintillating crystals (singles) to the detection of coincidences in PET. Simulation data results may be stored into multiple output files with different file formats. Time-dependence is taken into account at all steps of the simulation, so that realistic simulations of the acquisitions count rates and source decay can be achieved under dynamic configurations (e.g. rotation detectors or evolving bio-distributions).

2.2 Modeling the MicroPET® FOCUS 220

The microPET® FOCUS 220 system is a commercial scanner consisting in 4 detector rings: each ring is made of 42 detector blocks (Tai et al., 2005). Each detector block is composed of a matrix of 12×12 LSO crystals with the dimensions 1.5×1.5×10.0 mm^3. Its axial Field of View (FOV) is 7.6 cm and has a diameter of 26.0 cm. The FOCUS system has a volume resolution of 2.5 μL and an absolute sensitivity of 3.4%, both measured at the center of the FOV. The system is suitable for acquiring high-resolution images of small animal as rodents (mice and rats) and primates (macaque and small baboon).
The microPET® Focus 220 system was simulated in order to validate the use of GATE in the simulation of small animal PET. In order to do this, a model of the detection system and its geometry was developed. The accuracy of the developed detection model was tested through the comparison of simulated and measured results obtained from the FOCUS system for a number of performance protocols including spatial resolution, counting rate and contrast. Time dependence was introduced as a new feature to work with small animal imaging simulations. The geometry description of the microPET® scanner is illustrated in Fig. 1.
Accuracy and variability of quantitative values obtained for mouse imaging using the Focus system can be found in (Jan et al., 2004b).

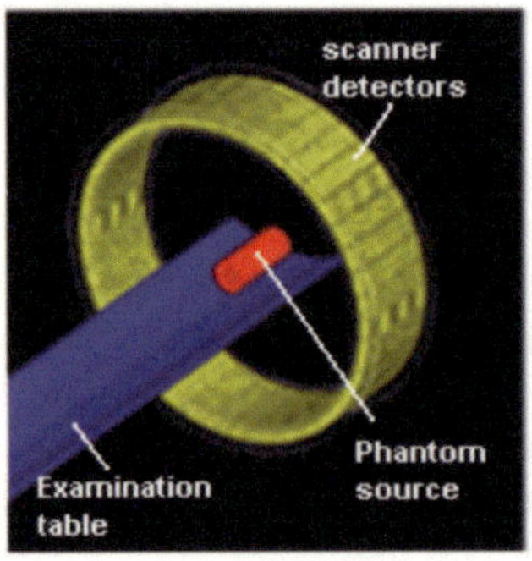

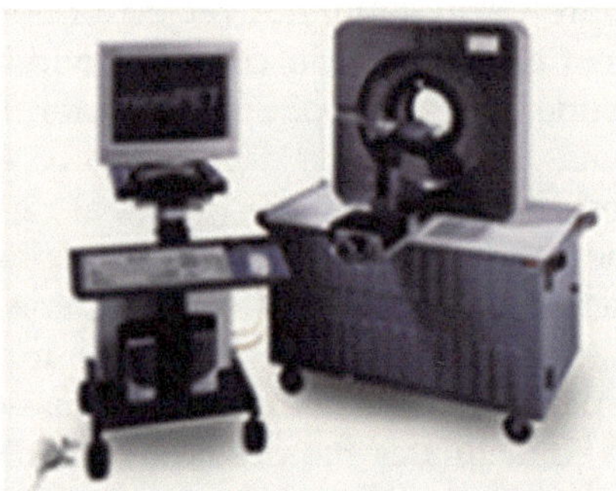

Fig. 1. MicroPET® FOCUS 220 geometry modeled by GATE (left) and the real system (right).

2.3 The MOBY phantom description within GATE

The MOBY mouse phantom combines the realism of a voxelized phantom, with the flexibility of a mathematical phantom, based on non-uniform rational B-splines (NURBS)

(Segars et al., 2004). The organ shapes are modeled with NURBS surfaces, widely used in three dimensional computer graphics to accurately describe complex 3D surfaces, providing the foundation for a realistic model of the 3D mouse anatomy. The phantom software could generate voxelized representations of the mouse anatomy at any user-defined resolution. Also, organs can be set to different tissue resolutions. The execution of the MOBY program generates 3D voxelized attenuation coefficient phantoms and 3D voxelized emission phantoms. These voxelized representations can be used as input in the GATE Monte Carlo platform.

The default whole body MOBY phantom consists of a matrix of 128×128×448 cubic voxels with 0.25 mm sides. We applied a resampling on the default MOBY matrix to reduce the voxel number to 40×40×124 voxels with a voxel unit size of 0.5×0.5×0.5 mm^3. This allowed to significantly reduce the computational time resulting from the particle tracking inside the simulated volume and took into account the spatial resolution of the scanner. The MOBY phantom includes 4D models of the mouse's cardiac and respiratory motions. Both motions were parameterized allowing changes on magnitude or rates of each motion to simulate many different variations, normal and abnormal. The MOBY respiratory motion was set up to be dependent on two time varying parameters: the change in the height of the diaphragm ($\Delta_{diaphr.}$) and the amount of chest expansion (Δ_{AP}). In the default MOBY configuration, the extent of diaphragmatic motion for normal breathing is set to be 1.0 mm while the chest expansion is 0.7 mm. These values correspond to a respiratory cycle with a period of 0.37 s. We manipulated these parameters to produce a "stress breathing" condition, in order to reproduce the respiratory motion of a mouse during a typical PET examination: the $\Delta_{diaphr.}(t)$ was set to 6.0 mm and the $\Delta_{AP}(t)$ was defined to 4.2 mm.

A spherical lung lesion was implemented in the middle region of the left lung and its motion modeled as a function of the non-normal tidal breathing condition. The motion of a specific spot of the lung is modeled as a two-way motion between two points in space, with same cycle of the diaphragm movement.

For a respiratory cycle with a typical period of 0.37 s, the diaphragm motion can be decided by:

$$\Delta_{diaphr.}(t)=\begin{cases} 0.5mm\cos\left(\frac{\pi}{0.16}t\right)+0.5 & 0\le t\le 0.16s \\ 0.5mm\cos\left(\frac{\pi}{0.24}(0.4-t)\right)+0.5 & 0.16\le t\le 0.4s \end{cases} \quad (1)$$

The $\Delta_{AP}(t)$ diameter of the chest was assumed to change a maximum of N mm's sinusoidally as shown in Equation:

$$\Delta_{AP}(t)=\begin{cases} -\frac{N}{2}\cos\left(\frac{\pi}{0.16}t\right)+\frac{N}{2} & 0\le t\le 0.16s \\ -\frac{N}{2}\cos\left(\frac{\pi}{0.24}(0.4-t)\right)+\frac{N}{2} & 0.16\le t\le 0.4s \end{cases} \quad (2)$$

The N parameter was adjusted according to the total amount of volume change in the lungs (0.15 mL for normal tidal breathing in the mouse).

Each respiratory cycle was divided into N bins (temporal frames), and one phantom was created for each of the N instances of the respiratory cycle. Based on Equations (1) and (2), a set of 10 temporal frames (gates) of 0.037 s was generated over a complete respiratory cycle of 0.37 s in addition to a non-gated data set. The 10 respiratory gated images were produced by the MOBY program for 10 different position of one respiratory cycle. The first 5 images correspond to the inhalation and the other 5 images to the exhalation process respectively. The modified MOBY phantom and the parameter curves for both respiratory and lesion motion are illustrated in Fig. 2 and Fig. 3.

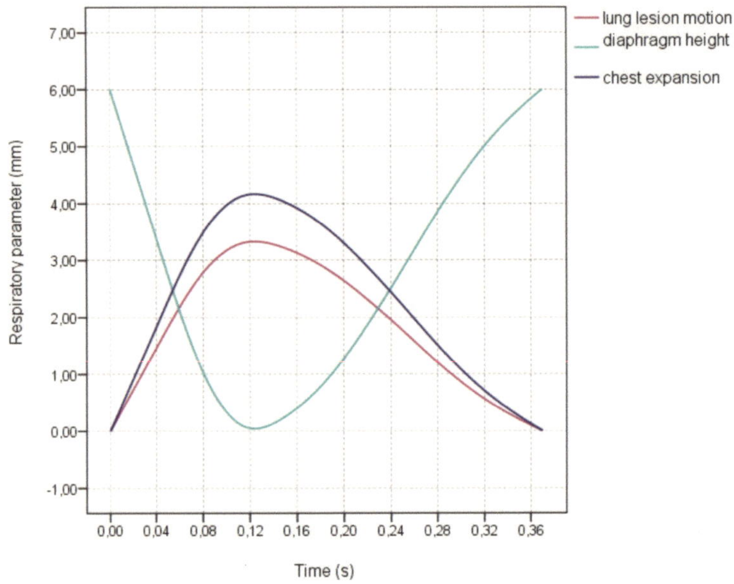

Fig. 2. Parameter curves and lesion motion for the "stress" breathing condition in the MOBY phantom.

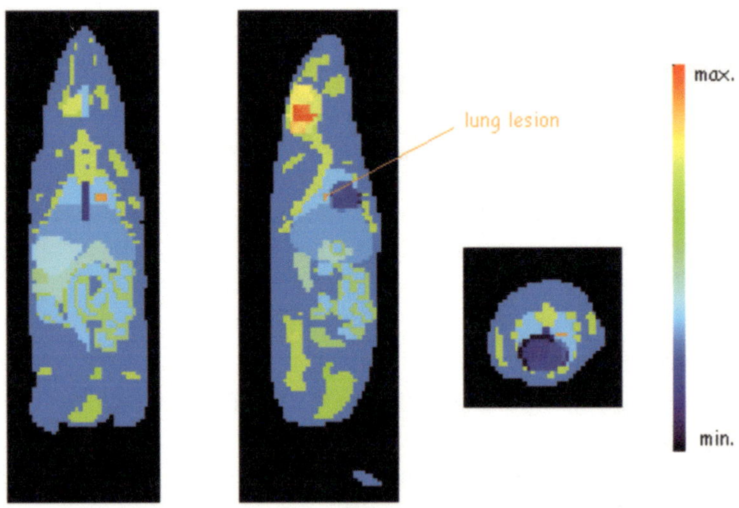

Fig. 3. Slices of the emission map of the MOBY phantom including a spherical lesion in middle region of the left lung, generated by the MOBY program.

For the studies without the inclusion of respiratory motion, simulations were carried out approximating clinical acquisitions of 15 minutes (last frame of a FDG acquisition) in order to provide whole-body images of variable statistical quality. For the simulations with respiratory motion, the acquisition time used in static simulation, T_{acqTot}, was divided by the number of respiratory cycles, N_{cycles}, and the number of bins, N_{bins}, per respiratory cycle to obtain the acquisition time at one instance (bin) of the respiratory cycle, T_{acqBin}:

$$T_{acqBin} = \frac{T_{acqTot}}{N_{cycles} N_{bins}} \tag{3}$$

In this way the total acquisition time remains the same for simulations with or without the inclusion of respiratory motion.

2.4 Metabolic imaging using FDG

The *2-Deoxy-[18F]fluoro-D-glucose* (FDG) is the most common radiotracer used for the study of cancer in the clinical setting. FDG is an analog of glucose and is taken up by living cells through the normal glucose pathway.

Tumor imaging with FDG is based on the fact that malignant tumors with high metabolic rates take up greater amounts of glucose and FDG than surrounding tissues (Couturier, 2004; Larson & Schwartz, 2006).

A dynamic whole body mouse FDG exam was used to generate an emission map that consist of a matrix of 104×61×95 voxels, which are of 0.46 mm along the x and y axis, and 0.80 mm along the z axis. The mouse was injected with an activity of 220 mCi and scanned during 90 minutes. Data was binned into 18 frames (5×60 s; 5×120 s; 3×300 s; 3×600 s; 2×900 s).

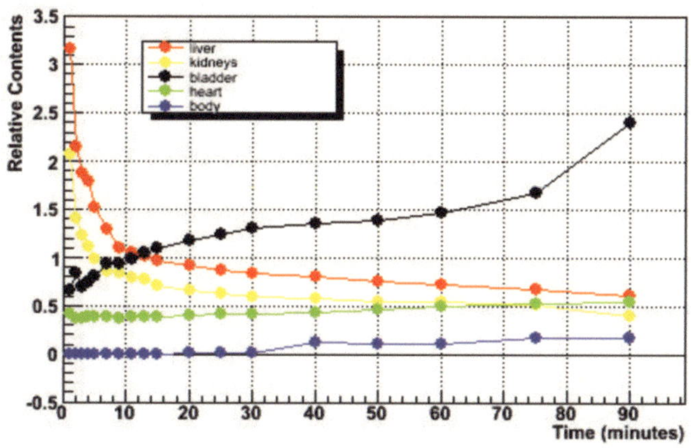

Fig. 4. Measured TACs used as input for the FDG uptake simulation.

The microPET images were employed in order to accurately model the variable FDG distributions. The FDG biodistribution is defined by the Time Activity Curves (TACs), which are assigned to different body structures. The dynamic FDG mouse exam was used to compute the FDG biodistribution, needed to set the activity distribution in each organ at each point of time in the simulation studies performed. Regions of Interest (ROIs) were drawn around the bladder, heart, liver, kidneys and whole body. The activity in each ROI was normalized to the total body activity in order to obtain a relative concentration in each organ at each time point. Fig. 4 shows the TAC for each organ at each time frame. The TACs for the function model of the FDG tracer are used to set the input activity function in each structure for the MOBY phantom.

2.5 Simulation and reconstruction set-up

In order to evaluate the effect of the respiratory motion in 3D and 4D microPET images, a set of static (non-gated MOBY data set without any motion associated) and dynamic (gated MOBY data set, where respiratory and lesion motions are present) FDG simulations were performed. Different lesion diameter (0.75 mm, 1.0 mm, 1.25 mm, 1.5 mm and 2.0 mm) were considered as well as different activity uptakes of FDG (0.01 μCi, 0.03 μCi, 0.05 μCi, 0.08 μCi, 1.08 μCi and 1.35 μCi), for the last time frame.

The gated and non-gated MOBY emission maps are integrated into GATE as voxelized sources to assign the activity to different anatomical structures, in order to obtain static and dynamic emission data sets.

The activity distribution in all of the other organs was defined according to the last acquisition time frame for an FDG exam (determined with a typical mouse FDG-PET exam). The concentration activity of the last frame (900 s of acquisition time) corresponds to a 131 μCi.

The FDG biodistribution was defined by the TACs obtained from real whole-body mouse PET exams, as described previous. The activity distribution, within the MOBY phantom, was set according to the activity distribution assigned to the different whole body structures for the FDG radiotracer. In all simulation protocols physical effects like positron range, gamma accolinearity and tissue attenuation were not taken into account in order to obtain the "best case scenario", which could be used as defining the optimal results that we could obtain with a dedicated scanner and a specific radiotracer. Simulated data were rebinned with the Fourier Rebinning algorithm (FORE) and reconstructed using the OSEM2D method (16 subsets and 4 iterations).

2.6 Evaluation of the respiratory motion in lung lesion quantification

With the goal of better understanding the effect of the respiratory motion we have investigated the combined effects of target size, target-to-background activity concentration ratio and extent of respiratory motion on signal recovery of spherical lesions (targets) in 3D and 4D microPET images.

Sets of static (non-gated MOBY data set without any motion associated) and dynamic (gated MOBY data set, where respiratory and lesion motions are present) FDG simulations were performed. Different lesion diameters (0.75 mm, 1.0 mm, 1.25 mm, 1.5 mm and 2.0 mm) were considered as well as different activity uptakes of FDG (0.1 mCi, 0.3 mCi, 0.5 mCi, 0.8 mCi, 1.08 mCi and 1.35 mCi), for the last time frame. The gated and non-gated MOBY emission maps are integrated into GATE as voxelized sources to assign the activity to different anatomical structures, in order to obtain static and dynamic emission data sets.

The activity distribution in all of the other organs was defined according to the last acquisition time frame for an FDG exam (determined with a typical mouse FDG PET exam). The concentration activity of the last frame (900 s of acquisition time) corresponds to 131 mCi.

The FDG biodistribution was defined by the TACs obtained from real whole-body mouse PET exams, has described previously. The activity distribution, within the MOBY phantom, was set according to the activity distribution assigned to the different whole body structures for the FDG radiotracer. In all simulation protocols, physical effects like positron range, gamma accolinearity and tissue attenuation were not taken into account in order to obtained the "best case scenario", which could be used as defining the optimal results that could be obtain with a dedicated scanner and a specific radiotracer.

2.7 Data analysis

Detection in PET images strongly depends on the ability to recognize the signal pattern in the presence of noisy background that in turn, is limited by the capability of the imaging system to detect objects with very low contrast relatively to the background level and to spatially resolve a focal uptake. In the following paragraphs, the general methodology to evaluate the signal detection capability of an imaging system is presented. Although only the basic concepts on signal detection theory will be introduced, its description is important to contextualize the adopted analysis using the simulated data acquired with the microPET® Focus 220 scanner model.

The spatial resolution was measured by the Full Width at Half Maximum (FWHM). The FWHMs of reconstructed lesion images were determined along the direction of lesion movement due to respiratory motion. The image statistics were evaluated by calculating the signal-to-noise ratio (SNR) and contrast-to-noise ratio (CNR). The SNR is defined as the ratio of the average activity concentration measured in the target to the standard deviation. The higher the SNR, the less obtrusive the noise is. SNR is often defined as:

$$SNR = \frac{T}{\sigma_T} \tag{4}$$

The CNR was calculated as:

$$CNR = \frac{T - B}{\sqrt{\sigma_T^2 + \sigma_B^2}} \tag{5}$$

where T and B are the average activity concentrations measured in the target (lung lesion) and background region in the reconstructed image, respectively. $\sigma_{T,B}^2$ are the variances of these activities (Lartizien et al., 2004).

In general, the "quality" of an image can be described (quantitatively) by its SNR. The SNR directly affects diagnostic and quantitative accuracy. In essence, then, a major goal of nuclear medicine equipment is to maximize the SNR in an image. The CNR refers to the ability in PET to distinguish between various contrasts in an acquired image and the inherent noise in the image. The mean signal recovery of SNR and CNR were evaluated as a function of the lesion size and the lesion activity uptake, using Equations (4) and (5).

The target-to-background ratio (TBR) is defined as the relation between the lesion activity to the background activity concentration. The TBR values are computed using the following relation:

$$TBR = \frac{T}{B} \tag{6}$$

The data recorded from the ROIs were used to compute the contrast (C) and the volume recovery coefficient (VRC). The evaluation of the contrast indicates how reliable the reconstructed image would be for lesion detection tasks in real situations. This result in the ability to evaluate the reconstruction algorithm used to recover a certain simulated contrast between a lesion and a background. The contrast between the simulated lesions and the surrounding organs in the reconstructed images was computed using the expression:

$$C = \frac{T - B}{T + B} \tag{7}$$

where T was the mean activity in the simulated spherical lesion ROI and B was the mean activity in the background region ROIs. Higher contrast values are often related with noisier images. In practice, this contrast is provided by the radiotracer's distribution. The goal of the imaging system is to preserve this contrast in the image. Contrast is maintained by avoiding blurring, which smears counts from higher activity regions into lower activity regions (and vice versa), thus reducing image contrast. In this way, spatial resolution and contrast are closely linked.
In order to determine temporal resolution, the VRC was defined as:

$$VRC = \frac{V_{measured}}{V_{true}} \tag{8}$$

where $V_{measured}$ is the measured lesion volume and V_{true} is the real lesion volume. To perform data analysis, and quantify VRC values, we have drawn a volume of interest (VOI) around the centroid of each lesion. The size of the drawn VOI depends on the lesion size, in order to include as many voxels as possible, to keep a good statistic, and, at the same time, to include only voxels that corresponded to the lesion. For each VOI we calculated the average number of counts in each voxel. Background values were obtained by drawing and merging circular VOIs around each lesion (within the surrounding soft tissues: lung and liver regions) and by calculating the average number of counts and the corresponding standard deviation within. These data was also used to calculate the mean percent error in the volume for each lesion. The mean percent error between the estimated volume and the true volume of the spherical lesions was given by:

$$\%error = \frac{V_{measured} - V_{true}}{V_{true}} \tag{9}$$

3. Results

3.1 Quantification considerations

Detection in PET images At the beginning of this discussion we stated that the results obtained for the higher diameter lesions (1.25 mm, 1.5 mm and 2.0 mm) in the dynamic mode (gated images) are not show due to lesion blending into the liver. Additionally, due to the limited spatial resolution of the scanner used the results obtained for the smallest lesion (0.75 mm) may be compromised by a decrease in the sensitivity of detection and thus statistics could not be accurately measured. Due to this, to evaluate the effects produced by the respiratory motion we choose to use the 1.0 mm lesion.
Concerning data analysis, a selected lesion ROI for each particular case was used to estimate T (average activity concentrations measured in the lesion) when positioned over a background region. In the present analysis, the mean lung lesion activity T was computed as the average pixel intensity in the spherical ROI located at the lesion. The ROIs were all

extracted from transaxial slices of the MOBY phantom passing through the different planes containing the lesion activity. The mean background activity B was estimated as the average pixel intensity within ROIs projected into reconstructed images without the lesion data added, however surrounding the lesion location. The placement of the lesion ROI for a 1.0 mm diameter lesion and background ROIs is illustrated in Fig. 5.

Fig. 5. Sagital slices through the MOBY phantom containing a 1.0 mm diameter lung lesion or only background, illustrating the placement of the background and lesion ROIs used for data analysis.

The statistical errors measured as the ratio standard deviation over mean for all ROIs considered for each lesion diameter, as function of the activity defined, are represented in Table 1. We found higher values in higher activity concentrations. This Table suggests that for the smaller lesion sizes (0.75 mm and 1.0 mm diameter) we have compromised results when compared to the statistical errors obtained for the other lesion sizes due to limited FOCUS system resolution. In addition, lower activity concentrations (0.1 mCi and 0.3 mCi) show the same behavior because lower activity concentrations significantly deteriorate the lesion signal recovery. The statistical errors for the ROIs considered in static simulation were found to be 18.92% and 22.44% for the dynamic simulations.

Activity (μCi)	Static Simulations					Dynamic Simulations
	Lesion Diameter					
	0.75 mm	1.0 mm	1.25 mm	1.5 mm	2.0 mm	1.0 mm
0.1	12.26%	21.0%	20.58%	14.56%	18.91%	11.81%
0.3	17.16%	33.92%	25.82%	16.98%	19.41%	9.11%
0.5	20.22%	43.43%	33.66%	31.72%	24.39%	11.88%
0.8	22.80%	49.65%	39.39%	37.25%	27.64%	14.54%
1.08	24.68%	51.74%	41.85%	40.35%	32.76%	19.54%
1.35	24.82%	55.46%	43.72%	42.67%	37.73%	20.71%

Table 1. Statistical error obtained for the defined ROIs in the lung lesion implementation in the MOBY phantom, from the static and the dynamic simulation modes.

3.2 Motion blurring versus spatial resolution

"Best case scenario" images are presented in Fig. 5 and Fig. 6, from static (non-gated data, without motion involved) and dynamic simulated data (gated data, where respiratory and lesion motions are present).

From Fig. 6 and Fig. 7 differences between the non-gated data set (static simulation) and the gated data set (dynamic simulation) can be seen. The extent of respiratory motion is evident between the 1st and the 10th frames in Fig. 7. The coronal slices shows the realistic motion of the various structures present in the thorax and upper abdomen due to the lungs expansion and contraction for the non normal tidal breathing configuration.

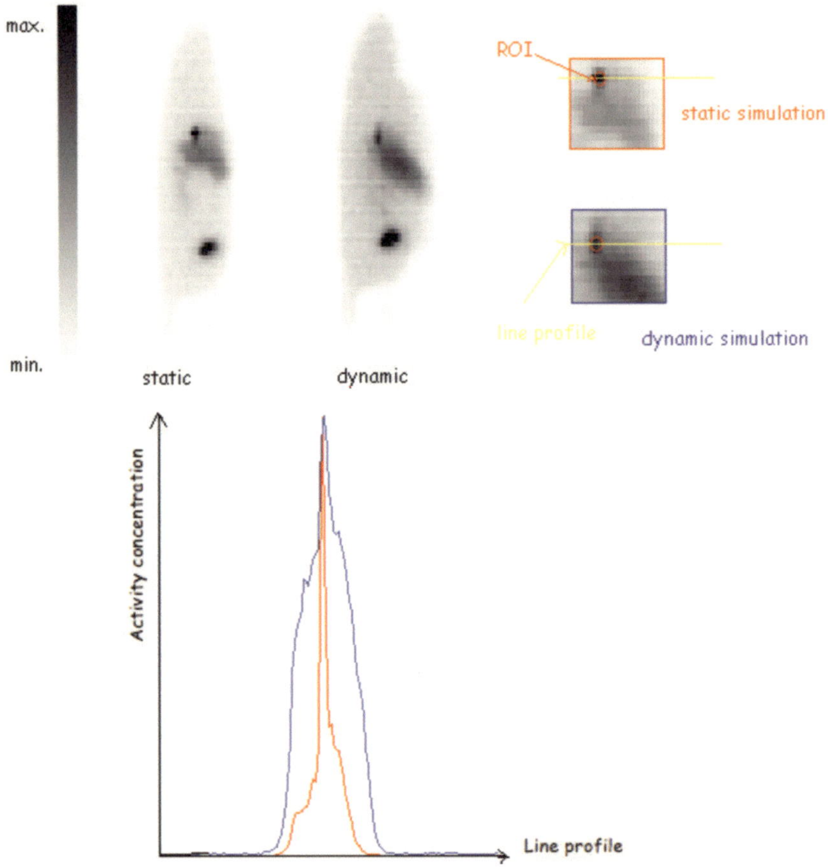

Fig. 6. Sagital slices, of the reconstructed MOBY phantom, for a static acquisition, where no motion was simulated, and for the simulation of a dynamic acquisition, where respiratory and lesion motions were considered, with a lung lesion of 1.0 mm diameter and an FDG uptake of 0.5 mCi. The maximum concentration profiles from 3D and 4D simulated exams: where the blurring or smearing effect induced by respiratory motion are represented in the right.

From the visual inspection of the static image, in Fig. 6, the lesion is clearly shown, keeping its spherical shape. However, for the dynamic image, in the same Figure, the lesion appears blurred and elongated as a consequence of the breathing movement. Consequently, respiratory motion may preclude the accurate detection of small lung lesions.

The motion vector defined in section 2.3 (Equation (1)) indicates more motion blurring within the transaxial plane than along axial (z) direction. Fig. 8 shows the difference of blurring along different directions. This result also indicates, due to respiratory motion, that a sphere lesion can be blurred to a shape with different size in different directions in 3D space. Additionally, the extent of blurring along different directions will depend on the motion vector at the position in the lung.

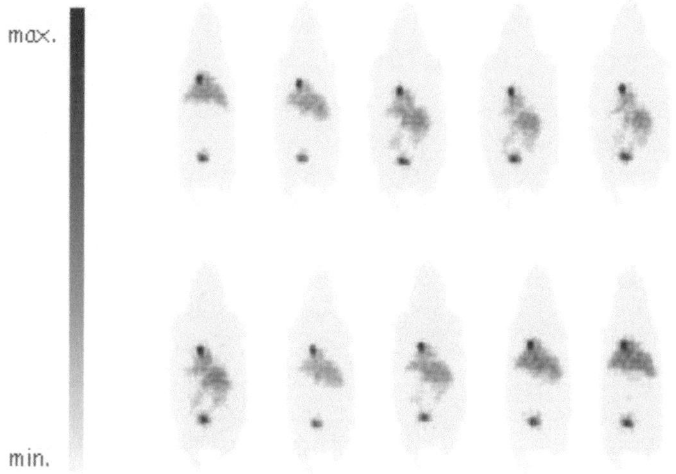

Fig. 7. Coronal slices of the MOBY phantom corresponding to the simulation of a "stress" condition breathing motion including a lung motion lesion of 1.5 mm diameter and an FDG uptake of 1.35 mCi. These coronal slices represent one respiratory cycle for an FDG exam in the last time frame. The dynamic 3D emission assumed an event collection during 900 s, where 5.65×10^9 particles were generated.

Fig. 8. Transaxial, coronal and sagital slices of the reconstructed lung lesion, in the MOBY phantom, with 2.0 mm diameter and an FDG uptake of 0.8 mCi. No motion was simulated.

The image spatial resolution was parameterized by the FWHM of Gaussian fits of the profiles taken over all lesions in the reconstructed images of the MOBY phantom. The results obtained for the static acquisitions are illustrated in Fig. 9. Spatial resolution improves most significantly for the smallest lesion diameter and at the same time for higher activity uptakes.

Fig. 10 shows the axial resolution of the lesion with 1.0 mm diameter for static and dynamic acquisitions, as a function of different FDG uptakes. It demonstrates that the blurring effect is lower for static acquisitions. It also demonstrates that when the FDG uptake increases the blurring decreases for dynamic and static acquisitions and consequently improves spatial resolution.

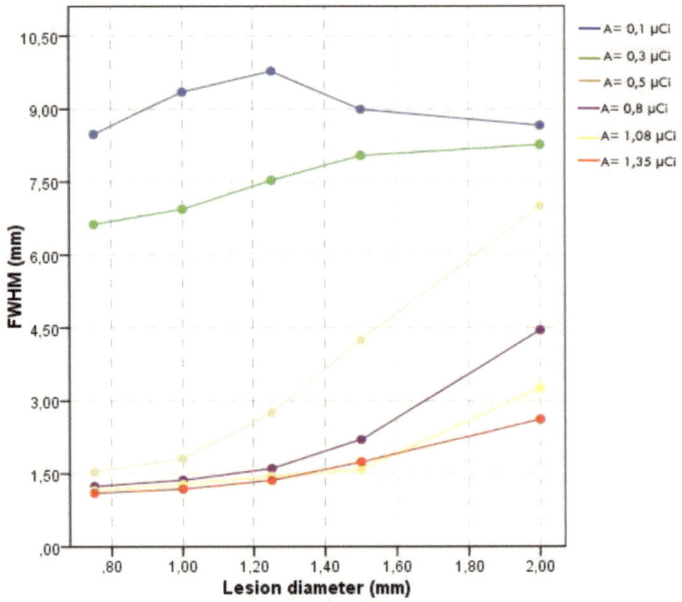

Fig. 9. FWHM of the line spread function through the lesion centroid as a function of the lesion diameter defined for the static acquisitions schemes.

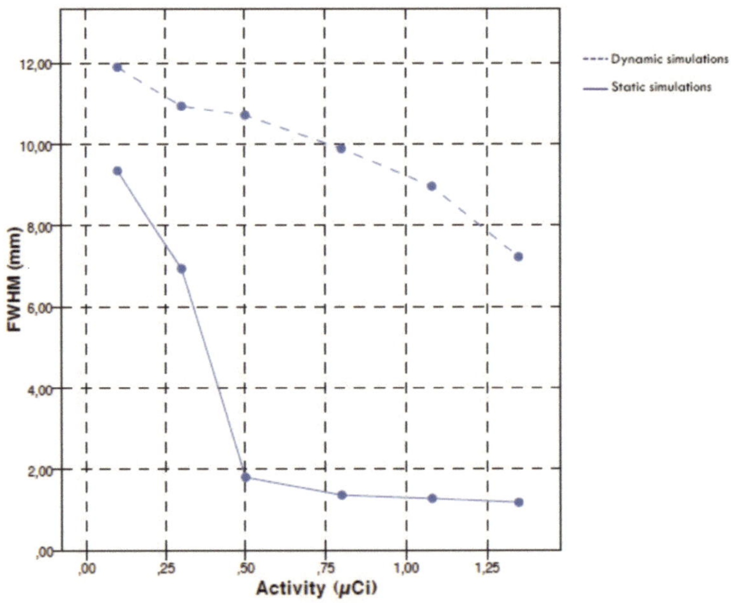

Fig. 10. FWHM of the line spread function through the lesion centroid as a function of the FDG activity defined for static and dynamic acquisitions schemes, for the 1.0 mm diameter lesion. Data from dynamic acquisitions are represented by dashed curves and static acquisition data are represented by solid curves.

3.3 Lesion detectability

Signal-to-noise (SNR) ratios are indicators of the visual utility of an image for detection purposes. The SNR directly affects diagnostic and quantitative accuracy (Sain & Barrett, 2003). The SNR describes the relative "strength" between the desired information and the noise in the image. The higher the SNR, the less obtrusive the noise is. The value SNR = 5 is the conventional value of detectability used in radiology, and as also been used in emission tomography images. Lesions for which $T - B > 5\sigma_T$ can be considered 100% visible (Cherry et al., 2003; Graham & Links, 2007). SNR values for the lower lesion activity concentration are in the vast majority of situations higher than the 100% detectability limit.

Fig. 11 show that the SNR depends strongly both on the lesion diameter and on the activity concentration. Nevertheless, the plots presented show that, for the highest activity values, most of the lesions converge to SNR values that are below the line of 100% visibility. In the case of higher activity concentrations, the smallest lesion diameter tend to converge to SNR values close to the 100% detectability line against SNR values that are significantly below that value for highest lesion diameter. However, according to the reconstructed images, the lesions with the considered diameters for all activity concentration ratios are all observable by visual inspection (some difficulties appear for the smallest lesions with lower activity concentrations, and the largest due to the lesion blending in the surrounding organs). This seems to indicate that the SNR = 5 criterion, from conventional radiology, might not be a good detectability criterion for emission tomography images. Keeping this in mind, we will, nevertheless, use this criterion as a reference for the quality of the images with respect to its SNR ratio.

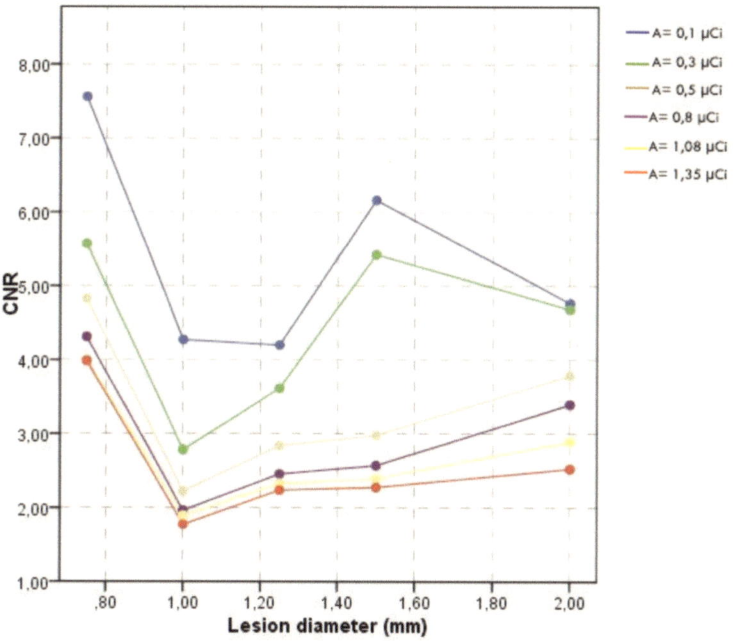

Fig. 11. SNR of the 0.1 mCi, 0.3 mCi, 0.5 mCi, 0.8 mCi, 1.08 mCi and 1.35 mCi FDG uptakes for the spherical lesions as a function of the lesion diameter. Results obtained for the static simulations.

Despite of the increase in the mean signal recovery, as a function of the FDG concentration increase, the standard deviation had also a significant increase. This result in a decrease of the SNR recovers values. We get the same behavior for the CNR values as a function of the activity concentration. These results can also be explained through the results obtained for the spatial resolution versus the motion blurring.

In respect to the CNR, when the size of a lesion is substantially larger than the limiting spatial resolution it can influence the detection ability, especially if the lesion has low contrast. The CNR is displayed in Fig. 12 as a function of the lesion diameter, and for different activity uptakes. Overall, CNR improves significantly as lesion contrast decreases and lesion size increases.

We need to have into account the same line of the results inspection: caused by the small size of lesions relative to scanner resolution (partial-volume effect) we got higher CNR values for the smallest lesion.

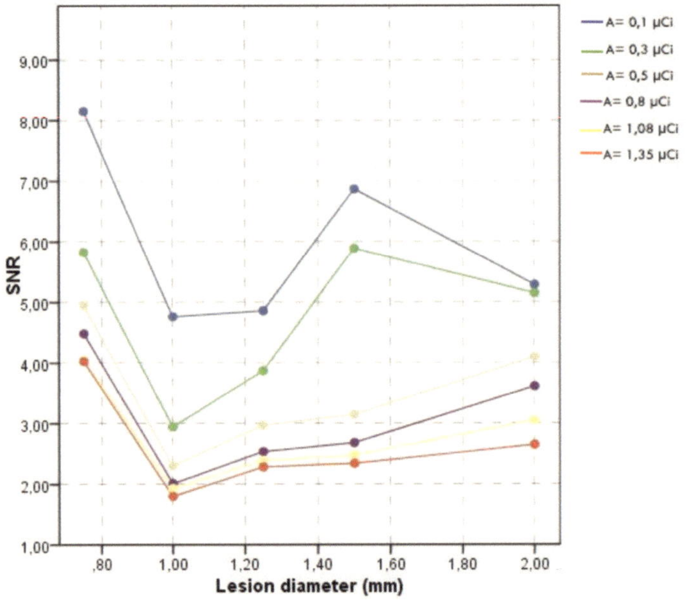

Fig. 12. CNR of the 0.1 mCi, 0.3 mCi, 0.5 mCi, 0.8 mCi, 1.08 mCi and 1.35 mCi FDG uptakes for the spherical lesions as a function of the lesion diameter. Results obtained for the static simulations.

Table 2 summarizes SNR and CNR values in the lesion with 1.0 mm diameter as a function of the FDG activity concentration. The first columns show the CNR and the SNR from the non-gated images of the phantom in a static mode. The other results correspond to data obtained from the gated images of the phantom in the dynamic mode. The dynamic simulations results in larger overestimations of SNR due to poor counting statistics and high image noise. This effect is more significant as the lesion activity concentration decreases, as it is shown in Table 2. However, the same table shows a slight improvement in CNR recovery for the dynamic acquisitions as the lesion activity increases. Respiratory motion has less of an effect on the peak lesion signal and thus could explain the improvement on the dynamic CNR results.

We expected improvements on the SNR and the CNR data as a function of the increase of the FDG activity (higher activities always provide better SNR and CNR). This is due to the fact that we defined the lesion motion as a function of the no normal tidal breathing and thus with a largest magnitude of motion. Because there is a higher motion in this condition then it is expected that we will get an improved signal recovery for the lower contrast lesions. As discussed before, the values obtained for the other dynamic acquisitions sets are quantitatively changed due to the lesion blending into the liver (in the case of the largest diameter lesions) and are not used in the comparative set. We decided to remove the comparative set for the smallest lesion because the statistical results may be compromise by the limited spatial resolution of the microPET® FOCUS 220.

	Static Simulations		Dynamic Simulations	
Activity (µCi)	CNR	SNR	CNR	SNR
0.1	4.274	4.764	0.213	8.465
0.3	2.785	2.948	2.405	10.975
0.5	2.225	2.303	2.407	8.419
0.8	1.966	2.014	2.920	6.880
1.08	1.897	1.933	2.823	5.117
1.35	1.766	1.803	2.968	4.829

Table 2. SNR and CNR values in the lesion with 1.0 mm diameter as a function of the FDG activity concentration. The first columns show the CNR and the SNR from the images of the phantom in a static mode. The other results correspond to data obtained from the images of the phantom in the dynamic mode.

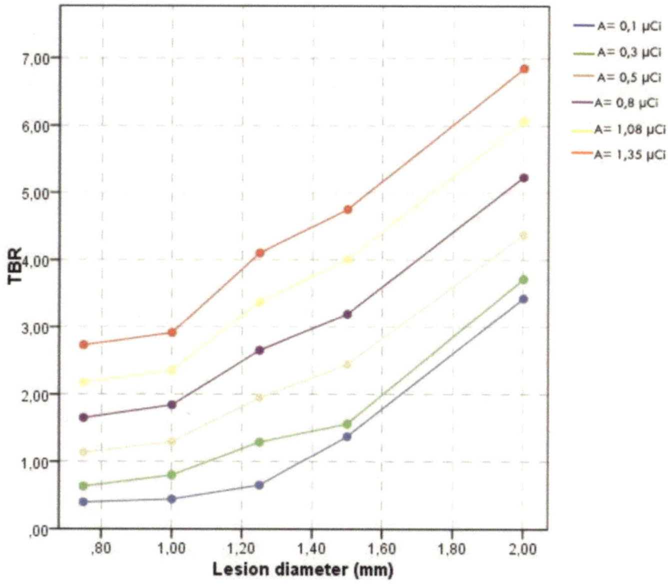

Fig. 13. TBR of the 0.1 mCi, 0.3 mCi, 0.5 mCi, 0.8 mCi, 1.08 mCi and 1.35 mCi FDG uptakes for the spherical lesions as a function of the lesion diameter. Results obtained for the static simulations.

Fig. 13 illustrates the relationship between contrast and activity concentration, TBR, as a function of the lesion diameter. The higher the contrast the higher is the detectability. Fig. 14 shows the TBR plot for a set of dynamic and static acquisitions as a function of the FDG activity concentration, for the lesion diameter of 1.0 mm. The curves show that the TBR increases as the activity concentration increases. Moreover, and as expected, the figure also illustrates that we achieved lower TBR values for the images of the moving lesions.

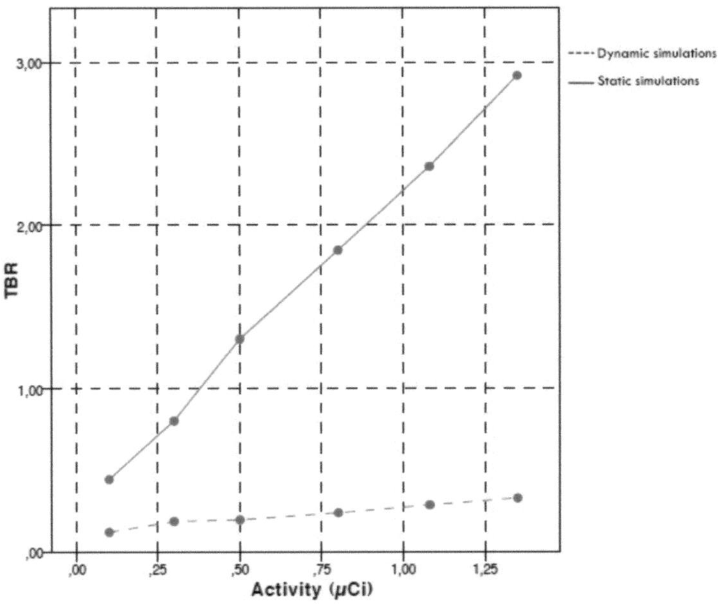

Fig. 14. TBR of a set of a dynamic and a static acquisition as a function of the FDG activity concentration for the 1.0 mm diameter lesion. Data from dynamic acquisitions are represented with the dashed curve and static acquisition data are represented by the solid curve.

3.4 Evaluation of the contrast and volume recovery coefficient

The Fig. 15 shows the trends of the contrasts, in the static acquisition simulations, against lesion diameter, for all the lesion activity uptakes considered. As it can be seen in these plots, the contrast values obtained in these studies are always high, even for the smallest lesion diameter. These plots highlight the fact that the contrast depends more strongly on the lesion diameter than it depends on the lesion to background considered. In fact, for a given diameter, the contrast is approximately the same for all the different activity uptakes. The strong dependence on lesion diameter illustrates a significant partial volume effect.

Fig. 16 illustrates the contrast of a set of dynamic and static acquisitions as a function of the FDG activity concentration for the 1.0 mm diameter lesion. We found higher contrast values from the dynamic data against the static data. We expected that the motion decrease the contrast in the reconstructed images, while images from static acquisitions can largely recover the signal lost due to motion. These results are influenced from the ROIs defined in the background level. However, the mean signal recover is higher in static data when compared to the dynamic data. These results suggest that the ROIs approach for the background level used probably was not the best choice (despite of the approach used in pre-clinical practice).

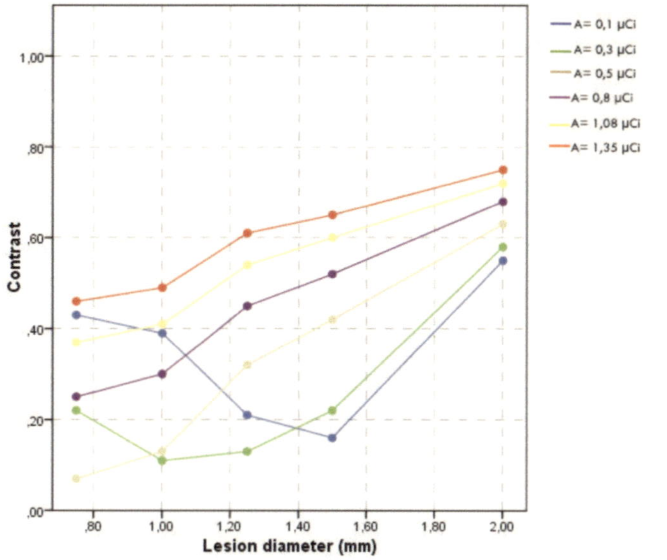

Fig. 15. Contrast of the 0.1 mCi, 0.3 mCi, 0.5 mCi, 0.8 mCi, 1.08 mCi and 1.35 mCi FDG uptakes for the spherical lesions as a function of the lesion diameter. Results obtained for the static simulations.

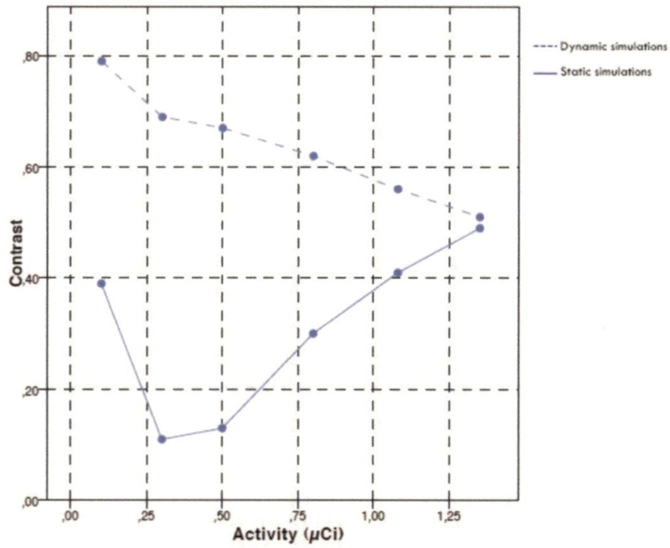

Fig. 16. Contrast of a set of dynamic and static acquisitions as a function of the FDG activity concentration for the 1.0 mm diameter lesion. Data from dynamic acquisitions are represented by the dashed curve and static acquisition data are represented by the solid curve.

Table 3 summarizes the VRC as a function of the lesion diameter, for static and dynamic acquisitions. As expected, with dynamic acquisitions the volumes of sphere were overestimated due to the smearing effect resulting from motion. For static acquisitions the VRC values are close to 1.0, which means that values were correctly recovered. The table also shows the mean percent errors in volume estimates measured on the simulated lesions as a function of the real lesion volume.

Lesion diameter (mm)	Static Simulations		Dynamic Simulations	
	VRC	% error	VRC	% error
0.75	1.629	61.30	3.259	225.88
1.0	1.120	12.02	2.930	192.98
1.25	1.098	9.83	N/A	N/A
1.5	0.987	1.27	N/A	N/A
2.0	0.995	0.54	N/A	N/A

Table 3. VRC in the static and dynamic acquisitions as a function of the lesion diameter. The mean percent errors in volume estimates measured on simulated lesions as a function of the real lesion volume are also shown.

(Note: N/A - "not available" - is this context means that the VRC value was not possible to measure due to the blurring and to the smearing effect resulting from the respiratory motion.)

4. Conclusions and perspectives

The FWHMs of reconstructed lesion images were determined alongside with the direction of movement due to respiratory motion for static and dynamic acquisitions. The results demonstrate how the respiratory motion would affect the blurring of a lung lesion along the direction of movement.

As expected, contrast-to-noise ratio (CNR) recovery improves for static acquisitions. The static images have a slightly greater CNR recovery compared to the dynamic images, which is due to the loss of resolution in the motion images. CNR recovery also improves as lesion size increases and lesion contrast decreases.

The results illustrates that the signal-to-noise ratio (SNR) deteriorate for motion data. Results for higher diameter lesions in the lung were influenced by lesion blending into the liver. However, results for the 1.0 mm lesion shown better SNR data induced by the respiratory motion. Concerning the static acquisitions we found better SNR for lower FDG uptakes and higher lesion sizes. The contrast depends more strongly on the lesion diameter than it depends on the lesion to background considered. Better temporal resolution (volume recover) was found in the non-gated data.

As discussed before, respiratory motion leads to reduced contrast and quantitative accuracy in terms of recovered contrast activity concentration and functional volumes. Several methodologies proposed for reducing the effects of respiratory motion have been based on the development of respiratory-gated acquisitions (Visvikis et al., 2006; Nehmeh et al., 2002; Dawood et al., 2006; Detorie & Dahlbom, 2006; Lamare et al., 2007a; Dawood et al., 2008; Bettinardi, 2009; Lamare et al., 2007b; Detorie & Dahlbom, 2008). However, in general, 4D PET images have low counting statistics and high image noise compared to static 3D PET images. Since the same number of coincidence events in 3D PET is divided into many different respiratory phase bins or time frames, the number of coincidence events per image bin is considerably reduced. This leads to higher image noise in 4D PET images, resulting in an even lower SNR of the reconstruction. Therefore, there is a trade-off between image noise and temporal resolution. Long duration time per frame gives low noise but blurred images resulting from the loss of temporal resolution (Park et al., 2008; Zhu et al., 2002). In order to determine the effect of the number of gating bins on image noise and temporal resolution, sets of 4D simulations will be performed for the MOBY phantom following the same line of reasoning of these studies.

Some other limitations of our research are related to the phantom's anatomy and breathing cycle. In future studies different phantoms anatomy can improve our quantitative evaluation. In our work, we produced a stress breathing condition on the respiratory motion cycle of the phantom, whereas variations in respiratory cycle from an animal to another and in time may also influence the observed effects. Moreover, variations in the amplitude of the diaphragm motion also influence the results. A reference to a real examination can be helpful to compare the results obtained. Therefore, there is still the need for a method that takes into account the effect of respiratory motion without, at the same time, affecting the quantification analysis on the reconstructed images. For that reason, this work is being complemented by accessing the impact of such motion in the quantification analysis using a dynamic VOI, placed around the centroid of each lesion, in 4D imaging studies.

This research contributes to evaluating the respiratory motion effect in the quantification of microPET images. A complete evaluation should also consider real dynamic FDG examinations that need to be compared against the results presented in this thesis. Moreover, the production of realistic images, where attenuation information (using the phantoms attenuation maps to set the different body structures and the correspondent attenuation information) and physical effects (using the isotope decay instead a gamma/gamma emission source) are included, was not done. Although this was not among the main goals of this work, its inclusion would allow evaluating the consequence of these physical effects on image sensitivity and quantification. Since the physical effects are not taken into account, further investigation is needed to accurately evaluate these effects on image quantification.

We have used the OSEM algorithm for image reconstruction with fixed parameters (16 subsets and 4 iterations). These parameters are normally used in pre-clinical standard protocols. However, there are several other image reconstruction algorithms and parameters including smoothing filters and the number of subsets and iterations that could affect the results (namely, lesion quantification may be inaccurate depending on the reconstruction algorithms used), but have not been addressed in this study. Further studies are required to investigate the effect of these parameters on signal and volume recovery.

In this research we have always used the same breathing condition to simulate respiratory motion.

However, image quantification is influenced by the amplitude and pattern of respiratory motion. This suggests that it may be beneficial to simulate different breathing motion conditions to obtain a reasonable estimate on image quantification under clinical conditions.

Background activity is unavoidable and it causes significant noise and contrast loss in PET images (Tai & Laforest, 2005). The effect of background activity concentration will be analyzed in the next phases of this research.

5. References

Andreo, P. (1991). Monte carlo techniques in medical radiation physics. Physics in Medicine and Biology, Vol. 36, No. 7, pp. (861–920).

Andreo, P., & Ljungberg, M. (1998). *Monte Carlo Calculations in Nuclear Medicine: Applications in Diagnostic Imaging*. Institute of Physics Publishing. Chap. General Monte Carlo Codes for use in Medical Radiation Physics, pp. (37–52).

Bettinardi, V. (2009). Number of partitions (gates) needed to obtain motion-free images in a respiratory gated 4D-PET/CT study as a function of the lesion size and motion displacement. *Medical Physics*, Vol. 36, No. 12, pp. (5547–5558).

Buvat, I., & Castiglioni, I. (2002). Monte Carlo simulations in SPECT and PET. *The Quarterly Journal of Nuclear Medicine*, Vol. 46, No. 1, pp. (48–61).

Buvat, I., Castiglioni, I., Feuardent, J. & Gilardi, M.-C. (2005). Unified description and validation of Monte Carlo simulators in PET. *Physics in Medicine and Biology*, Vol. 50, pp. (329–346).

Buvat, I., & Lazaro, D. (2006). Monte Carlo Simulations in Emission Tomography and GATE: an overview. *Nuclear Instruments and Methods in Physics Research A*, Vol. 569, pp. (323–329).

Chatziioannou, A. F. (2002). PET scanners dedicated to molecular imaging of small animal models. *Molecular Imaging and Biology*, Vol. 4, No. 1, pp. (47–63).

Cherry, S. R. (2004). In vivo molecular and genomic imaging: new challenges for imaging physics. *Physics in Medicine and Biology*, Vol. 49, pp. (R13–R48).

Cherry, S. R., & Gambhir, S. S. (2001). Use of positron emission tomography in animal research. *Institute for Laboratory Animal Research*, Vol. 42, No. 3, pp. (219–232).

Cherry, S. R., Sorenson, J. A., & Phelps, M. E. (2003). *Physics in Nuclear Medicine*. Saunders. Chap. Image Quality in Nuclear Medicine, pp. (253–272).

Couturier, O. (2004). Fluorinated tracers for imaging cancer with positron emission tomography. *European Journal of Nuclear Medicine and Molecular Imaging*, Vol. 31, No. 8, pp. (1182–1206).

Dawood, M., Lang, N., Jiang, X. & Schafers, K. P. (2006). Lung motion correction on respiratory gated 3D PET/CT images. *IEEE Transactions of Medical Imaging*, Vol. 25, No. 4, pp. (476–485).

Dawood, M., Buther, F., Jiang, X. & Schafers, K. P. (2008). Respiratory motion correction in 3D PET data with advanced optical flow algorithms. *IEEE Transactions on Medical Imaging*, Vol. 27, No. 8, pp. (1164–1175).

Detorie, N., & Dahlbom, M. (2006). Motion correction for respiratory gated PET images. *IEEE Nuclear Science Symposium Conference Record*, pp. (3273–3277).

Detorie, N. C., & Dahlbom, M. (2008). Quantitative evaluation of reconstruction algorithms for motion compensated PET. *Nuclear Science Symposium Conference Record*, pp. (5366–5372).

GATE. 2010. http://www.opengatecollaboration.org.

Graham, L. S., & Links, J. M. (2007). *Nuclear medicine and PET/CT: Technology and Techniques*. Mosby Elsevier. Chap. Instrumentation, pp. (59–104).

Jan, S., et al. (2004a). GATE: a simulation toolkit for PET and SPECT. *Physics in Medicine and Biology*, Vol. 49, No. 19, pp. (4543-4561).

Jan, S., Boisgard, R., Fontyn, Y., Eroukhmanoff, C., Comtat, C., & Trebossen, R. (2004b). Accuracy and variability of quantitative values obtained for mouse imaging using the microPET Focus. *Nuclear Science Symposium Conference Record*, Vol. 5, pp. (2934–2937).

Jan, S., Desbree, A., Pain, F., Guez, D., Comtat, C., Gurden, H., Kerhoas, S., Laniece, P., Lefebvre, F., Mastrippolito, R., & Trebossen, R. (2005). Monte Carlo simulation of the microPET Focus system for small rodents imaging applications. *IEEE Nuclear Science Symposium Conference Record*, Vol. 3, pp. (1653–1657).

Lamare, F., Carbayo, M. J. Ledesma, Cresson, T., Kontaxakis, G., Santos, A., Rest, C. Cheze Le, Reader, A. J., & Visvikis, D. (2007a). List-mode-based reconstruction for respiratory motion correction in pet using nonrigid body transformations. *Physics in Medicine and Biology*, Vol. 52, pp. (5187–5204).

Lamare, F., Cresson, T., Savean, J., Rest, C. Cheze Le, Reader, A. J., & Visvikis, D. (2007b). Respiratory motion correction for pet oncology applications using affine transformation of list mode data. *Physics in Medicine and Biology*, Vol. 52, pp. (121–140).

Larson, S. M., & Schwartz, L. H. (2006). ^{18}F-FDG PET as a candidate for qualified biomarker: Functional assessment of treatment response in oncology. *The Journal of Nuclear Medicine*, Vol. 47, No. 6, pp. (901–903).

Lartizien, C., et al. (2004). A Lesion Detection Observer Study Comparing 2-Dimensional Versus Fully 3-Dimensional Whole-Body PET Imaging Protocols. *Journal of Nuclear Medicine*, Vol. 45, pp. (714-723).

Ljungberg, M. (1998). *Monte Carlo Calculations in Nuclear Medicine: Applications in Diagnostic Imaging*. Institute of Physics Publishing. Chap. Introduction to the Monte Carlo Method, pp. (1–12).

Ljungberg, M. (2004). *Emission tomography: The fundaments of PET and SPECT*. Elsevier. Chap. Simulation Techniques and Phantoms, pp. (551–563).

Nehmeh, S. A., Erdi, Y. E., Ling, C. C., Rosenzweig, K. E., Schoder, H., Larson, S. M., Macapinlac, H. A., Squire, O. D. & Humm, J. L. (2002). Effect of respiratory gating on quantifying PET images of lung cancer. *Journal of Nuclear Medicine*, Vol. 43, No. 7, pp. (876–881).

Park, S.-J., Ionascu, D., Killoran, J., Mamede, M., Gerbaudo, V. H., Chin, L. & Berbeco, R. (2008). Evaluation of the combined effects of target size, respiratory motion and background activity on 3D and 4D PET/CT images. *Physics in Medicine and Biology*, Vol. 53, pp. (3661-3679).

Peter, J., Tornai, M. P., & Jaszczek, R. J. (2000). Analytical versus voxelized phantom representation for Monte Carlo simulation in radiological imaging. *IEEE Transactions on Medical Imaging*, Vol. 19, pp. (556–564).

Poston, J. W., Bolch, W., & Bouchet, L. (2002). *Therapeutic Applications of Monte Carlo Calculations in Nuclear Medicine*. Institute of Physics Publishing. Chap. Mathematical models of the human anatomy, pp. (108–132).

Riemann, B., Schafers, K. P., Schober, O., & Schafers, M. (2008). Small animal PET in preclinical studies: opportunities and challenges. *Quarterly Journal of Nuclear Medicine and Molecular Imaging*, Vol. 52, No. 3, pp. (215–221).

Rogers, D. W. O. (2006). Fifty years of Monte Carlo simulations for medical physics. *Physics in Medicine and Biology*, Vol. 51, pp. (R287–R301).

Rowland, D. J., & R., S. R. Cherry S. (2008). Small-animal preclinical nuclear medicine instrumentation and methodology. *Seminars in Nuclear Medicine*, Vol. 38, No. 3, pp. (209–222).

Sain, J. D., & Barrett, H. H. (2003). Performance evaluation of a modular gamma camera using a detectability index. *The Journal of Nuclear Medicine*, Vol. 44, No. 1, pp. (58–66).

Sang-June, P., et al. (2008). Evaluation of the combined effects of target size, respiratory motion and background activity on 3D and 4D PET/CT images. *Physics in Medicine and Biology*, Vol. 53, pp. (3661-3679).

Segars, W. P., et al. (2004). Development of a 4-D Digital Mouse Phantom for Molecular Imaging Research. *Molecular Imaging and Biology*, Vol. 6, No. 3, pp. (149-159).

Tai, Y.-C., & Laforest, R. (2005). Instrumentation aspects of animal pet. *Annual Review of Biomedical Engineering*, Vol. 7, pp. (255–285).

Tai, Y., et al. (2005). Performance Evaluation of the microPET FOCUS: A Third-Generation microPET Scanner Dedicated to Animal Imaging. *Journal of Nuclear Medicine*, Vol. 46, pp. (455-463).

Visvikis, D., Lamare, F., Bruyant, P., Boussion, N., & Le Rest, C. C. (2006). Respiratory motion in positron emission tomography for oncology applications: Problems and solutions. *Nuclear Instruments and Methods in Physics Research A*, Vol. 569, pp. (453–457).

Zaidi, H. (1999). Relevance of accurate Monte Carlo modeling in nuclear medical imaging. *Medical Physics*, Vol. 26, No. 4, pp. (574–608).

Zaidi, H. (2006). *Quantitative analysis in Nuclear Medicine Imaging*. Springer Publishing. Chap. Monte Carlo Modeling in Nuclear Medicine Imaging, pp. (358–390).

Zaidi, H., & Sgouros, G. (2002). *Therapeutic Applications of Monte Carlo Calculations in Nuclear Medicine*. Institute of Physics Publishing.

Zubal, I. G. (1998). *Monte Carlo Calculations in Nuclear Medicine: Applications in Diagnostic Imaging*. Institute of Physics Publishing. Chap. Anthropomorphic Phantoms, pp. 25–36.

Zaidi, H., & Tsui, B. M. W. (2009). Review of computational anthropomorphic anatomical and physiological models. *Proceedings of the IEEE*, Vol. 97, No. 12, pp. (1938–1953).

Zaidi, H., & Xu, X. G. (2007). Computational anthropomorphic models of the human anatomy: The path to realistic Monte Carlo modeling in radiological sciences. *Annual Review of Biomedical Engineering*, Vol. 9, pp. (471–500).

Zhu, Zhiyu, Tsui, B. M.W., & Segars, W. P. (2002). A simulation study of the effect of gating scheme on respiratory motion blurring in FDG lung PET. *IEEE Nuclear Science Symposium Conference Record*, pp. (1554–1558).

12

Fiber-optic Raman Probe Coupled with a Ball Lens for Improving Depth-resolved Raman Measurements of Epithelial Tissue: Monte Carlo Simulations

Zhiwei Huang
Optical Bioimaging Laboratory, Department of Bioengineering, Faculty of Engineering, National University of Singapore, Singapore

1. Introduction

Raman spectroscopy is a vibrational spectroscopic technique capable of optically probing biomolecular changes of tissue associated with neoplastic transformation, and has shown promise for the noninvasive, *in vivo* diagnosis and detection of epithelial precancer and cancer in various organs [1-3]. But analyzing Raman spectroscopic information emitted from tissue remains complicated for tissue diagnosis and characterization due to the reasons that the overall Raman signals acquired from the tissue surface usually contain a mixture of Raman information originating from different tissue depths [4, 5], while the changes of tissue morphology or biochemical constituents associated with disease transformation may be depth-dependent in biomedical systems [6]. For instance, the epithelial tissue usually consists of a superficial epithelium and an underlying stroma, the dysplasia-related changes (precancer) may be associated with the thickening of epithelial tissue, which results in the attenuation of the excitation light to penetrate into deeper areas of tissue and also the attenuation of Raman emission from deeper tissue regions (e.g., stroma) [7, 8]. On the other hand, the changes of other optical properties (e.g., absorption coefficient, scattering coefficient, anisotropic factor, refractive index) of tissue are also correlated with tissue physiologic/pathologic status, significantly affecting the overall Raman signal collection from biomedical tissue [9]. Hence, to better understand the origins of Raman signals collected from tissue surface for further improving the diagnosis of epithelial precancer or early cancer, it is highly desirable to develop a depth-resolved Raman spectroscopic technique for facilitating the wide applications of Raman spectroscopy in biomedical diagnosis.

A number of fiber-optic probe designs have been reported for depth-resolved optical spectroscopic measurements, but most work are centered on fluorescence and reflectance spectroscopy for tissue diagnosis [10-15]. The depth-resolved fiber probe designs can mainly be classified into two types: (i) single-fiber probe in which the same fiber is used for both light excitation and reflectance/fluorescence/Raman collection, and (ii) multiple-fiber probe in which separate fibers are used for light delivery and reflectance/fluorescence/Raman collection [8-12]. Although the single-fiber probe with a smaller aperture (i.e., core diameter) shows a high sensitivity of detecting spectral signal particularly emitted from superficial layer of epithelial tissue, its collection efficiency is much reduced when the fiber diameter decreases. With multiple-fiber probe designs, varying the excitation-collection fiber separations or the oblique angles between the excitation-collection fibers permit the depth-discrimination of fluorescence/Raman signals from tissue [11, 12]. Although the multi-fibers probe design has shown a better depth-selectivity for spectroscopic acquisitions, the bulky probe design is unsuited for endoscope-based biomedical applications. In this work, we propose a fiber-optic Raman probe design coupled with a ball lens for improving the collection efficiency of depth-resolved Raman measurements, particularly for probing subsurface regions of epithelial tissue. The use of ball lens as the illumination and collection optics of spectroscopic probes has proven to be efficient for epithelial tissue measurement [16]. Moreover, ball-lens probe shows advantages of compactness and short working distance which are in favor of *in vivo* tissue measurement. In this study, we employ the Monte Carlo (MC) simulation method to evaluate the performance of the ball-lens Raman probe designs under different optical configurations. Raman experiments of a ball lens Raman probe design on a layered tissue phantom are also tested.

2. Materials and methods

2.1 Raman probe configuration

Fig. 1 shows the schematic of a fiber-optic Raman probe design coupled with a ball lens for depth-resolved tissue Raman measurements [8]. The laser light can be coupled into the excitation arm of the Raman probe through a single fiber (200 μm, NA=0.22), and delivered

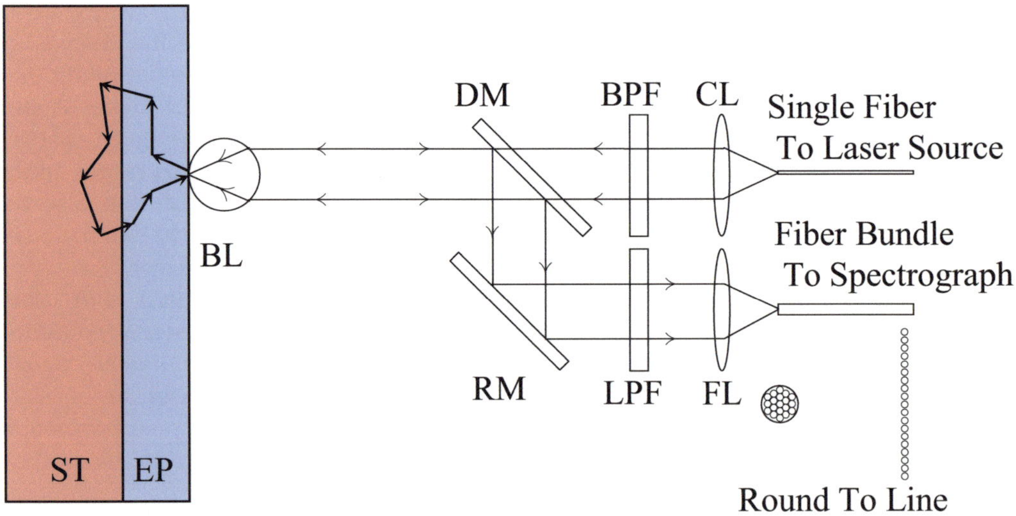

Fig. 1. Schematic of the Raman probe design and two-layer epithelial tissue model for Monte Carlo (MC) simulations. CL: collimating Lens; FL: Focusing Lens; BPF: Band Pass Filter; LPF: Long Pass Filter; DM: Dichroic Mirror; RM: Reflection Mirror; BL: Ball Lens; EP: Epithelium; ST: Stroma.

into the filtering module incorporated with a near-infrared (NIR) lens for collimating excitation light and a narrow band-pass (BP) filter for removing fiber fluorescence and laser noise. Then, the laser light is focused onto the tissue through a ball lens mounted on the tip of the Raman probe. The backscattered light is collected by the same ball lens and subsequently reflected back into the collection arm of the Raman probe through a dichroic mirror and a reflection mirror. The scattered light can be further filtered by an edge long-pass (LP) filter to block the Rayleigh scattered laser light while allowing Raman scattered light photons to get into the collection fiber bundles (28×50 μm arranged in line, NA=0.22) for tissue Raman signals detection [3].

2.2 Monte Carlo simulations

Monte Carlo simulations have been widely used to mimic light propagation in turbid media (e.g., biological tissue) [14, 15, 17], and also simulate the fluorescence generation and propagation in biological tissue [14, 15, 17-19]. With the development of MC simulation model to evaluate the fiber probe design coupled with a ball lens for depth-resolved fluorescence measurement on layered epithelial tissue [14, 15], we further modified the MC model to study Raman light generation and propagation in epithelial tissue as well as Raman signal collection with the use of ball lens fiber-optic Raman probe. The modified MC codes include the following modules: (i) excitation light propagation in ball lens and tissue; (ii) Raman photons generation and propagation in tissue; (iii) Raman photons collection by the ball lens and propagation in the ball lens; (iv) Raman photons collection by the focusing lens and subsequently by the collection fibers of the Raman probe.

In MC simulations, one hundred million excitation light photons are launched into the tissue through the ball lens. The photons are initialized as a uniform light beam with a beam diameter the same as the ball lens' diameter. When the excitation light photons are incident into the ball lens or the Raman photons pass through the ball lens, the direction of the refracted light is calculated using Snell's law. The photon weight is then updated as $w \leftarrow w(1-R)$, whereby the reflection coefficient, R, is calculated using Fresnel's formula:

$$R = \frac{1}{2}\left[\frac{\sin^2(\alpha_i - \alpha_t)}{\sin^2(\alpha_i + \alpha_t)} + \frac{\tan^2(\alpha_i - \alpha_t)}{\tan^2(\alpha_i + \alpha_t)}\right] \quad (1)$$

where α_i and α_t are the incident angle and the refracted angle, respectively. In this simulation, Raman generation is estimated with the probability (p) of the illumination light to be converted to Raman scattered light as follows [20,21]:

$$p = \left(\frac{\mu_s}{\mu_a + \mu_s}\right) \times QY \quad (2)$$

where μ_a is the absorption coefficient for generating Raman photons, μ_s is the scattering coefficient, and QY (<<1) is the Raman quantum yield. To determine the Raman photon generation at a particular scattering position, a random number between 0 and 1 is generated; if the probability yielded in Eq. (2) is larger than the random number, then Raman photon is produced; otherwise, no Raman photon is generated. In our MC programs, we presume that the radiation angle of Raman photons emitted from the Raman scatterers is isotropic [20] and the emitted Raman photons will not be reabsorbed by the Raman scatterers for generating secondary emission of Raman photons due to their extremely low intensity levels. The deflection angle (β) of each scattering in the medium is described by Henyey-Greenstein phase function as the following equation [17, 22]:

$$\cos\beta = \begin{cases} \dfrac{1}{2g}\left\{1+g^2-\left[\dfrac{1-g^2}{1-g+2g\xi}\right]^2\right\} & if \quad g>0 \\ 2\xi-1 & if \quad g=0 \end{cases} \tag{3}$$

where g is anisotropy factor and ξ is a random number between 0 and 1. The azimuthal angle ψ can be determined by 2πξ.

After escaping from tissue surface, Raman photons are collected by the ball lens within the collection cone angle [23]:

$$\theta = \sin^{-1}\left(\frac{2(n_b-1)}{n_b n_t}\right) \tag{4}$$

where θ is half-angle of the collection cone of the ball lens; n_b and n_t are the refractive indices of the ball lens and tissue, respectively. Tissue Raman photons which pass through the ball lens will be coupled into the collection fibers by a focusing lens (focal length, f=12 mm) of the Raman probe. Eventually, all those photons that reach the collection fibers within the collection cone angle of the collection fibers (NA=0.22) will be considered as the collected Raman photons by the Raman probe. The 2-D distributions of excitation light and the origins of the Raman photons collected from tissue will be given by MC simulations to evaluate the performance of the fiber-optic Raman probe design for depth-resolved tissue Raman measurements. In addition, the collection efficiency of the Raman probe defined as the ratio of the collected tissue Raman photon numbers to the incident excitation light photon numbers is also estimated by using MC simulations.

2.3 Two-layer epithelial tissue model

A two-layer tissue model which mimics the epithelial tissues is used for MC simulations of the excitation light and Raman photons propagation in tissue. Table 1 gives the optical properties (absorption coefficient, μ_a; scattering coefficient, μ_s; anisotropy factor, g; tissue refractive index, n_t, and tissue thickness, d) [24] of the modeled tissue. The wavelengths of excitation light and Raman scattered photon light are selected at 785 and 820 nm, respectively, for MC simulations [2, 3].

Tissue Layer	Wavelength (nm)	μ_a (cm^{-1})	μ_s (cm^{-1})	g	n_t	d (mm)
Epithelium	785 (excitation)	0.9	25	0.9	1.4	0.3
Stroma		0.45	165	0.9	1.4	3
Epithelium	820 (Raman)	0.8	24	0.9	1.4	0.3
Stroma		0.3	150	0.9	1.4	3

Table 1. Optical properties of the two-layer epithelial tissue model for MC simulations [14, 15, 24].

3. Simulation results and discussion

3.1 Effect of the refractive index of the ball lens on tissue Raman measurements

Fig. 2 shows the MC simulation results of the 785 nm excitation light distribution in epithelial tissue for the fiber-optic Raman probe designs with different refractive indices of the ball lens and a fixed diameter of 3 mm. Note that the indices selected for simulation correspond to different optical materials (1.46-UV fused silica; 1.51-Boro-crown glass; 1.63-Dense flint glass; 1.76-Sapphire; 1.83-Lanthanum flint glass). Overall, the excitation light exhibits higher intensity over the whole tissue when increasing the refractive index of the ball lens. A 1.1- to 1.5- fold increase in excitation intensity distribution in tissue is found for the use of ball lens at refractive indices of 1.51, 1.63, 1.76 and 1.83 as compared to the refractive index of 1.46. The corresponding excitation light distribution in the epithelium is approximately 1.1- to 2.7- fold stronger. This suggests that Raman probe with a larger refractive index of the ball lens achieves higher efficiency in focusing the excitation light photons into the tissue, especially in the epithelium layer of the tissue.

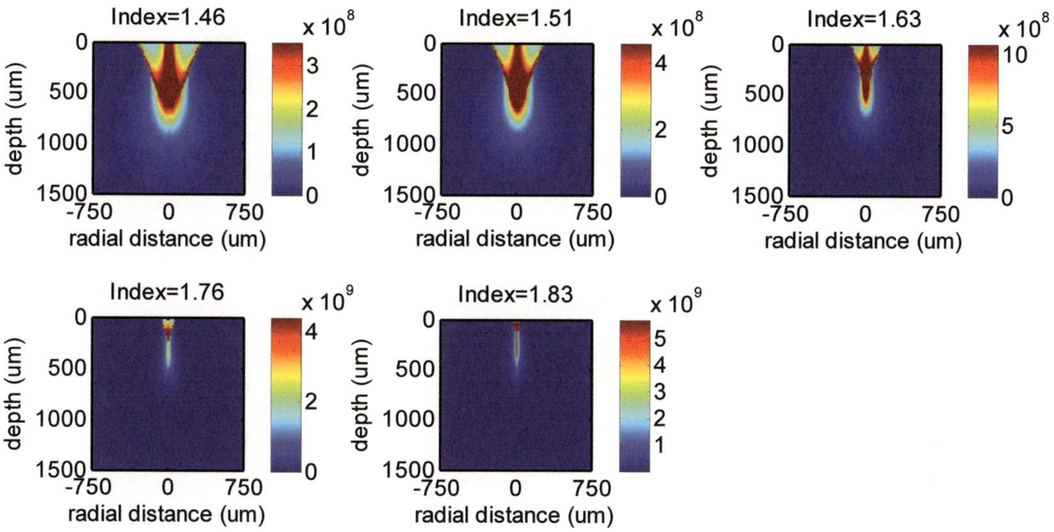

Fig. 2. The 785-nm excitation light distributions along the tissue depth and radial directions in tissue using the Raman probe designs with different refractive indices of the ball lenses (n= 1.46, 1.51, 1.63, 1.76 and 1.83).

Fig. 3 shows the 785-nm excitation light distributions along the tissue depth which are the sum of the excitation light distribution (Fig. 2) over the radial dimension at each tissue depth. Each depth profile is normalized to the integrated area under the profile for better comparison among different refractive indices of the ball lens in Raman probe. The excitation light undergoes a shorter penetration into tissue when increasing the refractive index of the ball lens. For instance, an intensity maximum of the excitation light in epithelium layer is observed around the focal plane of the ball lens when using the refractive index of 1.76 or 1.83 of the ball lens (Fig. 3). This suggests that increasing the refractive index of the ball lens of the Raman probe design makes the excitation light to be more tightly focused in the shallower regions of tissue (i.e., the epithelium). The findings above can be explained by the enhanced focusing ability of the ball lens attributed to the increase of refractive index. The ball lens focal length can be estimated using the following equations [23]:

$$BFL = EFL - \frac{D}{2}; \quad EFL = \frac{n_b D}{4(n_b - 1)} \tag{5}$$

where BFL is back focal length, representing the distance from the ball lens front tip to the focal point; EFL is effective focal length, representing the distance from the ball lens center to the focal point; D and n_b is the diameter and the refractive index of the ball lens, respectively. According to Eq. (5), if keeping diameter D constant, EFL and BFL are inversely proportional to refractive index n_b. That is why the ball lens with a larger refractive index leads to a shorter light penetration depth in tissue

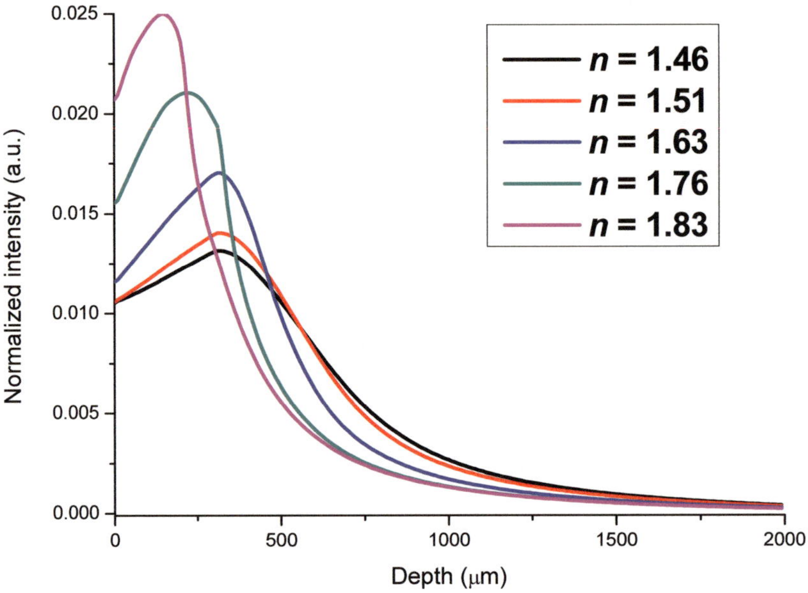

Fig. 3. The 785-nm excitation light distributions along the tissue depth using the Raman probe designs with different refractive indices of the ball lenses (n=1.46, 1.51, 1.63, 1.76 and 1.83).

Fig. 4 shows the calculated results of the origins of the Raman photons generated from different tissue locations of epithelial tissue. Similar to the excitation light distribution in tissue (Fig. 2), the Raman photons generated from different tissue depths are also dependent on the use of the refractive index of the ball lens in Raman probe designs. With the increase of the refractive index of the ball lens, Raman photons radiation tends to be more strongly coming from the shallower regions of the epithelium layer (e.g., ~5 orders of magnitude stronger in Raman intensity using the ball lens's refractive index of 1.83 as compared to that using the ball lens's refractive index of 1.46) (Fig. 4). This is due to the fact that excitation light is more tightly focused in the shallower layer of the epithelium, and the ball lens with a larger refractive index has larger collection cone angle (Eq. (4)), leading to the significant improvements of Raman signal collections from the epithelium in tissue. The findings above imply that increasing the refractive index of the ball lens in Raman probe design can effectively improve the collection efficiency of tissue Raman photons from the tissue, especially from the subsurface regions of the epithelium layer in tissue.

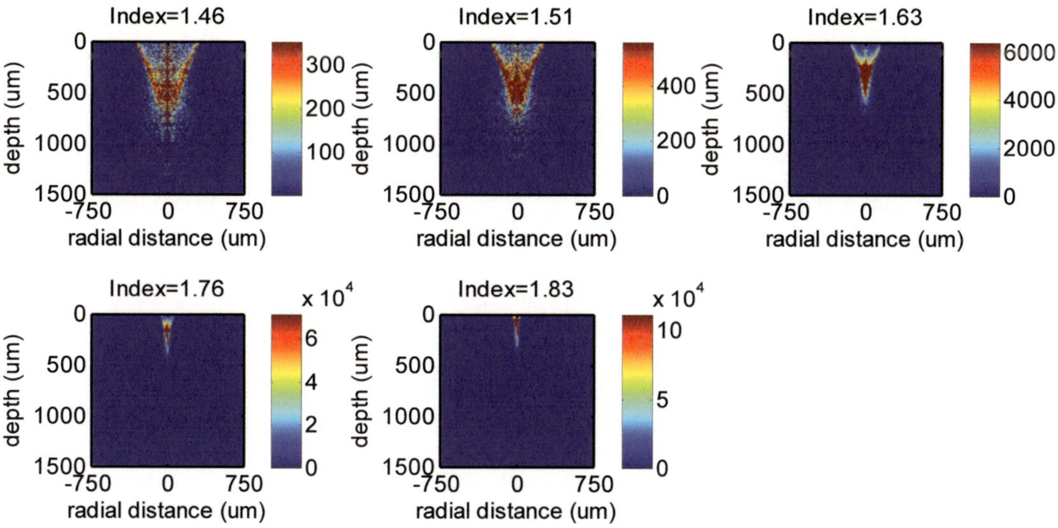

Fig. 4. Distributions of the Raman photons collected from different tissue depths using the Raman probe designs with different refractive indices of the ball lens (*n*=1.46, 1.51, 1.63, 1.76 and 1.83).

Fig. 5 shows the depth distribution of the origins of Raman photons collected from tissue for the use of different refractive indices of the ball lens in Raman probe designs. The depth distribution is created by integrating the 2-D distribution (Fig. 4) over the radial dimension at each tissue depth and is then normalized to the integrated area under the profile. It can be used to represent the relative contribution of Raman photons from different tissue depths to the overall collected Raman photons. The relatively weak Raman photons are generated throughout different tissue depths when using the ball lens with refractive indices of less than 1.63 (Fig.5); but stronger Raman photons generation tends to be arising from the epithelium layer in tissue when using the ball lens with larger refractive indices (e.g., n=1.76, 1.83). For instance, a maximum Raman radiation appears in the shallower region (~40 μm) of the epithelium layer in tissue for the use of ball lens with refractive index of 1.83 (Fig. 5). This indicates that the Raman probe design with the use of high refractive index ball lens is in favor of detecting Raman signal emitted from subsurface layer of the epithelial tissue.

We also evaluate the collection efficiency of the Raman probe versus the refractive index of the ball lens (Fig. 6). The collection efficiency of the Raman probe increases monotonously when increasing the refractive index of 1.46 up to 1.83. All the MC simulation results above confirm that Raman probe design with the use of a larger refractive index of the ball lens has the advantage of preferentially detecting the Raman signal from subsurface regions of the epithelium in tissue with high collection efficiency.

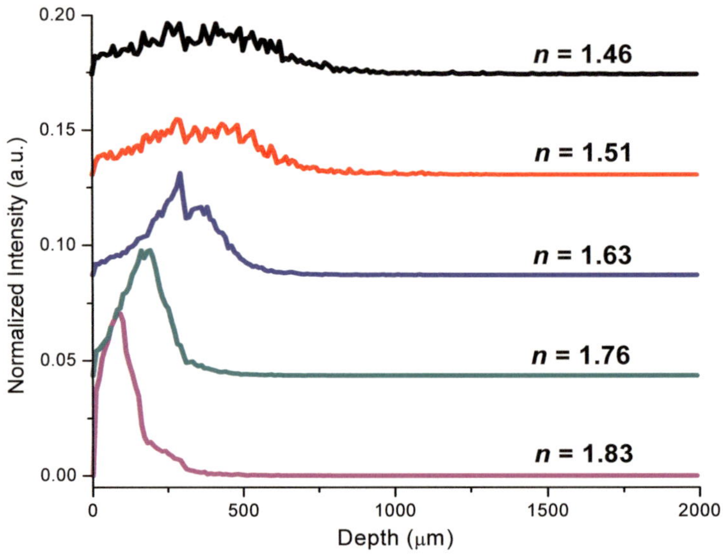

Fig. 5. Depth-resolved Raman photons collected from different tissue depths using the Raman probe designs with different refractive indices of the ball lens (n=1.46, 1.51, 1.63, 1.76 and 1.83). Note that for comparison purpose, the depth-resolved Raman intensity profiles with different refractive indices of the ball lens have been vertically shifted to different intensity levels.

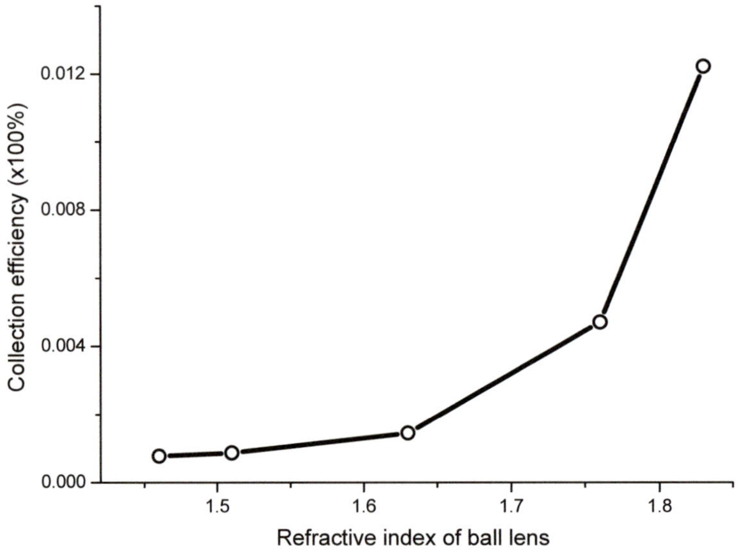

Fig. 6. Collection efficiency of the Raman probe as a function of the refractive index of the ball lens.

3.2 Effect of the ball lens diameter on tissue Raman measurements

Fig. 7 shows the MC simulation results of the 785 nm excitation light distribution in epithelial tissue for the fiber-optic Raman probe designs with different diameters of the ball lens (refractive index of 1.83). With the use of smaller diameters of the ball lens in Raman

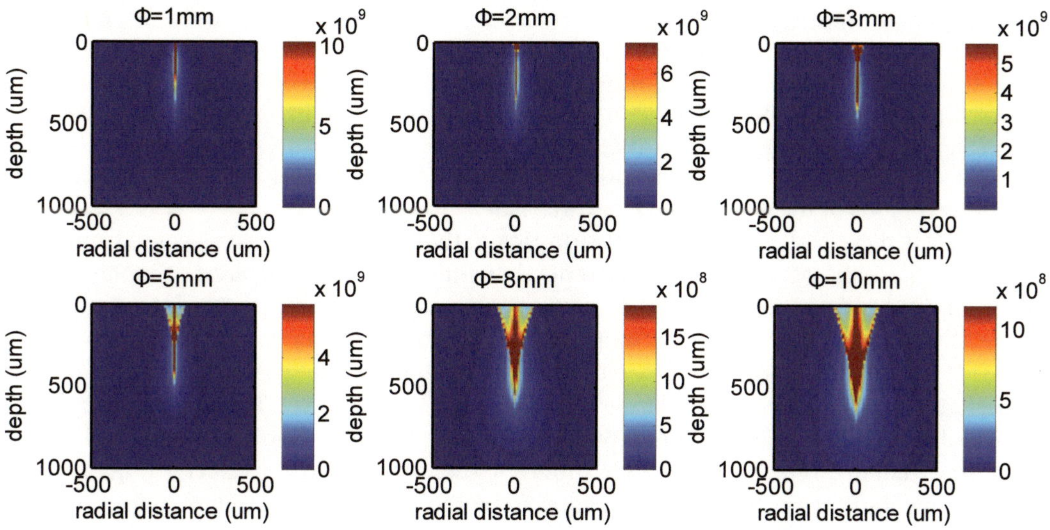

Fig. 7. The 785-nm excitation light distributions in tissue using the Raman probe designs with different diameters of the ball lens (Φ=1, 2, 3, 5, 8 and 10 mm).

probe design, the incident light is found to be more tightly focused into shallower regions of epithelial tissue with stronger incident light distribution as compared to the use of large diameters of the ball lens. This can be explained by the shortening of the ball lens focal length (Eq.5) [23] when using the ball lens with small diameters. Fig. 8 presents the depth distribution of the 785 nm excitation light in tissue calculated by integrating the 2-D intensity distribution (Fig. 7) over the radial direction at each tissue depth. The excitation light from the Raman probe appears to have a shorter penetration depth in tissue when

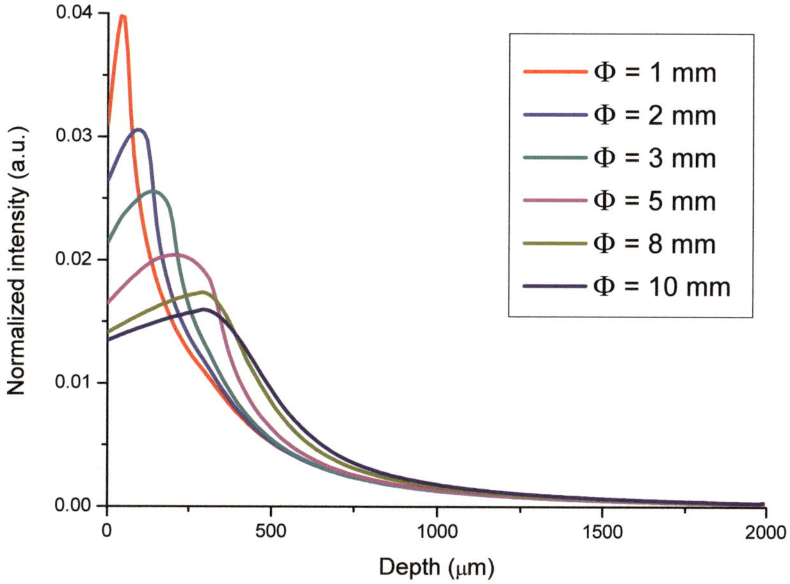

Fig. 8. The 785-nm excitation light distribution along the tissue depth using the Raman probe designs with different diameters of the ball lens (Φ=1, 2, 3, 5, 8 and 10 mm).

using a smaller diameter of the ball lens. For instance, an incident light intensity maximum occurs at the subsurface region (~50 um) of the epithelial tissue when the Raman probe uses the ball lens with a diameter of 1 mm, whereas the incident light tends to penetrate into deeper regions of the epithelial tissue when using the ball lens with larger diameters (e.g., 10 mm) (Fig. 8). Again, this implies that the Raman probe design with the use of smaller diameters of the ball lens can be more efficiently focusing the excitation light into the shallower regions of the epithelium layer in tissue.

Fig. 9 depicts the 2-D distributions of the origins of the Raman photons collected from tissue using the Raman probes with different diameters of the ball lens. Similar to the corresponding excitation light distribution in tissue (Fig. 7), the tissue Raman photons collected with the use of a small diameter of the ball lens in Raman probe design appears to be mostly originating from the shallower areas of the epithelium layer in tissue as compared to the Raman probe design with larger diameters of the ball lens. This can be more clearly displayed in the depth distribution of the origins of the Raman photons collected from tissue using the Raman probe designs with different diameters of the ball lens (Fig. 10). The relative contribution of the Raman photons from the epithelium becomes more dominant when reducing the ball lens' diameter in Raman probe design. For example, the Raman probe design with the use of 1 mm ball lens enables a detection of ~95% of Raman signal arising from the epithelium, while only about 25% of Raman signal originating from the epithelium can be detected if using the 10 mm ball lens. Hence, the Raman probe design with a smaller diameter of ball lens can efficiently improve the detection of the Raman signal originating from the epithelium layer in tissue.

MC simulations are also carried out to exhaustedly search for all the possible combinations of the diameters and the refractive indices sof the optimized Raman probe designs for improving depth-resolved Raman measurements. Fig. 11 describes the depth-resolved measurement performance of the probe design as a function of the combination of the ball lens' diameter and refractive index. The results show that the ball lens with a refractive

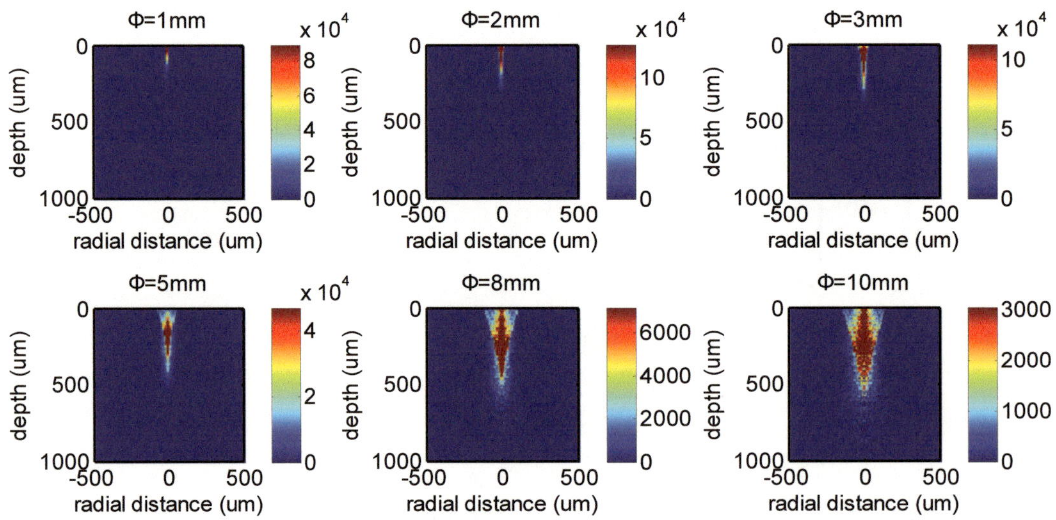

Fig. 9. Distributions of the origins of the Raman photons collected from tissue using the Raman probe designs with different diameters of ball lenses (Φ=1, 2, 3, 5, 8 and 10 mm).

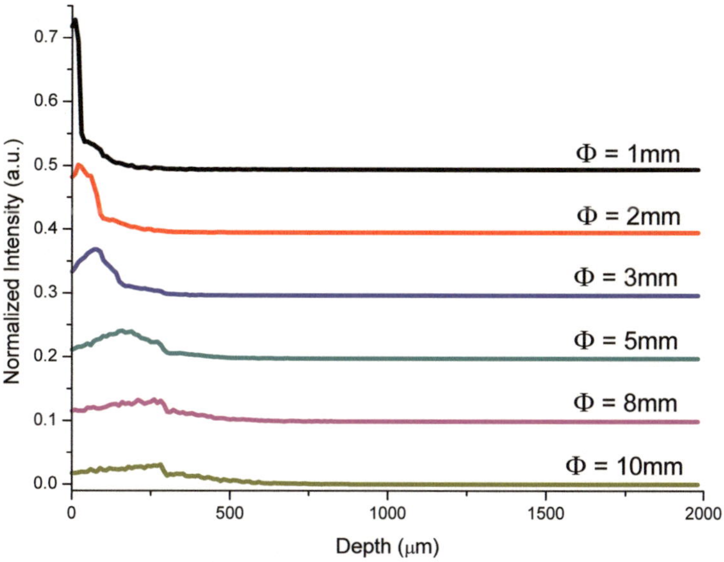

Fig. 10. Depth distribution of the origins of the Raman photons collected from tissue using the Raman probe designs with different diameters of the ball lens (Φ=1, 2, 3, 5, 8 and 10 mm).

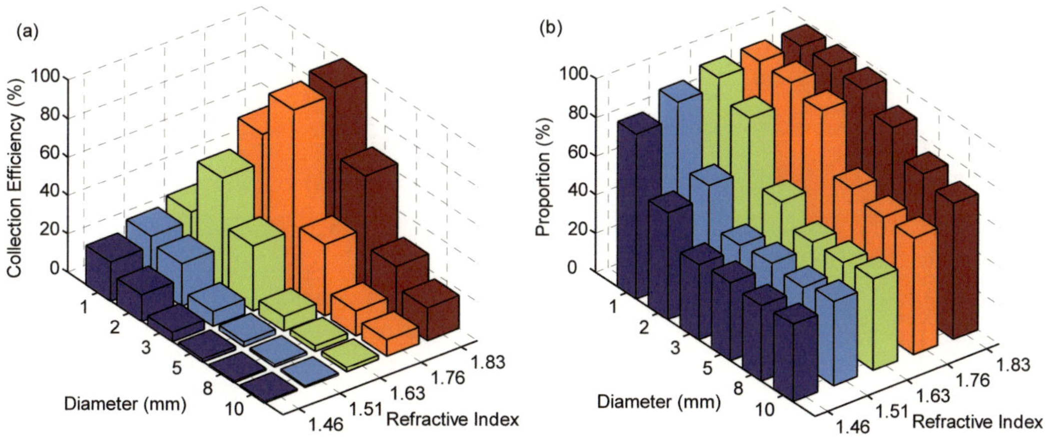

Fig. 11. The simulation results of the probe design based on various combinations of ball lens diameters (i.e., 1, 2, 3, 5, 8 and 10 mm) and refractive indices (i.e., 1.46, 1.51, 1.63, 1.76 and 1.83): (a) collection efficiency; (b) proportion of the Raman photons from the epithelium to the total collected Raman photons from the tissue surface.

index of 1.83 and diameter of 3 mm achieves the highest collection efficiency (Fig. 11a). With the use of this probe design, Raman photons originating in the epithelium of tissue cover 97% of the overall Raman photons collected from the surface of epithelial tissue as shown in Fig. 11b, indicating a good depth-selectivity to the epithelium. Although the depth-selectivity can be further improved by reducing the diameter of the ball lens down to 2 mm, the collection efficiency will drop by about 40%. This suggests that the Raman probe design with the use of a ball lens with the diameter of 3 mm and the refractive index of 1.83 is optimal for selectively detecting the Raman signal from the epithelial tissue. The above result indicates that Raman probe designs with a proper selection of the refractive index and diameter of the ball lens can improve both the collection efficiency and the ability to preferentially acquire the Raman photons emitted from the epithelium layer of epithelial tissue.

3.3 Effect of the probe-tissue distance on tissue Raman measurements

In practical tissue measurements, the probe-to-tissue distance may play a significant role in depth-resolved tissue spectroscopy [10, 11, 14, 15]. We comprehensively study the relationship of the collection efficiency of the ball lens Raman probe designs versus probe-tissue distances. Fig 12a shows an example of the collection efficiency versus probe-tissue distances using the Raman probe with the ball lens' diameter of 3 mm and refractive index of 1.83. The collection efficiency drops sharply with the increased probe-tissue distances (0 to 200 μm) and then the collection efficiency gradually decreases to a minimum (250 to 1000 μm). We also study the effect of the probe-tissue distance on the ratio of the Raman signal collected from the epithelium layer to the overall Raman signal from the entire epithelial tissue in depth-resolved Raman measurements (Fig. 12b). It is found that when the probe-to-tissue distances are in the range of 0 to 100 μm, Raman photons arising from the tissue epithelium layer account for over 90% of the total Raman photons of the entire epithelial tissue. The above results suggest that the collection efficiency and the depth-selectivity of the Raman probe design can be optimized by setting a proper gap between the probe and the tissue.

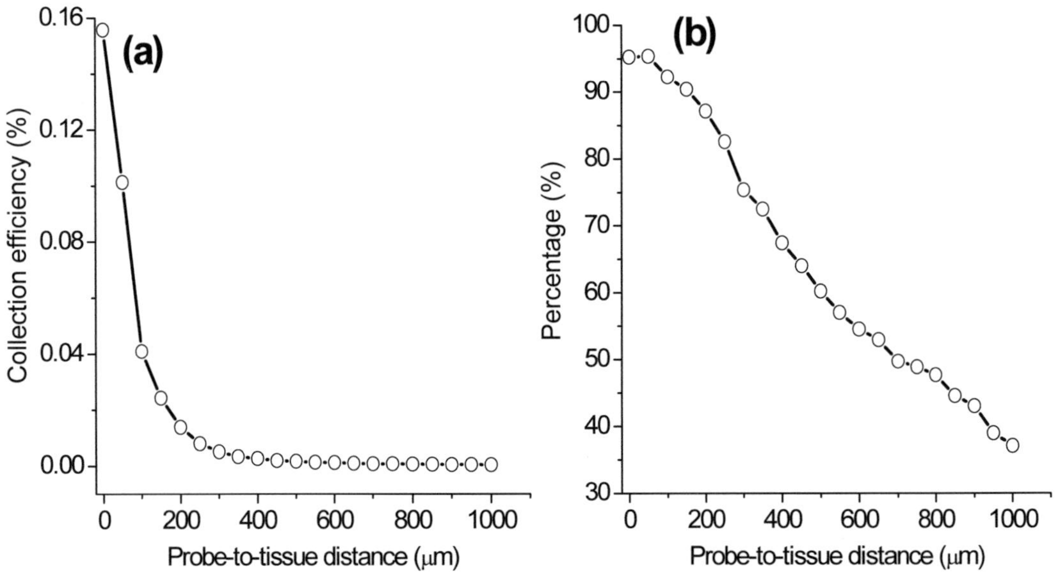

Fig. 12. (a) Collection efficiency of the Raman probe as a function of probe-tissue distances; (b) Percentage of the Raman signal collected from the epithelium layer to the overall Raman signal from the entire epithelial tissue. The refractive index and the diameter of the ball lens are 1.83, and 3 mm, respectively, in Raman probe design.

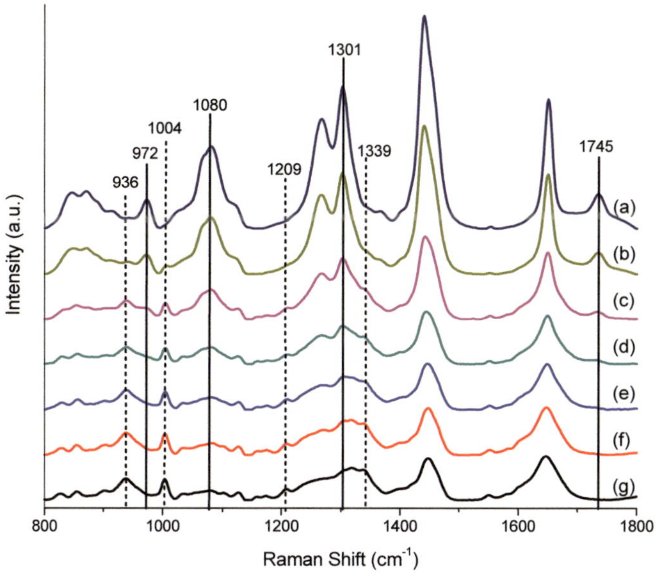

Fig. 13. Raman spectra acquired from chicken muscle and fat tissue, as well as from the two-layer tissue phantoms with the muscle tissue thickness of 0.3, 1.2, 2.1, 3 and 3.9 mm, respectively. Spectra: (a) fat tissue; (b)-(f): two-layer tissue phantoms with the muscle tissue layer of thickness of 0.3, 1.2, 2.1, 3.0 and 3.9 mm, respectively, overlaying on a fat tissue layer (thickness of 5 mm); (g) muscle tissue. Note that all tissue Raman spectra are acquired with an integration time of 1 s under the 785-nm excitation power of 1.5 W/cm^2. The dotted and solid lines indicated in Raman spectra stand for the distinctive Raman peaks originating from the muscle and fat chicken tissue, respectively.

3.4 Raman experiments on two-layer tissue phantom

We have also carried out tissue Raman measurements on a two-layer tissue phantom to evaluate the performance of a ball lens Raman probe design using a sapphire ball lens (refractive index of 1.76, and a diameter of 3 mm). The two-layer tissue phantom was constructed by overlaying different thicknesses of chicken muscle tissue on a chicken fat tissue: the thickness of fat tissue layer was fixed to be 5 mm, while the thickness of the muscle tissue layer varied from 0.3 to 3.9 mm. Fig. 13 shows Raman spectra acquired from chicken muscle and fat tissue, as well as from the two-layer tissue phantoms with the muscle tissue thickness of 0.3, 1.2, 2.1, 3 and 3.9 mm, respectively. It is observed that chicken muscle and fat tissue show distinctively different Raman spectral features. For instance, the Raman spectrum of muscle tissue shows distinct Raman peaks at 936 (C-C stretching of proteins), 1004 (C-C stretching of phenylalanine), 1209 ($C-C_6H_5$ stretching of tryptophan and phenylalanine), and 1339 cm^{-1} (CH_3CH_2 wagging of collagen). In contrast, the Raman spectrum of fat tissue exhibits four different unique peaks at 972 (Calcium-phosphate stretching of cholesterols/lipids), 1080 (C-C/C-O stretching of phospholipids), 1301 (CH_2 twisting and wagging modes of lipids, triglycerides (fatty acids)) and 1745 cm^{-1} (C=O stretching of ester (phospholipids)) [2, 8]. With the thickness of muscle tissue layer increasing from 0 to 3.9 mm in the two-layer tissue phantom, the Raman intensity at 1004 cm^{-1} for muscle tissue increases by 2.1 to 5.6 folds, whereas the Raman signal at 1745 cm^{-1} for fat tissue undergoes a 28 to 1.6 fold reduction in intensity (Fig. 14). This implies that the

Raman signal contribution of the surface muscle layer to the overall Raman signal increases as the muscle tissue thickness increases, while the signal contribution of the deeper fat tissue layer reduces concomitantly. The results above indicate the potential of the ball lens Raman probe design for effective depth-selective Raman measurements in layered tissue.

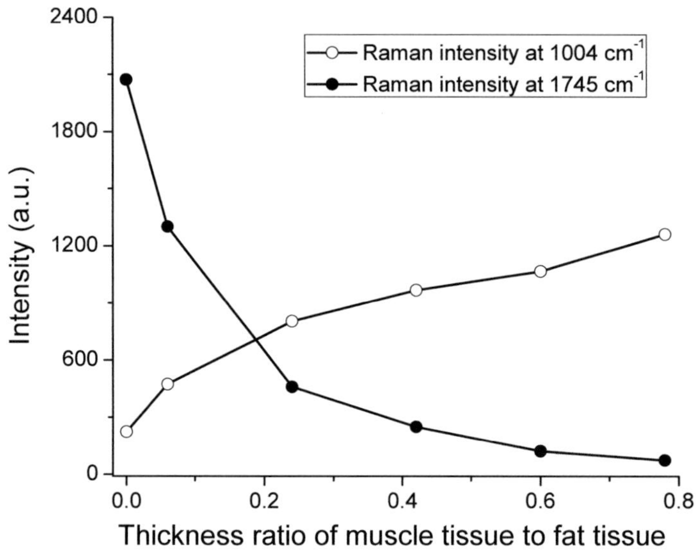

Fig. 14. Raman peaks intensities at 1004 and 1745 cm^{-1} as a function of thickness ratios of the muscle tissue layer to the fat tissue in a two-layer tissue phantom.

4. Conclusions

We have proposed a fiber-optic Raman probe coupled with a ball lens for improving depth-resolved Raman measurements of epithelial tissue. We have comprehensively evaluated the effects of optical configurations of the ball lens Raman probe design on depth-resolved Raman measurements using Monte Carlo simulations. The MC calculation results show that depth discriminations of Raman signals are achievable by changing either the refractive index or diameter of the ball lens, or the ball lens-tissue distances. The Raman probe design by increasing the refractive index or reducing the diameter of the ball lens is in favor of probing Raman signals particularly arising from the shallower regions of the epithelium layer of tissue. Experimental evaluation of a ball lens probe design confirms its ability for efficient depth-resolved measurement on layered tissues. The simulations results can serve as a guideline to optimize the optical configurations of the Raman probe design aiming at improving the detection efficiency of layered tissue Raman measurements, which may facilitate the applications of depth-resolved Raman technique in early diagnosis and detection of precancer or early cancer at the molecular level.

5. Acknowledgements

This work was supported by the Biomedical Research Council, the National Medical Research Council, and the Faculty Research Fund from the National University of Singapore.

6. References

[1] N. Stone, C. Kendall, N. Shepherd, P. Crow, and H. Barr, "Near-infrared Raman spectroscopy for the classification of epithelial pre-cancers and cancers," J. Raman Spectrosc. 33, 564-573 (2002).

[2] Z. Huang, A. McWilliams, H. Lui, D. I. McLean, S. Lam, and H. Zeng, "Near-infrared Raman spectroscopy for optical diagnosis of lung cancer," Int. J. Cancer 107, 1047-1052 (2003).

[3] Z. Huang, H. Zeng, I. Hamzavi, D. I. McLean, and H. Lui, "Rapid near-infrared Raman spectroscopy system for real-time in vivo skin measurements," Opt. Lett. 26, 1782-1784 (2001).

[4] M. G. Shim, B. C. Wilson, E. Marple, and M. Wach, "Study of fiber-optic probes for in vivo medical Raman spectroscopy," Appl. Spectrosc. 53, 619-627 (1999).

[5] Z. Huang, S. K. Teh, W. Zheng, J. Mo, K. Lin, X. Shao, K. Y. Ho, M. Teh, and K. G. Yeoh, "Integrated Raman spectroscopy and trimodal wide-field imaging techniques for real-time in vivo tissue Raman measurements at endoscopy," Opt. Lett. 34, 758-760 (2009).

[6] R. Drezek, C. Brookner, I. Pavlova, I. Boiko, A. Malpica, R. Lotan, M. Follen, and R. Richards-Kortum, "Autofluorescence microscopy of fresh cervical-tissue sections reveals alterations in tissue biochemistry with dysplasia&para," Photochem. Photobiol. 73, 636-641 (2001).

[7] F. Abdul-Karim, Y. S. Fu, J. W. Reagan, and W. B. Wentz, "Morphometric study of intraepithelial neoplasia of the uterine cervix," Obstet. Gynecol. 60, 210-214 (1982).

[8] J. Mo, W. Zheng, J. J. H. Low, J. Ng, A. Ilancheran, and Z. Huang, "High wavenumber Raman spectroscopy for in vivo detection of cervical dysplasia," Anal. Chem. 81, 8908-8915 (2009).

[9] W. C. Shih, K. L. Bechtel, and M. S. Feld, "Intrinsic Raman spectroscopy for quantitative biological spectroscopy part I: theory and simulations," Opt. Express 16, 12726-12736 (2008).

[10] T. J. Pfefer, K. T. Schomacker, M. N. Ediger, and N. S. Nishioka, "Light propagation in tissue during fluorescence spectroscopy with single-fiber probes," Selected Topics in Quantum Electronics, IEEE Journal of 7, 1004-1012 (2001).

[11] T. J. Pfefer, K. T. Schomacker, M. N. Ediger, and N. S. Nishioka, "Multiple-fiber probe design for fluorescence spectroscopy in tissue," Appl. Opt. 41, 4712-4721 (2002).

[12] L. Nieman, A. Myakov, J. Aaron, and K. Sokolov, "Optical sectioning using a fiber probe with an angled illumination-collection geometry: evaluation in engineered tissue phantoms," Appl. Opt. 43, 1308-1319 (2004).

[13] R. A. Schwarz, D. Arifler, S. K. Chang, I. Pavlova, I. A. Hussain, V. Mack, B. Knight, R. Richards-Kortum, and A. M. Gillenwater, "Ball lens coupled fiber-optic probe for depth-resolved spectroscopy of epithelial tissue," Opt. Lett. 30, 1159-1161 (2005).

[14] F. Jaillon, W. Zheng, and Z. Huang, "Beveled fiber-optic probe couples a ball lens for improving depth-resolved fluorescence measurements of layered tissue: Monte Carlo simulations," Phys. Med. Biol. 53, 937-951 (2008).

[15] F. Jaillon, W. Zheng, and Z. Huang, "Half-ball lens couples a beveled fiber probe for depth-resolved spectroscopy: Monte Carlo simulations," Appl. Opt. 47, 3152-3157 (2008).

[16] J. T. Motz, M. Hunter, L. H. Galindo, J. A. Gardecki, J. R. Kramer, R. R. Dasari, and M. S. Feld, "Optical Fiber Probe for Biomedical Raman Spectroscopy," Appl. Opt. 43, 542-554 (2004).

[17L. Wang, S. L. Jacques, and L. Zheng, "MCML--Monte Carlo modeling of light transport in multi-layered tissues," Comput. Methods Programs Biomed. 47, 131-146 (1995).

[18] A. J. Welch, C. Gardner, R. Richards-Kortum, E. Chan, G. Criswell, J. Pfefer, and S. Warren, "Propagation of fluorescent light," Lasers Surg. Med. 21, 166-178 (1997).

[19] G. M. Palmer, and N. Ramanujam, "Monte-Carlo-based model for the extraction of intrinsic fluorescence from turbid media," J. Biomed. Opt. 13, 024017-024019 (2008).

[20] W. C. Shih, K. L. Bechtel, and M. S. Feld, “Intrinsic Raman spectroscopy for quantitative biological spectroscopy part I: theory and simulations,” Opt. Express 16(17), 12726–12736 (2008).

[21] K. L. Bechtel, W. C. Shih, and M. S. Feld, “Intrinsic Raman spectroscopy for quantitative biological spectroscopy part II: experimental applications,” Opt. Express 16(17), 12737–12745 (2008).

[22] L. G. Henyey, and J. L. Greenstein, "Diffuse radiation in galaxy," Astrophys. J 93, 70-83 (1941).

[23] M. J. Riedl, *Optical design fundamentals for infrared systems* (SPIE Press, Bellingham, Wash., 2001).

[24] S. K. Chang, D. Arifler, R. Drezek, M. Follen, and R. Richards-Kortum, "Analytical model to describe fluorescence spectra of normal and preneoplastic epithelial tissue: comparison with Monte Carlo simulations and clinical measurements," J. Biomed. Opt. 9, 511-522 (2004).

13

Monte Carlo Simulations of Powerful Neutron Interaction with Matter for the Goals of Disclosure of Hidden Explosives and Fissile Materials and for Treatment of Cancer Diseases versus their Experimental Verifications

V.A. Gribkov[1,2,3], S.V. Latyshev[1], R.A. Miklaszewski[2], M. Chernyshova[2], R. Prokopowicz[2], M. Scholz[2], K. Drozdowicz[4], U. Wiącek[4], B. Gabańska[4], D. Dworak[4], K. Pytel[5], A. Zawadka[5], M. Ramos Aruca[6], F. Longo[7], G. Giannini[7] and C. Tuniz[3]
[1]*A.A. Baikov Institute of Metallurgy and Material Sciences, Russian Ac. Sci., Moscow,*
[2]*Institute of Plasma Physics and Laser Microfusion, Warsaw,*
[3]*The Abdus Salam International Center for Theoretical Physics, Trieste,*
[4]*Institute of Nuclear Physics, Polish Academy of Sciences, Krakow,*
[5]*Institute of Atomic Energy, Otwock-Swierk,*
[6]*Institute of Nuclear Science, Miramar # 502, Havana,*
[7]*University of Trieste and INFN, Trieste,*
[1]*Russian Federation*
[2,4,5]*Poland*
[6]*Cuba*
[3,7]*Italy*

1. Introduction

One of the most significant task in unveiling of illegal transportation of *explosive or fissile materials*, e.g. inside an airplane luggage, in a car, in a long-distance train carriage or at a sea container, is to disclose of the above illicit materials and explosives *as fast as possible*, probably *during a process of their transportation.*

The method proposed by us lies in a wider group of approaches [1, 2, 3a] that make use of an interaction of neutrons (fast or thermal) with different materials. As a result of such interaction a field of scattered neutrons is formed. This field appears because of elastic and inelastic scattering of primary neutrons by nuclei of irradiated matter. The information on elemental composition of the object can be obtained from spectra of the scattered neutron fields and from amplitudes of peaks corresponding to nuclei of various elements.

The so-called Fast Neutron Scattering Analysis (FNSA) developed lately by Buffler et al. [3*a*] makes use of a train of *nanosecond* pulses of fast neutrons having low intensity (of the order of $10^2...10^3$ neutrons per pulse, supplied by the Van de Graaff accelerator). The necessary data about a chemical content of the substance under interrogation are obtained from an analysis of a spectrum of the *elastically* scattered neutrons registered with a help of a photo-multiplier tube with a scintillator (the time-of-flight - TOF - method). The above authors have demonstrated a possibility to determine relative concentration of the elements H, C, N, and O (very common to different types of explosives) in small (0.2-1.0 kg) samples providing for this goal *a few billions* of the neutron pulses. The main reasons for production of such a huge number of pulses are the necessity to reach exhaustive statistics at the collection of the recoil protons produced by neutrons within a scintillator and to increase a signal-to-noise ratio to a satisfactory level. Other concepts [3*b*...*g*] use also relatively low-intensity ($\leq 10^6...10^8$ n/pulse) *long-duration* pulses (1-10 μs) generated by neutron sources. They demand many shots during long interrogation time (from few minutes till half an hour with the overall fluence above 10^{11} through 10^{13} neutrons emitted by the sources in the full solid angle during this examination) and result in high activation of an object under unveiling.

We proposed [6] to bring into play a neutron source based on a *plasma accelerator* of the Dense Plasma Focus type (DPF), which generates pulses of almost monochromatic neutrons of the energy $E_0 \approx 2.5$ or $E_0 \approx 14.0$ MeV with $\Delta E/E_0 \approx 1...3\%$ in the nanosecond (ns) range of their durations but producing at the same time a very large number of neutrons per pulse – $10^8...10^{11}$. It gave us an opportunity to provide *all measurements* in TOF technique by means of just a *single* nanosecond pulse, i.e. *during one millionth of a second or less*. Due to the pulse duration used in the proposed method the TOF base can be restricted just by a few meters. The technique that uses a single very bright neutron pulse of nanosecond time duration is named "Nanosecond Impulse Neutron Investigation System" (NINIS).

Our neutron pulse having duration in the range 2...50 ns depending on the DPF size occupies in a space in the direction of its propagation a distance of about 4-50 cm (in fact the neutron pulse from a DPF chamber spreads into space as an almost spherical shell of the above thickness). This distance is approximately the same as the distance of neutron's penetration depth into suspicious materials (e.g. explosives). Because of the unique characteristics of the neutron source the *signal-to-noise ratio* will be increased just proportionally to the decreased number of shots (e.g. one pulse instead of billions compared with the case of the Van de Graaff source [3a]) whereas *neutron fluence* necessary to characterize hidden objects will be reduced by 2-4 orders of magnitude compared with [3]. It results in low activation of items under interrogation.

However, for this very promising technique to be proved theoretically and then verified experimentally it is needed to provide a very accurate preliminary numerical modeling of neutron scattering in real geometries. Sometimes (in particular in the cases of *inelastic* scattering of neutrons by *fissile* materials - see below) we have to know the resulted spectrum beforehand. These simulations can be produced with the help of Monte-Carlo codes.

2. Numerical modeling of the NINIS method by use of MCNP5 and FLUKA codes

We applied MCNP™ – a general-purpose Monte Carlo N-Particle code that can be used for neutron, photon, electron, or coupled neutron/photon/electron transport calculations [4] (MCNP, MCNP5, and "MCNP Version 5" are trademarks of the Regents of the University of California, Los Alamos National Laboratory). The code treats an arbitrary three-dimensional configuration of materials in geometric cells bounded by first- and second-degree surfaces and fourth-degree elliptical tori. Pointwise cross-section data are used. For neutrons, all reactions given in a particular cross-section evaluation (such as ENDF/B-VI) are accounted for. Thermal neutrons are described by both the free gas and S(α, β) models. Important standard features include a powerful general source; both geometry and output tally plotters; a rich collection of variance reduction techniques; a flexible tally structure; and an extensive collection of cross-section data.

We undertake attempts to simulate scattering of 2.45-MeV neutrons from various objects by means of full MCNP calculations. We used MCNP5 [4b], the 5-th version of the MCNP, which takes into account the whole process of neutron scattering by dissimilar objects and allows to model signals registered by virtual detectors with high precision. As an example we present here usage of this MCNP5 code to simulate scattering of neutrons from *long objects* (Fig.1).

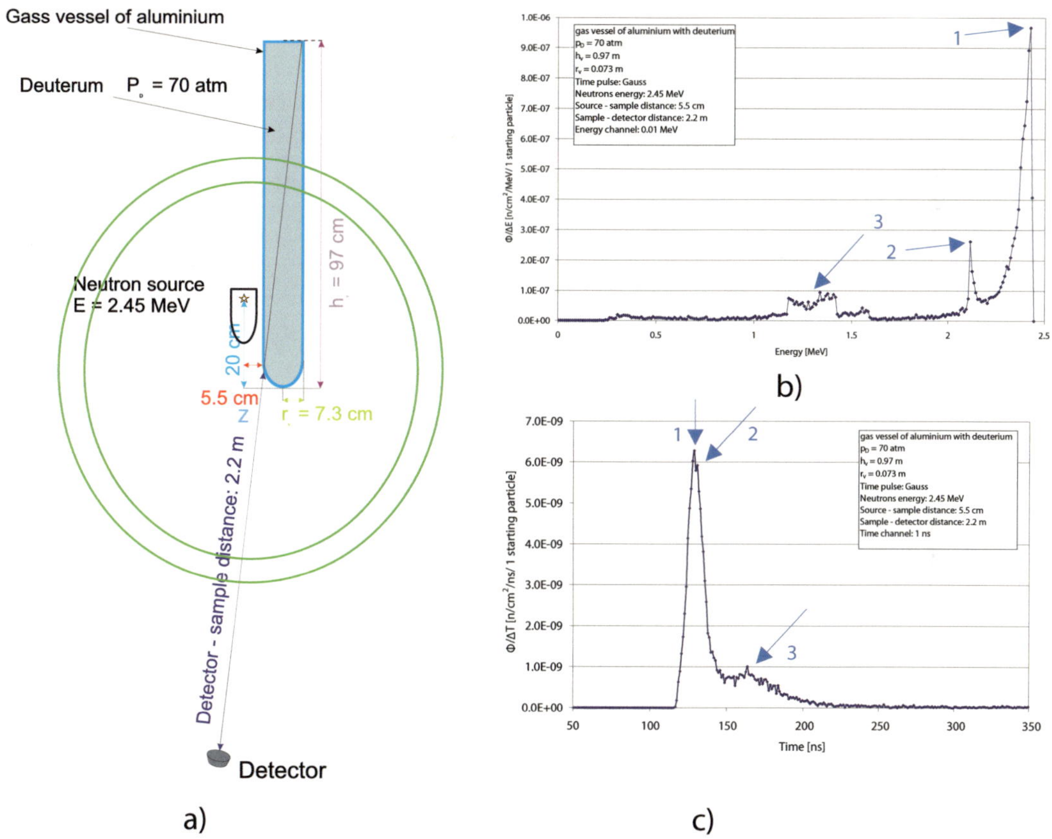

Fig. 1. Scheme of numerical experiment (*a*), energetic distribution (*b*) and temporal behaviour (*c*) of neutrons coming to the detector: 1 – direct neutrons (2.45 MeV), 2 – neutrons scattered by aluminium, 3 – neutrons scattered by deuterium

In this picture there is a scatterer – a 1-meter high-pressure aluminium cylinder filled with deuterium at 70 atm. – and a DPF-based neutron source (Fig. 1a). The energy distribution (spectrum) of "direct" and scattered neutrons is presented in Fig. 1b whereas the resulting time-of-flight signal (the expected oscilloscope trace) is shown in Fig. 1c.

These our computational works were aimed also at elaboration of the theoretical basis for the *fissile materials detection concept* and to verify expected experimental results.

The first part of them applies a FLUKA code [5] to investigate detailed interaction of neutrons with localized objects (explosives and fissile materials as well as everyday use materials). The FLUKA code is described further in the text. The calculations were provided in the idealized geometry shown in Fig. 2.

Neutrons from DPF irradiate the target (a fission fuel element) as a parallel beam along Z-axis. The beam has a diameter 7 cm which is equal to the diameter of the fuel element. The target was *a fuel element MR-6/80%*, which consists of 6 concentric tubes (internal tube in some calculations was substituted by a rod made of aluminium). The area of the cross-section of the neutron beam is 38 cm^2. The total area of the whole fission fuel element is 7 cm × 100 cm = 700 cm^2. Thus the neutron beam irradiates only a small part of the overall fuel element.

Neutrons and X-Ray photons are registered on the surface of a sphere surrounding the target and having a radius equal to 200 cm. The sphere is divided into zones occupied by detectors. Each zone has a width equivalent to 20 cm. Thus all detectors are "seen" by particles escaping the target within the same angle equal to 5.73° except the last detector #32 (backside of the neutron beam), which has the angle of particles' collection slightly higher.

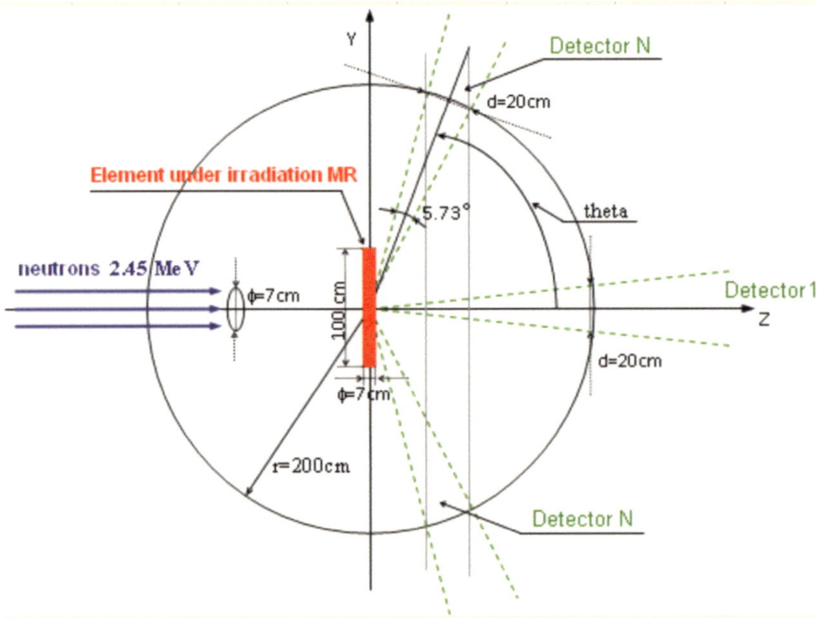

Fig. 2. Idealized geometry of the neutron beam and positioning of a sample under irradiation and neutron detectors

Below we present a table contenting results of our calculations and two pictures (Fig. 3 *a* and *b* correspondingly) demonstrating one example of energy distributions of neutrons and photons escaping the target at a certain angle (i.e. for a certain detector) after irradiation. Solid line in red color shows results for original fuel elements MR. Green dashed line presents results obtained for pure aluminium, i.e. at the substitution of uranium fuel layers by aluminium layers to show clearly an effect of the „aluminium background". Boundary energy is energy of the irradiating neutron beam, above which every neutron originates only from fission of uranium in the fuel layer. Due to this feature fission neutrons are seen especially clear.

FNSA-2009: Fuel element MR-6/80% placed perpendicularly to the beam of 2.45-MeV neutrons. Number of simulated histories – 100 mln of neutrons from the source.
Estimator: Boundary crossing absolute FLUENCE one-way estimator

DET	theta [deg]	Neutrons (*)	Photons (*)	N<2.466 (*)	N>2.466 (*)	%N>2.466 [%]
1	0.00	2.19E-03	1.74E-07	2.19E-03	3.37E-09	1.54E-04
2	5.73	5.62E-07	1.73E-07	5.59E-07	2.97E-09	5.28E-01
3	11.46	3.29E-06	1.72E-07	3.29E-06	2.89E-09	8.77E-02
4	17.20	1.81E-06	1.70E-07	1.81E-06	2.80E-09	1.54E-01
5	22.93	6.44E-07	1.69E-07	6.41E-07	2.80E-09	4.35E-01
6	28.66	3.68E-06	1.70E-07	3.67E-06	2.79E-09	7.59E-02
7	34.39	6.88E-07	1.69E-07	6.85E-07	2.77E-09	4.02E-01
8	40.12	3.12E-07	1.67E-07	3.09E-07	2.87E-09	9.20E-01
9	45.86	2.27E-06	1.66E-07	2.26E-06	2.82E-09	1.24E-01
10	51.59	5.84E-07	1.65E-07	5.82E-07	2.73E-09	4.68E-01
11	57.32	7.10E-07	1.62E-07	7.07E-07	2.82E-09	3.98E-01
12	63.05	8.47E-07	1.59E-07	8.44E-07	2.75E-09	3.25E-01
13	68.78	7.26E-07	1.56E-07	7.23E-07	2.65E-09	3.66E-01
14	74.52	3.94E-07	1.52E-07	3.91E-07	2.64E-09	6.71E-01
15	80.25	4.22E-07	1.47E-07	4.19E-07	2.50E-09	5.92E-01
16	85.98	4.49E-07	1.43E-07	4.46E-07	2.43E-09	5.42E-01
17	91.71	3.09E-07	1.42E-07	3.06E-07	2.44E-09	7.90E-01
18	97.44	3.16E-07	1.46E-07	3.14E-07	2.46E-09	7.79E-01
19	103.18	3.48E-07	1.51E-07	3.46E-07	2.63E-09	7.54E-01
20	108.91	2.92E-07	1.55E-07	2.90E-07	2.61E-09	8.93E-01
21	114.64	1.70E-07	1.59E-07	1.67E-07	2.70E-09	1.59E+00
22	120.37	2.47E-07	1.62E-07	2.44E-07	2.74E-09	1.11E+00
23	126.10	5.93E-07	1.65E-07	5.90E-07	2.78E-09	4.69E-01
24	131.84	2.67E-07	1.67E-07	2.64E-07	2.77E-09	1.04E+00
25	137.57	2.36E-07	1.68E-07	2.33E-07	2.89E-09	1.22E+00
26	143.30	2.16E-07	1.70E-07	2.14E-07	2.71E-09	1.25E+00
27	149.03	6.62E-07	1.70E-07	6.60E-07	2.75E-09	4.15E-01
28	154.76	3.33E-07	1.73E-07	3.30E-07	2.88E-09	8.66E-01
29	160.50	3.76E-07	1.73E-07	3.73E-07	2.94E-09	7.82E-01
30	166.23	7.01E-07	1.74E-07	6.98E-07	2.97E-09	4.24E-01
31	171.96	4.04E-07	1.73E-07	4.01E-07	2.88E-09	7.12E-01
32	180.00	8.42E-07	1.76E-07	8.39E-07	3.13E-09	3.71E-01

(*) – units: [particles/cm^2/one beam neutron]
N<2.466 – number of neutrons with energy E<2.466 MeV (lower limit of energy of beam neutrons)
N>2.466 – number of neutrons with energy E>2.466 MeV (unambiguously coming from fission)
%N>2.466 – percentage of neutrons having energy E>2.466 MeV (ratio of columns 6 to 3)

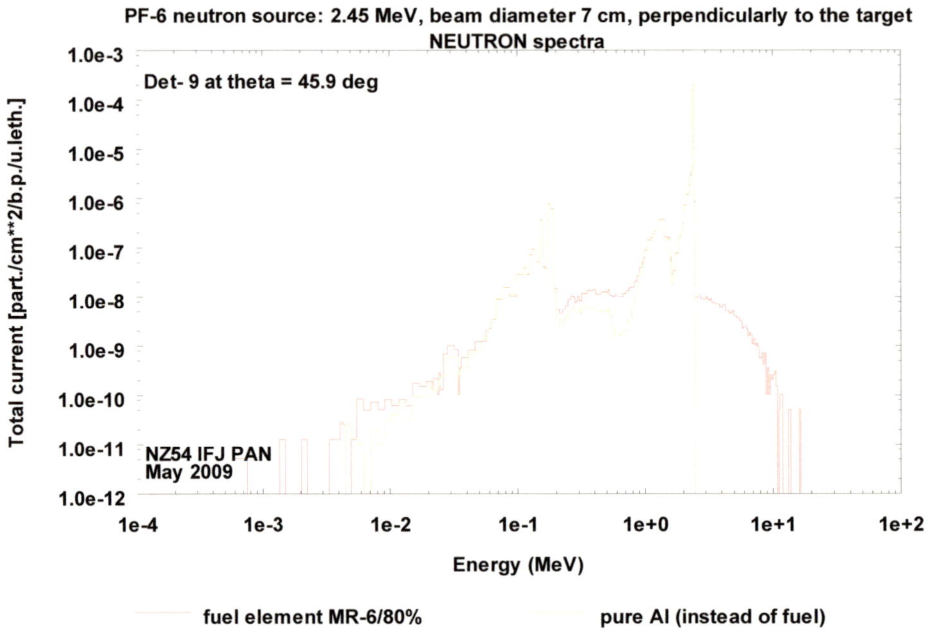

a)

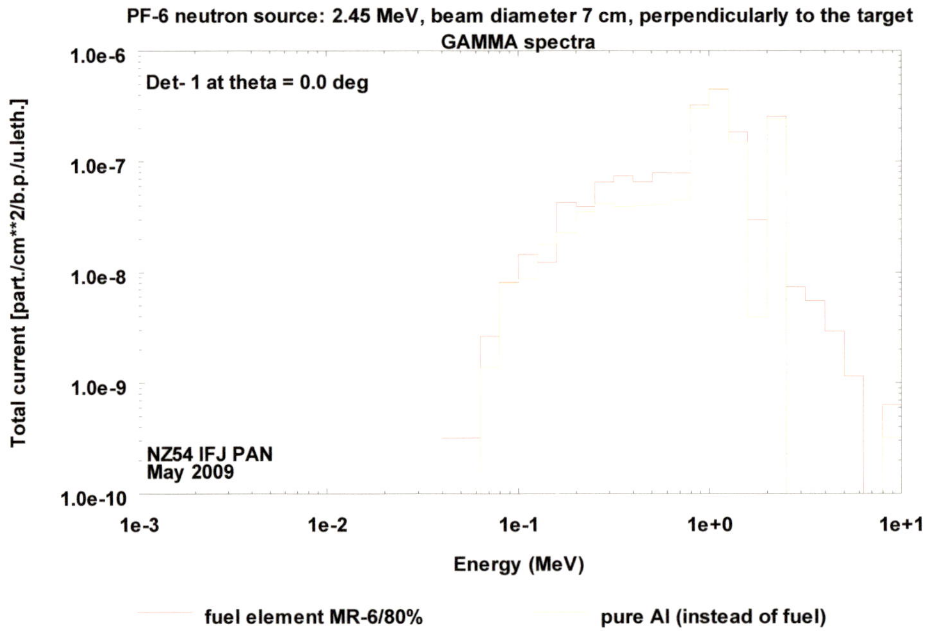

b)

Fig. 3. Number of neutrons and gamma-photons produced due to fission processes in the fuel element MR-6/80% (red colour); note neutrons whose energy exceeds the energy specific for the DPF device (on the right-hand side)

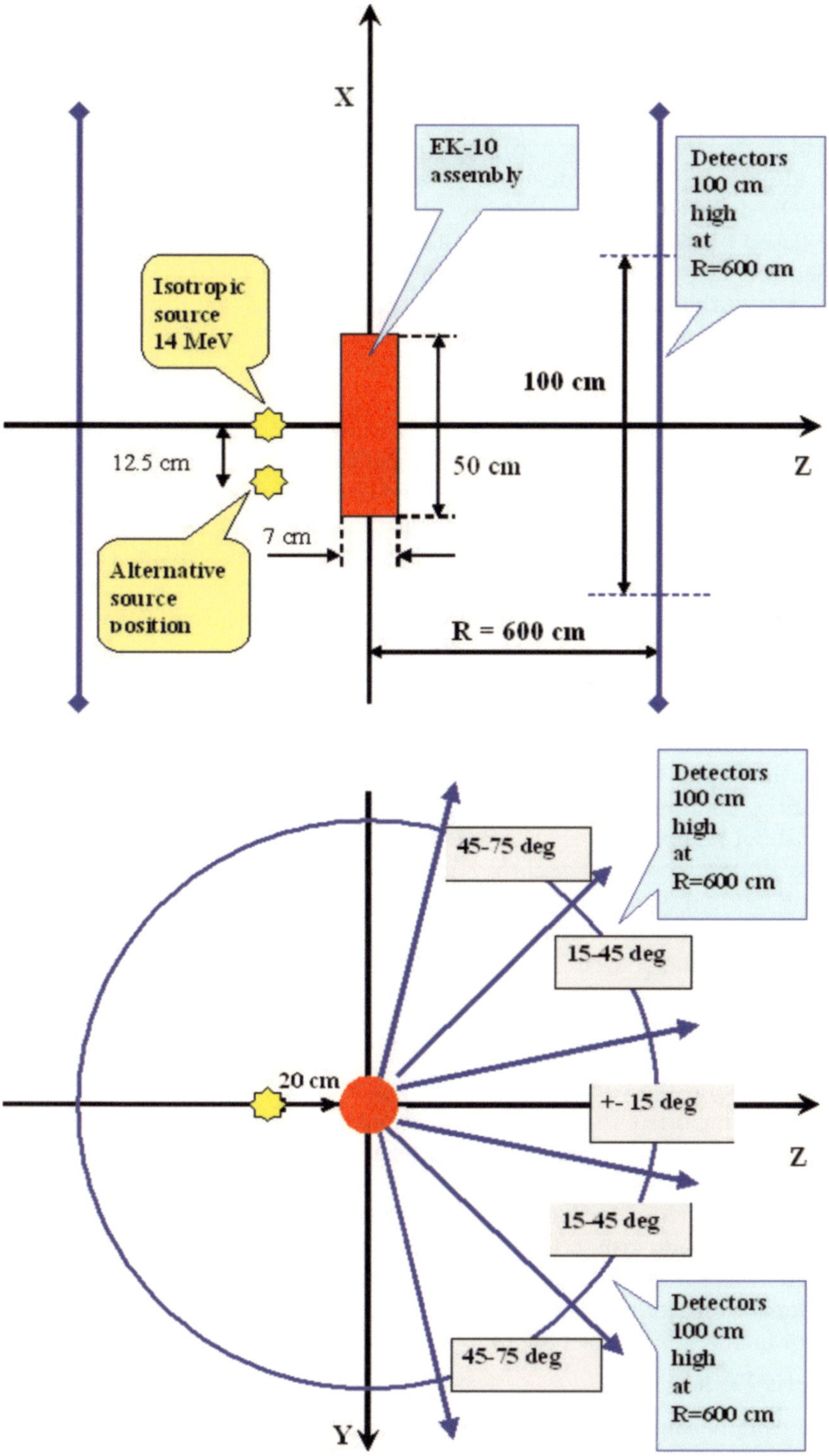

Fig. 4. Geometry of the experiment for 14-MeV neutrons irradiating fuel element EK-10

One may see that the number of fission neutrons may amount a few percent of the "low-energy" scattered neutrons. However taking into consideration that our DPF devices (PF-6 [4]) can produce neutron yield for E_0 ~ 2.466-MeV neutrons (i.e. operating with pure deuterium as a working gas) on the level 10^9 neutrons per pulse only, one may see that the number of high-energy (i.e. fission) neutrons coming to the detector's scintillator that has a 10-cm width in the above idealized geometry under consideration (Fig. 2) is not high enough to be detected them confidently. Thus we have to come to shorter distances between the DPF-based neutron source and the fuel element (compared with the above 2 meters), to wider neutron beams. Also we must use 14-MeV neutrons from DPF operated with DT mixture as a working gas. In this configuration the total neutron yield of PF-6 in a single shot is two orders of magnitude higher for this device (10^{11} n/pulse). However in this case spectrum of fission neutrons will have energies less compared with the energy of primary, i.e. 14-MeV neutrons.

Thus the next step in our simulation works was done in geometry (Fig. 4) more close to our real experiments produced with the PF-6 device and described below. The device was operated in the experiments with the DT-filled chamber.

With this geometry we provided numerical modelling by use of the FLUKA code again. This code has been developed for many years at CERN and Milan. The code distinguishes "high energy neutrons" and "low energy neutrons". The border is at 20 MeV. All neutrons with energy lower than 20 MeV are called "low-energy neutrons" and they are calculated separately and differently than other particles. To solve these low-energy neutron transport problems FLUKA applies the so-called multigroup method. This widely known approach is similar to that applied in famous MORSE MC code - one of the progenitors of modern MC calculations in radiation transport. In the case of FLUKA the whole low-energy neutron range, starting from neutron energy E = 20 MeV down to E = 1.0E-5 eV, is divided into 260 neighbouring, contiguous energy groups. Afterwards, due the course of calculations we don't say about neutron energy but rather about neutron group. In this way energy of each neutron is determined with accuracy to the group limits. Group numbers go always in descending mode (bigger group no. means lower energy). The TOF spectra are obtained by simple recalculation of neutron energies to time of flight – for distance 6 m in this case.

In this modelling the source is very simple. It is mono-energetic (14 MeV), point, instant, and fully isotropic source. For this reason one cannot observe in the spectra a peak at 2.45 MeV originated from the D-D reaction taking place inside the DPF chamber and seen in the real oscilloscope traces (see below).

Generally speaking the code doesn't distinguish elastic and non elastic collisions. All this information is included in the so-called transfer matrix. For each material (nucleus) the transfer matrix includes integrated cross-sections for all energy groups - recalculated to probabilities. Simply speaking, for each material and neutron energy group the probability distribution exists. These probabilities say: what is the chance that after a collision a neutron falls down into a given group. In other words, from this distribution the final (after collision) neutron group is sampled. Sampling of fission neutrons is made additionally after collision with fissionable materials. If we have a mixture of many nuclei a neutron chooses the nucleus for interaction on the base of total, macroscopic cross-sections.

Fuel assembly EK-10

Fuel composition is mixed UO_2 and Mg (73.33g of U-238, 8.05g of U-235, 13.03g of Mg).

An individual fuel element is a cylinder: 50 cm high and 7 mm in diameter, which makes 19.24 cm^3 of the total volume.

Element	Atomic number	Atomic weight [u]	Proportion by number [%]	Proportion by weight [g/cm³]
U-235	92	235.044	2.19	0.4184
U-238	92	238.051	19.71	3.8113
O	8	15.999	43.80	0.5693
Mg	12	24.305	34.30	0.6772

Fuel density: 5.4762 g/cm³

Fuel *assembly* was modelled as 16 cylindrical fuel pipes. Each pipe is 50 cm high and has an external diameter equal to 10 mm (7 mm of fuel + 2 x 1.5 mm of aluminium wall). The pipes are parallel to each other and they form sort of a ring bundle. Looking at the bundle cross sections (at YZ plane) the centres of these 16 pipes are on the ring with diameter 6 cm, and go around, thus the pipes are almost close to each other. In this way we can say that the „external diameter" of this ring of the pipes (whole assembly) is equal to 7 cm (and internal diameter 5 cm). Fig. 5 shows results of these calculations for spectra of 14-MeV neutrons scattered by several elements composing the fuel element.

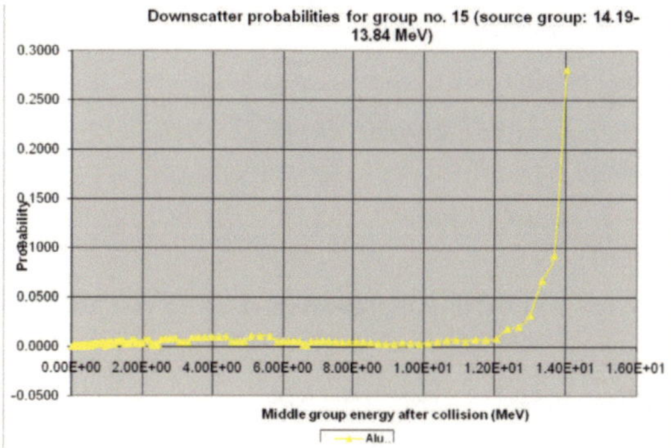

(a) Aluminum

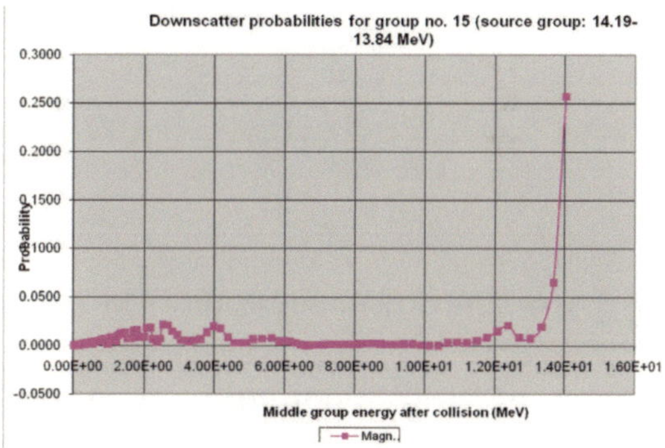

(b) Magnesium

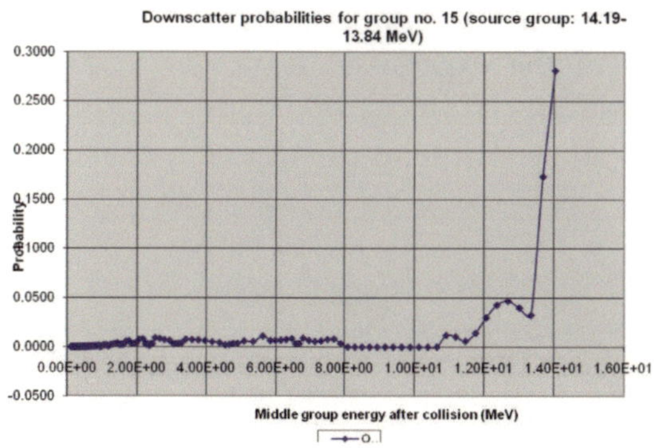

c) Oxygen

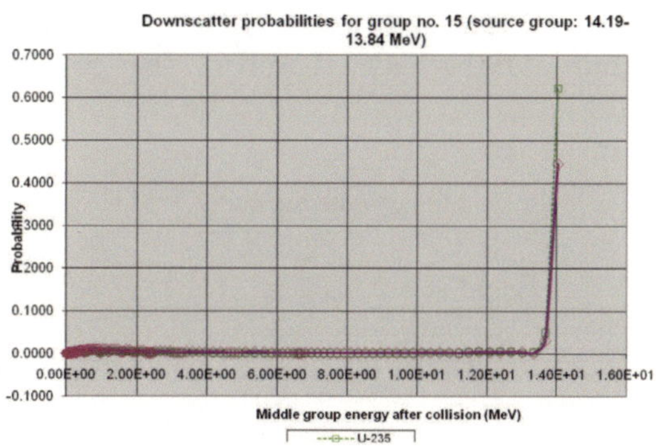

d) Uranium U-235 (□) and U-238 (○)

Fig. 5. Results of FLUKA-code calculations for spectra of 14-MeV neutrons scattered by several nuclei composing the fuel element

In the below results of calculations one may see peaks at different energies specific for each element's nucleus. Vast majority of neutrons are scattered *elastically* by the elements, and this peak merges with the main peak of primary neutrons: after scattering in given material, for instance Oxygen, of a neutron in energy group 15, the probability of getting a neutron in the same group (15) is 28.10%; that to get a neutron in the following group (group 16) is 17.34%, in group 17 it is 3.25% etc.

In Fig. 6 one may see spectrum of neutrons scattered on uranium nuclei with an enlargement of the region where we have to have our inelastically scattered (fission) neutrons (with spectrum centred near 0.5…1.5 MeV).

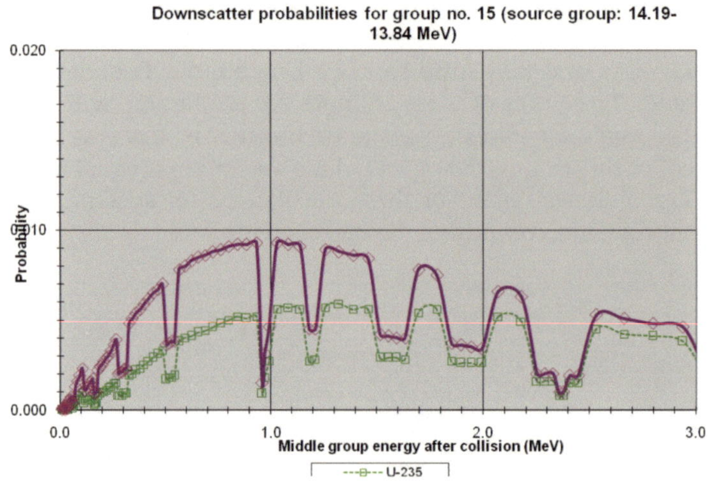

Fig. 6. Spectrum of neutrons scattered by uranium nuclei U-235 (□, green) and U-238 (◊, violet)

3. Tests of NINIS technique – "proof-of-principle" experiments

a. For a verification of our MCNP simulations we provide in our first session a *"proof-of-principle" experiment* investigating scattering of neutrons by 1-liter bottles of ethanol (C_2H_5OH) [6], methanol (CH_3OH) and phosphoric acid (H_3PO_4) positioned in a very close vicinity to the DPF chamber. The geometry of the experiment is shown in Fig. 7.

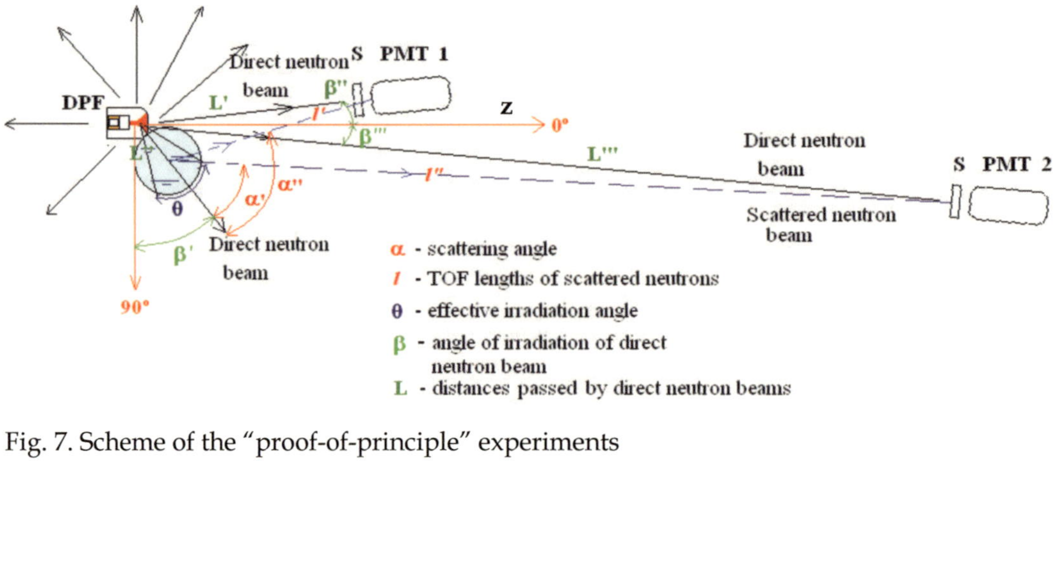

Fig. 7. Scheme of the "proof-of-principle" experiments

In the first cases we used in PF-6 the discharge chamber producing 10^9 of 2.45-MeV neutrons per shot (E_{bank} = 7 kJ) whereas later we operated with the DPF bank energy on the level of about 4-5 kJ with neutron output of the device ~ 3×10^8 neutrons per pulse. Our scintillator used for the PMT probe had a diameter 10 cm with its length of 10 cm. Our fast channels (photomultiplier tubes with scintillators - PMT+S) had in these experiments temporal resolution 3.12 ns. We used two channels placed in L' = 1.0-m and L'' = 18.5-m distances from the DPF. A typical result obtained with them for the second case is presented in Fig. 8. The lowest trace is the same as the middle one but taken with a higher sensitivity of the oscilloscope.
Preliminary testing shots made with the PF-6 device (IPPLM) have shown that the hard X-Ray pulse (HXR, photon energy $h\nu$ > 60 keV) always has its rise-time shorter than the temporal resolution of our PMT+S channels.

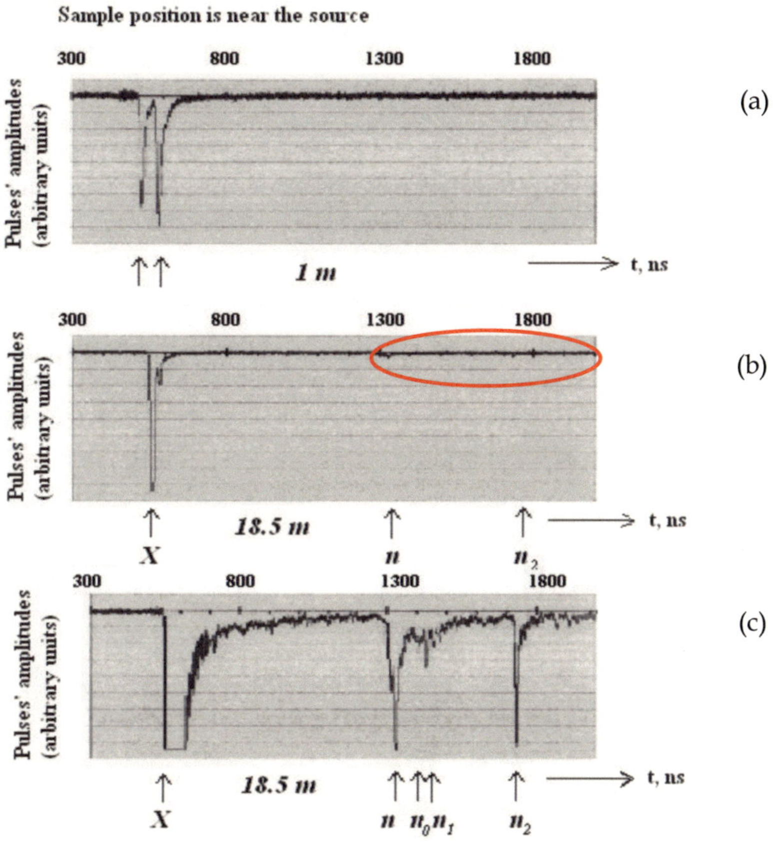

Fig. 8. Oscilloscope traces of PMTs placed at 1.0 and 18.5 meters from the target

At the same time a set of 100 successive shots made during this experiment simultaneously with two PMT+S placed at 3.5 and 7.5 meters from the DPF chamber in the same direction (along Z-axis) has shown that *inside the chamber* the neutron pulse follows the HXR pulse with the delay of 8 ns +/- 2 ns [6]. And what's more, the broadening of the same neutron pulse at the distance of 7.5 meters compared to the pulse measured at 3.5 meters shows that the neutron spectrum in Z-axis direction is monochromatic: $\Delta E/E \approx 1…3\%$.

In the oscilloscope trace of Fig. 8 (*c*) for the PMT+S positioned at 18.5-m distance a sequence of pulses is seen, which demonstrates different energies because of their delay time in relation to the hard X-Ray pulse.
First of all a calculation of neutrons' energy of the first pulse ("*n*"), seen in Fig. 8 and provided by use of time-of-flight (TOF) data with the help of formula:

$$E\,[\text{MeV}] = (L[\text{m}]\ /\ t\,[\text{ns}])^2 \times 5.23 \cdot 10^3,$$

has shown that the medial magnitude of the energy of these neutrons is ≈ 2.6 MeV. This value is a typical one for neutrons generated in a DPF in forward direction, i.e. with the small angle in relation to Z-axis of its chamber ("head-on" neutrons). However the so-called "side-on" neutrons generated at the angle 90° to Z-axis of a DPF chamber have energy 2.45 MeV.
To calculate the real position of neutron pulses "n_0" and "n_1" in the oscilloscope trace and consequently their TOF and energy we have to perform the following procedures:

1. To move to the left on the oscilloscope trace the hard X-Ray pulse by its TOF of 18.5 m (62 ns). It will be the moment of the appearance of the HXR pulse inside the chamber.
2. To move to the right on the oscilloscope trace the above point by 8 ns - it will be the moment for neutrons to top out their maximum inside the DPF chamber.

After the above procedure we shall have the *reference point*, from which we can calculate all time intervals needed for direct or scattered beams of neutrons to reach our PMT. Taking into consideration that our target is placed at a distance of 20 cm to the DPF chamber center and in the "side-on" position, we have to perform all calculations for the neutrons *having energy 2.45 MeV* and in the conditions that their direct TOF from the centre of the DPF chamber till the target is 10 ns. Effective angle of the bottle's irradiation was $\theta \approx 10°$.
Kinematics of elastic scattering of neutrons by different nuclei gives the diagram of the dependence of lost energy at collisions in relation to the neutron laboratory scattering angle (Fig. 9).

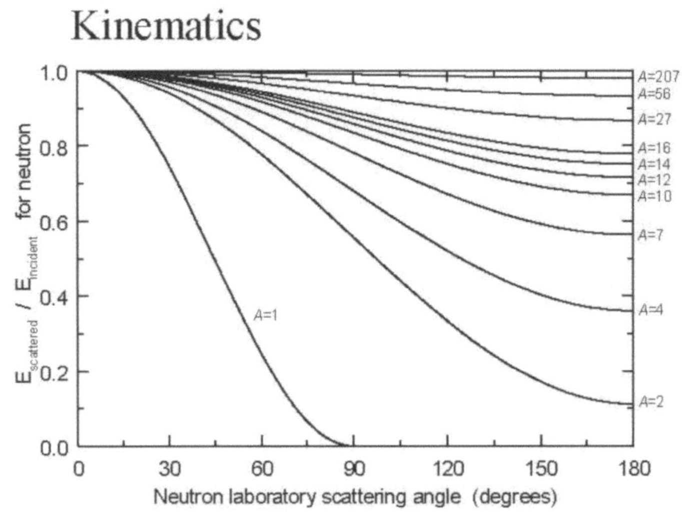

Fig. 9. Graph showing the ratio of energy of neutrons scattered by nuclei of various elements to the initial energy of neutrons of the irradiating beam in dependence of scattering angle

Our PMT+S probe was placed at the angle α of about 80° to the direction of the neutron beam passing through the centre of the bottle with methanol. From kinematics of scattering and in our experimental geometry one can see that our two peaks on the oscilloscope trace – "n_0" (908 - 10 = 898 ns) and "n_1" (925 - 10 = 915 ns) – may be attributed to the scattering of the *2.45-MeV neutrons* on the *oxygen* and *carbon* nuclei accordingly (Fig. 10). Uncertainty is resulted from neutron pulse's duration (τ), time resolution of detectors, from a precision of measurements of the peak's position on the trace, and due to TOF of neutrons through the bottle. It shows that in principle scattering on nitrogen nuclei can be distinguishable in this experiment as well.

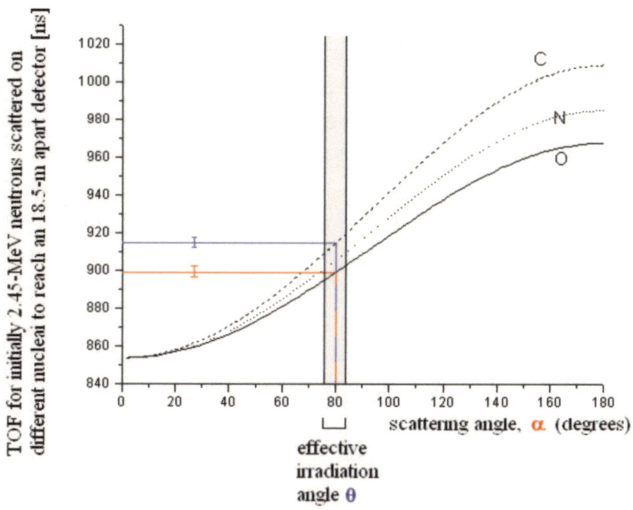

(a)

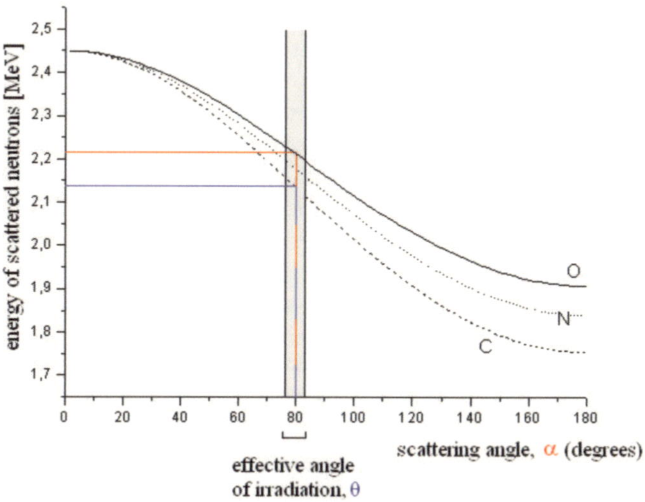

Fig. 10. TOF for 18.5 m (*a*) and energy (*b*) measurements plotted for the scattering scheme presented in Fig. 7

It appears also that our high-pressure 10-litre 1-m by height cylinder made of aluminium and filled with deuterium at a *high pressure* ≈ 150 atm. is responsible for "n_2" pulse. It was placed at 1 m from the DPF chamber. It has rather *small diameter* of about 14 cm (less compared with the space occupied by the neutron pulse in the propagation direction) and it was positioned *vertically* that resulted in a short scattering pulse.
It is interesting to compare cross-sections of 2.45-MeV neutrons, elastically scattered by nuclei of the above materials, and of 2.6-MeV neutrons – on a 20-cm *Teflon* cylinder (positioned in the direction of the PMT+S and blocking neutrons i.e. forming a sort of a "screen" for the strait-forward beam of neutrons). It appears that this figure is equal to 1.5 barns for nuclei of ^{12}C, whereas the related magnitude for ^{16}O, which is going to a minimum at 2.35 MeV (relatively narrow) in this range of $\sigma(E)$ is equal to 0.6 barns at its slope. Cross-sections of elastic scattering on deuterium and aluminium are 2.35 and 2.2 barns correspondingly. For fluorine and 2.6-MeV neutrons it is on the level of 1.5 barns. These figures together with the geometrical factors and chemical formulas of the substances under irradiation are very well fitted to the relative ratio for the amplitudes of the peaks "n", "n_0", "n_1", and "n_2".
b. Our next experiment was devoted to the clarification of the *restrictions of the method implied by distances and neutron yield* of the device. A 1-litre bottle with phosphoric acid (H_3PO_4) was used as a target in this very case. Diameter of the bottle was 10 cm. It was installed tightly with the DPF chamber, and the geometry of our experiments was the same as above with $\beta' \approx 35°$, $\beta'' \approx \beta''' \approx 27°$, L′=2.2 m, L″ = 8 cm, $\theta \approx 10°$, L‴ = 7 m. In these tests we have experienced an opportunity to use much lower bank energy (~2…3 kJ), smaller DPF chamber, and decreased neutron yield (~ 10^8 n/shot) which results in much lower activation of objects under interrogation and in shorter TOF base as well (2.2 meters). We used here 2 PMT of the SNFT type (2.5 ns time resolution) placed in two different distances from the scatterer in each experiment. In this case the neutron pulse duration detected at a close vicinity to the DPF chamber became 5-8 ns. Thus the longitudinal dimension occupied by the pulse in the direction of its propagation (or a "thickness" of an almost spherical neutron "shell" spreading from the DPF chamber into space) is about 10-15 cm.
Two typical oscilloscope traces taken at the experiments with a bottle of phosphoric acid obtained from S+PMT-1 for two different situations – when direct neutron beam to the PMT-1 from the DPF chamber was almost completely blocked by a screen and conversely when it irradiated a scintillator freely – are shown accordingly in Fig. 11 *a* and *b*.
Because the neutron detector signals contain an essential noise component in this case of a low dose of neutrons we used a Wavelet method suggested by MATLAB Wavelet Toolbox. We used De-noising 1-D. We considered the noise to be un-scaled white. The signal was presented by 2048 numerical points. We used soft fixed form of the threshold method. Fig. 11 *c* and *d* shows the de-noising of the signals, where a number of wavelets were used for real oscilloscope traces *a* and *b*. Different variants of wavelets give the same result with good accuracy. Thus one can see that the results of the wavelet de-noising allow identifying reliably peaks 1, 2, and 3. Same procedure as above has shown that peaks 2 and 3 belong to neutrons scattered by nuclei of phosphorus and oxygen.
Taking into account cross-sections and number of atoms in the acid's molecule we have verified why both peaks are almost equal by their amplitudes (difference is 1.2 times). Of course, to compare these amplitudes one has to subtract background from the overall signal as it is shown by vertical bars (red lines) in Fig. 11 *c* and *d*. Thus these sets of tests has shown

that even ~ 10^8 neutrons per pulse and TOF base equal to about 2 meters can still serve in certain cases in our NINIS technique.

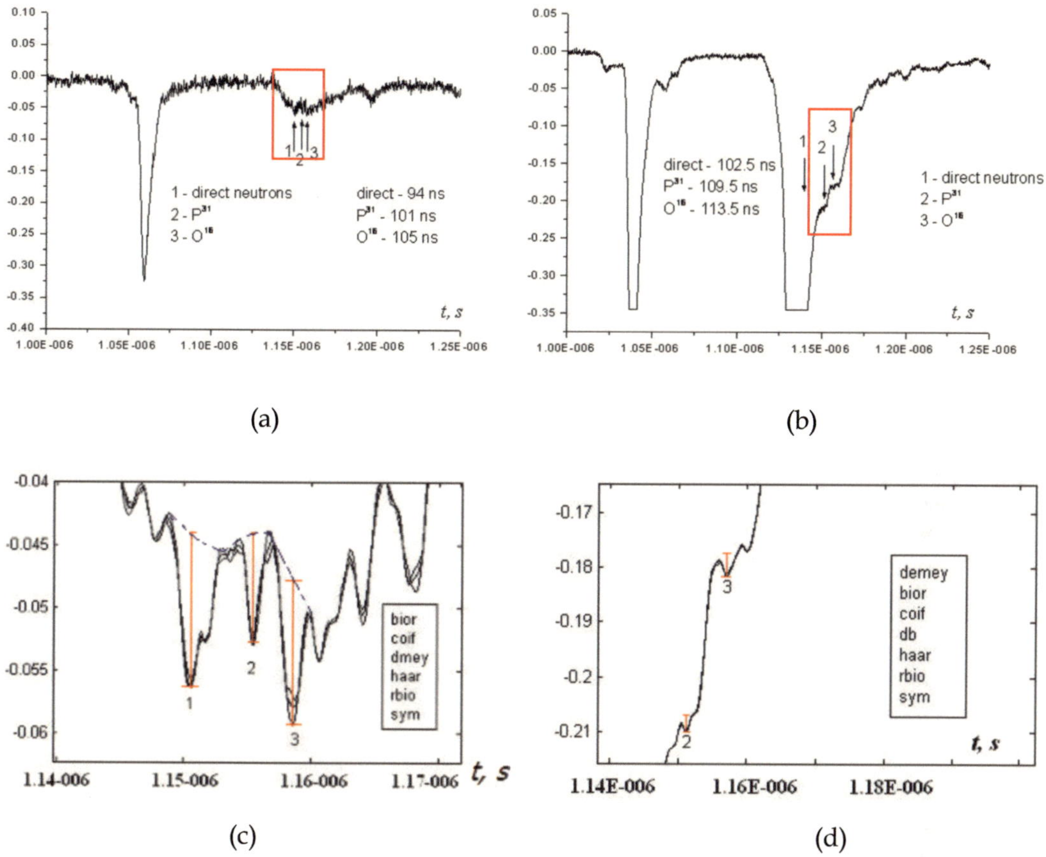

Fig. 11. Oscilloscope traces for the cases when direct beam of neutrons (1) was blocked almost completely by a neutron screen (*a*) and without screening (*b*); de-noising signals obtained with different wavelet types, level 2: (*c*) for (*a*) and (*d*) for (*b*)

c. Our next experimental session was devoted to *lengthy objects*. We used our high-pressure cylinder made by aluminium and filled with deuterium with the pressure of 70 atm. in this case. The geometry of the experiment was the same as shown in our MCNP simulations (Fig. 1a). Typical oscilloscope traces are shown in Fig. 12.

Difference in time lags between these experimental results and our simulation oscilloscope trace (Fig. 1c) is small. It comes from the fact that in our numerical modeling we supposed that DPF irradiates 2.45-MeV neutrons in *all* directions. In our real situation neutrons irradiated along Z-axis have energy 2.6 MeV. That is why they come to the detector slightly earlier. It is clearly seen also that the pulse of neutrons, scattered by deuterium, has the *same rise-time* as the neutron pulse from DPF. However it obeys *much longer tail* compared with the pulse of direct neutrons. It comes from the fact that the length of our object (~ 1 m) is about 4-5 times *higher* compared with the "thickness" of our neutron shell (≈ 20 cm).

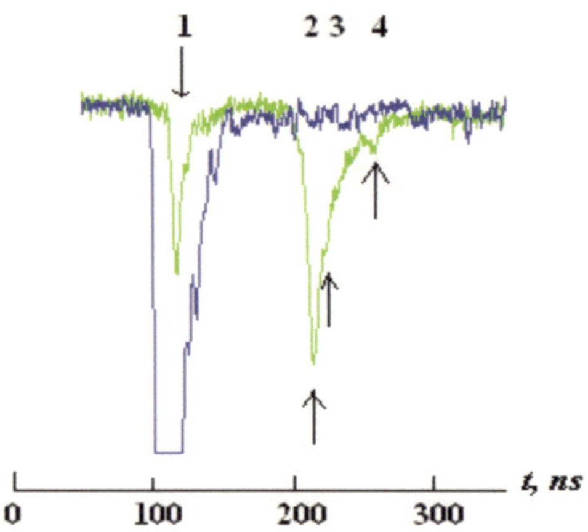

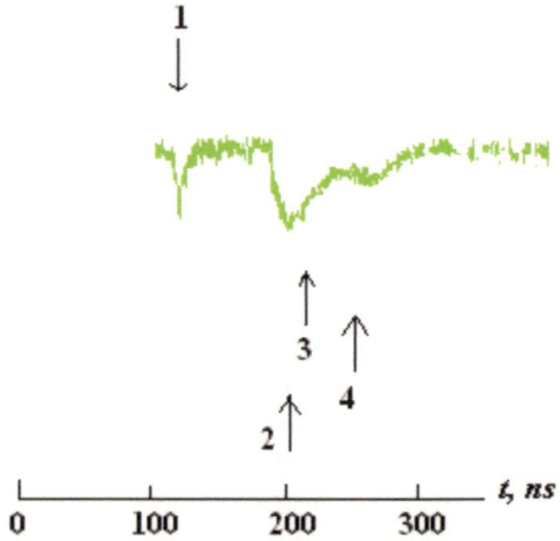

Fig. 12. Oscilloscope traces without a screen (a) and with it (b) blocking partially X-Rays (1) and direct neutrons (2) but not blocking neutrons scattered by Al (3) and D_2 (4) nuclei

Mean free path (MFP) of neutrons in deuterium at 70 atm. is:

$$L_D = 1/n\sigma = 1/2\times2\times2.7\times10^{19}\times70\times2.3\times10^{-24} \approx 100 \text{ cm},$$

where L_D – *MFP*, n – nuclei (atoms) concentration in 1 cm³, 2.7×10^{19} – Loschmidt's number, pressure p = 70 atm, and σ – cross-section of elastic scattering, i.e. L_D is about the length of our high-pressure cylinder l = 1 m. Thus this short single-pulse technique can characterize *geometry of objects*.

At the same time the pulse of neutrons scattered by aluminium wall of the cylinder is short. It reflects the fact that our PMT+S was oriented *along* the cylinder's wall, so neutrons scattered by the most distant part of the aluminium wall were *absorbed* by closer parts of it. Indeed the MFP of 2.45-MeV neutrons in aluminium is 20 cm:

$$L_{Al} = 1/n\sigma = 1/1.7\times10^{22}\times3\times10^{-24} \approx 20 \text{ cm},$$

with $n = \rho/u\times m_p = 2.7/27\times1.67\times10^{-24}$, where ρ – specific density of aluminium, u – unified atomic mass unity, m_p – proton's mass. So MFP here is much less compared with the cylinder length: $L_{Al} << l$. Thus our detector shows the neutrons scattered only by the part of the cylinder closest to the detector. However this MFP value in aluminium is about the same as the "thickness" of our neutron shell.

d. In the next session we used 14-MeV neutrons in preliminary experiments devoted to irradiation of *fissile materials* (*Fuel assembly EK-10*).

We have provided our experiments in the same geometry as it is presented in Fig. 4. Our preliminary estimations and examination of the above Fig. 5 and 6 as well as our experimental oscilloscope traces from our DPF operated with DT mixture as a working gas gave us the following moments for peaks *expected* in our TOF oscilloscope traces:

1. Main neutron energy peaks from the DPF source originating from D-T nuclear reactions according to our previous measurements: 1-st pulse – 14.0 MeV, 2-nd – 13.7 MeV, 3-rd – 12.5 MeV

2. ${}^{8}_{16}O$: 12.5; 11.0; 8.0…5.0; 2.5 MeV
3. ${}^{13}_{27}Al$: 5.5; 4.0; 2.7 MeV
4. ${}^{12}_{24}Mg$: 12.5; 5.5; 4.0; 2.3; 2.0; 1.8; 1.6 MeV
5. Neutron energy peaks from the DPF source originating from D-D nuclear reactions (having about 2 orders of magnitude lower amplitude compared with the 1st peaks) according to our previous measurements: 2.5…2.7 MeV
6. ${}^{92}_{238}U$ and ${}^{92}_{235}U$: 12.7; 3.5…(1.5-1.0)…0.5 MeV.

One may see that some of the above-mentioned peaks are overlap.

Taking into consideration that the hard X-Ray peak is generated inside the DPF chamber about 10-20 ns earlier compared with the maximum of the main pulse of 14-MeV neutrons we estimate positions of the most important pulses in the TOF oscilloscope traces estimated (recalculated from the above energies to time of flight) - for PMT+S detector placed at the distance 6 m in this case:

- HXR top - 0 ns,
- 14-MeV (direct) neutrons - 115 ns,
- 3-MeV D-D and elastically scattered neutrons - 250 ns,
- 1.5 MeV - 350 ns, 1.0-MeV - 433 ns, 0.5-MeV - 618 ns (fission neutrons),

and we found that these peaks in the oscilloscope traces of Fig. 13 and 14 are coincided with the above estimations and as well as with our modelling simulations presented in Fig. 6.

We have to mention here that one may see several additional peaks on the oscilloscope traces having nothing with our object under interrogation. They results from the neutron elastic scattering due to various elements of our DPF device such as DPF chamber (Cu), current collector (Cu), 4 transformers, 4 capacitors filled with castor oil, polyethylene and Teflon plates, cables, etc. They are positioned on different distances from the neutron source (usually further compared with the position of our bottle) and at dissimilar angles. However we know where we have to expect *the peaks of our interest* in the oscilloscope traces (usually first pulses of the chain) beforehand, and we found them namely in these time positions. Fortunately in this case we have no overlapping of these peaks with peaks from other elements as it was proved by the amplitude analysis.

e. Now it is interesting to understand *how many scattered neutrons can reach and can be captured by our scintillator*. Let us make estimations for the most doubtful case of scintillator having 50 cm in diameter and 50 cm by length when DPF irradiate only 10^8 2.45-MeV neutrons per pulse (case ***b***)). From geometry of the experiment it is easy to calculate that our bottle (10 cm in diameter and 15 cm by height placed at a distance 7.75 cm) encompasses ~1/7 part of the solid angle thus giving a figure for total number of neutrons irradiated it equal to about 14%. The above-mentioned cross-sections give evidence that the majority of neutrons coming to the bottle will be scattered by it. It means that the total number of scattered neutrons will be: $10^8 \times 0.17 \cong 1.7 \times 10^7$. At the distance of 2.2 meters where we have our S+PMT-1 the neutron flux density will be equal to 25 n/cm^2.

Taking into consideration that the neutron-receiving surface of the scintillator is 2×10^3 cm^2 and that almost a half of our neutrons ($E_n \sim 2.5$ MeV) will be captured by the scintillator of this thickness we obtain for the number of neutrons forming two our pulses (scattered by O and N nuclei) the figure more than 10^5 neutrons (note that nuclei of hydrogen do not scatter neutrons in this our geometry). This is a reasonable body for the two pulses of acceptable quality (i.e. we obtain rather good statistics).

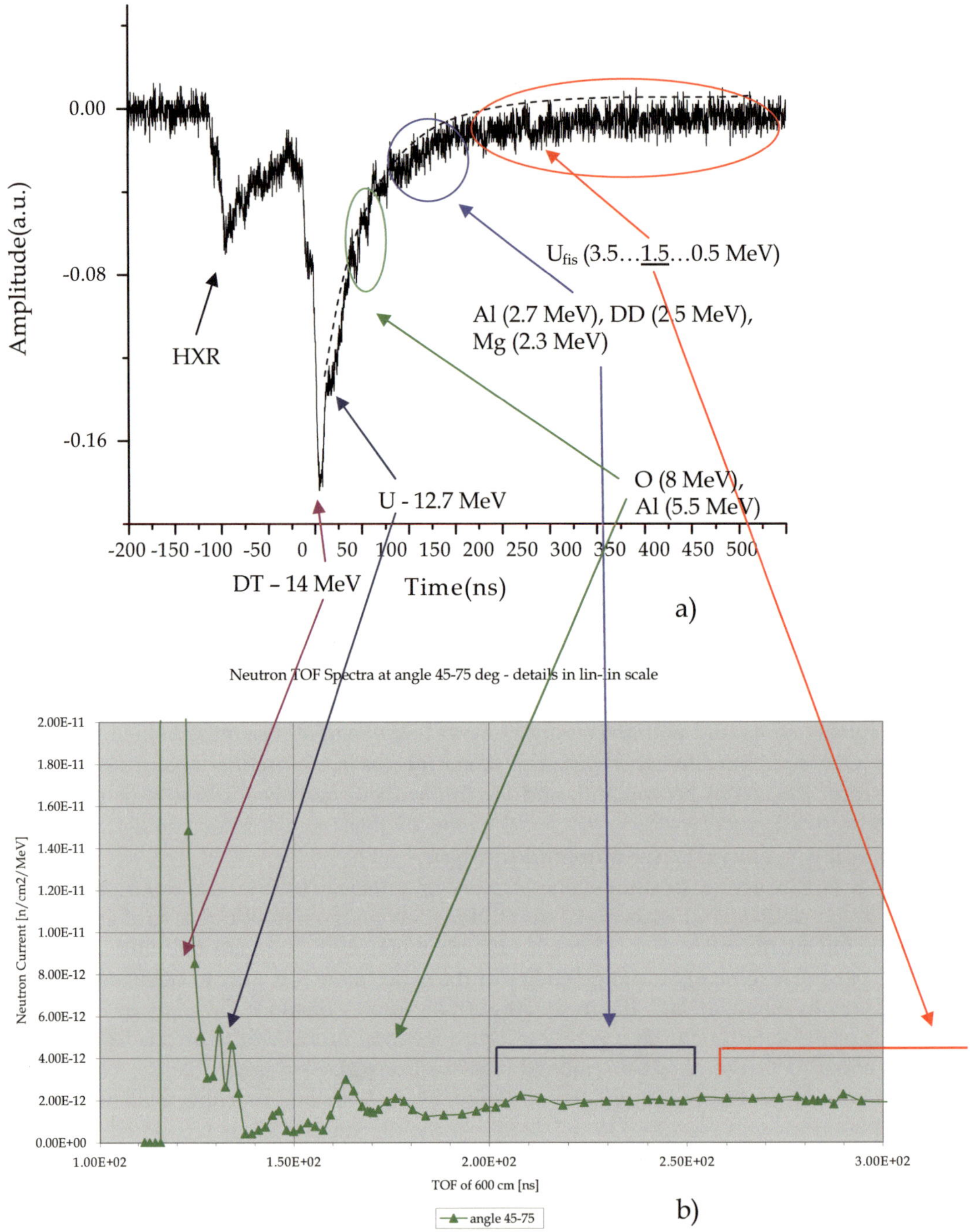

Fig. 13. Experimental oscilloscope traces (*a*) showing: 1) peaks of neutrons scattered by nuclei composing fission fuel element (U, O, Mg, Al); 2) sufficiently broader peak around 1.5 MeV belonging to fission neutrons; and 3) their comparison with numerical modelling made with the help of FLUKA code (*b*)

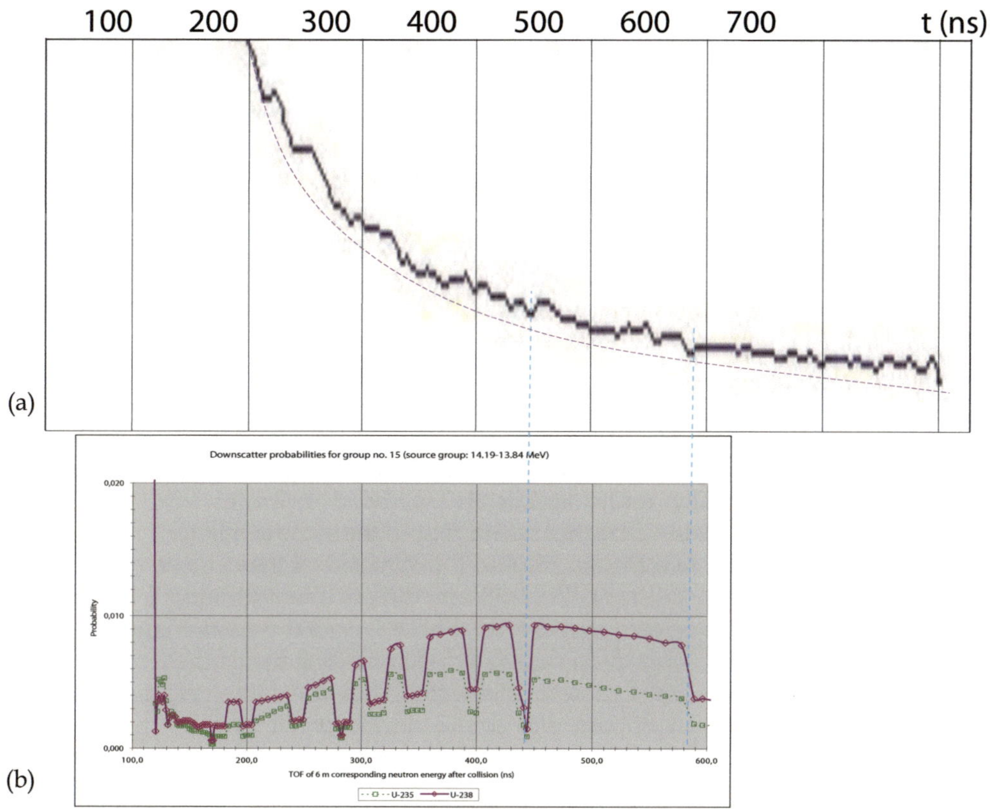

Fig. 14. Part of the oscilloscope trace related to the spectrum range of inelastically scattered by nuclei of U-235 and U-238 (i.e. fission) neutrons cleaned from noises by a Wavelet technique in relation to the TOF signal calculated by FLUKA code

f. Restrictions of the method

The method proposed has of course some restrictions. As it was shown in many works all explosive substances have in their contents hydrogen (a.w. = 1), carbon (a.w. = 12), nitrogen (a.w. = 14), oxygen (a.w. = 16) (and sometimes potassium (a.w. = 39). At the same time the main feature, which differs explosives from another substances, is *the almost equal percentage* of the above 4 main elements (H, C, O, and N) within them in contrast to common materials (see e.g. [1]). It means that taking into account cross-sections of elastic scattering of neutrons by the above nuclei we can expect the *predictable* (almost equal) amplitudes of the three peaks of neutrons scattered backward from C, O, N and separated one from another by the *predictable* time-delays as well as one peak of about the same amplitude scattered forward from H nuclei (at a proper choice of the scattering angles). Namely, presence of these 4 peaks at two PMT' oscilloscope traces will be a "signature" of an explosive in a box under interrogation.

Of course it is possible that some other elements positioned at another distance (and/or at another angle) may give a scattering peak, which overlap one of our peaks. In these circumstances still we shall have 3 suspicious peaks yet of distorted amplitudes. This is one of the restrictions of the method. However in this case we may repeat our shot making it at a different angle (rotating the object under interrogation). After this procedure we shall distinguish our peaks perfectly. Or we may use the 3-rd (or even 4-th) PMT+S placing it at a different angle to an object. Then we may compare our suspicious peaks *in the same shot*.

g. Perspectives

We believe that the perspectives of the NINIS method (an increase of its reliability in unveiling of illicit items and a decrease of its fault preditions) lie in the following additional techniques that may be exploited in the same single shot of the DPF device:

- use of both 2.45- and 14-MeV neutrons simultaneously (i.e. in filling of DPF by DT-mixture as a working gas) with measurements of elastically scattered neutrons of *both* energies,
- in measurements (additionally to scattered neutrons) of the *characteristic photons* appeared due to (n,γ) inelastic neutron scattering (both prompt and delayed),
- in application of hard X-Ray *imaging* of an object during the same DPF shot by use of an X-Ray flash produced by DPF (see e.g. Fig. 8),
- in elaboration of *automated* (computer-aided) procedure of the identification of chemical content of details (sub-items) of an object using X-Ray image in combination with data obtained from elastically and inelastically scattered neutrons and photons (n,γ) appeared due to (n,γ) inelastic neutron scattering in the same single DPF shot, and
- in exploiting of the fact that the spatial size ("thickness" of the neutron shell irradiated by a DPF device) is in the range 10…50 cm for an interrogation of large (e.g. sea containers) objects; having as a monitor the PMT+S system we shall know precisely at each moment the *configuration of our neutron shell* spreading inside the item, i.e. we shall know the distance between scatterers (elements inside the container) and the neutron source; it will give us an opportunity for identification of every pulse of scattered neutrons in the manner described above; use of a couple of 2D matrix of the PMTs ensures a characterization of the suspicious large-scale object with a spatial precision ("voxel") of the above-mentioned 10...50 cm.

However this *single-shot nanosecond technique* gives something more (as it was mentioned in the preface). We believe that this feature is very important and forms for NINIS its special niche between other methods. We mean the following aspect of the method. If a car of a suicide bomber fully loaded with explosives moves to its target with the speed 100 km per hour (as it happened by the spring of the year 2009 during the attempt on the life of the president of Ingushetia Yunus-Beck Evkurov in southern Russia) it passes during our *10-ns* neutron pulse a distance equal to 1 micrometer only. Thus for a DPF's neutron pulse it is a *static* object. Such a car can be interrogated and eliminated *before* it strikes the goal. Same opportunity may be important for interrogation of a train during its movement.

Second unique opportunity is connected with the fissile materials. Being almost monochromatic the nanosecond pulses of neutrons with energy around 2.45 MeV (for DD reactions) or 14.0 MeV (for DT reactions) irradiated by DPF may unveil these substances practically instantly with the distance of irradiation of a suspicious object from the DPF chamber just of the order of a meter. In this method fast measurements of both over-running neutrons and specific features of the induced fission neutron spectrum may be used.

Third opportunity is connected with the low-dose aspect of the NINIS technique. It is easy to estimate that at the pulse with the total number of 2.45-MeV neutrons equal to 10^9 per shot (which is perfect for NINIS) an object (e.g. a suicide bomber) at the airport standing at a distance of 1 meter from the DPF chamber and having a half-square-meter area will obtain a dose equal to a three-days background irradiation on the Earth surface or a dose equal to those absorbed by him during his planned flight.

4. Pulsed neutron source for Boron Neutron Capture Therapy - initial simulation results

The use of short and powerful neutron pulses for Boron Neutron Capture Therapy (BNCT) potentially could reduce the total dose absorbed by the patient. A Dense Plasma Focus device (DPF) emits very short (in the nanosecond range) and extremely intense pulses of X-Rays and fast neutrons (2.5- or 14-MeV neutrons energy from D-D or D-T nuclear reactions respectively). It was demonstrated that interaction of very powerful beam of X-Rays with bio-test objects during few nanoseconds can produce diverse effects on the biochemical functions of the cells [7]. The induction of the synergetic effects within the cells, e.g. producing a high concentration of secondary particles (free radicals, ions, and electrons) during a time interval short compared with the periods of durations of chemical reactions with the above particles, may result in a collective action of them.

Nevertheless there is no evidence up to now of the use of pulse neutron flash in BNCT, but it is known [8] that the use of nanosecond X-Ray pulses in radiation chemistry and biology could produce the desiderate effect with a considerable less total absorbed dose. At the same time in the work [9] it was shown that spectrum of neutrons where not only thermal but also fast neutron component is presented improves cancer treatment. From the other side in the paper [10] it was studied a possibility of using pulsed radiation of high-power in biological applications and its potential advantages.

The biological effects of radiation depend on the dose, the dose power and the spatial distribution of the microscopic energy deposition. To verify the recent studies of the interactions of pulsed radiation with biological tissues [11] in the context of BNCT treatment, we introduced in our model the effects of the temporal profile of the beam (pulsed versus continuous radiation).

In this work we focus on the development of a detailed simulation of interaction of short-pulse radiation generated by a DPF with tissue to estimate the absorbed dose by the cells for this dynamic case. The simulation was carried out by means of the Geant4 code [12], a toolkit to simulate the interaction of radiation with matter, originally developed for nuclear and particle physics. The experimental simulation was developed in three fundamental steps. The first consists in the modeling of the pulsed neutron source itself. The second is devoted to modeling of the interaction of fast mono-energetic neutrons with a moderator specific for BNCT. The third one is the development of a biological model to quantify the interaction of the pulsed neutron beam with a tissue.

4.1 Model

The simulation process includes: geometry of the system, materials involved, and physical processes governing particle interactions.

In the first stage a DPF was simulated. Using the Geant4 for the simulation of the system geometry, DPF was implemented following the features for the DPF construction (Fig. 15). The neutron source was taken with neutrons produced from the D-D reaction, i.e. with energy E = 2.45 MeV, and it had a flux $\Phi=10^9$ neutron/cm^2 on the wall of the discharge chamber of a DPF. It means that the overall neutron yield of the device is about 10^{12} neutrons/pulse in full solid angle. Several such DPF devices were in operation since the beginning of 70's [13]. With a present day technology [14] such neutron yield may be generated by this device having energy in their capacitor bank about 100...200 kJ, current on the level of 2.5...3 MA and with a footprint of the device (including its battery) about 5 m^2. In the case when a D-T mixture is used as a working gas this device may produce a flash of 14-MeV neutrons with the yield two orders of magnitude higher compared with pure deuterium working gas [15].

In the Geant4 model, the pulsed neutron radiation was generated. The specific capability of G4 to keep track of temporal evolution of the different processes was used to verify the temporal evolution signature of short neutron pulses at different distances from the source.

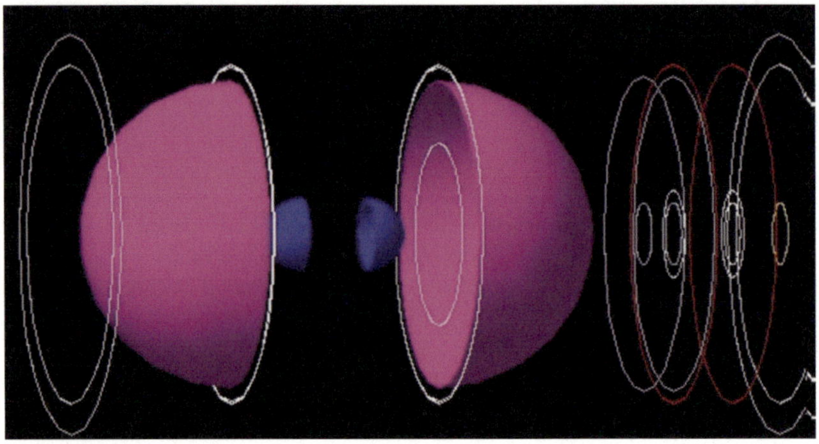

Fig. 15. Plasma Focus Device geometry simulated in Geant4. The internal diameter of the spherical anode (blue) of the device's chamber is 60 mm. The external diameter of the spherical cathode (pink) of the device's chamber is 120 mm

Important problem arising at the interaction of powerful pulses of neutrons with living tissues is the time duration of their interaction. In real experiment it has to depend on neutron interaction process with a moderator (second step) and then with a human phantom (third stage).

Neutron thermalization was studied in detail. For this case, a point neutron source surrounded by a water sphere with 0.5 cm radius was considered. An energy detector was placed at the sphere surface. The resulting neutron spectrum was calculated and subsequently used in the simulation of the interaction process of them with the cells cluster at the second stage of our computing.

This model includes also the development of a human phantom placed at 3 meters from the pulsed neutron source, and the evaluation of Dose deposition in a phantom produced by each neutron pulse. The energy deposition is found placing a detector in the phantom to measure the energy deposited in the body.

Another set of calculations was provided for the special case where we tried to preserve as much as possible the short duration of the neutron pulse generated by a DPF.

These neutrons (D-D fusion neutrons with energy of 2.45 MeV and D-T fusion neutrons with energy of 14 MeV) need to be moderated to the optimal neutron energy spectrum for BNCT. Moderating the neutrons to near the optimal energy of 10 keV [16] can be performed in two stages. In the above-mentioned study [16] the best results were achieved with iron and Fluental™ moderator materials. Fluental™ (69% AlF_3/30% Al/1% LiF) is a neutron moderator material developed at VTT in Finland. The material combination of Fluental™ is ideal to decrease the neutron flux to the desired energy range of 10 keV without over-moderation. This particular energy (10 keV) is good for cancer therapy from three points of view - relatively long penetration depth of these neutrons into human body (a few cm), favorite (as it was shown in [9]) neutron spectrum enriched by fast neutrons, and still a high cross-section of neutrons' absorption by boron nuclei (for applicability of BNCT). In Fig. 16 we present geometry of our moderator's assembly.

Fig. 16. Moderator's assembly: copper layers (white), Fluental™ material (blue), iron (yellow), plasma column, producing neutrons inside the DPF discharge chamber (red)

However a problem is raised here: whether this moderation process (being in any case much more preferable in comparison with moderation by hydrogen-containing substances like water) will preserve the pulse duration τ of the neutron radiation from DPF still much shorter than the duration of reactions with e.g. free radicals (i.e. $\tau \ll 1$ μs)?

4.2 Geometry of the modeled cell's cluster

A closed packed structure of 14 spheres made from homogeneous material, whose composition was defined using the parameters of table (1) from ICRU [11] was used. The arrangement of the cells in the cluster was optimized to use less space [17] (see Fig. 17). Each cell had a diameter of 13 μm. The cell composition used in our model was that defined by ICRU [11] (table1), but we included a Boron with the concentration of 30 ppm of boron nuclei per tissue's molecules.

Composition of the Cell Medium						
	Hydrogen	Carbon	Nitrogen	Oxygen	Phosphorus	Boron
Tissue	59.59 %	11.109 %	4.039 %	24.239 %	1.009 %	0.0029 %

Table 1.

4.3 Dose distribution and number of tracks through the cluster

Geant4 calculates the neutron interaction with the cell's atoms using a Monte Carlo algorithm and tracks of the resultant particles produced by the nuclear reactions, including also the secondary reactions of the resultant's particles. The energy deposition is found placing a detector in the cytoplasm to measure the energy deposited in the cell. The dose (in Grays) and the mean track length of the particles (in micrometers) are then evaluated.

4.4 Results

In this section we present general results obtained with our simulations.

The pulsed simulated neutron spectrum was calculated with its initial time spread of 10 ns. Its moderated spectrum was found in general agreement with the predictions, given the amount of moderation material in front of the neutron source. The relative amount of quasi-thermal neutrons (with energy less than 1 MeV) was found to increase with the amount of fluental material. A preliminary tradeoff of the desired neutron spectrum with the optimal pulse spread was calculated.

Fig. 17. Image of cell cluster as simulated by G4. Dimension of the cell cluster is around 26 μm of diameter, arranged in order to minimize the space by each cell. The cells in the cluster were surrounding by water

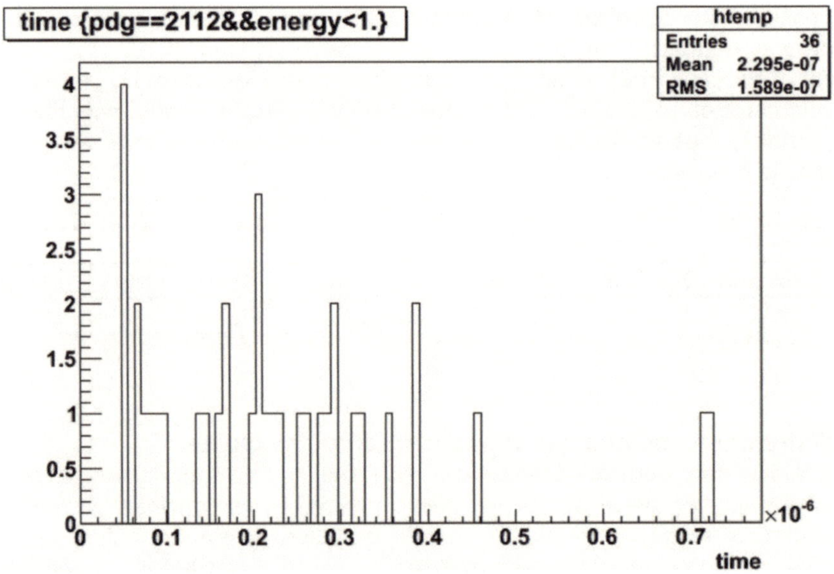

Fig. 18. Temporal shape of a 50-ns pulse of 2.5-MeV neutrons after its moderation by means of the assembly shown in Fig. 16

Similar studies were performed with a large iron/fluental moderator (see Fig. 16), where a larger moderation is obtained while keeping the neutron pulse within the time scale much less than 1 microsecond. The resulting spectrum was found to be much more thermal than the previous one. In these calculations we used a 50-ns neutron pulse. The final pulse shape width (FWHM) was found to be 200 nanoseconds, only a factor of 4 more than the initial neutron pulse width (see Fig. 18).

The resulting spectrum is then moderated by a large water sphere to simulate an isotropic flux as the one delivered to treated cells. The dose delivered to small cells was then preliminary evaluated. First, we have found that the dose is distributed homogeneously among the cells within the cluster. Second, we found small differences in dose deposition between the cells of the cluster. These differences arise mostly from the differences in a number of tracks through each cell; therefore the number of neutrons will be more important in determining the number of tracks through the cells rather than the energy of the neutrons. The preliminary results we obtained at this level need to be validated since the ability of Geant4 to track neutrons inside the cell cluster at such small scales has to be demonstrated. We will plan dedicated measurements to validate our results. The result from this model suggests that one should plan the *in vitro* experiment in mammalian cells using pulsed neutron source taking into account that the dose deposition will be homogeneously distributed around tissue.

5. Acknowledgments

The work was partly supported by grants from: Polish Ministry of Science and Higher Education No. O N202 049735 and from NATO Science for Peace Programme, SfP-981118.

6. References

[1] J. Csikai "Neutron-based techniques for the detection of concealed objects", *Proc. of the enlargement workshop on "Neutron Measurements and Evaluations for Applications"*, 5-8 November 2003, Budapest, Hungary, Report EUR 21100 EN

[2] A.M. Pollard, C. Heron, Archaeological chemistry, Cambridge, Royal Society of Chemistry (1996)

[3] a) F.D. Brooks, A. Buffler, M.S. Allie, K. Bharuth-Ram, M.R. Nchodu and B.R.S. Simpson "Determination of HCNO concentrations by fast neutron scattering analysis", *Nuclear Instruments and Methods in Physics Research* A 410 (1998) 319 - 328

b) G. Nebbia, S. Pesente, M. Lunardron, S. Moretto, G. Viesti "Use of neutron based technique in the control of illicit trafficking of fissile and explosive material", *S. Apikyan and D. Diamond (eds.), Countering Nuclear and Radiological Terrorism,* 271-290 (2006) Springer, Printed in the Netherlands

c) Yigang Yang, Yuanjing Li, Haidong Wang, et al. "Explosives detection using photoneutrons produced by X-rays", *Nuclear Instruments and Methods in Physics Research* A 579 (2007) 400–403

d) Kiyoshi Yoshikawa, Kai Masuda, Teruhisa Takamatsu, Seiji Shiroya, Tsuyoshi Misawa, Eiki Hotta, Masami Ohnishi, Kunihito Yamauchi, Hodaka Osawa, Yoshiyuki Takahashi "Research and development of a compact discharge-driven D–D fusion neutron source for explosive detection" *Nuclear Instruments and Methods in Physics Research* B 261 (2007) 299–302

e) E.T.H. Clifford, J.E. McFee, H. Ing, H.R. Andrews, D. Tennant, E. Harper, A.A. Faust "A militarily fielded thermal neutron activation sensor for landmine detection", *Nuclear Instruments and Methods in Physics Research* A 579 (2007) 418–425

f) G. Vourvopoulos, P. C. Womble "Pulsed fast/thermal neutron analysis: A Technique for Explosives Detection"; www.wku.edu/API/research/explo.htm - PELAN

g) "GIOS: Gerät zur Identifizierung Organischer Substanzen", I.U.T. (Institut für Umwelttechnologien) GmbH (brochure); http://www.iut-berlin.de/

[4] a) MCNP - A General Monte Carlo N-Particle Transport Code, Version 5, X-5 Monte Carlo Team, Diagnostics Applications Group, Los Alamos National Laboratory, "MCNP Homepage", http://mcnp-green.lanl.gov/index.html
b) „MCNP5 Homepage", http://mcnp-green.lanl.gov/about_mcnp5.html
[5] a) G. Battistoni, S. Muraro, P.R. Sala, F. Cerutti, A. Ferrari, S. Roesler, A. Fasso`, J. Ranft, "The FLUKA code: Description and benchmarking", *Proceedings of the Hadronic Shower Simulation Workshop 2006*, Fermilab 6--8 September 2006, M. Albrow, R. Raja eds., AIP Conference Proceeding 896, 31-49, (2007)
b) A. Fasso`, A. Ferrari, J. Ranft, and P.R. Sala, "FLUKA: a multi-particle transport code", CERN-2005-10 (2005), INFN/TC_05/11, SLAC-R-773
c) "FLUKA Homepage", http://www.fluka.org/fluka.php
[6] a) V.A. Gribkov, R. Miklaszewski "On a possibility of the single-shot detection of hidden objects by using nanosecond impulse neutron inspection system", *Acta Phys. Chim. Debr.* XXXVIII-XXXIX (2005) 185-193
b) V.A. Gribkov, R.A. Miklaszewski "Nanosecond Radiation Pulses for Rapid Detection of Explosives", *"Combined Devices for Humanitarian Demining and Explosives Detection"*, http://www-pub.iaea.org/MTCD/publications/PDF/Pub1300_label.pdf, *Proc. of an IAEA Tech. Meeting, Padova,* 2006, IAEA-TM-29225, A-03
[7] V.A. Gribkov, M.A. Orlova, "Enzyme Activation and Inactivation Induced by Low Doses of Irradiation", *Applied Biochemistry and Biotechnology*, vol. 88, pp. 243-255, 2000
[8] V.A. Gribkov, A.V. Dubrovsky, M.A. Orlova, M. Scholz, "Opportunities Afforded by New Generation of Pulsed Radiation Sources in Flash Radiation Physics and Chemistry", *Research Journal of Chemistry and Environment*, vol. 9 (4), Dec., pp. 11-19, 2005
[9] T.A. Buchholz , J.S. Rasey, G.E. Laramore, J. Livesey, L. Chin, R. Reisler, A. Spence, T.W Griffin, "Concomitant boron neutron capture therapy during *in vivo* fast neutron radiation of a rat glioma", *Radiology,* 191 (3) (1994) 863–867
[10] V. A. Gribkov, A. V. Dubrovsky, M. Scholz, et al., "PF-6 – an effective plasma focus as a source of ionizing radiation and plasma streams for application in material technology, biology and medicine", *Nucleonika*, 51, No.1 (2006) 55-62
[11] ICRU, Tissue Substitutes in Radiation Dosimetry and Measurements, Report 44, International Commission on Radiation Units and Measurements, Bethesda, MD, 1989
[12] A. Agostinelli et al., "Geant4 - a simulation toolkit", *Nuclear Instruments and Methods in Physics Research,* A 506 (2003) 250-303
[13] A. Bernard et al., "Scientific status of plasma focus research", *Journal of the Moscow Phys. Soc.*, 8, No. 2 (1998) 93-170
[14] V.A. Gribkov, L. Karpinski, P. Strzyzewski, M. Scholz, A. Dubrovsky, "New efficient low-energy dense plasma focus in IPPLM", *Czechoslovak Journal of Physics*, 54, Suppl. C (2004) C191-C197
[15] a) V.P. Vyskubov, V.A. Gribkov, L.M. Zhogov et al., "On the DPF Operation with the D-T Mixture", *P.N. Lebedev Physical Institute Reports*, M: FIAN, No. 12 (1979) 37-41
b) All-Russia Research Institute of Automatics (VNIIA), "VNIIA homepage": http://www.vniia.ru
[16] H. Koivunoroa, D.L. Bleuela, U. Nastasib, et al., "BNCT dose distribution in liver with epithermal D-D and D-T fusion-based neutron beams", *Applied Radiation and Isotopes*, 61 (2004) 853–859
[17] V.J. Petteri, L. Juha, K. Antti, I. Sami, S. Jiri, S. Sauli, "Comparison of different cell-cluster models for cell-level dosimetry", *Acta oncologica*, 40, No. 1 (2001) 92-97

14

HERWIG: a Monte Carlo Program for QCD at LHC

Giuseppe Marchesini
University of Milano–Bicocca and INFN Sezione di Milano–Bicocca, Milano
Italy

1. Introduction

Monte Carlo programs could be used for the partial description of particle physics production at high energy. These particles are hadrons, such as proton, neutron, pion and many others. They are described by QCD (quantum chromodynamics). At perturbative level QCD is formulated as gauge interaction of quarks and gluons which have color number force. They produce hadrons as physical bound states, see for instance (1). At non perturbative level, controlled numerically by computer simulations, QCD produces physical hadrons. The mass of the proton is about 1.672×10^{-27} kg $\simeq 0.937$ GeV.
The FermiLab machine, see (2), has proton and antiproton running in the center of mass with an energy of 2 TeV. It was intensively operating in the last years. The FermiLab is located near Chicago.
The LHC (large hadron collider) machine is located at CERN, see (3). The machine is made of two round circles which are 27 km long. Here particles are running near Geneva between France and Switzerland. The two protons are running here one against the other with an energy of 3.5 TeV c^2 so that the total mass of the colliding system is of 7 TeV. This machine started at the end of 2009. It operates until 2011 and then it will start again at a double of its present total colliding mass.
The LHC total colliding energy discloses a key point of the Standard model for particle physics, the presence of the Higgs meson which is expected with a mass between hundred and hundred and fifty time the proton mass, i.e. M_{Higgs} between 100 and 150 GeV. The Higgs meson is needed to give a simple description of the present Standard model. His absence should generate a substantial problem to this theory which unifies all elementary particle physics. A major point of the Higgs field is that it gives a mass to the weak boson Z and $W^{\pm}$. The above limit on Higgs mass are obtained from intense studies of present data on particle experiments at FermiLab, see (2), and at CERN, see (3).
The Standard model is the present theory for elementary particles, except for gravitational forces. This theory includes QCD and involves electroweak particles such as leptons (electron, muon and tau) and corresponding neutrinos. It involves photons and massive electroweak bosons as Z and $W^{\pm}$.
QCD is the theory one uses for hadron interactions. Hadrons are strong interaction particles such as barions (as proton, nucleon etc) and mesons (as pions etc.). By perturbative description these fields interact via a gauge Lagrangian. Fields are given by partons, i.e. quark, antiquark and gluon. Hadrons are made of bound states of these elementary fields. The perturbative formulation does not allow to generate hadrons which are color singlet states of partons (color is one of parton index). QCD hadrons are generated as bound states of quarks

and gluons acting near the initial or final states. They are not reconstructed by perturbative order.

At perturbative level one needs to introduce an artificial scale M_0. Above this scale quark and gluon interaction is well definite and perturbative analysis can be done. But at low scale one has divergences for $M_0 \to 0$ and one needs to introduce hadrons. Such an impossibility forces one to maintain a finite scale of M_0. It could be fixed by perturbative analysis and its effective value is of the order of the proton mass. Below that infrared scale M_0 one has that non perturbative effects need to be involved to give hadrons in the initial or final states, but this generation of hadrons could be treated only numerically and no clear theory is still known.

One expects at the infrared scale M_0 hadrons are composed as bound states of quarks and gluons. They are single states composed as color space (i.e. singlet in color space). They have a small mass and could be used to generate hadrons. Since no clear theory exists at the moment, hadrons are generated artificially. Their states are mainly close in space-time.

The perturbation theory is intensively considered in many details here. It is the basis for the Monte Carlo program called HERWIG (hadron reaction with interfering gluons). See (4). Other similar models for particle generations in these events are given in two reports in (5).

1.1 LHC processes and the HERWIG model

The HERWIG Monte Carlo model is essentially based on many results of perturbative QCD. It generates quarks and gluons in processes which are at short momentum distances. As we discussed above, HERWIG involves partons with an infrared artificial scale M_0. These are the relevant programs for many physical processes involving Higgs boson generation as we shall see.

An important part of the HERWIG program is the study of Higgs field which is needed to generate the mass of intermediated weak bosons Z and $W^{\pm}$. Later we will comment on this model.

The HERWIG Monte Carlo program for LHC starts from the collision of a pair of protons and generates hadrons in the final state process. It could be generalized to include general Standard model particles. Here we consider again simplifications by using only QCD processes, see later for extensions.

The Monte Carlo program is characterized by analysing processes which are at short distances or large momentum Q_{hard}. They are very important for QCD and specific for Higgs search, see later.

Each incoming proton is fragmented into three quarks at a scale M_0. One of this quarks starts the hard process by generating further partons via successive radiation which are characterized by the hard scale Q_{hard}. Later the produced final partons recombine to generate the final hadron states as recombination of final partons at soft scale M_0. HERWIG processes are then characterized by the hard physical scale Q_{hard} and the artificial scale M_0. A general picture of these collisions is then given in Fig. 1.

Here the two incoming protons are represented as black lines. Both protons have initial state emissions. Each proton emits an interacting quark of virtual mass M_0 which undergoes successive emissions of quarks and gluons considered later for parton reconstruction at the end of the full cascade (see green box).

All these collisions are characterized by the hard scale Q_{hard} which enters in the hard event. The hard parameter Q_{hard} is here the momentum of emitted hard parton with respect to the incoming proton. Hard partons are generated in the hard collision at the center of this picture.

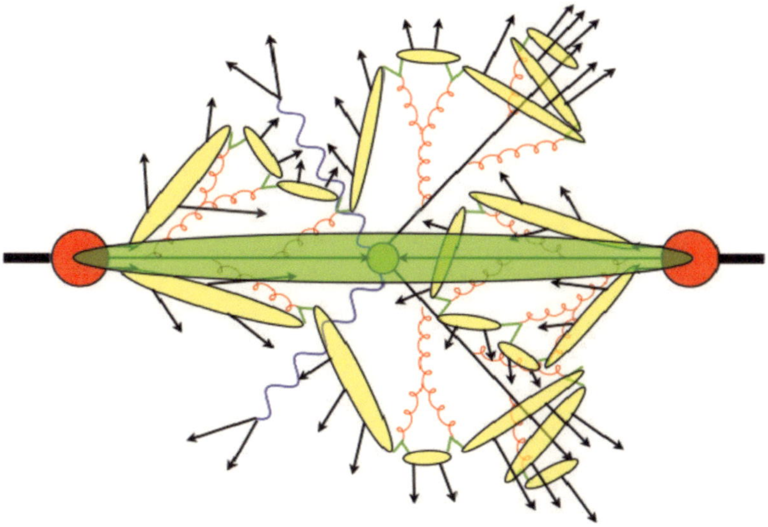

Fig. 1. LHC Monte Carlo evolution described by HERWIG program. Two protons are incoming. A proton is made of three quarks. A generation of Standard model particles is produced. Quarks are yellow and gluons are red

These partons and all other partons emitted in the initial state branching undergo successive branching into softer partons. The final emitted partons have an artificial scale M_0. They need to go under final hadron reconstructions. In the cascade a quark (a black line) undergoes gluon cascade (yellow line) which emits again gluons or quarks and antiquarks. They decay in the cascade to the soft mass M_0.
In hard collision photons are generated (green lines) and decay into a pair of electrons and positrons.
The preconfinement model force all emissions to construct hadrons in the final state (see the yellow boxes). For this reconstruction model see reference (6). Notice that incoming partons emitted by one of the incoming proton are used to reconstruct final hadrons.
One has that parton evolution and hard scattering are within perturbative QCD physics (at least to leading order). What is not included in hard QCD is the parton decay and recombination here represented as green boxes. Here hadrons are generated as from Particle Data Book, see (7).
The next picture in Fig. 2 represents the HERWIG model for the CERN machine for e^+e^- collisions. First one has the e^+e^- collision emitting a γ which dacays into $q\,\bar{q}$ starting the final state branching. Here one sees $q \to qg$ and $g \to gg$. Then, after $q\bar{q}$ formation out of each final state gluon at M_0 one generates color singlet $q\bar{q}$. They form color singlets of small mass (see later) which cluster into hadrons which may decay. Here hadrons are generated as from Particle Data Book in (7).

1.2 Some indications on general evens

Complications to involve other processes in QCD or in more general theories could be here included, see (3). They could involve the full electroweak model. First of all one could generate electrons, positrons and photons and study their successive decay. Or one studies the production of weak bosons such as Z and $W^\pm$ and their decay. In the same way one

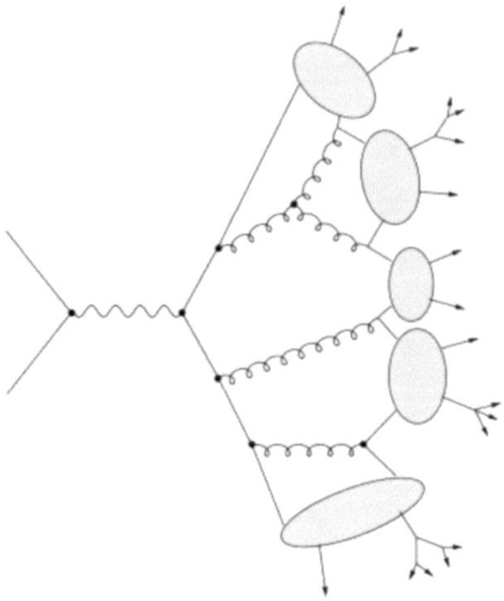

Fig. 2. e^+e^- Monte Carlo evolution in HERWIG program

involves neutrinos and antineutrinos. Finally one could include the Higgs production with its decay. This is actually the most studied program at LHC.
One could extend the model to study in HERWIG non electroweak processes as previewed by extension beyond the Standard model.
The HERWIG program has been intensively used for various processes involving other initial state particles.

1.2.0.1 FermiLab machine for $p\bar{p}$ collision.

The HERWIG program was used to study proton and antiproton entering the collisions as in the collider near Chicago operating at 2 TeV. Many results have been obtained here and the HERWIG program was heavily used. See (2).

1.2.0.2 DESY machine for *pe* collision.

The HERWIG program has been used to study other type of processes. One is the electron-proton collision at DESY near Hamburg. There is an electron ring of 30 GeV running against a proton ring of 820 GeV. Here the events are studied by using essentially the HERWIG program with a different organization with one electron (or positron) as incoming particle instead of a proton in LHC. This machine proved quite well many basis of QCD, the Standard model and analyzed models beyond the Standard one. See (8).

1.2.0.3 CERN machine for e^+e^- collision.

The HERWIG program was also intensively used for LEP (large electron positron) at the electron-positron collision with a total energy of about 100 and 200 GeV. See (9). This e^+e^- collider was at CERN and now it is replaced by the LHC machine. Many aspects of QCD have been studied. The same for the Standard model and models beyond the Standard one. Here the electroweak particles have been intensively studied.
In all these studies HERWIG was used to consolidate the theory and in particular its strong forces. It is very interesting that many properties of perturbative QCD can be extended to all of these hard processes. Again, the missing point of the hadron formation involving the soft scale M_0 are missed theoretically. They are represented as parton formation by preconfinement. For a generalization to present energies at LHC see (10).

2. The LHC accelerator

The LHC is a proton-proton accelerator at 7 TeV in the center of mass (it will move to 14 TeV). One of its main aim is the discovery of the neutral Higgs boson with a mass between hundred and hundred and fifty time the proton mass, i.e. between 100 and 150 GeV. In Fig. 3 one has the CERN accelerator.

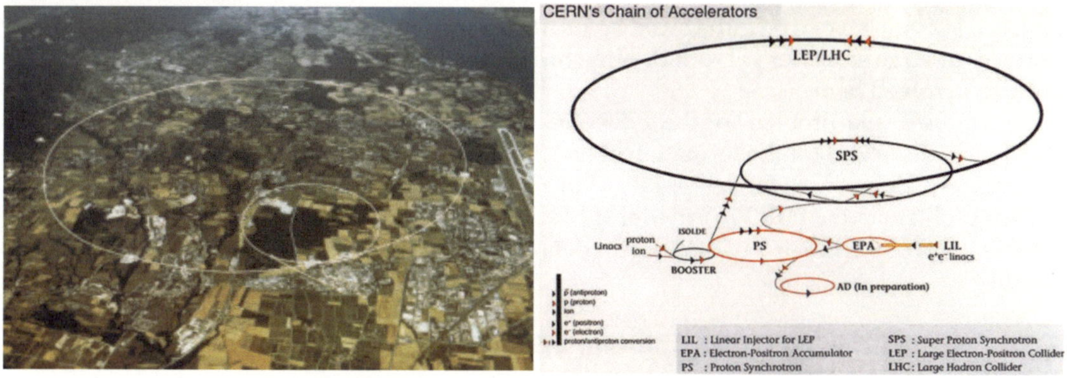

Fig. 3. The LHC accelerator at CERN

The first picture represents the structure of the accelerator which is a ring of 27 km near Geneva. The two proton beams run into two bunches one against the other. This machine started measurements at the end of 2009. The construction is schematically represented in the second picture with various other accelerators, see (3). The two proton bunches are running in opposite directions and colliding in four places. The ATLAS and CMS detectors are the two important data measurements on Standard model and beyond physics. Both collaborations have more than 3000 peoples of many countries of all continents. The other two detectors are LHCb, specialized in particular on b-meson physics measurement and ALICE, specialized on soft physics studies. See (3).

All recent CERN detectors are constructed underground, depending. The LHC/LEP machines are placed at least at 50 m underground. Similarly for the measuring four detectors.

In Fig. 3 one sees the old CERN accelerator LEP (large electron positron) which was running up to 200 GeV. Now it has been replaced by the LHC accelerator. Magnets have been changed along these years.

One sees also the SPS machine for p and $\bar{p}$ hard collider which is now used mostly for neutrino creation and collisions at Gran Sasso detector, see (12). In the past it was used as proton antiproton accelerator as $Sp\bar{p}s$ at 650 GeV and used for Z and $W^{\pm}$ discoveries, see (3). We do not comment on the other small machines presented in the second part of in Fig. 3.

2.0.0.4 The LHC measurements.

At the LHC collider in Fig. 3 the ATLAS and CMS detectors are studying the Standard model physics and its possible developments. First one has the search of the Higgs boson at a supposed mass between hundred and hundred and fifty times the proton mass. The role of this "particle is to break" the gauge structure of the theory and give the measured mass to Z ($M_Z = 91.2$ GeV) and $W^{\pm}$ ($M_W = 80.3$ GeV). All these studies are essentially done at large scale Q_{hard}. The machines used are the LEP $e\bar{e}$ collider at 100 GeV at CERN and the FermiLab $p\bar{p}$ collider at 2 TeV.

If this neutral Higgs meson is not found one should consider complications of the Standard model. These complications are at the moment introduced to make the Standard model more acceptable on basis of principle. Indeed the model has no theoretical control on the masses of all particles as the hadrons and electroweak particles. An important example is the very low mass of neutrinos. This can be explained within the Standard model with complications.
The HERWIG program allows the study of many processes within the Standard model and beyond. Masses have to be introduced according to PDB in (7). In particular one searches new particles at large scale not yet found. High order in QCD are also considered. New collisions are also involved here.
As mentioned one problem of the HERWIG program is the presence of the soft scale M_0 previously discussed for the formation of hadrons. This is one of the key point of the HERWIG program which involves the possibility of predictions of particle emission.
A final problem in the HERWIG model at LHC is the presence of soft collision contribution at high $Q_{\rm hard}$. They will not be discussed in detail in the following, but they are very important, see (3).

3. The HERWIG Monte Carlo program: original structure

The HERWIG Monte Carlo is based on a first perturbative order of QCD analysis of re-summed contributions to all orders of the emission of partons (quark, antiquark and gluon). It involves a large ultraviolet scale $Q_{\rm hard}$ and can be applied to all processes. They are:

- $e\,p$ collider at DESY with respective energy 30 and 820 GeV, see (8);
- e^+e^- collisions at CERN with energy around 100 and 200 GeV, see (9):
- $p\,\bar{p}$ collider at FermiLab with total energy of 2 TeV, see (2);
- $p\,p$ collider at LHC with 7 TeV, see (3).

The QCD program to first order involves elementary vertexes as

$$q \to qg,\ \bar{q} \to \bar{q}g,\ g \to gg,\ g \to q\bar{q}\,. \tag{1}$$

In general two loop orders are also partially considered in HERWIG. Examples are two loops in parton splitting, next order in running coupling, higher order in parton hard collisions, etc. Important extensions are the studies of QCD infrared correction to emissions. As we shall see later they involve for instance the discussion on the scale of the running coupling.
In this paper we concentrate on a simplified form of hard QCD radiation, see (1). Complications are of course typically used in (10).
Here we mainly consider LHC collisions with proton-proton interaction. This is the running machine at CERN which will explore for instance the presence of Higgs meson. As mentioned, in LHC the total incoming momentum of the two colliding protons is now given by 7 TeV. In the future it will be 14 TeV.
One studies typically the process needed for the identification of the Higgs meson. Here one selects a large value of the ultraviolet scale $Q_{\rm hard}$, typically a transverse momentum of an emitted system of particles. Many other hard scales could be involved to study specific objects or specific processes or particle production. As mentioned, both the Standard model is involved and also its extensions.
Dealing with perturbative QCD we need to introduce a soft scale M_0 which is an artificial cutoff that characterizes the formation of incoming or emitting hadrons made of hard quark and gluon. This fundamental parameter characterizes our missing pieces

for the understanding of QCD. This parameter has to be fixed by perturbative analysis. Phenomenologically it turns out to be larger than the proton mass.
The picture of HERWIG program for LHC is schematically described as follows. All these pieces are at QCD perturbative order to some degree and partially extended to other models (see later).

3.0.0.5 Initial state cascade of proton.

We consider first the incoming quark k_0 emitted by the incoming proton. Later this quark branches into additional partons $k_1\, k_2 \cdots k_n$ which are either quarks, antiquarks or gluons. This branching is described by equations (1). The first incoming quark k_0 has a negative mass Q_0^2. In the fragmentation an off shell quark or gluon k_1 is emitted at a positive square mass $-Q_1^2$. One finishes with $|Q_0^2| \ll |Q_1^2|$. The incoming parton k_1 undergoes a successive initial state branching into partons $k_2, \cdots k_n$. Here one has an ordered succession of decay processes with $|Q_0^2| \ll |Q_1^2| \ll \cdots \ll |Q_n^2|$. These decays are repeated to all possible orders. Ordering is defined by Sudakov distributions of quark or gluon fragmenting (see later). The lower value is fixed at the soft scale $M_0^2 = |Q_0^2|$. The higher value is characterized by the hard scale $|Q_n^2| < Q^2_{\text{hard}}$.

3.0.0.6 Hard collision.

One finds the final emitted partons p_1 and p_2 of both incoming protons. They have large square momenta $|Q_n^2|$ and $|Q_m^2|$. Note that the indices n and m are the final emitted partons in the two proton decays. They undergo a hard collision giving two partons p_3 and p_4

$$p_1 + p_2 \rightarrow p_3 + p_4 \,. \tag{2}$$

This process is computed in perturbative order and than needs a perturbative calculation (first at leading order). Outgoing momenta p_3 and p_4 are at large positive square momenta Q_3^2 and Q_4^2 which are again characterized by Q^2_{hard}, depending on the selected HERWIG process. This can be generalized to include high order emission processes.

3.0.0.7 Final state parton branching.

At the end of the previous cascades, as described by (1), one ends up with many outgoing momenta generated in the initial stage of the fragmentation of both incoming quarks and in the outgoing momenta p_3 and p_4. All these momenta are off shell as required by the cascade process. All of them will fragment by processes as $a \rightarrow bc$ with a the successive incoming parton and b and c the outgoing partons. During this decay all partons decrease their off shell mass and via Sudakov form factors they reach the off shell artificial scale M_0.

3.0.0.8 Final state emission at M_0^2.

Note that the soft scale M_0^2 that characterizes the final emitted parton is positive. Instead the soft scale Q_0^2 involved at the beginning of initial state emission of incoming protons is negative. However we set the same soft scale $M_0^2 = -Q_0^2$ even for initial emission. In the HERWIG program the soft initial scale and the final scale are taken to be similar, but for simplicity we unify them to be the same M_0.

3.0.0.9 Hadron formation via preconfinement.

At the end of all these cascades one finishes with partons which are at the scale M_0. All of them form color singlets via preconfinement (see later in Fig. 7. They are parton systems which could be converted into the measured particles (mesons or baryons). This conversion is outside a perturbative analysis and is based on intuition of the non perturbative expression of QCD.

3.0.0.10 Other processes.

Considerations on other processes in QCD, Standard model or non-Standard models will be discussed later.

3.1 The decaying incoming quark

One starts with the fragmentation of each incoming proton into three quarks. One of these is the incoming quark q_0 with an artificial space-like scale with $M_0^2 = -Q_0^2$ positive. The other two quarks are spectators and they will be considered at the end of the general branching.
The quark q_0 undergoes a branching given by $q \to qg$. The successive branching of q_0 is given by (1) and is also scaled with successive negative mass.
Consider the first process in which q at the original square scale $|Q_0^2|$ decays into q' and g. As before they are selected according to Sudakov decomposition (see also later). There are two cases according to the fact that the quark q' or the gluon g is the second outgoing parton after the q branching.
In the first case the decaying process is $q \to q'g$ with q' the incoming emitted quark with negative square mass $|Q_1^2| \gg |Q_0^2|$. Here g is the off shell emitted momentum to be discussed later for the final state emission. The distribution to one loop is given by

$$\hat{P}_{q\to qg}(z) = C_F \frac{1+z^2}{1-z} \,. \tag{3}$$

Here z is the fraction of the outgoing quark q' with respect to the incoming quark q.
In the second case the decaying process is the symmetric one $q \to gq'$ with g acquiring a negative square mass $|Q_2^2|$ which is larger then $|Q_0^2|$. Here the emitted quark q' is an outgoing emitted quark and will be considered later. In this case one has equation (3) but $1-z$ is the fraction of the incoming gluon g with respect to the incoming quark q.
The chosen processes which involves q' or g are selected again by the Sudakov form factor. This expression is determined by the exponentiation of the fragmentation distribution in (2) so that the problem is here normalized in a self consistent way.
In the evolution it enter α_s, the QCD running coupling. Its argument will be discussed later.

3.2 Fragmentation function for incoming parton

Consider an intermediated process in which the parton a_ℓ with negative square momentum $-Q_\ell^2$ is fragmenting into two partons $a_{\ell+1}$ and $b_{\ell+1}$. Here $q_{\ell+1}$ is a harder emitted initial parton. This is given by

$$a_\ell \to a_{\ell+1}\, b_{\ell+1} \,, \tag{4}$$

with a_ℓ and $a_{\ell+1}$ the ordered incoming momenta with negative squared masses $|Q_\ell^2| \ll |Q_{\ell+1}^2|$. Here $b_{\ell+1}$ is the emitted parton with positive square momentum entering the final states to be considered later.
In conclusion the incoming initial quark q_0 branches accord (1). Its initial state successively emitted partons $q_1, \cdots q_n$ are bounded by the rule $|Q_0^2| \ll |Q_1^2| \ll \cdots \ll |Q_n^2|$. Finally they will stop at a maximum value $|Q_n^2| \ll Q_{\text{hard}}^2$, the ultraviolet scale setting the transverse momentum of final event. The QCD vertices considered at low perturbative orders are parton decay into two partons, see (1). The Sudakov form factor is again here involved, see later.

The general splitting functions for $a \to bc$ are given by

$$\begin{aligned} \hat{P}_{q\to qg}(z) &= C_F\,\frac{1+z^2}{1-z}\,, \\ \hat{P}_{g\to q\bar{q}}(z) &= \frac{n_f}{2}\,(z^2+(1-z)^2)\,, \\ \hat{P}_{g\to gg}(z) &= 2C_A\left(\frac{1-z}{z}+\frac{z}{1-z}+z(1-z)\right), \end{aligned} \tag{5}$$

with z the energy fraction of $a_{\ell+1}$ with respect to the incoming hadron momentum. The coefficients $C_F = \frac{N_c^2-1}{2N_c} = \frac{4}{3}$ and $C_A = N_c = 3$ are given by the Casimir operators of the theory. Here n_f is the number of quark lines involved, typically less than $n_f \leq 6$ for the $SU(3)$ theory. Of course all these rules are valid when the quark q is replaced by the antiquark $\bar{q}$.
The Sudakov form factors define all these selections of momenta. They are needed to satisfy sum rules. They are defined by

$$\ln S_a(Q, M_0) = -\sum_b \int_{M_0^2}^{Q^2} \frac{dq^2}{q^2} \int_{\frac{M_0}{Q}}^{1-\frac{M_0}{Q}} dz\, \frac{\alpha_s}{2\pi}\, \hat{P}_{a\to bc}(z)\,. \tag{6}$$

The sum extends to all QCD channels. One has introduced a square momentum q^2 integrated between the hard momentum Q^2 (see later) and the soft one M_0^2. Also the z integration requires similar scale. In general they are integrated between $z > \frac{M_0}{Q}$ and $z < 1 - \frac{M_0}{Q}$ to cut off the possible singularities in the P-functions. As we will see these rules fix the appropriated sum rules for the distributions. For the soft scale M_0 entering in the Sudakov factor and in the evolution, see later.
All described events are determined by leading order evolution in hard QCD. Of course higher orders need to be explored.
All descriptions are represented above by starting from the incoming momentum of the quark entering the incoming proton. In reality (see (3)) the mathematical process is fixed in an opposite way. One considers the hard scale Q^2_{hard} of the searched process. Then one fixes via Sudakov form factor the negative square scale of the last of incoming parton with momentum q_n. When $|Q_n^2|$ is found by using (5) one starts again to determine the previous incoming momentum $|Q_{n-1}^2|$ with similar procedure. Then one ends up to the original incoming momentum $|Q_0^2|$. The original branching is then fully determined by using appropriated Sudakov form factor and the selected distributions in (5).

3.3 General initial state evolution

Consider the fragmentation of an incoming parton a into an outgoing harder parton b. This process goes to a successive emission of intermediate incoming partons. All masses are arranged as increasing from a to b. This inclusive distribution is described as $D_{ba}(x, Q^2)$. Here Q^2 is the hard (positive) squared momentum much larger then the soft scale M_0^2. Here x is the fraction of momentum of outgoing momentum b with respect to the incoming original parton a. The general fragmentation process assumes the general evolution equation found in (11) given by

$$Q^2 \frac{\partial}{\partial Q^2} D_{ba}(x, Q^2) = \sum_{cd} \int_x^{1-\frac{M_0}{Q}} \frac{dz}{z}\, \frac{\alpha_s}{\pi}\, P_{b\to cd}(z)\, D_{ca}\left(\frac{x}{z}, Q^2\right)\,, \tag{7}$$

where the distributions $P_{a\to bc}(z)$ are the ones described above to one loop with virtual corrections coming from $S_a(Q, M_0)$. They are given by

$$\begin{aligned}
P_{q\to qg}(z) &= \hat{P}_{q\to gg}(z) - \delta(1-z)\int_0^{1-\frac{M_0}{Q}} dy\, C_F\frac{1+y^2}{1-y}\,,\\
P_{q\to gq}(z) &= \hat{P}_{q\to qg}(1-z)\,,\\
P_{g\to q\bar{q}}(z) &= \hat{P}_{g\to q\bar{q}}(z)\,,\\
P_{g\to gg}(z) &= \hat{P}_{g\to gg}(z) - \delta(1-z)\left(\int_0^{1-\frac{M_0}{Q}} dy\, 2C_A\frac{y}{1-y} + \frac{C_A+2n_f}{6}\right),
\end{aligned} \tag{8}$$

where a cut off M_0/Q has to be set at the maximum of z in (5) and y in (8). Note that the distributions $P_{a\to bc}(z)$ have a M_0/Q dependence. A similar dependence appears in the distribution$D_{ab}(z,Q)$. This is removed when $M_0 \to 0$ limit is taken. Here the limits at $z = 1$ corresponds to the presence of the Sudakov form factors in the evolution equation (7). Equation (7) could be improved with two loop corrections. The running coupling α_s dependence on the scale will be described below.

The Sudakov factors are defined by requiring the following sum rules. The first is the conservation of parton number when all events are generated. The second refers to the conservation of the total momentum in the same conditions. The contributions depend on the soft scale M_0^2 but the sums are independent of M_0^2 for small values. Of course the various sums do not depend on the hard scale Q^2.

There are various distributions for various channels. They are the following

$$D_{qq},\ D_{\bar{q}q},\ D_{q\bar{q}},\ D_{pg},\ D_{gp},\ D_{gg}\,. \tag{9}$$

Again here one has the $q \to \bar{q}$ symmetry. All these channels are active in the normal parton evolutions. They contribute to the various channels and could be directly measured. There are various measurements and comparisons with (7). At high energy the agreement with data is quite good. Also the sum rules are quite reliably satisfied.

Later we will discuss also the distribution for the final state evolutions. They are not different from the ones in (7) at one loop but they change both for higher loops and for the running coupling dependence on the hard scale

3.4 The hard collisions

At this point two partons of momenta p_1 and p_2 are entering our collision in (2) with negative square masses. They could be either quarks or gluons. Here p_1 and p_2 are the result of the successive emissions out of the two incoming protons in LHC. Here they collide according to the maximal hard scale $Q_{\rm hard}$ selected for this process.

As given in (2) they generate the hard collisions giving outgoing partons p_3 and p_4. They could be either quarks or gluons. At this level the theory predicts, at the large scale here considered, only vertices with emissions as in (1). Other events could be used with more than two emitted partons. In all these events the partons p_3 and p_4 have hard momenta given by $Q^2_{\rm hard}$.

The distribution (2) in QCD is taken to the perturbative order at least to zero order. Indeed the distribution is controlled by the hard scale for the process and then only low orders are relevant. Complications to higher order are also considered. One could also consider non QCD production as in the Standard model or beyond.

3.5 The recombination

Consider the two proton collisions in the LHC process. At this point they undergo a hard collision $p_1 p_2 \to p_3 p_4$ as in (5). In the Monte Carlo evolution one ends with:

- partons emitted by initial state radiation leading to p_1 and p_2. They are off shell and have mass much smaller then Q_{hard};
- partons p_3 and p_4 emitted in the hard collision. They have momentum much smaller than Q_{hard}.

In addition to all these off shell partons p_3 and p_4 and the radiation of p_1 and p_2 one has to consider their final state emission. According to QCD rules all these partons decay as in the usual rule with successive decaying processes $a \to b\,c$ with a, b and c given by quarks, antiquarks or gluons. Here they have positive mass. Their radiate by emitting additional partons according to QCD rules in (4). They radiated masses here are both positive and decrease down to M_0. This is done according to QCD rules as in (7).
As before they are selected by the Sudakov decomposition. The results are again obtained by the usual rules $\hat{P}_{a\to bc}(z)$. At one loop they are given in (5). Here z is the fraction of the intermediate parton momentum with respect to the incoming parton emitted by initial legs. Notice that the two outgoing momenta z and $1-z$ are here involved, see (5).
The Sudakov form factors are given by the exponential integrations of $\hat{P}_{a\to bc}(z)$. They are given in (6). It is interesting that all these expressions as the parton distributions $P_{a\to bc}(z)$ and the Sudakov factors are the same as the incoming distributions, see by (5) and (6). However the emission distributions $P_{a\to bc}(z)$ and Sudakov form factors $S_a(Q, Q_0)$ differ at next to leading order in initial states and in final emissions. They have different expressions depending on the facts that they change for the z dependence and the running coupling expressions (as it would be mentioned later).
Finally one ends with many partons emitted in the final state with low momentum M_0 described above. They are partons which are generated by the radiation of p_3 and p_4 partons in the hard collision (2). To them one adds the partons generated by decay of the hard partons $k_1 \cdots k_n$ radiated by the intermediate emissions out of initial states. As a result all final state emissions are depending on the hard physical scale Q_{hard} and the infrared artificial M_0^2. To these final partons emitted at scale M_0^2 one needs to add the pair of quark generated in the initial proton fragmentation.
Summarizing all the evolutions, one finds a succession of final states parton emitted at scale M_0^2. They come from

- splitting of finally emitted partons p_3 and p_4 in (2);
- splitting of $k_1 \cdots k_n$ which are partons emitted by incoming legs;
- final sate evolutions of spectator partons emitted from the two protons.

All of these final state partons are obtained by the $a \to bc$ distributions in (5) and the Sudakov form factors in (6).

3.6 Color recombination into hadrons

In QCD all emitted quarks and antiquarks have a color index $N_c = 3$. For formal large color index N_c one has that all systems of emitted q and $\bar{q}$ from color singlet could be converted into hadrons which do not have color index.
Consider an example of final state emission with quark and antiquark with mass close to M_0. Take such a final state emission:

- consider a quark q_{n-1} decaying into a quark q_n and a gluon g. Suppose that outgoing quark q_n has a final state mass M_0;
- then consider the gluon g decaying into an antiquark $\bar{q}_n$ and a quark. Suppose that outgoing antiquark $\bar{q}_n$ has a final state mass M_0;
- for large color N_c one has that the quark and antiquark q_n and $\bar{q}_n$ form a large color singlet. Its mass results of the same order as M_0. This will be soon proved;
- the emitted final quark and antiquark q_n and $\bar{q}_n$ have a color singlet for large N_c. One has that these quark and antiquark form a color singlet and could be ready to generate a hadron system (meson as quark and antiquark). Similarly for the formation of barion (out of three quarks) or antibarion (out of three antiquarks).

So this is the basis for HERWIG formation of hadron final states. Without entering into this perturbative analysis of QCD once could give the necessary information for preconfinement, see (6).
Consider two final state partons q_a and p_b emitted in QCD with low off-shell mass M_0. Let us assume that we do not fix the color index of p_a and p_b we sum over all of them. Their square mass $m_{ab}^2 = (p_a + p_b)^2$ is arbitrary and simply smaller than the kinematical boundary. There are no conditions from Sudakov factor since they cancel in the real emission distribution $P(x)$ and the Sudakov factor $S(Q, Q_0)$.
The situation changes when one considers two partons q_n and $\bar{q}_n$ which are near in color as the ones described above. Here one could follow the color line of quark q_n and one ends into the anti-color of antiquark $\bar{q}_n$ (for large color). The presence of this color separation generates a Sudakov form factor of (6) with M_0 dependence.
As usual this is not cancelled by a compensation coming from the evolution vertices $P(z)$. This is enough to force parton q_n and $\bar{q}_n$ to be close in momentum. This fact, resulting from the Sudakov factors in QCD, are enough to force the two partons to be close in momentum with a mass of order of M_0.

3.7 The physics generation

At the end of the evolution one finishes with systems of partons. They are organized in color systems of small mass of order of M_0 and ready to form hadrons. Here one assumes that only quarks and antiquarks are generated in the final state. The HERWIG program is then organized in such a way to reconstruct hadrons out of these systems by using Particle Data Book in (7).
There are complications when the Sudakov distribution generates color singlet partons with mass not small enough. Here one needs to assume cluster formation according to simple rules given in (7). Of course this hadron generation is not constructed on the basis of QCD but based on reasonable principles grounded on physical considerations.
Of course other types of hadron generations are considered. They are generated in cluster of small mass color singlets of partons, see also (5).

3.8 Other processes

>From previous description it is clear that the HERWIG program could be extended to include other particle data, at least on perturbative level. They are for instance the followings:

- Higgs production are considered with large mass. This is one of the most important part of the Standard model which needs to be tested. They are based on the Standard model or its extensions;

- add electrodynamics predictions involving photon emission or recoils. This involves recoil of hadron or photon emission out of partons;
- the Standard model prediction with emission of weak bosons, that is $q \to Zq$ or $q \to W^{\pm}q$;
- similarly one could consider in HERWIG the decay of Z and $W^{\pm}$ into partons, photons, fermions, neutrinos, etc.

Many more extensions could be considered by taking into account also non Standard model physics.

4. The HERWIG Monte Carlo program: relevant details

Here we consider some important details in QCD theory. Most of these considerations are based on perturbative analysis. The derivations of these studies are actually based on analytical studies and included in HERWIG program. An important point in this HERWIG analysis is the presence of the infrared cutoff M_0 which enters all analysis. One recalls that this is due to our ignorance of non perturbative QCD converting all parton studies into hadrons. The other important point is that processes in HERWIG program are considered by including the physical scale Q_{hard} which enters in all hard processes.

4.0.0.11 The running coupling.

An important object to consider in QCD is the fact that the coupling is running in the ultraviolet region, i.e. for large momentum Q. This is universal up to two loops and given by

$$Q\frac{\partial}{\partial Q}\alpha_s(Q) = -\frac{\beta_0}{2\pi}\,\alpha_s^2(Q) - \frac{\beta_1}{4\pi^2}\,\alpha_s^3(Q) + \cdots \tag{10}$$

with $\beta_0 = 11 - \frac{2}{3}\,n_f$ and $\beta_1 = 51 - \frac{19}{3}\,n_f$. Here n_f is the number of flavors and Q is the hard physical momentum. High order corrections have higher powers of β_n with $n \geq 3$.
At large momentum Q gives

$$\alpha_s(Q) = \frac{4\pi}{\beta_0 \ln Q^2/\Lambda^2}\left(1 - \frac{2\beta_1}{\beta_0^2}\frac{\ln\ln(Q^2/\Lambda^2)}{\ln(Q^2/\Lambda^2)} + \ldots\right) \tag{11}$$

This function is decreasing at large $Q^2 \gg \Lambda^2$ as inverse power of $\ln Q/\Lambda$. The coefficient of this power is fixed by the two first orders of the expansion (10).
The parameter Λ is obtained from phenomenological calculation and is of order $\Lambda_{\overline{MS}} = 200$ MeV for $n_f = 5$. This is valid in the $\overline{\text{MS}}$ scheme one of the most used scheme in QCD. It is interesting that in the Monte Carlo HERWIG program the value of Λ is larger than the value at $\overline{\text{MS}}$ scheme by a factor 1.57 for $n_f = 5$. It has been computed directly in the HERWIG Monte Carlo scheme by perturbative calculations valid at large x. This expression holds both for positive and negative Q^2. It is defined by (11) at two loops.
The form of $\alpha_s(Q)$ is represented in the first part of Fig. 4. Comparison with data in various processes is given such as in e^+e^- collisions, in hadronic collisions, in heavy quark events. The maximal scale of Q considered is up to $Q = 200$ GeV.
In the second part of Fig. 4 one has the average $\alpha_s(M_z)$ at the mass $M_Z = 91.2$ GeV. Various measurements are here represented.
Here the $\alpha_s(Q)$ determination is valid for Q larger than few GeV. The determination of $\alpha_s(Q)$ is reduced at large Q. Here one expects that at large momentum in LHC the determination of $\alpha_s(Q)$ will be rather good.

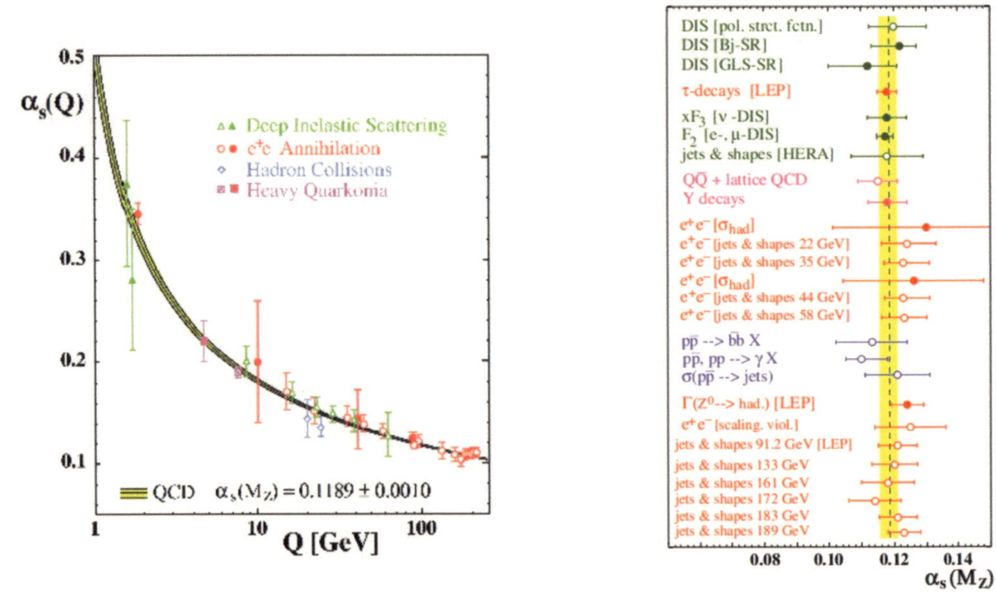

Fig. 4. Parton evolution in QCD. First part:the running coupling $\alpha_s(Q)$ as function of Q. Second part: average $\alpha_s(M_z)$

4.0.0.12 Parton evolutions in initial states.

Consider the initial state evolution with energy fraction x of final parton b. Here parton density $D_{ba}(Q^2, x)$ evolves as in (5) and one needs to define the running coupling dependence on Q^2. QCD analysis at present scales defines Q as the transverse momentum of emitted initial state parton b. This is found from initial sate emission at limited scale used by present machines, see (1).
At larger momenta one should use a more complex variable corresponding essentially to Q given by angle of emitted parton with respect to the incoming original one given by proton momentum. Experimental evidence of the relevance of this scale for Q is clear from various analysis, see (1).
There are complications when one reduces x to very small values, well below $x \simeq 10^{-4}$. Here the evolution is more complex than the one given in (14). The new equation in this region is more complex and involves more degree of freedom. The new formulation is described in (14) which is not considered in the HERWIG program.

4.0.0.13 Parton evolutions in final states.

Consider now the final state evolution with energy fraction x of emitted parton b. Here parton density $D_{ba}(Q^2, x)$ evolves as in (5). One needs to define the running coupling with respect to Q^2. QCD analysis at present scales defines Q as given by p_{bt} rescaled by incoming e_b and final energy E, i.e. $Q = p_{b\,t} \times e_b/E \simeq e_b\,\theta_b$. Here θ_b is the angle of emitted parton b. This means that the new scale is essentially, for small momentum, of the order of the emitted parton transverse momentum. This rescaling is due to QCD calculations accounting for soft emitted gluon coherence, see (15).
This selection of the final state emission has been defined for many QCD quantities. The important point here is that the scale Q decreases as one decreases the emitted angle θ_b and

the energy e_b. This last dependence is the crucial one. It is for instance responsible for the dependence on the multiplicity that we discuss now, see (1).

4.0.0.14 Multiplicity.

In e^+e^- emission at energy E the parton multiplicity has been computed, see (15), and is given by

$$< N(Q) > \simeq N_0 \left(\ln \frac{Q^2}{\Lambda^2} \right)^{\frac{\sqrt{N_c}}{2\pi\beta_0}} \exp \sqrt{\frac{2N_c}{\pi\beta_0} \ln \frac{Q^2}{\Lambda^2}} \tag{12}$$

with Λ the QCD scale. Here N_0 is a normalization constant to be defined experimentally. It is the multiplicity evaluated at a scale Q_0. This involves again the QCD scale discussed before. In this expression we have neglected the two loop formulation. This is one of the most measured quantity in QCD, see Fig. 5.

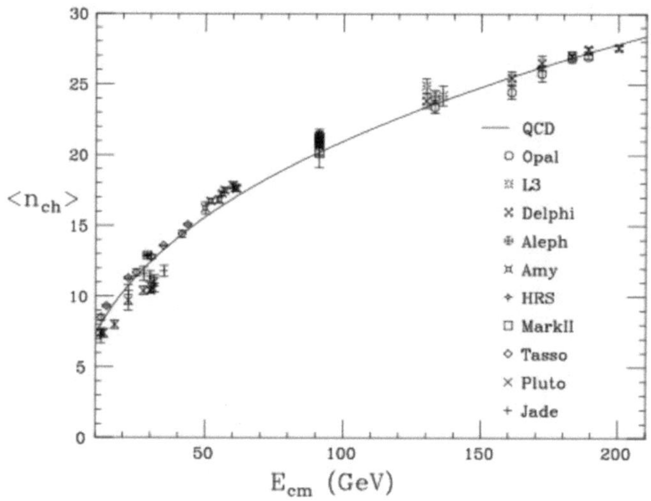

Fig. 5. Multiplicity

Total multiplicities will be measured at LHC for various channels. The agreement of data with (12) is expected to be very good.

4.0.0.15 Preconfinement and hadron formation.

In the Monte Carlo evolutions many partons are produced in the final state. They have a color and they could generate hadrons made of color singlets. Then an important question is how these partons are organized in the final state and how color singlet partons are organized with small mass to form hadrons.

The reason that makes the mass of color singlet partons in QCD small, of order of M_0, is the presence of a Sudakov form factor which damps the mass. Indeed, the singlet emission of color partons (in the infinite N_c limit) contains this form factor which is fastly decreasing with total momentum. In this way one finds that color singlet partons could form a system of combined hadrons.

One checks by QCD evaluation, see (6), that in QCD color singlet partons are actually generated with small mass of order of M_0. In this case one could implement into HERWIG

calculation a reconstruction of hadrons. This reconstruction is reasonable but out of a formal treatment of QCD calculations.
To construct hadrons out of color singlet partons in HERWIG one uses this QCD property and looks into the Particle Data Book property, see (7), and identifies clusters of color singlet parton system.

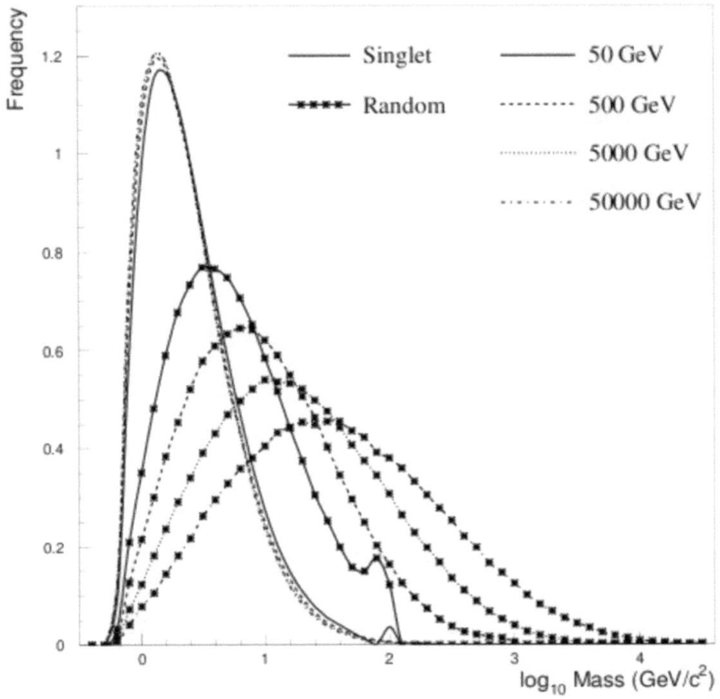

Fig. 6. Preconfinement

In Fig. 6 one sees the distribution in the mass of two partons in e^+e^- machine at various energies. The left line gives the distribution in the mass of color singlet. As one sees changing the total energy E the curves do not move and the distribution remains centered at $M_0 = 2$ GeV.
The situation is different for the other lines which cluster two generic partons with no selection of color charge. They move as the total energy E increases and no hadron cluster could be formed.

4.0.0.16 Non perturbative QCD assumptions.

After the described process of hadron formation in QCD, in HERWIG evolution one could explore other particle formations. They could involve Standard model processes as leptons, neutrinos and weak boson formations. One of the most important case is the Higgs boson generation with mass of order of hundred or hundred and fifty times the proton mass. They will confirm the simplest case of the Standard model. I recall that the Higgs meson is so important that is responsible for the formation of the mass of the weak bosons Z and $W^{\pm}$. Without the Higgs boson one has serious difficulties with the present version of the Standard model.

Other important processes which can be explored in HERWIG are non Standard model processes. They involves the supersymmetric models or generalization of the Standard model to implement new physics. See (16).

4.0.0.17 Single proton distribution.

The data on W^+W^- production distribution is given at FermiLab up to total momentum $p_t \simeq$ 70 GeV, see Fig. 7. Here one plots the inclusive distribution $\frac{d\sigma}{dp_t}$ in the transverse momentum of WW pair. See (2).
The curves are again compared with the analytical behavior. The agreement with experiments is quite well. One expects a similar behavior at LHC energy.

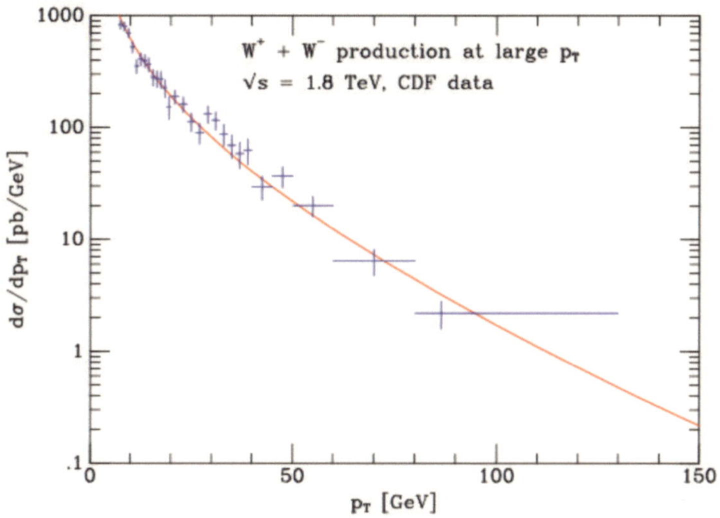

Fig. 7. WW inclusive distribution at FemiLab

4.0.0.18 Particle clustering.

Consider the shape of the particle jet in Fig. 8 Measurements were done at e^+e^- machine at CERN. The jets are defined by giving a definite opening angle $y_{\rm cut}$. This is defined by fixing momentum clustering as follows:

- given two emitted particles of momentum p_i and p_j one computes the variable $y_{ij} = 2\min\{E_i^2, E_j^2\}$ with E the energy of p;
- if $y_{IJ} = \min\{y_{ij}\} < y_{\rm cul}$ with all previously analyzed momenta p_i and p_j, then particles I and J are put in a single particle k with $p_k = p_I + p_J$ as a new momentum;
- replace until $y_{ij} < y_{\rm cul}$. This defines the order of jets with previous resolution.

Jets are resolved according to parameters which define the number of jets given in first point above. Here one considers jet resolution given for 2, 3, 4, 5 jets. They are distributed according to Monte Carlo programs HERWIG and PYTIA. Data are taken from OPAL in e^+e^- collider at CERN, see (9).
The first distribution is done according to the resolution parameter $y_{\rm cut}$ given above. Mass is fixed at $E = 91$ GeV at Opal at CERN, see Fig. 8. As one sees the average number of

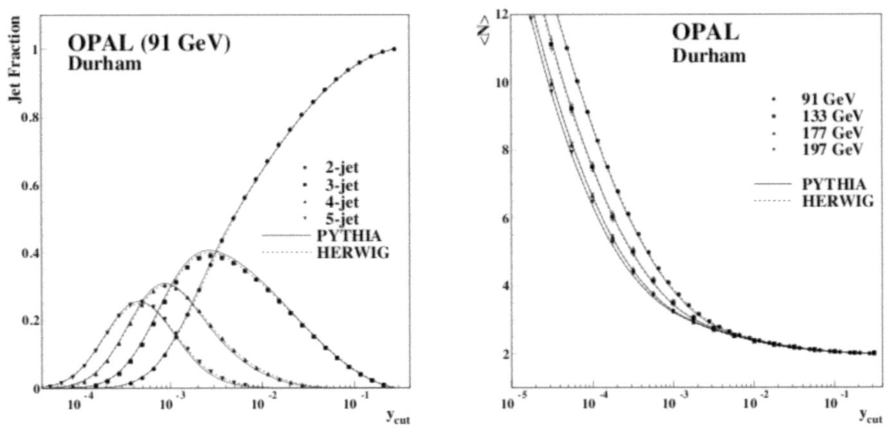

Fig. 8. Jet distribution at $e+e-$ accelerator.

jets increases as one decreases the resolution y_{cut}. That is the number of jets, as expected, increases as one decreases the resolution. The plots are computable in perturbation theory as for HERWIG. Of course, there is a minimum limit in the resolution y_{cut} to avoid particle identification.
The second plot represents the average values of jet resolution with respect to energy for the detector at 91, 133, 177, 197 GeV. The average number of jets decreases as one increases the total energy E.

4.0.0.19 The Higgs boson.

The experimental observation of one or several Higgs bosons will be fundamental for a better understanding of the mechanism of electroweak symmetry-breaking. In the Standard model these are various expressions for the Higgs meson. This means to give a mass to Z and $W^{\pm}$. In particular there are indications from previous experiments at FermiLab and CERN for e^+e^- colliders that one has a Higgs meson mass between 100 and 150 GeV.
Here there are some important examples for the decay of standard Higgs meson. These data are taken from ATLAS studies, see (3);

- $H \to \gamma\gamma$ direct productions;
- $H \to \gamma\gamma$ from the associated production of $W+H$, $W+Z$ and $t\bar{t}+H$;
- $H \to b\bar{b}$ from the observed production $W+H$, $Z+H$ and $t\bar{t}+H$:
- $H \to ZZ \to$ and Z into two leptons;
- $H \to ZZ \to$ and ZZ into two leptons and two neutrinos;
- $H \to W^+W^-$ and $H \to ZZ$ with Standard model decays.

In Fig. 9 we consider possible rates for Higgs production and decay. We report the determinations of the frequencies of the various channels by changing the H energy. The estimation is done by ATLAS group, see (1).

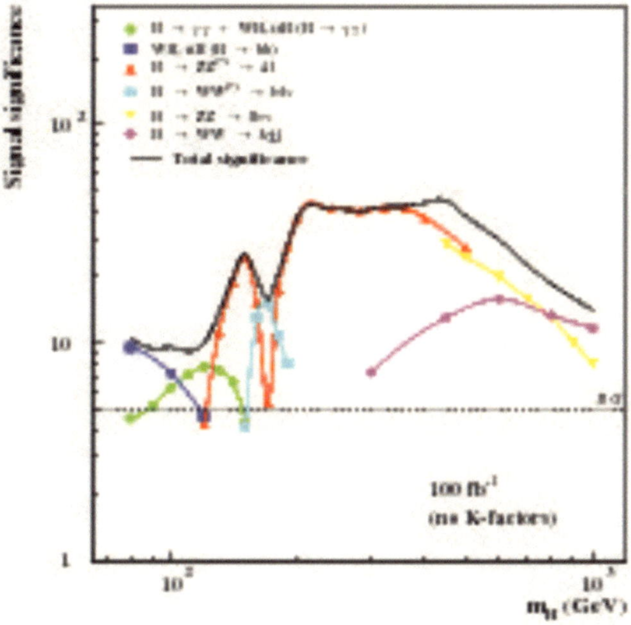

Fig. 9. Preview of particle measurements

4.0.0.20 The Higgs boson in SUSY physics.

The supersymmetric standard model is a usual way to generalize the Standard model by including Supersymmetry, i.e. by adding a symmetry between bosons and fermions, see (16). The curves in the first part of Fig. 10 give $1/\alpha(Q)$ for the normal Standard model. As one sees here in the case of the Standard model the three curves do not meat. They are close at an energy $Q \sim 10^{15}$ GeV but do not meet. See details close to the expected mixing point.
In the case of SUSY model, see the second curve, data on $1/\alpha(Q)$ are given for the three curves. At $Q = 10^{15}$ GeV they actually meet and the model in principle can be unified. Actually the unification energy is rather high. There are various analysis of the SUSY model and there are various generalizations. See details near the mixing point.
The generalization of the Standard model and its analysis with HERWIG is used and analyzed in principle. Important generalizations involve theories beyond the Standard model. We do not enter here. See for example (17).

4.0.0.21 Associated soft interactions.

In all hard collisions also soft interactions are involved and need to be considered for many measurements. These collisions are not considered here and could be found in the relevant references, see (4; 5).

5. Summary

The original formulation of the HERWIG program was stated in 1983, see (4). Later it was developed for various accelerators by using various QCD rules and their generalizations to the Standard model and beyond. At the moment it is used for the LHC accelerator. Large momenta are here involved to select very specific distributions. The search of Higgs is one

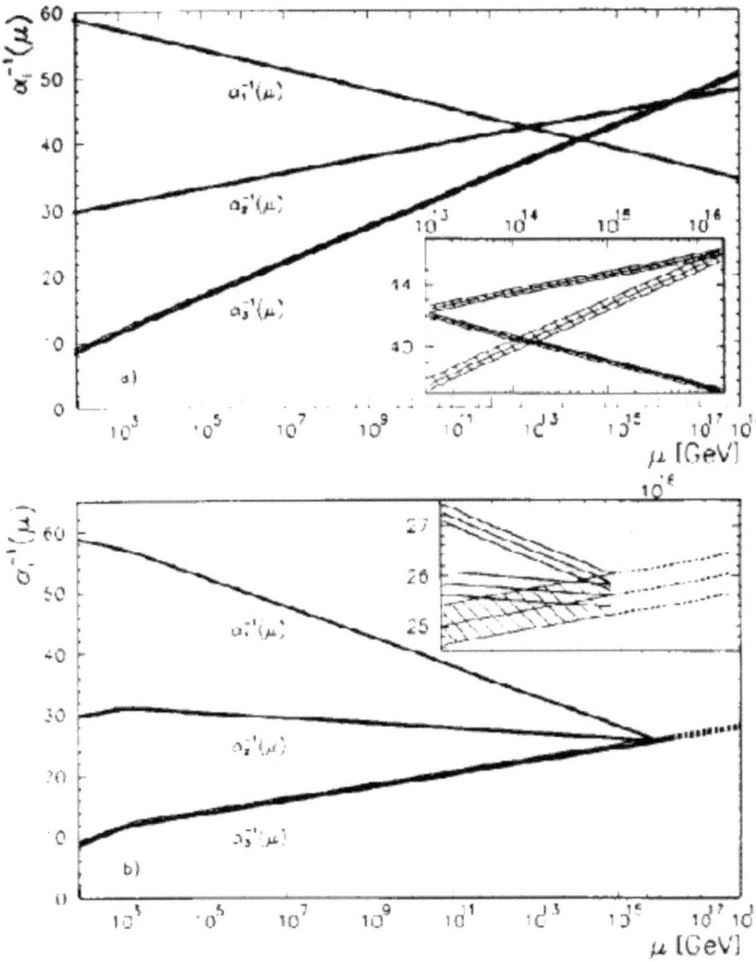

Fig. 10. SUSY unification for α_s

of the major point for the HERWIG program. It is important for setting the Standard model and the masses of Z and $W^{\pm}$. Very important at this LHC scale are the observations of other possible observables such as non QCD distributions in the Standard model and beyond.
All QCD perturbative calculations involved in the HERWIG program are obtained at leading level. Some important non leading corrections are here included in many computed quantities. Some important additions are discussed here.
The important point here is the presence of the hard scale Q_{hard}. These selected hard processes are under control of perturbative QCD analysis. Important processes are selected in this way. Higgs search is one of the crucial point which was intensively discussed here. Extensions to Standard model are easily treated here. Similarly for simple example beyond the Standard model.
An important point is the presence of the artificial parameter of the infrared cutoff M_0. It forces the absence of infrared divergences and is effectively close to the proton mass. This

parameter forces one to implement the presence of the physical hadrons. They are generated artificially by constructing hadron generation out of small mass color singlets of partons, see (4). The HERWIG program is actually based on this reconstruction of hadrons. Actually one can use different methods to generate hadrons but the essential basis are the same.
One element not considered in this study is the contributions from aspects that are beyond perturbative QCD such as the role of soft interaction within hard collisions. Their behavior is beyond perturbative QCD and then related to still not known quantities. They affect hard interactions and are clearly controlled.
Many pictures here shown are obtained from Bryan Webber transparencies. He was very important for my contribution to HERWIG.

6. References

[1] Alfred H. Mueller, Phys.Rev.D4:150-155,1971;
Yuri L. Dokshitzer, Dmitri Diakonov, S.I. Troian, Phys.Rept.58:269-395,1980;
Guido Altarelli, Phys.Rept.81:1,1982;
Antonio Bassetto, Marcello Ciafaloni, Giuseppe Marchesini, Phys.Rept.100:201-272,1983.

[2] See for instance http://www.fnat.gov

[3] See for instance http://www.cern.ch
See also:
http://atlas.web.cern.ch/Atlas
http://cms.web.cern.ch/cms

[4] G. Marchesini, B.R. Webber, Nucl. Phys. B238 (1984) 1;
G. Marchesini, B.R. Webber, Nucl. Phys. B310 (1988) 461;
G. Marchesini, B.R. Webber, G. Abbiendi, I.G. Knowles, M.H. Seymour and L. Stanco, Phys. Commun. 67 (1992) 465,
G. Corcella, I.G. Knowles, G. Marchesini, S. Moretti, K. Odagiri, P. Richardson, M.H. Seymour and B.R. Webber, JHEP 0101 (2001) 010.

[5] T. Sjostrand, S. Mrenna, P.Z. Skands, JHEP 0605:026,2006,
A. Buckley, J. Butterworth, L. Lonnblad, H. Hoeth, J. Monk, H. Schulz, J. E. von Seggern, F. Siegert, L. Sonnenschein, arXiv:1003.0694.

[6] D. Amati and G. Veneziano, Phys.Lett. B82 (1979) 87;
A. Bassetto, M. Ciafaloni, G. Marchesini, Phys. Lett. B83 (1979) 207.

[7] See the Particle Data Group at http://pdg.web.cern.ch/pdg/ The Review includes a compilation and evaluation of measurements of the properties of the elementary particles. Evaluations of these properties are abstracted in summary tables.

[8] HERA (Hadron-Electron Ring Accelerator) was an electron and positron accelerator at DESY. Its operation started in 1992 and finished in 2007. The two machines where H1 and Zeus. Electron energy was up to GeV and proton energy up to GeV.

[9] The collider for e^+e^- was built at CERN. The total center of mass energy was used up to about 200 GeV. It operated from 1989 until 2000. Then it was replaced by LHC. There where four detectors: Aleph, Delphi, Opal and L3. See for instance the first part of (3).

[10] S. Gieseke, D. Grellscheid, K. Hamilton, A. Ribon, P. Richardson, M.H. Seymour, P. Stephens, B.R. Webber, arXiv:hep-ph/0609306v1

[11] V.N. Gribov, L.N. Lipatov. Sov.J.Nucl.Phys.15:438 (1972),
G. Altarelli and G. Parisi. Nucl.Phys.B126:298 (1977),
Yu. L. Dokshitzer. JETP, 46:641 (1977).

[12] see for instance http://www.cern.ch and http://www.lngs.infn.it/

[13] S. Catani, G. Marchesini, B.R. Webber, Nucl.Phys.B349:635-654,1991.
[14] E.A. Kuraev, L.N. Lipatov, V.S. Fadin, Sov.Phys.JETP 45:199-204,1977;
I.I. Balitsky, L.N. Lipatov, Sov.J.Nucl.Phys.28:822-829,1978;
V.S. Fadin, L.N. Lipatov, Phys.Lett.B429:127-134,1998;
M. Ciafaloni, D. Colferai, Phys.Lett.B452:372-378,1999.
[15] A.H. Mueller, Phys. Lett. B104 (1981) 116;
B.I. Ermolayev, V.S. Fadin, JETP Lett.33(1981) 269;
A. Bassetto, M. Ciafaloni, G. Marchesini, A.H, Mueller, Nucl.Phys. B207 (1982) 189;
Yu.L. Dokshitzer, V.S. Fadin,V.A. Khoze, Z.Phys.CI5 (1083) 325.
[16] Examples of discussions of physics Beyond the Standard Model are discussed for instance in the first reference in (3).
[17] See for instance U. Amaldi, W. de Boer, H. Furstenau, Phys.Lett.B260:447-455,1991.

15

Monte Carlo Simulation of TLD Response Function: Scatterd Radiation Application

Seied Rabie Mahdavi[1] Ph.D., Alireza Shirazi[2] Ph.D.,
Ali Khodadadee[3] BS.c., Mostafa Ghaffory[4] MS.c. and Asghar Mesbahi[5] Ph.D
[1]*Dept. of Medical Physics, Faculty of Medicine, Iran University of Medical Sciences, Tehran*
[2]*Dept. of Medical Physics, Faculty of Medicine, Tehran University of Medical Sciences, Tehran*
[3]*Azad Research and Science University, Tehran*
[4]*Secondary Standard Dosimetry Laboratory (SSDL), Iranian Organization of Atomic Energy, Karaj*
[5]*Dept. of Medical School, Tabriz University of Medical Science, Tabriz, Iran*

1. Introduction

Thermoluminescence dosimetry (TLDs) are routinely used for in-vivo dosimetry as well as other application in medicine and industry [1, 2]. The most commonly used TLD material is Lithium flouride based doped with small quantities of Mg and Ti that is denonted by LiF:Mg,Ti (TLD-100). This popularity is due, in part, to approximate tissue equivalence and low signal fading [3].

Knowledge of TL response, especially at commonly used photon energies, is useful to estimate the uncertainty of dosimetry system, and experimental methodology has elsewhere been regarded as the most reliable option [4].

TLDs are relative dosimeters and therefore have to be calibrated against absolute dosimetry systems such as a calibrated ion chamber. In radiotherapy application it is convenient to calibrate them in ^{60}Co γ-ray beam or in a low-energy megavoltage x-ray beam of ^{137}Cs γ-rays [4, 5] . It is therefore important to know quality dependence and energy correction factors that should be applied if the TLDs are used in photon beams other than calibration beam such as scattered beams [4].

In the present study, quality dependence of TLD-100 response was measured in different beam qualities followed by mcnp simulation. It was done to model the behaviour of dosimetry at low energy x-ray beams to improve the TLD usage in scattered radiation field.

2. Materials and methods

We used fourthy cubic chips of lithium fluoride (LiF) crystals doped with Magnesium (Mg) and Titanium (Ti) presented at concentrations of 200 and 10 ppm by weight, respectively. Chips sizes were 3.1×3.1×1 mm^3 with density of 2.64 g cm^{-3} and manufactured by Harshaw

company. Our protocol for using TLD-100 was described in detail by Mckeever [2]. Briefly, The chips were first annealed at 400°C for 1h, followed by a second annealing at 100°Cfor 2h. After irradiation, and before reading, the TLDs were stored for 24h at room temperature (20°C) to clear the low energy traps. To produce radiation beams with different energies, Co-60 radiotherapy and orthovoltage x-ray therapy machines were used as specified in Table 1.
To determine the sensitivity of each individual TLD efficient correction coefficient (ECC) were obtained by the following equation after irradiation on a perspex holder.

$$Ecc_i = \frac{R_i}{\overline{R}} \tag{1}$$

where ECC_i is the ECC of each TLD, R and R_i are individual reading and average reading of the total TLDs, respectively.
The TLDs were calibrated against an ionization chamber at depth of 5 cm of water phantom at a distance of 50 cm from the radiation source. Water absorbed dose of $^{60}Co\ \gamma$-rays was measured by using IAEA protocol 277 [6]. To obtain absorbed dose calibration factors in cGy/ Count, TLD chips in groups of three or four were irradiated with different beam qualities(120 kVp- 300 kVp). Then, the average counts (corrected for background counts) of the TLDs at each dose group were determined. Calibration factor at each energy quality was defined as the inverse of the tangent of TLD absorbed dose response curve. This factor allows to convert the TL signal to the received dose:

$$(CF)_q = \text{CalibrationDose} / \text{TL} \tag{2}$$

Where "calibration dose" is the given dose for calibration of TLD and TL is the dosimeter response in columbs after irradiation with beam quality of "q" [7]. The quality dependence factor $\left(F_{Co}^{X}\right)$ is then defined as:

$$F_{Co}^{X} = \frac{TL(X) / D_{med}(X)}{TL(Co) / D_{med}(Co)} \tag{3}$$

Where $TL(X) / D_{med}(X)$ is the light output of material TL per unit dose for the x-ray beam quality or inverse of calibration factor for the each beam quality. $TL(Co) / D_{med}(Co)$ is the light out put per unit dose in the same medium for ^{60}Co gamma-rays or inverse of calibration factor for the ^{60}Co gamma-rays. Assuming the D_{LiF} to be the dose of TLD material that is directly proportional to the output light of TL(X) at any x-ray beam quality, F_{Co}^{X} can also be written as:

$$F_{Co}^{X} = \frac{(D_{med} / D_{LiF})_{Co}}{(D_{med} / D_{LiF})_{X}} \tag{4}$$

To measure the absorbed dose cavity theory defines the relation between the dose absorbed in a medium (D_{med}) and the average absorbed dose in the detector or cavity $\overline{D}_{cav}$:

$$D_{med} = \overline{D}_{cav}\ f_{med,cav} \tag{5}$$

Where $f_{med,cav}$ is a factor that varies with energy, radiation type, medium, size and composition of the cavity. For a cavity that is large enough in comparison to the range of electrons, the dose in the medium can be obtained from the mass energy-absorption coefficient ratio of that medium to the cavity material:

$$f_{med,cav} = \left(\frac{\mu_{en}}{\rho} \right)_{med,cav} \tag{6}$$

Where $\left(\frac{\mu_{en}}{\rho} \right)_{med,cav}$ is the ratio of the mass-energy absorption coefficient of medium to the cavity, averaged over the photon energy fluence spectrum present in the medium. This expression completely neglects any perturbation effects or interface effects that may be occur by the introduction of the detector material into the uniform medium [8].

As a consequence, for kilovoltage x-rays the dose ratio of water to LiF is equal the mass energy-absorption coefficient of water to Lif. This is justified as the range of electrons generated by kilovoltage x-rays are very short compared to the smallest distance across the cavity in the beam direction. From equation 5 quality dependence was re-designed as:

$$\frac{\left((\mu_{en}/\rho)_w / (\mu_{en}/\rho)_{\text{LiF}} \right)_{Co}}{\left((\mu_{en}/\rho)_w / (\mu_{en}/\rho)_{\text{LiF}} \right)_Q} \tag{7}$$

The mass energy absorption coefficients for water and LiF are taken from Hubble (1982) [9].

3. Monte Carlo simulation

MCNP-4C Monte Carlo system was used for all simulations reported in this study. Monte Carlo calculation did not show any difference in behaviour of pure LiF and TLD-100 in kilovoltage or megavoltage x-ray ranges. This is expected since the concentration of Ti and Mg by weight is negligible in TLD-100 [10]. The TLD chips were represented by 3.1 mm ×3.1 mm×1 mm. In all cases the phantom material was represented by a 20cm×20cm×12cm cube of water same as experimental method. The incident photons were transported in a water medium and the dose scored in a water cube of the same dimension as the TLD placed with its center at a particular depth. The depth of irradiation of the TLD in kV x-rays and ^{60}Co gamma-rays was 5 cm. We used energy cut-off variance reduction technique in this simulation. Electron and photon transport were terminated at 10 keV and 1 keV, respectively. The photons were assumed to be perpendicularly incident on the flat surface of the chip. Non-divergent beam and field size of 6cm×8 cm were applied to simulatethe exprimental method. The recent publishing photon beam spectra for theratron 780 E cobalt machine was also used as input. Kilovoltage spectra was taken from results of our previous investigation.

The mean energies simulation shown in the table 1 were calculated from the expression:

$$E_{mean} = \left(\sum_{l}^{n} \phi(E_i) E_i \Delta E_i \right) \left(\sum_{l}^{n} \phi(E_i) \Delta E_i \right)^{-1} \tag{8}$$

where E_i is the phantom energy and $\phi(E_i)$ is the number of photons in the energy bin of width ΔE_i at phantom surface.

The uncertainty was estimated by dividing the calculations into ten batches as well as calculating the variance on the mean. Each simulation was terminated when the uncertainty reached to lower than %1 and fo this it needed between 3×10^7 to 2×10^8 x-ray photons.

(Radiation qualities)		Mean energy (MCNP)
(Applied Kilovoltage)	(HVL)	
120 kVp	0.2 mm Cu	58keV
180 kVp	0.5 mm Cu	74keV
200 kVp	1.0 mm Cu	88.6keV
250 kVp	2.0 mm Cu	114.5keV
300 kVp	3.2 mm Cu	140.2keV
1.25MeV (average Co-60 energy)	1.1 mm Pb	1.08MeV

Table 1. Specifications of X or γ -ray beams that were used for measurements and calculations in this research

4. Results

The calibrated siemens stabilipan II superficial/orthovoltage therapy unit was used to irradiation TLDs with kilovoltage therapy beams as shown in Table 1. Table 2 shows the calibration factor values of the TLD's which obtained as explained in method section.

Photon specifications		Calibration factor (cGy/ Count)
Qualities	HVL	
120 kVp	0.2 mm Cu	0.00718
180 kVp	0.5 mm Cu	0.00740
200 kVp	1.0 mm Cu	0.00795
250 kVp	2.0 mm Cu	0.00862
300 kVp	3.2 mm Cu	0.00894
1.25MV (Co-60)	1.1 mm Pb	0.00923

Table 2. Calibration factors of different x-ray qualities were tabulated

Table 3 demonstrates the experimental quality dependence factor of different x-ray qualities and ^{60}Co gamma rays. The data in Table 3 shows the experimental quality dependence factors of TLD at different beam qualities and ^{60}Co gamma rays.

The data in Table 3 shows the experimental quality dependence factors of TLD at different beam qualities. Calculating the absorbed dose to water for different test beams based on the ^{60}Co calibration factor shows some deviations in comparison to the related beam calibration factor. Table 4 shows the deviation between calculated absorbed dose to water based on ^{60}Co calibration factor. Maximum deviation observed in the 120 kVp irradiation field.

Beam quality	HVL	Qulality dependence factor	Correction dependence factor
120 kVp	0.2 mm Cu	1.28	0.70
180 kVp	0.5 mm Cu	1.24	0.80
200 kVp	1.0 mm Cu	1.16	0.86
250 kVp	2.0 mm Cu	1.07	0.93
300 kVp	2.5 mm Cu	1.03	0.97
1250keV	1.1mm Pb	1	1

Table 3. Experimental quality dependence factors and their respective energy correction factors against Co-60 calibration factor were tabulated.

Qualities	HVL	Mean diff.(%)	Standard deviation
120 kVp	0.2 mm Cu	19.9	2.1
180 kVp	0.5 mm Cu	13.78	4
200 kVp	1.0 mm Cu	8.46	3.51
250 kVp	2.0 mm Cu	3.60	2.64
300 kVp	2.5 mm Cu	1.25	1.14
1250keV	1.1mm Pb	-	-

Table 4. The mean ± SD of error absorbed dose to water reading of TLDs at different beam qualities when they are calibrated with the energy of Co-60 ($p<0.02$).

For calculation of Monte Carlo quality dependence factor, we obtained the ratio of absorbed dose in water and LiF (cavity) (D_W / D_{LiF}). Figure 1 shows the changes of the mass energy - absorption coefficient ratio and the Monte Carlo calculated dose ratio of water to LiF from 120 kVp to1250 keV x-ray beams. It shows that experimental calibration factor varies as Monte Carlo calibration factor (D_W / D_{LiF}) changes.

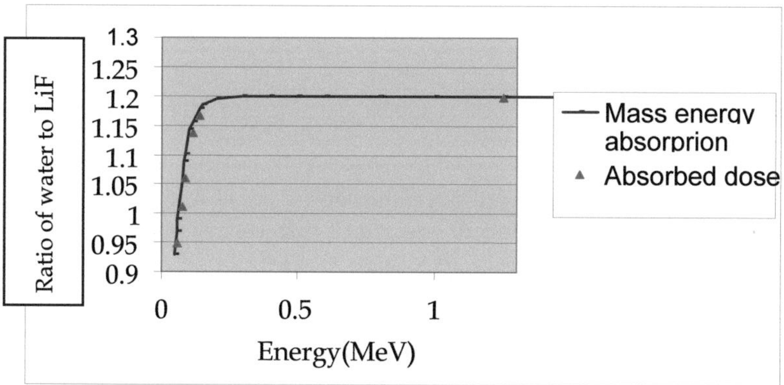

Fig. 1. TLD-100 in kV x-ray beams and ^{60}Co gamma rays:comparison of the monte carlo derived dose ratio, water to LiF, with the mass energy - absorption coefficient ratios, as a function of the maximum tube voltage in kV beams and ^{60}Co gamma rays.

The low and medium energy radiation of orthovoltage and superficial Siemens stabilipan were simulated by Monte Carlo calculation. The ratio of absorbed dose scored in water and LiF TLD (D_W / D_{LiF}) was calculated by Monte Carlo method. We also obtained the theoretical prediction of the (D_W / D_{LiF}) by the definition of cavity theory for LiF TLDs. Table 5 shows the different values of (D_W / D_{LiF}) obtained from Monte Carlo calculation and theoretical prediction by means of cavity theory for different beam qualities

Qualities	HVL	D_W / D_{LiF} (Monte Carlo)	D_W / D_{LiF} (Cavity theory)
120 kVp	0.2 mm Cu	0.91	0.97
180 kVp	0.5 mm Cu	1.00	1.05
200 kVp	1.0 mm Cu	1.05	1.09
250 kVp	2.0 mm Cu	1.13	1.15
300 kVp	2.5 mm Cu	1.16	1.17
1250keV	1.1mm Pb	1.196	1.20

Table 5. The ratio of absorbed dose in water and LiF TLDs by monte carlo calculation and prediction of cavity theory were shown.

In Table 6 the results of quality dependence factor obtained from Monte Carlo calculation, experimental study and cavity theory method were shown. The differneces between experimental and mcnp values were also obtained. It was illustrated that calculated values of quality dependence factor by Monte Carlo and cavity theory predictions are more comparable at higher mean energies

Qualities	Qulality dependence factor	Quality dependence factor (MonteCarlo)	Diff.(%)	Quality dependence factor (Cavity theory)
120 kVp	1.28	1.134	-11.41	1.237
180 kVp	1.24	1.196	+58.06	1.142
200 kVp	1.16	1.139	-1.81	1.100
250 kVp	1.07	1.052	-1.68	1.043
300 kVp	1.03	1.034	+0.04	1.018
1250keV	1	1	0.00	1

Table 6. Value of quality dependence factors obtained by measurement, Monte Carlo calculation and cavity theory were shown. Percent of differences between measured values of quality factors and mcnp calculated factors were also tabulated

5. Discussion

The precision in TL dosimetry is very critical when the quality of radiations are to be considered. It is generally accepted that ±5% uncertainty in dose delivery to the target volume can be considered as a safe limit causing no severe radiotherapy treatment consequences [11]. The quality dependence factor is necessary if LiF TLDs are calibrated using a ^{60}Co photon beam but are used in lower or higher energy photon beams.

In dosimetry it is frequently assumed that the quality dependence of thermonuminescence LiF:Mg,Ti detectors such as TLD-100, follows the ratio of the energy absorption coefficient for the LiF and water. It has been shown by Mobit et al (1998), that the quality dependence factor for LiF-TLD in kilovoltage x-rays relative to $^{60}C_0$ gamma-rays ranges from 1.36 for 50 kV x-rays to 1.03 for 300 kV which are comparable with our results [10]. Kearfott et al (1990) observed an quality dependence factor of LiF TL ribbon from 1.045 (50 keV) to 1.353 (100 keV) [12]. Study of Kron et al (1998) has also shown the quality dependence factor of 1.47 at 27 keV from synchrotron radiation [4]. Esteban et al (2003) reported results from experimental and cavity theory studies of LiF TLD in 20-29 photon beams ,where the measured value of correction factor (approximately 0.78) are more comparable to the value determined from cavity theory for the effective energies of 25 keV and 29 keV [13].

We experimentally obtained the absorbed dose calibration factor (CF) for x-ray range of 120 to 1250 keV. The calibration factor varies from 0.00718 to 0.00923 cGy/Count for 120 kVp-1250 keV and quality dependence factor were in the range of 1.000 to 1.28 for Co-60 to 120 kVp x-rays respectively (Table 3). It shows that quality dependence factor decreases with increasing the beam energy and it reaches to the normalized one (in this case to the CF of Co-60). This is an important points for dosimetry out of primary radiation field. TLDs are used for dosimetry of scatterd radiations and in such cases the calibration factor quality dependency may be a major consideration.

Finding dose ratio of water to LiF ($D_{W/}D_{LiF}$) and the mass energy absorption coefficient ratio, more comparable with increasing mean energy. This is reasonable because with increasing energy added filtration also increased and low energy portion of the spectrum is filtered out so that values of ($D_{W/}D_{LiF}$) obtained by two methods are more comparable. Same phenomenon was experienced by Esteban et al for LiF-TLD [13]. Quality dependence factors obtained from Monte Carlo method are in good agreement with exprimental method except for 180 kVp and to a lesser degree for 120 kVp. The difference between quality factors at 180 kVp is about 3.5% wich may be due to more exposure rate beam quality so that made its control more difficult. There is a significant difference of qualty dependence factors between cavity theory and Monte Carlo quality dependence factors. As shown this difference decrease with increasing beam filtration. The same effect was also reported by Esteban and et al (2003) that may be explained by attenuation of low energy photons [13].

Modelling the calibration factor of detectors can be used to predict the quality dependence factor. This model is to provide a tool for evaluation and not a physical explanation for the calibration factor. The energy model decrease with decreasing energy. The change of calibration factor with energy followed the equation:

$$CF = B_0 + B_1E + B_2E^2 + B_3E^3 \tag{9}$$

Where CF and E are calibration factor and energy (in keV), respectively. B_0, B_1, B_2 and B_3 are 0.0058, 1.8E-5, 1.3E-8 and 1.2E-1. Equation 9 was fitted to the changes of calibration factors for diferent beam qualities.

Low energy x-rays are the major part of the scattered radiations which may arise partly from the primary irradiation field and partly from the any scatterer medium in the path of the primary beam. Using the data of the curve over the low energy range based on the equation 9 can lead to the more precise results in TL dosimetry. Our finding also showed significant difference between dose values when TLDs are calibrated at Co-60 beam. The greatest difference was equal to 19.9 ±2.1% for beam quality of 120 kVp.

6. Conclusions

In conclusion, our study showed that the quality dependence of TLDs should be considered if LiF is calibrated in different beam quality than really wanted to be used. Dosimetry of non-primary radiation fields need more attention beacause of wide range of low energy photons contribution to dose formation. Obtaining a dose response curve may be helpful to calculate the calibration factor with more precision. The simplest way is to calibrate the chips against an ionization chamber using the beam quality that is to be used for the measurement

7. References

[1] Attix F. H., 1986. *Introduction to Radiological Physics and Radiation Dosimetry*. (New York: Wiely)

[7] Banjade D. P., Aloysius Raj T., Ng B.S., Xavier S., Tajuddin A. A. and Shukri A., 2003. *Entrance dose measurement: A simple and reliable technique*. Medical Dosimetry, 28, 73–78

[8] Carlson A. G., 1973, *Dosimetry at interfaces theoretical analysis and measurement by means of thermoluminescent* LiF.Acta. Radiol. Suppl. 332

[13] Esteban J., Ibbott G., Hanson W., Horton J., White A. and Cho S., 2003. *Energy Dependence of TLD System for Characterizing Low Energy Brachytherapy Sources* (WIP), Medical Physics, 30(6): 1349

[9] Hubbell J. H., 1982. *Photon mass attenuation and energy absorption coefficient for 1 keV to 20 MeV* .Int. J. Appl. Radiat. Isot., 33, 1171-6

[6] IAEA, 1997. *Absorbed dose determination in photon and electron beams*.Report 277, 3-4

[11] ICRU, 1993. *Prescribing, recording and reporting photon beam therapy*. Report No. 50

[12] Kearfott K. J., Nabelssi B. K., Rucker R. H., Klingler G. W., 1990. *Evaluation of two thermoluminescencent detection systems for medical imaging environment.* Health Phys. 59, 827-37

[4] Kron T., Dugan L., Smith T., Rosenfeld A., Buston M., Kaplan G., Howlett S., Hydoo K., 1988. *Dose response of various radiation detectors to syncchotron radiation*. Phys.Med. Biol.43, 3235-59

[3] Massillon-JL G., Gamboa-deBuen I. and Brandan M. E., 2006. *Onset of suprelinear response in TLD-100 exposed to* ^{60}*Co gamma-rays*. J. Phys. D: Appl.Phys. 39, 262-268

[2] McKeever S. W. S., Moscovitch M. and Townsend P. D., 1995. *Thermoluminescence Dosimetry Materials:Properties and Uses*(Ashford,England:Nuclear Technology Publishing)

[10] Mobit P. N., Nahum A. E. and Maylest Ph., 1998. *A Monte Carlo study of the quality dependence factors of common TLD materials in photon and electron beams*. Phys. Med. Biol. 43, 2015-2032

[5] Spanne P., Carlsson C. A. and Alm Carlsson G., 1984. *International intercomparison of standards for low collision kerma rates in air by means of low dose TLD techniques*. Radiat. Prot. Dosim., 6, 261-4

16

Monte Carlo Implementations of Two Sex Density Dependent Branching Processes and their Applications in Evolutionary Genetics

Charles J. Mode[1], Towfique Raj, Ph.D.[2] and Candace K. Sleeman, Ph.D.[3]
[1]*Professor Emeritus of Mathematics, Drexel University Philadelphia, PA 19104*
[2]*Postdoctoral Research Fellow, & Harvard Medical School and Brigham Women's Hospital, & Boston, MA 02115*
[3]*Manager Of Engineering, NAVTEQ Corporation, Malvern, PA 19355*
USA

1. Introduction

Branching processes are a class of stochastic processes that deals with the dynamics of evolving populations and have an extensive literature dating back one hundred years or more. Some references to this early literature may be found in the book of Harris (1963) (7) as well as in the book Mode (1971) (9) on mulitype branching process and their applications. Other books on branching processes include those on Athreya and Ney (1972) (2), Jagers (1975) (8), Asmussen and Hering (1983) (1) and Haccou et al.(2007 (6), which contains discussions of classes of stochastic processes and their applications to biology and other fields. Fisher (1958), in Dover reprint of an edition of book first published in the late 1920's, was the first to apply what is now known as a Galton-Watson process to the study of the survival of mutations in biological evolution. Mode and Gallop (2008) (11) in a review paper on the applications of Monte Carlo simulation methods in the study and analysis of the widely used Wright-Fisher process of evolutionary genetics suggested that multitype branching processes could be used to eliminate the assumptions of constant population size which characterizes most applications of this process in the study of biological evolution.
Despite this extensive literature, little attention has been paid to two sex process as well as processes that are density dependent and evolve on a time scale of discrete generations. By definition, two sex branching processes entail the formation of couples consisting of a female and male, who produce offspring of both sexes. By a density dependent process, we mean that the expected number of offspring produced by a couple as well as the survival of offspring may depend on total population size in every generation. In this chapter such processes will be referred to as self regulating branching processes. In most classes of branching processes considered in the literature heretofore, total population size increases stochastically at a geometric rate so that there is no finite bound on total population size. This property is objectionable, because in real biological populations, the size of a population cannot increase indefinitely due limitations of resources and the environment. As will be shown by examples in subsequent sections, in the class of self regulating branching processes described in this

chapter and elsewhere this objectionable property of classical branching processes has been removed.
Two sex processes also allow for the inclusion of multitypes such as three or more genotypes at some autosomal locus that provide a framework for the study of several components of natural selection. Among these components are sexual selection, different expectations of the number of offspring among couple types and the differential survival by genotypes of the offspring. Sexual selection will be characterized in terms of probabilities of a female or male selecting a mate according to genotype or phenotype of its prospective partner. Differential expectations of the number of offspring among couple types as well survival of the offspring will be expressed as functions of total population size. A preliminary version of the two sex process described in this chapter may be found in Mode (1995) and more developed versions of this process may be found in the forthcoming book Mode and Sleeman (2010-2011) (13) chapter 11. The formulation developed in this book is at a general level in an attempt to provide a framework within which many versions of the process may be considered. However, the version of the two sex self regulating process described in this chapter is a simplified version of a more general process, which entailed an almost complete rewrite of the material in the forthcoming book. This rewrite is sufficient to make this chapter self contained without laborious references to yet unpublished literature.
The class of branching processes just described would be very difficult to analyze if an investigator had to resort to only the methods of classical mathematics. But thanks to the continuing development of powerful Monte Carlo simulation methods, such processes can be described algorithmically and analyzed by conducting Monte Carlo simulation experiments and summarizing the simulated data statistically. In this chapter, an outline of the algorithms involved in the computer implementation of such processes will be given and the results of a few illustrative Monte Carlo simulation experiments will be presented as exercises in the predictive implications of the model. Another property that is included in the formulation is that of embedding of non-linear deterministic models in the stochastic process, which make it possible to compare the predictive performance of the stochastic and deterministic models in any computer experiment. It should also be mentioned that all the computer experiments reported in this chapter were motivated by the book Wells (2008) (16), which presents evidence based on mutations in mitochondrial and Y chromosome DNA that all humans existing on planet earth today are descendants of small groups of hominids that migrated out of Africa 50,000 to 60,000 years ago.

2. Parameterization of couple formation processes

In the two sex branching process under consideration, offspring of the next generation are produced by couples consisting of a female and male. The first step in the formulation of this class of stochastic processes is to describe the couple formation process, which, among other things, may involve a type of sexual selection in which females or males have preferences as to the genotype or phenotype of their prospective sexual partners. When one includes genetics in a formulation, it will also be necessary to describe the set of genotypes under consideration in some suitable notation. For example, let $\mathfrak{G} = (i, j, k, \cdots)$ be the set of gametes under consideration with respect to some autosomal locus or set of autosomal loci. A diploid genotype will be denoted by the ordered pair (i, j), where i is the gamete contributed by the female parent and j is the gamete contributed by the male parent. Let $\mathfrak{T}_f = ((i, j) \mid i \in \mathfrak{G}, j \in \mathfrak{G})$ denote the set of female genotypes and define the set $\mathfrak{T}_m$ similarly for males. Elements of these sets will be denoted by τ_f and τ_m, respectively. A couple will be of type $\kappa = \left(\tau_f, \tau_m\right)$ if the female is of genotype τ_f and the male is of genotype τ_m and let $\mathfrak{K}$ denote the set of all couple types. Either females or males who are not members of couples will be called singles. In practice, singles in some generation will consist of all offspring of the couple types present in that generation.

For the sake of simplicity, in this paper only one autosomal locus with two alleles will be under consideration. For this case the set of gametes will be denoted by $\mathfrak{G} = (A, a)$ so that if the gametes contributed by the maternal and paternal parents are distinguished, then the set of genotypes $\mathfrak{T}_f$ for females would contain 4 elements, and, similarly, the set $\mathfrak{T}_m$ of genotypes for males would also contain 4 elements. For this case, it follows that the set $\mathfrak{K}$ of couple types would contain 16 elements.

Let the random function $X\left(n; \tau_f\right)$ denote the number of single females present in the population in generation $n = 0, 1, 2, \cdots$ of genotype τ_f, and similarly let the random function $Y\left(n; \tau_m\right)$ denote the number of single males of genotype τ_m in generation n. Given these numbers of single females and males, let the random function $N_C\left(n; \kappa\right) \geq 0$ denote the potential number of couples formed in generation n from the single females and males. A helpful way of thinking about the random function $N_C\left(n; \kappa\right)$ is that it represents the maximum number of couples that could be formed, given the interactions of single females and males in their searches for mates in generation n.

Let the random function $Z\left(n; \kappa\right)$ denote that actual number of couples of type κ formed in generation n. Then, in the formulation under consideration, it will be assumed that $Z\left(n; \kappa\right)$ is a realization of a binomial random variable with index $N_C\left(n; \kappa\right)$ and probability $p\left(\kappa\right)$ for all $\kappa \in \mathfrak{K}$. From this assumption, it follows that $0 \leq Z\left(n; \kappa\right) \leq N_C\left(n; \kappa\right)$ with probability one for all $\kappa \in \mathfrak{K}$ and generations n. As will be demonstrated subsequently, this condition plays an essential role in showing that the random functions $Z\left(n; \kappa\right)$ satisfy a set of necessary constraints imposed by the number of single females and males eligible to form couples in any generation n with probability one.

A basic component of the formulation under consideration is that of social contact probabilities among single females and males in their searches for mates. Given a single female of genotype $\tau_f \in \mathfrak{T}_f$ in generation n, let $\gamma_f\left(n; \tau_f, \tau_m\right)$ denote the conditional probability that she has contact with a single male of genotype $\tau_m \in \mathfrak{T}_m$. The conditional contact probability $\gamma_m\left(n; \tau_m, \tau_f\right)$ for single males of genotype $\tau_m \in \mathfrak{T}_m$ in generation n is defined similarly. Subsequently, it will be shown that these contact probabilities for single females and males will be constructed in every generation from, among other things, the frequencies of the genotypes within the female and male subpopulations of singles. In this construction, all probabilities will belong to the closed interval $[0, 1]$, and for females, for example, will satisfy the condition

$$\sum_{\tau_m \in \mathfrak{T}_m} \gamma_f\left(n; \tau_f, \tau_m\right) = 1 \tag{2.1}$$

for all $\tau_f \in \mathfrak{T}_f$ and generations n. An analogous condition holds for the contact probabilities of single males.

Let

$$\gamma_f\left(n; \tau_f\right) = \left(\gamma_f\left(n; \tau_f, \tau_m\right) \mid \tau_m \in \mathfrak{T}_m\right) \tag{2.2}$$

denote a vector of contact probabilities for single females of genotype τ_f in generation n and let $\gamma_m\left(n; \tau_m\right)$ denote a similar vector for single males in generation n. For single females of genotype τ_f in generation n, let the random function $Z_f\left(n;\tau_f,\tau_m\right)$ denote the number of single males of genotype τ_m selected as potential sexual partners, and let

$$\boldsymbol{Z}_f\left(n;\tau_f\right)=\left(Z_f\left(n;\tau_f,\tau_m\right)\mid\tau_m\in\mathfrak{T}_m\right) \tag{2.3}$$

denote a vector of these random functions. Given the number $X\left(n;\tau_f\right)$ of single females of genotype τ_f in generation n, it will be assumed that the vector $\boldsymbol{Z}_f\left(n;\tau_f\right)$ has a conditional multinomial distribution with index $X\left(n;\tau_f\right)$ and probability vector $\gamma_f\left(n;\tau_f\right)$. In symbols,

$$\boldsymbol{Z}_f\left(n;\tau_f\right)\sim CMultinom\left(X\left(n;\tau_f\right),\gamma_f\left(n;\tau_f\right)\right). \tag{2.4}$$

Similarly, let $\boldsymbol{Z}_m\left(n;\tau_m\right)$ denote the corresponding vector of random functions for single males of genotype τ_m in generation n. Then, it will also be assumed that

$$\boldsymbol{Z}_m\left(n;\tau_m\right)\sim CMultinom\left(Y\left(n;\tau_m\right),\gamma_m\left(n;\tau_m\right)\right). \tag{2.5}$$

Having defined the distributions of the vectors $\boldsymbol{Z}_f\left(n;\tau_f\right)$ and $\boldsymbol{Z}_m\left(n;\tau_m\right)$ in (2.4) and (2.5), it is now possible to state how realizations of the random function $N_C\left(n;\kappa\right)$ in any generation n and couple type $\kappa=\left(\tau_f,\tau_m\right)$ will be computed. Because the potential number of pair-wise contacts of type $\left(\tau_f,\tau_m\right)$ cannot exceed the number of single females of genotypes τ_f seeking single males of genotype τ_m and similarly the number of single males of genotype τ_m seeking singly females of genotype τ_f, it follows that a plausible choice for the random function $N_C\left(n;\kappa\right)$ is

$$N_C\left(n;\kappa\right)=\min\left(Z_f\left(n;\tau_f,\tau_m\right),Z_m\left(n;\tau_m,\tau_f\right)\right), \tag{2.6}$$

for all $\kappa\in\mathfrak{K}$ and generations n, where $\kappa=\left(\tau_f,\tau_m\right)$. As shown above, if the random function $Z\left(n;\kappa\right)$ is the actual number of couple of type κ realized in generation n, then $Z\left(n;\kappa\right)\leq N_C\left(n;\kappa\right)$ for all $\kappa\in\mathfrak{K}$ and generations n. Also note that from (2.4) it follows that

$$\sum_{\tau_m\in\mathfrak{T}_m}Z_f\left(n;\tau_f,\tau_m\right)=X\left(n;\tau_f\right) \tag{2.7}$$

with probability one for all genotypes $\tau_f\in\mathfrak{T}_f$ and generations n. Therefore, from (2.6) is can be seen that

$$\sum_{\tau_m\in\mathfrak{T}_m}N_C\left(n;\tau_f,\tau_m\right)\leq\sum_{\tau_m\in\mathfrak{T}_m}Z_f\left(n;\tau_f,\tau_m\right)=X\left(n;\tau_f\right) \tag{2.8}$$

for all generations n and genotypes $\tau_f\in\mathfrak{T}_f$. Therefore, the total number of females of genotype τ_f in couples of the types $\left(\tau_f,\tau_m\right)$ such the $\tau_m\in\mathfrak{T}_m$ will not exceed the number of single females of this genotype $X\left(n;\tau_f\right)$ present in the population prior to the time the couple formation process occurred. By a similar argument, it can be shown that

$$\sum_{\tau_f\in\mathfrak{T}_f}N_C\left(n;\tau_f,\tau_m\right)\leq\sum_{\tau_f\in\mathfrak{T}_f}Z_m\left(n;\tau_m,\tau_f\right)=Y\left(n;\tau_m\right) \tag{2.9}$$

with probability one for all $\tau_m \in \mathfrak{T}_m$ and generations n. Thus, the number of couples with males of genotype $\tau_m \in \mathfrak{T}_m$ will never exceed the number of single males $Y(n;\tau_m)$ of this genotype present in the population before the couple formation processes occurred in every generation n with probability one.

The last step in the formulation of the couple formation process is that of defining a procedure for calculating the contact probabilities for single females and males, which will depend on acceptance probabilities for both females and males. For example, given a single female of genotype $\tau_f \in \mathfrak{T}_f$, let $\alpha_f\left(\tau_f,\tau_m\right)$ denote the conditional probability that she finds a single male of genotype $\tau_m \in \mathfrak{T}_m$ acceptable as a sexual partner. Similarly, for a single male of genotype τ_m, let $\alpha_m\left(\tau_m,\tau_f\right)$ denote the conditional probability that he finds a single female of genotype τ_f acceptable as a sexual partner. These acceptance probabilities will be discussed in more detail subsequently.

All contact probabilities will depend on the frequencies of the genotypes in the single populations of females and males prior to the beginning of the couple formation process. By definition, the frequency of genotype τ_f in the single female population in generation n is

$$U_f\left(n;\tau_f\right) = \frac{X\left(n;\tau_f\right)}{X\left(n;\circ\right)}, \tag{2.10}$$

where

$$X\left(n;\circ\right) = \sum_{\tau_f\in\mathfrak{T}_f} X\left(n;\tau_f\right) \tag{2.11}$$

and $X(n;\circ) > 0$. If $X(n;\circ) = 0$, then $U_f\left(n;\tau_f\right) = 0$. Similarly, let $U_m(n;\tau_m)$ denote the frequency of genotype $\tau_m \in \mathfrak{T}_m$ in the male population of singles in generation n.

By the law of total probability, the probability that a single female of genotype $\tau_f \in \mathfrak{T}_f$ has contact with some single male is

$$\sum_{\tau_m\in\mathfrak{T}_m} U_m\left(n;\tau_m\right)\alpha_f\left(\tau_f,\tau_m\right). \tag{2.12}$$

By an application of Bayes' formula, it follows that conditional probability that a single female of genotype τ_f in generation n has contact with a single male of genotype τ_m is

$$\gamma_f\left(n;\tau_f,\tau_m\right) = \frac{U_m\left(n;\tau_m\right)\alpha_f\left(\tau_f,\tau_m\right)}{\sum_{\tau_m\in\mathfrak{T}_m} U_m\left(n;\tau_m\right)\alpha_f\left(\tau_f,\tau_m\right)}. \tag{2.13}$$

Similarly, the conditional probability that a single male of genotype τ_m has contact with a single female of genotype τ_f in generation n is

$$\gamma_m\left(n;\tau_m,\tau_f\right) = \frac{U_f\left(n;\tau_f\right)\alpha_m\left(\tau_m,\tau_f\right)}{\sum_{\tau_f\in\mathfrak{T}_f} U_f\left(n;\tau_f\right)\alpha_m\left(\tau_m,\tau_f\right)}. \tag{2.14}$$

From these equations, it can be seen that if there are positive constants such that $\alpha_f\left(\tau_f,\tau_m\right) = a$ and $\alpha_m\left(\tau_m,\tau_f\right) = b$ for all types of contacts, $\left(\tau_f,\tau_m\right)$ and $\left(\tau_m,\tau_f\right)$, then

$$\gamma_f\left(n;\tau_f,\tau_m\right) = U_m\left(n;\tau_m\right) \tag{2.15}$$

and

$$\gamma_m \left(n; \tau_m, \tau_f\right) = U_f \left(n; \tau_f\right) . \tag{2.16}$$

When these conditions hold, the mating system is, by definition, random.
For a case of one autosomal locus with two alleles under consideration, the defining and numerical assignments of the acceptance probabilities for both single females and males reduce to considering 9 acceptance probabilities for each sex. Let

$$\mathfrak{T} = (AA, Aa, aa) = (1,2,3) \tag{2.17}$$

denote the set of genotypes for each sex. Then, for the case of single females, the matrix of acceptance probabilities takes the form

$$\boldsymbol{A}_f = \begin{pmatrix} \alpha_f(1,1) & \alpha_f(1,2) & \alpha_f(1,3) \\ \alpha_f(2,1) & \alpha_f(2,2) & \alpha_f(2,3) \\ \alpha_f(3,1) & \alpha_f(3,2) & \alpha_f(3,3) \end{pmatrix} . \tag{2.18}$$

There is also a similar matrix of acceptance probabilities for single males. At first sight, it may strike a reader that assigning numerical values of 18 probabilities may be an insurmountable task. But, in subsequent sections, it will be shown that meaningful genetic examples may be considered in computer simulation experiments by assigning numerical values to as few as two parameters for each sex.
Another version of a couple formation process described in this section for the case of sexually transmitted diseases may be found in the book Mode and Sleeman (2000) (12).

3. Gamete and offspring distribution for couples

In the class of two sex processes under consideration, describing the evolution of a diploid population on a discrete time scale of generations, genes are passed on in the offspring of those couples who reproduce. For, example consider a couple of type $\kappa = \left(\tau_f, \tau_m\right)$, where the genotype of the female is τ_f and that of the male is τ_m. For the autosomal locus with two alleles under consideration each of these genotypes will belong the to set (AA, Aa, aa). From now on for the sake of simplicity, the parental origin of the gametes making up a genotype will not be distinguished as to whether it is maternal or paternal. Given a couple of type $\kappa = \left(\tau_f, \tau_m\right)$ in some generation, let $p(\kappa; \tau)$ denote the conditional probability that the couple produces an offspring of genotype $\tau \in (AA, Aa, aa)$. Initially, the sex of the offspring will be ignored, but, subsequently, it will be taken into account in the formulation.
One of the significant processes underlying evolution is that of mutation. For the sake of simplicity, it will be assumed that mutations occur only among the two alleles in the set $(A, a) = (1,2)$. Let μ_{12} denote the conditional probability per meiosis that allele A mutates to allele a, and, similarly, let μ_{21} be the conditional probability that allele a mutates to allele A per meiosis. In what follows, it will be helpful to represent mutation probabilities in the form of the 2×2 matrix

$$\mathfrak{M} = \begin{pmatrix} \mu_{11} & \mu_{12} \\ \mu_{21} & \mu_{22} \end{pmatrix} \tag{3.1}$$

where the diagonal elements are chosen such that each row of this matrix sums to one. Observe that μ_{11} is the conditional probability that allele A does not mutate per meiosis, and, similarly, μ_{22} is the conditional probability that allele a does not mutate per meiosis.

The next step in the formulation is to derive the gametic distribution for each genotype under the assumption that mutation occurs. Let $p_g(\tau;\nu)$ denote the conditional probability that a genotype $\tau \in (AA, Aa, aa) = (1,2,3)$ produces a gamete of type $\nu \in (A,a) = (1,2)$ during meiosis. To illustrate the procedure for deriving these probabilities, suppose $\tau = AA = 1$ and $\nu = A = 1$. Then the probability that the left allele in the genotype AA is contributed to the gene pool of the population without mutation is $\mu_{11}/2$. Similarly the right allele in the genotype AA is contributed to the gene pool of the population without mutation is $\mu_{11}/2$. Thus, $p_g(1;1) = \mu_{11}$ and by a similar argument it may be shown that $p_g(1;2) = \mu_{12}$. By using this argument repeatedly, it can be shown that $p_g(2;1) = (\mu_{11} + \mu_{21})/2, p_g(2;2) = (\mu_{12} + \mu_{22})/2, p_g(3;1) = \mu_{21}$ and $p_g(3;2) = \mu_{22}$.

Next consider a couple of type $\kappa = \left(\tau_f, \tau_m\right)$ and let $p_c(\kappa;\tau)$ denote the conditional probability that a couple of type κ produces an offspring of genotype $\tau = (\nu, \nu')$. Then, under the assumption that female and male gametes unite independently to form a zygote, it follows that

$$p_c(\kappa;\tau) = p_g\left(\tau_f;\nu\right) p_g\left(\tau_m;\nu'\right) \tag{3.2}$$

for all couple types $\kappa \in \mathfrak{K}$ and genotypes $\tau = (\nu, \nu') \in (AA, Aa, aa)$. The collection of probabilities in (3.2) as τ varies over the set (AA, Aa, aa) will be referred to as the offspring distribution for a couple type $\kappa \in \mathfrak{K}$. Note that for each couple type $\kappa \in \mathfrak{K}$ there corresponds an offspring distribution. For the case under consideration in which the parental origin of the gametes making up an individual is not accounted for, it is easy to see that there would be 9 types of couples. In what follow, it will be helpful to let the vector

$$\boldsymbol{p}_c(\kappa) = (p_c(\kappa;\tau) \mid \tau \in (AA, Aa, aa)) \tag{3.3}$$

denote the offspring distribution for a couple of type $\kappa \in \mathfrak{K}$.

Up to now in our formulation, the only component of natural selection that has been accommodated in the formulation is that of sexual selection. Another component of natural selection that will be accommodated in the model is that of reproductive success of each couple type $\kappa \in \mathfrak{K}$. Let $N(\kappa)$ denote a random variable, taking values in the set $(m \mid m = 0, 1, 2, \cdots)$ of nonnegative integers, be defined for each couple type $\kappa \in \mathfrak{K}$, and let $W(\kappa;\tau)$ denote a random variable representing the number of offspring of genotype τ produced by a couple of type $\kappa \in \mathfrak{K}$ in any generation. To simplify the notation, it will also be helpful to let

$$\boldsymbol{W}(\kappa) = (W(\kappa;\tau) \mid \tau \in (AA, Aa, aa)) \tag{3.4}$$

denote a vector representing the number of offspring of each of the three genotypes produced by a couple of type κ under consideration in some generation. It will be assumed that, given a realization of the random variable $N(\kappa)$, the random vector $\boldsymbol{W}(\kappa)$ has a multinomial distribution with an index $N(\kappa)$ and probability vector $\boldsymbol{p}_c(\kappa)$. In symbols,

$$\boldsymbol{W}(\kappa) \sim CMultinom(N(\kappa), \boldsymbol{p}_c(\kappa)) \ . \tag{3.5}$$

To complete the formulation of this module of the model, it will be assumed that each random variable $N(\kappa)$ has a Poisson distribution with parameter $\lambda(\kappa)$, where $\kappa \in \mathfrak{K}$. For the case under consideration, there are three genotypes $(AA, Aa, aa) = (1,2,3)$ and 9 couple types. Let $\lambda(i,j)$ denote the Poisson parameter for a couple of type $\kappa = (i,j)$. Then, the nine Poisson parameters under consideration may be represented in the form of a 3×3 matrix

$$\mathbf{\Lambda} = \begin{pmatrix} \lambda(1,1) & \lambda(1,2) & \lambda(1,3) \\ \lambda(2,1) & \lambda(2,2) & \lambda(2,3) \\ \lambda(3,1) & \lambda(3,2) & \lambda(3,3) \end{pmatrix} . \tag{3.6}$$

When faced with models with many parameters, it is always of interest to find ways in which the number of parameters to be considered may be reduced. For the case of the matrix in (3.6) it seems reasonably to assume that the matrix $\mathbf{\Lambda}$ is symmetric. That is $\lambda(i,j) = \lambda(j,i)$ for all pairs. In terms of the genotypes of the female and male making up a couple, it seems reasonable to assume that couples of type (AA, aa) or (aa, AA) would on average produce the same number of offspring per generation. Of course, it may also be plausible to assume that mothers of genotype AA are more successful in producing offspring than those of genotype aa, but the exploration of such questions in computer experiments will be left to readers.

4. A Self regulating stochastic population process

In this section some algorithms will be described for computing realizations of the two sex stochastic process under consideration. The aim of these algorithms is set up a procedure such that, given some number of generations G such as four to six thousand, a number $M \geq 1$ of replications of the stochastic evolution of the process for G generations may be computed. This sample of M realizations of the process will then be summarized statistically and will be used as a graphic description of the variability among the realizations of the process for G generations of evolution. In any generation n, for $n = 0, 1, 2, 3, \cdots$, let $X\left(n; \tau_f\right)$ and $Y(n; \tau_m)$ denote, respectively, the number of single females and males in the population with genotypes τ_f and τ_m. In any simulation experiment, the initial numbers $X\left(0; \tau_f\right)$ and $Y(0; \tau_m)$ will be assinged by an experimenter. Given these numbers of single females and males in some generation n, let the random function $Z(n; \kappa)$ denote the number of couples of type $\kappa = \left(\tau_f, \tau_m\right)$ formed in generation n from the single females and males.

In generation $n \geq 1$, let the random function $T(n; \kappa; \tau)$ denote the total number of individuals of genotype $\tau \in \mathfrak{T} = (AA, Aa, aa)$ produced by couples of type κ in generation. For, given $Z(n; \kappa) \geq 0$, let $(W_\nu(\kappa; \tau) \mid \nu = 1, 2, \cdots, Z(n; \kappa))$ be a collection of conditionally independent random variables whose common distribution is that of the random variable $W(\kappa; \tau)$ in (3.5). Then, $T(n; \kappa; \tau)$ is the random sum

$$T(n; \kappa; \tau) = \sum_{\nu=1}^{Z(n;\kappa)} W_\nu(\kappa; \tau) , \tag{4.1}$$

where $T(n; \kappa; \tau) = 0$ if $Z(n; \kappa) = 0$. Let the random function $V(n; \tau)$ denote the total number of offspring of genotype τ produced in generation n. Then,

$$V(n; \tau) = \sum_{\kappa \in \mathfrak{K}} T(n; \kappa; \tau) . \tag{4.2}$$

The sex of each genotype will be considered subsequently. The total number of offspring produced by couples in generation n is given by the random function

$$T(n) = \sum_{\tau \in \mathfrak{T}} V(n; \tau) , \tag{4.3}$$

which will play a role in the survivability of each offspring in generation n.
At this point in the discussion, the sex of each offspring will be taken into account. Let p_f denote the probability that an offspring is female and let p_m denote the probability that an offspring is male. Then, given $V(n;\tau)$, the total number of females offspring of genotype $\tau_f = \tau$, say $X_T(n;\tau)$, is given by a realization of a conditional binomial random variable with index $V(n;\tau)$ and probability p_f. In symbols,

$$X_T(n;\tau) \sim CBinom\left(V(n;\tau), p_f\right) \tag{4.4}$$

and the number of male offspring of genotype $\tau_m = \tau$ is given by $Y_T(n;\tau) = V(n;\tau) - X_T(n;\tau)$.
If at this point in the description of the algorithms, a reader may concerned as to the validity of these computations, because it would make more sense to simulate whether an offspring is female or male for each couple type. In this connection, it is suggested that the following property of a sum of independent binomial random variables X_k with respective indices N_k for $k = 1, 2, \cdots, M$ with a common probability p_f be recalled. For in this case, the random variable $Y = X_1 + X_2 + \cdots X_M$ has a binomial distribution with index $N = N_1 + N_2 + \cdots + N_M$ and probability p_f. Hence, the computational procedure indicated in (4.4) is justified, and, moreover, it is more efficient from the computational point of view than doing the computation for each couple type separately.
At this point in the formulation of the model, another component of natural selection will be taken into account; namely, the ability of the female and male offspring of generation n to survive, form couples and contribute offspring to generation $n+1$. For a female of genotype $\tau_f \in \mathfrak{T}$ in generation n, let $s\left(n; T(n), \tau_f\right)$ denote the conditional probability that she survives to reproduce in generation $n+1$, given $T(n)$. Then, it will be assumed that $s\left(n; T(n), \tau_f\right)$ has a parametric form of a Weibull survival function

$$s_f\left(n; T(n), \tau_f\right) = \exp\left(-\left(\beta_f\left(\tau_f\right) T(n)\right)^{\alpha_f(\tau_f)}\right) \tag{4.5}$$

for every $\tau_f \in \mathfrak{T}$, where $\beta_f\left(\tau_f\right)$ and $\alpha_f\left(\tau_f\right)$ are positive parameters. The corresponding survival function $s_m(n; T(n), \tau_m)$ for males of genotype τ_m is defined similarly with parameters $\beta_m(\tau_m)$ and $\alpha_m(\tau_m)$.
Let the random functions $X\left(n+1; \tau_f\right)$ and $Y(n+1; \tau_m)$, respectively, denote the number of single females and males in generation n of genotypes τ_f and τ_m who survive to produce the offspring of generation $n+1$. Then, it will be assumed that

$$X\left(n+1; \tau_f\right) \sim CBinom\left(X_T\left(n; \tau_f\right), s_f\left(n; T(n), \tau_f\right)\right) \tag{4.6}$$

for every $\tau_f \in \mathfrak{T}$. Similarly, it will be assumed that

$$Y(n+1; \tau_m) \sim CBinom\left(Y_T(n; \tau_m), s_m(n; T(n), \tau_m)\right) \tag{4.7}$$

for every $\tau_m \in \mathfrak{T}$.
Given realizations of the random functions in (4.6) and (4.7), the algorithms developed in section 2 may be applied to compute realization of the collection of random functions $(Z(n+1; \kappa) \mid \kappa \in \mathfrak{K})$ for generation $n+1$. It should also be observed that, because the

parameters in the Weibull survival function depend on sex and genotype, values of these parameters may be assigned by sex, genotype or a combination of sex and genotype. Thus, in implementation of the formulation under consideration, the α and the β parameters may differ among genotypes in each sex. In subsequent computer experiments, examples of these differences will be given.

5. Non-linear deterministic equations embedded in the stochastic population process

Some stochastic formulations start with a deterministic set of equations, such as difference or differential equations in continuous or discrete time, and then proceed to extend them to stochastic model by adding a stochastic "error" term or some other random components. In this section, however, a different approach will be followed in that, given a stochastic process, a set of recursive non-linear difference equations will be embedded in the stochastic process discussed in the previous section by a procedure that entails the idea of estimating the sample functions of the process. To illustrate the idea of estimating the sample function of a stochastic process, let the sequence of random variables $X_1, X_2, X_3, \cdots$ denote some Markov process in discrete time and suppose each random variable in this sequence has a finite expectation.
It is well known that if one is considering a Markovian sequence of random variables, then the best estimate, in the sense of mean square error, of the sample function X_{n+1} based on some function of the random variable X_n is to find some function of X_n, say $f(X_n)$, such that the conditional expectation

$$E\left[(X_{n+1} - f(X_n))^2 \mid X_n\right] \tag{5.1}$$

is a minimum. By using well known properties of conditional expectations, it can be shown that

$$f(X_n) = E[X_{n+1} \mid X_n] \tag{5.2}$$

Thus, if we let $\widehat{X}_{n+1}$ denote the best estimate of X_{n+1}, then

$$\widehat{X}_{n+1} = E[X_{n+1} \mid X_n] \ . \tag{5.3}$$

Observe that the conditional expectation on the right is a random variable, since it is a function of the random variable X_n. Quite often, the conditional expectation on the right is a non-linear function of the random variable X_n so that finding a useful expectation of this random variable if often difficult or nearly impossible. But, if one knows that the value of an initial random variable X_0, then the estimate

$$\widehat{X}_1 = E[X_1 \mid X_0] \tag{5.4}$$

is known exactly. Next consider the estimate

$$E[X_2 \mid X_1] \ , \tag{5.3}$$

which is also a non-linear function of the X_1. But, an estimate of X_1 is given in (5.4). Thus, it seems reasonable, to choose

$$\widehat{X}_2 = E\left[X_2 \mid \widehat{X}_1\right] \tag{5.4}$$

as an estimate of X_2. By continuing this procedure, one arrives at the recursive system

$$\widehat{X}_{n+1} = E\left[X_{n+1} \mid \widehat{X}_n\right] \tag{5.5}$$

for $n = 0, 1, 2, \cdots$. In subsequent sections of this chapter, trajectories that have been computed using a non-linear difference equation or equations of form (5.5) will be compared graphically with a statistical summarization of a sample of realizations of the stochastic population process discussed in the preceding section.

As a first step in applying the ideas just discussed, let the symbol $\mathfrak{B}(n)$ denote a realization of the sample functions of the population process in generation n. Then, from (4.6) and (4.7) it follows that for any arbitrary genotype $\tau \in \mathfrak{T}$

$$E\left[X(n+1;\tau) \mid \mathfrak{B}(n)\right] = s_f(n; T(n), \tau)\, X_T(n;\tau) \ . \tag{5.6}$$

Similarly,

$$E\left[Y(n+1;\tau) \mid \mathfrak{B}(n)\right] = s_f(n; T(n), \tau)\, Y_T(n;\tau) \ . \tag{5.7}$$

From these equations, it can be seen that the random variables $T(n), X_T(n;\tau)$ and $Y_T(n;\tau)$ will have to be estimated. From (4.4) it follows that

$$E\left[X_T(n;\tau) \mid \mathfrak{B}(n)\right] = p_f V(n;\tau) \ , \tag{5.8}$$

and

$$E\left[Y_T(n;\tau) \mid \mathfrak{B}(n)\right] = p_m V(n;\tau) \ . \tag{5.9}$$

Thus, the random function $V(n;\tau)$, which denotes the total number of offspring of genotype τ produced by couples in generation n, will also have to be estimated.

From (4.1) and (4.2) it can be seen that the first step in estimating the random function $V(n;\tau)$ is that of estimating the random function

$$T(n;\kappa;\tau) = \sum_{\nu=1}^{Z(n;\kappa)} W_\nu(\kappa;\tau) \ . \tag{5.10}$$

Observe that for every $\nu = 1, 2, \cdots, Z(n;\kappa)$, it follows from (3.2) and (3.5) that

$$E\left[W_\nu(\kappa;\tau)\right] = \lambda(\kappa)\, p_c(\kappa;\tau) \ . \tag{5.11}$$

Therefore, from (5.10) it can be seen that

$$E\left[T(n;\kappa;\tau) \mid \mathfrak{B}(n)\right] = Z(n;\kappa)\, \lambda(\kappa)\, p_c(\kappa;\tau) \ . \tag{5.12}$$

From this equation, it follows that the random function $Z(n;\kappa)$ needs to be estimated.

To estimate this random function, section 2 should be consulted. From this section, it can be seen that

$$E\left[Z(n;\kappa) \mid \mathfrak{B}(n)\right] = N_c(n;\kappa)\, p(\kappa) \ , \tag{5.13}$$

where $p(\kappa)$ is the probability that a couple of type $\kappa \in \mathfrak{K}$ is formed during any generation n. From (2.6) it can be seen that the random function $N_c(n;\kappa)$ is computed from the random functions $Z_f\left(n; \tau_f, \tau_m\right)$ and $Z_m\left(n; \tau_m, \tau_f\right)$ for couples of type $\kappa = \left(\tau_f, \tau_m\right)$. But, these random functions are, respectively, elements of random vectors of multinomial distributions with probability vectors $\gamma_f\left(n; \tau_f\right)$ and $\gamma_m(n; \tau_m)$ and indices $X\left(n; \tau_f\right)$ and $Y(n; \tau_m)$, see (2.1) – (2.5) for details. From the properties of multinomial distribution, it follows that

$$E\left[Z_f\left(n; \tau_f, \tau_m\right) \mid \mathfrak{B}(n)\right] = X\left(n; \tau_f\right) \gamma_f\left(n; \tau_f, \tau_m\right) \tag{5.14}$$

and
$$E\left[Z_m\left(n;\tau_m,\tau_f\right) \mid \mathfrak{B}(n)\right] = Y(n;\tau_m)\,\gamma_m\left(n;\tau_m,\tau_f\right) . \quad (5.15)$$

Observe that the probabilities $\gamma_f\left(n;\tau_f,\tau_m\right)$ and $\gamma_m\left(n;\tau_m,\tau_f\right)$ are computed from the realized random functions in every generation n, see (2.10) – (2.15) for details. In particular, in the initial generation 0 integers are assigned to the initial values $X(0;\tau)$ and $X(0;\tau)$ for all $\tau \in \mathfrak{T}$. Given these initial values, $\gamma_f\left(0;\tau_f,\tau_m\right)$ and $\gamma_m\left(0;\tau_m,\tau_f\right)$ could be calculated. Thus, the estimate of the random function $Z_f\left(n;\tau_f,\tau_m\right)$ in generation 0 would be computed according to the formula

$$\widehat{Z}_f\left(0;\tau_f,\tau_m\right) = X\left(0;\tau_f\right)\gamma_f\left(0;\tau_f,\tau_m\right) , \quad (5.16)$$

and similarly
$$\widehat{Z}_m\left(0;\tau_m,\tau_f\right) = Y(0;\tau_m)\,\gamma_m\left(0;\tau_n,\tau_f\right) . \quad (5.17)$$

Finally, the random function $N_c(n;\kappa)$ would be estimated in generation $n = 0$ by using the formula
$$\widehat{N}_C(0,\kappa) = \min\left(\widehat{Z}_f\left(0;\tau_f,\tau_m\right), \widehat{Z}_m\left(0;\tau_m,\tau_f\right)\right) \quad (5.18)$$

for every couple of type $\kappa = \left(\tau_f,\tau_m\right) \in \mathfrak{K}$.
Given these estimates, the random function $V(n;\tau)$ denoting the total number of offspring of genotype τ produced in generation $n = 0$ would be estimated using the formula

$$\widehat{V}(0;\tau) = \sum_{\kappa\in\mathfrak{K}} \widehat{N}_C(0,\kappa)\,p(\kappa)\,\lambda(\kappa)\,p_c(\kappa;\tau) . \quad (5.19)$$

Therefore, from (5.6) – (5.9) it follows that

$$\widehat{X}(1;\tau) = s_f\left(0;\widehat{T}(0),\tau\right)p_f\widehat{V}(0;\tau) , \quad (5.20)$$

and
$$\widehat{Y}(1;\tau) = s_m\left(0;\widehat{T}(0),\tau\right)p_m\widehat{V}(0;\tau) \quad (5.21)$$

for all $\tau \in \mathfrak{T}$.
Now suppose the procedure just described in continued recursively so that in generation $n \geq 2$ we arrive at the collection of estimates

$$\widehat{\mathfrak{B}}(n) = \left(\widehat{X}(n;\tau), \widehat{Y}(n;\tau) \mid \tau \in \mathfrak{T}\right) . \quad (5.22)$$

Then the estimates of these random functions in generation $n+1$ would be computed using the equations
$$\widehat{X}(n+1;\tau) = s_f\left(n;\widehat{T}(n),\tau\right)p_f\widehat{V}(n;\tau) , \quad (5.23)$$

and
$$\widehat{Y}(n+1;\tau) = s_m\left(n;\widehat{T}(n),\tau\right)p_m\widehat{V}(n;\tau) . \quad (5.24)$$

As can be seen form the derivation just completed, the pair of equations (5.23) and (5.24) are purely deterministic and depend on the numerical values that are assigned to the parameters of the model in any computer experiment as well as the initial conditions. Given these parameter assignments in generation $n = 0$ and the initial conditions, trajectories based on the embedded deterministic model could be computed for generations $n = 1, 2, \cdots, G$, where G is some preassigned integer. It would also be possible to compute a sample of $M \geq 2$ of Monte Carlo replications of realizations of the process for G generations, which could then be statistically summarized in the form of quantile and mean trajectories over G generations. In such experiments, an interesting question to ask is: do the predictions for the evolution of a population for G generations computed by using the embedded deterministic model compare in some favorable or unfavorable sense with the predictions of the stochastic process? In subsequent sections of this chapter, the results of a number of computer experiments will be reported in an attempt to provide some answers to this question.

6. Failure of deterministic model to predict the evolution of the stochastic process

Among the conceptual schemes of evolution is the idea that many existing populations evolved from a small founder population and beneficial mutations among them and their descendants led to significant genetic transformations as the population evolved. For the case of the present of the world wide human population, a reader may wish the consult the interesting book by Wells (2006) (16) in which evidence is presented for the idea that various sub-populations of man making up the present world population evolved from a small founder population that migrated out of Africa in successive waves about 50,000 to 60,000 years ago. Another related theme is that humans also evolved in genetically significant ways with the development of agriculture during the last 10,000 years, which provided a means to gather in communities in which further cultural evolution occurred at various geographic regions around the world. Cultural evolution in turn, which progressed on a shorter time scale than biological evolution, made it possible for populations to grow to unprecedented sizes, which increased the probability that beneficial mutations would emerge and become established in a population. For an extensive account of this view that human populations have undergone significant genetic changes during the last 10,000 years, the interesting book of Cochran and Harpending (2009) (3) with the title, "The 10,000 Thousand Year Explosion" may be consulted.

The views just discussed motivated the computer experiment that will be reported in this section, using the stochastic framework described in the preceding sections of this chapter. To implement the embedded deterministic model described in section 5, 4,000 generations of evolution were considered. If one assumes that in humans, the length of a generation is 15 years, the age most human females become fertile, then 4,000 generations would represent about $4,000 \times 15 = 60,000$ years, which falls within the "out of Africa" hypothesis. If, however, a generation is assumed to be 20 years, then 4,000 generations would represent $4,000 \times 20 = 80,000$ years. Thus, under both assumptions as to the time length of a generation, 4,000 generations are adequate to cover the evolutionary time periods under consideration. As indicated in previous sections of this chapter, the genetic evolution of a population will be considered with respect to an autosomal locus with two alleles with the set $\mathfrak{T} = (AA, Aa, aa) = (1, 2, 3)$ of genotypes common to both sexes.

In the experiment reported in this section, two components of natural selection were considered. The first was that sexual selection was in force among males so that the matrix of acceptance probabilities for males were given the assinged values

$$\boldsymbol{A}_m = \begin{pmatrix} 0.1 & 0.1 & 0.9 \\ 0.1 & 0.1 & 0.9 \\ 0.1 & 0.1 & 0.9 \end{pmatrix}. \tag{6.1}$$

Observe that according to this matrix, males of all genotypes 1, 2, and 3, prefer females of genotype $3 = aa$ as sexual partners. By assumption sexual selection among females was neutral in the sense that each element in the matrix of acceptance probabilities $\boldsymbol{A}_f$ was assigned the value 1. It was also assumed that the probability per generation that the probability $p(\kappa)$ that a pair of type κ formed a couple was $p(\kappa) = 0.9$ for all $\kappa \in \mathfrak{K}$.
Another component of natural selection considered in this experiment was that of differential reproductive success as expressed in terms the matrix of expected values

$$\boldsymbol{\Gamma} = \begin{pmatrix} 3 & 3 & 3 \\ 3 & 3 & 3 \\ 4 & 4 & 4 \end{pmatrix} \tag{6.2}$$

for Poisson distributions. According to these assignments of values, all those couples in which the females were of genotype $3 = aa$ were most successful reproductively in the sense that such couples produced an expected number of 4 offspring per generation; whereas the other couple types produced on average only 3 offspring per generation.
Among the driving forces of evolution is that of mutation among the two alleles under consideration. To take mutation into account is was assumed that the mutation matrix had the numerical form

$$\mathfrak{M} = \begin{pmatrix} \mu_{11} & 10^{-6} \\ 10^{-7} & \mu_{22} \end{pmatrix}, \tag{6.3}$$

where the diagonal elements μ_{11} and μ_{22} were chosen such that the sum of each row the matrix $\mathfrak{M}$ was 1. Observe that by assumption the mutation $A \rightarrow a$ occurred with probability 10^{-6} per generation, but the back mutation $a \rightarrow A$ occurred with probability 10^{-7} per generation.
With respect to the survival of the offspring for each generation, it was assumed that natural selection was neutral in the sense that all parameters in the Weibull survival functions were the same, see formula (4.5). Let $\boldsymbol{\beta}_f = \left(\beta_{f1}, \beta_{f2}, \beta_{f3}\right)$ denote the vector of alpha parameters for each of the three female genotypes and let $\boldsymbol{\beta}_m$ denote the corresponding vector of parameters for males. Throughout of all experiments reported in this chapter, the beta parameters for females and males were assigned the common values $(2, 2, 2)$. Let alpha parameters for females and males be denoted by the vectors $\boldsymbol{\beta}_f$ and $\boldsymbol{\beta}_m$, respectively. For the experiment reported in this section, both the beta vectors of the Weibull survival function were assigned the common values $\boldsymbol{\beta}_f = \boldsymbol{\beta}_m = \left(10^{-7}, 10^{-7}, 10^{-7}\right)$. Another way of viewing these parameter assignments was that the environment in which the population evolved could support about 10,000,000 individuals of each sex in any generation.
It was also assumed that the evolution of the hypothetical population under consideration evolved from a small founder population with the initial number of 100 females of genotypes $1 = AA$ as symbolized by the vector $\boldsymbol{X}(0) = (100, 0, 0)$ and that the initial population vector for males had the form $\boldsymbol{Y}(0) = (105, 0, 0)$, indicating that only genotype $3 = AA$ was present in the initial female and male populations. Finally, it was assumed the p_f, the probability an offspring was female, had the value $p_f = 100/205$ and that for males had the value $p_m = 105/205$. Throughout all experiments reported in this chapter, it was assumed that the initial conditions and values of parameters stated in this paragraph were in force.
Presented in Figure 1 are the graphs of the trajectories of the three genotypes, which were computed using the embedded deterministic model described in section 5. In this figure, the horizontal axis is expressed in generations and the vertical axis denotes the estimated number of individuals of each genotype present in the population in each of the 4,000 generations.

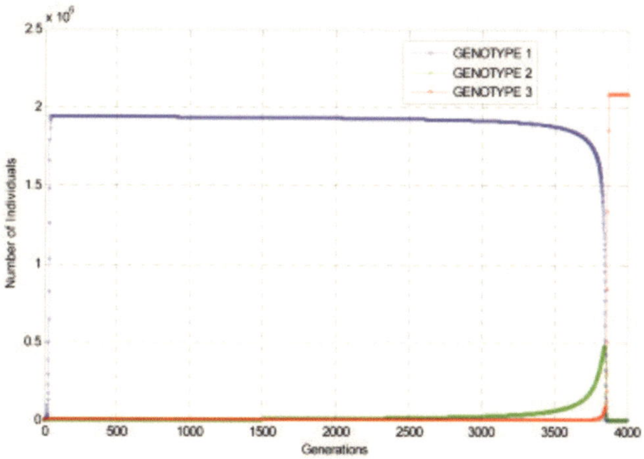

Fig. 1. Graphs of the Trajectories for the Three Genotypes as Computed by the Deterministic Model for the Female Population

As can be seen from this figure, the trajectory for genotype $1 = AA$ rises to a little less that 2×10^6 individuals in less than 500 generations into the evolutionary time period considered in the experiments; whereas the heterozygote, genotype $2 = Aa$, did not rise to noticeable numbers until about 2,000 generations of evolution. But, on the other hand, genotype $3 = aa$, which had selective advantages from the point of view of sexual selection and reproductive success, did not rise to noticeable numbers in the population until a little less than 4,000 generations when it rose to predominance among the three genotypes. By generation 4,000 the numbers of individuals of this genotype appear to have converged to a constant with a value greater than 2×10^6, while the numbers of the other two genotypes fell to values near zero. It should also be mentioned that the deterministic graphs for the male population were similar to those presented in 1.

The experiment just described was also carried out with the same parameter values and initial numbers as those used for the deterministic projections displayed in 1, using the two sex stochastic population stochastic process described in foregoing sections of this chapter. In this Monte Carlo simulation experiment 100 replications of 4,000 generations of evolution were computed and summarized statistically as described in Mode and Gallop (2008). Furthermore, the random number generators described in that paper were also used in this and all other Monte Carlo simulation experiments that are reported in this and subsequent sections of this chapter. Curiously, in this Monte Carlo experiment, it was observed that none or very few individuals of genotype $3 = aa$ arose in either the female or male sub-populations among the 100 replications of 4,000 generations of evolution.

This observation came as a surprise, because in other Monte Carlo simulation experiments conducted with this model, it was observed that deterministic predictions based on the embedded deterministic model were reasonable predictors for the stochastic process in the long run, even though it would miss entirely the high levels of variation or stochasticity that were observed among the 100 realizations of the process, during the beginning generations of experiments. Similar very high levels of stochasticity in Monte Carlo simulation experiments were also observed during those time periods of evolution when one genotype started its evolution to predominance over the others. Consequently, the contrary observations made in this experiment motivated a search of the parameter space of the model to find examples of chosen parameter values such that the embedded deterministic model was a better predictor for the trajectories of the stochastic process in the long run. It is also important to mention that without a formulation in which deteministic and stochastic approaches to modeling were considered simultaneously within one structure, this discrepancy between the predictions of a deteministic and a stochastic process would never have been realized. It is also very interesting to note that if Monte Carlo simulation techniques had not been developed with the help of many investigators over several decades, it would have been impossible to carry out the computer experiments reported in this chapter.

7. A Case in which the Deterministic model was a better predictor of the stochastic process

In the computer experiment reported in this section, all parameter values assigned in the experiment reported in the preceding section were in force except that the vectors of beta parameters $\boldsymbol{\beta}_f$ and $\boldsymbol{\beta}_m$ were assigned different values. In particular, the values chosen for these vectors were $\boldsymbol{\beta}_f = \boldsymbol{\beta}_m = \left(10^{-9}, 10^{-9}, 10^{-9}\right)$ so that in this experiment the carrying capacity of the environment for each sex and genotype was about 10^9 or one billion individuals. The value of 10^{-9} was chosen, because in the experiment reported in the preceding section, where the beta value 10^{-7} was used for all genotypes in both sexes, it was thought that in the Monte Carlo simulation experiment the number of individuals of genotype $1 = AA$ in the female population did not become sufficiently large to ensure that genotype $3 = aa$ would occur with sufficiently high probability. As will be seen subsequently, the beta value 10^{-9} was sufficient to ensure that the genotype $3 = aa$ arose in the early generations of the experiment and in the long run became the predominant genotype in the population. It should be mentioned that, even by today's standards, a population of a billion people or more people would be considered large and may be distributed over a geographic area which would encompass several countries.
Presented in Figure 2 are the trajectories for the three genotypes, which were computed using the deterministic model embedded in the stochastic process for the first 200 generations of a computer simulation experiment simulating 4,000 generations of evolution.

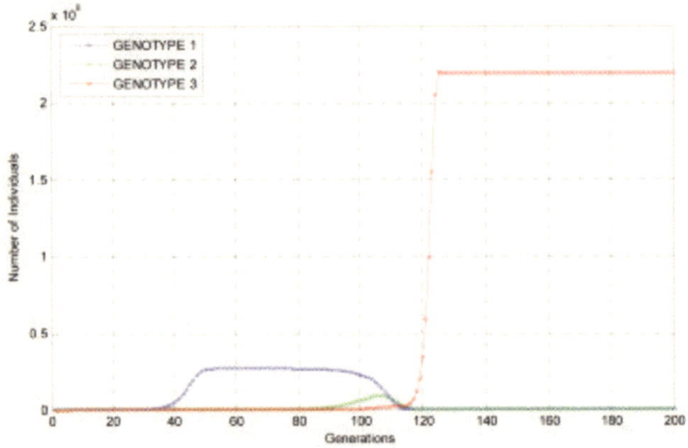

Fig. 2. Deterministic Trajectories for the Three Genotypes in the Male Population for the First 200 Generations

As can be seen from 2, genotype $3 = aa$ rose to predominance in the male population in many fewer generations than that shown in 1 for the population of females. In this figure, it can be seen that by about 50 generations of evolution, the number of individuals of genotype $1 = AA$ had risen to about $0.4 \times 10^8 = 40,000,000$ individuals, which was sufficiently large to ensure that the genotype $3 = aa$ did appear the in population after of about 120 generations of evolution. After appearing in the population, this genotype quickly rose to predominance and reached a constant value of over 2^8 individuals in the male population. It should also be mentioned that, had the graphs for the female population been plotted, they would have been very similar to those for the male population displayed in 2. In this experiment, the numbers of individuals of each of the three genotypes converged to constants, which has been the case for most experiments conducted with the embedded deterministic model.
Presented in Figure 3 are the $Min, Q50, Max, Mean$ and SD of the trajectories for the population of individuals of genotype $3 = aa$, which were estimated from the first 200 generations of a sample Monte Carlo realizations of the stochastic process based on 100 replications of evolution for 4,000 generations. By way of definitions, the symbols $Min, Q50, Max, Mean$ and SD represent, respectively, the minimum, median, maximum, mean and standard deviation of 100 realizations of the process at each of the 200 generations shown in 3.

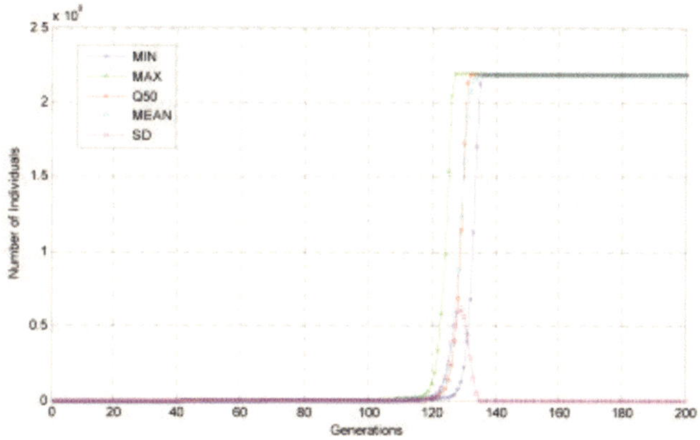

Fig. 3. Estimated Statistical Trajectories for Individuals of Genotype aa **in the Male Population in the First 200 Generations of Evolution**

As can be seen from this figure, summarizing the results of a Monte Carlo simulation experiment, genotype $3 = aa$ did not begin to appear in the population until about 100 generations into the projection as indicated by the Max trajectory, in contrast the experiment reported in the previous section in which a significant number of the genotype did not appear during 4,000 generations of evolution. At somewhat more than 120 generations, the Min trajectory for the genotype $3 = aa$ begins its ascent to higher values and the $Q50$ and $Mean$ trajectories, which lie between the Min and the Max also begin their ascent to higher values. At about 140 generations of evolution, all trajectories are close to each other and settle in to values over 2×10^8 individuals. It is also very interesting to note that during of the period between about 120 and 140 generations the trajectory for the standard deviation, SD, rises to a maximum of about 0.5×2^8 individuals before it declined to small values at about 140 generations of evolution. This rise and fall of the SD trajectory is a signature of the presence of high levels of stochasticity during the evolutionary period that genotype $3 = aa$ was rising to predominance in the population. If one relied only on the trajectories computed using the deterministic model, this high level of stochasticity would have been missed entirely. In should also be mentioned in passing, that if trajectories for the female population had been plotted, they would have been very similar to those in 3.

It is also of basic interest to mention that the close proximity of the Min, Q50, Max and Mean trajectories after about 140 generations of evolution is indicative of a stochastic process converging to a quasi-stationary distribution for which the level of variation among the realizations of the process is low as indicated by small values of the SD trajectory after about 140 generations of evolution. No formal treatment of this statement will be given here, except to mention that the stochastic process under consideration may be viewed as a Markov chain with a state space that will not be described here. But, if a reader is interested pursuing the subject of quasi-stationary distributions further, it is suggested that this phrase be typed into a search engine for the internet, where many references to this concept may be found.

If a generation time in human population is in the range of 15 to 20 years, then 200 generations would consist of $200 \times 15 = 3,000$ to $200 \times 20 = 4,000$ years of evolution. The notion that a case for sexual selection in humans may be made was the thought that in some populations males preferred female sexual partners with blue eyes, which are inherited as a recessive homozygous autosomal genotype aa. Of course, if it were assumed that females or both females and males prefer sexual partners with blue eyes, the results of such computer experiments would not have differed much from the one reported in this section. Consequently, the experiment reported in this section lends credence to the notion advanced by Cochran and Harpending (2009) (3) and others that during the last 10,000 years as agriculture developed and populations became large, blue eyes may have risen by mutation and rose to significant frequencies in some human populations due to the process of sexual selection or perhaps some other form of selection. Computer simulation experiments, such as the one reported in this section, are supportive of this notion.

8. Competitive advantage for one genotype is a sufficient condition for evolutionary predominance

In the computer experiment reported in this section, all acceptance probabilities in the matrices $\boldsymbol{A}_f$ and $\boldsymbol{A}_m$ were chosen as 1 so that, by definition, the mating system was random. It was also assumed that each couple type, consisting of a female and male of given genotypes, produced 4 offspring per generation; thus no genotype was had reproductive advantage over the others. All other parameters of the model were the same as those used in the experiment in section 7 except for the beta parameters that were assigned to each genotype for both sexes. In the experiment reported in section 6, it was observed that when the probability of the mutation $A \rightarrow a$ was assigned the value $\mu_{12} = 10^{-6}$, the reverse probability of mutation was assigned the value $\mu_{21} = 10^{-7}$ and all beta parameters were assigned the value 10^{-7}, then the mutant genotype $3 = aa$ rose to predominance in the population when the embedded deterministic model was used to compute the evolutionary trajectories for each of the three genotypes. In the corresponding Monte Carlo simulation experiment, however, only very small numbers of the mutant genotype $3 = aa$ appeared among the 100 replications of 4,000 generations of evolution.

Similar results were observed in a preliminary experiment in which the beta parameters were assigned the values $\beta_f = \beta_m = \left(10^{-7}, 10^{-7}, 10^{-8}\right)$ for both sexes, which, by assumption, gave the mutant genotype $3 = aa$ a competitive edge over the other genotypes. In an attempt to avoid the case in which the deterministic model was not a good predictor for the

evolutionary behavior of stochastic model, the beta parameters for both sexes were chosen as $\beta_f = \beta_m = (10^{-8}, 10^{-8}, 10^{-9})$ in the experiment reported in this section. As will be shown in what follows, these choices of parameter values were sufficient to show that after a rather large number of generations of evolution, the mutant genotype $3 = aa$ rose to predominance in the population according to both the deterministic and stochastic models.
Presented in Figure 4 are the evolutionary trajectories for the three genotype in the male population as computed using the deterministic model. As can be seen form this figure, the competitive advantage for genotype $3 = aa$ was sufficient for this genotype to become predominant in the population at about 1,800 generations into the projection. In this deterministic projection, the number of individuals of genotype $3 = aa$ converged to a constant with a value greater than 2×10^8.

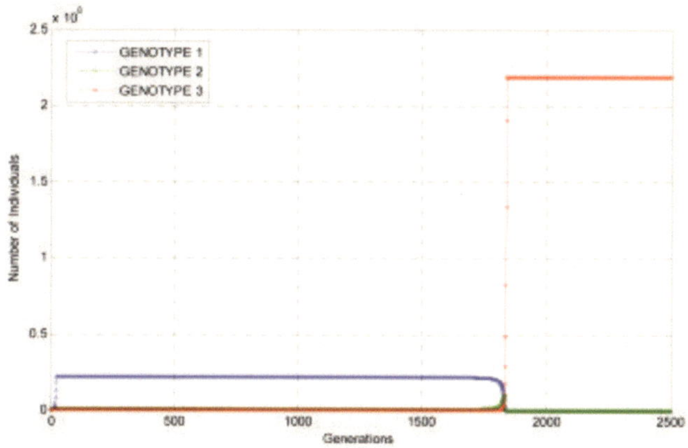

Fig. 4. Trajectories for the Three Genotypes in the Male Population for the First 2,500 Generations in an Experiment with 4,000 Generations

In Figure 5, the trajectories *Min*, *Q*50, *Max*, *Mean* and *SD* are plotted using for the first 2,500 generations of Monte Carlo simulation data consisting of 100 replications of 4,000 generations of evolution.

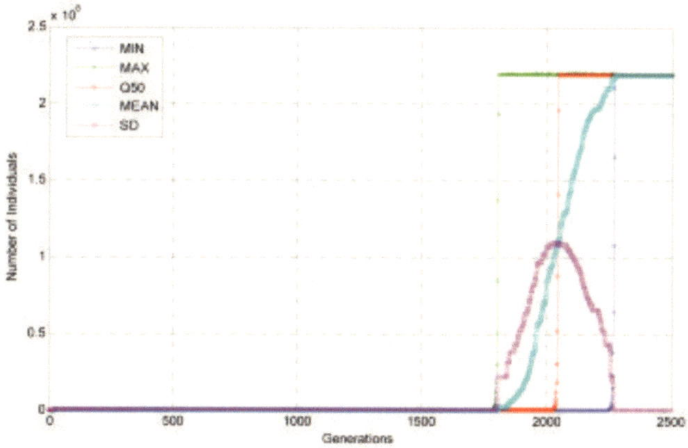

Fig. 5. Estimated Statistical Trajectories for Individuals of Genotype aa **in the Male Population in the First 2,500 Generations of Evolution**

As can be seen from this figure, significant numbers of genotype $3 = aa$ did not appear in the population until about 1,800 generations into a stochastic projection of 4,000 generations as can be seen from the Max trajectory as it begins its nearly vertical rise for a level greater than 2×10^8. Unlike the experiment reported in section 7, the level of variability or stochasticity was higher in this experiment in that the Min trajectory did not begin its steep rise until about 2,250 to 2,300 generations into the stochastic projection. Interestingly, the $Q50$ trajectory begins its steep rise at a little more than 2,000 generations, which is approximately the midpoint between the steep rise of the Max and Min trajectories. That the level of stochasticity among the realizations of the process was high can be seen by observing that the SD trajectory had a maximum greater than 1×10^8 at about 2,000 generations of evolution. Another interesting feature of 5 is that, unlike previous experiments with the stochastic model, the $Q50$ and *Mean* trajectories are distinct, during the evolutionary period when genotype $3 = aa$ was rising to predominance in the population. The coalescence of all trajectories in this figure at about 2,500 generations is indicative of a stochastic process converging to a quasi-stationary distribution with relatively low levels of variability among the realizations of the stationary process.
When compared with the experiment reported in section 7, the pace of evolution in this experiment was rather slow. For example, if in humans a generation time is in the interval 15 to 20 years, then the period of evolutionary time covered in the above figures was in the range $2,500 \times 15 = 37,500$ to $2,500 \times 20 = 50,000$ years. It is interesting to note that this range is within the estimated range of the "Out of Africa Hypothesis", in which it is postulated that all humans that inhabit the earth today are descendants of waves of human migration out Africa about 50,000 to 60,000 years ago.

9. An Example of slow evolution when mutation probabilities are small

In the experiment reported in this section, all values of parameters used in the experiment in section 8 were retained except that the probabilities of mutation per generation were chosen to be much smaller and the capacities to compete with other individuals for resources, which depended on the genotype, were chosen to be orders of magnitude smaller. In particular, the mutation probabilities per generation were assigned the values $\mu_{12} = 10^{-8}$ and $\mu_{21} = 10^{-9}$ and the beta parameters for both sexes were assigned the values $\beta_f = \beta_m = (10^{-10}, 10^{-10}, 10^{-12})$. Observe in this experiment, the beta values 10^{-10} were two orders of magnitude smaller than the mutation probability $\mu_{12} = 10^{-8}$ of the mutation $A \to a$, which was analogous to the values used in the experiment reported in section 8. In terms of actual population size, these choices of beta parameters indicate, by assumption, that individuals of genotypes $1 = AA$ and $2 = Aa$ of either sex could compete for resources only in populations of sizes up to about 10^{10} individuals; whereas individuals of genotype $3 = aa$ of either sex could compete for resources successfully in populations of sizes up to 10^{12} individuals. It is suggested that reader compare these numbers with the estimated size of the present world population of humans, which is thought to lie in the interval 6 to 7 billion individuals.
In preliminary experiments with the deterministic model, it was observed that no individuals of genotype $3 = aa$ appeared in the population after 10,000 generations of evolution. Consequently, it was decided to do an experiment which simulated 20,000 generations of evolution based on the deterministic model. As can be seen from 6 below, mutant genotype $3 = aa$ did not rise to predominance in the population until about 18,000 generations of evolution when its numbers rose almost vertically to a constant number of individuals with a value of over 2×10^{11}.

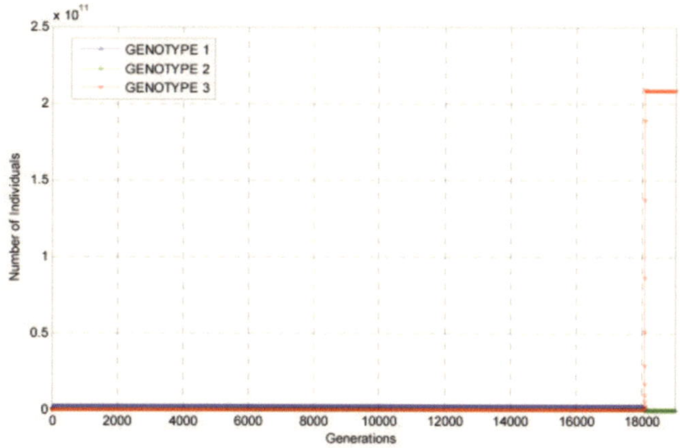

Fig. 6. Evolutionary Trajectories for the Three Female Genotypes as Computed Using the Deterministic Model

In terms of human evolution with generation times of 15 to 20 years, the time period of evolution covered in this experiment was in the range $20,000 \times 15 = 300,000$ to $20,000 \times 20 = 400,000$ years. It is thought that Homo erectus, a hominid species ancestral to man, evolved in Africa about 1.8 million years ago and spread out of Africa to as far as China. For further information on this extinct species, it is suggested that the internet be consulted. When compared to 1.8 million years of evolution time periods of 300,000 to 400,000 years are relatively short. Even though in terms of recent evolutionary history of the hominid line, it is doubtful whether population sizes ever attained those considered in this experiment, but it is plausible that other combinations of numerical values of parameters could be found such that genotype $3 = aa$, with a superior ability to compete for resources, could rise to predominance in a population within 300,000 to 400,000 years. With reference to human evolution, it is plausible that a superior ability to compete for resources would be associated with increased cognitive abilities, which may be in turn associated with enhanced neural networks in the brains of individuals.

No attempt was made to do a stochastic version of the experiment reported in this section by computing Monte Carlo simulations of the process for 100 replications of 20,000 years of evolution, because it was doubtful that such an experiment could be completed in an acceptable period of time. It was also doubtful if the desk top computers available to do such an experiment had sufficient memory capacity to store the rather large arrays that would have been generated.

10. Discussion

From the experiments reported in the preceding sections on the evolution of an autosomal locus with two alleles by mutation and selection, a general conclusion that may be drawn is that whether a beneficial mutation becomes established in a population depends not only the probability of mutation per generation that an ancestral form of a gene mutates to a more beneficial form but also on the ability of a mutant genotype to compete with other individuals for available resources. At the molecular level many mechanisms may underlie the ability of a mutant genotype to compete with other individuals, but in this section attention will be focused only on two mechanisms that may be involved in this component of natural selection.

One mechanism that comes to mind is that a mutant genotype may be able to process available sources of food more efficiently, which may, for example, involve some change in the chemical mechanisms of digestion such that an individual of a mutant genotype can extract more calories from the same amount food than as an individual with an ancestral genotype and would thus have more energy to expend in the search for food and other activities. Another mechanism that may be involved in a beneficial mutation is that individuals of a mutant genotype may have increased cognitive abilities, which result in the invention of technologies and methods to greatly expand the amount of food that can be extracted from a given geographical region. Another beneficial impact of increased cognitive abilities is that such individuals may be more adept at passing on information from generation to generation and would thus increase the survivability of individuals with such genotypes over many generations. It is beyond the scope of this chapter to further pursue the evolution of the human brain, but, it is suggested that an interested series of lectures on this and other subjects by Sapolsky (2005) (14) be consulted.

One of the limitations of the class of branching processes described in this chapter is that attention has been focused only on discrete generations of individuals and not on accommodating the existence of many birth cohorts in a population at any time, which provides a milieu for the passing of information from the older to younger individuals. This passing of information and techniques from older to younger individuals is among the defining characteristics of human populations, and there is little doubt that this educational process has played a significant role in the development of civilization as we know it today. An example of the outcome of this type of activities in human populations are the inventions of techniques and the passing on of information from generation to generation in man as agriculture developed during the last 10,000 years. It is also beyond the scope of this chapter to give a detailed account of the evolution of agriculture and the rise of urban communities, but it is suggested that an interested reader consult a series of lectures by Sojka (2009) (15), where this and other related subjects are treated in more detail.

In chapter 12 of the forthcoming book, Mode and Sleeman (2010-2011) (13), the two sex branching process described in this chapter has been extended to an age dependent process in a preliminary formulation that accommodates over lapping generations or the presence of many birth cohorts in a population at any time. Within the framework of this formulation, many more components of natural selection can be considered than in the formulation described in this chapter. Among these components is a parametric survival function for long lived species such as humans, which provide a means for calculating conditional probabilities of death or survival for each sex, given an age group to which an individual belongs. In principle, these parameterized conditional probabilities provide a means for changing the conditional probabilities of death or survival for infants and the elderly as a population evolves in a simulation experiment as conditions for survival either improve or decline over time. Within this age dependent framework, components of natural selection involving altruism may also be included in the formulation in terms of parental care of the young, which increases their probabilities of survival. This age dependent formulation also has the self regulating property in the sense that whether an individual of any age group or sex survives to reproduce also depends of total population size as described in this chapter and elsewhere. Although the case that age dependence should be included in mathematical models of human evolution that accommodate age dependence is easy to justify, including age groups in a formulation as well as a set of possible genotypes leads to the necessity of processing large arrays in a computer, which can be problematic even if networks of computers are available to an investigator or team of investigators. Among the problems that arise is the need to consider many couple types, which give rise to very large arrays, particularly when sexual selection according to age as well as genotype or phenotype are included in a formulation. These problems become particularly acute when computing samples of Monte Carlo realizations of the process and inventing procedures for informative statistical summarizations of Monte Carlo simulation data of high dimension. For these reasons, in the preliminary computer experiments reported in chapter 12 of the forthcoming book (13) attention has been confined to the deterministic model embedded in the stochastic process. Even in this deterministic case, a special sub-case in which females choose male sexual partners without couple formation was implemented to avoid the necessity of processing large arrays that arise when all possible couple types are considered. Some cases were also implemented when the evolution of a hypothetical species may be described in terms of only a few age groups. These cases served as a "proof of principle" that the formulation could be implemented on a computer even though much more work needs to be done on the age dependent formulation. It is hoped that in the future other investigators will join in the quest to develop stochastic age dependent self regulating population processes that may be implemented on computers. Even though these age dependent formulations involve high dimensional structures, the implementation of Monte Carlo simulation methods will play an essential role in developing an understanding of these models.

There is one other property of the embedded deterministic model considered in this chapter as well as those described in the forthcoming book Mode and Sleeman (2010-2011) (13) that should be mentioned. Without exception, when some combinations of numerical values of parameters are considered in computer experiments, the trajectories, which were computed using a deterministic model, become chaotic after a small number of generations of evolution. If a reader in interested in the subject chaos in deterministic systems, it is suggested that the book Gulick (1992) (5) and others be consulted. In chapter 9 of the forthcoming book, Mode and Sleeman (2010-2011) [13], examples of chaotic behavior of the embedded deterministic model are presented along with statistical trajectories estimated from samples of Monte Carlo simulation for a case of only one type of individual. As it turned out, in some cases the behavior of the statistical trajectories displayed more regularity than the chaotic deterministic trajectories. It is suggested that an interested reader consult chapter 9 of the forthcoming book for more details on cases of chaotic behavior in one type self regulating branching processes. For the sake of simplicity, no cases of chaotic behavior in the embedded deterministic model have been included in this chapter.

11. References

[1] Asmussen, S. and Hering, H. (1983), Branching Processes. Birkhauser, Boston, Basel, and Stuttgart.

[2] Athreya, K. B. and Ney, P. (1972), Branching Processes. Springer-Verlag, Berlin, Heidelberg, New York.

[3] Cochran, G. and Harpending, H. (2009) The 10,000 Year Explosion - How Civilization Accelerated Evolution Basic Books. New York.

[4] Fisher, R. A. (1958) The Genetical Theory of Natural Selection - Second Revised Edition. Dover Publications, New York, N.Y.

[5] Gulick, D. (1992), Encounters With Chaos. McGraw-Hill, New York, London

[6] Haccou, P., Jagers, P. and Vatutin, V. A. (2007) Branching Processes - Variation, Growth and Extinction of Populations. Cambridge University Press, The Edinburgh Building, Cambridge, CB2 8Ru, UK

[7] Harris, T. E. (1963), The Theory of Branching Processes. Springer-Verlag, Berlin, Heidelberg, New York.

[8] Jagers, P. (1975), Branching Processes with Biological Applications. John Wiley and Sons, London, New York, Sydney, Toronto.

[9] Mode, C. J. (1971), Multitype Branching Processes - Theory and Applications. American Elsevier, New York, Toronto.

[10] Mode, C. J. (1995) An Extension of the Galton-Watson Process to a Two Sex Density Dependent Genetic Model. Proceeding of the First World Conference on Branching Processes. Edited by C. Heyde, Springer Lecture Notes in Statistics. 99:152-168.

[11] Mode, C. J. and Gallop, R. J. (2008) A Review on Monte Carlo Simulation Methods as They Apply to Mutation and Selection as Formulated in Wright-Fisher Models of Evolutionary Genetics. Mathematical Biosciences 211: 205-225.

[12] Mode, C. J. and Sleeman, C. K. (2000) Stochastic Processes in Epidemiology - HIV/AIDS, Other Infectious Diseases and Computers. World Scientific, New Jersey, London, Hong Kong.

[13] Mode, C. J. and Sleeman, C. K. (2010-2011) Stochastic Processes in Genetics and Evolution - Computer Experiments in the Quantification of Mutation and Selection. World Scientific, New Jersey, London, Hong Kong.

[14] Sapolsky, R. (2005) Biology and Human Behavior: The Neurological Origins of Individuality The Teaching Company. Chantilly, Virginia, USA. www.teach12.com.

[15] Sojka, G. A. (2009) Understanding the Human Factor: Life and its Impact The Teaching Company. Chantilly, Virginia, USA. www.teach12.com.

[16] Wells, S. (2006) Deep Ancestry - Inside the Genographic Project. National Geographic Society, Washington, D. C. , U.S.A.

17

Monte Carlo Modeling of Light Propagation in Neonatal Skin

J.A. Delgado Atencio[1], S.L. Jacques[2] and S. Vázquez y Montiel[1]

[1]Instituto Nacional de Astrofísica Óptica y Electrónica,
[2]Oregon Health & Science University-Dermatology/Biomedical Engineering,
[1]México
[2]USA

1. Introduction

The origin of the "Monte Carlo method" historically comes from Los Alamos National Laboratory in the early years after the Second World War and is related with two important events that took place in 1945: the successful test at Alamogordo and the building of the first electronic computer (the ENIAC) (Metropolis, 1987). After the review of the ENIAC results held in the spring of 1946 at Los Alamos, Stanislaw Ulam realized that statistical techniques in combination with the surprising speed and the versatility of this electronic computer could lead to a powerful tool in theoretical calculations (Metropolis, 1987). On March 11, 1947, John von Neumann in a handwritten letter included a detailed outline of a possible statistical approach (incorporating Stanislaw´s idea) to solving the problem of neutron diffusion in a spherical core of fissionable material surrounded by a shell of tamper material. At that time, Nick Metropolis suggested the name "Monte Carlo" for the re-emerging sampling technique (Metropolis, 1987).

However, a previous work performed by Enrico Fermic in neutron diffusion in Rome in the early thirties, incorporated the essential principles of the Monte Carlo method when he was studying the moderation of neutrons (Metropolis, 1987). Another example of the previous use of this sampling technique is an ancient problem in geometric probability: "The Buffon's needle problem" which was stated in 1733 and solved (solution published in 1777) by Geroges Louis Leclerc, Comte de Buffon (1707-1788) (Weisstein, accessed September 2010). In this problem the probability of the needle crossing a line (in a table marked with equidistant parallel lines) is proportional to the inverse of the number π provided that the length of the needle is less than the space between lines. The repetition of this experiment many times results into the assessment of π.

During the post-war period the Monte Carlo (MC) method spread into many fields of knowledge such as astrophysics, solid state, optics, etc. One example in astrophysics is the study of the transfer of visible radiation through terrestrial clouds using a MC computer program that incorporated the Henyey-Greenstein phase function to describe the scattering process of water droplet clouds (Danielson et al., 1969). Another illustration of this method appears in the book "The Monte Carlo Methods in Atmospheric Optics" (Marchuk et al., 1980) which had a first Russian edition in 1974. In the preface of this book an acceptable definition of the MC method is given which is reproduced here:

"The most universal method for solving the above mentioned problems is the Monte Carlo method, which is a numerical simulation of the radiative-transfer process. This process can be regarded as a Markov chain of photon collisions in a medium, which result in scattering or absorption. The Monte Carlo technique consists in computational simulation of that chain and in constructing statistical estimates of the desired functionals".

In 1983 the MC method was applied for the first time to determine light distribution in biological tissues (Wilson & Adam, 1983), and it was specially designed to predict the distribution of absorbed dose in homogeneous tissues irradiated either by external beam light or by mean of interstitial optical fibers. After this pioneer work, various MC approaches to deal with light propagation in turbid media has been developed and applied to specific problems in the field of biomedical optics (Hasegawa et al., 1991; Graff et al., 1993; Wang et al., 1995; Wang et al., 1997). Currently, new improvements regarding the reduction of the intrinsic high computation time of Monte Carlo codes have been performed (Alerstam et al., 2008; Lo et al., 2009) by either an FPGA (field-programmable gate arrays) or GPU (graphics processing units) based platform. The significance of the results obtained so far is that this new platform may potentially enable real-time treatment planning in interstitial Photodynamic Therapy (PDT). It is interesting to observe that the same application (interstitial photodynamic therapy (PDT)) in which the MC method was applied for the first time to light distribution in tissues in 1983, is nowadays one of the most outstanding field of continuous development in biomedical optics.

The application that this chapter presents is based on the use of the so-called Monte Carlo code MCML (Wang et al., 1995) to simulate the light propagation in neonatal skin affected with different grades of hyperbilirubinemia. The neonatal jaundice (hyperbilirubinemia) can have its origin in the accumulation of the bilirubin in the serum of the blood since the liver not yet has developed totally enzymes to oxidize the bilirubin. Hyperbilirubinemia (total level of serum bilirubin TSB>1.0 mg/dL) appears in almost all newborns, whereas significant hyperbilirubinemia (TSB > 12.9 mg/dL) and excessive hyperbilirubinemia appear in only 5 to 6% of the healthy population of newborns (Bhutani et al., 2000). An excessive level of bilirubin in neonates blood (29.2 mg/dL < TSB < 47.5 mg/dL) can induce changes in the mitochondria of the basal ganglia resulting in alterations of cerebral metabolism and producing permanent damage (Groenendaal et al., 2004). The subcommittee of hyperbilirubinemia of the American Academic of Pediatry (AAP) elaborated a clinical practical guideline for the management of hyperbilirubinemia in the newborn infant (Maisels et al., 2004). The third key element of the recommendations provided by this guideline states that clinicians should measure the total serum bilirubin (TSB) or transcutaneous bilirubin (TcB) level on infants jaundiced in the first 24 hours. Transcutaneous bilirubin levels have been measured non-invasively, for instance with the transcutaneous device BiliCheck (Respironics, Marietta, GA) in a multicenter evaluation study (Rubaltelli et al., 2001) and with the transcutaneous jaundice meter model JM-103 (Minolta) in a multiracial population study of 849 newborns >**35** weeks of gestation (Maisels et al., 2004). One remarkable conclusion in this multicenter study is that BiliCheck can be used as a reliable substitute of TSB assessment whereas the JM-103 bilirubinometer correlates well with TSB levels for the entire population with the exception of black newborn infants where TcB levels are rather overestimated (Maisels et al., 2004). Two classical papers (Jacques et al., 1997, Delcher, et al. accessed April, 2007) contain the working principles of BiliCheck, presenting the basics underlying development of an optical fiber spectrometer for measurement of TcB levels in newborn infants. The working principle of this measurement accounts for variations in dermal scattering, melanin content and cutaneous blood content by using the spectrum of visible light 380-760 nm for a total of 221 spectral points (Kolman et al., 2007).

This chapter reports on the use of Monte Carlo modeling to numerically simulate the diffuse reflectance spectrum of neonatal skin in the spectral region 400-700 nm. The Monte Carlo code MCML (Wang et al., 1995) can accurately consider the multiple layers of a complex structure like the skin which is modeled in this study as a three layer optical medium: epidermis, dermis and subcutaneous tissue. In order to implement the spectral simulation of diffuse reflectance, two codes in Matlab were developed to facilitate this task. Simulation results considering the influence of factors such as: bilirubin content, grade of epidermis pigmentation, content of blood and slight variation of refractive index of skull and subcutaneous layer are presented. The significance of this study is that from MC simulations in a wide spectral region is deduced the potential possibility of using the narrow spectrum of visible light from LEDs to design and develop a low cost bilirubin meter for clinical applications in developing countries.

2. Materials and methods

2.1 Programming codes

The MC program MCML is written in standard C for modeling of the photon transport in multi-layered media, where the optical properties (μ_a, μ_s, g, n) and thickness (d) of each layer are known parameters (Wang et al., 1995). This simulation code describes the transport of an infinitely narrow photon beam perpendicularly incident on the multi-layered medium. The response of a multi-layered tissue system, speaking in terms of the simulated quantities, due to this interaction is called the impulse response or Green's function (Wang & Jacques, 1992-1998). The reflectance, transmittance, photon absorption and fluence, are the physical quantities simulated with this code. The MCML simulation records the escape of photons at the top Rd(r, α) and bottom Tt(r, α) surfaces of a multi-layered tissue slab as local radial reflectance and transmittance, respectively. Here α is the angle between the photon exiting direction and the normal to the tissue surfaces. In this work, we are only interested in simulating the total diffuse reflectance R_d of neonatal skin since this physical quantity or a fraction of it can be easily measured in-vivo.

One important feature of simulating with MCML code is the possibility to prepare a single input data file for multiple and independent runs where the number of runs is not limited by the memory capacity of the computer. We took advantage of this distinct property to naturally implement the spectral simulation of diffuse reflectance R_d (λ_i) by linking optical properties (μ_a, μ_s, g, n) at a discrete wavelength λ_i with the ith independent run. Therefore, there will be as many independent runs in the input data file as discrete wavelengths in the spectral region of interest. Another distinguishing characteristic of this software is that for each independent run defined in the input file there will be only one output data file which will contain all the above mentioned simulated quantities. So, the code will generate as many output file as discrete wavelengths of interest have been defined by the user.

Based on the main features described in previous paragraphs, the code MCML was combined with two programs in Matlab developed by us in order to facilitate the task of spectral simulations over a relatively wide spectral range (400-700 nm) with 31 spectral points and 10 nm of increment. The first Matlab program is called MCinput (see Appendix 1) and is used to prepare the input data file with extension .mci for multiple runs of the MCML

program. In this case each run corresponds to optical and geometrical parameters given at a specific wavelength as stated above. The second program is called MCoutput (see Appendix 1) and is used to read the recorded total diffuse reflectance Rd from the multiple output data files with extension .mco corresponding to each wavelength of the spectral range.
A total of $5x10^4$ photons were launched for each specified wavelength in order to simulate the diffuse reflectance with the adequate precision. This number of launched photons is more than one order of magnitude higher than the required typical number of photons (3000) for modelling the total diffuse reflectance from a turbid medium of specified optical properties (Wang & Jacques, 1992-1998).

2.2 Optical model of neonatal skin

The model mimics the body site were TcB measurements are performed in clinical applications: the forehead. In this site we considered the skin formed by three flat and infinite layers that lie on the frontal bone of the infant being the air and skull the top medium and the bottom medium, respectively as it is shown in figure 1.

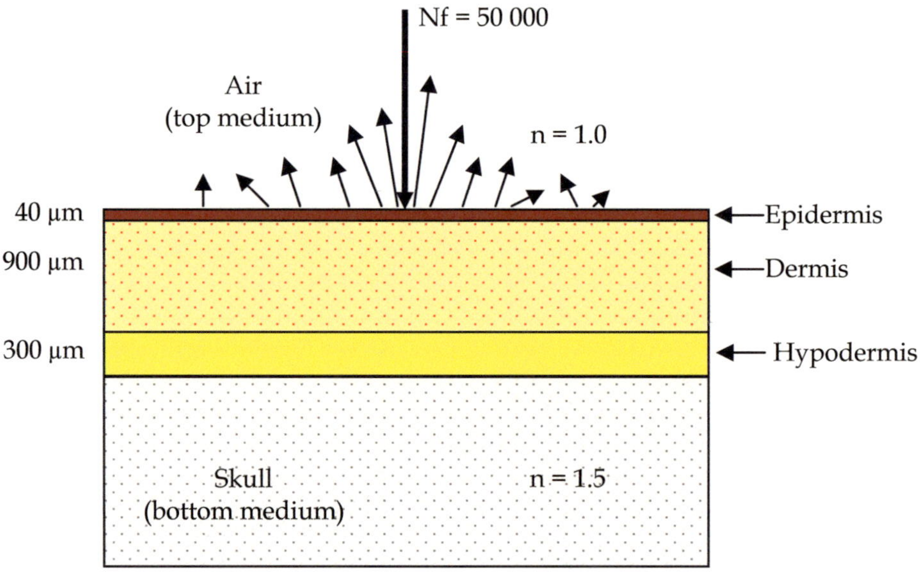

Fig. 1. Schematic representation of the tree-layer skin model of the forehead of newborn infants. The skin is considered as a 3-D half-infinite medium divided into three layers: epidermis, dermis and subcutaneous tissue (or hypodermis). The top medium is the air surrounding epidermis and the bottom medium is the skull.

The most external layer is epidermis where melanin is the only absorber and is considered as being uniformly distributed in epidermis thickness of about 40 μm. The volume fraction of melanosomes in this layer is denoted by f_{me} and its absorption coefficient is calculated as:

$$\mu_{a\_epidermis}(\lambda) = f_{me}\mu_{a\_me}(\lambda) \quad (1)$$

here $\mu_{a\_me}(\lambda) = 6.6 \times 10^{11} \lambda^{-3.33}$ is an approximate analytical expression for the absorption coefficient of the interior of a melanosome (Jacques, 1998).

The second layer, from the surface to the depth, is the dermis. We considered in this layer two primary absorbers, the blood and the bilirubin, which are both assumed to uniformly distribute in the dermis (900 μm). The volume fraction of blood vessels containing whole blood is denoted by f_{bl}. Collagen fibers are considered as the only elements to determine the scattering coefficient in epidermis and dermis. Scattering coefficient is considered the same for both epidermis and dermis (Jacques, 1998). Bilirubin concentration in the blood, C_{bi} [g/L], the extinction coefficient $\varepsilon_{bi}(\lambda)$ [cm^{-1}/(moles/L)] and the gram molecular weight P_{Mbi} [g/moles] of bilirubin molecule are put together into equation (2) with a numerical factor, ln(10), such that absorption coefficient due to bilirubin was

$$\mu_{a\_bi}(\lambda)=\ln(10)\frac{C_{bi}}{P_{Mbi}}\varepsilon_{bi}(\lambda) \tag{2}$$

Then equation (2) was scaled by a fixed partition coefficient f_{bi} (kept constant at 0.20, in reality, should vary nonlinearly as C_{bi} exceeds holding capacity of serum albumin), to account for the fact that bilirubin enters the dermis at a fraction of its concentration, C_{bi}, in blood vessels. The volume fraction of whole blood in skin is f_{bl}, which scales the absorption coefficient of whole blood, μ_{a_blood}, based on 150 g haemoglobin per liter blood. Hence, the total dermis absorption is:

$$\mu_{a\_dermis}(\lambda) = f_{bl}\mu_{a\_blood} + f_{bi}\mu_{a\_bi}(\lambda) \tag{3}$$

The first and second terms in equation (3) are the average absorption coefficient of the dermis due to blood and bilirubin, respectively. In turn, the absorption coefficient of blood, μ_{a_blood}, is calculated as

$$\mu_{a\_blood}(\lambda) = S\mu_{a\_oxy} + (1-S)\mu_{a\_deoxy} \tag{4}$$

here S is the oxygen saturation of blood and μ_{a_oxy} and μ_{a_deoxy} are the absorption coefficients of oxy-hemoglobin (HbO_2) and deoxy-hemoglobin (Hb), respectively. A similar expression to equation (2) is used for these coefficients:

$$\mu_{a\_oxy}(\lambda) = \ln(10)\frac{C_{bl}}{P_{Mbl}}\varepsilon_{oxy}(\lambda),\ \mu_{a\_deoxy}(\lambda)=\ln(10)\frac{C_{bl}}{P_{Mbl}}\varepsilon_{deoxy}(\lambda) \tag{5}$$

Extinction coefficient for bilirubin $\varepsilon_{bi}(\lambda)$, oxy-hemoglobin $\varepsilon_{oxy}(\lambda)$ and deoxy-hemoglobin $\varepsilon_{deoxy}(\lambda)$ used in dermis layer were taken from tabulated data published by Dr. Prahl (Prahl, accessed September 2010). The wavelength dependence of the anisotropy factor, g, was adopted from published optical properties (van Gemert et al., 1989) for epidermis and dermis of neonatal skin:

$$g(\lambda) = 0.62 + 0.29 * 10^{-3}\lambda \tag{6}$$

where the wavelength, λ, is in nanometres. This linear relationship yields values of g in the range 0.736-0.823 for the spectral region 400-700 nm used in this study.
The third layer included in the model is the subcutaneous tissue which is considered as a highly scattering and low absorption layer with a thickness of 300 μm. The absorption coefficient and the anisotropy factor were set as constant along the entire wavelength range with a value of 600 cm^{-1} and 0.8, respectively following published data (Tsumura et al.,

accessed January, 2006). The reduced scattering coefficient for epidermis and dermis was considered the same and was calculated following the expression reported in a published PhD thesis for a gestational age of 39 weeks (Randeberg, 2005) :

$$\mu_s'(\lambda) = C_{Mie}(1 - 1.745 * 10^{-3}\lambda + 9.844 * 10^{-7}\lambda^2) + C_{Rayleigh}\lambda^{-4} \tag{7}$$

where $C_{Mie} = 6800$ [m^{-1}], and $C_{Rayleigh} = 9.5 * 10^{13}$ [nm^4/m] are the Mie and Rayleigh constants, respectively and the wavelength is given in [nm].

2.3 Simulations

The first simulation focused on the dependence of the diffuse reflectance spectrum on the serum levels (C_{bi}) of bilirubin. The serum levels of the bilirubin were chosen as: 0, 5, 10, 15, 20 and 25 mg/dL while f_{bl} and f_{me} were held constant at 0.002 and 0.020, respectively.

The second simulation investigated the influence of the epidermal melanin pigment on the diffuse reflectance spectrum of a typical jaundice neonate (C_{bi} = 10 mg/dL = 0.10 g/L) with blood content f_{bl} = 0.002. Here the content of melanin was changed according to the values of f_{me} = 0 (amelanotic skin), 0.02 and 0.04 (lightly pigmented skin).

The third simulation was dedicated to the analysis of the dependence of the spectral diffuse reflectance with the blood content f_{bl}. The values of volume fraction of blood f_{bl} were chosen as: 0.001, 0.002, 0.01 and 0.02 while f_{me} and C_{bi} were held constant at 0.02 and 10 mg/dL, respectively. The maturity of the skin was assumed to be 39 weeks which specified the dermal scattering properties of neonatal skin. Hemoglobin concentration of 150 g/L, oxygen saturation S = 0.70 and a refractive index of 1.5 for neonatal skull, respectively, were assumed in all simulations above.

The fourth and fifth simulations were performed to investigate how variations in the refractive index of skull and fatty tissue would affect the diffuse reflectance spectrum of skin, respectively. There is not abundant literature about the refractive index of neonatal skull (Gibson et al., 2001). Therefore, we assumed that this bone has a refractive index similar to the refractive index reported in published literature concerning techniques for dissection and measurement of refractive index of osteones with different grade of mineralization (Ascenzi & Fabry, 1959). To study the effect of skull refractive index on reflectance spectrum we assumed this parameter to vary in the range 1.5-1.56 with an increment of 0.02. On the other hand to investigate the influence subcutaneous tissue refractive index on reflectance spectra this parameter was varied in the range 1.44-1.50 with an increment of 0.02.

3. Results and discussions

The total absorption coefficient of dermis for the first and third simulation described in subsection 2.3 is plotted in figure 2 following equations of subsection 2.2. In figure 3 is shown the total absorption coefficient of epidermis according to specifications of the second simulation.

In figure 2 A) are shown the resulting absorption spectra of dermis at different bilirubin concentrations. It is observed, as expected according to equations (2) and (3) that the total absorption coefficient of dermis is linearly increased with bilirubin concentration, C_{bi}. In addition, the absorption profile goes comparatively from a narrow curve for the lowest concentration (C_{bi} = 0, only blood is absorbing) to a wide spectral shape for the highest bilirubin concentration (C_{bi} = 0.25 g/L) which corresponds to an extremely dangerous physiological concentration. In figure 2 B) are shown the resulting absorption spectra of dermis at different values of the blood volume fraction. It is observed, as expected according to equations (3), (4) and (5) that the total absorption coefficient of dermis is linearly increased with blood content, f_{bl}. The monotonically decreasing behavior of total absorption coefficient of epidermis is depicted in figure 3 and is a direct consequence of the analytical expression for the absorption coefficient of the interior of a melanosome (Jacques, 1998) and equation (1).

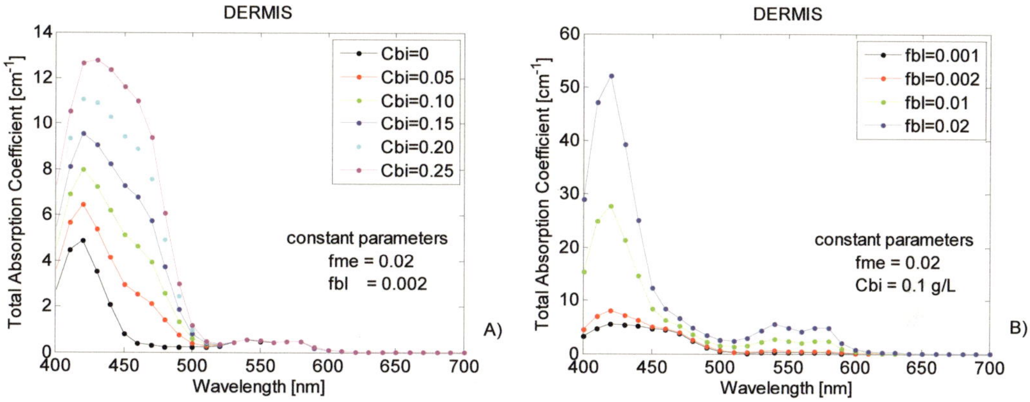

Fig. 2. Absorption coefficient of dermis for the optical model presented in subsection 2.2. A) The bilirubin concentration in the blood, C_{bi}, is varied. B) The volume fraction of blood vessels, f_{bl}, is varied.

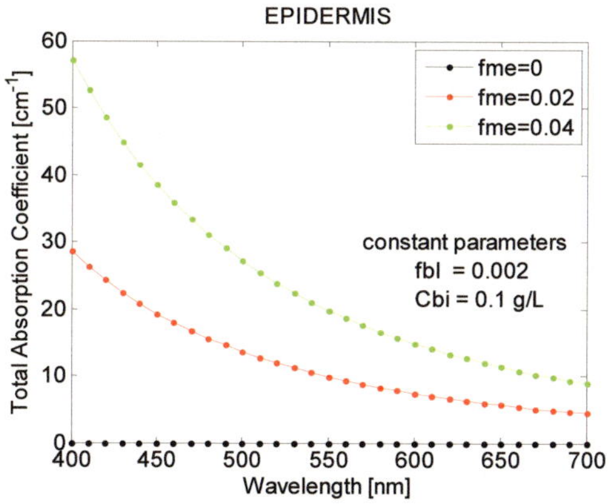

Fig. 3. Absorption coefficient of epidermis for the optical model as the volume fraction of melanosomes, f_{me}, is varied.

In figure 4 A) is shown diffuse reflectance spectra for several bilirubin concentrations. It is observed that the spectra change their shape in the range of 400-520 nm with the amount of added bilirubin. It is also important to note the non- linear relationship between bilirubin concentration and diffuse reflectance in the 400-520 nm spectral region. The decrease in diffuse reflectance with added bilirubin is not proportional to bilirubin, which is an important factor during the development of algorithms to assess the bilirubin concentration *in-vivo* in jaundiced neonates.

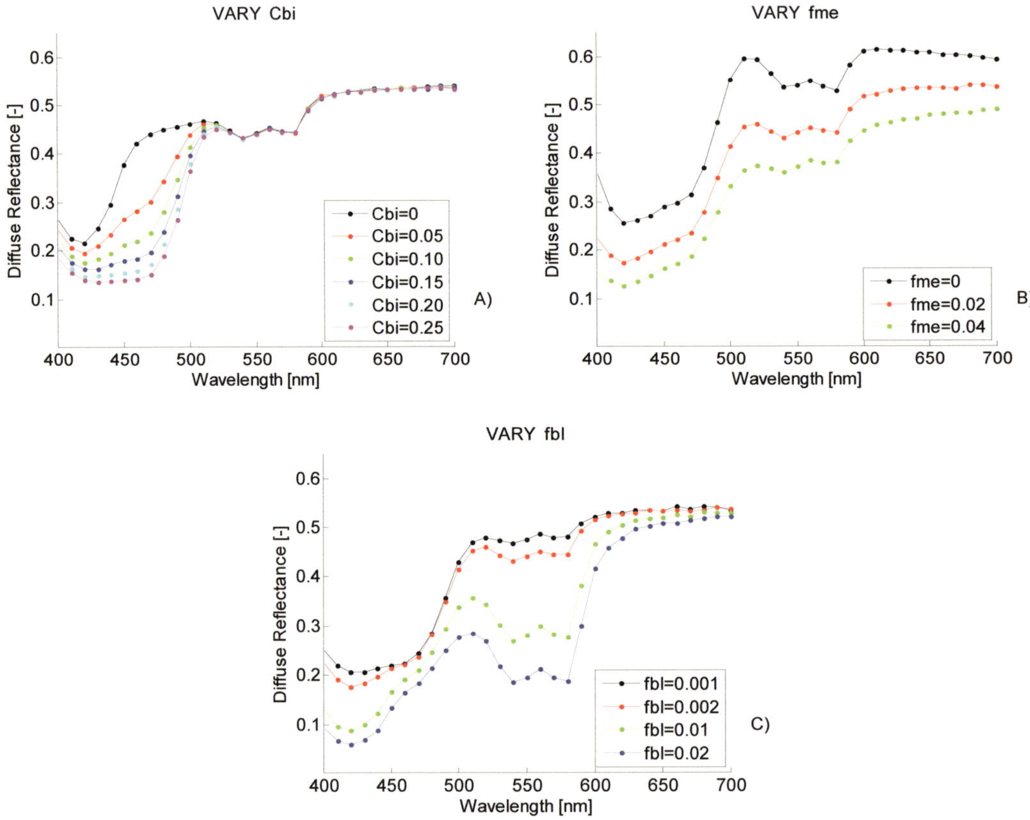

Fig. 4. Diffuse reflectance spectra that result from the Monte Carlo simulation for the three simulated situations. A) First simulation: bilirubin concentration is varied. B) second simulation: volume fraction of melanosomes is varied. C) Third simulation: blood vessels volume fraction is varied.

Figure 4 B) shows the diffuse reflectance spectra when the epidermal melanin pigmentation is varied. In this case, for the same concentration of bilirubin (10 mg/dL, representing a typical jaundiced neonate) a remarkable change in the diffuse reflectance occurs across the whole spectral range (400 to 700nm).

It is important to take into account this result when designing and developing the devices and methods to determine bilirubin levels based on spectroscopic, imaging or color techniques because they mainly record and process the spectral diffuse reflectance.

We consider that in order to make a more complete study further simulations are required to evaluate the dependence of this result for volume fraction of melanosomes that are representative of neonates with moderately and darkly pigmented skin.

In figure 4 C) is shown reflectance spectrum of skin when the content of blood f_{bl} is varied. For a relatively small change of this parameter (from 0.002 to 0.001) the most notable influence on diffuse reflectance is located near the following central wavelengths: 420, 542 and 578 nm. It is important to note that for the ranges 450-500 nm and 600-700 nm the reflectance practically do not change with this small change in blood. However, when a relatively greater change of f_{bl} is used, for instance from 0.002 to 0.01 or 0.02, a considerable change occurs in the reflectance spectrum for the 450-500 nm spectral region and in general in the whole spectral region 400-650 nm. It is observed from this figure that the impact of blood on Rd(λ) is minimal in the 650-700 nm range (red light). A tendency to minimal change of reflectance for near infrared wavelengths is expected. So in a future work MC simulations should be performed considering an extension of the visible spectral region used in this work.

It is easy to see the so called characteristic "W" pattern (Angelopoulou, 1999) that appears within the 500-600 nm range and the pronounced valley at 420 nm for the larger values of f_{bl} (0.01 or 0.02). This result expresses the importance of considering the individual variability of blood content during the assessment of transcutaneous bilirubin levels by optical methods. The simulation reproduces qualitatively the results reported by Jacques using diffusion theory to simulate reflectance spectrum of jaundiced newborns (Jacques et al., 1997).

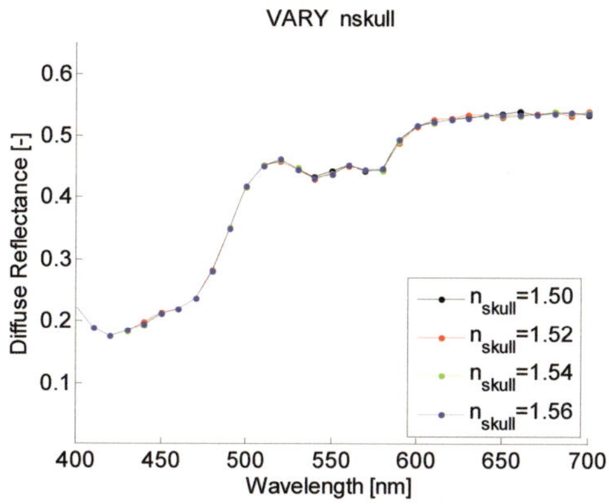

Fig. 5. Diffuse reflectance spectra of neonatal skin when the refractive index of skull is varied while the remaining parameters (C_{bi} = 0.1 g/L, f_{bl} = 0.002, f_{me} = 0.02 and n_{fat} = 1.44) of the model are kept constant.

In figure 5 is shown the reflectance spectra when the refractive index of skull is varied. As can be observed from this figure the variation of skull refractive index, n_{skull}, in a realistic range (1.50-1.56) does not affect the diffuse reflectance spectrum for the three-layer model presented in this study. From the individuality of the growing and expansion processes of brain and skull in neonates it could be expected that at birth differences of mineralization and ossification could be present and hence the refractive index of skull might change accordingly to these processes. The significance of the result summarized in figure 5 is precisely that attention should not be paid to individual variation of skull refractive index when the diffuse reflectance is measured in the visible spectral range. Therefore, a correction factor is not necessary to be included in the algorithm of determination of transcutaneous bilirubin level to account for the different grade of maturity of neonate's skull. This picture dramatically changes when the fat refractive index of subcutaneous tissue (fatty tissue) is changed in this model as we will comment in next paragraph.

Figure 6 illustrates the reflectance spectra for various refractive indexes of subcutaneous layer, n_{fat} . For $\lambda < 500$ nm there is a null difference among reflectance spectra whereas for wavelengths in the region 500 nm $<\lambda <$ 600 nm there is a slight increase of the difference among reflectance spectra. The spread of reflectance spectra is maximal for $\lambda>600$ nm where maximum difference between spectrum for n_{fat} =1.44 and the spectrum for n_{fat} =1.54 is about 4% with respect to the average spectral curve. A closer view of this spectral region reveals that there is a trend of reflectance spectrum to diminish as the fat refractive index, n_{fat}, is increased.

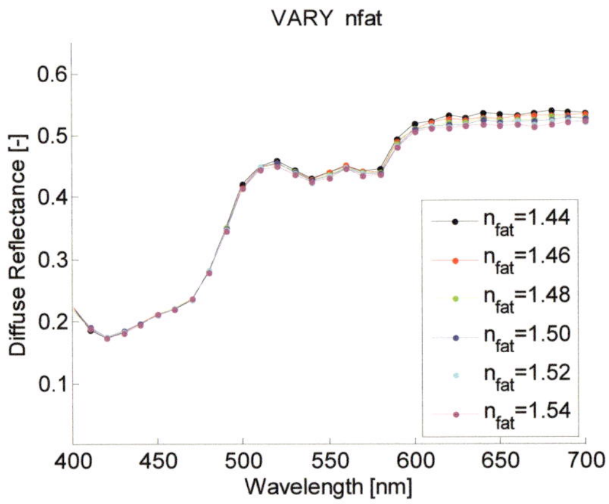

Fig. 6. Diffuse reflectance spectra of neonatal skin for various refractive index of subcutaneous tissue while the remaining parameters (C_{bi} = 0.1 g/L, f_{bl} = 0.002, f_{me} = 0.02 and n_{skull} = 1.50) of the model are kept constant.

One important and general observation is done here. If we turn reflectance spectra into optical density OD or absorption spectra A:

$$A(\lambda) = -\log_{10} R(\lambda) \tag{8}$$

a linear analysis can be used to interpret $A(\lambda)$ in terms of the melanin, blood and bilirubin concentrations. On the other hand, a relatively simple inversion algorithm could be implemented based on the combination of the main results presented in figure 4 (section 3) with a diffusion approximation theory for light transport in tissue to solve the inversion problem. The basic ideas of this problem are briefly discussed in next section and detailed information will appear in a forthcoming research work.

4. Inverse problem

So far we have just analyzed the direct problem, that is how physiological parameters: bilirubin concentration, Cbi; blood content, fbl; melanin pigmentation content, fme; and refractive indexes of skull, and fat layer, respectively affect the simulated diffuse reflectance spectrum of a given optical model for neonatal skin. However, what is more important for practical purposes is to solve the inverse problem: determining bilirubin levels in jaundiced newborns from spectra despite the variation of melanin and blood. Especially it is encouraging not to use the whole spectra to solve this problem but rather to use few reflectance values at specific wavelengths. That is precisely what will be presented in the next paragraphs.

4.1 Principles of the inverse algorithm

The inverse algorithm is based on the use of an approximate diffusion theory expression for the total diffuse reflectance:

$$Rd(\lambda) = \exp(-\mu_a(\lambda)8d(\lambda)) \quad (9)$$

where $d = \sqrt{D / \mu_a}$ and $D = 1/(3(\mu_a + \mu_s'))$ are the optical depth penetration coefficient and the diffusion coefficient, respectively. These coefficients are in turn calculated from the basic optical parameters of the tissue which are wavelength dependent as it is well known.

The main steps of the algorithm are briefly outlined:

Step 1. {Cbi, fbl, fme}

Generate the dependence $R_{700}=F_1(fme)$ and using the inverse function $fme= F_1^{-1}(R_{700})$ determine the melanin content fme from a "measurement" of diffuse reflectance for the wavelength of 700 nm (R_{700}). Hence, the main output of this step is the extracted value of melanin content, fme_ext.

Step 2. {Cbi, fbl, fme_ext}

Generate the dependence $R_{578}=F_2(fbl)$ and using the inverse function $fbl=F_2^{-1}(R_{578})$ determine the blood content fbl from a "measurement" of diffuse reflectance for the wavelength of 578 nm (R_{578}). Therefore, the principal output of this step is the extracted value of blood content, fbl_ext.

Step 3. {Cbi, fbl_ext, fme_ext}

Generate the dependence $R_{460}=F_3(Cbi)$ and using the inverse function $Cbi=F_3^{-1}(R_{460})$ determine bilirubin concentration Cbi from a "measurement" of diffuse reflectance for the wavelength of 460 nm (R_{460}). So, the principal goal of this step is the extracted value of bilirubin content, Cbi_ext.

The above steps were programmed in matlab programming language and saved into a code called Inverse_MAIN.m which contains several subroutines to perform the steps described above. The program yields the extracted values: fme_ext, fbl_ext, and Cbi_ext from a test spectrum of known physiological parameters fme_true, fbl_true and Cbi_true.

4.2 Case study

In this section we test the accuracy of the recovery of Cbi parameter as function of the grade of hyperbilirubinemia. In order to do this, we consider a set of spectra corresponding to known serum levels of bilirubin (Cbi_true) chosen as: {0.015, 0.045, 0.075, 0.105 g/L} and {0.155, 0.205, 0.255 g/L} to include jaundice cases classified as hyperbilirumemia and excesive hyperbiliruminemia, respectively. These spectra were synthesized corresponding to a population of high melanin pigmentation fme = 0.20 (20%) following the criterion that appears in published literature (Jacques, 1998). The blood content, fbl was held constant at 0.002 (0.2%) which corresponds to a typical value of this parameter for human skin. Therefore, seven synthetic spectra were generated and saved for the above described physiological parameters. The use of synthetic spectra for which true physiological parameter (Cbi, fbl, fme) values are known allows quantitative estimation of the recovery accuracy of the algorithm proposed. The figure of merit to quantify this accuracy is the recovery relative error, which is calculated as the ratio of the difference between the extracted and true parameter to the true parameter, (extracted - true)/true. This recovery error is expressed in percentage.

The spectra as defined above were loaded into the inverse Matlab algorithm (Inverse_MAIN.m) in order to perform the extraction of bilirubin concentration (Cbi_extracted). The results of extracted values are shown in figure 7. From figure 7 A) it is qualitatively observed that, our algorithm retrieves the bilirubin content, Cbi, correctly which is based on the proximity between the obtained result and the expected ideal result plotted values. This is quantitatively represented in figure 7 B) where the extraction error of

Cbi is showed as function of true Cbi values. From this last figure is concluded that with bilirubin content, Cbi, in the range 0.045-0.255 g/L the extraction error of our recovery algorithm is less than 6%.

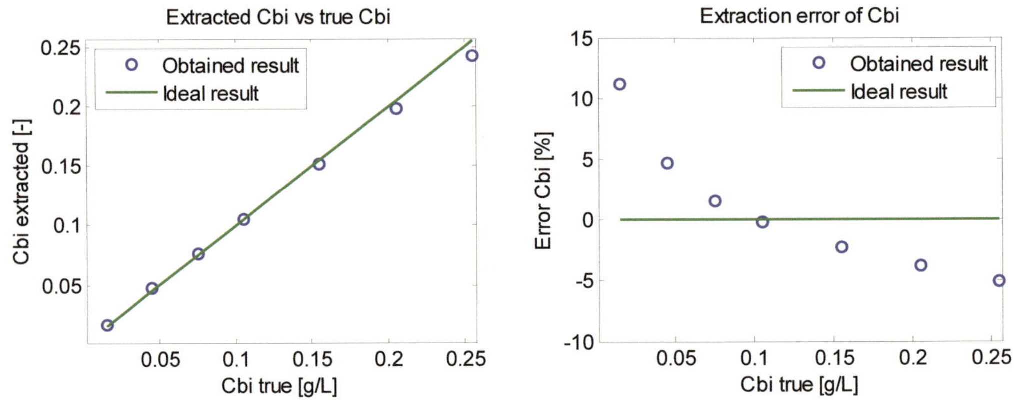

Fig. 7. Result of the inverse algorithm for the case study presented in subsection 4.2 A) Cbi extracted value vs Cbi true value. B) Extraction error vs true Cbi value.

5. Concluding remarks

The Monte Carlo code (MCML) used in this chapter in combination with the simplified optical model proposed for neonatal skin predicts the behavior of reflectance spectra of a jaundiced skin when bilirubin, melanin and blood content are variable physiological parameters. Regarding this fact three direct conclusions are drawn as follows: First, the effect of melanin (homogeneosly distributed in a 40 μm epidermis layer) on Rd(λ) is strong in the 650-700 nm range (red light), while blood and bilirubin have no effect. Therefore, the deep red wavelength range can specify the epidermal melanin content. Second, the impact of blood on Rd(λ) is maximal in the 540-580 nm range (green/yellow/orange light), while bilirubin has no effect in this spectral region. Hence the yellow wavelength range, after correcting for melanin, can specify the dermal blood content. Third, the influence of bilirubin on Rd(λ) is maximum around 460 nm (blue light). So the blue wavelength range, after correcting for melanin and blood, can specify the bilirubin content of dermal skin.

On the other hand the simulation results suggest that there is a wide range over which the refractive index of neonatal skull has a null effect on the reflectance curves whereas a more significant influence on reflectance spectra was observed when the fat refractive of the subcutaneous layer was allowed to change.

The practical significance of the above conclusions is that a simple low-cost hand-held bilirubin meter can be built with three LEDs (red, yellow and blue light-emitting diodes), to specify bilirubin levels despite variations in the melanin or blood content of a newborn's skin. Such a device would have a tremendous impact on the world-wide health of newborns, with minimal cost. This last idea is reinforced in this study by a preliminary implementation of an inverse algorithm to recover the bilirubin concentration, Cbi, from discrete measurement of diffuse reflectance at specific wavelengths in the visible spectrum, namely 460 nm, 578 nm and 700 nm.

The combination of Matlab codes presented in this chapter (MCinput.m and MCoutput.m) and MCML Monte Carlo code can serve as a valuable tool for the spectral simulation of other physical quantities within the output data file generated by the MCML code. To do this only a precise knowledge of the structure this file and slight modifications of Matlab codes are required. In order to make more realistic simulations the work presented in this chapter should be improved by considering the extent and geometry of real LEDs beams, the emission-detection geometry and spectral feature of LEDs and detector, among other parameters.

Finally to conclude, some issues relating to the simulation are noted here. The direct Monte Carlo simulation of diffuse reflectance in neonatal skin is based on the use of spectral libraries of tabulated molar extinction coefficient for hemoglobin in water and bilirubin dissolved in chloroform, respectively (Prahl, accessed September 2010) but neither haemoglobin nor bilirubin in human skin are exactly dissolved in these conditions. Therefore a more realistic molar extinction coefficient should be determined to improve the reliability of future simulations. A fixed partition coefficient f_{bi} (kept constant at 0.20) was considered when, in reality, it should vary nonlinearly as C_{bi} exceeds holding capacity of serum albumin. This issue should be investigated in more detail to be included properly in next simulations. The recovery algorithm was based on the use of diffusion theory and in future work we will explored the possibility of an easy implementation of this algorithm using MC simulations to reformulate the three step method described in this chapter.

Appendix 1 Matlab codes MCinput.m and MCoutput.m

A) The code MCinput.m

```
%%%%%%%%%%%%%%%%%%%%%%%%%%%%%%%%%%%%%%%%%%%%%%%%%%%%%%%
% MCinput.m is a matlab script
% to generate several input data files with extension .mci
% when bilirubin content, Cbi, is varied as the vector below:
% CBi = [0 0.05 0.1 0.15 0.20 0.25]
%%%%%%%%%%%%%%%%%%%%%%%%%%%%%%%%%%%%%%%%%%%%%%%%%%%%%%%
% by J.A.Delgado Atencio
% Instituto Nacional de Astrofísica Óptica y Electrónica (INAOE), Puebla, México
% September 3, 2010
%%%%%%%%%%%%%%%%%%%%%%%%%%%%%%%%%%%%%%%%%%%%%%%%%%%%%%%
clear all
for l=1:6
CBi = [0 0.05 0.1 0.15 0.20 0.25]; CBi=CBi(l);          % Bilirubin content in [g/L]
H1='C:\INTECH Book_2010\WORKSHOPS\'                      % files address
H2=sprintf('Cbi_%d-APPENDIX.mci',l); H=[H1 H2];          % Name of input data files
% 1 SIMULATION PARAMETERS-I ---> The grid and number of photons
Nf=50000                                                 % No. of photons
dz=20E-4 , dr=20E-4                                      % dz, dr of the grid
Nz=62 , Nr=200 , Na=1                                    % No. of dz, dr & da.
% 1 SIMULATION PARAMETERS-II---> Geometrical and optical properties of layers
nc=3;                                                    % Number of layers
nabove=1.00;                                             % Refractive index TOP medium
n1=1.37,d1=40E-4;                                        % Layer 1 of 3
n2=1.37,d2=900E-4;                                       % Layer 2 of 3
n3=1.44,d3=300E-4;                                       % Layer 3 of 3
nbelow=1.5;                                              % Refractive index BOTTOM medium
fme=2/100;                                               % MELANIN content kept constant
```

```
fbl=0.2/100;                                  % BLOOD   content kept constant
fbi=20/100;                                   % Partition number
S =70/100;                                    % Oxygen saturation
Cbl =150;                                     % Typical Hb concentration [g/L]
P_Mbl=64500;                                  % Molecular weight of Hb [g/moles]
CM1=Cbl/P_Mbl;                                % Constant, see equation (5)
CM2=Cbl/P_Mbl;                                % Constant, see equation (5)
P_Mbi=585;                                    % Molecular weight of Bi in [g/moles]
CM3=CBi/P_Mbi;                                % Constant, see equation (2)
% 1 SIMULATION PARAMETERS-III---> Spectral data
lambdai=400;lambdaf=700,step=10;              % Spectral region and increment
numruns=((lambdaf-lambdai)/step)+1;           % Number of runs
lambda=lambdai:step:lambdaf;                  % Discret wavelengths
format long
% 2 OPTICAL PROPERTIES
% ABSORPTION and SCATTERING in <<EPIDERMIS>>
miuame=(6.6*10^11)./(lambda.^3.33);           %Absorption coefficient of melanosome
mua1= fme*miuame;                             % Epidermis absorption coefficient
g=0.62 + (0.29E-3).*lambda;                   % Anisotropy factor
miuspN= 68*(1-(1.745*10^(-3)).*lambda + (9.8443*10^(-7)).*lambda.^2 ) +
(9.5*10^(11)).*(lambda.^(-4));
mus1=miuspN./(1-g);                           % Epidermis scattering coefficient
% ABSORPTION and SCATTERING  in <<DERMIS>>
kindexi=((lambdai-350)/2)+1;                  % Measurement step= 2nm
kindexf=((lambdaf-350)/2)+1;
kindex=(kindexi:step/2:kindexf);
load MEHemoglobin.txt -ascii                  % Load Hb extinction coefficient
MEHemoglobin;
ExtHbO2=MEHemoglobin(:,2);
ExtHb    =MEHemoglobin(:,3)
E1=ExtHbO2(kindex);
E2=ExtHb(kindex)
miuasangreHbO2=CM1*(log (10)).*E1;            % See equation (5)
miuasangreHb    =CM2*(log (10)).*E2;          % See equation (5)
mindexi=(lambdai-350)/(0.25)+1;               % Measurement step= 0.25nm
mindexf=(lambdaf-350)/(0.25)+1
mindex=(mindexi:step/0.25:mindexf);
load MEBilirubin.txt -ascii;                  % Load bilirubin extinction coefficient
MEBilirubin;
ExtBi=MEBilirubin(:,2);
E3=ExtBi(mindex)
miuabilirubin=CM3*(log (10)).*E3;
mua2= fbl.*(S.*[miuasangreHbO2'] + (1-S).*[miuasangreHb'])+ fbi.*([miuabilirubin']);
color='krgbcm'; color=color(l);
% Verification of dermal absorption by plotting
plot(lambda,mua2,color);
hold on
mus2=miuspN./(1-g);
```

```
% ABSORPTION and SCATTERING in <<HYPODERMIS>>
mua3=1
mus3=600
g3=0.8
% 3 WRITE INPUT DATA FILES FOR EACH WAVELENGTH
fout= fopen(H,'wt');
fprintf(fout,'####\n');
fprintf(fout,'# Template of input files for Monte Carlo simulation (mcml).\n');
fprintf(fout,'# Anything in a line after "#" is ignored as comments.\n');
fprintf(fout,'# Space lines are also ignored.\n');
fprintf(fout,'# Lengths are in cm, mua and mus are in 1/cm.\n');
fprintf(fout,'####\n\n');
fprintf(fout,'1.0\t\t\t\t\t\t# file version\n');
fprintf(fout,'%1d\t\t\t\t\t\t# number of runs\n\n',numruns);
for k=1:numruns
fprintf(fout,'### Specify data for run %2d\n',k);
fprintf(fout,'%d.mco\t\tA\t\t\t\t# output filename, ASCII/Binary\n',lambda(k));
fprintf(fout,'%2d\t\t\t\t\t\t# No. of photons\n',Nf);
fprintf(fout,'%5.4f\t%5.4f\t\t\t\t\t# dz, dr\n',dz,dr);
fprintf(fout,'%1d\t%2d\t%2d\t\t\t\t# No. of dz, dr & da.\n\n',Nz,Nr,Na);
fprintf(fout,'%1d\t\t\t\t\t\t# No. of layers\n', nc);
fprintf(fout,'# n\tmua\tmus\tg\td\t\t# One line for each layer\n');
fprintf(fout,'%3.2f\t\t\t\t\t\t# n for medium above.\n',nabove);
fprintf(fout,'%3.2f\t%5.3f\t%5.3f\t%3.4f\t%5.4f\t\t# layer
1\n',n1,mua1(k),mus1(k),g(k),d1);
fprintf(fout,'%3.2f\t%5.3f\t%5.3f\t%3.4f\t%5.4f\t\t# layer
2\n',n2,mua2(k),mus2(k),g(k),d2);
fprintf(fout,'%3.2f\t%5.3f\t%5.3f\t%3.4f\t%5.4f\t\t# layer 2\n',n3,mua3,mus3,g3,d3)
fprintf(fout,'%3.2f\t\t\t\t\t\t# n for medium below.\n\n\n',nbelow);
end
fclose(fout)
end
```

B) The code MCoutput.m

```
%%%%%%%%%%%%%%%%%%%%%%%%%%%%%%%%%%%%%%%%%%%%%%%%%%%%
% MCoutput.m is a matlab script
% to read diffuse reflectance from six folders (ncarp=6) called
% CBi_1 , CBi_2....CBi_6 where each of them contain 31 MC ouput files called
% 400.mco, 410.mco.......700.mco
% CBi = [0 0.05 0.1 0.15 0.20 0.25]
%%%%%%%%%%%%%%%%%%%%%%%%%%%%%%%%%%%%%%%%%%%%%%%%%%%%
% by J.A. Delgado Atencio
% Instituto Nacional de Astrofísica Óptica y Electrónica (INAOE), Puebla, México
% September 3, 2010
%%%%%%%%%%%%%%%%%%%%%%%%%%%%%%%%%%%%%%%%%%%%%%%%%%%%
clear all
name='Cbi';                          % Name of the folders to open
ncarp=6;                             % Number of folders
```

```
for j=1:ncarp
 fname1=sprintf('Diffuse_reflectance_%d.txt',j);        % Name of saved spectra files
 address1='C:\INTECH Book_2010\WORKSHOPS\';
 namecarp= [name ,'_%d']; folder1=sprintf(namecarp,j); slasht1='\';
 total1= [address1 , folder1, slasht1, fname1];
 fid_w= fopen(total1, 'wt');                            % Open file .txt to write spectrum
 for k=400:10:700
 fname=sprintf('%d.mco',k);
 total = [address1, folder1, slasht1, fname];
 fid_r= fopen(total, 'rt');                             % Open file .mco to read reflectance
 for i=1:13
   line = fgetl(fid_r);                                 % Get the name of output file .mco
   end
   name1   = sscanf(line,'%sc');
   bindex=(1:1:3);
   I=double(name1);
   m=I(bindex);
   s=char(m);
   lambda=str2num(s);
   for i=14:28
   line = fgetl(fid_r);                                 % Get the reflectance from file .mco
   end
   Rd    = sscanf(line,'%f');
   fprintf(fid_w,'%f\t',lambda);                        % Write wavelength and the reflectance
   fprintf(fid_w,'%f\n',Rd);                            % to the opened file .txt
   fclose(fid_r);                                       % Close file .mco
 end
fclose(fid_w);                                          %Close file .txt
end
% Plotting  comparative spectra to reproduce figure 4 A) of this chapter
format long
for m=1:ncarp
 fname3=sprintf('Diffuse_reflectance_%d.txt',m);
 folder3=sprintf(namecarp,m);
 total3= [address1, folder3, slasht1, fname3];
 fid3 = fopen(total3 ,'rt');
 B  = fscanf(fid3, '%f %f', [2 inf]);
 B  = B';
 fclose(fid3);
    hold
 X1=B(:,1);                                             % Wavelength [nm]
 Y1=B(:,2);                                             % Diffuse reflectance [-]
 figure(1)
 C1='krgbcm'; C1=C1(m);
 C2='......'; C2=C2(m);
 C3='------'; C3=C3(m); C=[C1,C2,C3];
 plot(X1,Y1,C)
 sz=14;
```

```
  set(gca,'fontsize',sz)
  axis([400 700 0.003 0.65]);
  xlabel('Wavelength [nm]');
  ylabel('Diffuse Reflectance [-]');
  state='VARY  '; superior= [state , name];
  label1=sprintf(superior,j);
  title (label1)
  legend('Cbi=0','Cbi=0.05','Cbi=0.10','Cbi=0.15','Cbi=0.20','Cbi=0.25',4);
hold
end
```

5. Acknowledgment

The authors of this work would like to thanks to INAOE and CONACYT, México for the support for the development of this research work.

6. References

Metropolis, N. (1987). "The Beginning of the Monte Carlo Method." Los Alamos Science. Especial Edition, 125-130.

Weisstein, E.W. "Buffon's Needle Problem." from MathWorld A Wolfram Web Resource. http://mathworld.wolfram.com/BuffonsNeedleProblem.html, accessed April 5, 2007.

Danielson, R.E., Moore, D.R., van de Hulst, H.C. (1969). "The Transfer of Visible Radiation Through Clouds." Journal of the Atmospheric Science. Vol.10, No 6, 1078-1087.

Marchuk, G.I. et al, "The Monte Carlo Methods in Atmospheric Optics". English edition © Springer-Verlag Berlin Heidelberg 1980. Original Russian Edition 1974.

Wilson, B.C. & Adam, G. (1983). "A Monte Carlo Model for the absorption and flux distributions of light in tissues." Medical Physics. Vol.10, No 6, 824-830.

Hasegawa, Y., Yamada, Y., Tamura, M., Nomura, Y. (1991). "Monte Carlo simulation of light transmission through living tissues." Appl. Optic. Vol. 30, Issue 31, pp. 4515-4520.

Graaff, R., Koelink, M.H., de Mul, F.F.M., Zijlstra, W.G., Dassel, A.C.M and Aamoudse, L.G. (1993) "Condensed Monte Carlo simulations for the description of light transport" Appl. Opt. Vol. 32, pp. 426-434.

Wang, L., Jacques, S.L, Zheng L. (1995). "MCML-Monte Carlo modeling of light transport in multi-layered tissues". Computers Methods and Programs in Biomedicine 47, 131-146.

Wang, L., Jacques, S.L., Zheng L. (1997). "CONV-Convolution for responses to a finite diameter photon beam incident on multi-layered tissues". Computers Methods and Programs in Biomedicine 54, 141-150.

Alerstam, E., Svensson, T., Andersson-Engels, S. (2008). "Parallel computing with graphics processing units for high-speed Monte Carlo simulation of photon migration." J Biomed Opt; 13(6):060504.

Lo, W., Redmond, K., Luu, J., Chow, P., Rose, J., Lilge. (2009). "Hardware acceleration of a Monte Carlo simulation for photodynamic therapy treatment planning." Journal of Biomedical Optics, vol. 14, p. 014019.

Bhutani, V. K., Gourley, G.R., Adler, S., Kreamer, Bill., Dalin, Chris., Johnson, L.H. (2000). "Noninvasive measurement of total serum bilirubin in a multiracial predischarge newborn population to assess the risk of severe hyperbilirubinemia" Pediatrics Vol. 106 No. 2, 1-9.

Groenendaal, F., van der Grond, J., de Vries, L.S. (2004). "Cerebral metabolism in severe neonatal hyperbilirubinemia" Pediatrics Vol. 114 No. 1, 291-294.
Maisels, M.J et al. (Subcommittee on hyperbilirubinemia), (2004). "Management of hyperbilirubinemia in the newborn infant 35 or more weeks of gestation " Pediatrics Vol. 114; 297-316.
Rubaltelli, F.F., Gourley, G.R., Loskamp, N., et al. (2001). "Transcutaneous bilirubi measurement: a multicenter evaluation of a new device". Pediatrics. Vol. 107:1264–1271.
Maisels, M.J., Ostrea, E.J., Touch, S., et al. (2004). "Evaluation of a new transcutaneous bilirubinometer". Pediatrics. Vol. 113:1638–1645.
Jacques, S.L., Saidi, I., Ladner., A., Oelberg, D. (1997). "Developing an optical fiber reflectance spectrometer to monitor bilirubinemia in neonates". SPIE Proceedings 2975:115-124, Laser-Tissue Interactions, San Jose, CA Feb.
Delcher, H.K., Newman, G., Bambot, S., Jacques, S.L. "Transcutaneous bilirubin measurement in a mixed population: clinical evaluation of a new device." http://www.spectrx.com/techdata/bilirubin/paperweb.pdf ., accessed April 5, 2007.
Kolman, K.B., Mathieson, K.M., Frias, C. (2007) "A Comparison of transcutaneous and total serum bilirubin in newborn hispanic infants at 35 or more weeks of gestation"
Wang, L., & Jacques, S.L. (Copyright © 1992 - 1998). "Monte carlo modeling of light transport in multi-layered tissues in standard C", http://omlc.ogi.edu/pubs/pdf/man_mcml.pdf.
Jacques, S.L. (1998). "Skin optics", http://omlc.ogi.edu/news/jan98/skinoptics.html. accessed January 5, 2006.
Prahl, S.A. "Tabulated molar extinction coefficient for hemoglobin in water", http://omlc.ogi.edu/spectra/hemoglobin/summary.html. Accessed September 19, 2010.
Prahl, S.A. "Tabulated molar extinction coefficient for bilirubin dissolved in chloroform", http:// omlc.ogi.edu / spectra / PhotochemCAD / html / bilirubin.html. Accessed September 19, 2010.
van Gemert M.J.C., Jacques, S.L., , Sterenborg, H.J.C.M., Start, W.M. (1989). "Skin Optics" IEEE Transaction on biomedical engineering, Vol. 36. No.12.
Tsumura, N., Kawabuchi, M., Haneishi, H., Miyake, Y. "Mapping pigmentation in human skin by multivisible-spectral imaging by inverse optical scattering technique" http://www.mi.tj.chiba-u.jp/~tsumura/Tsumura/papers/CIC8_oxygen.pdf, accessed January 5, 2006.
Randeberg, L.N. (2005) "Diagnostic applications of diffuse reflectance spectroscopy". Doctoral thesis, Norwegian University of Science and Technology, Trondheim, June 2005, ISBN 82-471-7077-9
Ascenzi, A. & Fabry, C.(1959),"Technique for Dissection and Measurement of Refractive Index of Osteones" http://www.ncbi.nlm.nih.gov/pmc/articles/PMC2229768/pdf/139.pdf, Accessed September 19, 2010.
Gibson, A., Yusof, R.M., Dehghani, H., Riley, J., Everdell, N., Richards, R., Hebden, J. C., Schweiger, M., Arridge, S.R. and Delpy, D.T. (2003)"Optical tomography of a realistic neonatal head phantom". Applied Optics, Vol. 42, No. 16, 3100-2116.
Angelopoulou, E. (1999) "The Reflectance Spectrum of Human Skin". Technical Report MS-CIS-99-29.http://repository.upenn.edu/cgi/viewcontent.cgi?article=1616& context=cis_reports. Accessed September 27, 2010.

18

Monte-Carlo Simulation of Ionizing Radiation Tracks

Ianik Plante and Francis A. Cucinotta
NASA Johnson Space Center, Houston, TX
USA

1. Introduction

Ionizing radiation comprises several types of energetic particles such as electrons, ions, and neutrons and energetic photons (X-rays or γ-rays). They are widely used in medicine for diagnosis and for cancer radiotherapy either as a curative or adjunctive treatments. Ionizing radiation is also known to increase cancer risk and other late risks include cataracts, heart disease and central nervous system effects. While the biological pathways involved in the effects of radiation are numerous and complex, they are initiated by physical, physico-chemical and chemical interactions of the radiation with the medium.

Because of the stochastic nature of radiation interactions, Monte-Carlo simulations techniques are very convenient not only to help our understanding of the mechanisms of interaction of ionizing radiation with matter, but they are also used in practical applications such as in microdosimetry, accelerator design and radiotherapy treatment planning. Therefore, several Monte-Carlo simulation codes of radiation tracks have been developed with different purposes (reviewed in Nikjoo et al., 2006).

In this chapter, the Monte-Carlo techniques used in particle transport related to energy deposition will be reviewed first. In the second part, the concept of *cross section* will be discussed. The cross sections are of particular importance for radiation transport, because they represent the probability of interaction of radiation with the medium. The *differential cross sections* are used to find the energy of the interaction and the direction of the particles afterward. The *total cross sections* are needed to calculate the mean free path between two interactions of the radiation. Therefore most of the discussion will be on the interaction cross sections for electrons, ions and photons, their sampling and their use in radiation transport codes.

2. Monte-Carlo techniques used in particle transport

Before discussing of the simulation of ionizing radiation tracks, some basic Monte-Carlo techniques used for particle transport will be introduced.

2.1 Random numbers

Monte Carlo simulations require large quantities of random numbers. A random number is defined as a particular value of a continuous random variable distributed uniformly in the interval [0,1]. The most commonly used type of random number generator is the so-called *congruential generator*. A sequence of random numbers is generated from the integer number I_i by

$$I_{i+1} = (aI_i + c)\mathrm{mod}(b) \tag{1}$$

where mod is the remainder of the division of aI_i+c by b. To obtain a number between 0 and 1, the result is divided by b: $R_i=I_i/b$. For example, setting a=7, c=3 and b=11 and an initial value I_i of 1 would give the sequence

$$1, 10, 7, 8, 4, 9, 0, 3, 2, 6, 1, 10,\ldots \tag{2}$$

An intial value of I_i, usually called *seed*, will always generate the same sequence of numbers. As illustrated in this example, this generator is not perfect since 5 is not in the sequence. The couple of successive points are also located along parallel lines on a 2D plot (sequential correlation), which would not be the case for a true random sequence. In fact, the algorithms used today fail statistic tests of randomness at some point (Devroye, 1986). Nevertheless, the congruential generator is widely use because of its simplicity and a period of ~10^9 when used with appropriate values of a,b and c (Press et al., 2000) which is sufficient for most purposes.

2.2 Sampling in a table

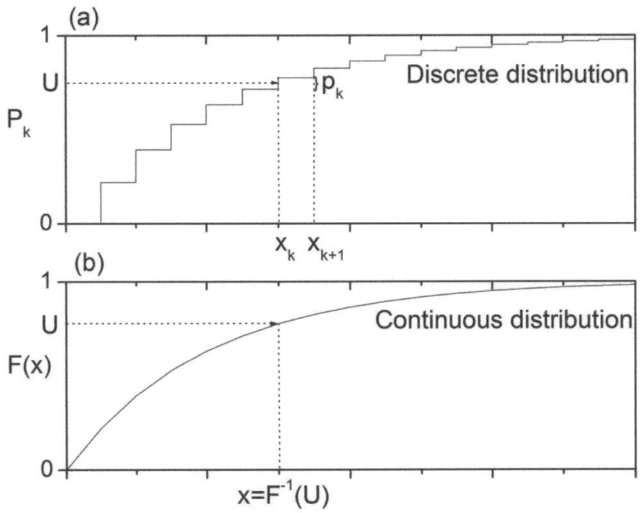

Fig. 1. Cumulative probability distributions for (a) a discrete distribution and (b) a continuous distribution.

In the theory of probability and statistics, a *probability distribution* is a function that maps events to real numbers (random variable). The distributions can be either discrete or continuous. A *discrete probability distribution* can only assume a finite or countably infinite random number of values. An example of this is the simulation of a toss of a dice. The N events for a dice are the numbers 1 to 6, each with $p_i=1/6$. The probabilities are normalized:

$$\sum_{i=1}^{N} p_i = 1 \tag{3}$$

The cumulative probabilities P_k are obtained by summing the p_i values from i=1 to i=k :

$$P_k = \sum_{i=1}^{k} p_i \tag{4}$$

Consider now the problem of obtaining computer generated random samples from uniform probability distributions. To simulate the toss of a dice, a random number in the interval [0,1] is drawn. Then the value of k which verifies $P_k < U \le P_{k+1}$ is found as illustrated in Figure 1a. The random number U is placed on the left axis. The value of k is obtained by using the cumulative probability distribution. The value of k determines which event occurs.

2.3 Inversion method

In *continuous probability distributions*, the random variable can take an infinite number of possible values (for example, a position on the X axis). The probability to find a number between x and x+dx is described by the distribution f(x)dx. This distribution is normalized:

$$\int_{-\infty}^{\infty} f(x')dx' = 1 \tag{5}$$

The cumulative probability distribution F(x) is obtained by integration:

$$F(x) = \int_{-\infty}^{x} f(x')dx' \tag{6}$$

Let U be a random number uniformly distributed between 0 and 1 and X a random number distributed according to the density f(x). If F(x) is easy to obtain and invert, a value of X can be generated by invertion of the cumulative probability distribution:

$$F(X) = \int_{-\infty}^{X} f(x')dx' = U \tag{7a}$$

$$X = F^{-1}(U) \tag{7b}$$

The classical example to illustrate this method is the exponential distribution, which is also very important in particle transport. This distribution can be written:

$$f(x) = \lambda^{-1}\exp(-x/\lambda)\,,\ x\geq 0,\ \lambda>0 \tag{8}$$

The integration and inversion of the cumulative probability distribution gives:

$$X = -\lambda \log(1-U) \text{ or } X = -\lambda \log(U) \tag{9}$$

because 1-U is also an uniform distribution between 0 and 1. The inversion method is, as illustrated on Figure 1b, the continuous limit of sampling in a table.

2.4 Rejection method

It is not always be possible to apply the direct (or inversion) method of sampling. Another well established method is the so-called *rejection sampling* technique. The name comes from the fact that not all of the random samples generated are retained, some are rejected on the basis of a criterion which are now specified. Let f(x), the probability distribution to sample. Let further assume that f(x) can be written in the form

$$f(x) = g(x)\rho(x) \tag{10}$$

where g(x) is a probability distribution normalized and easy to sample such as the exponential and $\rho(x)$ is a function bounded by a constant $c \geq 1$ ($\rho(x) \leq c$). Random numbers distributed as f(x) can be generated by the following algorithm:

Algorithm 1: Rejection method
REPEAT
{
    Generate a random X distributed as g(x)
    Generate a uniform random number U (between 0 and 1)
}
UNTIL $cU > \rho(X)$
RETURN X ■

This method can be understood intuitively by looking at Figure 2. A point (X, cU) is generated in the plane. By selecting only the points which verifies the condition $cU \leq \rho(X)$, X is distributed as f(x).

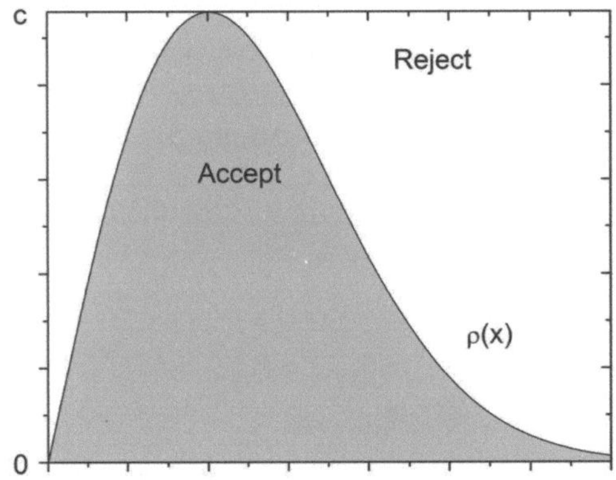

Fig. 2. Rejection method. A point (X,cU) is generated in the plane bounded by the constant c.

2.5 Composition method

The target density f(x) can sometimes be decomposed in a combination of probability distributions such as:

$$f(x) = \sum_{i=1}^{n} p_i g_i(x) \rho_i(x) \tag{11}$$

where the p_i form a probability vector (i.e. $p_i \geq 0$ for all i and $\Sigma p_i=1$) and $\rho_i(x)$ are normalized probability distributions which can be sampled by inversion. Then the following algorithm may be used to generate X distributed as f(X):

Algorithm 2: Composition method
REPEAT
{
    Generate uniform independent random numbers U_1, U_2 and U_3 (between 0 and 1)
    Find the value of i for which $p_{i-1} < U_1 < p_i$
    $X=\Theta_i^{-1}(U_2)$
}
UNTIL $U_3>g_i(X)$
RETURN X ■

In this algorithm, $\Theta_i(x)$ is the cumulative probability distribution of $\rho_i(x)$. The random number U_1 determines which probability distribution is sampled. The distribution $\rho_i(x)$ is then generated by the rejection method described in the previous section.

3. Generalities in particle transport

The Monte-Carlo simulation of particle transport is basically following the trajectory of a particle in a medium and of all its interactions. A particle will be followed until it leaves the volume of interest, its energy decreases below a cutoff energy or disappears by a physical process (for example, a photon is absorbed by photoelectric effect). Of course, many other particles such as secondary electrons are generated and should also be followed. In this section, several important concepts used in particle transport for all radiation types are discussed: the direction vector, the cross sections and mean free path, the choice of an interaction and the change of direction following an interaction.

3.1 Coordinate system and direction vector

The particles used in radiation transport codes are usually attributed several characteristics such as an energy E, a position x,y,z and a direction given by θ and φ in a spherical coordinates system, which are the angles between the direction vector and the axis Oz and the azimutal angle in the plane Oxy. The direction vector is given by the direction cosines

$$\vec{v} = \begin{bmatrix} \sin(\theta)\cos(\varphi) \\ \sin(\theta)\sin(\varphi) \\ \cos(\theta) \end{bmatrix} \quad (12)$$

This coordinate system is shown on Figure 3.

3.2 Cross sections and mean free path

Let a flux of particles of intensity I and energy E interact with a layer of matter of density N and of width dx (Figure 4). After going through the layer, the intensity of the incident flux of particles is reduced by

$$dI = -\sigma(E)NIdx \quad (13)$$

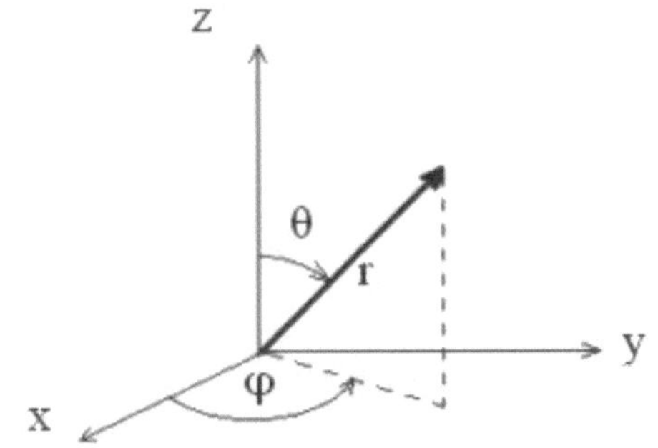

Fig. 3. Coordinate system in spherical coordinates. Here $0 \leq \varphi \leq 2\pi$ and $0 \leq \theta \leq \pi$.

Here, $\sigma(E)$ is the total interaction cross section by target atom (units: 1 barn=10^{-24} cm^2) or *microscopic cross section*. The *macroscopic cross section,* which is defined as $\Sigma(E)=N\sigma(E)$ (units: cm^{-1}), is also seen in some texts.

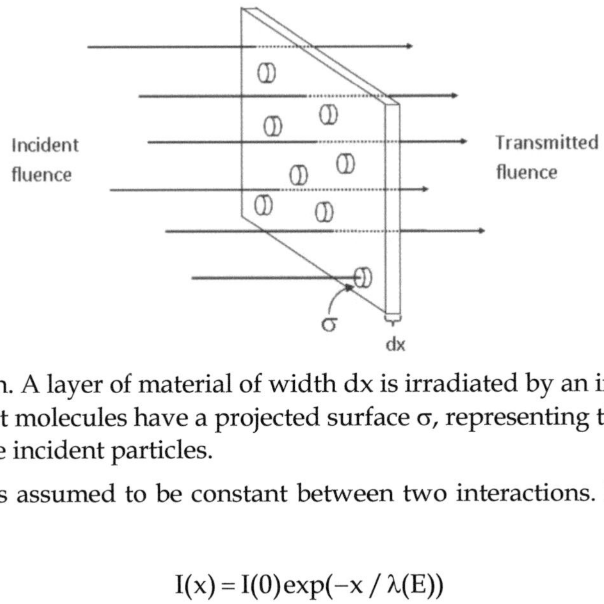

Fig. 4. Cross section. A layer of material of width dx is irradiated by an incident fluence of particles. The target molecules have a projected surface σ, representing their probability of interaction with the incident particles.

The cross section is assumed to be constant between two interactions. Hence equation (13) can be solved:

$$I(x) = I(0)\exp(-x / \lambda(E)) \tag{14}$$

Where $\lambda(E)=1/(N\sigma(E))$ is the mean free path (units : cm). Therefore the probability to find a particle which has not interacted at distance x from its original position is distributed exponentially. In particle transport codes, a distance s between two interactions is usually sampled by using the inversion method for the exponential distribution:

$$s = -\lambda \log(U) \tag{15}$$

Therefore, the next interaction of the particle will be at the position (x′,y′,z′):

$$\begin{aligned} x' &= x + s\sin(\theta)\cos(\varphi) \\ y' &= y + s\sin(\theta)\sin(\varphi) \\ z' &= z + s\cos(\theta) \end{aligned} \tag{16}$$

We conclude this section by mentioning that the cross sections discussed yet are the *total cross sections*. They are often found by integrating the *differential cross section* in angle and/or in energy.

3.3 Choice of interaction

In general, the total interaction cross section is the sum of several interaction cross sections. The total cross section is used to find the distance between two interactions. The ratio between the cross section for a given type of interaction to the total cross section represents the probability for a type of interaction to occur. Therefore, the sampling in a table technique may be used to determine the type of interaction. Of course, since a particle loses energy at each inelastic interaction, the cross sections should be updated at each timestep.

3.4 Change of direction following an interaction

After an interaction, the direction of the trajectory of a particle change. Let the direction of the trajectories before and after the interaction described by the vectors $\vec{v}_0$ and $\vec{v}_1$:

$$\vec{v}_0 = \begin{bmatrix} v_{0_x} \\ v_{0_y} \\ v_{0_z} \end{bmatrix} = \begin{bmatrix} \sin(\theta_0)\cos(\varphi_0) \\ \sin(\theta_0)\sin(\varphi_0) \\ \cos(\theta_0) \end{bmatrix} ; \vec{v}_1 = \begin{bmatrix} v_{1_x} \\ v_{1_y} \\ v_{1_z} \end{bmatrix} = \begin{bmatrix} \sin(\theta_1)\cos(\varphi_1) \\ \sin(\theta_1)\sin(\varphi_1) \\ \cos(\theta_1) \end{bmatrix} \quad (17)$$

The angles θ_0, φ_0, θ_1 and φ_1 are the angles of the trajectory of the particle in the laboratory frame in spherical coordinates (Figure 3). We also define

$$A_{1,0} = \sin(\theta_0)\cos(\varphi_0) \quad (18a)$$

$$A_{2,0} = \sin(\theta_0)\sin(\varphi_0) \quad (18b)$$

Following an interaction from which the trajectory is deflected by the angles θ and φ relatively to the initial trajectory, the new trajectory of the particle $\vec{v}_1$ should be found in the laboratory frame (R). To do so, a rotation to a reference frame (R'') in which $\vec{v}_0$ is oriented along the z'' axis is performed. Therefore a transformation to go from the referential R'' to R and its inverse is needed. The transformation R→R'' is as follows:

1. A rotation of φ_0 around the z axis to bring $\vec{v}_0$ in the plane Ox'z'.
2. A rotation of θ_0 around the y' axis to bring $\vec{v}_0$ in the direction z''

These transformations can be written by using the (inverse) rotation matrix:

$$\vec{v}_0^{\,'} = \begin{bmatrix} v_{0_x}^{'} \\ v_{0_y}^{'} \\ v_{0_z}^{'} \end{bmatrix} = \begin{bmatrix} \cos(\theta_0) & 0 & \sin(\theta_0) \\ 0 & 1 & 0 \\ -\sin(\theta_0) & 0 & \cos(\theta_0) \end{bmatrix} \begin{bmatrix} v_{0_x}^{''} \\ v_{0_y}^{''} \\ v_{0_z}^{''} \end{bmatrix} = \begin{bmatrix} v_{0_x}^{''}\cos(\theta_0) + v_{0_z}^{''}\sin(\theta_0) \\ v_{0_y}^{''} \\ -v_{0_x}^{''}\sin(\theta_0) + v_{0_z}^{''}\cos(\theta_0) \end{bmatrix} \quad (19a)$$

$$\vec{v}_0 = \begin{bmatrix} v_{0_x} \\ v_{0_y} \\ v_{0_z} \end{bmatrix} = \begin{bmatrix} \cos(-\varphi_0) & \sin(-\varphi_0) & 0 \\ -\sin(-\varphi_0) & \cos(-\varphi_0) & 0 \\ 0 & 0 & 1 \end{bmatrix} \begin{bmatrix} v_{0_x}^{'} \\ v_{0_y}^{'} \\ v_{0_z}^{'} \end{bmatrix} = \begin{bmatrix} v_{0_x}^{'}\cos(\varphi_0) - v_{0_y}^{'}\sin(\varphi_0) \\ v_{0_x}^{'}\sin(\varphi_0) + v_{0_y}^{'}\cos(\varphi_0) \\ v_{0_z}^{'} \end{bmatrix} \quad (19b)$$

Combining these equations gives

$$\vec{v}_0 = \begin{bmatrix} v_{0_x} \\ v_{0_y} \\ v_{0_z} \end{bmatrix} = \begin{bmatrix} (v''_{0_x}\cos(\theta_0) + v''_{0_z}\sin(\theta_0))\cos(\varphi_0) - v''_{0_y}\sin(\varphi_0) \\ (v''_{0_x}\cos(\theta_0) + v''_{0_z}\sin(\theta_0))\sin(\varphi_0) + v''_{0_y}\cos(\varphi_0) \\ -v''_{0_x}\sin(\theta_0) + v''_{0_z}\cos(\theta_0) \end{bmatrix} \tag{20}$$

In the R'' system, the direction vector after the interaction is given by

$$\vec{v}''_1 = \begin{bmatrix} v''_{1_x} \\ v''_{1_y} \\ v''_{1_z} \end{bmatrix} = \begin{bmatrix} \sin(\theta)\cos(\varphi) \\ \sin(\theta)\sin(\varphi) \\ \cos(\theta) \end{bmatrix} \tag{21}$$

To calculate $\vec{v}_1$ in the laboratory frame, the transformation R''→R is applied. After some calculations, we find

$$\cos(\theta_1) = \cos(\theta)\cos(\theta_0) - \sin(\theta)\cos(\varphi)\sin(\theta_0) \tag{22a}$$

$$\cos(\varphi_1) = \frac{1}{\sin(\theta_1)}\left[(\sin(\theta)\cos(\varphi)\cos(\theta_0) + \cos(\theta)\sin(\theta_0))\cos(\varphi_0) - \sin(\theta)\sin(\varphi)\sin(\varphi_0)\right] \tag{22b}$$

$$\sin(\varphi_1) = \frac{1}{\sin(\theta_1)}\left[(\sin(\theta)\cos(\varphi)\cos(\theta_0) + \cos(\theta)\sin(\theta_0))\sin(\varphi_0) + \sin(\theta)\sin(\varphi)\cos(\varphi_0)\right] \tag{22c}$$

This gives the algorithm for the change of direction. $A_{1,0}$, $A_{2,0}$, A_3, A_4 and A_5 are calculated first:

$$A_{1,0} = \sin(\theta_0)\cos(\varphi_0) \tag{23a}$$

$$A_{2,0} = \sin(\theta_0)\sin(\varphi_0) \tag{23b}$$

$$A_3 = \sin(\theta)\cos(\varphi) \tag{23c}$$

$$A_4 = A_3\cos(\theta_0) + \cos(\theta)\sin(\theta_0) \tag{23d}$$

$$A_5 = \sin(\theta)\sin(\varphi) \tag{23e}$$

After the interaction, A_1 and A_2 becomes

$$A_{1,1} = A_4\cos(\varphi_0) - A_5\sin(\varphi_0) \tag{24a}$$

$$A_{2,1} = A_4\sin(\phi_0) + A_5\cos(\phi_0) \tag{24b}$$

The angles θ_1 and φ_1 can now be calculated in the laboratory frame:

$$\cos(\theta_1) = \cos(\theta_0)\cos(\theta) - A_3 \sin(\theta_0) \quad (25a)$$

$$\sin(\theta_1) = \sqrt{1 - \cos^2(\theta_1)} \quad (25b)$$

$$\cos(\varphi_1) = A_{1,1} / \sin(\theta_1) \quad (25c)$$

$$\sin(\varphi_1) = A_{2,1} / \sin(\theta_1) \quad (25d)$$

4. Simulation of ionizing radiation tracks

The energy deposition by radiations is strongly dependent on the type and energy of radiation. Most damage induced by radiation to biomolecules leading to biological consequences are not caused by the direct impact of the primary radiation but are induced by secondary electrons and chemical species generated by the primary ionizing particle (O'Neill & Wardman, 2009). In fact, secondary electrons are produced in large quantities by the attenuation of all energetic primary ionizing radiations such as β- and α-particles, heavy ions, X-rays and γ-rays (Pimblott & LaVerne, 2007). These secondary electrons also cause additional ionization and excitations in the medium, leading to the formation of radiation chemical spurs(1) (Mozumder & Magee, 1966). Therefore the simulation of electron tracks is a very important subject, which is part of every radiation transport code. In this section, the cross sections used in the code RITRACKS (Plante & Cucinotta, 2008; 2009) are shown. The cross sections used in RITRACKS are relativistic, but the discussion will be limited here to the non-relativistic energy range. Moreover, since the sampling of the cross sections for electrons and ions was discussed in (Plante & Cucinotta, 2008; 2009), only the sampling of the cross sections for photons will be detailed here.

4.1 Electrons

A large portion of the secondary electrons created by ionizing radiation have low energy (<100 eV) (Pimblott & LaVerne, 2007). These electrons are very important since they have been shown to create irreversible damage to DNA and other molecules as well (Boudaïffa et al, 2000). Some secondary electrons may have energies in the MeV region depending on the initial radiation type and energy. These electrons can travel several millimeters in biological media (Meesungnoen et al., 2002) and affect cells far away from the trajectory of the radiation track. Electrons interact with matter by ionizations, excitations, elastic collisions and dissociative attachment.

4.1.1 Ionization

Ionization is the most important process for energy loss by electrons >10 eV. The molecular orbitals of water are $^1b_1$, $^3a_1$, $^1b_2$, $^2a_1$ and $^1a_1$. A convenient expression for the cross sections is given by the Rudd's semi-empirical equation (Rudd, 1990):

$$\frac{d\sigma_{ion}^{i}}{dw} = \frac{d\sigma_{ion}^{i(1)}}{dw} + \frac{d\sigma_{ion}^{i(2)}}{dw} \quad (26a)$$

---

[1] A *spur* is a cluster of chemical species produced by the radiolysis of water

$$\frac{d\sigma_{ion}^{i(1)}}{dw} = \frac{S_i}{I_i} F_1(t) \left[\frac{1}{(1+w)^3} + \frac{1}{(t-w)^3} - \frac{1}{(1+w)^{3/2}(t-w)^{3/2}} \right] \tag{26b}$$

$$\frac{d\sigma_{ion}^{i(2)}}{dw} = \frac{S_i}{I_i} F_2(t) \left[\frac{1}{(1+w)^2} + \frac{1}{(t-w)^2} - \frac{1}{(1+w)(t-w)} \right] \tag{26c}$$

The differential cross section is written as a function of $t=T/I_i$ and $w=W/I_i$, where T is the energy of the primary electron, W is the energy of the ionized electron and I_i is the binding energy of the molecular orbital. The multiplicative factor $S_i = 4\pi a_0^2 N_i (\Re / I_i)^2$, a_0 is Bohr's radius (5.3×10^{-11} m), $\Re$ is Rydberg energy (13.6 eV) and N_i is the number of electrons in the orbital, which is 2 in every case. The functions $F_1(t)$ and $F_2(t)$ are given by:

$$F_1(t) = A_1 \frac{\ln(t)}{t+B_1}; F_2(t) = \frac{A_2}{t+B_2} \tag{27}$$

The parameters A_1, A_2, B_1 and B_2 (Table 1) were determined by fitting experimental data.

Parameter	External shells	Internal shells
A_1	0.94	1.31
A_2	1.13	0.37
B_1	2.30	0.00
B_2	22.0	0.00

Table 1. Parameters used in Rudd's equation for electrons

The total cross section is calculated by integrating the differential cross section over W:

$$\sigma_{ion}^{i} = \int_0^{E_{max}+I_i} \frac{d\sigma_{ion}^{i}}{dW} dW \tag{28}$$

This integral can be evaluated analytically. The maximum energy transfer (E_{max}) for classical or relativistic electrons it T/2, because the incident and secondary electron are indiscernable. Replacing E_{max} by T/2, the result of the integral can be written:

$$\sigma_{ion}^{i} = S_i F_1(t) \frac{t-1}{2t^2} \left(t+1 - \frac{4\sqrt{t}}{3+t} \right) + S_i F_2(t) \left(1 - \frac{1}{t} - \frac{\ln(t)}{t+1} \right) \tag{29}$$

The ionization cross sections by electron for each orbital are shown on Figure 5. The differential cross section for the ionization of the orbital $^1b_1$ of water by 0.1, 1, 10 and 100 keV electrons is obtained by sampling in a table.

The orbital $^1a_1$ is an internal orbital of the water molecule. The ionization of this orbital is much less frequent than ionization of external shells. The vacancy created result in a reorganization of the molecule, leading to the emission of an Auger electron. Finally, Rudd's equation does not applies to electrons with relativistic energies (>150 keV). In this case, Seltzer's equation may be used (Uehara et al., 1992; Nikjoo et al., 2008; Plante and Cucinotta, 2009).

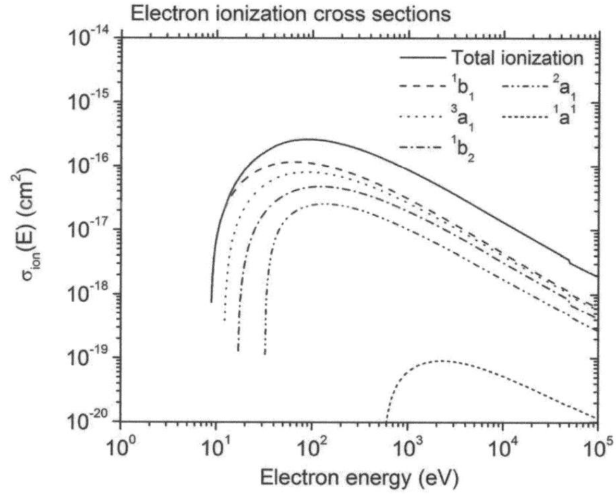

(a)

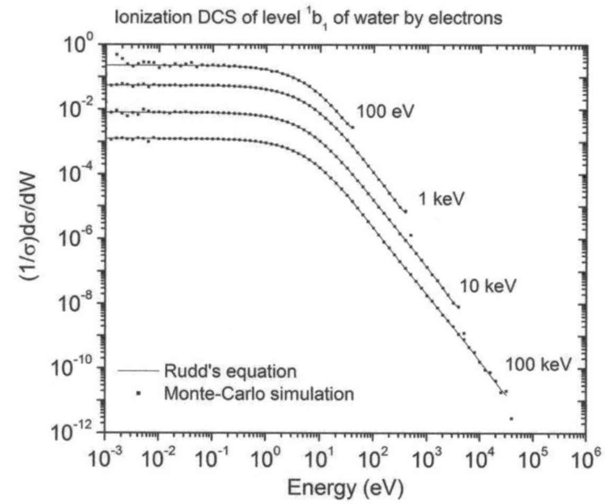

(b)

Fig. 5. a) Total electron ionization cross section for water calculated by Rudd's formula for energy <50 keV for excitation levels $^1b_1$, $^3a_1$, $^1b_2$, $^2a_1$ et $^1a_1$. b) Energy distribution of ionized electrons calculated by Rudd's formula for 10^2, 10^3, 10^4 and 10^5 eV incident electrons for the molecular orbital $^1b_1$ of water.

4.1.2 Excitations

Excitation cross sections are about an order of magnitude lower than the ionization cross sections, except at low energy. The relative contribution of the excited states $\tilde{A}^1B_1$, $\tilde{B}^1A_1$, Rydberg series A+B and C+D, diffuse band and plasmon (collective) excitation is controversial (Dingfelder et al., 1999; Nikjoo et al., 2006). In RITRACKS, only the states $\tilde{A}^1B_1$, $\tilde{B}^1A_1$ and plasmon excitation are included (Cobut et al., 1998).

A model of differential cross section for the energy loss W by excitation in liquid water was proposed by Kutcher & Green (1976):

$$\frac{d\sigma_{ex}^{i}}{dW} = \rho(W)Wf_i(W)\ln\left[\frac{\alpha(T)T}{W}\right] \quad (30)$$

Here, T is the energy of the incident electron, ρ(W) is the differential cross section for charged particles interacting with electron at rest and $f_i(W)$ are functions to be defined later. The parameter α(T) was introduced by Cobut (1993) to link the cross sections at high and low energy. The cross section ρ(W) is given by

$$\rho(W) = \frac{e^4}{8\pi\varepsilon_0^2 mv^2W^2} = \frac{4\pi a_0^2}{T}\left(\frac{\Re}{W}\right)^2 \quad (31)$$

In this equation, a_0 is Bohr's radius, ε_0 is vacuum permittivity, $\Re$ is Rydberg energy and m, v and e are the mass, velocity and charge of the electron. The parameter α(T) is given by

$$\alpha(T) = 4 - 3\exp[-(W - W_{0,i})/\alpha_i] \quad (32)$$

where $\alpha_j = E_{min}(\beta^* - 1)/\ln(2)$, $\beta^*=5$ and $E_{min}=7.34$ eV (Cobut et al., 1998). When $T \rightarrow W_{0,i}$, $\alpha(T) \rightarrow 1$; when $T \rightarrow \infty$, $\alpha(T) \rightarrow 4$. This parameter varies slowly between 1 and 4. The functions $f_i(W)$ for the excitation levels $\tilde{A}^1B_1$ and $\tilde{B}^1A_1$ are Gaussian:

$$f_i(W) = f_{o,i}\sqrt{\frac{\alpha_i}{\pi}}\exp\left[-\alpha_i(W - W_{0,i})^2\right] \quad (33)$$

For plasmon excitation, $f_i(W)$ is given by:

$$f_i(W) = f_{o,pl}\alpha_{pl}\frac{e^{\tau}}{(1+e^{\tau})^2} \quad (34)$$

where $\tau = \alpha_{pl}(W - W_0)$. The parameters $f_{0,i}$, α_i et $W_{0,i}$ are given in table 2.

	$\tilde{A}^1B_1$	$\tilde{B}^1A_1$	Plasmon
f_{0i}	0.0187	0.0157	0.7843
α_i	3 (eV^{-2})	1 (eV^{-2})	0.6 (eV^{-1})
W_{0i} (eV)	8.4	10.1	21.3

Table 2. Parameters used to calculate the functions $f_i(W)$

The excitation cross section for the excitation level i is calculated by integrating numerically the differential cross section:

$$\sigma_{ex}^{i} = \int_{7.34}^{\min(100,T)} \rho(W)Wf_i(W)\ln\left[\frac{\alpha(T)T}{W}\right]dW \quad (35)$$

The inferior limit of integration is 7.34 eV, which is the minimal energy transferred by excitation. The superior limit is the lowest value between 100 eV and the energy of the incident electron. These limits covers the domain where the functions $f_i(W)$ are significant, which are very narrow peaks between [7.18, 9.63] and [7.98,12.2] eV for the levels $\tilde{A}^1B_1$ and $\tilde{B}^1A_1$ and between [12.5-30.1] eV for plasmon excitation.

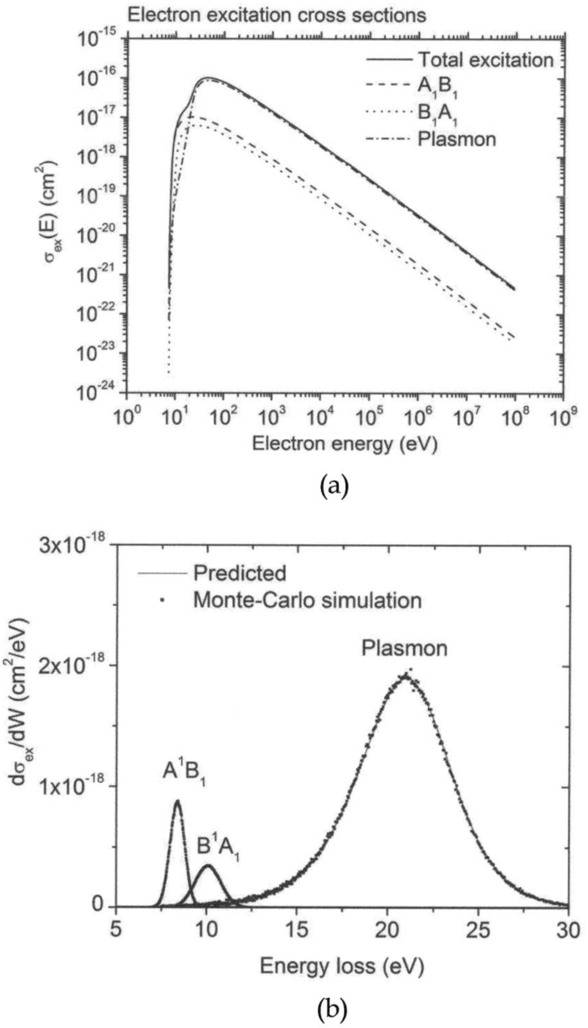

Fig. 6. a) Excitation cross sections for levels $\tilde{A}^1B_1$, $\tilde{B}^1A_1$ and plasmon excitation. Right: DCS of the energy loss of 1 MeV electron by excitation for levels $\tilde{A}^1B_1$, $\tilde{B}^1A_1$ and plasmon excitation in liquid water. The area is proportional to the cross section. b) Sampling of the energy loss by a 1 keV electron by excitation.

4.1.3 Excitation of vibration and rotation levels

Experiments by Michaud et al. (2003) for 1-100 eV electrons have shown that it is possible to excite vibration and rotation levels of water molecules. Contrary to the excitation described in the previous section, they do not lead to the dissociation of the water molecule. These cross sections have been included in the code RITRACKS. Several vibration and rotation level exists, but they will not be detailed here (See Michaud et al., 2003).

4.1.4 Dissociative electron attachment

Attachment of an electron with a water molecule leads to the following sequence of events:

$$H_2O + e^- \rightarrow H_2O^- \rightarrow H^- + {}^{\bullet}OH \tag{36}$$

This process is the dissociative attachment. In water, H^- is very unstable and reacts with a neighbor water molecule to give non-captable molecular hydrogen (Jay-Gerin & Ferradini, 1999).

$$H^- + H_2O \rightarrow H_2 + OH^- \tag{37}$$

The dissociative attachment has been observed experimentally (Rowntree et al., 1991). It happens only at low energy (~6-7 eV).

4.1.5 Elastic collisions

During an elastic collision, there is no loss of energy by the electron. Therefore, only the deflection angle should be determined when an elastic collision occurs.

Electrons of energy below 200 eV

For energies below 200 eV, the experimental elastic cross section of Michaud et al. (2003) is used. When an elastic scattering event occurs, the semi-empirical DCS parameterized by Brenner & Zaider (1983) is used to sample the angle of deflection. It can be written as:

$$\frac{d\sigma_{el}}{d\Omega} = \alpha(T)\left\{\frac{1}{\left[1+2\gamma(T)-\cos(\theta)\right]^2} + \frac{\beta(T)}{\left[1+2\delta(T)+\cos(\theta)\right]^2}\right\} \tag{38}$$

where T is the energy of the electron, $\alpha(T)$ is a proportionality constant, $\beta(T)$, $\gamma(T)$ and $\delta(T)$ are parametric functions in the form of exponentials and polynomials, θ is the angle of deflection and $d\Omega=2\pi\sin(\theta)d\theta$ is the differential solid angle element in the direction θ.

Electrons of energies over 200 eV

For electrons with energies over 200 eV, the Rutherford cross section with a screening parameter η (Uehara et al., 1992) are used in RITRACKS:

$$\frac{d\sigma_{el}}{d\Omega} = \frac{Z(Z+1)r_e^2}{(1-\cos(\theta)+2\eta)^2}\frac{1-\beta^2}{\beta^4} \tag{39}$$

Here, r_e is the classical electron radius and β is the relativistic velocity (v/c). This equation is relativistic and can be used at high energies. The screening parameter η depends of the atomic number (Z) of the target.

$$\eta = \eta_c \frac{1.7 \times 10^{-5} Z^{2/3}}{\tau(\tau+2)} \tag{40}$$

Integration over $d\Omega$ yields the total elastic cross section:

$$\sigma_{el} = \int_0^{\pi} 2\pi \frac{d\sigma_{el}}{d\Omega}\sin(\theta)d\theta = \frac{\pi Z(Z+1)r_e^2}{\eta(\eta+1)}\frac{1-\beta^2}{\beta^4} \tag{41}$$

For a molecular target like water, an effective value Z_{eff} is used instead of Z. The values proposed by Uehara et al. (1992) have been tried to join the experimental results at 200 eV.

The value Z_{eff}=7.22 have been chosen. The total elastic cross section used in RITRACKS is shown on Figure 7 and compared with calculations (Dingfelder et al., 2008; Uehara et al., 1992; Pimblott et al., 1996) and experimental data (Powell et al., 2005; Katase et al., 1986; Danjo & Nishimura, 1985).

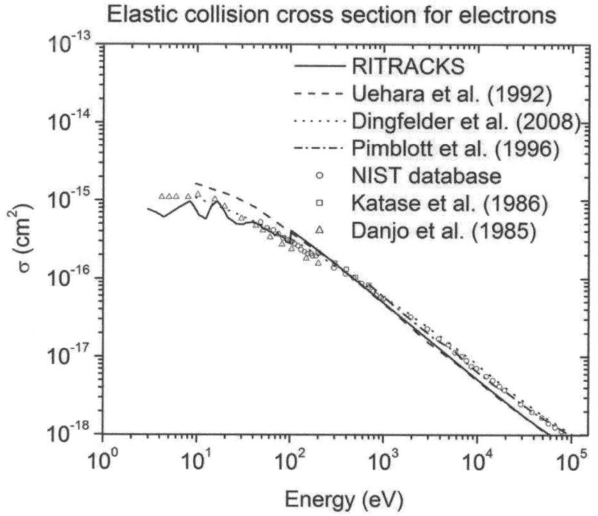

(a)

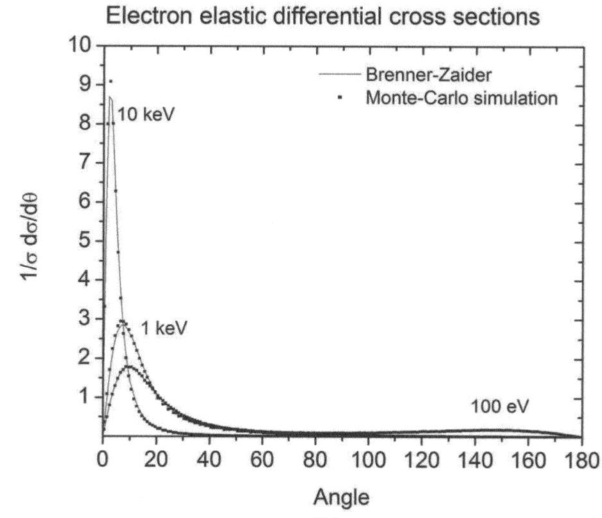

(b)

Fig. 7. a) Elastic cross sections. The cross section from Michaud et al. (2003) are used for energies < 100 eV. For energies > 100 eV, the Rutherford cross section with the screening parameter η (see text) is used. The elastic cross section used by Dingfelder et al. (2008), Uehara et al. (1992) and Pimblott et al. (1996) are also shown. Experimental data: NIST Database (Powell et al., 2005), Katase et al. (1986) and Danjo & Nishimura (1985). b) Elastic DCS calculated with the parameterization of Brenner & Zaider (1983). The lines are the analytical models; the small dots are obtained by sampling the DCS.

4.2 Ions

Heavy ions of all charges from proton to uranium are present in space, the great majority being protons and α-particles. Their energies cover a large spectrum extending from a few MeV/nucleon to nearly 10^{15} MeV/nucleon, with a peak at ~1 GeV/amu. Heavy ions are shielded by the Earth's magnetosphere and atmosphere. In space, however, high charged (Z) and energy (HZE) particles such as $^{56}Fe^{26+}$ are very penetrating and may collide with nuclei of the atoms they encounter, fragmenting either the target and/or the projectile, which produces several secondary particles. Therefore it impossible to completely shield astronauts from these radiations and they are of concern for a long term space mission such as the 3-years Mars mission which would lead to whole-body dose of about 1 Sievert (Sv) or more. On travelling to Mars, it is estimated that every cell nucleus in an astronaut's body would be hit by a proton or secondary electron (eg, electrons of the target atoms ionized by the HZE ion) every few days and by an HZE ion about once a month (Cucinotta & Durante, 2006). Energy deposition by HZE ions is highly heterogeneous, with a localized contribution along the trajectory of every particle and lateral diffusion of energetic electrons (i.e. δ-rays, the target atom electrons ionized by the incident HZE ion and emitted at high energy) many microns from the path of the ions. These particles are therefore densely ionizing along the primary track (e.g. the track followed by the incident heavy ion, the so-called *core*); moreover, they are surrounded by a region (*penumbra*) comprising the high-energy electrons ejected by ions. As heavy ions slow down, they lose a larger part of their energy. Before they stop, heavy ions deposit a high fraction of their energy in a small region, named the *Bragg peak*. Therefore, heavy ions are gaining importance in radiotherapy, because of their advantageous dose profile which allows the deposition a larger amount of dose to the tumor and sparing of normal tissue.

4.2.1 Ionization

Rudd (1990) have also proposed a semi-empirical equation for the differential ionization cross sections of the molecular orbitals $^1b_1$, $^3a_1$, $^1b_2$, $^2a_1$ et $^1a_1$ of liquid water by protons:

$$\frac{d\sigma_{ion}^{i}}{dw} = \frac{S_i}{I_i} \frac{F_1(v) + wF_2(v)}{(1+w)^3 \left\{1 + \exp[\alpha(w - w_{c_i})/v]\right\}} \tag{42}$$

As for electrons, i is the index of the orbital, I_i is the binding energy, $w=W/I_i$, W is the secondary electron energy and $S_i = 4\pi a_0^2 N_i (\Re / I_i)^2$. Furthermore, $T=E_p(m/M_p)$, M_p and E_p are the mass and energy of the incident proton, m is the electron mass, and $v=\sqrt{T/I_i}$ and $w_c = 4v^2 - 2v - \Re / 4I_i$. The functions $F_1(v)$ and $F_2(v)$ are defined as:

$$F_1(v) = L_1 + H_1 \; ; \; F_2(v) = \frac{L_2 H_2}{L_2 + H_2} \tag{43}$$

where

$$L_1 = \frac{C_1 v^{D_1}}{1 + E_1 v^{D_1+4}} \; ; \; H_1 = \frac{A_1 \ln(1+v^2)}{v^2 + B_1 / v^2} \tag{44a}$$

$$L_2(v) = C_2 v^{D_2} \; ; \; H_2 = A_2 / v^2 + B_2 / v^4 \tag{44b}$$

The parameters $A_1, B_1 \ldots B_2 .. D_2$ and α were determined by fitting experimental data (Table 1).

Parameter	External orbitals	Internal orbitals	Parameter	External orbitals	Internal orbitals
A_1	0.97	1.25	A_2	1.04	1.10
B_1	82.0	0.50	B_2	17.3	1.30
C_1	0.40	1.00	C_2	0.76	1.00
D_1	-0.30	1.00	D_2	0.04	0.00
E_1	0.38	3.00	α	0.64	0.66

Table 4. Parameters used in Rudd's equation for protons

The total ionization cross section is found by numerically integrating

$$\sigma^i_{ion} = \int_0^{E_{max}+I_i} \frac{d\sigma^i_{ion}}{dW} dW \tag{45}$$

Here, E_{max} is the maximal energy transfer in a single collision. In classical mechanics, this energy is given for an ion of mass M and energy E by (Turner, 2007):

$$E_{max} = \frac{4mME}{(M+m)^2} \cong 4\frac{m}{M}E \tag{46}$$

The total ionization cross section for the molecular orbitals $^1b_1$, $^3a_1$, $^1b_2$, $^2a_1$ and of water and the differential cross section for ionization of orbital $^1b_1$ by protons are shown on Figure 8.

4.2.2 Excitations

The excitation cross section is about one order of magnitude lower than the ionization cross section at a given energy. As for electrons, the relative contributions of each discrete electronic excitation levels so-called $\tilde{A}^1B_1$, $\tilde{B}^1A_1$, Ryd A+B, Ryd C+D (Rydberg series), diffuse bands and plasmon excitation (collective excitation) is currently debated (Nikjoo et al., 2006). The expression of these discrete excitation levels can be calculated by using the semi-empirical formulation shown in Dingfelder et al. (2006) or in Kutcher and Green (1976). In the former, for reasons that are discussed in Cobut et al. (1998), only the excitation levels $\tilde{A}^1B_1$, $\tilde{B}^1A_1$, and plasmon are considered. The differential cross section can also be written with the semi-empirical equation of Kutcher and Green (1976):

$$\frac{d\sigma^i_{ex}}{dW} = \rho(W)W\, f_i(W)\ln\left(\frac{4T}{W}\right) \tag{47}$$

where

$$\rho(W) = \frac{Z^2e^4}{8\pi\varepsilon_0^2 mv^2W^2} = \frac{4\pi a_0^2 Z^2}{T}\left(\frac{\Re}{W}\right)^2 \tag{48}$$

Here, W is the energy loss by excitation, $\rho(W)$ is the differential cross section for charged particle scattering on free electrons at rest, T=E(m/M), a_0 is the Bohr radius, ε_0 is vaccuum permittivity, m is electron mass and M, E, v and Z are the mass, energy, velocity and charge of the incident ion. Note that the definition of W and v are different from the previous section. The functions $f_i(W)$ are the same as those defined previously for electrons. The total excitation cross section is calculated by integrating numerically equation (47):

$$\sigma_{ex}^{i} = \int_{0.01}^{100} \rho(W) W f_i(W) \ln\left[\frac{4T}{W}\right] dW \tag{49}$$

The integration limits used here are empirical; as for electrons, they are chosen to cover the domain for which the functions $f_i(W)$ are significant. These cross sections are shown on Figure 9.

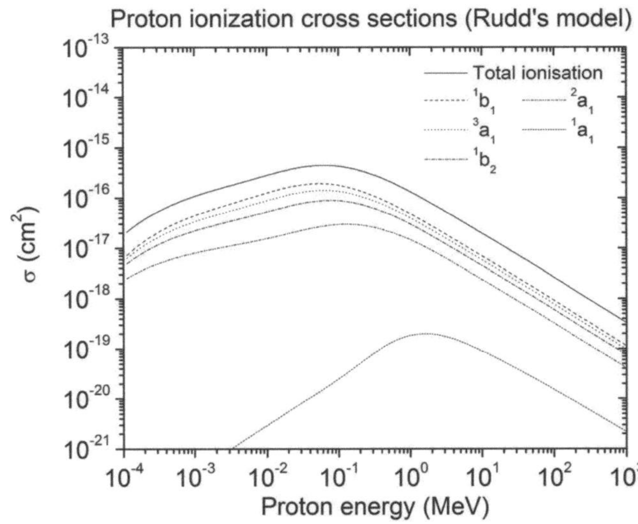

(a)

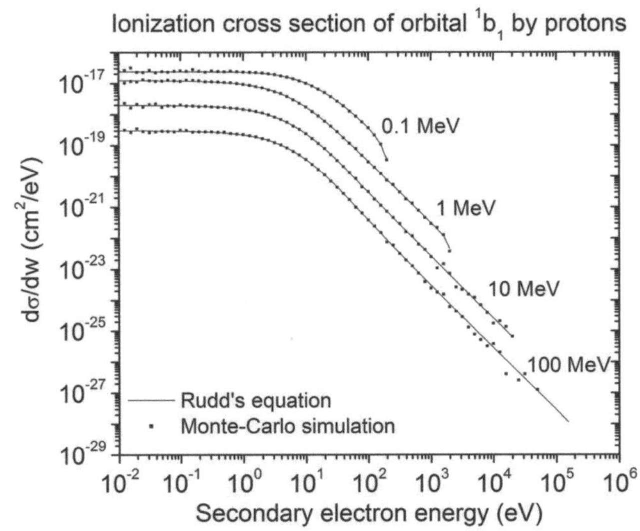

(b)

Fig. 8. a) Ionization cross sections for ionization of the molecular orbitals $^1b_1$, $^3a_1$, $^1b_2$, $^2a_1$ and $^1a_1$ of liquid water by protons. b) Sampling of the differential ionization cross section of the orbital $^1b_1$ by protons of 0.1, 1, 10 and 100 MeV and comparison with Rudd's equation.

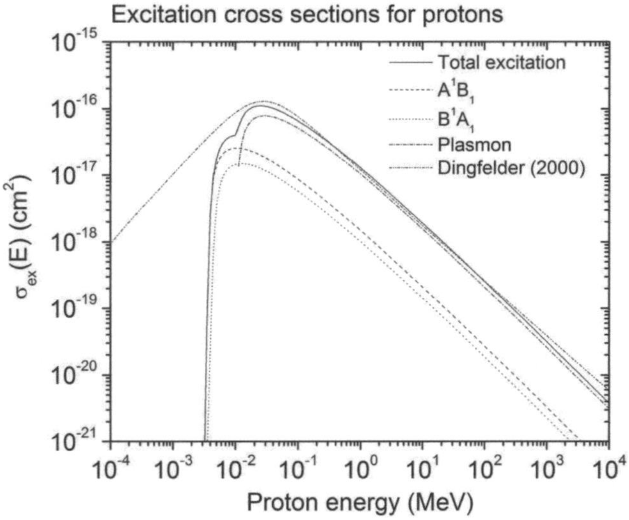

(a)

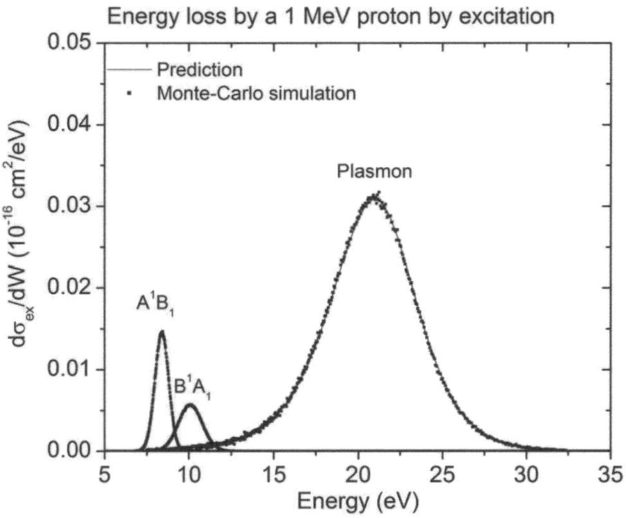

(b)

Fig. 9. a) Excitation cross sections for levels $\tilde{A}^1B_1$, $\tilde{B}^1A_1$ and plasmon excitation of water molecule by protons. b) DCS of the energy loss of 1 MeV proton by excitation for levels $\tilde{A}^1B_1$, $\tilde{B}^1A_1$ and plasmon in liquid water. The area is proportional to the cross section.

4.2.3 Heavy ions cross sections

A heavy ion of mass M_{ion} with kinetic energy $E_{ion} = (M_{ion} / m_p)E_p$ has the same velocity of a proton (mass m_p) with kinetic energy E_p. This is true for both non-relativistic and relativistic ions (Dingfelder, 2006). Therefore, within the first order plane wave Born approximation, the interaction cross section for bare heavy ions of velocity v are obtained from proton interaction cross sections by scaling the differential cross section for a proton with the same velocity v by the square of the charge Z_0 of the ion (Dingfelder et al., 2006):

$$\frac{d\sigma_{ion}(v)}{dW} = Z^2 \frac{d\sigma_{proton}(v)}{dW} \tag{50}$$

Heavy ions at small energies have electrons attached and thus have a reduced charge $Z_{eff}<Z$. If Z_{eff} is defined to give the correct observed stopping power, it is not equal to the mean charge per particle of a beam leaving an absorber (Tai et al., 1997). An equation from Barkas (1963) is commonly used for the effective charge:

$$Z_{eff} = Z[1 - \exp(-125\beta Z^{-2/3})] \tag{51}$$

4.3 Photons

Photons such as γ-rays or X-rays have been used for decades in radiotherapy and are still widely used today. Over last years, several techniques such as stereotactic radiosurgery, 3D conformal radiotherapy (3DCRT) and Intensity-Modulated Radiation Therapy (IMRT) have evolved to deliver radiotherapy more efficiently and reducing secondary effects (Reynaert et al., 2007).

In the energy range between 100 eV to 2 MeV, photons interact with medium mainly by Compton effect, which results in the emission of a Compton electron and a photon with smaller energy. Photons of low energy are usually absorbed by photoelectric effect, resulting in the emission of a photoelectron. Therefore, photons also lead to production of electrons in the medium. Pair production (creation of an electron and a positron) can also occur, but only at energies greater than 1.022 MeV. Since the probability of pair production is small in the energy range under consideration, it will be neglected in this discussion. The photonuclear reactions are also neglected because the energy threshold for these reactions is above a few MeV and their cross section is relatively small (Anderson, 1984). For this work, the absorption coefficients given by Storm & Israel (1967) are used (figure 10).

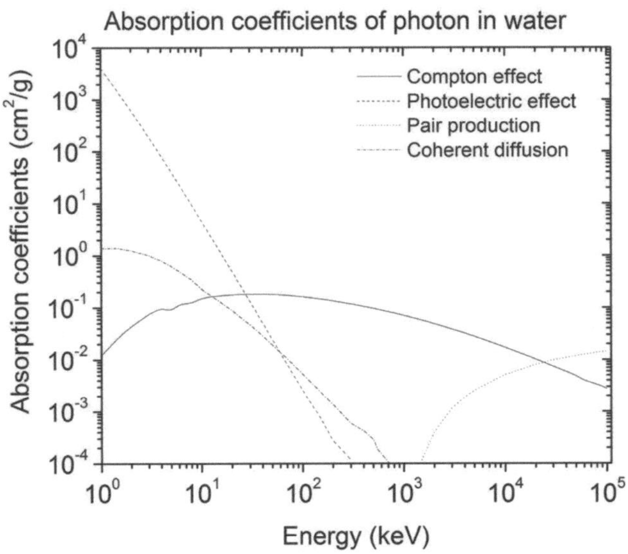

Fig. 10. Absorption coefficients for Compton effect, photoelectric effect, pair production and coherent diffusion for photons in water.

4.3.1 Compton effect

The Compton effect is the interaction of a photon with an electron. The initial photon has an energy hν. A part of this energy is transferred to the electron and a new photon of energy hν′ is scattered. For this work, the notation of Davisson & Evans (1952) is used.

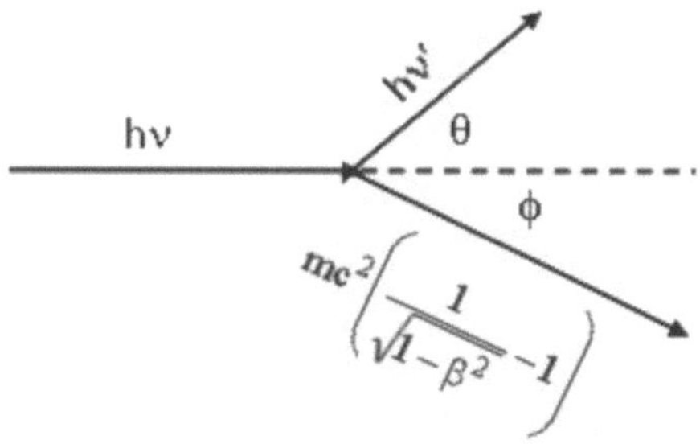

Fig. 11. Compton effect. A photon with initial energy hν interacts with an electron. The electron is ejected at angle ϕ with an energy $mc^2[(1-\beta^2)^{-1/2}-1]$ and a photon is emitted at angle θ with energy hν′ (Davisson & Evans, 1952).

The laws of conservation of energy and momentum can be used to write the following relationships between the angles and energies of the Compton electron and diffused photon:

$$h\nu' = \frac{h\nu}{1+\alpha(1-\cos(\theta))} \tag{52a}$$

$$E_{\text{electron}} = h\nu\left(1 - \frac{1}{1+\alpha(1-\cos(\theta))}\right) \tag{52b}$$

$$\cos(\theta) = 1 - \frac{2}{(1+\alpha)^2\tan^2(\phi)+1} \tag{52c}$$

$$\tan(\phi) = \frac{1}{1+\alpha}\sqrt{\frac{2}{1-\cos(\theta)}-1} \tag{52d}$$

Here, $\alpha = h\nu/mc^2$, h is the Planck's constant, υ is the incident photon frequency, m is the electron rest mass and c is the speed of light.

Klein-Nishina cross section

When a Compton interaction occurs, the energy and angle should be determined for the diffused photon and for the Compton electron. All these quantities are linked by equations (52). The probability of a photon and an electron to diffuse in directions θ and ϕ is function of the energy of the initial photon and was obtained by Klein & Nishina (1929) by solving Dirac's equation for a free electron:

$$\frac{d\sigma_{KN}(\theta)}{d\Omega} = k(\theta) = \frac{r_0^2}{2}\left\{\frac{1}{\left[1+\alpha(1-\cos(\theta)\right]^2}\left[1+\cos^2(\theta)+\frac{\alpha^2(1-\cos(\theta))^2}{1+\alpha(1-\cos(\theta))}\right]\right\} \tag{53}$$

where σ_{KN} is the Klein-Nishina cross section and $r_0=e^2/mc^2=2.82\times10^{-13}$ cm[(2)]. Another important quantity is the differential cross section for Compton electrons. The laws of conservation state that probability of an electron to be deflected in the solid angle $d\Omega'$ in the direction ϕ is the same as the probability for a photon to diffuse in the solid angle $d\Omega$ in direction θ:

$$d\sigma_{KN} = k(\theta)d\Omega = k(\phi)d\Omega' \quad \text{or} \quad k(\phi) = k(\theta)(d\Omega / d\Omega') \tag{54}$$

By using relationship between angles, it can be shown that:

$$\frac{d\Omega}{d\Omega'} = -\frac{\sin(\theta)(1+\cos(\theta))}{(1+\alpha)\sin^3(\phi)} = -4\frac{(1+\alpha)^2\cos(\phi)}{\left[(1+\alpha)^2 - \alpha(2+\alpha)\cos^2(\phi)\right]^2} \tag{55}$$

Therefore $k(\phi)$, the angular distribution of Compton electron, can be calculated from Klein-Nishina differential cross section. The cross section for the Compton effect is obtained by integrating the Klein-Nishina cross section over all solid angles. This calculation gives:

$$\sigma_{KN} = 2\pi r_0^2\left[\frac{\alpha+1}{\alpha^2}\left\{\frac{2(\alpha+1)}{1+2\alpha} - \frac{1}{\alpha}\ln[1+2\alpha]\right\} - \frac{1+3\alpha}{(1+2\alpha)^2} + \frac{1}{2\alpha}\ln[1+2\alpha]\right] \tag{56}$$

Atomic form factor

The Klein-Nishina cross section was obtained by assuming that the photon interacts with an electron at rest. In reality, electrons are bound to atoms and molecules; therefore, the entire atom interacts with the incident photon. To take this into account, an *atomic form factor* S(q,Z) is introduced (Chibani, 1994):

$$\frac{d\sigma}{d\Omega} = \frac{d\sigma_{KN}}{d\Omega}S(q,Z) \tag{57}$$

where

$$q = k\sin(\theta/2) = \frac{h\nu(\text{MeV})\sin(\theta/2)}{12.3885\times10^{-3}} \tag{58}$$

Here k is the momentum of the photon, θ is the diffusion angle of the incident photon and q is the momentum transferred to the electron ($Å^{-1}$). The function S(q,Z) increase with q, with a maximum value of Z. The effect of this form factor is to reduce the Klein-Nishina cross section. S(q,Z) also disfavor diffusion at small angles. The values of S(q,Z) were tabulated by Hubell et al. (1975) for Z from 1 to 100 and for q between 0 and 10^9 $Å^{-1}$. If a material is composed by elements Z_n in proportions p_n, S(q,Z) is replaced by:

$$S_T(q) = \sum_n p_n S(q,Z_n) \tag{59}$$

The effect of this form factor on the cross section is shown on Figure 12. It has no effect over 20 keV for ^{1}H and over 100 keV for ^{8}O.

---

[2] r_0 is also referred to as the *classical electron radius*, the radius of a spherical shell whose total electrostatic energy equals the electron rest mass

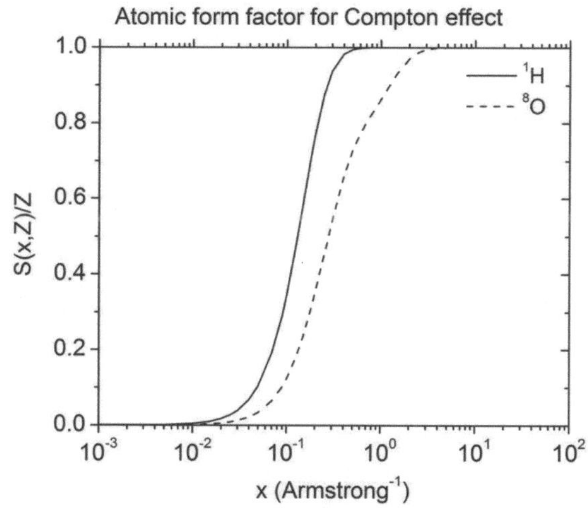

(a)

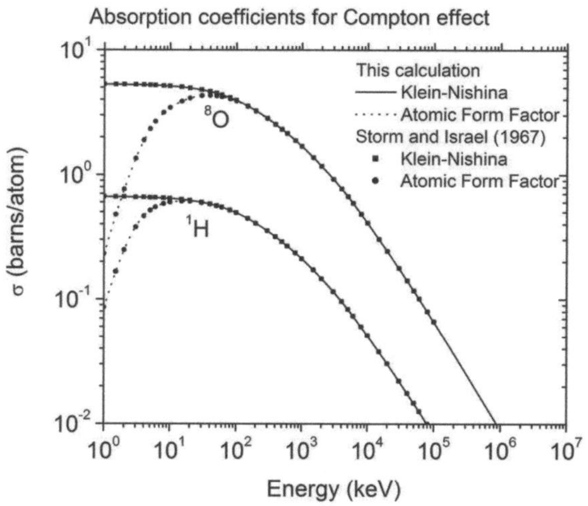

(b)

Fig. 12. (a) Atomic form factors for ^{1}H and ^{8}O for Compton effect (Hubbell et al., 1975). (b) Effect of the atomic form factor on the Compton effect cross sections for ^{1}H and ^{8}O. The data are obtained by integrating numerically the Klein-Nishina cross section multiplied by the form factor. The results are compared to the tabulated data of Storm & Israel (1967).

Sampling of the differential cross section

A method to generate angles distributed according to the Klein-Nishina cross section multiplied by the atomic form factor is needed for transport codes. If there were no atomic form factor, the algorithm of Kahn described in Raeside (1976) could be used. The following algorithm will be used instead (Plante, 2009). Let

$$x = 1 + \alpha(1 - \cos(\theta)) \tag{60}$$

The variable x varies between 1 (θ=0) and 1+2α (θ=π). The cross section may be written

$$\frac{d\sigma(\theta)}{d\Omega} = \frac{r_0^2}{x^2}\left[1 - \frac{\sin^2(\theta)}{2} + \frac{(x-1)^2}{2x}\right] \quad (61)$$

This can be sampled by rejection. The distribution $1/x^2$ (normalized) is generated from a random number U by inversion:

$$x = \frac{1+2\alpha}{1+2\alpha U} \quad (62)$$

The function between brackets is the rejection function, for which the maximum value is $(1+2\alpha)/2$. Since the rejection constant should be greater than or equal to 1, it is chosen to be 1 for $\alpha < 1/2$, or $(1+2\alpha)/2$ for $\alpha \geq 1/2$. The angle θ is calculated by using the definition of x:

$$\cos(\theta) = 1 - \frac{x-1}{\alpha} \quad (63)$$

The values of x and θ are introduced in the rejection function (RF):

$$RF = 1 - \frac{\sin^2(\theta)}{2} + \frac{(x-1)^2}{2x} \quad (64)$$

This gives algorithm 3:

Algorithm 3: Sampling of the angles for Compton effect for a photon of a given energy, given by the Klein-Nishina cross section multiplied by the form factor. The definition of x is used to calculate θ.

CALCULATE FFMax=S(E,π,Z)
IF α<1/2 { RC=1 } **ELSE** { RC=(1+2α)/2 }
REPEAT
{
Generate two random numbers R_1 and R_2 between 0 and 1

$$X = \frac{1+2\alpha}{1+2\alpha U_1}$$

$$\Theta = \cos^{-1}\left(1 - \frac{X-1}{\alpha}\right)$$

$$FR = 1 - \frac{\sin^2(\Theta)}{2} + \frac{(X-1)^2}{2X}$$

$$FF = S(E,\Theta,Z)$$

}
WHILE FFxFR < U_2xRCxFFMax
RETURN Θ ■

From the angle θ obtained with this algorithm, the energy of the scattered γ and the angle and energy of the Compton electron can be calculated. The algorithm was used 1 000 000 times to generate the distribution of angles θ and ϕ (Figure 13). The calculations were performed for five energy values and stored in normalized histograms. There is no difference between the sampling results and the analytical curves. For the energy values used in Figure 13a, the form factor has no effect. The difference appears at low energies, such as shown on Figure 13b.

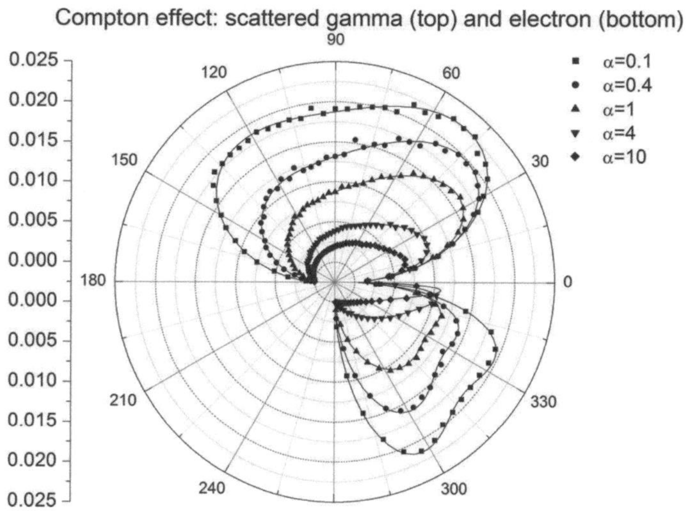

(a)

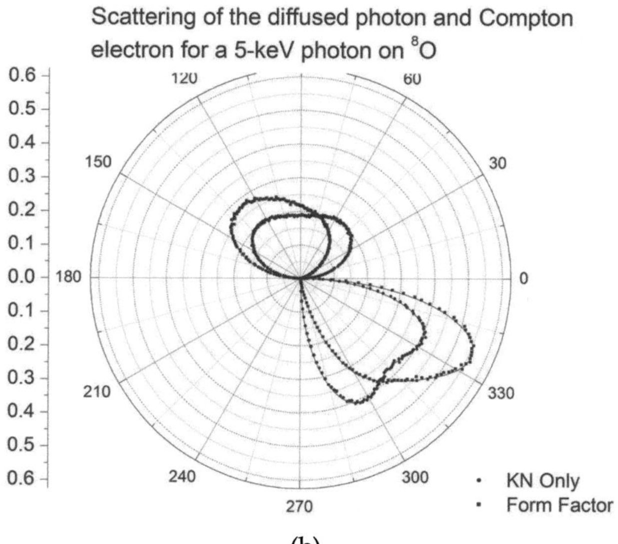

(b)

Fig. 13. a) Angular distribution of the scattered photon (top) and of the Compton electron (bottom) for initial photon energies of 0.0511 MeV, 0.2044 MeV, 0.511 MeV, 2.044 MeV and 5.11 MeV. b) Effect of the atomic form factor on the angular distributions of the scattered photon (top) and Compton electron (bottom). As usual, the lines are the analytical predictions, and the dots are given by Monte-Carlo sampling.

An important quantity that can be obtained is the energy distribution of the Compton electrons (Figure 14). The form factor is important only for low-energy photons (<100 keV).

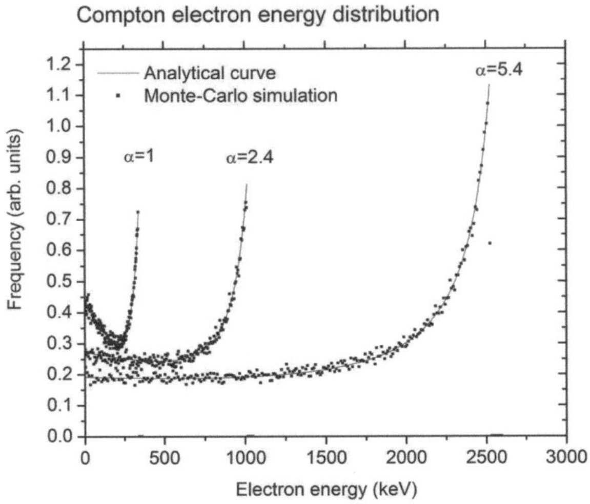

(a)

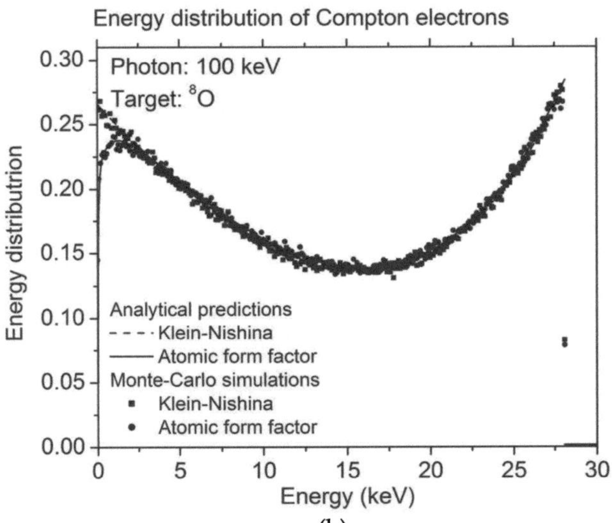

(b)

Fig. 14. a) Distribution of Compton electron energy for photons of initial energies of 0.511 MeV, 1.226 MeV and 2.76 MeV. b) Effect of the atomic form factor on the distribution of Compton energy for photons of MeV. The lines are the analytical predictions, and the dots are obtained by Monte-Carlo simulation.

4.3.2 Coherent diffusion

When an electromagnetic wave is incident on a charged particle, the electric and magnetic components of the wave exert a Lorentz force on the particle, setting it into motion. Therefore, energy is absorbed from the incident wave by the particle and re-emitted as electromagnetic radiation. Such a process is equivalent to the scattering of the electromagnetic wave by the particle. Its differential cross section is given by:

$$\frac{d\sigma_T}{d\Omega} = \frac{r_0^2}{2}\left[1+\cos^2(\theta)\right] \tag{65}$$

The total cross section σ_T[3] is calculated by integrating $d\sigma_T/d\Omega$ over all solid angles:

$$\sigma_T = \int \frac{d\sigma_T}{d\Omega} d\Omega = 2\pi \int_0^{\pi} \frac{r_0^2}{2}[1+\cos^2(\theta)]\sin(\theta)d\theta = \frac{8\pi r_0^2}{3} \tag{66}$$

Atomic form factor

According to equation (66), the coherent diffusion cross section is not function of the photon energy, which is obviously not the case (see absorption coefficients). As for Compton effect, an atomic form factor should be introduced (Chibani, 1994):

$$\frac{d\sigma_T}{d\Omega} = \frac{r_0^2}{2}[1+\cos^2(\theta)]\left|F(q,Z_n)\right|^2 \tag{67}$$

The values of F(q,Z) were tabulated by Hubell & Øverbø (1979). If a material is composed of elements Z_n in proportions p_n, $|F(q,z)|^2$ is replaced by:

$$F_T(q) = \sum_n p_n \left|F(q,z_n)\right|^2 \tag{68}$$

The effect of the atomic form factor on the cross sections is shown on Figure 15.

Sampling of the coherent diffusion cross section

An algorithm to generate angles corresponding to the coherent diffusion cross section is needed. The differential cross may be written

$$\frac{d\sigma_T}{d\theta} = r_0^2[1+\cos^2(\theta)]\left|F(q,Z_n)\right|^2 \frac{\sin(\theta)}{2} \tag{69}$$

The distribution $\sin(\theta)/2$ is normalized; therefore, a random number Θ with such distribution can be generated by the inversion method (R is an uniform random number between 0 and 1):

$$\Theta = \cos^{-1}(1-2R) \tag{70}$$

The rejection function is therefore

$$RF = \left(\frac{F(q,Z)}{Z}\right)^2 \left(\frac{1+\cos^2(\theta)}{2}\right) \tag{71}$$

This gives the algorithm to generate angles distributed as coherent diffusion.

---

[3] σ_T is the Thompson cross section

Algorithm 4: Algorithm to sample the coherent diffusion angles. The maximal value of F(q,Z) is Z.
REPEAT
{
Generate two random numbers R_1 and R_2 between 0 and 1

$$\Theta = \cos^{-1}(1 - 2R_1)$$

$$FR = \left(\frac{F(q,Z)}{Z}\right)^2 \left(\frac{1+\cos(\Theta)}{2}\right)$$

}
WHILE $FR*R_2>R_1$
RETURN Θ ■

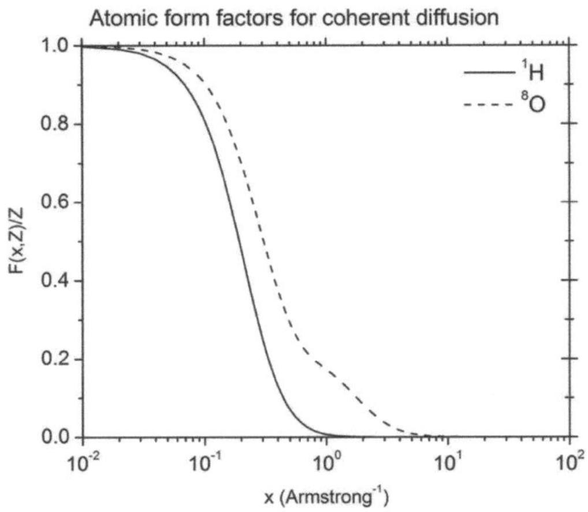

(a)

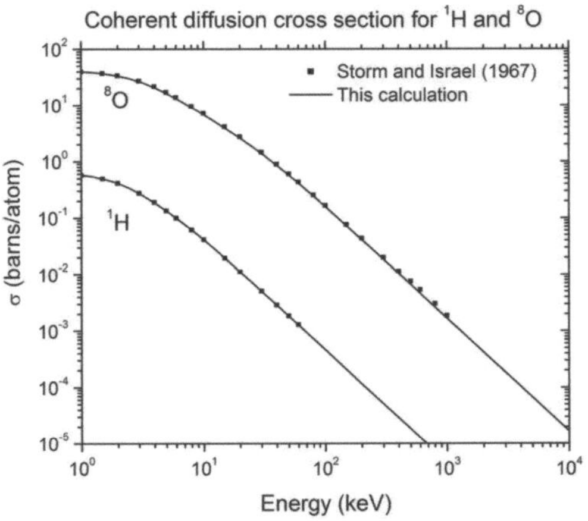

(b)

Fig. 15. a) Atomic form factors for coherent diffusion on ^{1}H and ^{8}O. (Hubbell et al., 1975). b) Coherent diffusion cross section for ^{1}H and ^{8}O calculated by integrating numerically the differential cross section multiplied by the atomic form factor. The results are compared with tabulated data of Storm & Israel (1967).

Simulation results (dots) are compared with the analytical curves of Figure 13. The dots are so close to the analytical functions that the lines are not seen.

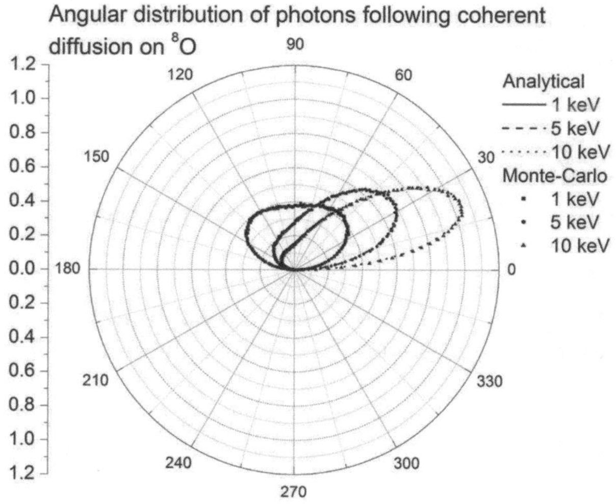

Fig. 16. Sampling of the angular distribution for photon of 1 keV, 5 keV and 10 keV on ^{8}O, taking the atomic form factor into consideration. The dots are obtained by Monte-Carlo simulation by sampling the algorithm 1000000 times. The lines are the analytical predictions.

4.3.3 Photoelectric effect

Photoelectric effect is the process by which an orbital electron absorbs the energy of an incident photon and is ejected. The energy of the electron is the photon energy minus the binding energy of the electron. The photons that have an energy greater than the binding energy of the K shell of Oxygen, I_K=539.7 eV, interacts only with those electrons. Otherwise, the binding energy I_L =19.6 eV is assumed.

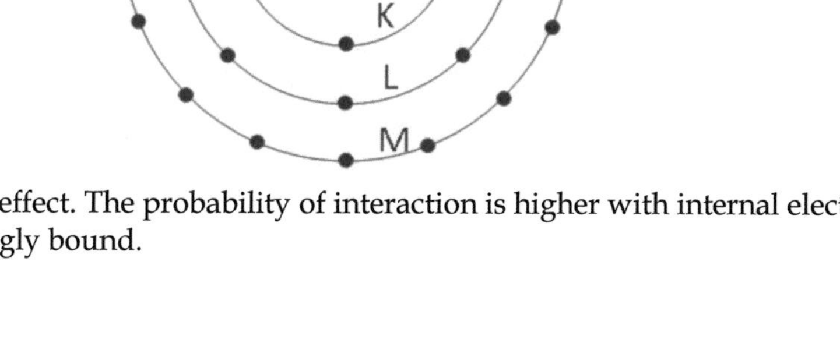

Fig. 17. Photoelectric effect. The probability of interaction is higher with internal electrons, which are more strongly bound.

Since a free electron cannot absorb a photon (this is not allowed by the laws of conservation of momentum and energy), photoelectric effect can only occur on a bound electron. In fact, the probability of photoelectric effect increases with the binding energy of the electron (Heitler, 1954). In (Anderson, 1984; Storm & Israel, 1967), an empirical formula gives the ratio of the total photoelectric cross section (σ_τ) to K layer photoelectric cross section (σ_K):

$$\sigma_\tau / \sigma_K = 1 + 0.01481(\ln(Z))^2 - 0.00079(\ln(Z))^3 \tag{72}$$

For oxygen, if $\sigma_\tau=\sigma_K+\sigma_L$, the calculation gives $\sigma_L=0.057\sigma_K$. Some authors (Hill & Smith, 1996; Turner et al., 1980) assumed that photons which energy is higher than the binding energy of the K shell of oxygen, I_K=539.7 eV, interact only with these electrons. For lower energy, the binding energy I_L =19.6 eV is assumed. When an electron of the K shell is emitted, an Auger electron of energy E_{Auger}=520.1 eV is also emitted (Hill & Smith, 1996). Note that Turner et al. (1980), which has performed similar calculations, have used I_K=532 eV, I_L=12 eV and E_{Auger} = 508 eV.

The cross section for the photoelectric effect is harder to calculate analytically than in the case of Compton effect, because Dirac's equation should be solved for bound electrons. In this work, Sauter's formula for the angular distribution of photoelectrons is used (Sauter, 1931). It can be written (Tseng et al, 1978):

$$\frac{d\sigma_\tau}{d\Omega} = \frac{\lambda \sin^2(\theta)}{[1-\beta\cos(\theta)]^4}\{1+\kappa[1-\beta\cos(\theta)]\} \tag{73}$$

Where

$$\kappa = \gamma\left(-\frac{1-\sqrt{1-\beta^2}}{2\sqrt{1-\beta^2}} + \frac{\left(1-\sqrt{1-\beta^2}\right)^2}{2(1-\beta^2)}\right) = \frac{\gamma(\gamma-1)(\gamma-2)}{2} \tag{74}$$

$$\lambda = \frac{4Z^5\alpha\beta(\gamma+1)}{(\gamma-1)^4\gamma^3} = \frac{4Z^5\alpha\beta(\gamma+1)n^4}{\gamma^3} \tag{75}$$

Here, $\alpha = e^2 / \hbar c$ is the structure fine constant, EB is the binding energy of the electron, n is the energy in units of electron rest mass ($n=h\upsilon/mc^2$) and

$$\gamma = \frac{1}{\sqrt{1-\beta^2}} = \frac{h\nu - E_B + mc^2}{mc^2} 1 + 1/n \tag{76}$$

The total cross section is calculated by integrating $d\sigma_\tau/d\Omega$ over all solid angles. This yields the results given in Davisson & Evans (1952):

$$\sigma_\tau = \frac{3}{2}\varphi_0 \frac{Z^5}{(137)^4} n^5(\gamma^2-1)^{3/2}\left[\frac{4}{3} + \frac{\gamma(\gamma-2)}{\gamma+1}\left[1 - \frac{1}{2\gamma\sqrt{\gamma^2-1}}\ln\left(\frac{\gamma+\sqrt{\gamma^2-1}}{\gamma-\sqrt{\gamma^2-1}}\right)\right]\right] \tag{77}$$

The photoelectric cross section cannot reproduce properly the absorption cross section of photoelectric effect for water. This difference comes from the fact that Z varies with energy (Anderson, 1984). However, using a variable exponent in the calculation of σ_τ, the cross section is very similar to the data of Storm & Israel (1967). This is illustrated on Figure 18.

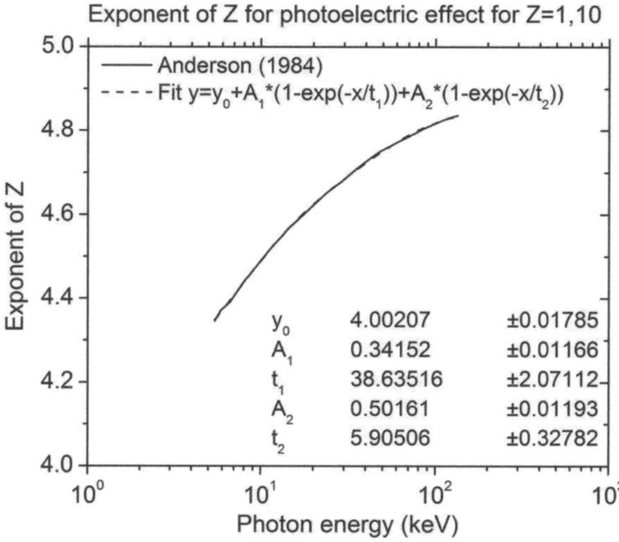

(a)

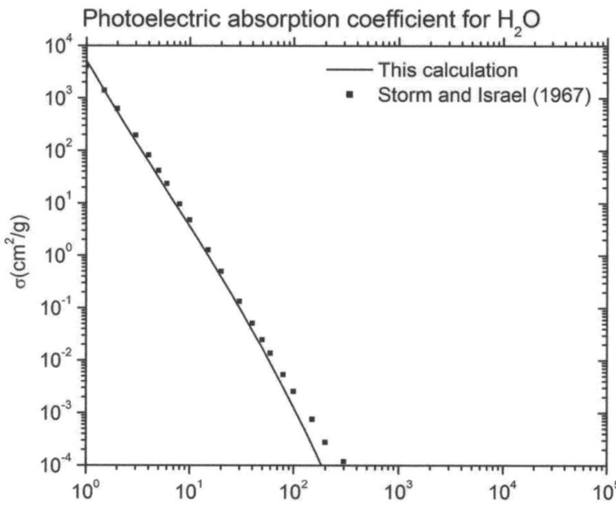

(b)

Fig. 18. a) Exponent Z as a function of the photon energy for photoelectric effect.
b) Photoelectric absorption coefficients calculated from Sauter's formula, including the variation of the exponent as function of the energy.

To find the angular distribution of photoelectrons, Sauter's distribution is written as:

$$d\sigma_\tau = \frac{2\pi\lambda\sin^3(\theta)}{[1-\beta\cos(\theta)]^4}\{1+\kappa[1-\beta\cos(\theta)]\}\,d\theta \tag{78}$$

Introducing $u=\cos(\theta)$, the distribution takes a simpler form:

$$f(u) \propto \frac{1-u^2}{(1-\beta u)^4}\left[1+\kappa(1-\beta u)\right] \tag{79}$$

This function can be sampled by rejection. We define g(u) and h(u), such as $f(u) \propto g(u)h(u)$, g(u) is normalized and $h(u)\geq 1$:

$$g(u) = \frac{1}{2\gamma^2(\kappa+\gamma^2)}\frac{\left[1+\kappa(1-\beta u)\right]}{(1-\beta u)^3} \tag{80}$$

$$h(u) = \frac{\gamma-1}{2\gamma}\left(\frac{1-u^2}{1-\beta u}\right) \tag{81}$$

The function g(u) can be sampled by inversion, by solving the following equation for Y:

$$R = \int_{-1}^{Y}\frac{1}{2\gamma^2(\kappa+\gamma^2)}\frac{\left[1+\kappa(1-\beta u)\right]}{(1-\beta u)^3}du \tag{82}$$

The integral yields[4]:

$$R = \frac{1}{4\beta\gamma^2(\kappa+\gamma^2)}\left[\frac{1}{(1-\beta Y)^2}+\frac{2\kappa}{(1-\beta Y)}-\frac{1}{(1+\beta)^2}-\frac{2\kappa}{(1+\beta)}\right] \tag{83}$$

By completing squares, we find:

$$R = \frac{1}{4\beta\gamma^2(\kappa+\gamma^2)}\left[\left(\kappa+\frac{1}{1-\beta Y}\right)^2-\left(\kappa+\frac{1}{1+\beta}\right)^2\right] \tag{84}$$

It is now possible to isolate Y (Kawrakow & Rogers, 2003):

$$Y = \frac{1}{\beta}\left[1-\left(\sqrt{4\beta\gamma^2(\kappa+\gamma^2)R+\left(\kappa+\frac{1}{1+\beta}\right)^2}-\kappa\right)^{-1}\right] \tag{85}$$

This gives the algorithm 5, which may be used to sample the photoelectrons angular distribution.

---

[4] The normalization of g(u) is verified by using Y=1 in the equation, i.e. $\int_{-1}^{1} g(u)du = 1$

Algorithm 5: Sampling of the Sauter's angular distribution of photoelectrons. The quantities β, γ and κ are defined in the text.

CALCULATE β, γ and κ

REPEAT

{

Generate two random numbers R_1 and R_2 uniformly disbributed between 0 and 1

$$Y = \frac{1}{\beta}\left[1-\left(\sqrt{4\beta\gamma^2(\kappa+\gamma^2)R_1+\left(\kappa+\frac{1}{1+\beta}\right)^2}-\kappa\right)^{-1}\right]$$

$$h(Y) = \frac{\gamma-1}{2\gamma}\left(\frac{1-Y^2}{1-\beta Y}\right)$$

}

WHILE $R_2>h(Y)$

RETURN $\Theta = \cos^{-1}(Y)$ ■

The angular distribution obtained by using the preceding algorithm is compared to Sauter's distribution on Figure 19.

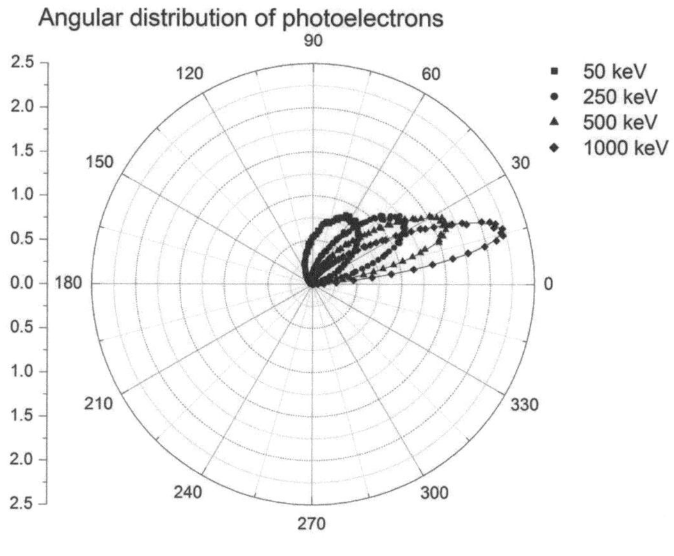

Fig. 19. Angular distribution of photoelectrons obtained by sampling Sauter's formula 100000 times with the algorithm. The dots are obtained by Monte-Carlo simulation. The lines are the analytical predictions (Sauter's distribution).

5. Simulation results

In this section, simulation results obtained with the Monte-Carlo transport code RITRACKS are shown.

5.1 Electrons

5.1.1 Electron range

The range of electrons of energies up to 150 keV in liquid water has been calculated by Meesungnoen et al. (2002) and up to 100 keV by Uehara & Nikjoo (2006). Figure 20 displays the computed values of the electron penetration as a function of initial electron energy from 0.1 eV to 10 MeV calculated with RITRACKS by using the relativistic and the non-relativistic cross sections. Experimental results from Konovalov et al. (1988) are also shown.

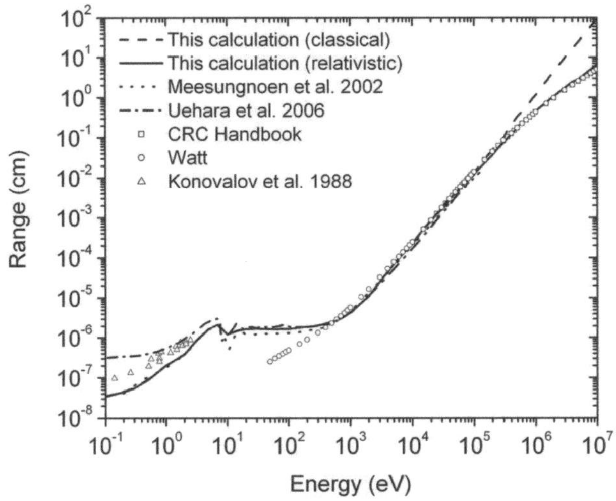

Fig. 20. Electron range in liquid water. The calculations have been performed using the classical and relativistic cross sections. Data from Meesungnoen et al. (2002), Uehara and Nikjoo (2006), Watt (1996), the CRC Handbook (Brodsky, 1978) and Konovalov et al. (1988) are also shown.

The results obtained below 150 keV are similar to those from Meesungnoen et al. (2002); the reader is thus referred to this article for a more detailed discussion of this curve below 150 keV. Only major points will be recalled here. In the subexcitation electron energy range (<7.3 eV), the penetration range is often called the "thermalization distance". It increases from ~0.35 nm at 0.1 eV to ~18 nm at 7.3 eV. This problem has been extensively studied (Goulet et al. 1990); the results of RITRACKS are in good agreement with the reported values. Three minimas in the electron range curve are reported by Meesungnoen et al. (2002) at ~11, 22 and 30-35 eV; however, they are not clearly seen in figure 11 because the energy steps used between each point is too large. Between 30 and 300 eV, the calculated range increases very slowly, also in agreement with the calculation from Meesungnoen et al. (2002). To our knowledge, there are no experimental data between ~5-50 eV, where the minimas are predicted by Meesungnoen et al. (2002) and by Uehara and Nikjoo (2006). Between 300 eV and 150 keV, there is an excellent agreement of our calculations with the values from the CRC Handbook (Brodsky, 1978) and the book of Watt (1996). Over ~150 keV, the difference in the electron range calculated with the relativistic and the non-relativistic cross sections appears. This is discussed in Plante & Cucinotta (2009). At high energy, the relativistic cross sections needs to be used to have the calculation of the electron range in agreement with data from Watt (1996) and the CRC Handbook (Brodsky, 1978)

5.1.2 Stopping power

The stopping power[5] is another very important quantity that was used to validate the RITRACKS code. The calculation has been performed by Gümüş (2005) and Paretzke (see Dingfelder et al., 2008). Stopping power data are found in the CRC handbook (Brodsky, 1978); Watt, 1996; ICRU 37 (1984), ICRU 16 (1970) and IAEA (1995). The available data for stopping power exists with and without the bremsstrahlung. The stopping power was calculated by RITRACKS (figure 21) with Rudd's formulae for energies <150 keV. At higher energies, relativistic corrections to cross sections and bremsstrahlung needs to be added, but this will not be discussed here (see Plante & Cucinotta, 2009). There is excellent agreement of the results with the existing data in all range, but the agreement is the best between ~1 keV and ~100 keV.

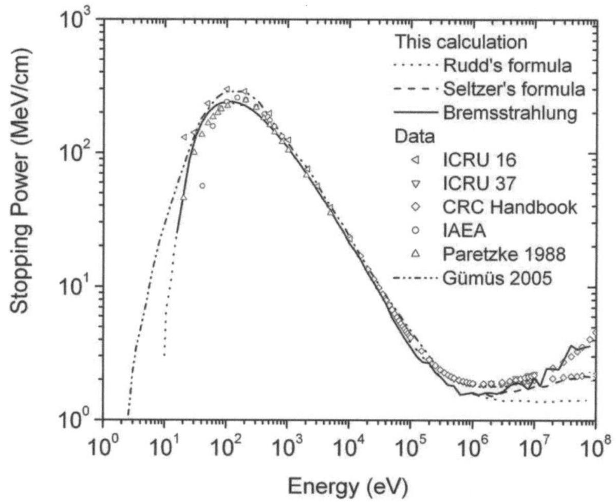

Fig. 21. Electron stopping power, calculated without bremsstrahlung using Rudd's relativistic formula and Seltzer's formulae. Data without bremsstrahlung from CRC Handbook (Brodsky, 1978), Gümüş (2005), Paretzke (Dingfelder et al., 2008), ICRU 16 (1970) and ICRU 37 (1984) and with bremsstrahlung from CRC Handbook (Brodsky, 1978) are also shown.

5.2 Ions

5.2.1 Tracks

On Figure 22, XY plane projections of track segments calculated at ~10^{-12} s are shown for $^{4}He^{2+}$, $^{12}C^{6+}$, $^{28}Si^{14+}$ and $^{56}Fe^{26+}$ ions (LET ~150 keV/µm). Even if the ions have the same LET, their structure are very different. The central region of the track is the so-called *core* of the track, and results from the dense ionization created by the ion. The peripherical region, the *penumbra,* is created by the trajectories of the secondary electrons ionized by the primary ion. As discussed previously, the maximum energy that can be transferred to an electron is proportional to the energy per nucleon of the ion. This is exactly what is observed here: the higher the energy per nucleon, the more energetic are the secondary electrons and the larger the penumbra.

---

[5] The stopping power is closely related to the linear energy transfer (LET), except that the LET does not include radiative loss (such as bremsstrahlung).

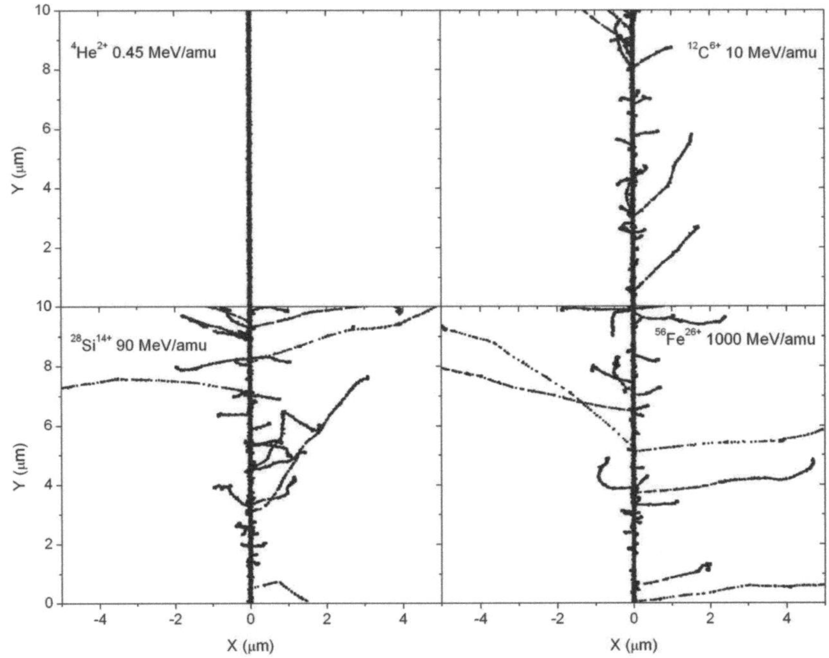

Fig. 22. Projections over the XY plane of simulated tracks segments (calculated at ~10^{-12} s) for the following impact ions: $^{4}He^{2+}$ (0.45 MeV/amu), $^{12}C^{6+}$ (10 MeV/amu), $^{28}Si^{14+}$ (90 MeV/amu) and $^{56}Fe^{26+}$ (1 GeV/amu). Ions are generated at the origin along the Y axis in liquid water at 25 °C under identical LET conditions (~150 keV/μm). Each dot represents a radiolytic species.

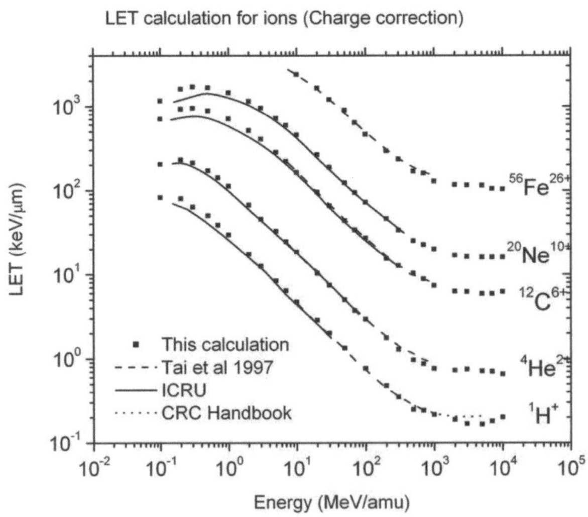

Fig. 23. Calculation of the LET as a function of the energy for $^{1}H^{+}$, $^{4}He^{2+}$, $^{12}C^{6+}$, $^{20}Ne^{10+}$ and $^{56}Fe^{26+}$ using the cross sections shown above and including charge effects and relativistic corrections.

5.2.2 Stopping power

The stopping power (or LET) was calculated as function of the energy for the ions $^1H^+$, $^4He^{2+}$, $^{12}C^{6+}$, $^{20}Ne^{10+}$ and $^{56}Fe^{26+}$ (Figure 23). In general, results are in good agreement with the calculations derived from other codes (Tai et al., 1997), ICRU values (ICRU 1993) and CRC Handbook values (Brodsky, 1978), for all ions and the energy range considered (~10^{-1}-10^4 MeV/amu).

5.2.3 Radial dose

The radial dose is of interest for microdosimetric applications and was also used to validate the results of the RITRACKS code. It is calculated by recording the energy deposited and the radial distance from the Y axis of the energy loss events. The energy deposited in each differential volume element is then divided by its volume and converted to Gy. The calculated radial dose for a 1-MeV $^1H^+$ ion (Figure 24) are in good agreement with previous amorphous tracks calculations (Cucinotta et al. 1998). Radial dose profiles for other ions are shown in (Plante & Cucinotta, 2008).

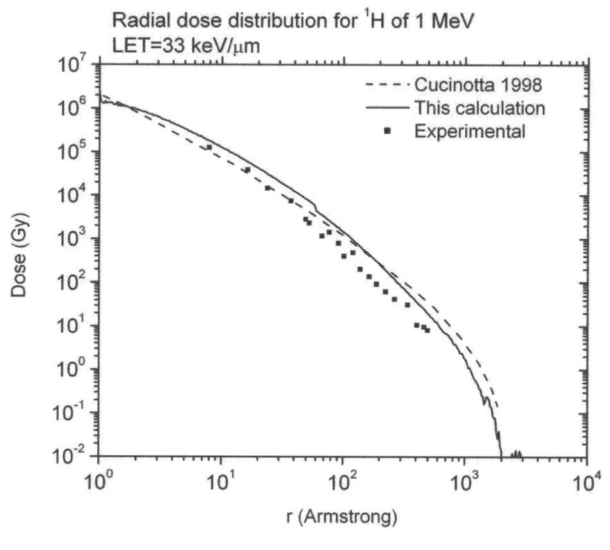

Fig. 24. Calculation of radial dose profiles for $^1H^+$, 1 MeV (LET~33 keV/μm). Amorphous track calculations and experimental data from Cucinotta et al. (1998) are also shown.

5.3 Photons

5.3.1 Number of electrons emitted per photon

Simulations have been performed with photons of energies up to 2 MeV. Figure 25 shows the number of electrons generated per incident photon. This calculation is compared with previous results from Turner (1980). The curve seems to plateau at about 17 electrons per photon. This is explained by the fact that the Compton electrons spectra is more intense near the maximal energy transfer, with is a more important fraction of the initial energy when the initial photon energy is large. Thus, a photon will lose an important fraction of its energy during the first collisions. At low energies, we note that at least two electrons are emitted. This is due to the emission of the Auger electron.

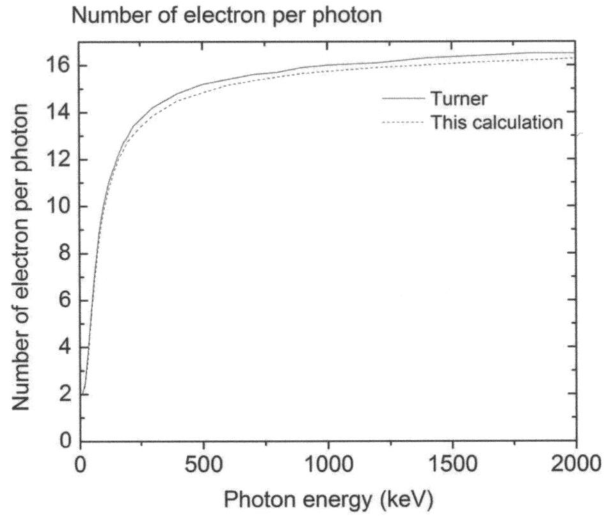

Fig. 25. Number of electrons emitted per photon, as function of the initial photon energy.

5.3.2 Energy distribution of the secondary electrons

A very important quantity that is calculated by the program is the distribution of the energy of the secondary electrons, resulting from the slowing down of photons. The calculation has been performed for 50 keV, 200 keV, 1 MeV, 1.2 MeV, 1.4 MeV, 1.6 MeV, 1.8 MeV and 2.0 MeV. Our results are shown on Figure 26 and compared with results from Turner et al. (1980). Although a very different approach has been used by Turner to sample the cross sections, the results are similar in all cases. The peak that is seen at 500 eV corresponds to Auger electrons.

6. Conclusion

Ionizing radiations comprises several types of energetic particles such as electrons, protons, α-particles and photons (X-rays or γ-rays). They are produced by natural processes and by man-made devices and are widely used in medical applications for diagnostic procedures and cancer treatment. In space, HZE particles are also present and may be a concern for long-term manned missions.

Several health risks are associated with radiation exposure. The increase in cancer risk is the most studied; however, ionizing radiation may also increase the risk of degenerative diseases of the cardio-vascular and central nervous systems. The biological pathways involved in the effects of radiations are complex, but they are initiated by physical, physico-chemical and chemical interactions with the medium. Therefore much effort has been invested over last decades to understand these processes.

Because of the stochastic nature of radiation interactions, Monte-Carlo simulations are very useful to study ionizing radiations. They have greatly helped our understanding of the physical interactions of radiation with matter. Over the years, they have also become more accessible thanks to the availability of computer power and storage capacity. As new cross sections data become available, the models of radiation interaction are continuously improving over time. Therefore, Monte-Carlo simulations are now indispensable tools that are used in many applications such as in radiotherapy treatment planning and in fundamental research.

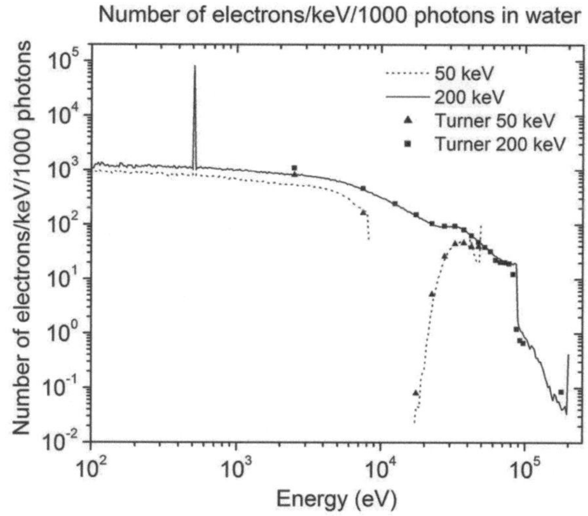

(a)

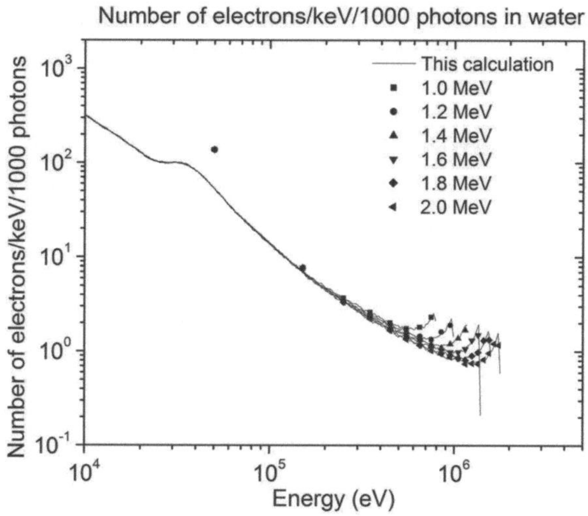

(b)

Fig. 26. Distribution of the energy of the secondary electrons created by irradiation of liquid water with photons. This calculation (lines) and results from Turner (1980).

7. Acknowledgements

We would like to thank Prof. Jean-Paul Jay-Gerin (University of Sherbrooke) for helpful discussions.

8. References

Anderson, D.W. (1984). *Absorption of Ionizing Radiation*, University Park Press, ISBN: 083911821X, Baltimore, Md.

Barkas, H. (1963). *Nuclear Research Emulsions Vol. 1*, Chapter 9, p. 371, Academic Press, ISBN: 0120783010, New York, NY

Boudaïffa, B.; Cloutier, P.; Hunting, D.; Huels, M.A. & Sanche, L. (2000). Resonant formation of DNA strand breaks by low energy (3 to 20 eV) electrons. *Science*, 287, 1658-1659. ISSN: 0036-8075

Brenner, D.J. & Zaider, M. (1983). A computationally convenient parameterisation of experimental angular distributions of low energy electrons elastically scattered off water vapour. *Phys. Med. Biol.*, 29 443-447. ISSN: 0031-9155.

Brodsky, A.B. (1978). *CRC Handbook of Radiation Measurement and Protection*. CRC Press, ISBN: 9780849337703, West Palm Beach, Fl.

Chibani, O. (1994). *Simulation du transport de particules (Photons, électrons et positrons) – Le système GEPTS*. Ph.D. thesis, Université Paul Sabatier, Toulouse, France.

Cobut, V. (1993). *Simulation Monte Carlo du transport d'électrons non relativistes dans l'eau liquide pure et de l'évolution du milieu irradié: rendements des espèces créées de 10^{-15} à 10^{-7} s*. Ph.D. thesis, Université de Sherbrooke, Québec, Canada.

Cobut V.; Frongillo, Y.; Patau, J.P.; Goulet, T.; Fraser, M.-J. & Jay-Gerin, J.-P. (1998). Monte-Carlo simulation of fast electron and proton tracks in liquid water - I. Physical and physicochemical aspects. *Radiat. Phys. Chem.*, 51, 229-243. ISSN: 0969-806X

Cucinotta, F.A. & Durante, M. (2006). Cancer risk from exposure to galactic cosmic rays: implications for space exploration by human beings. *Lancet Oncol.*, 7, 431-435. ISSN: 1470-2045

Cucinotta, F.A.; Katz, R. & Wilson, J.W. (1998). Radial distribution of electron spectra from high-energy ions. *Radiat. Env. Biophys.*, 37, 259-265. ISSN : 0301-634X

Danjo, A. & Nishimura, H. (1985). Elastic scattering of electrons from the H_2O molecule. *J. Phys. Soc. Jpn.*, 54, 1224-1227. ISSN: 0031-9015

Davisson, C.M. & Evans, R.D. (1952). Gamma rays absorption coefficients. *Rev. Mod. Phys.*, 24, 79-107. ISSN: 0034-6861

Devroye, L. (1986). *Non-Uniform Random Variate Generation*. Springler-Verlag, New York. ISBN: 978-0387963051

Dingfelder, M.; Jorjishvili, I.G.; Gersh, J.A. & Toburen, L.H. (2006). Heavy ion track structure simulation in liquid water at relativistic energies. *Radiat. Prot. Dosim.*, 122, 26-27. ISSN: 0144-8420

Dingfelder, M.; Ritchie, R.H.; Turner, J.E.; Friedland, W.; Paretzke, H.G. & Hamm, R.N. (2008). Comparisons of calculations with PARTRAC and NOREC: transport of electrons in liquid water. *Radiat. Res.*, 169, 584-594. ISSN: 1938-5404

Goulet, T.; Patau, J.-P. & Jay-Gerin, J.-P. (1990). Thermalization and recombination of subexcitation electrons in solid water. *Radiat. Prot. Dosim.*, 31, 33-36. ISSN: 0144-8420

Gümüş, H. (2005) Simple stopping power formula for low and intermediate energy electrons. *Radiat. Phys. Chem.*, 72, 7-12. ISSN: 0969-806X

Hill, M.A. & Smith, F.A. (1996). Is the response of the Fricke dosimeter constant for high energy electrons and photons? *Radiat. Phys. Chem.*, 47, 637-647. ISSN: 0969-806X

Hubbell, J.H.; Veigele, W.J.; Briggs, E.A.; Brown, R.T.; Cromer, D.T. & Howerton, R.J. (1975). Atomic form factors, incoherent scattering functions and photon scattering cross sections. *J. Phys. Chem. Ref. Data*, 4, 471-538. ISSN: 0047-2689

Hubbell, J.H. & Øverbø, I. (1979). Relativistic atomic form factors and photon coherent scattering cross sections. *J. Phys. Chem. Ref. Data*, 8, 69-106. ISSN: 0047-2689

ICRU (1984). *Stopping Powers and Ranges for Electrons and Positrons*. ICRU Report 37. International Commission on Radiation Units and Measurements, Bethesda, Md.

ICRU (1970). *Linear Energy Transfer*. ICRU Report 16. International Commission on Radiation Units and Measurements, Bethesda, Md.

ICRU (1993). *Stopping Powers and Ranges for Protons and Alpha Particles*. ICRU Report 49. International Commission on Radiation Units and Measurements, Bethesda, Md.

IAEA (1995). *Atomic and Molecular Data for Radiotherapy and Radiation Research*. IAEA-TECDOC-799, IAEA, Vienna

Jay-Gerin, J.-P. & Ferradini, C. (1999). La radiolyse de l'eau et des solutions aqueuses: historique et actualité. *Can. J. Chem.* 77, 1542-1575. ISSN: 0008-4042

Kawrakow, I. & Rogers, D.W.O. (2003). *The EGSnrc Code System: Monte Carlo Simulation of Electron and Photon Transport.* NRCC Report PIRS-701.

Katase, A.; Ishibashi, K.; Matsumoto, Y.; Sakae, T.; Maezono, S.; Murakami, E.; Watanabe, K. & Maki, H. (1986). Elastic scattering of electrons by water molecules over the range 100-1000 eV. *J. Phys. B*, 19, 2715-2734. ISSN: 0022-3700

Klein, O. & Nishina, Y. (1929). Über die Streuung von Strahlung durch freie Elektronen nach der neuen relativistischen Quantendynamik von Dirac. *Z. Phys.*, 52, 853-868. ISSN: 0044-3328

Konovalov, V.V.; Raitsimring, A.M. & Tsvetkov, Yu.D. (1988). Thermalization lengths of "subexcitation electrons" in water determined by photoinjections from metals into electrolyte solutions. *Radiat. Phys. Chem.*, 32, 623-632. ISSN: 0969-806X

Kutcher, G.J. & Green, A.E.S. (1976). A model for energy deposition in liquid water. *Radiat. Res.*, 67, 408-425. ISSN: 1938-5404

Meesungnoen, J.; Jay-Gerin, J.-P.; Filali-Mouhim, A. & Mankhetkorn, S. (2002). Low-energy electron penetration range in liquid water. *Radiat. Res.,* 158, 657-660. ISSN: 1938-5404

Michaud, M.; Wen, A. & Sanche, L. (2003). Cross sections for low-energy (1-100 eV) electron elastic and inelastic scattering in amorphous ice. *Radiat. Res.*, 159, 3-22. ISSN: 1938-5404

Mozumder, A. & Magee, J.L. (1966). Theory of radiation chemistry, VII. Structure and reaction in low LET tracks. *J. Chem. Phys.*, 45, 3332–3341. ISSN: 0021-9606

Nikjoo, H.; Uehara, S., Emfietzoglou, D. & Cucinotta, F.A. (2006). Track-structure codes in radiation research. *Radiat. Meas.*, 41, 1052–1074. ISSN: 1350-4487

Nikjoo, H.; Uehara, S.; Emfietzoglou, D. & Brahme, A. (2008). Heavy charged particles in radiation biology and biophysics. *New J. Phys.*, 10, 1-28. ISSN: 1367-2630

O'Neill, P. & Wardman, P. (2009). Radiation chemistry comes before radiation biology. *Int. J. Radiat. Biol.*, 85, 9-25. ISSN: 0955-3002

Pimblott, S.M. & LaVerne, J.A. (2007). Production of low-energy electrons by ionizing radiation. *Radiat. Phys. Chem.*, 76, 1244-1247. ISSN: 0969-806X

Plante, I. & Cucinotta, F.A. (2008). Ionization and excitation cross sections for the interaction of HZE particles in liquid water and application to Monte-Carlo simulation of radiation tracks. *New J. Phys.* 10, 125020. ISSN: 1367-2630

Plante, I. & Cucinotta, F.A. (2009). Cross sections for the interactions of 1 eV - 100 MeV electrons in liquid water and application to Monte-Carlo simulation of HZE radiation tracks. *New J. Phys.*, 11, 063047. ISSN: 1367-2630

Plante, I. (2009). Développement de codes de simulation Monte-Carlo de la radiolyse de l'eau par des électrons, ions lourds, photons et neutrons. Applications à divers sujets d'intérêt expérimental. Ph.D. thesis, Université de Sherbrooke, Québec, Canada.

Powell, C.J.; Jablonski, A. & Salvat, F. (2005). NIST databases with electron elastic-scattering cross sections, inelastic mean free paths, and effective attenuation lengths *Surf. Interface Anal.*, 37, 1068-1071. ISSN: 0142-1421

Press, W.H.; Teukolsky, S.A.; Vetterling, W.T. & Flannery, B.P. (1992). *Numerical Recipes in Fortran*. 2nd Edition, Cambridge University Press, ISBN: 978-0521880688, Cambridge.

Raeside, D.E. (1976). Monte-Carlo principles and applications. *Phys. Med. Biol.*, 21, 181-197. ISSN: 0031-9155.

Reynaert, N.; van der Marck, S.C.; Schaart, D.R.; Van der Zee, W.; Van Vliet-Vroegindeweij, C.; Tomsej, M.; Jansen, J.; Heijmen, B.; Coghe, M. & De Wagter, C. (2007). Monte Carlo treatment planning for photon and electron beams. *Radiat. Phys. Chem.*, 76, 643-686. ISSN: 0969-806X

Rowntree, P.; Parenteau, L. & Sanche, L. (1991). Electron stimulated desorption via dissociative attachment in amorphous H_2O. *J. Chem. Phys.*, 94, 8570-8576. ISSN: 0021-9606

Rudd, M.E. (1990). Cross sections for production of secondary electrons by charged particles. *Radiat. Prot. Dosim.*, 31, 17-22. ISSN: 0144-8420

Sauter, F. (1931). Über den Atomaren Photoeffekt in der K-Schale nach der Relativistischen Wellenmechanik Diracs. *Ann. Phys.*, 11, 454-488. ISSN: 0003-4916

Storm, E. & Israel, H.I. (1967). *Photon Cross Sections from 0.001 to MeV for Elements 1 through 100*. Los Alamos Scientific Laboratory report 3753, New Mexico.

Tai, H.; Bichsel, H.; Wilson, J.W.; Shinn, J.L.; Cucinotta, F.A. & Badavi, F.F. (1997). Comparison of stopping power and range databases for radiation transport studies. NASA technical paper 3644.

Tseng, H.K.; Pratt, R.H.; Yu, S. & Ron, A. (1978). Photoelectron angular distributions. *Phys. Rev. A*, 17, 1061-1079. ISSN: 1050-2947

Turner, J.E.; Hamm, R.N.; Wright, H.A.; Módolo, J.T. & Sordi, G.M.A.A. (1980). Monte Carlo calculation of initial energies of Compton electrons and photoelectrons in water irradiated by photons with energies up to 2 MeV. *Health Phys.*, 39, 49-55. ISSN: 0017-9078

Uehara, S.; Nikjoo, H. & Goodhead, D.T. (1992). Cross-sections for water vapour for the Monte Carlo electron track structure code from 10 eV to the MeV region. *Phys. Med. Biol.*, 37, 1841-1858. ISSN: 0031-9155.

Uehara, S. & Nikjoo, H. (2006). Monte Carlo simulation of water radiolysis for low-energy charged particles. *J. Radiat. Res.*, 47, 69-81. ISSN: 0449-3060

Watt, D.E. (1996). *Quantities for Dosimetry of Ionizing Radiations in Liquid Water*. Taylor & Francis, ISBN 0-203-21095-6, London, UK

19

Monte Carlo Simulation Tool of Evanescent Waves Spectroscopy Fiber – Optic Probe for Medical Applications (FOPS 3D)

Daniel Khankin[1,2], Shlomo Mark[1,2] and Shaul Mordechai[3]
[1]*Negev Monte Carlo Research Center (NMCRC), Sami Shamoon College of Engineering (SCE), Bialik/Basel Sts. Beer Sheva, 84100,*
[2]*Software Engineering Department, Sami Shamoon College of Engineering (SCE), Bialik/Basel Sts. Beer Sheva, 84100,*
[3]*Department of Physics, Ben-Gurion University, Beer-Sheva 84105, Israel*

1. Introduction

Fiber-optics evanescent wave spectroscopy has become a common technique for IR absorbance spectroscopy. Evanescent waves are formed when waves travelling in a medium undergo total internal reflection, which is the basis for the attenuated total reflectance (ATR) sampling technique [1,2]. Evanescent waves decrease exponentially as they propagates further away into the sample. Optical fibers which are transparent in the mid - IR are used as the ATR elements. The more reflections which cause the evanescent fields, the more efficient will be the measurement. Hence the curvature of the fiber and the radius of the uncladded part of the fiber, which brought in contact with the sample, play an important role in the efficiency of the measurement.

In this work, we describe a simulation tool (FOPS 3D) which can simulate full three dimensional geometrical structure of the fiber and the propagation of the light beam through the fiber. The simulation tool has been developed as a two iteration process of three steps each: alpha, beta, and release. The first iteration was a C# module (NMCRC-FEWs) [3] serving as an independent confirmation tool. After a "Software Test Plan", "Description", and "Report", the program moved (second iteration) to Java platform (FOPS 3D) and passed all the testing phases (requirements, design, program installation and regression testing). In addition, the FOPS 3D program favorably passed a black-box testing phase process of validation and verification.

This application tool has the facility to freely bend the fiber, what gives the possibility to create any possible curvature folded fiber. Folding the fiber increases the number of beam hits in the uncladded part by slowing down the beam's propagation. A second feature of the tool is the possibility to change the radius of the uncladded part individually, specifically decreasing the radius relative to the fiber's radius, which increases the number of beam hits in the uncladded section. In addition, the fiber can be deformed and clay modeled, what gives the possibility to create different alternative geometrical shapes and inspecting their efficiency as ATR elements [2,3,4].

The simulation tool uses Monte Carlo methods for different parts of the simulation. There are two kinds of light emitters, an isotropic emitter and a Gaussian distribution oriented emitter. The simulation history is defined as a light beam, which hits the uncladded part and successfully travels through the fiber up to the light sensor. The number of successful histories is an estimator for the efficiency of the simulated fiber shape. The unbiased mean value of hits in successful histories is used for calculating the Fresnel transmission coefficients [1] being the absorption property of the simulated shape.

Thus, we first computed the relation between the radius of the uncladded part and the resultant absorption value. In order to find the most efficient geometrical shape, we then computed the relation between different folded fiber slopes with a constant radius of the uncladded section and the deduced absorption values.

The software engineering process for creating a simulation product is designed to systematically lead us from an initial conception of what the software is meant to do, to an implementation that correctly meets the objectives assigned to it [5].

When preparing or acquiring software for the simulation of fiber evanescent wave spectroscopy (FOPS 3D) processes, software engineering practices are invoked to force the software developer to recognize and confront issues before errors become embedded in a software product that does not work as a result. The preparation of software simulating a process begins with a problem to be solved, an environment representing the world in which the problem is to be formulated, a collection of stakeholders representing the diverse interests in the problem and successive reformulations of the problem as it moves from an imprecise "real world" form, to the resulting software product.

Developing a simulation tool invokes us to create a mathematical model for the process, a real - life or hypothetical situation in order to estimate its characteristics or solve problems in terms of the model. By changing states or variables of the model, we can predict the behavior of the system. With the advancement of computers and the improvement in ease of programming languages, computer simulation became a useful part of modeling systems, in variety of fields. In this article we present a simulation tool for optimizing fiber-optic probe structure for use in evanescent wave spectroscopy.

Evanescent wave spectroscopy is a very useful technique for inspecting and examining the properties of materials, mostly in the IR range. Due to the attenuated total reflection phenomenon, a ray which is completely reflected within the medium leaves an evanescent wave on the interface between the medium and an adjacent sample. The more reflections in the fiber, the more evanescent waves would be created, hence more signal will be absorbed. It is known that spectra of benign lesions and malignant cancerous regions have biochemical differences [2]. Thus, fiber evanescent wave spectroscopy is applied in biomedical skin diagnosis.

An important factor is the utilization of the spectroscopic method. Fiber wave spectroscopy is intensified if the absorbance of the fiber is increased. There are two ways to accomplish this. First it is possible to taper the untapped part of the fiber. It was investigated by [3] and by [4], who provided a correlation between the absorbance and the thickness of the untapped part. In other words, we would like to find the optimal width, d, of the untapped part.

Secondly, it's possible to bend the fiber about the untapped part. This action will make it harder for the light beam to progress and will make more hits in the untapped part, which will create more evanescent waves, thus increasing the absorption intensity. Briefly, we would like to find the optimal bending angle of the fiber with some constant width.

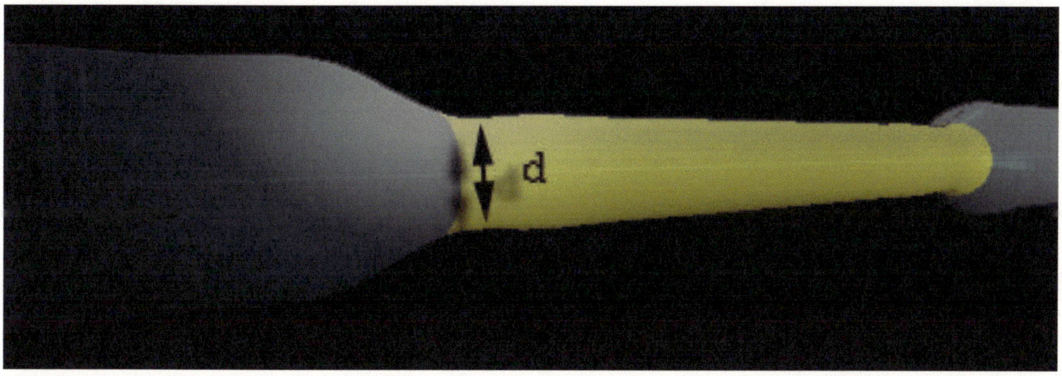

Fig. 1.

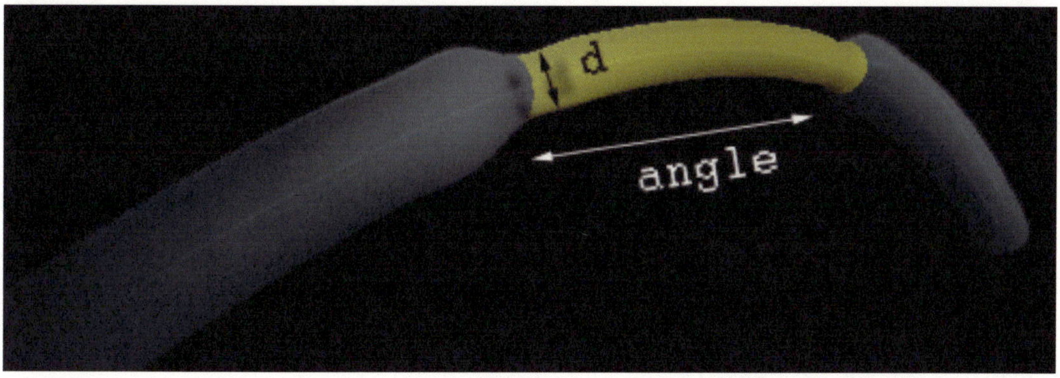

Fig. 2.

2. System description

The whole system consists of the simulated fiber, with properties such as the length, radius, reflection coefficients, and curvature radius of the midsection that can be set by user. There's an infrared simulated source, which emits rays according to a radial Gaussian distribution, uniform distribution and isotropous distribution.

The tool will simulate the advancement of the light beam through the fiber. The simulation will be based on Monte Carlo methods. Monte Carlo methods have been successfully applied in Chemistry, Physics, Medicine, or prediction of realistic behavior of an industrial system. The Monte Carlo methods approach, while simulating physical phenomena, is to create very large samples of random occurrences to recreate the dynamics of a system.

The purpose of the simulation is to measure the utilization of certain fiber geometry configuration. The simulation will estimate the probability of rays to successfully pass through the fiber in current geometry.

3. Physical background

The principle application of fiber evanescent wave spectroscopy in use is an IR source emits rays into a flexible optical fiber focused by a microscope objective. The radiation exits at the distal end of the fiber into an FTIR detector. The cladding of the middle section to be applied to the region of interest is removed and immersed in a fluid. The taper is conical, narrowing down to a thinner cylindrical midsection, with index of refraction of the core n_1, the liquid index of refraction n_2, and n_{cl} of the cladding. To describe and sampling each incoming ray we need the radial distance r and angle θ relative to the z axis. When r is a Gaussian distribution for a beam waist given by [8]:

$$I(r) = I_0 e^{-8r^2/r_0^2} \tag{1}$$

r_0 is the radius of the laser aperture and I_0 is the irradiance at the center of the aperture.
The incidence angles of the rays must be less than $\theta_{cl} = \sin^{-1}(\sqrt{n_1^2 - n_{cl}^2})$ when θ_{cl} is the critical angle of the cladded section, and sampled from the angular distribution that given by [9]

$$P(\theta) \propto \begin{cases} \sin\theta / \cos^3\theta & \theta < \theta_{crl} \\ 0 & \theta \geq \theta_{crl} \end{cases} \tag{2}$$

According to the Beer-Lambert Law The transmitted power P(z) along a fiber is given by

$$P(z) = P_0 e^{-\gamma z} \tag{3}$$

Where P_0 is the power at the input face of the fiber, and γ is the effective evanescent absorption coefficient (varies for different orientations of the ray), which obey [10]:

$$\gamma(\theta) = \frac{\alpha \lambda n_2 \cos\theta \cot\theta}{2\pi r n_1^2 \cos^2\theta_c \sqrt{(\sin^2\theta - \sin^2\theta_c)}} \tag{4}$$

Where θ_c is the critical angle of the unclad section:

$$\theta_{cl} = \sin^{-1}\left(\sqrt{n_1^2 - n_{cl}^2}\right) \tag{5}$$

And α is the bulk specific absorption coefficient of the cladding material at the given wavelength λ [11]

$$\alpha = A e^{-\gamma v / v_0} \tag{6}$$

v is the optical wavenumber (1/λ) and A, γ, and v_0 are constants given in data tables [12].
For a simple tube of constant radius, $\gamma(\theta)$ can be computed by integration of Equation 4 over the power distribution of Equation 2. This is very difficult and inapplicable in a condition where the incidence angles change at each collision with the interfacing surface, especially when we use a non-point source emitted rays. Thus, in our Monte Carlo approach we have used Ruddy's equation [10]

$$\gamma = NT \tag{7}$$

where N is the number of reflections per unit length and T is the Fresnel transmission coefficient for an evanescent wave, which, for any angle θ_z relative to the core axis, is:

$$T(\theta_z) = \frac{\alpha \lambda n_2 \sin\theta_z}{\pi n_1^2 \sin^2\theta_c \sqrt{(\cos^2\theta_z - \cos^2\theta_c)}} \tag{8}$$

Where,

$$\theta_c = \cos^{-1}(n_2 / n_1)$$

is the complementary critical angle.
These formulas apply only to rays above the critical angle. The conical section, however, reflects many incident rays below the critical angle. In these cases, the ray is quickly attenuated completely, as the Fresnel power coefficient for rays not completely reflected is:

$$\begin{aligned}\frac{I_r}{I_0} &= \frac{(n_1\cos\theta_1 - n_2\cos\theta_2)^2}{(n_1\cos\theta_1 + n_2\cos\theta_2)^2} \\ &+ \frac{(n_2\cos\theta_1 - n_1\cos\theta_2)^2}{(n_1\cos\theta_2 + n_2\cos\theta_1)^2}\end{aligned} \tag{8}$$

Where, I_r is the intensity of the reflected ray and I_0 of the incident ray.
In the Monte Carlo simulation, rays are fired into the fiber according to the radial and angular distributions of Equations 1 and 2, respectively.
The ray movement is defined by five variables: Three Cartesian coordinate - to define the particle location, and two angles defining the direction of movement, or alternatively using three Cartesian coordinate and the projection on each axis. In order to define the new location we define three variables:

1. Location, defined by the vector $\vec{r}$, when $\vec{r} = (x_{old}, y_{old}, z_{old})$
2. Direction of movement $\vec{u}$, when $\vec{u} = (u_{in}, v_{in}, w_{in}) = (\sin\theta\cos\phi, \sin\theta\sin\phi, \cos\theta)$ where the angles θ, ϕ defined relative to the Z.
3. Distance to the geometric boundary ds.

Thus, $\vec{r} = \vec{r} + \vec{u}\cdot ds$, when $\vec{r} = (x_{new}, y_{new}, z_{new})$, therefore

$$\begin{aligned}x_{new} &= x_{old} + u_{in}\cdot ds \\ y_{new} &= y_{old} + v_{in}\cdot ds \\ z_{new} &= z_{old} + w_{in}\cdot ds\end{aligned}$$

At the geometric boundary we get changes in the direction, and the new directions are defined by new scattering angles Θ, Φ.
In order to define the new direction we have to use the operator

$$\Re = \begin{pmatrix} \cos\theta\cos\phi & -\sin\phi & \sin\theta\cos\phi \\ \cos\theta\sin\phi & \cos\phi & \sin\theta\sin\phi \\ -\sin\theta & 0 & \cos\theta \end{pmatrix}$$

Therefore the new projections are

$$(u_{new}, v_{new}, w_{new})$$

$$\begin{aligned}u_{new} &= u_{old}\cdot\cos\Theta + \sin\Theta\cdot(w_{old}\cdot\cos\Phi\cos\phi - \sin\Phi\sin\phi) \\ v_{new} &= w_{old}\cdot\cos\Theta + \sin\Theta\cdot(w_{old}\cdot\cos\Phi\sin\phi + \sin\Phi cos\phi) \\ w_{new} &= v_{old}\cdot\cos\Theta - \sin\Theta\cdot(\sin\theta\cdot\cos\Phi)\end{aligned}$$

The simulation process is based on realization of the beam movement in a three dimensional virtual fiber. We outline the Monte Carlo approach to fiber evanescent wave spectroscopy by firing rays according to a given distribution into an optical fiber with a ROI (the unclad section) and ended with a detector. In the Monte Carlo tool we modeled the absorbance at each point of reflection, and the net absorption of the ROI - if θ is above the critical angle of the unclad section, the ray is discarded; otherwise, the number of collisions encountered within the unclad section are counted and multiplied by γ/α to provide its absorbance "weight". This is averaged over a large amount of rays fired (histories) into the fiber to yield the average relative absorbance.

4. Development process

The development process is a very important aspect, especially in heavy computational applications. In addition to the common problems inherent in software development, this simulation tool goes under the category of scientific software. Scientific software is addressed towards scientific computations [7]. The purpose of which is usually some reconstruction or prediction of phenomena or process from science. It is also another way to study a phenomena besides theory and experiment. Scientific software is susceptible to complex scientific loads. Furthermore, it requires a knowledgeable user, who should know how to use and operate the software. Consequently, he should also understand the input for the software and the output. One more important requirement is a knowledgeable tester. Person, who is responsible for testing the software, obviously should also be aware to the mathematical models being used. The software engineering process for creating a simulation product is meant to systematically lead us from an initial conception of what the software is meant to do, to an implementation that correctly meets the objectives assigned to it [5]. In the initial step of the software engineering process, project initiation document, difficulties could be seen. It is very unclear what exactly has to be done, and how the simulation tool has to work. Proceeding to the software requirement specifications document (SRS) didn't solve the issues. It's very unclear what exactly the client wants, for the reason that the user has strong knowledge in physics, usually, as opposed to the developer. The developer may understand what the client says, and understand the formulae but he doesn't grasp their exact meaning, and the conclusions they predict. On the other hand, the client is not thoroughly knowledgeable about constraints and difficulties the developer has. Some of them are very significant, such as floating point precision, round off errors, parallel computations, running time, and complexity of implementing algorithm. They may constitute to correct working of application or vice versa be the reason for failure. It's like a big gap between the developer and the client, two separated worlds. One understands the words of the other but doesn't understand their supposed meaning. Hence, different approach must be taken. Specifically, the Agile software development methodology was chosen to be the basis for working on the project. Short on words, agile methodology governs important rules. The whole task must be broken into small units with minimal planning. Each unit development involves full software development cycle. Contact with the client on daily basis, preferably face to face over documents. Collaborative work with the customer (doesn't has to be the client). Secondly, test driven development methodology should be incorporated (TDD). TDD states, that the test cases should be created first, and only afterwards codes the functionality which will pass the test case. Code requirements must be defined before writing the code. The tests will contain assertions that either true or false. Since the whole work was broken into small units, Black Box testing was easily adapted.

Taking an external perspective of the test object, which is one unit of work, to derive test cases. Tests are usually functional, treating the unit as black box with no knowledge of internal structure. Tests determine correct output on valid or invalid input. FOPS3D was developed on Java, for portability of the application and independence of floating point calculations in hardware. Furthermore, for the developer to waste less time on memory managements and generic algorithms development, what could be in the case of using C++. The software was developed under the requirements and conditions of Object Oriented Analysis Design and Programming with particular attention to practical techniques such as UML (Unified Modeling Language) diagramming and design patterns. The use of iterative design, parallel development and high modularity all enhance maintain ability, ease of verification and code reusability. To ensure a high quality program and improve reliability, FOPS3D has passed all the software testing and verification phases and methods - requirement phase testing, design phase testing, program phase testing, automated black box testing, walkthrough, and white box testing. The last verification came when the results showed agreement with previous experimental and with the analytical calculations. After we achieved those agreements we could say that FOPS3D present a powerful tool for analyzing Fiber-Optics probe, where detailed experiments are too cumbersome to undertake.

5. Development characterization

The simulation tool was developed in Java language, utilizing object oriented and event driven concepts of the language. Furthermore, with the help of Java standard API, it was possible to concentrate on the mathematical model and development of the simulation tool itself using the native abstract data structures and collections which are part of the Java platform. The graphics was programmed using OpenGL API, without decreasing the portability of Java. The computations of the fiber's surfaces and geometrical structure, and of the ray beam advancement and collision, were distributed among multiple threads, in order to achieve maximal CPU utilization.

6. Application structure

The program is categorized into logical packages subdivision. There are a total of five packages:

Package Name	*Package Description*
common	Contains objects, data structures and interfaces used through the application.
forms	Contains GUI elements.
graphics	Contains graphic objects, and the rendering engine.
math	Contains the mathematical model for fiber construction, mathematical
root	Application loader.

The fiber entity is represented with the help of two data structures contained in two classes. The 'Fiber' class and the 'FiberPart' class which composes the Fiber. The 'FiberPart' class represents the smallest section of the fiber. There, all fiber parts are connected among themselves to construct the whole fiber. In order to implement the geometrical elasticity effect, the fiber was uniquely designed. Among the central axis, control points were positioned, and an interpolation was made to pass a curve through those control points. The fiber surface is built around this curve. This gives the possibility to bend the fiber. As soon as the user moves one of the control points, the curve is re-interpolated and the fiber's surface is rebuilt. On the fiber's surface different control points are placed. With the same principle, another curve is passed through those control points. This curve sets every fiber part's shape, by determining the radius of every fiber part independently. By moving the exterior control points, the radius of the fiber parts is altered appropriately, what gives the possibility to freely model the fiber's geometrical structure.

The ray is implemented by the 'Ray' class. The ray class samples the initial emission angles, and performs the computation for ray movement and collisions.

During the simulation process, no graphics are displayed in the sake of centralizing all CPU time on simulation computations.

Those are the main classes of the simulation application:

Fiber

Fiber class which is responsible for the fiber structure, and holds all the data structures which combine the fiber. In addition, the visual representation of the fiber is implemented in this class.

FiberPart

It's a data structure which hierarchically combines the fiber, and holds the normal vectors to the fiber's surface. This data structure plays an essential part in the simulation's computations.

Ray

Class which holds the entire ray beam data regarding of its spatial position points and its visual representation.

RayWorker

Worker class which is responsible for the calculation of the advancement and reflections of a ray beam. For each ray the calculations is performed on different thread.

FiberSurfaceWorker

Worker class which is responsible for the mathematical model of the fiber, the calculation and recalculation of fiber surface and shape as the user performs deformation of the fiber's surface and bends it. The calculation of the fiber's shape is done on different thread.

SimulationEngine

The engine of the simulation application, the engine connects all different parts of the simulation and responsible for the whole procedure of the simulation.

The visual and the computational modules are isolated from each other and controlled by the simulation unit.

7. Simulation results

The simulation ran for different tapered midsection radii and different bending angles while the midsection's radius is constant. For every different setting of fiber, the simulation ran for 1,000,000 histories or for $\rho \leq 0.1$. The midsection type for both simulations was radial and the results were compared with the results from [3].

The first results are when the fiber is not bent, and the simulation ran for different midsection radii while the radius of the fiber is constant.

Those results are in accordance with those presented in [3], where tapped midsection was used. It's possible to see that the results are slightly different, because of the different

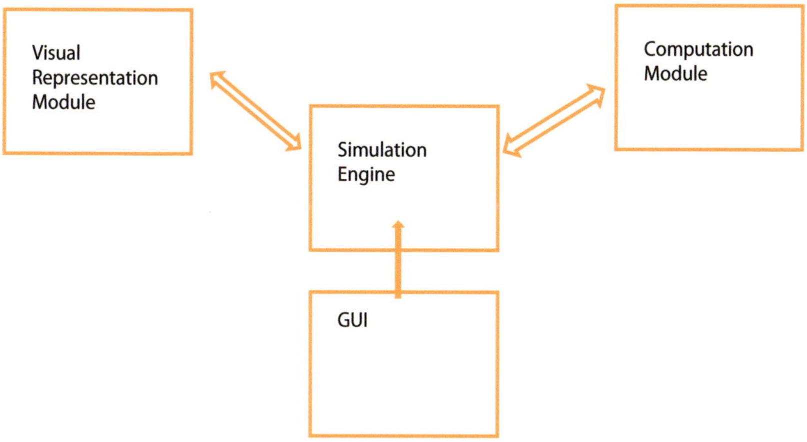

Fig. 3.

midsections used in the simulation. Thus, our results clearly indicate that using thinner tapered midsection radii may increase the absorbance intensity dramatically and improve spectral signal to noise ratio.

Property	Value
Fiber radius	0.9mm
Midsection radius	0.2mm - 0.36mm
n_1	1.457
n_2	1.357
Fiber length	10cm
Midsection length	5cm
Histories	1,000,000

The results are shown in Fig. 4.

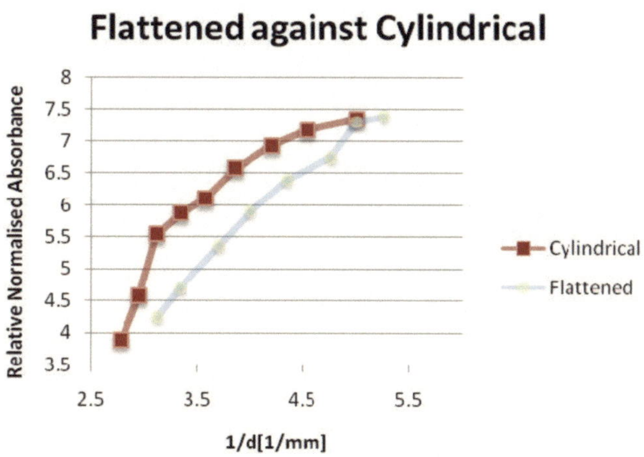

Fig. 4.

Program user manual

1. Popup menu

Right clicking the mouse bring a popup menu, in which the user can select one of the three modes: View Perspective Change, Bend Fiber, Deform Fiber.

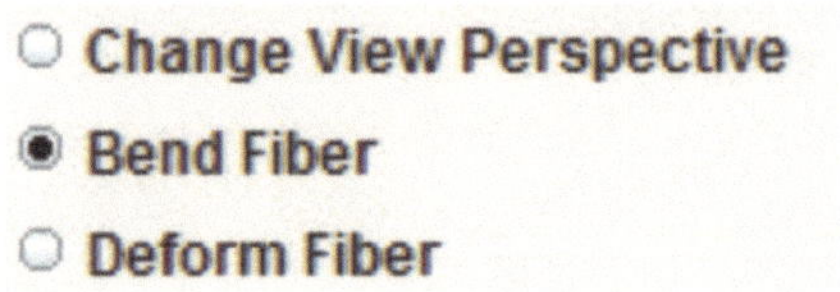

1.1 Perspective Change

The fiber being simulated exists in a 3D world, in a right-handed coordinate system, i.e. the negative Z axis points into the screen, the positive Y is pointing up and the positive X axis is pointing right. The user can rotate the viewing position about the X and Y axis and zoom in/out.

1.1.1 Viewpoint rotation

while holding the left mouse button and moving the mouse left or right will rotate the viewing position about the Y-axis accordingly. Moving the mouse up or down will rotate the viewing position about the X axis accordingly.

1.1.2 Zoom In/Out

Using the mouse wheel, the user can zoom in or out. Rotating the wheel forward will zoom in and rotating the wheel backward will zoom out.

1.1.3 Fiber bending

For bending the fiber the user should move the big control points. When the user moves the mouse over one of those control points they will highlight for letting know that they can now be moved. When the control point is highlighted, hold left mouse button to grasp the control point. Moving the mouse will also move the control point causing the fiber to bend itself. There are total four control points for bending the fiber. One at each end of the fiber, and two among the body of the fiber.

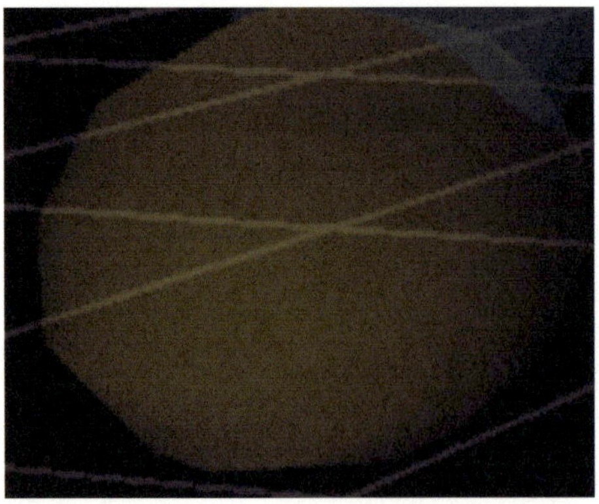

It's possible to bend the fiber from a spinner component and setting the bending angle.

1.1.4 Fiber deformation

For deforming the fiber the user should move the small control points. When the user moves the mouse over the small control point it will highlight for letting know that they can now be moved. When the control point is highlighted, hold left mouse button to grasp the control point. Moving the mouse will also move the control point cause the fiber to deform its shape. The control points are among the top edge of the fiber.

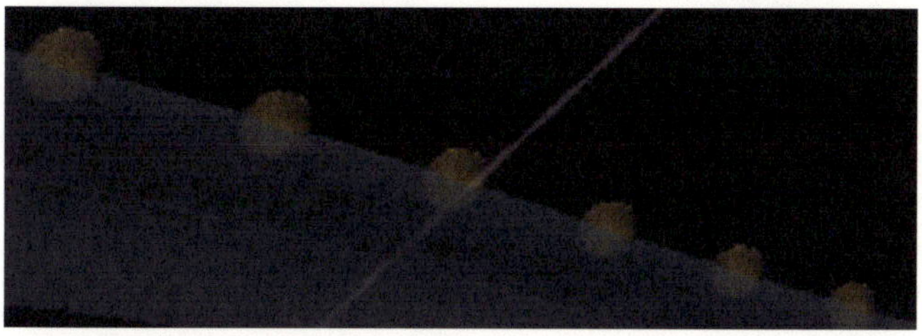

1.1.5 Fiber and/or midsection radius

The fiber's radius can be set using the spinner component.

For midsection part, it's possible to change its radius from a spinner component.

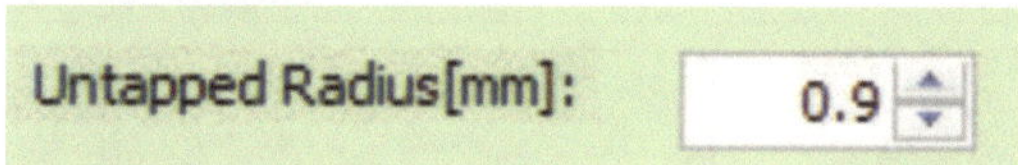

1.2 Simulation properties

1.2.1 Fiber properties

Fiber properties of the simulated fiber which can be changed are:
the refractive index of the cylindrical core n_1, the refractive index of the cladding n_2, the fiber's inner radius, fiber length, untapped part length, untapped part radius.

1.2.2 Simulation properties

The number of iterations (histories) can be changed and its number would be accounted in the overall calculation.

1.2.3 Midsection type

From menu, positioned at the bottom, it's possible to choose whether the midsection is radial or flattened.

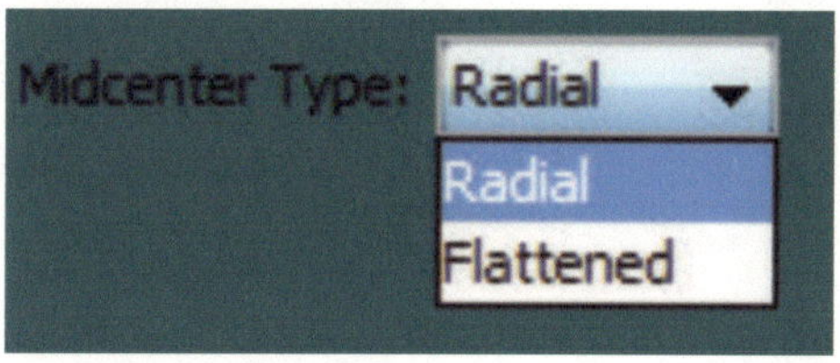

1.3 Selecting untapped part

For the simulation to begin, the untapped part must be set. This can be done in either the fiber bending mode or the fiber deformation mode. While in one of those modes, select a small control point by left clicking with the mouse. Its color will be changed to notify that it's selected. Clicking the right mouse button will bring a popup menu where the user can set whether the selected control point is the left end of the untapped part either the right end.

After setting both left and right ends, the untapped part of the fiber will be marked in different color. Afterwards, the simulation can be started.

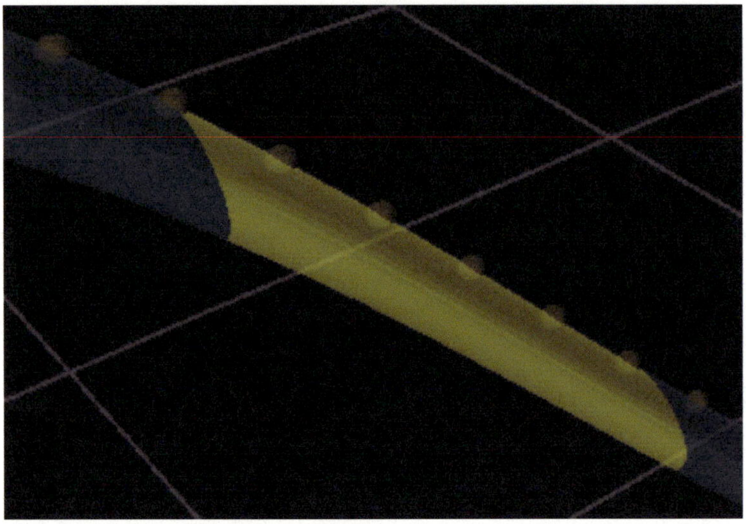

1.4 Starting simulation

Clicking the start button  will start the simulation by sending beams of light, which advancement can be tracked in two types of animation window, 3rd person view and 1st person view. The animation can be turned off to offload the CPU. Before starting the simulation, it's necessary to set the number of iterations.

1.5 Pausing the simulation

The simulation can be paused at any moment by clicking the pause button , and clicking it again will resume.

1.6 Managing rays

On the left part of the screen, a table is shown with every ray which is being in the fiber at the moment and its advancement progress.

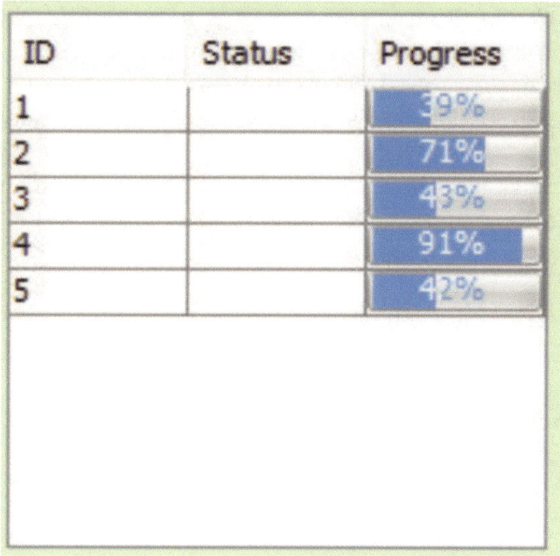

ID	Status	Progress
1		39%
2		71%
3		43%
4		91%
5		42%

8. Reference

A. Messica, A. Greenstein, and A. Katzir, *Theory of fiber – optic evanescent wave spectroscopy and sensors. Applied Optics*, Vol. 35, Issue 13, pp. 2274-2284 (1996).

Y. Raichlin, L. Fel, and A. Katzir. *Evanescent-wave infrared spectroscopy with flattened fibers as sensing elements*. Optics Letters, Vol. 28, Issue 23, pp. 2297-2299 (2003)

Mann MP, Mark S, Raichlin Y, Katzir A and Mordechai S., *Optimization of fiber-optic evanescent wave spectroscopy: a Monte Carlo approach*. Appl Spectrosc. 2009 Sep;63(9):1057-61.

B. D. Gupta, C.D. Singh, A. Sharma, *Fiber optic evanescent field absorption sensor: effect of launching condition and the geometry of the sensing region*, Optical Engineering, Volume 33, No. 6, pgs. 1864-1868, June (1994)

Sommerville, I, Software engineering, 7th edition, New York: Addison Wesley, (2004)

A Dubi, *Monte Carlo Applications in Systems Engineering*: John Wiley & Sons, 2000.

Daniel Khankin, Alan D Solomon, Yosef Shpungin, Yoram Shtoland, and Shlomo Mark, "A Monte Carlo Package for Optimizing Fiber - Optic Evanescent Wave Spectroscopy as a Test Case for Scientific Programming" in *SMRLO*, Beer Sheva, Israel, 2010.

E. Hecht, *Optics*, Addison Wesley 2002

A. W. Snyder and J. D. Love, Optical Waveguide Theory (Chapman and Hall, London, 1983).

V. Ruddy, B. D. MacCraith, and J. A. Murphy, J. Appl. Phys. 67, 10 (1990).

T. F. Deutsch, J. Phys. Chem. Solids 34, 2091 (1973).

R. Waynant and M. Ediger, Electro-Optics Handbook (McGraw Hill Professional, New York, 2000), 2nd ed.

Strain Effects in p-type Devices using Full-Band Monte Carlo Simulations

Valérie Aubry-Fortuna, Karim Huet*, T.T. Trang Nghiêm, Arnaud Bournel, Jérôme Saint-Martin and Philippe Dollfus
Institut d'Électronique Fondamentale, CNRS UMR 8622, Bât. 220, Univ. Paris-Sud, 91405 Orsay cedex,
**now at Excico France, 13-21 quai des Grésillons, Bât. B7, 92230 Gennevilliers, France*

1. Introduction

The particle-based Monte Carlo (MC) technique is acknowledged as a powerful method for accurately describing the carrier transport in semiconductor materials and devices within the semi-classical approximation, i.e. the Boltzmann transport equation (BTE) for the distribution function. It has been developed by many groups to study a wide variety of transport problems in many kinds of devices, to such a point that it is impossible to summarize here the most significant examples of its applications. The accuracy of the semiclassical transport description is then given by the models used for the band structure and the scattering mechanisms.

Hole transport properties in realistic Si devices are particularly affected by the strong anisotropy of the valence band (Thomson et al., 2006), which is further increased by the presence of strain. Analytic approximations fail to describe the valence band structure of Si, and an accurate or « full » description of the energy dispersion is then needed to describe hole transport correctly. In this work, the valence band structure is calculated thanks to a stress-dependent 30-band *k.p* model (Rideau et al., 2006). With this accurate valence band description, « Full-Band » Monte Carlo simulation becomes an appropriate tool to study various (unstrained or strained) p-type devices. Beyond the description of the model in Section 2, we show here two typical examples of application of the full-band Monte simulator to strain effects in p-type devices.

In Section 3, the influence of mechanical stress on Double Gate p-MOSFET performance is be investigated. Multiple gate structures are now recognized as promising architectures to overcome short channel effects in nanometer scaled MOSFET. Double Gate MOSFETs (DGMOS) are found to reach the best performance among SOI-based transistors (Saint Martin et al., 2006). In addition, mechanical stress is used as a technological performance booster for CMOS technology. The impact of stress on carrier transport is then of great importance and is both studied experimentally (Huet et al., 2008 ; Suthram et al., 2007) and theoretically (Huet et al., 2008a; Bufler et al., 2008; Pham et al., 2008). In this work, device performance of strained Si p-DGMOS is studied considering uniform biaxial and uniaxial stresses in the channel. The effect of strain is analyzed *via* some of the main usual figures of merit for device comparison: on-state and off-state currents, subthreshold slope and intrinsic gate delay.

In Section 4, the giant piezoresistance effect is investigated in p-type silicon. The piezoresistance is defined as the change in electrical resistance under the effect of mechanical stress (Smith, 1954). Recently, an unexpected giant piezoresistance effect has been demonstrated experimentally in p-type Si nanowires (He & Yang, 2006). It could be used to achieve high performance MEMS sensors. High piezoelectric coefficients (up to about 3500×10^{-11} Pa^{-1}) were obtained for structures of high resistivity (i.e. lightly doped) and small diameter. It opens the way to the design and implementation of very small piezoresistive sensors, 5 to 10 times smaller than current MEMS components, with performance at least equal or even superior to those of the state of art. Some studies have attempted to explain the origin of this giant piezoresistance effect (Cao, 2008; Nakamura, 2009) which is not fully understood yet at the microscopic level. Hence, the theoretical understanding of this phenomenon by means of accurate simulation is of practical importance.

2. Monte Carlo and *k.p* models

2.1 Band structure calculations

Ab initio methods, such as the density functional theory, allow calculating the bandstructure from first principles (without any fitting parameters) to the price of large computational resources. More efficient semi empirical methods, involving fitting parameters, such as empirical pseudo-potentials (EPM), tight-binding (TB) or *k.p*, are more commonly used. The *k.p* method is based on the perturbation theory and some symmetry considerations (Rideau et al., 2006; Luttinger & Kohn, 1955, Cardona & Pollak, 1966; Richard et al., 2004). For a periodical lattice, the wave functions Φ_{nk} can be expressed in a periodical Bloch function basis (u_{nk}):

$$\Phi_{nk} = \exp(i\mathbf{k}.\mathbf{r})\, u_{nk}(\mathbf{r}) \tag{1}$$

where n is the band number, **k** the reciprocal lattice vector and **r** the real space position vector of the atoms.

Using Bloch theorem and assuming the eigenfunctions (wave functions) and eigenvalues (energies) at state **k** = 0 are known, the Schrödinger equation writes:

$$H_k u_{nk} = \left(H_0 + \frac{\hbar}{m_0}\mathbf{k}.\mathbf{p} + \frac{\hbar^2 |\mathbf{k}|^2}{2m_0} \right) u_{nk} = E_{nk} u_{nk} \tag{2}$$

where H_0 is the Hamiltonian at **k** = 0, m_0 the free carrier mass, **p** the carrier momentum and E_{nk} the energy associated with carrier wave vector **k** and band n.

The Hamiltonian H is projected on a truncated basis, here a given number N of the Zinc-Blende Γ-centered Bloch functions, and the resulting matrix is diagonalized to obtain the eigenenergies and wave functions at **k** for the N bands. Adding spin-orbit interaction gives a better description of the bandstructure but doubles the size of H. The matrix elements of H depend on interband coupling parameters and eigenenergies at **k** = 0. The empirical parameters used are the band gap and known effective masses around specific **k**-points. The accuracy and the **k**-space range of validity of the resulting bandstructure depend on the number of bands taken into account (i.e. the number of Bloch functions of the truncated basis). When "full-zone" *k.p* methods are considered, including up to 30 bands or more with spin-orbit coupling as done in this work, a great number of interband coupling parameters is needed. Due to the lack of experimental data, they are determined by comparison to ab initio calculations. To include mechanical stress in the calculation, the other band methods (EPM, TB) treat the strained crystal as a new system. However, taking strain into account in the *k.p* formalism, as first introduced by Bir and Pikus (Bir & Pikus, 1974), is straightforward using correctly adjusted deformation potentials (Rideau at al., 2006).

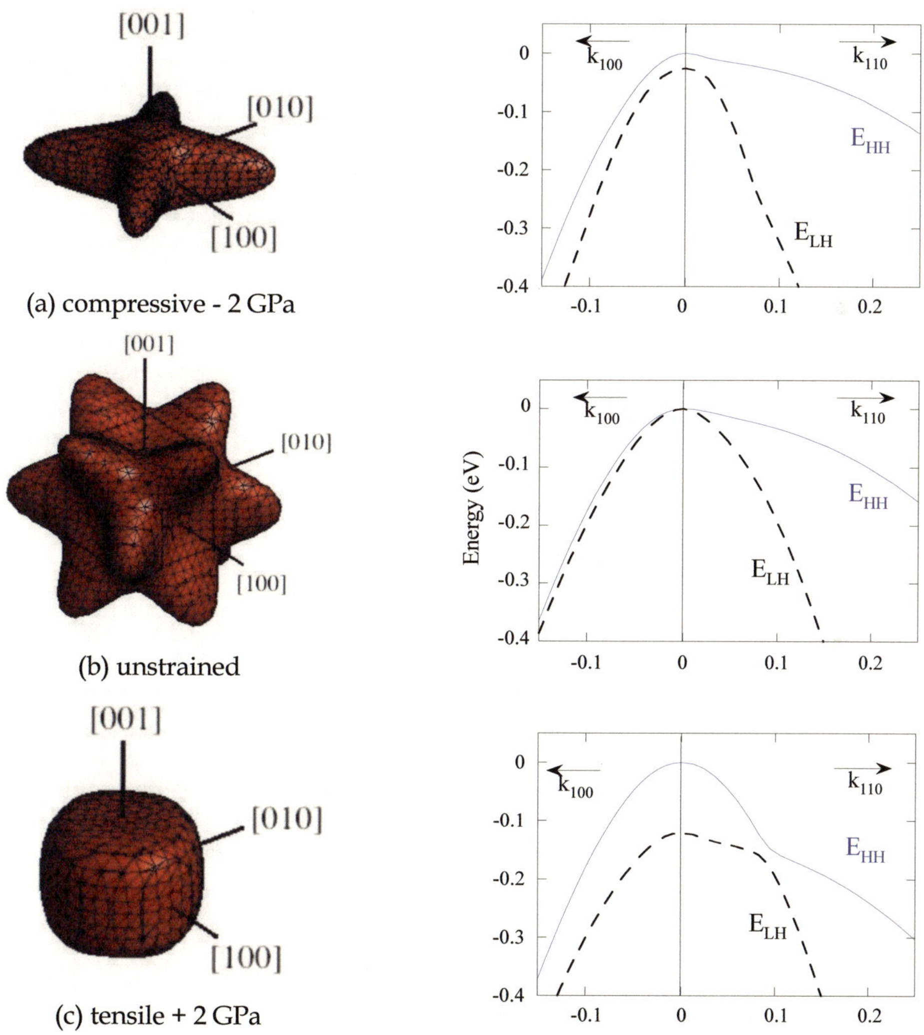

Fig. 1. Si bandstructures obtained using 30 band *k.p* method with and without strain. On the left: constant energy surface at 40 meV from band edge for the 1st hole band (heavy holes). On the right: corresponding E(k) (eV) in [100] and [110] directions for the 1st (HH) and 2nd (LH) bands. (a) Compressive strain - 2 GPa, (b) unstrained, (c) tensile strain + 2 GPa.

The influence of biaxial strain can be seen on Fig. 1. For unstrained Si, the "heavy hole" (HH) band (hereafter called the 1st band) shape is very anisotropic and the "light hole" (LH) band (hereafter called the 2nd band) shape is more isotropic. Under strain, the degeneracy at the Γ point is lifted. For compressive strain, the nature of the bands is similar to the unstrained case. For tensile strain, the nature of the bands is inverted at low energy and returns to the unstrained case shape at higher energies. For the 2nd band, the effective mass in the [100] direction does not vary significantly with strain. For the 1st band, it shows a 20% decrease under compressive strain and a 3% decrease under tensile strain.

2.2 Monte Carlo code

MONACO is a self consistent particle MC device simulator (Aubry-Fortuna et al., 2006) coupled with a 2D Poisson equation solver. We consider scattering mechanisms related to elastic acoustic phonons, inelastic optical phonons, ionized impurities and SiO_2/Si surface roughness. The latter is accounted for via an empirical combination of diffusive and specular reflections (50% of diffusive reflections for holes). The Newton propagation equations during free flights are solved numerically with a first order Runge Kutta scheme (Laux & Fischetti, 1991). The anisotropy of the bandstructure is taken into account in the choice of the state after scattering by considering the "local" density of states in reciprocal space as done in (Jungemann et al., 1999).

The phonon scattering rates are energy-dependent and proportional to the density of states calculated from the full bandstructure. The optical phonon energy is 63 meV. The acoustic ($D_{AC}/c_s = 7.72\ 10^{-4}$ eV.m^{-1}.s, c_s being the average sound velocity in bulk Si) and optical ($D_{OP} = 7.1\ 10^{8}$ eV.cm^{-1}) phonon deformation potentials have been slightly adjusted to reproduce the experimental velocity as a function of applied field characteristics of bulk unstrained Si (Ottaviani et al., 1975; Huet et al., 2008b). The impurity scattering rate is calculated using an analytical approximation as in (Aubry-Fortuna et al., 2006).

3. p-DGMOS performance

The typical simulated device characteristics are the following: gate length L_G = 21 nm, channel length L_{ch} = 19 nm, physical gate oxide thickness T_{ox} = 1 nm, Si body thickness T_{Si} = 8 nm, metallic midgap gate material with a workfunction Φ_m = 4.56 eV, supply voltage V_{DD} = 0.9 V. The undoped channel is <100> or <110>-oriented on a (001) wafer. The N+ doping level in the source and drain extensions is 10^{20} cm^{-3} and abrupt doping profiles at source-channel and channel-drain junctions are considered. The source (or drain) access length L_{spac} is 80 nm, which corresponds to a total access resistance of about 230 Ω.cm. The simulations of the devices have been performed considering a uniform biaxial strain in the (100) plane or a uniaxial strain along <110> or <-110>, with stress values ranging from -0.5 GPa (compressive) to +1 GPa (tensile).

3.1 Current-voltage characteristics

Drain current I_D as a function of gate voltage $-V_{GS}$ characteristics at low drain voltage V_{DS} (= -0.05 V) and high V_{DS} (= $-V_{DD}$ = -0.9 V) have been simulated for all devices. The threshold voltage V_T is determined from the $I_D(-V_{GS})$ curves, using the constant current method with I_D = 10 μA/μm as the reference current obtained at low V_{DS} (-0.05 V) and not in saturation (-0.9 V). To clearly evidence the impact of strain, values of the on-state current I_{on} are compared at the same gate overdrive (V_T - V_{GS}), which corresponds exactly to V_{GS} = -0.9 V in the case of unstrained device. Some of the typical $I_D(V_T - V_{GS})$ characteristics at $V_{DS} = 0.9V$ are reported in Fig. 2.

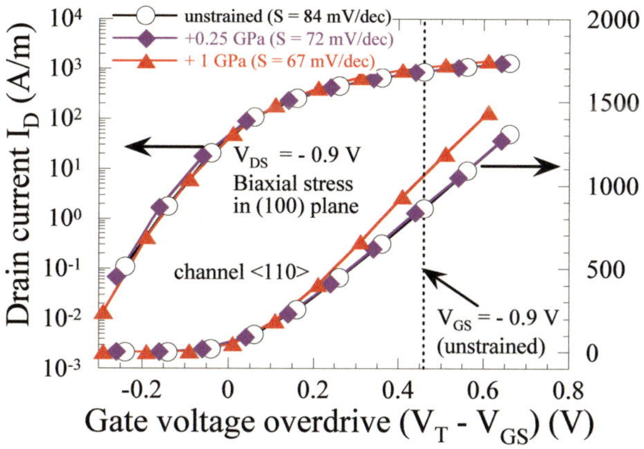

(a)

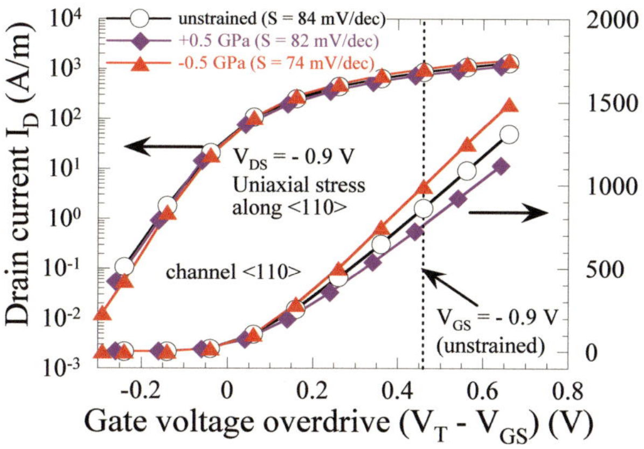

(b)

Fig. 2. $I_D(V_T - V_{GS})$ characteristics at high V_{DS} for: (a) a biaxial stress in the plane (100) and (b) a uniaxial stress along <110>. The channel is oriented along the <110> direction. Values of subthreshold slopes are indicated in the legends.

According to these results and to the other characteristics not shown here, the strain - biaxial or uniaxial, tensile or compressive - is systematically beneficial to the subthreshold slope S, certainly due to strained-induced splitting of valence bands. The lowest improvement of S is obtained for a uniaxial stress along <110> with a <110>-oriented channel: S varies from 84 mV/dec for unstrained to 82 mV/dec for +0.5 GPa (as indicated in Fig. 2b). However, in the case of a biaxial stress with the same channel orientation, S is strongly improved and decreases down to 67 mV/ dec for +1 GPa (see Fig. 2a). In Fig. 3, on-state currents (at the same gate overdrive) are reported as a function of stress for all studied devices. Under a tensile biaxial strain (Fig. 3a), the current I_{on} always increases and the highest values are obtained for a <100>-oriented channel. Indeed, in the unstrained case, due to the anisotropy of the valence band stucture, the heavy hole mass is lower in the <100> direction than in the <110> one, which is advantageous for transport and yields a higher on-state current (see the symbols at 0 GPa in Fig. 3a). Applying a biaxial stress in the plane (001) induces an important degeneracy lift between heavy hole (HH) and light hole (LH) bands (30 meV for +0.5 GPa and ≈ 55 meV for +1 GPa (Huet, 2008)). It also makes the HH band more isotropic with lower HH masses than in the unstrained case, leading to a systematic improvement in current (as it can be seen in Fig. 3a). In addition, quasi-ballistic transport has been previously studied in such devices (Huet et al., 2008b). The hole transport is obviously non-stationary. The fraction of ballistic holes (non-scattered holes when crossing the channel), also called intrinsic ballisticity, is quite low in these devices (about 10%) and remains nearly strain independent (maximum of 12%). The average number of scatterings N without strain is also low (N ≈ 4) and variations with strain is less than 10% (for more details, see (Huet, 2008)). Hence, in the case of a tensile biaxial stress, the drive current variation is mostly due to band curvature improvement.

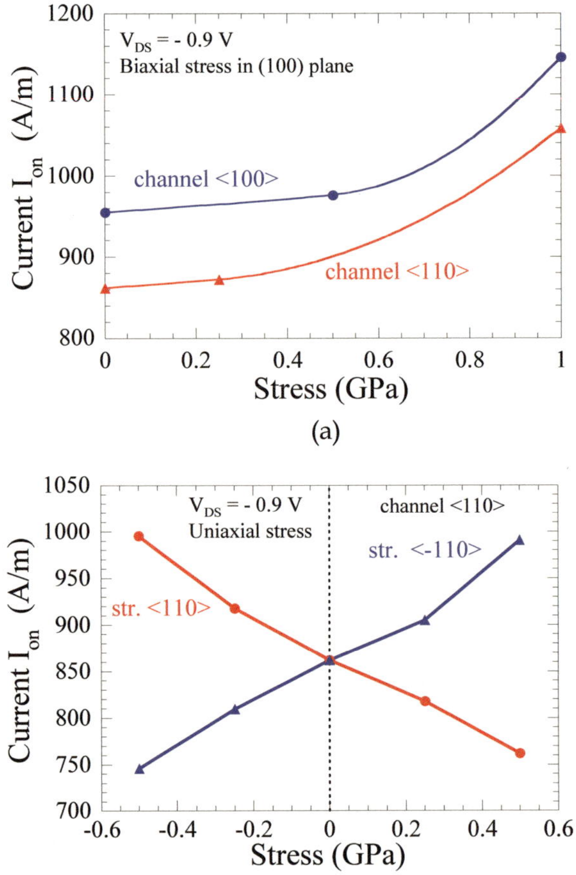

Fig. 3. Variation of the on-state current I_{on} at the same gate overdrive as a function of: (a) biaxial stress in the (100) plane (the two channel directions are represented), and (b) uniaxial stress along <110> and <-110> (the channel direction is <110>).

Under uniaxial stress (Fig. 3b), both compressive stress along <110> (channel direction) and tensile stress along <-110> improve the on-state current. The opposite behaviour is observed under tensile and compressive stress, respectively. The behaviour of the on-state current as a function of stress is also related to hole mass variations. For example, for a uniaxial stress along <110>, the valence band structure remains anisotropic and the compressive stress is the most advantageous case, while it greatly decreases the heavy hole mass in the <110> direction (compared to the tensile one). Concurrently, the compressive stress increases the LH mass, but due to the degeneracy lift (≈ 25 meV for -0.5 GPa), it remains beneficial for hole transport and is then responsible for the I_{on} improvement shown in Fig. 3b. In addition, the number of scattering events has been analyzed. For the same example as previously (uniaxial stress along <110>) and contrary to the biaxial stress case, the intrinsic ballisticity decreases progressively when tuning the stress from -0.5 GPa to +0.5 GPa. As a consequence, the average number of scatterings N varies from ≈ 3.5 to ≈ 6 in the same stress range. The average mean free path of holes, defined as L_{ch}/N, decreases and is then perfectly correlated to the on-state current (Huet, 2008). Unlike the biaxial stress case, the variation of interband phonon scattering with strain (correlated to band splitting) plays a role as important as the band curvatures on the enhancement or degradation of on-state current.

3.2 Comparison with experimental mobilities and currents

On-state current variations have been compared to experimental data (Huet et al., 2008a; Rim et al., 2003) and the results are reported in Fig. 4. For uniaxial stress, variations of mobility and of on-state current are similar though quantitatively different. In addition, for stress along <110>, the calculated I_{on} variations are in fairly good agreement with experimental currents obtained for long channel transistors under bending (Fig. 4b, red diamonds) (Huet et al., 2008a). For biaxial stress, variations of mobility and I_{on} are quite different.

First, as observed in ultra-short devices, on-state current variations are often lower than the long-channel mobility ones (see e.g. (Aubry-Fortuna et al., 2006) for the impact of biaxial strain in bulk n-MOS). Second, using the Kubo-Greenwood formalism (KG), mobilities in inversion layers have been previously calculated and compared to results from wafer bending experiments (Huet et al., 2008a). The experimental trends are correctly reproduced using a 3D hole gas description (KG 3Dk) for uniaxial stresses along <110> and <-110> in <110>-oriented channels, but it was shown that quantum confinement (KG 2Dk) has to be taken into account in the calculation to fit with long-channel mobility variations in the biaxial case. Using full-band simulation including quantization, I-V characteristics have been very recently reported for uniaxially-strained short-channel p-DGMOS but for a high stress value (-2 GPa), which makes the comparison with our results difficult (Pham et al., 2008). The problem of the actual influence of quantization effects in strained transistors is thus still open. Nevertheless, it was shown that, in ultra-short devices with highly non-stationary transport quantum, confinement effects are small except in the case of biaxial tensile strain (Wang et al., 2006) for which bulk band results may overestimate the strain influence. Therefore, the results for biaxial strain should be considered cautiously. It is shown at least that, though it remains a modelling issue, in the early phase of technology development of aggressively scaled DGMOS including strain-engineering, the key figures can be given by standard full-band Monte Carlo simulation.

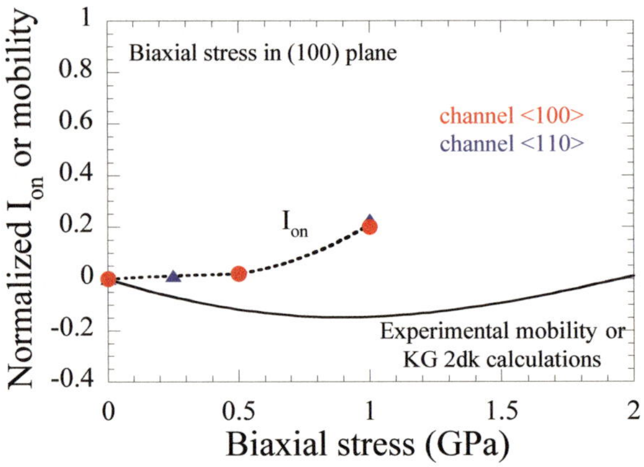

(a)

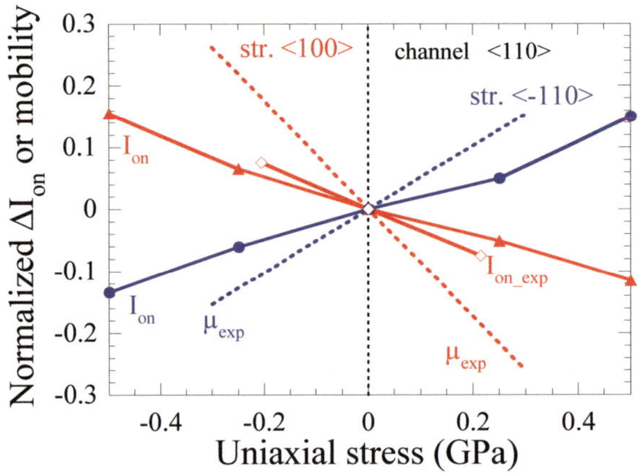

(b)

Fig. 4. Normalized I_{on} (relative to unstrained device) as a function of: (a) biaxial strain with experimental mobility from (Rim et al.,2003) and Kubo-Greenwood 2dk calculations (Huet et al.,2008); and (b) uniaxial strain with experimental mobility and current from (Huet et al., 2008).

3.3 Figures of merit

Intrinsic gate delay $C_G V_{DD}/I_{on}$ and off-state current I_{off} are considered as important figures of merit for CMOS applications. The intrinsic gate capacitance C_G is extracted from the Monte Carlo simulation results, as the derivative of the total charge in the device with respect to V_{GS} at low V_{DS}. The off-state current is determined at the same gate overdrive (V_T - V_{GS}), which corresponds to V_{GS} = 0 V in the case of unstrained device and is then equal to -0.44 V. Intrinsic gate delays and off-currents are often compared to ITRS specifications (ITRS, 2008) which fix the device performance objectives (Fig. 5). Nevertheless, it is to be noted that ITRS delay values are for n-MOSFET and the ones for p-MOSFET should be probably higher.

All off-state currents are lower than the maxima defined by the ITRS specifications. Most of the devices exhibit delay values lower than the LSTP40 specifications, except the two ones that have the lowest on-state currents as shown in Fig. 3b (tensile stress along <110> and compressive stress along <-110>). Performance of the unstrained and strained devices studied here is quite satisfactory according to the 2008 ITRS recommendations. Let's remark that the ITRS access resistance for source and drain access is estimated to be around 180-190 Ω.µm. The total access resistance in our simulations is higher (230 Ω.µm), which leads to under-estimated on-state currents, and then to overestimated delay values.

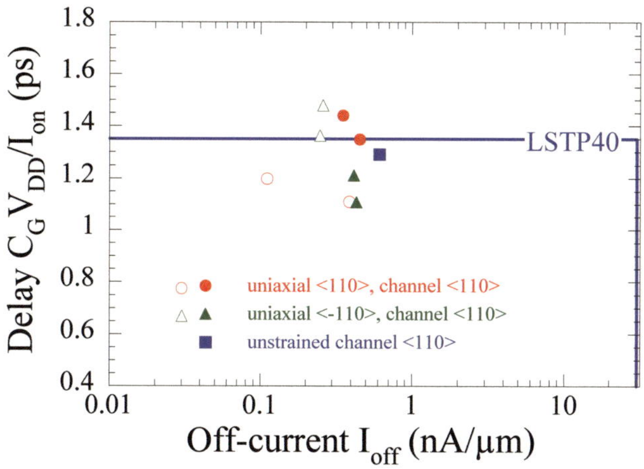

Fig. 5. $C_G V_{DD}/I_{on}$ variations for all uniaxially stressed p-DGMOS. Specifications of ITRS'2008 are also reported. Open symbols are for various compressive stresses and solid ones for various tensile stresses.

4. Giant piezoresistance effect in p-Si nanowires

A nanowire is essentially a three-dimensional object. However, in a first approach to the problem of giant piezoresistance and to reduce the computation time, we restricted ourselves to the consideration of silicon nano-layers of infinite width described in 2D real space. The effect of stress on the surface potential is applied on both sides of the nano-layer. In nanostructures, the size quantization effects may be very important. Several works on silicon nanowires have shown that these effects may influence substantially their electrical and mechanical properties. In particular, for diameter smaller than 20 nm, many physical quantities such as the Young's modulus, the Poisson ratio, the electron and hole effective mass, the band gap and the mobility are strongly affected with respect to bulk data (Leu et al., 2006; Leu et al., 2008; Ghetti et al., 2007). However, in this study, to compare with available experimental data, we simulated structures with minimum thicknesses of 80 nm which is much larger than the critical size mentioned above. Quantization effects are thus safely neglected here.

4.1 Simulated structures

All simulated structures have an effective length of 500 nm. The thickness d is 80 nm, 100 nm or 150 nm. The p-type Si layer is doped to 10^{18} cm^{-3}, 2.7×10^{17} cm^{-3} or 1.49×10^{16} cm^{-3}, which corresponds to a bulk resistivity of 0.044 Ω.cm, 0.1 Ω.cm and 1 Ω.cm, respectively. At both ends, the Si layer is overdoped to 10^{19} cm^{-3} and contacted by an Ohmic contact which injects/ detects the flux of particles flowing through the structure. The uniaxial stress is uniformly applied along the [110] transport direction. The surface potential φ is defined as the difference in the top of valence band between the surface and the volume of the material where neutrality is assumed to be recovered. The effect of stress is modeled along the line proposed by Rowe who investigated the giant piezoresistance effect in Si nanowires using a very simple approach of transport (Rowe, 2008). For a uniaxial stress X, the surface potential φ varies according to the law

$$\frac{d\varphi}{dX} = 0.5 \text{ meV/MPa} \tag{3}$$

considering that for unstrained Si, φ_0 = 0.54 eV. The nano-layers are simulated under a bias voltage of 0.5 V for stresses ranging from 0 to ± 100 MPa applied along the <110> crystallographic direction.

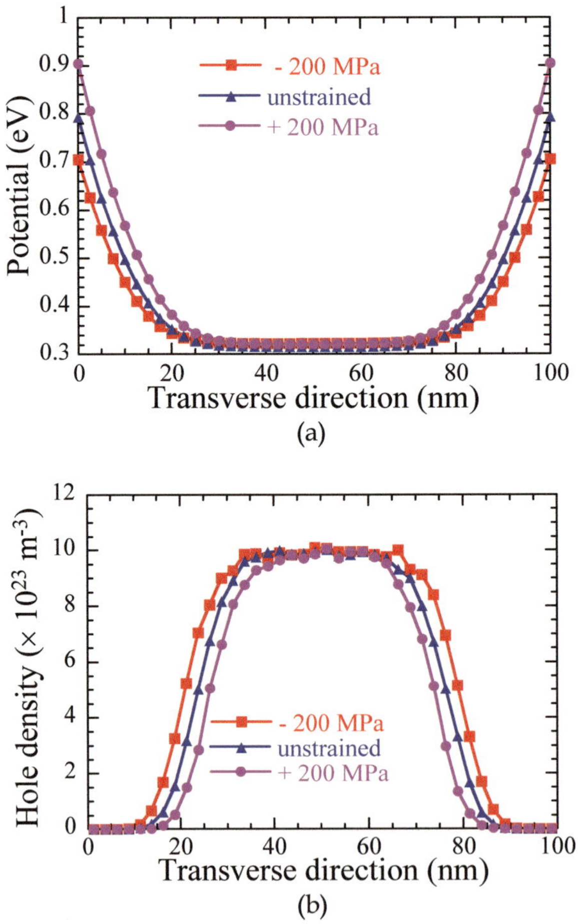

Fig. 6. (a) Potential and (b) hole density profiles in a 100 nm-thick Si layer of resistivity 0.044 Ω.cm for three stress conditions.

4.2 Potential and hole density profiles

According to Eq.(3), the surface potential is reduced under tensile strain while it is enhanced under compressive strain. Fig. 6a shows the typical potential profile in the middle of the device along the transverse direction for three values of stress and a small resistivity $\rho = 0.044\ \Omega$.cm. The stress essentially modulates the depth of the surface depleted region, while the potential in the center of the structure remains unchanged and equal to its equilibrium position. Accordingly, the maximum hole density remains equal to the impurity concentration in the central region. The stress controls only the width of this neutral region, i.e. the conductive area, as shown in Fig. 6b. The situation is different for a higher resistivity $\rho = 0.1\ \Omega$.cm, as shown in Fig. 7. Due to lower doping concentration, the depleted region extends more deeply in the structure and the potential does not fully recover its equilibrium position (Fig. 7a). Accordingly, there is no longer any neutral region in the device and the stress not only controls the width of the conductive area but also the height of the potential barrier for holes and the maximum hole density (Fig. 7b). These results are in qualitative agreement with experimental C-V measurements on nanowires (Garnett et al., 2009).

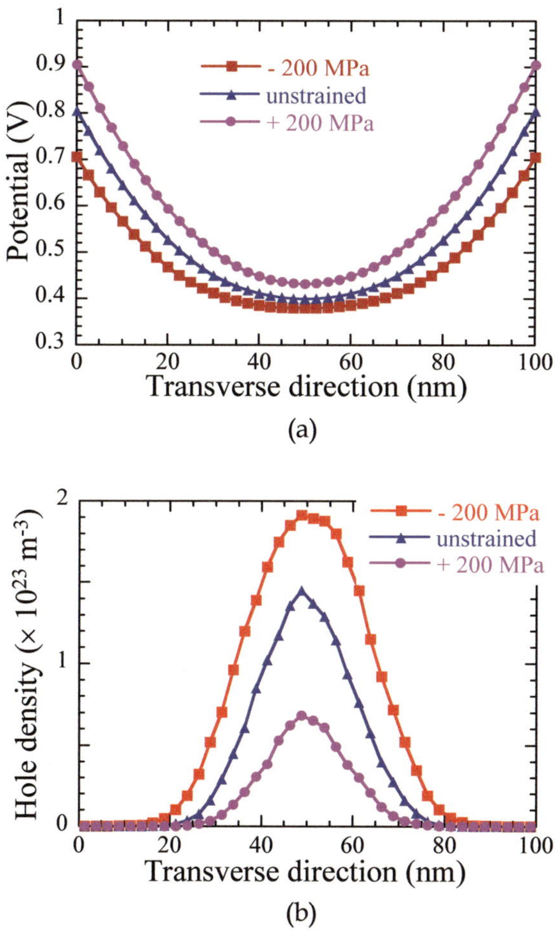

Fig. 7. (a) Potential and (b) hole density profiles in a 100 nm-thick Si layer of resistivity 0.1 Ω.cm for three stress conditions.

4.3 Current and piezoresistive coefficients

Fig. 8 shows the current in the nano-layers as a function of stress for a thickness of 100 nm and various resistivity values. In the low-resistivity structure (ρ = 0.044 Ω.cm), the current is controlled by the width of the conductive area and is linearly dependent on stress. For higher resistivities (ρ = 0.1 Ω.cm and 1 Ω.cm), the current is much smaller and controlled by the height of the potential barrier in the centre of the structure, which leads to a quasi-exponential dependence of the current as a function of stress.

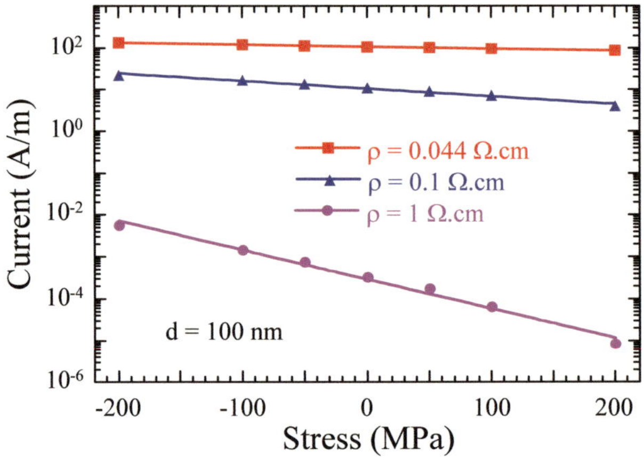

Fig. 8. Current versus stress in nano-layers of 100 nm-thickness for different resistivities. For the two highest resistivities, the solid lines are exponential fitting curves.

To quantify the piezoresistive phenomenon, the most relevant factors of merit are the relative variation of conductivity $\Delta\sigma/\sigma_0$ and the longitudinal piezoresistive coefficient π_1^{σ}. The relative change in conductivity $\Delta\sigma/\sigma_0$ for <110> nanowires is directly deduced from the relative change in conductance $\Delta G/G_0$ using the following equation (see Supplementary Information of (He & Yang, 2006)):

$$\frac{\Delta\sigma}{\sigma_0} = \frac{\Delta G}{G_0} + (0.84 \times 10^{-11}\,\mathrm{Pa}^{-1})X \qquad (4)$$

Some results of relative change in conductivity $\Delta\sigma/\sigma_0$ as a function of stress are shown in Fig. 9 for three thicknesses of 80, 100 and 150 nm and three resistivities of 0.044, 0.1 and 1 Ω.cm.

To separate the contributions of stress-induced changes in the valence band structure and in the surface potential, we first considered the only effect of surface potential modulation while keeping the band structure of unstrained Si. The effect of stress on the band structure was considered in a second stage. The comparison of the solid and dashed lines in Fig. 9a shows that both contributions of the potential surface variation and of the change in bands must be taken into account, though the latter smaller, especially in the case of thin layers. The change in conductivity is not always linear and depends strongly on both the doping level and the thickness (that is to say, the diameter in the case of a nanowire). At a given resistivity, the variation $\Delta\sigma/\sigma_0$ as a function of stress is higher and more nonlinear when reducing the layer thickness. The amplitude of variation of conductivity obviously increases when increasing the resistivity (see Fig. 9b).

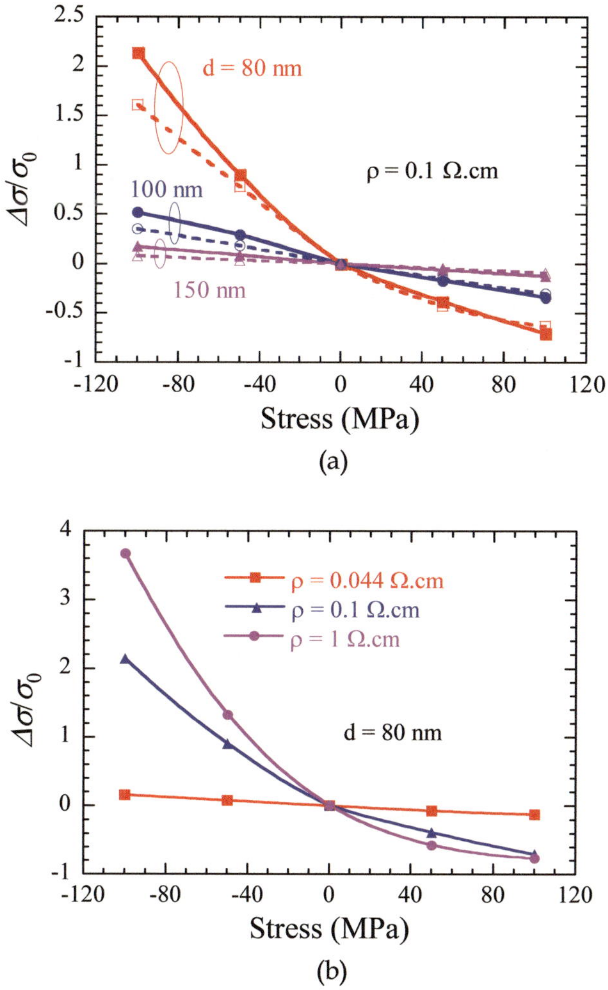

Fig. 9. Relative variation of conductivity $\Delta\sigma/\sigma_0$ as a function of stress for different thicknesses and resistivities, and with (solid lines) or without (dashed lines) change in band-structure. (a) $\rho = 0.1\ \Omega$.cm and (b) d = 80 nm.

For a high resistivity of 1 Ω.cm, the relative change of conductivity as a function of stress seems to be nearly independent of the layer thickness, as shown in Fig. 10. This is probably associated with the fact that the current in a quasi-fully-depleted region is exponentially controlled by the potential barrier whatever the thickness, which makes the stress-dependent change of relative conductivity weakly dependent of thickness. Overall, these results are in agreement with trends observed experimentally by He and Yang for nanowires (He & Yang, 2006).
The corresponding piezoresistive coefficients were calculated around X = 0 using the following expression

$$\pi_1^{\sigma} = \frac{1}{\sigma_0}\frac{d\sigma}{dX} \tag{5}$$

where σ_0 is the conductivity under zero stress.
The resulting piezoresistive coefficients are summarized in Table 1. As expected, they are strongly dependent on the nano-layer thickness and resistivity. A large piezoresistive coefficient of 1750×10^{-11} Pa^{-1} is obtained for a 80 nm thick layer with resistivity of 1 Ω.cm. The results obtained are quite consistent with experimental results of He and Yang (He & Yang, 2006). For instance, they obtained a first order piezoresistive coefficient of 660×10^{-11} Pa^{-1} for a 75 nm thick <110> oriented nanowire with resistivity of 0.3 Ω.cm. The highest piezoresistive coefficient measured was 3100×10^{-11} Pa^{-1} for a nanowire with resistivity of 102 Ω.cm. Accurate MC calculation in such a high resistivity layer is very difficult because of very small current level.

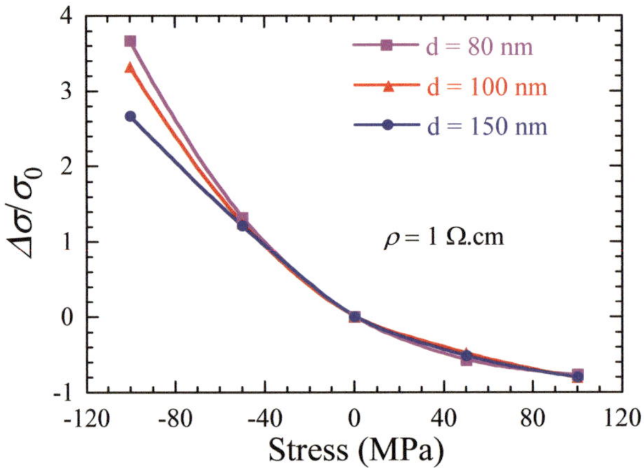

Fig. 10. $\Delta\sigma/\sigma_0$ as a function of stress for the resistivity of 1 Ω.cm and for different thicknesses.

Thickness	Piezoresistive	coefficients	(x 10^{-11} Pa^{-1})
d (nm)	ρ = 0.044 Ω.cm	ρ = 0.1 Ω.cm	ρ = 1 Ω.cm
80	141	842	1750
100	111	420	1589
150	80	149	1564
200	60	105	1505

Table 1. Piezoresistive coefficients in p-type <110>-oriented Si nano-layers for different thicknesses and resistivities.

5. Conclusion

We have presented a full-band particle Monte Carlo simulator based a 30 band *k.p* bandstructure calculation, and two typical applications to p-type silicon nanodevices. First, the advantage of introducing compressive and tensile stresses in ultra-thin p-type Si DGMOS has been discussed in the case of biaxially and uniaxially strained <100> and <110>-oriented channels. The strain-induced improvement of device performance has been highlighted when devices are compared at the same gate overdrive. The performance indicators agree quite well with specifications of the updated 2008 ITRS defined for LSTP40 technology node. Second, we have investigated the giant piezoresistance effect in p-type Si nanolayers of 80 - 150 nm thickness which are assumed to behave as nanowires. This effect is mainly due to the strain-induced modulation of the surface potential. The effective conduction area, wide in the case of compression, becomes much narrower in the case of tensile strain. Taking into account the effects of stress on both the surface potential and the valence band, the relative variation of conductivity depends on both the thickness and the resistivity. Through this modulation, the effect of giant piezoresistance has been shown in p-type nanolayers. The results are in satisfying agreement with experimental data available for nanowires.

In conclusion, it is shown that the full-band Monte Carlo approach of semiclassical simulation semiconductor devices allows us to include all the complexity of the silicon band structures, especially in the presence of strain, and all non stationary transport phenomena which occur in modern nanodevices.

6. References

Aubry-Fortuna, V., Bournel, A.; Dollfus, P. & Galdin-Retailleau, S. (2006). Ultra-short n-MOSFETs with strained Si: device performance and the effect of ballistic transport using Monte Carlo simulation, *Semicond. Sci. Technol.*, Vol. 21, pp. 422-428.

Bir, G.L. & Pikus, G.E. (1974). *Symmetry and Strain-induced Effects in Semiconductors*, Wiley, New York.

Bufler, F.M.; Gautschi, R. & Erlebach, A. (2008). Monte Carlo stress engineering of scaled (110) and (100) bulk pMOSFETs. *IEEE Elect. Dev. Lett.*, Vol. 29, pp. 369-371.

Cardona M. & Pollak F.H. (1966). Energy-band structure of germanium and silicon : the *k.p* method. *Phys. Rev.*, Vol. 142, pp. 530-543.

Garnett, E.C. ; Tseng, Y.-C. ; Khanal, D.R. ; Wu, J. ; Bokor, J. & Yang, P. (2009). Dopant profiling and surface analysis of silicon nanowires using capacitance--voltage measurement. *Nature Nanotech.*, Vol. 4, pp. 311-314.

Ghetti, A.; Carnevale, G. & Rideau, D. (2007). Coupled Mechanical and 3-D Monte Carlo Simulation of Silicon Nanowire MOSFETs. *IEEE Trans. on Nanotech.*, Vol. 6, pp. 659-666.

He, R. & Yang, P. (2006). Giant piezoresistance effect in silicon nanowires. *Nature nanotech.*, Vol. 1, pp. 42-46.

Huet, K; Feraille, M; Rideau, D; Delaware, R.; Aubry-Fortuna, V.; Kasbari, M.; Blayac, S.; Rivero, C.; Bournel, A.; Tavernier, C.; Dollfus, P. & Jaouen, H. (2008a). Experimental and theoretical analysis of transport in uniaxially strained pMOSFETs. *Proceedings of the ESSDERC'2008*, pp. 234-237, Edimburg (United Kingdom), 15-19 september.

Huet, K. (2008). Modeling of carrier transport in sub-65nm CMOS transistors under mechanical stress (text in French), PhD Thesis, Université Paris-Sud, September 29.

Huet, K. ; Chassat, C. ; Nguyen D.-P. ; Galdin-Retailleau, S. ; Bournel, A. & Dollfus, P. (2008b). Full Band Monte Carlo study of ballistic effects in nanometer-scales strained P channel Double Gate MOSFETs. *Physica Status Solidi (c)*, Vol. 5, pp. 43-46.

ITRS (2008). http://www.itrs.net/Links/2008ITRS/Home2008.htm

Jungemann, C. ; Keith, S. ; Bartels, M. & Meinerzhagen, B. (1999). Efficient Full-Band Monte Carlo simulation of silicon devices. *IEICE Trans. Electron.*, Vol. E82-c, p. 870-879.

Laux, S.E. & Fischetti, M.V. (1991). Numerical aspect and implementation of the DAMOCLES Monte Carlo devices. Simulation program, In : *Monte Carlo device simulation: Full Band and Beyond*, K. Hess, pp. 1- 26, Kluwer, Dordrecht.

Leu, P.W. ; Shan, B. & Cho, K. (2006). Surface chemical control of the electronic structure of silicon nanowires: density functional calculations. *Phys. Rev. B*, Vol. 73, pp. 195320-195325.

Leu, P.W ; Svizhenko, A. & Cho, K. (2008). Ab initio calculations of the mechanical and electronic properties of strained Si nanowires. *Phys. Rev. B*, Vol. 77, pp. 235305-235319.

Luttinger, J.M. & Kohn, W. (1955). Motion of electrons and holes in perturbed periodic fields. *Phys. Rev.*, Vol. 97, pp. 869-883.

Ottaviani, G.; Reggiani, L.; Canali, C.; Nava, F. & Alberigi-Quaranta, A. (1975), *Phys. Rev. B*, Vol. 12, pp. 3318-3329.

Pham, A.T.; Jungemann, C.; Meinerzhagen, B. (2008). Deterministic multisubband device simulations for strained double gate PMOSFETs including magnetotransport. *Proceedings of the IEDM Technical Digest*, pp. 895-898, San Francisco (USA), 15-17 december.

Richard, S.; Aniel, F. & and Fishman, G. (2004). Energy-band structure of Ge, Si and GaAs. *Phys. Rev. B*, Vol. 70, p. 235204-235206.

Rideau, D.; Feraille, M.; Ciampolini, L.; Minondo, M.; Tavernier, C.; Jaouen, H. & Ghetti A. (2006). Strained Si, Ge and $Si_{1-x}Ge_x$ alloys modeled with a first-principles-optimized full-zone *k.p* method. *Phys. Rev. B*, Vol. 74, pp. 195208-195227.

Rim, K.; Chan, K.; Shi, L & al. (2003). Fabrication and mobility characteristics of ultra-thin strained Si directly on insulator (SSDOI) MOSFETs. *Proceedings of the IEDM Technical Digest*, pp. 311-314, Washington DC (USA), 8-10 december.

Rowe, A. C. H. (2008). Silicon nanowire feel the pinch. *Nature Nanotech.*, Vol. 3, pp. 311-312.

Saint Martin, J.; Bournel, A.; Dollfus, P. (2006). Comparison of multiple-gate MOSFET architectures using Monte Carlo simulation. *Solid-State Electr.*, Vol. 50, pp. 94-101.

Smith, C. S. (1954). Piezoresistance effect in germanium and silicon. *Phys. Rev.*, Vol. 94, pp 42-49.

Suthram, S; Ziegert, J.C.; Nishida, T. & Thomson, S.E (2007). Piezoresistance coefficients of (100) Silicon nMOSFETs measured at low ans high ($\approx$ 1.5 GPa) channel stress. *IEEE Elect. Dev. Lett.*, Vol. 28, pp. 58-61.

Thompson, S.E.; Guangyu, S.; Youn Sung, C. & Nishida, T. (2006). Uniaxial-process-induced strained-Si: extending the CMOS roadmap. *IEEE Trans. Electron Dev*, Vol. 53, pp. 1010-1020.

Wang, E.X. ; Matagne, P. ; Shifren, L. ; Obradovic, B. ; Kotlyar, R. ; Cea, S. ; Stettler, M. & Giles, M.D. (2006). Physics of hole transport in strained Silicon MOSFET inversion layers. *IEEE Trans. on Electron Devices*, Vol. 53, pp. 1840-1851.

21

Utilizing Monte Carlo Simulation for Valuation: the Case of Barrier Options under Stochastic Interest Rates

Snorre Lindset
Trondheim Business School
Norway

1. Introduction

In this chapter we propose a Monte Carlo approach for pricing barrier options when analytical pricing formulas are unavailable. Barrier options are among the most commonly used options in the financial market and our approach should therefore be of interest. Based on numerical examples presented in the chapter, it seems likely that our approach reduces the computation time by a factor between 236,000 and 94,000,000.[1] To put this in perspective, assume we have a computer that uses one second to estimate the price using our proposed pricing algorithm. To obtain comparable price estimates using standard Monte Carlo simulations would require a computation time between three days and three years!

Plain vanilla put and call options give the owner the right to sell or buy an asset at a pre specified price at some future point in time. Barrier options are either of knock-out or knock-in type. If the price of the underlying asset crosses some barrier H, a knock-out option becomes worthless, i.e., the option contract is canceled. For a knock-in option the option is invoked when the underlying asset crosses the barrier. Thus, a knock-in option expires worthless if the price of the underlying asset never crosses the barrier during the option's life.

Analytical pricing formulas for barrier options are readily available when the value of the underlying asset follows a geometric Brownian motion and interest rates are deterministic. Here we have in mind a situation where the underlying asset follows a process that precludes the derivation of an analytical pricing formula for the option. In particular we focus on the situation where interest rates are stochastic. Other situations could be where the underlying asset follows more complicated price processes.

We propose a Monte Carlo approach to value the barrier option. Estimating the market value of barrier options by Monte Carlo simulations is know to be rather time consuming (see e.g., Broadie et al. (1997)). First, a relatively high number of simulations is needed in order to reduce the standard error of the price estimates. Second, since the barrier option is path-dependent, the whole price path for the underlying asset is needed to determine whether the barrier H has been crossed or not. Approximating the price path with few monitoring points, results in biased estimates. In fact, somewhat surprisingly many monitoring points is needed to get unbiased price estimates. Both these facts make estimation of barrier option

[1] Using other parameter values will change these factors, but we think they give a reasonable picture of the merits of our simulation approach.

prices by Monte Carlo simulation very computational intensive. Our simulation approach *simultaneously* handles these two issues. We exploit the analytical pricing formula for the option when the underlying asset follows a geometric Brownian motion and interest rates are deterministic, and include this price as a control variate in the simulations. This gives a significant reduction in the number of simulations needed to get estimates with a given level of the standard error. Also, and more important, by including the control variate the number of monitoring points needed to reduce the problem with biased estimates is considerably reduced. These two effects make the proposed Monte Carlo approach highly efficient. It is also easy to implement. Related use of the control variate technique for Asian options is considered in Fu et al. (1998) and for different price processes by Lindset & Lund (2007).

The chapter is organized as follows: In section 2 we present the economic set-up. In section 3 a short description of barrier options is given. The simulation approach is described in section 4, while the barrier option under stochastic interest rates is analyzed in section 5. Numerical examples are given in section 6 and the chapter is concluded in section 7.

2. The economic model and preliminaries

We assume a frictionless financial market with two primary traded assets; a non-dividend paying stock and a money market account.[2] We further assume that there exists a unique equivalent martingale measure Q, also known as the risk-neutral measure. The price dynamics of the stock under the equivalent martingale measure Q are given by[3]

$$dS_t = r_t S_t dt + \boldsymbol{\sigma}(t)^\top S_t d\mathbf{W}_t^Q,$$

where r_t is the short-term interest rate at time t, $\boldsymbol{\sigma}(t)$ is a d-dimensional, possibly time dependent volatility function, $\mathbf{W}_t^Q$ is a standard d-dimensional Brownian motion under the equivalent martingale measure Q, and $^\top$ means transpose. In what follows we let $d = 2$.

It will be convenient to divide the time interval $[0, T]$ into N time periods of equal length. We let time period n be the interval $[t_{n-1}, t_n]$, where in particular $t_0 = 0$ and $t_N = T$. The accumulated log-return on the stock over the future time period $n \in \{1, 2, \ldots, N\}$ is given by

$$\delta_n = \int_{t_{n-1}}^{t_n} \left(r_v - \frac{1}{2} ||\boldsymbol{\sigma}(v)||^2 \right) dv + \int_{t_{n-1}}^{t_n} \boldsymbol{\sigma}(v)^\top d\mathbf{W}_v^Q,$$

where $||\cdot||$ is the Euclidean norm.

Let $f(t,s)$, $t \le s$, be the instantaneous forward rate at time s prevailing at time t. Intuitively, we can think of $f(t,s)$ as the interest rate we can agree upon at time t to be paid on "very short-term" borrowing or received from "very short-term" deposits at time s. Adopting the framework of Heath et al. (1992), we have that the arbitrage free dynamics of the forward rate are given by

$$df(t,s) = \boldsymbol{\sigma}_f(t,s)^\top \int_t^s \boldsymbol{\sigma}_f(t,u) du dt + \boldsymbol{\sigma}_f(t,s)^\top d\mathbf{W}_t^Q,$$

where $\boldsymbol{\sigma}_f(t,s)$ is a time dependent d-dimensional volatility function. The short-term interest rate is obtained by setting $s = t$, i.e., $r_t = f(t,t)$. The money market account is an asset that accrues the short-term interest rate and has the following price dynamics

$$dM_t = r_t M_t dt, \qquad M_0 = 1.$$

[2] Strictly speaking, we also assume that there is a continuum of zero-coupon bonds traded in the market.
[3] Vectors and matrices are written in bold fonts.

Note that the accumulated log-return on the money market account over the future time period n is given by

$$\beta_n = \int_{t_{n-1}}^{t_n} r_v dv = -\ln F(0, t_{n-1}, t_n) + \frac{1}{2}\sigma^2_{\beta_n} + \sum_{k=1}^{n-1} c_{k,n}$$
$$+ \int_0^{t_{n-1}} \Big(\int_{t_{n-1}}^{t_n} \boldsymbol{\sigma}_f(v,u)du \Big)^\top d\mathbf{W}_v + \int_{t_{n-1}}^{t_n} \Big(\int_v^{t_n} \boldsymbol{\sigma}_f(v,u)du \Big)^\top d\mathbf{W}_v,$$

where

$$F(0, t_m, t_n) = \frac{B(0, t_n)}{B(0, t_m)},$$
$$\sigma^2_{\beta_n} = \int_0^{t_{n-1}} || \int_{t_{n-1}}^{t_n} \boldsymbol{\sigma}_f(v,u)du||^2 dv + \int_{t_{n-1}}^{t_n} || \int_v^{t_n} \boldsymbol{\sigma}_f(v,u)du||^2 dv,$$

and

$$c_{m,n} = \int_0^{t_{m-1}} \Big(\int_{t_{m-1}}^{t_m} \boldsymbol{\sigma}_f(v,u)du \Big)^\top \Big(\int_{t_{n-1}}^{t_n} \boldsymbol{\sigma}_f(v,u)du \Big) dv$$
$$+ \int_{t_{m-1}}^{t_m} \Big(\int_v^{t_m} \boldsymbol{\sigma}_f(v,u)du \Big)^\top \Big(\int_{t_{n-1}}^{t_n} \boldsymbol{\sigma}_f(v,u)du \Big) dv.$$

Here $B(t, T)$ is the time t market value of a zero coupon bond maturing at time $T \geq t$ with unit face value, i.e., $B(T, T) = 1$, $\sigma^2_{\beta_n}$ is the variance of β_n, and $c_{m,n}$ is the covariance between β_m and β_n, $1 \leq m < n$.
Future cashflows (defined under the equivalent martingale measure Q) to be received from the options at time T are discounted back to present (time 0) with the discount factor $e^{-\sum_{i=1}^N \beta_i}$.
To obtain numerical results, we need a closer functional specification for the volatility structure. Throughout the chapter we assume that

$$\boldsymbol{\sigma}(t) = \sigma_S \begin{bmatrix} 1 \\ 0 \end{bmatrix}$$

and

$$\boldsymbol{\sigma}_f(v,u) = \sigma e^{-\kappa(u-v)} \begin{bmatrix} \varphi \\ \sqrt{1-\varphi^2} \end{bmatrix},$$

where σ_S, σ, κ, and φ are constants. This specification corresponds to the model of Hull & White (1990), also known as the extended Vasicek (1977) model, and is Gaussian since the volatilities are only time dependent. Here κ is the force at which the short-term interest rate reverts to some long-term mean level.
For technical details, see e.g., Heath et al. (1992) and Amin & Jarrow (1992).

3. Barrier options

There are four types of plain barrier options:

1. down and out option

2. down and in option
3. up and out option
4. up and in option.

In this chapter we have chosen to focus on the first of these; a down and out option, or more precisely, a down and out call. The results we present apply equally well, given appropriate adjustments, for the other three options.

A down and out call is a regular call option with the extra feature that it is knocked out if the value of the underlying stock at some point in time during the option's life crosses the barrier H from above. When the option matures at time T, the payoff of the option is $B_T = \max(S_T - X, 0)\mathbb{I}$, where X is the exercise price and

$$\mathbb{I} = 1 \qquad \text{if} \quad \min_{t \in [0,T]} S_t > H$$

and $\mathbb{I} = 0$ otherwise. Let B_0 be the time zero market value of the barrier option and C_0 the corresponding call value. It is then the case that $B_0 = C_0 - J_0$, where J_0 is the non-negative knock-out discount.[4]

Assuming constant interest rates, the market value of the barrier option can be calculated in closed form. Once we allow for stochastic interest rates, there is, to the best of our knowledge, no known analytical formula for the market value of the option. We therefore turn to numerical methods to estimate the market value. More precisely, we use Monte Carlo simulations.

As is well known in the literature (see e.g., Broadie et al. (1997)), estimating the market value of barrier options by Monte Carlo simulations can be extremely computational intensive. To see if the option is knocked out, and therefore has zero value, requires the entire sample path for the stock price over the option's life time to be observed. By simulation, the best we can do is to have discrete observations of the price path. We can therefore possibly miss observing where the stock price crosses the barrier (at least) twice between two monitoring points. Simulating many stock prices for each price path is more time consuming than simulating few stock prices. However, simulating few stock prices gives a higher probability of missing stock prices that cross the barrier. This results in problems with bias. For a knock-out option, the expected bias in the estimated option price is positive but decreases in the number of monitoring points. In figure 1 we illustrate the relative slow convergence rate in terms of number of monitoring points for the case with deterministic interest rates.[5]

Of course, if we only have one monitoring point (at the maturity date for the option, i.e., at time T), this corresponds to the plain European call option. As we see from figure 1, even 1,000 (10^3) and 10,000 (10^4) monitoring points lead to some bias.

4. The simulation procedure

Under the equivalent martingale measure Q, the stock price at time t_n, $n \in \{1, 2, \ldots, N\}$ is given by

$$S_{t_n} = S_{t_{n-1}} e^{\delta_n}.$$

[4] Expressions for B_0, C_0, and J_0 can be found in books on option pricing, for instance in Musiela & Rutkowski (1997).

[5] The calculations are performed using Ox, see e.g., Doornik (1999).

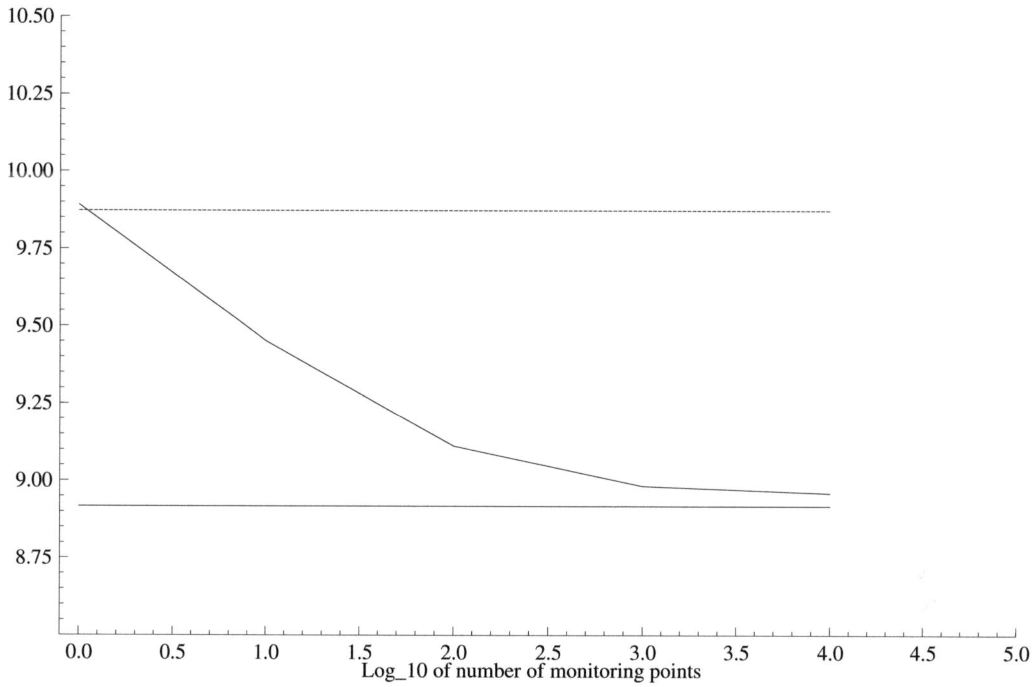

Fig. 1. The figure shows the estimated market value of the barrier option for different number of monitoring points when interest rates are deterministic (downward sloping line). The upper straight line shows the market value of the corresponding European option, while the lower straight line shows the market value of the barrier option (both estimated with analytical pricing formulas). Parameter values are: $S_0 = 100$, $X = 95$, $H = 90$, $r = 0.05$, $\sigma = 0.2$, and $T = 0.5$, where X is the exercise price and H is the knock out barrier. The prices are estimated using 1,000,000 simulations.

Notice that the log-return on the stock in period n can be written as

$$\delta_n = \underbrace{\beta_n}_{a_n} \underbrace{- \frac{1}{2}\int_{t_{n-1}}^{t_n} ||\boldsymbol{\sigma}(v)||^2 dv + \int_{t_{n-1}}^{t_n} \boldsymbol{\sigma}(v)^\top d\mathbf{W}_v}_{b_n}.$$

Both a_n and b_n are random variables with Gaussian distributions. In order to simulate price paths for the stock and the discount factor, we *simultaneously* simulate all the $2N$ random variables a_n and b_n, $n \in \{1, 2, \dots, N\}$. To this end, we first calculate the variance-covariance matrix, $\boldsymbol{\Sigma}$, for the $2N$ variables and Cholesky decompose this matrix into a new matrix $\mathbf{A}$, i.e.,

$$\boldsymbol{\Sigma} = \mathbf{A}\mathbf{A}^\top.$$

Each of the variables has a deterministic part that we denote D. We include the $2N$ Ds in a $2N$-dimensional vector $\mathbf{D}$. Finally, letting $\mathbf{R}$ be a vector containing all the random variables, we calculate $\mathbf{R}$ as follows:

$$\mathbf{R} = \mathbf{D} + \mathbf{A}\boldsymbol{\varepsilon},$$

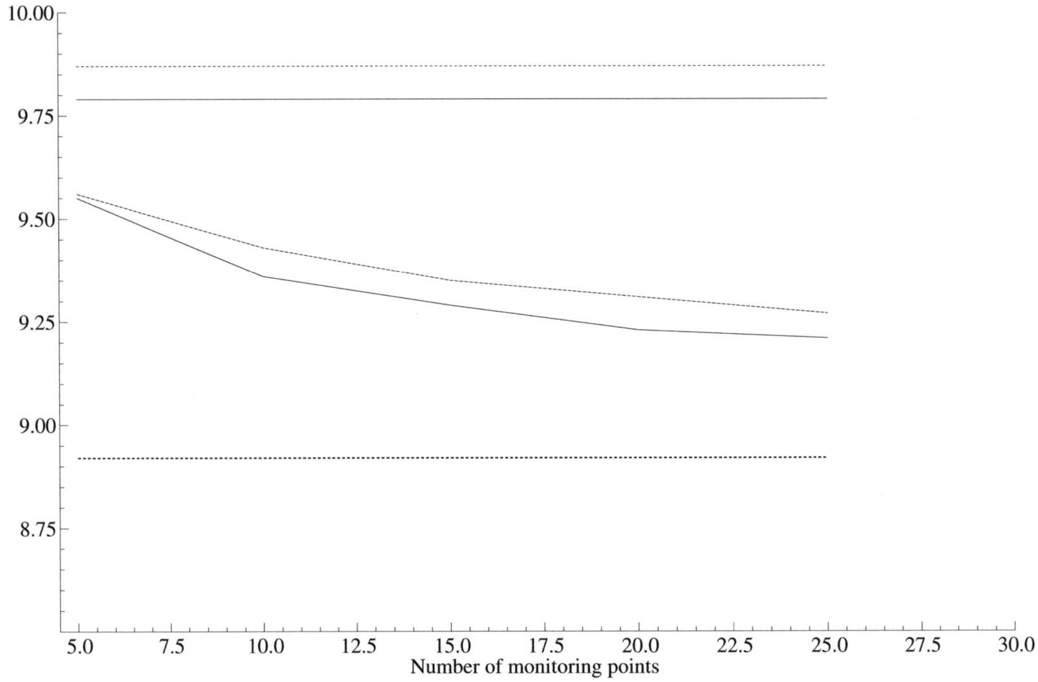

Fig. 2. The figure shows the estimated market value of the barrier option for different number of monitoring points (the two downward sloping lines). The dotted lines are option prices under deterministic interest rates, while the solid lines are under stochastic interest rates. The two straight lines at the top show the market values of European options, while the lower straight line shows the market value of the barrier option (these are estimated by analytical pricing formulas). Parameter values are: $S_0 = 100$, $X = 95$, $H = 90$, $\sigma_S = 0.2$, $\sigma = 0.03$, $\kappa = 0.1$, $\varphi = -0.5$ and $T = 0.5$. The initial term structure of interest rates is assumed flat and equal to 0.05. The prices are estimated using 1,000,000 simulations (they are also reported in table 1).

where ε is a $2N$-dimensional vector with nth element $\varepsilon_n \sim \mathcal{N}(0,1)$ and where ε_n and ε_m, $n \neq m$, are independent.

5. Barrier options and stochastic interest rates

As already mentioned, we are not aware of any analytical pricing formulas for barrier options in the presence of stochastic interest rates, and a simulation approach for estimating the option value can therefore make sense. As figure 2 illustrates, also under stochastic interest rates the convergence rate is slow (note that we do not know the true value of the barrier option). Notice in particular that the differences between the price estimates under deterministic and stochastic interest rates are about the same for different number of monitoring points.

The idea in this chapter is to exploit the analytical pricing formula that exists under deterministic interest rates when we simulate under stochastic interest rates. We use the case with deterministic interest rates as a control variate for the estimation of the option value under stochastic interest rates. We benefit from the control variate in two ways.

First, for realistic parameter values the major part of the uncertainty in the state variable, i.e., in the future stock prices, comes from the b_n-parts, not the a_n-parts. Under deterministic interest rates the a_n-parts are of course non-random. Thus, future stock prices will be highly correlated under stochastic and deterministic interest rates, and so will also the discounted future payoffs from the options be. As we show later in the chapter, this gives a significant reduction in the standard errors of the price estimates.

Second, let g be the option price calculated under deterministic interest rates with the analytical pricing formula. Let further f_i and g_i be the ith simulated *unbiased* discounted payoff of the barrier option under stochastic and deterministic interest rates, respectively. The ith simulated value using the control variate then becomes

$$f_i(b) = f_i - b(g_i - g), \tag{1}$$

for some constant b. From figure 2 we remember that the price estimates behave somewhat similarly under deterministic and stochastic interest rates when the number of monitoring points changes. Let g_i' and f_i' be the ith simulated discounted payoff of the barrier options that are *biased* because too few monitoring points are used. Let further ϕ_i and γ_i be the bias under stochastic and deterministic interest rates, respectively. These biases are defined as $\phi_i = f_i' - f_i$ and $\gamma_i = g_i' - g_i$. The expected biases in the price estimates are $\phi = E_Q[\phi_i]$ and $\gamma = E_Q[\gamma_i]$. Let $f_i'(b)$ be the ith simulated value when using the control variate and the biased values f_i' and g_i'. We then have that

$$\begin{aligned} f_i'(b) &= f_i' - b(g_i' - g) \\ &= (f_i + \phi_i) - b((g_i + \gamma_i) - g) \\ &= f_i - b(g_i - g) + (\phi_i - b\gamma_i). \end{aligned}$$

In the special case where $\phi = b\gamma$, it is clear that $E_Q[f_i'(b)] = E_Q[f_i(b)]$ is an unbiased estimator for the value of the barrier option under stochastic interest rates. It seems difficult to analyze the bias analytically, and we therefore have to rely on numerical calculations. We show by numerical examples that the use of the control variate in the simulations makes it possible to reduce the number of monitoring points. The computation time increases quadratically in the number of monitoring points. Thus, including the control variate in the simulations has the potential to severely reduce the computation time. In figure 3 we illustrate the computation time as a function of the number of monitoring points.

The optimal b (see equation (1)) is usually found by regressing the simulated f_is on the simulated g_is. The optimality criterion is then to minimize the standard error of the price estimate. In our setting, as long as $|\phi - b\gamma| < \phi$, the control variate also helps reduce the problem with bias. The optimal choice of b is now more complicated; one has to balance increased speed because of variance reduction and because of bias reduction. How to balance this must be determined by the user of the algorithm. In this chapter we have for simplicity set $b = 1$.

6. Numerical examples

In this section we present numerical examples illustrating the use of our proposed pricing algorithm. As our base-case we use the following parameter values: $S_0 = 100$, $X = 95$, $H = 90$, $\sigma_S = 0.2$, $\sigma = 0.03$, $\kappa = 0.1$, $\varphi = -0.5$, and $T = 0.5$. The initial term structure of interest rates is assumed flat and equal to 0.05. In table 1 we present the results for the base-case parameters.

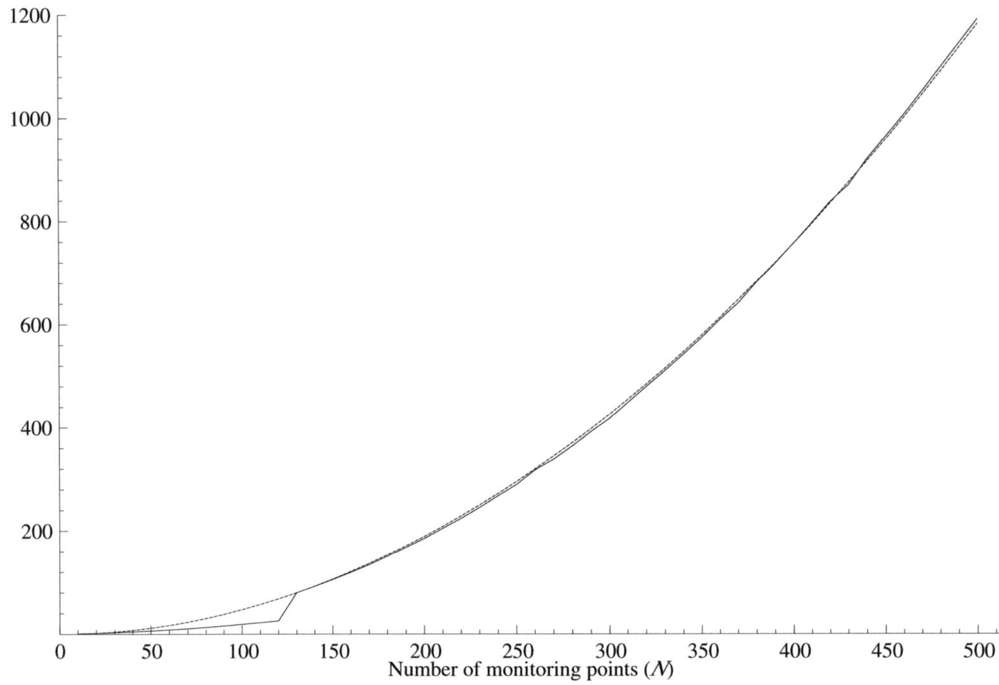

Fig. 3. The figure shows the normalized computation time (ct) for different number of monitoring points (solid line).The computation time for 10 monitoring points is set to one. The dottet line shows the fittet function $ct(N) = 0.004732N^2$ with $R^2 = 0.9995$.

We then change the parameter values that are related to the interest rates (σ (table 2), κ (table 3), and φ (table 4)).

The simulation results in table 1 indicate that in order to obtain estimates with standard errors of the same order of magnitude, we only have to do about 4,000 to 5,000 simulations when including the control variate, compared to 1,000,000 when using standard Monte Carlo simulations.[6] Thus, in terms of standard errors, standard Monte Carlo simulation has about 200 to 250 times higher computation time than when the control variate is included. Furthermore, it seems like we can reduce the number of monitoring points from 500 to 10 or 20 and still obtain about the same price estimates. Keep in mind that we are not able to come up with a good benchmark price to compare our results with. For instance, with $T = 0.5$, the Cholesky decomposition failed for 600 monitoring points. However, given the similarity between the pricing problem under deterministic and stochastic interest rates and the results in figure 1, we may project that to get unbiased price estimates as much as 10,000 or more monitoring points are needed if raw Monte Carlo simulations are performed in the model with stochastic interest rates. When we take into account that the computation time grows quadratically in the number of monitoring points, we estimate that by *not* including the control variate in the simulations increases the computation time by a factor between

[6] The squared ratio of the standard errors are about $(\frac{0.0113}{0.0007})^2 \approx \frac{1,000,000}{4,000}$.

Number of Observation Points	Deterministic Interest Rates		Stochastic Interest Rates		Stochastic Interest Rates Control Variate	
1	9.8727*	–	9.7901*	–	–	–
5	9.5563	(0.01137)	9.5460	(0.01123)	8.9019	(0.00119)
10	9.4273	(0.01140)	9.3626	(0.01127)	8.8438	(0.00078)
15	9.3472	(0.01142)	9.2898	(0.01129)	8.8322	(0.00069)
20	9.3061	(0.01143)	9.2320	(0.01130)	8.8294	(0.00067)
25	9.2688	(0.01143)	9.2096	(0.01133)	8.8279	(0.00067)
100	9.1066	(0.01147)	9.0432	(0.01135)	8.8274	(0.00070)
500	9.0215	(0.01150)	8.9266	(0.01136)	8.8269	(0.00073)
∞	8.9175*	–	–	–	–	–

* Estimated by analytical pricing formula.

Table 1. The table shows price estimates for barrier options for different number of monitoring points for the case with deterministic interest rates, stochastic interest rates, and for our proposed approach using the control variate. Parameter values are: $S_0 = 100$, $X = 95$, $H = 90$, $\sigma_S = 0.2$, $\sigma = 0.03$, $\kappa = 0.1$, $\varphi = -0.5$, and $T = 0.5$. The initial term structure of interest rates is assumed flat and equal to 0.05. The prices are estimated using 1,000,000 simulations. Standard errors are reported in parenthesis.

236,000 and 94,000,000![7] If we only use 5,000 simulations with 10 or 20 monitoring points, the calculations are fast (takes only a fraction of a second).

As we can see from table 2, increasing the interest rate volatility to 0.08, which is much higher than what we observe in most economies, the option prices decrease and the standard errors for the cases where the control variate has been used increase. The explanation for the first observation is that increasing interest rate volatility actually leads to decreased volatility for the return on the stock under the equivalent martingale measure Q. The second observation follows because the stock price under deterministic and stochastic interest rates becomes less correlated. I.e., the interest rate volatility becomes more important. When the price of the two stocks becomes less correlated, the effect of using the control variate decreases and the standard errors therefore increase. Notice that the algorithm still reduces the bias and only using 10 or 20 monitoring points is likely to be sufficient.

By comparing the results in table 1 and table 3 it is clear that doubling the value of the parameter κ from 0.1 to 0.2 has a negligible impact on the price estimates.

Finally, from table 4 we see that by imposing a positive correlation between the stock return and the interest rates (i.e., by setting $\varphi = 0.5$), the option prices under stochastic interest rates increase. The reason is that the overall volatility in the stock return now increases. However, most importantly for our analysis is that the standard errors by including the control variate still are significantly reduced and that we also can use a significantly lower number of monitoring points.

Finally, it should be mentioned that $\sigma = 0.2$ is a low parameter value if the underlying asset is a share of stock. This value would be more typical for a stock index where most of the idiosyncratic risk in individual stock returns is diversified away. By using a higher volatility,

[7] The first number is estimated as $0.004732 \cdot 500^2 \cdot 200 = 236,600$, where the number 200 comes from the variance reduction. The second number assumes that 10,000 monitoring points are needed: $0.004732 \cdot 10,000^2 \cdot 200 = 94,640,000$.

Number of Observation Points	Deterministic Interest Rates		Stochastic Interest Rates		Stochastic Interest Rates Control Variate	
1	9.8727*	–	9.6694*	–	–	–
5	9.5563	(0.01137)	9.4194	(0.01102)	8.7743	(0.00169)
10	9.4273	(0.01140)	9.2313	(0.01105)	8.7149	(0.00146)
15	9.3472	(0.01142)	9.1578	(0.01108)	8.7007	(0.00141)
20	9.3061	(0.01143)	9.0994	(0.01108)	8.6986	(0.00143)
25	9.2688	(0.01143)	9.0765	(0.01112)	8.6950	(0.00143)
100	9.1066	(0.01147)	8.9053	(0.01112)	8.6917	(0.00146)
500	9.0215	(0.01150)	8.7993	(0.01114)	8.6883	(0.00148)
∞	8.9175*	–	–	–	–	–

* Estimated by analytical pricing formula.

Table 2. The table shows price estimates for barrier options for different number of monitoring points for the case with deterministic interest rates, stochastic interest rates, and for our proposed approach using the control variate. Parameter values are: $S_0 = 100$, $X = 95$, $H = 90$, $\sigma_S = 0.2$, $\sigma = 0.08$, $\kappa = 0.1$, $\varphi = -0.5$, and $T = 0.5$. The initial term structure of interest rates is assumed flat and equal to 0.05. The prices are estimated using 1,000,000 simulations. Standard errors are reported in parenthesis.

Number of Observation Points	Deterministic Interest Rates		Stochastic Interest Rates		Stochastic Interest Rates Control Variate	
1	9.8727*	–	9.7914*	–	–	–
5	9.5563	(0.01137)	9.5474	(0.01123)	8.9033	(0.00119)
10	9.4273	(0.01140)	9.3642	(0.01127)	8.8438	(0.00077)
15	9.3472	(0.01142)	9.2913	(0.01129)	8.8340	(0.00068)
20	9.3061	(0.01143)	9.2480	(0.01131)	8.8307	(0.00065)
25	9.2688	(0.01143)	9.1873	(0.01130)	8.8315	(0.00067)
100	9.1066	(0.01147)	9.0417	(0.01133)	8.8297	(0.00071)
500	9.0215	(0.01150)	8.9283	0.01136)	8.8285	(0.00072)
∞	8.9175*	–	–	–	–	–

* Estimated by analytical pricing formula.

Table 3. The table shows price estimates for barrier options for different number of monitoring points for the case with deterministic interest rates, stochastic interest rates, and for our proposed approach using the control variate. Parameter values are: $S_0 = 100$, $X = 95$, $H = 90$, $\sigma_S = 0.2$, $\sigma = 0.03$, $\kappa = 0.2$, $\varphi = -0.5$, and $T = 0.5$. The initial term structure of interest rates is assumed flat and equal to 0.05. The prices are estimated using 1,000,000 simulations. Standard errors are reported in parenthesis.

say 30%-50%, the b_n-parts increase in importance relative to the a_n-parts. Thus, using a higher (and more realistic) volatility benefits the relative merits of the pricing algorithm proposed in this chapter.

Number of Observation Points	Deterministic Interest Rates		Stochastic Interest Rates		Stochastic Interest Rates Control Variate	
1	9.8727*	–	9.9627*	–	–	–
5	9.5563	(0.01137)	9.7303	(0.01153)	9.0806	(0.00118)
10	9.4273	(0.01140)	9.5551	(0.01156)	9.0231	(0.00077)
15	9.3472	(0.01142)	9.4646	(0.01158)	9.0145	(0.00068)
20	9.3061	(0.01143)	9.4283	(0.01160)	9.0130	(0.00065)
25	9.2688	(0.01143)	9.3852	(0.01160)	9.0118	(0.00067)
100	9.1066	(0.01147)	9.2266	(0.01162)	9.0136	(0.00071)
500	9.0215	(0.01150)	9.1236	(0.01164)	9.0147	(0.00072)
∞	8.9175*	–	–	–	–	–

* Estimated by analytical pricing formula.

Table 4. The table shows price estimates for barrier options for different number of monitoring points for the case with deterministic interest rates, stochastic interest rates, and for our proposed approach using the control variate. Parameter values are: $S_0 = 100$, $X = 95$, $H = 90$, $\sigma_S = 0.2$, $\sigma = 0.03$, $\kappa = 0.1$, $\varphi = 0.5$, and $T = 0.5$. The initial term structure of interest rates is assumed flat and equal to 0.05. The prices are estimated using 1,000,000 simulations. Standard errors are reported in parenthesis.

7. Conclusions

We have in this chapter proposed an algorithm for pricing barrier options when analytical pricing formulas are unavailable. We have analyzed the special case where interest rates are stochastic and showed that our approach, compared to standard Monte Carlo simulations, reduces the computation time by a factor of 236,000 to 94,000,000 for realistic parameter values. Although we have focused on the case with stochastic interest rates, the approach we propose should also have potential for being used when the underlying asset follows more complicated price processes. We leave such extensions for future research.

8. References

Amin, K. I. & Jarrow, R. (1992). Pricing options on risky assets in a stochastic interest rate economy, *Mathematical Finance* 2(4): 217–237.

Broadie, M., Glasserman, P. & Kou, S. (1997). A continuity correction for discrete barrier options, *Mathematical Finance* 2(4): 325–348.

Doornik, J. (1999). *Object-Oriented Matrix Programming Using Ox*, Timberlake Consultants Press and Oxford (www.nuff.ox.ac.uk/Users/Doornik), London.

Fu, M. C., Madan, D. B. & Wang, T. (1998). Pricing continuous asian options: a comparison of monte carlo and laplace transform inversion methods, *Journal of Computational Finance* 2(2): 49–74.

Heath, D., Jarrow, R. & Morton, A. (1992). Bond pricing and the term structure of interest rates: A new methodology for contingent claims valuation, *Econometrica* 25(1): 77–106.

Hull, J. & White, A. (1990). Pricing interest-rate-derivative securities, *Review of Financial Studies* 3(4): 573–592.

Lindset, S. & Lund, A.-C. (2007). A technique for reducing discretization bias from monte carlo simulations: Option pricing under stochastic interest rates, *European Journal of Finance* 13(6): 545–564.

Musiela, M. & Rutkowski, M. (1997). *Martingale Methods in Financial Modeling*, Springer Verlag, Berlin Heidelberg.

Vasicek, O. A. (1977). An equilibrium characterization of the term structure, *Journal of Financial Economics* 5(2): 177–188.

22

A rapidly Mixing Monte Carlo Method for the Simulation of Slow Molecular Processes

V. Durmaz, K. Fackeldey, M. Weber
Zuse Institute Berlin
Germany

1. Introduction

Since the middle of the last century, the continously increasing computational power has been adopted to molecular modeling and the simulation of molecular dynamics as well. In this field of research, one is interested in the dynamical behaviour of molecular systems. In contrast to the beginnings when only single or very few atoms could be simulated, the systems under consideration have grown to the size of macromolecules like proteins, DNA, or membrane structures nowadays resulting in high-dimensional conformational spaces. This development is triggered by permanently increasing computational power, the utilization of massively parallel hardware as well as improved algorithms and enhanced molecular force fields, covering chemical and especially biological molecular systems at a progressive rate. Applications basing on molecular modeling help to understand and predict molecular phenomena in various fields of applications providing information on e. g. molecular conformations and recognition, protein folding, drug-design, or binding affinities. Typical fields benefiting from their usage are pharmacy, medicine, chemistry and materials research.

Unfortunately, often the atomistic structure is so complex that a satisfactory mapping of the processes can hardly be realized, due to the large number of atoms and in particular, the difference in time scales. More precisely, for the molecular function of a protein for example, its folding is a key issue. In contrast to this folding event that may last up to several seconds or even minutes, the time step of an ordinary trajectory based molecular simulation is linked to the fastest molecular oscillation which occurs in case of the chemical $H - C$ bond with a time period around few 10^{-15} seconds. Even today, exorbitant computational effort and time need to be invested in order to capture such interesting processes.

2. Atomistic simulations

The molecular simulation methods can be divided into two classes: the deterministic and the stochastic approaches. The first one is also known as the classical molecular dynamcis (MD), which relies on classical mechanics as described by Newton's Equations of motion (e.g. Frenkel & Smit (1996); Griebel et al. (2007)). The latter class is known as Monte Carlo Methods (e.g. Binder & Landau (2000)). Both methods have celebrated a great success in various applications. For an overview, we refer to Leach (2001) and Schlick (2002).

In the forthcoming we will briefly introdcue the molecular dynamics and then give a more detailed introdcution into the Monte Carlo method within its framework. Later on, we will eploit the commonalities between both simulation methods in order to explain the hybrid Monte Carlo method.

2.1 Deterministic molecular simulations

The basic idea of molecular dynamics is to calculate trajectories containing spatial coordinates of atoms evolved in time. Let us assume, a state $x = (q, p) \in \mathbb{R}^{6n}$ of a molecular system with n atoms is given in a $6n$-dimensional phase space. Here, $q \in \Omega \subset \mathbb{R}^{3n}$ and $p \in \Gamma \subset \mathbb{R}^{3n}$ denote the position coordinates in the position space Ω and the momentum cooridnates in the momentum space Γ, respectively. For a classical description of molecular motion with conservative forces, Newton's second law is given by the equation

$$M\ddot{q} = f(q),$$

where $M \in \mathbb{R}^{3n \times 3n}$ is a diagonal matrix of atomic masses, $f(q) \in \mathbb{R}^{3n}$ is a vector of internal and external forces acting on the atoms at position q, and $\ddot{q}$ stands for the acceleration as the second time derivative of q. The total energy of the system under consideration, i.e. the Hamiltonian H is given by

$$H(p, q) = V(q) + K(p), \tag{1}$$

where $K(p) = \frac{1}{2} p^T M^{-1} p$ and $V(q)$ represent the kinetic and the poteintial part, respectively. Since the kinetic part only depends on the momenta and the potential part on the positions only, the Hamiltonian is separable, leading to the following equations of motion:

$$\dot{q} = \frac{\partial H(p,q)}{\partial p} = \frac{\partial K(p)}{\partial p} = M^{-1}p \tag{2a}$$

$$\dot{p} = \frac{\partial H(p,q)}{\partial q} = \frac{\partial V(q)}{\partial q} = -\nabla_q V(q). \tag{2b}$$

Inserting these two time derivatives $\dot{q}$ and $\dot{p}$ into the time derivative of the Hamiltonian

$$\frac{\mathrm{d}H(p,q)}{\mathrm{d}t} = \underbrace{(\nabla_q H)}_{=-\dot{p}}\dot{q} + \underbrace{(\nabla_p H)}_{=\dot{q}}\dot{p} = -\dot{p}\dot{q} + \dot{p}\dot{q} = 0 \tag{3}$$

shows that the total energy according to Hamilton is constant over time, i. e. $H(q(t), q(t)) = H(q(0), q(0))$ for $t \in (-\infty, \infty)$. Time discretization during simulation is achieved by applying a constant step size integrator like the Sörmer-Verlet (Verlet (1967)) or leap-frog (Hockney (1970)) integrator for which the time step size Δt is determined by the shortest oscillation period of bonds in a molecule, namely some femtoseconds. In addition, a time integration for a sampling scheme as represented by Equation (2) has to fulfil certain properties like reversibility and symplecticity. Besides the fact that the time step is confined to a small size, the total time span τ, i.e. the time of the simulation, has to be chosen carefully as well. More precisely, for a given initial state $x(0)$ and a slightly perturbated state $x^*(0)$ it can be shown:

$$\|x(t) - x^*(t)\| \sim \|x(0) - x^*(0)\| \exp(\lambda_{\max} t)$$

which means that the error $\|x(t) - x^*(t)\|$ depends exponentially on the time, where $\lambda_{\max}$ is the maximal Lyapunov characteristic exponent. It has been shown by Deuflhard et al.

(1999), that for molecular dynamics λ_{max} may be very large such that only trajectories of some 10^{-13} seconds are correlated with the initial state. Due to the large λ_{max} value, molecular dynamics is chaotic. However, if one is interested in the probability of rare events during this chaotic process, e. g. protein folding, the deterministic trajectory based approach seems not favourable. Here, we do not focus on these aspects and refer to Leimkuhler & Reich (2004) for details.
Having briefly scetched the idea of the classical molecular dynamics, we now change our point of view to the concept of statistical dynamics and investigate ensembles of molecular systems.

2.2 Statistical molecular simulations

In statistical molecular dynamcis, we are not interested in the movement or speed of each particle but in averaged macroscopic properties of the atoms. The advantage of this approach lies in the fact that many physical properties in which we are interested, like energies, enthalpies and entropies do not depend strongly on a detailed dynamical movement of each particle but on a collection of particles. In other words, we are no longer interested in each particle but in a system of particles and its probability to be in a certain state. In order to describe this state, we need the term "ensemble" which is an imaginary collection of systems described by the same Hamiltonian where each system is in a unique mircoscopic state at any given instant time.
In an (n, V, T)-ensemble, each subsystem, in our example of section 4 it is a single molecule in vacuum, has the same macroscopic properties volume V and temperature T. Furthermore, neither chemical reactions take place nor do particles escape which means that the number n of atoms is also kept constant. The subsystems can only exchange energy with their surroundings and therefore, have different states $x = (q, p)$ to which Boltzmann statistics can be applied. For a detailed derivation of the Boltzmann distribution which is defined as the most probable distribution of states in an (n, V, T)-ensemble and is also called *canonical ensemble* μ_{can}, see Schäfer (1960), pp. 5–11. Via the Hamiltonian $H(\cdot)$, the probability that a molecule attains the state x is

$$\mu_{can}(x) = \frac{1}{Z} \exp(-\beta H(x)),$$

where Z is a corresponding normalization. β is the inverse temperature

$$\beta = \frac{1}{k_B T},$$

where T is measured in Kelvin and $k_B \approx 1.38066 \cdot 10^{-23}\,\mathrm{J\,K^{-1}}$ is the Boltzmann constant.

2.2.1 Partition functions

For separable Hamiltonian functions, the Boltzmann distribution of molecular states $x = (q, p)$ in the canonical ensemble $\mu_{can}(x) = \pi(q)\eta(p)$ has the following splitting into a distribution of momenta and position states:

$$\eta(p) = \frac{1}{Z_p} \exp(-\beta K(p)), \quad \pi(q) = \frac{1}{Z_q} \exp(-\beta V(q)).$$

$\eta(\cdot)$ represents a Gaussian distribution for each of the $3n$ momenta coordinates, because K is a quadratic function with the diagonal matrix M.

Therefore, creating a sequence of momenta numerically (sampling) according to their Boltzmann distribution $\eta(p)$ is simple, see e.g. Allen & Tildesley (1987). The spacial factor $\pi(\cdot)$ is a more complex distribution function. Whereas the exponential function $\exp(-\beta V(q))$ can be computed pointwise, the normalization constant (also denoted as *spatial partition function*[1])

$$Z_q = \int_\Omega \exp(-\beta\, V(q))\, dq \tag{4}$$

is unknown. For a sampling of points $q \in \Omega$ according to a distribution which is known except for a normalization constant, the Metropolis-Hastings algorithm can be applied, see section 3.

2.2.2 Bracket notation

A macroscopic measurement is always carried out for a snapshot of a molecular ensemble, where molecular states are distributed according to the Boltzmann distribution. A spatial observable $\langle A \rangle_\pi$ of a function $A : \Omega \to \mathbb{R}$ in configuration space, e. g. potential energies or torsion angles, is therefore measured as an ensemble mean, i. e. an expectation value

$$\langle A \rangle_\pi = \int_\Omega A(q)\, \pi(q)\, dq, \tag{5}$$

where A is μ-Lebesgue integrable w. r. t. the measure $\mu(dq) := \pi(q)\, dq$. In the following, these bracket notations for observable and inner products will be often used abbreviations.

2.2.3 Importance sampling

In Equation 5 the dimension of the space Ω is proportional to the number of degrees of freedom. The evaluation of this integral leads to a high-dimensional numerical integration problem. Thus, a regular or equidistant grid in the phase space combined with a standard deterministic integration scheme, such as Simpsons rule cannot be used (see Table 1).

Method	Convergene
Trapeziodal	$N^{-2/d}$
Simpson	$N^{-4/d}$
Monte Carlo	$N^{-1/2}$

Table 1. The convergence behaviour of the determinstic quadrature rules (Simpson and Trapezoidal) depend on the dimension: With increasing number of dimension, the convergence rate growth. In contrast, the convergence behavior of the Monte Carlo method does not depend on the dimension

In a Monte Carlo method one solves numerically

$$\int_\Omega g(x) dx \approx \frac{1}{N} \sum_{i=1}^{N} g(x_i).$$

The key issue in a Monte Carlo method, is that the evaluation points $x_1, ..., x_N$ are statistically selected. There are many ways how to distribute the points. If they are distributed uniformly, it is called a simple sampling.

[1] Z_q is a function of temperature, volume and number of particles of an ensemble. For the canonical ensemble Z_q is a constant. The total partition function $Z = Z_q Z_p$ is the key to calculating **all** macroscopic properties of the system.

However, for complex functions like $\pi(q)$, a simple sampling is inappropriate since the uniform distribution of particles might lead to an insufficient reproduction of the function (see center distribution of Fig. 1). Fig. 1 illustrates well that it is not easy to generate a good distribution of particles in a reasonable amount of computer time. In the importance sampling, the integrand is modified in order to yield an expectation of a quantity that varies less than the original integrand over the region of integration. In order to solve Equation (5), one applies Monte Carlo integration methods with an importance sampling routine, i.e.

$$\langle A \rangle_\pi \approx \frac{1}{N} \sum_{i=1}^{N} A(q_i), \quad q_i \propto \pi, \tag{6}$$

where N position states $q_i \in \Omega$ are sampled according to their Boltzmann distribution π. Hence, the expectation value of an observable can be simply approximated by its arithmetic mean. For introductory literature of Monte Carlo integration methods see Hammersley & Handscomb (1964) and Robert & Casella (1999).

Since the major part of the conformational space Ω is physically irrelevant due to high potential energies $V(q)$, only few conformations have a probability substantially larger than zero. Instead of creating independent points q_i, in practice, one starts with a physically relevant position state $q_1 \in \Omega$ and generates further states via a Markov chain

$$q_1 \to q_2 \to \ldots \to q_N. \tag{7}$$

Summing up, both approaches have advantages and disadvantages. In classical molecular dynamics simulations the motion of each individual particle can be described deterministically. However, long simulations are hardly feasible. On the other hand, the statistical molecular simulation is capable of handling large molecular systems but lacks of a trajectory.

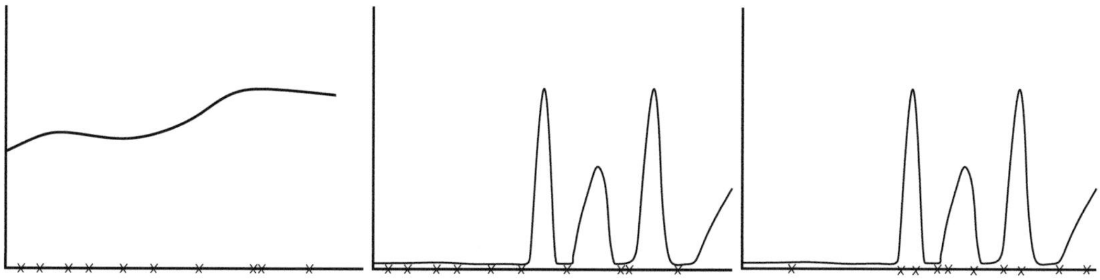

Fig. 1. Left: A simple sampling with a uniformly distributed set of particles fitting a nearly constant function. Center: A simple sampling inappropriate for unconstant distribution functions. Right: A suitable distribution of points well fitting the desired function (importance sampling).

3. Hybrid Monte Carlo method (HMC)

The conclusion of the forgoing section is a motivation to construct a method which profits from either of the two approaches. This has been done in the hybrid Monte Carlo method. Roughly speaking, this method can be seen as a combination of deterministic molecular dynamics combined with stochastic impulses. So far we have elucidated the basic framework of statistical simulations but not their numerical realization in detail. This will be done in the next prargraphs.

3.1 Detailed balance criterion

A sufficient condition for a correct sampling via Monte Carlo Simulation in the situation of Equation 7 is the detailed balance condition with the desired Boltzmann distribution π. This condition holds, if the conditional probability density function $\mathbf{P}(q \rightarrow \widetilde{q})$ for a transition $q \rightarrow \widetilde{q}$ in Equation 7 meets

$$\pi(q)\,\mathbf{P}(q \rightarrow \widetilde{q}) = \pi(\widetilde{q})\,\mathbf{P}(\widetilde{q} \rightarrow q) \tag{8}$$

where the occurrence of a certain position state q in 7 is proportional to te probability $\pi(q)$. Equation 8 describes the thermodynamic equilibrium of a molecular system with two (or more) possible states/conformations q and $\widetilde{q}$. The probability of being in state q and switching over to state $\widetilde{q}$ is equal to the probability for the reverse way. For the sufficient and necessary "balance condition" which is less rigorous than Equation 8, see Manousiouthakis & Deem (1999).

3.2 Metropolis-Hastings algorithm

In the following, we use a Metropolis-Hastings type algorithm (Metropolis et al. (1953)) where the transition probability density function $\mathbf{P}$ in Equation 8 is split into two factors

$$\mathbf{P}(q \rightarrow \widetilde{q}) = \mathbf{P}_{pr}(q \rightarrow \widetilde{q})\,\mathbf{P}_{\text{ac}}(q \rightarrow \widetilde{q}). \tag{9}$$

Here is the corresponding sampling scheme:

- In Equation 9, $\mathbf{P}_{\text{pr}}$ is a proposal probability density function, i.e. the probability that after $q \in \Omega$ a position state $\widetilde{q} \in \Omega$ is proposed as candidate for the next step in the Markov chain (see Equation 7).
- With an acceptance probability of $\mathbf{P}_{\text{ac}}$, the next step in the chain is $\widetilde{q}$, with a probability of $1 - \mathbf{P}_{\text{ac}}$ the step q is repeated in Equation 7. For a numerical realization of the acceptance probability, one computes a uniformly distributed random number $r \in [0,1]$ and accepts $\widetilde{q}$ if $r \leq \mathbf{P}_{\text{ac}}(q \rightarrow \widetilde{q})$.

With Equation 8 a sufficient condition for a correct sampling according to this scheme is:

$$\pi(q)\,\mathbf{P}_{\text{pr}}(q \rightarrow \widetilde{q})\,\mathbf{P}_{\text{ac}}(q \rightarrow \widetilde{q}) = \pi(\widetilde{q})\,\mathbf{P}_{\text{pr}}(\widetilde{q} \rightarrow q)\,\mathbf{P}_{\text{ac}}(\widetilde{q} \rightarrow q).$$

For a given (ergodic) proposal probability density function $\mathbf{P}_{\text{pr}}$, a possible choice for $\mathbf{P}_{\text{ac}}$ satisfying the latter equation is for example the Metropolis dynamics:

$$\mathbf{P}_{\text{ac}}(q \rightarrow \widetilde{q}) = \min\left\{1, \frac{\pi(\widetilde{q})\,\mathbf{P}_{\text{pr}}(\widetilde{q} \rightarrow q)}{\pi(q)\,\mathbf{P}_{\text{pr}}(q \rightarrow \widetilde{q})}\right\}. \tag{10}$$

Metropolis dynamics provides a chain of the form of Equation 9 with minimal asymptotic variance and is therefore the most popular one (see Peskun's theorem in Peskun (1973)).

3.3 Combination of MCMC and MD.

The transition probabilities $\mathbf{P}(q \rightarrow \widetilde{q})$ doesn't need to have any physical meaning in order to meet Equation 8, but for a good acceptance ratio $\mathbf{P}_{\text{ac}}$, a combination of the Metropolis-Hastings algorithm for Markov chain Monte Carlo integration (MCMC) with molecular dynamics simulations (MD) is useful.

Starting in 1980, a variety of hybrid methods have been developed, which take the advantages of both MD and MCMC (Andersen (1980); Duane et al. (1987)). These so-called HMC algorithms where originally developed for quantum chromo-dynamics, but they have been used successfully for condensed-matter systems (Clamp et al. (1994); Forrest & Suter (1994); Gromov & de Pablo (1995); Irbäck (1994); Mehlig et al. (1992)) and also for biomolecular simulations (Fischer et al. (1998); Hansmann et al. (1996); Zhang (1999)). HMC combines the large steps of MD in phase space with the property of MCMC to ensure ergodicity by altering orbits in phase space and to eliminate inaccuracies in the numerical computation of the Hamiltonian dynamics. In the following the HMC method is explained according to Fischer (1997).

3.4 Proposal step

HMC is a Metropolis algorithm, in which the proposal step $q \longrightarrow \tilde{q}$ is based on a molecular dynamics simulation with simulation length τ. To compute $\tilde{q}$ out of a given q, we first determine a start momentum vector $p \in \mathbb{R}^{3n}$, where n is the number of atoms. The start momentum vector is taken from the Boltzmann distribution $\eta(p)$ according to the simulation temperature (see Allen & Tildesley (1987), Section 5.7.2 for algorithmic details). Then, with some numerical integrator a trajectory of total length τ is computed. The starting point is given by (q, p), let the end point be denoted as $(\tilde{q}, \tilde{p}) = \Phi_h^\tau(q, p)$.
Due to determinism in the integration scheme, the probability for a proposition $\mathbf{P}_{\text{pr}}(q \longrightarrow \tilde{q})$ only depends on the choice of the initial momenta p, which is $\mathbf{P}_{\text{pr}}(q \longrightarrow \tilde{q}) \propto \exp(-\beta K(p))$.

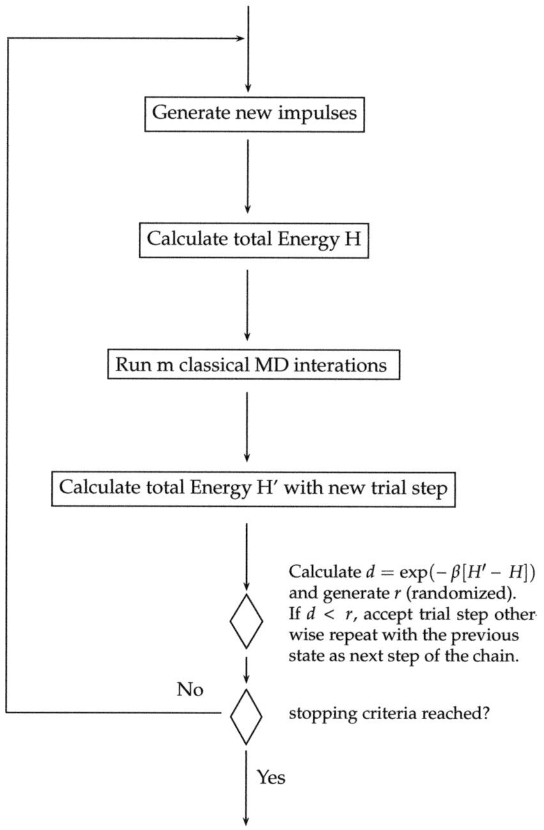

Fig. 2. The HMC Algorithm.

If the numerical integrator is momentum-reversible, then for the reverse step $\widetilde{q} \longrightarrow q$, we have to choose the start momentum vector $-\widetilde{p}$, which transfers the starting point $(\widetilde{q}, -\widetilde{p})$ to $(q, -p)$ in time span τ. This means, $\mathbf{P}_{\mathrm{pr}}(\widetilde{q} \rightarrow q) \propto \exp(-\beta K(-\widetilde{p}))$. In Equation 8, the two terms are integrated over the Lebesgue measure $dq \wedge d\widetilde{q}$. After transformation into the momenta space, the left hand side depends on $dq \wedge dp$ and the right had side on $d\widetilde{q} \wedge d\widetilde{p}$. But this does not change anything in Equation 10 because the mapping $(\widetilde{q}, \widetilde{p}) = \Phi_h^\tau(q, p)$ is area preserving. Both measures are equivalent. Inserting these results into 10 yields

$$\begin{aligned}\mathbf{P}_{\mathrm{ac}}(q \rightarrow \widetilde{q}) &= \min\left\{1, \frac{\pi(\widetilde{q})\exp(-\beta K(-\widetilde{p}))}{\pi(q)\exp(-\beta K(p))}\right\} \\ &= \min\left\{1, \frac{\exp(-\beta V(\widetilde{q}))\exp(-\beta K(\widetilde{p}))}{\exp(-\beta V(q))\exp(-\beta K(p))}\right\} \\ &= \min\left\{1, \exp(-\beta(H(\widetilde{q}, \widetilde{p}) - H(q, p)))\right\}, \qquad (11)\end{aligned}$$

i.e. the acceptance probability of the HMC proposal step is based on the change of the total energy during a numerical integration of the Hamiltonian. A reversible and area-preserving numerical integrator is necessary and sufficient for a correct sampling. For a rigorous proof, see also Mehlig et al. (1992), Section III.

3.5 Choice of the numerical integrator

Table 2 shows some algorithmic details of HMC and related methods. It shows, which Hamiltonian the methods are based upon, the acceptance probabilities and eventually a necessary pointwise re-weighting of the sampling trajectory in order to be mathematically rigorous.

3.5.1 "Exact" flow

As we have seen in the derivation of the acceptance probability, a reversible and area-preserving numerical integrator is necessary and sufficient for a correct sampling, no matter how bad its state space solution is. However, if we could apply an "exact" integrator the total energy would be constant during simulation, and therefore, the acceptance probability according to Metropolis dynamics would be 1. Adaptive integrators can be used with a pre-defined deviation from the exact flow. An example for an adaptive integrator for Hamiltonian dynamics is DIFEX2, an extrapolation method based on Störmer discretization, see Deuflhard (1983) and Deuflhard (1985). For DIFEX2, area-preservation and reversibility cannot be shown directly, but as the extrapolation method approximates the real flow, it inherits these properties from Φ^τ. Other adaptive integration methods and Fortran codes can be found in the book of Hairer et al. (1993). See also the first row of Table 2.

	Hamiltonian	**accept**	**re-weight**
"exact" flow	H	1	no
orig. HMC	H	$e^{-\beta \Delta H} < 1$	no
SHMC (idea)	$\widetilde{H}$	1	$\widetilde{H} \rightarrow H$
SHMC	$\widetilde{H}_{app}$	$e^{-\beta \Delta \widetilde{H}_{app}} \approx 1$	$\widetilde{H}_{app} \rightarrow H$

Table 2. Possible approaches for a correct sampling according to the HMC method. Algorithmic consequences.

3.5.2 Original HMC

Instead of solving the real dynamics, one can apply an arbitrary area-preserving and reversible integrator. In this case, the mean acceptance ratio decreases exponentially with system size n and the time step discretization h in the numerical integration Φ_h^{τ}. See Gupta et al. (1990) and Kennedy & Pendleton (1991) for an analytic study of the computational cost of HMC. It is a general opinion that HMC methods are only suitable for small molecular systems (see e.g. Section 14.2 in Frenkel & Smit (2002)). The reason is that in order to keep the mean acceptance probability constant for increasing system size, the time step h of the symplectic integrator has to decrease accordingly. Instead of time step refinements, one can also increase the order of the integration method. Using Hamilton's principle of a stationary action integral, Wendlandt & Marsden (1997) derived a systematical scheme for creating so-called *variational integrators*. With these higher-order numerical integrators the acceptance ratio of HMC can be improved due to better approximation properties. By omitting the constant step size h in variational integrators, one can even get symplectic *and* energy preserving integration schemes for the price of lower numerical efficiency. For an excellent overview of these methods, see Lew et al. (2004). See also the second row of Table 2.

3.5.3 Shadow HMC (SHMC)

Another approach uses the fact that some symplectic numerical integrator solves the dynamics of a modified Hamiltonian $\widetilde{H}$ *exactly* (see Hairer et al. (2004) or Skeel & Hardy (2002)). If one accepts each proposal step of the numerical dynamics simulation, this is like computing the density of the modified Hamiltonian (see third row of Table 2). In order to get the right distribution in configuration space, one has to re-weight the resulting position states accordingly. This is only possible, if the modified Hamiltonian is known. Fortunately, $\widetilde{H}$ can be approximated up to arbitrary accuracy. For algorithmic details, see Izaguirre & Hampton (2004).

3.5.4 Approximated SHMC

Approximating the modified Hamiltonian as exactly as possible, is numerically expensive. Therefore, one would like to truncate the Taylor expansion of $\widetilde{H}$ after a finite number of terms in order to yield $\widetilde{H}_{app}$. This method is part of the TSHMC method of Akhmatskaya & Reich (2004). Again, an acceptance rule is introduced which zeroes out the numerical error of truncation (see the last row of Table 2). This method seems to be very promising for larger molecules, because the acceptance probability is almost 1, the method is mathematically rigorous and numerically efficient (extra cost for computation of $\widetilde{H}_{app}$ is negligible).

4. Example: Brominated flame retardant hexabromocyclododecane

1,2,5,6,9,10-Hexabromocyclododecane (HBCD) is a widely used additive brominated flame retardant (BFR) to plastic materials as upholstery textiles, styrene-acrylonitrile resins or polystyrene foams (EPS, XPS) for the building sector with fractional percentages varying between 0.8 and 4% (Barda et al. (1985); de Witt (2002); Janak et al. (2005)). In the face of a world market demand of about 22000 metric tons in the year 2003 (Köppen et al. (2008)), HBCD is among a the most popular BFRs, especially in Europe (Janak et al. (2005)).
However, it is regarded as a persistent organic pollutant (POP) and has been detected increasingly in the environment during the last decades, e. g. in sewage sludges and sediments (see de Wit et al. (2006); Hale et al. (2006); Vos et al. (2003)) as well as in diverse tissues of both

terrestric and aquatic organisms (Janak et al. (2005); Tomy et al. (2004)). Even in the lipid phase of human breast milk of women from diverse european countries and the USA traces of HBCD and other BFR have been detected (Covaci et al. (2006); Johnson-Restrepo et al. (2008)).

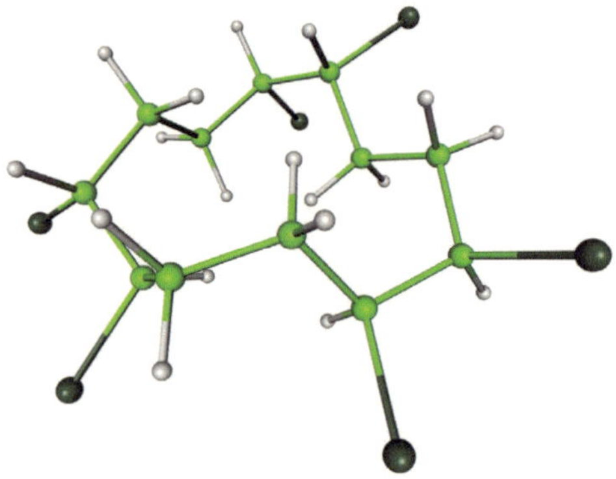

Fig. 3. 3-dimensional chemical structure of $(-)$-α-HBCD with six dark colored bromine atoms.

4.1 Technical and structural properties of HBCD

Technical HBCD is produced by bromination of the precursor 1,5,9-cyclododecatriene (CDT) unavoidably resulting in the formation of six stereocenters (Becher (2005); Heeb et al. (2004)). Theoretically, this yields 16 different HBCD diastereomers, six pairs of enantiomers and four mesoforms (Heeb et al. (2008)). But starting especially with the precursor (1Z,5E,9E)-CDT, the technical production results in a racemic mixture of three enantiomeric pairs ($\pm$)-α-, -β-, -γ-HBCD) and two mesoforms (δ-, ϵ-HBCD). The latter two will be neglected in the present work due to their negligible amounts in both the technical and the environmental mixture. The technical composition containing $(+)$-γ-HBCD mainly (Janak et al. (2005)) is presented in Table 3. See Fig. 5 for a graphical overview of the six main HBCD isomers. They are all characterized by a (R,R) or (S,S) configuration on their C_1Br–C_2Br-moiety and an (S,R) or (R,S) configuration on the C_5Br–C_6Br- and C_9Br–C_{10}Br-moieties. On the former moiety, α- and γ-HBCD feature C_2-symmetry, implying identical energetical properties for the latter two moieties, whereas the β-diastereomer does not possess any rotational symmetries.

In contrast to the technical mix, a completely different composition was found in the abiotic and biotic environment, which are always by far predominated by α-HBCD (Becher (2005); Heeb et al. (2008); Tomy et al. (2004)) with slightly differing concentrations and even enantioselective accumulation (Tomy et al. (2004)). Certainly, these observations raise the question of their cause. On the one hand, this might arise from variability in physicochemical properties such as dipole moment or solubility in water. The latter with respect to α-, β-

Diastereomer	CIP nomenclature of both enantiomers	Molar fraction	
		Technical	Equilibrium
($\pm$)-α-HBCD	1S,2S,5R,6S,9S,10R-HBCD, 1R,2R,5S,6R,9R,10S-HBCD	10 – 13 %	78 %
($\pm$)-β-HBCD	1S,2S,5R,6S,9R,10S-HBCD, 1R,2R,5S,6R,9S,10R-HBCD	1 – 12 %	14 %
($\pm$)-γ-HBCD	1R,2R,5R,6S,9S,10R-HBCD, 1S,2S,5S,6R,9R,10S-HBCD	75 – 89 %	8 %

Table 3. CIP names of HBCD isomers and their fraction in the technical mix and at equilibrium.

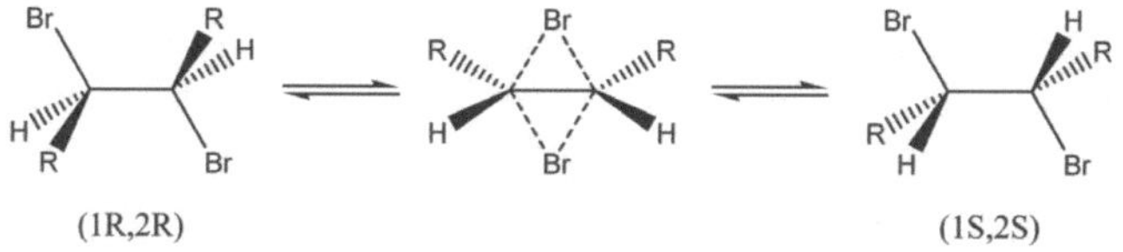

Fig. 4. Cyclic-concerted interconversion mechanism. A necessary condition for the quantum-chemically induced process is the *anti* positioning of two vicinal bromine atoms which leads to double-bonded bromines and five-bonded carbons during transition (center structure) caused by a nucleophilic attack of bromine. The interconversion results in a change of the involved chiralities.

and γ-HBCD is relatively low and was measured to be 48.8, 14.7, and 2.1 μg/L, respectively (Hunziker et al. (2004)).

On the other hand, differing diastereomeric ratios might be triggered by stereoselective uptake and metabolism. Indeed, there seems to be strong evidence for a biologically induced interconversion of HBCD stereoisomers (Hamers et al. (2006); Law et al. (2006a)). According to Vos et al. (2003), Hamers et al. (2006), and Meerts et al. (2000), some BFRs such as HBCD or its metabolite pentabromocyclododecaene (PBCD) are suspected to cause endocrine disruption

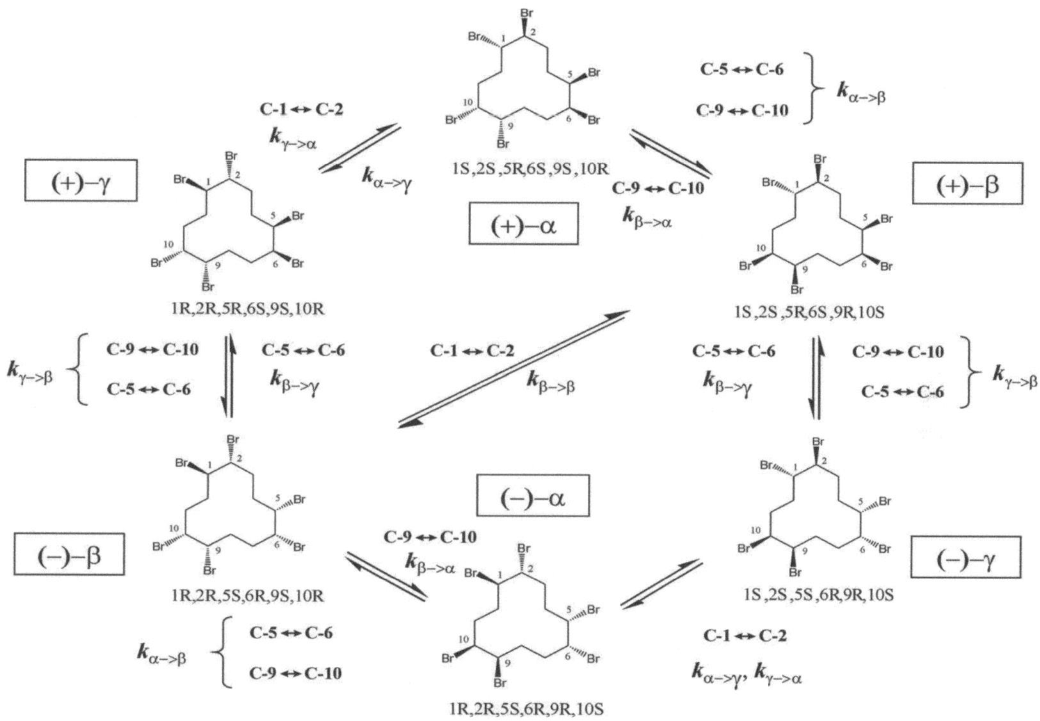

Fig. 5. Graphical overview of all possible interconversions between any connected two of the six main HBCD diastereomers taken from Köppen et al. (2008). The bromine *anti* conformation of any C_iBr–$C_{i+1}Br$-moiety of the starting diastereomers triggers the inversion to another diastereomer depending on the couple of concerned bromine atoms, i. e. depending on the value of index i with $i \in \{1, 5, 9\}$. This transition process with rate $k_{x \rightarrow y}$ is denoted as cyclic-concerted interconversion.

due to competition with thyroxine (T_4) for binding to the human transthyretin receptor (hTTR). Recently, Schriks et al. (2006) observed effects on the cell proliferation of Xenopus laevis induced by HBCD and another BFR denoted as BDE206 (brominated diphenyl ether). Temperatures above 160° C (433 K), which is close to the melting point of crystalline HBCD at 188 − 191° C, induce a isomerization process denoted as cyclic-concerted interconversion (Köppen et al. (2008)) described in detail below. As shown in Table 3, the equilibrium distribution of the HBCD diastereomers after thermal rearrangement is dominated by α-HBCD with a fraction of 78 % followed by β- and γ-HBCD with percentages of 13 % and 9 %, respectively (Peled et al. (1995)). Temperatures exceeding 200° C lead to HBCD decomposition (Barontini et al. (2003)).

4.2 Interconversion kinetics of HBCD

Any pair of vicinal bromine atoms each bonded with a chiral carbon (C_iBr–C_{i+1}Br-moiety) is able to undergo a stereo-isomerization process denoted as cyclic-concerted interconversion resulting in complementary chirality (Fig. 4) of both involved carbons (Köppen et al. (2008)). The transition state which is quantum-chemically motivated requires both bromine atoms to be *anti*-positioned and to form a second bond whith the respective vicinal chiral carbon atoms which switch from sp_3 to sp_2 hybridization and to a five-bonded state during transition (Fig. 4, center graphic).

Fig. 5 shows all possible interconverions between the six main diastereomers depending on the concerned C_iBr–C_{i+1}Br-moiety with $i \in \{1,5,9\}$. For example, if the C_1Br–C_2Br-moiety of $(+)$-γ-HBCD forms a *anti*-conformation of the bromines, which will happen with a certain probability in terms of statistical thermodynamics, the chirality of C_1Br–C_2Br will change from (1R,2R) to (1S,2S) resulting in $(+)$-α-HBCD.

As already mentioned above, the system of diastereomers moves towards a thermodynamical equilibrium dominated by $(+)$-α-HBCD. Recently, rate constants $k_{x\rightarrow y}$ have been determined by Köppen et al. (2008) at 160° C via high performance liquid chromatography (HPLC) using a chiral column. The results are presented in Table 4 and graphically in Fig. 6. It is worth mentioning that the rates are supposed to be the same for the enantiomeric counterparts in this thermally induced process. The fastest interconversion after these results is the one from γ-HBCD to α-HBCD, closely followed by the interconversion from β-HBCD to its enantiomeric counterpart. Both reactions occur on the C_1-C_2-moiety. By far, the lowest rate was measured in case of the interconversion from α- to β-HBCD.

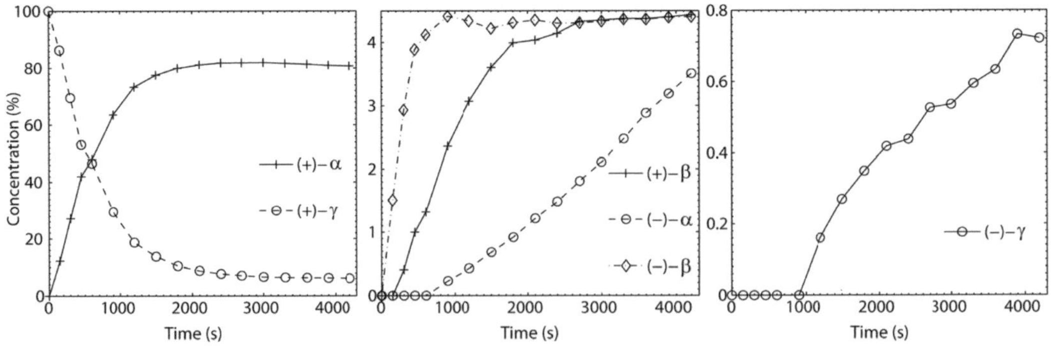

Fig. 6. Experimental determination on the isomerization of HBCD at 160° C starting with 100 % $(+)$-γ-HBCD. The tests were carried out by Köppen et al. (2008).

Interconversion	C_iBr–C_{i+1}Br-moiety	Rate constant k $\left[\frac{\text{mol}(\%)}{\text{s}}\right]$
$k_{\alpha\to\beta}$	C_5-C_6/C_9-C_{10}	$1.88 \pm 0.01 \times 10^{-5}$
$k_{\alpha\to\gamma}$	C_1-C_2	$1.42 \pm 0.01 \times 10^{-4}$
$k_{\beta\to\alpha}$	C_9-C_{10}	$1.20 \pm 0.01 \times 10^{-4}$
$k_{\beta\to\beta}$	C_1-C_2	$1.10 \pm 0.03 \times 10^{-3}$
$k_{\beta\to\gamma}$	C_5-C_6	$1.70 \pm 0.01 \times 10^{-4}$
$k_{\gamma\to\alpha}$	C_1-C_2	$1.50 \pm 0.01 \times 10^{-3}$
$k_{\gamma\to\beta}$	C_5-C_6/C_9-C_{10}	$1.46 \pm 0.01 \times 10^{-4}$

Table 4. Rate constants $k_{y\to z}$ with $y, z \in \{\alpha, \beta, \gamma\}$ for the cyclic-concerted interconversion process of HBCD at 160° C.

5. Simulation of HBCD interconversion rates

As already mentioned in section 4, the six main HBCD diastereomers underly a isomerization process at temperatures between 433 and 473 K denoted as cyclic-concerted interconversion (see Fig. 5) which is quantum-chemically motivated and results in complementary chirality of both concerned vicinal brominated carbon atoms. Nevertheless, this section presents an approach for estimating transition rates of such processes in terms of classical mechanics. It is due to the matter of time scale and the complexity of electronic densities, that the interconversion can hardly be investigated by quantum-chemical methods without enormous computational costs.
Due to high rotational barriers, high-temperature simulations are inevitable in order to avoid trapping effects. Hence, the adoption of these results to lower temperatures requires a reweighting strategy which has been developed within the framework of these investigations. Afterwards, the interconversion rates are approximated on the basis of free energy calculations in combination with the *Arrhenius* equation and by applying the transition state theory (TST). Fortunately, experimental data of the interconversion kinetics is available and will be compared to the theoretical results obtained here.

5.1 Classical model for the interconversion

A necessary condition for the transition state of interconversion processes is the *anti*-positioning of two vicinal bromine atoms in liquid phase, that we will call an "active state". It is assumed to occur more likely with lower rotational barriers between *anti* and *gauche* conformations and vice versa. The rate of the transition is considered to depend on both, the probability of such an activated state, which can be described in terms of classical thermodynamics and the velocity of the quantum-chemically motivated transition itself. The latter may simply be neglected due to the assumption of its identity in case of all HBCD diastereomers. Therefore, a qualitative definition of interconversion rates in terms of free energy differences only between two subsets Ω_{anti} and $\Omega_{\text{gauche}} \in \mathbb{R}^{3n}$ of the conformational space $\Omega \in \mathbb{R}^{3n}$ turns out to be a suitable approach.
Initially, a sampling of the conformational space had to be performed with the HMC method at an artificially high temperature $T = 1500$ K (i. e. with the *Boltzmann* factor $\beta_0 = 0.0802$ mol/kJ and in vacuum, neglecting mutual interactions with other HBCD molecules or with a solvent such as water and therefore, reducing computational costs. We decided to utilize the *Merck molecular force* □*eld* (mmff) designed by Halgren (1996) for our simulations. For each diastereomer, five trajectories were constructed each consisting of 100.000 MC steps with 60 MD steps per MC step. The MD integration step was set to 1.3 fs. Convergence was

checked in accordance with Gelman & Rubin (1992) on the basis of the five *Markov* chains. The *conjugate gradient* (CG) minimization method (Hestenes & Stiefel (1952)) was used for energy optimization of the sampled geometries in order to identify all local and thus, global minima. The free energy $A(\beta)$ is defined in terms of the partition function

$$A(\beta) = -\frac{1}{\beta}\ln\left(\int_{\Omega}\exp\left(-\beta V\left(q\right)\right)\mathrm{d}q\right). \tag{12}$$

Note, that the kinetic part $K(p)$ of the total energy $H(q,p)$ is missing due to the assumption of its idendity for both conformational subsets at identical temperature. In this section, we will only consider the potential energy fraction $V(q)$ of the separable Hamiltonian. It is not possible to approximate the integral in Equation 12; however, free energy differences $\Delta_{\text{ga}}A(\beta)$ (a $=$ *anti*, g $=$ *gauche*) of two conformational subsets Ω_{anti} and Ω_{gauche} may be approximated. Due to *importance sampling* (compare Equation 5 with 6), the number of geometries containing *anti-* (N_{anti}) and *gauche*-conformation $\left(N_{\text{gauche}}\right)$, respectively, according to the $C_iBr–C_{i+1}Br$-moiety under consideration is sufficiant in order to approximate

$$\Delta_{\text{ga}}A(\beta) \approx -\frac{1}{\beta}\ln\left(\frac{N_{\text{gauche}}}{N_{\text{anti}}}\right). \tag{13}$$

A dihedral angle θ between two vicinal bromine atoms was defined as *anti* if $|\theta| > 120°$, i. e. if the lower bromine atom remained in the grey-coloured segment as depicted in Fig. 7, whereas an angle $120 \geq \theta \geq -120\,°$ was defined as *gauche*.

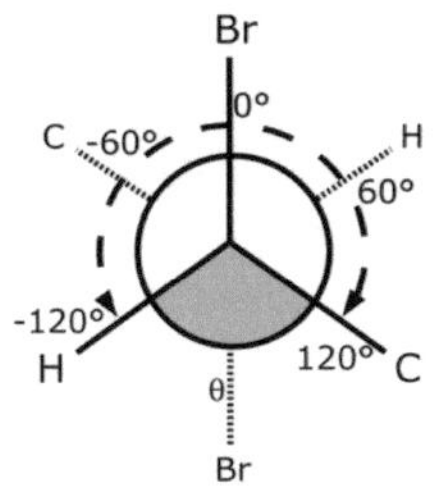

Fig. 7. For the interconversion anlysis, the bromine's conformation was defined as *anti* if the dihedral θ was greater than $120\,°$ and less than $-120\,°$ (lower bromine within the grey segment).

These free energy differences were calculated for each $C_iBr–C_{i+1}Br$-moiety of all $(+)$-HBCD enantiomers. The lower the free energy difference, the more the state indicated by the first index ($g =$ *gauche*) is preferred.

In the followings, we will additionally need another thermodynamic quantity derived from the simulated data, namely the mean potential energy $\langle V\rangle$ defined as a function of temperature β

$$\langle V\rangle(\beta) = \int_{\Omega} V\left(q\right)\frac{\exp\left(-\beta V\left(q\right)\right)}{\int_{\Omega}\exp\left(-\beta V\left(q\right)\right)\mathrm{d}q}\mathrm{d}q \tag{14}$$

which can be approximated by the arithmetic mean of all potential energy values from the HMC sampling. Again, the energy difference $\Delta_{\text{ga}}\langle V\rangle$ was determined for each $C_iBr–C_{i+1}Br$-moiety of all $(+)$-HBCD enantiomers, after having partitioned the conformational space Ω into *gauche* and *anti* subsets and having calculated their respective mean potential energies.

5.2 Thermodynamical energy reweighting

The HMC sampling had been performed at temperature $T = 1500\,\mathrm{K}$ ($\beta_0 = 0.0802\,\mathrm{mol/kJ}$) due to convergence reasons. However, we are interested in the energy distribution at $T = 433\,\mathrm{K}$ ($\beta_1 = 0.2778\,\mathrm{mol/kJ}$) which marks the melting point of HBCD. Usually, reweighting is understood in a point-wise way, reweighting the complete distribution to the temperature of interest and, therefore, statistically weighting up a relatively small number of points in the overlap region of both the high- and the low-temperature distribution (see grey coloured area in Fig. 8).

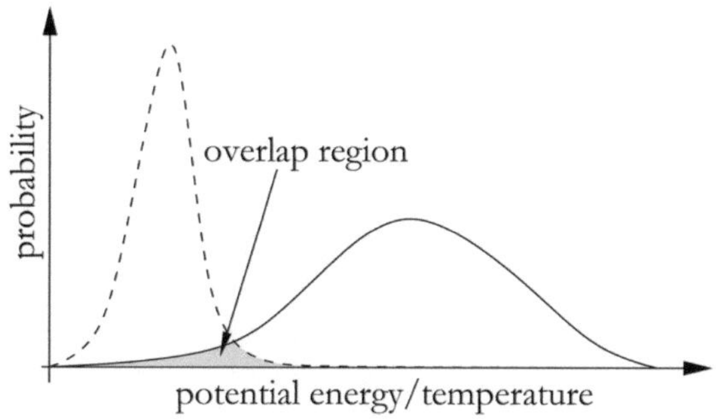

Fig. 8. Overlap region between high and low potential energy distributions relevant for point-wise reweighting.

Here, we apply a thermodynamical approach instead of a point-wise one, making use of the temperature-dependency of the distribution's mean value, i. e. its dependency on β. In analogy to the mean kinetic energy $\langle K \rangle$, we assume a linear dependency of the mean potential energy $\langle V \rangle$ on the temperature T (i. e. on β^{-1})

$$\Delta_{\mathrm{ga}} \langle V \rangle (\beta) = \frac{\left[\Delta_{\mathrm{ga}} \langle V \rangle (\beta_0) - \Delta_{\mathrm{ga}} \langle V \rangle (\infty)\right] \beta_0}{\beta} + \Delta_{\mathrm{ga}} \langle V \rangle (\infty). \tag{15}$$

$\Delta_{\mathrm{ga}} V(\infty)$ denotes the difference of the global minimal energies of both subspaces at absolute zero $T = 0\,\mathrm{K} \Leftrightarrow \beta = \infty$. Since the system moves towards the global optimum with decreasing temperature, a conjugate gradient minimization was applied to the complete canonical high-temperature ensembles of HBCD geometries. Again, each C_iBr–C_{i+1}Br-moiety of all (+)-HBCD enantiomers underwent this procedure after having been separated according to their *anti/gauche*-isomerization. In addition and via Equation 15, mean potential energies and their differences for each C_iBr–C_{i+1}Br-moiety can now be interpolated to the temperature of interest which is the melting point of HBCD at 433 K. See Fig. 9 for a graphical representation of the linear model.

However, in order to determine interconversion rates as described in the next section, free energy differences for each C_iBr–C_{i+1}Br-moiety at the desired temperature needed to be estimated as well. This was achieved by first differentiating Equation 12 and inserting Equation 14

$$\frac{\mathrm{d}}{\mathrm{d}\beta} \Delta_{\mathrm{ga}} A(\beta) = -\frac{1}{\beta} \Delta_{\mathrm{ga}} A(\beta) + \frac{1}{\beta} \Delta_{\mathrm{ga}} \langle V \rangle (\beta). \tag{16}$$

Inserting the linear model (Equation 15) instead of the last term of Equation 16 leads to the ordinary differential equation

$$\frac{\mathrm{d}}{\mathrm{d}\beta} \Delta_{\mathrm{ga}} A(\beta) = -\frac{1}{\beta} \Delta_{\mathrm{ga}} A(\beta) + \frac{\left[\Delta_{\mathrm{ga}} \langle V \rangle (\beta_0) - \Delta_{\mathrm{ga}} V(\infty)\right] \beta_0}{\beta^2} + \frac{\Delta_{\mathrm{ga}} V(\infty)}{\beta}. \tag{17}$$

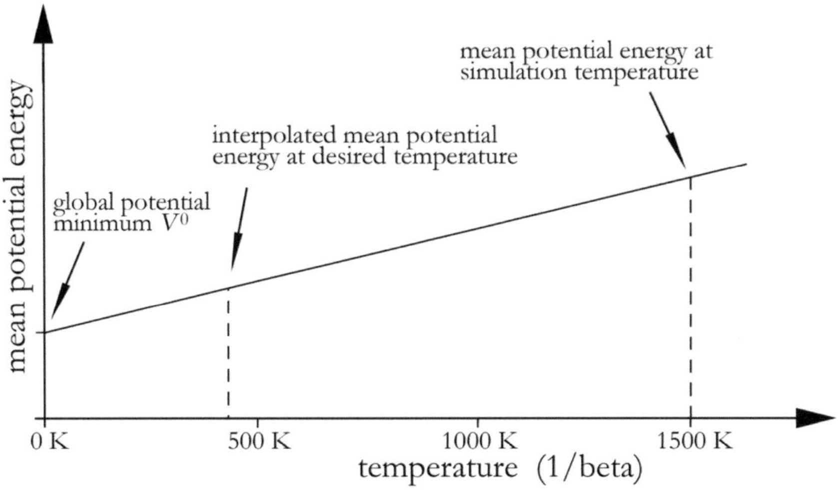

Fig. 9. A linear model for the thermodynamical reweighting of mean potential energies to temperatures between the one used for high-temperature simulations and absolute zero.

which can be solved analytically, such that

$$\begin{aligned}\Delta_{\mathrm{ga}} A(\beta) &= \frac{\beta-\beta_0}{\beta}\Delta_{\mathrm{ga}}\langle V\rangle(\infty) \\ &+ \frac{\beta_0}{\beta}\ln\left(\frac{\beta}{\beta_0}\right)\left[\Delta_{\mathrm{ga}}\langle V\rangle(\beta_0) - \Delta_{\mathrm{ga}}\langle V\rangle(\infty)\right] + \frac{\beta_0}{\beta}\Delta_{\mathrm{ga}} A(\beta_0).\end{aligned} \tag{18}$$

Equation 18 allows to interpolate free energy differences for temperatures such as the desired one at $T = 433\,\mathrm{K}$.

5.3 Rate matrix and interconversion kinetics

Basically, the estimation of interconversion rates rested upon the combination of the *Arrhenius* equation (Göpel & Wiemdörfer (2000)) with the transition state theory (TST) (Weber (2007)). According to *Arrhenius*, the reaction rate k depends on the temperature T (respectively β) and on the activation energy E_A as follows

$$k = A \cdot \exp(-\beta E_A) \tag{19}$$

with a prefactor A. In this work, the activation energy for the interconversion process at a certain C_iBr–C_{i+1}Br-moiety requiring *anti* conformation was approximated by the free energy difference between the respective subspaces of the conformational space, due to an obvious dependency of the interconversion rate k from the free energy difference $\Delta_{ag}A = -\Delta_{\mathrm{ga}}A$. In other words, the higher the free energy difference between the *gauche* and *anti* subspace is, the more likely the system is to form *anti* conformations and, therefore, the larger the interconversion rate will be. Hence, we propose this correlation such that

$$k \propto \exp\left(-\beta\Delta_{\mathrm{ag}}A\right) \tag{20}$$

neglecting the prefactor from Equation 19 which needs to be determined experimentally and marks an upper bound for the maximal reaction rate. As we do not expect to gain quantitative, but qualitative interconversion rates, the prefactor does not play any role for our purposes.

These rates were used now to fill up non-zero entries of the squared matrix $K \in \mathbb{R}^{6\times6}$ with one dimension per HBCD diastereomer in the order $(+)$-α, $(+)$-β, $(+)$-γ, $(-)$-α, $(-)$-β, $(-)$-γ. For example, the element of the third row ($(+)$-γ = educt) and the first column ($(+)$-α = product) of K is determined by

$$k_{3,1} = k_{(+)\gamma\rightarrow(+)\alpha} = \exp\left(-\beta\Delta_{ag}A\right) \tag{21}$$

where $\Delta_{ag}A$ is the free energy difference for *anti* and *gauche* conformations of the according C_1Br–C_2Br-moiety, derivable from Fig. 5. Note, that the interconversion from α- or γ- to β-HBCD is associated with two C_iBr–C_{i+1}Br-moieties (C_5Br–C_6Br and C_9Br–C_{10}Br). Here, both respective free energy differences must be summed up before being inserted into Equation 21.
K is a stochastic matrix with the row sums needing to be scaled to 1. It is also denoted as *embedded Markov chain* playing a central role in the TST, particularly for the computation of the rate matrix $Q \in \mathbb{R}^{6\times6}$ we are interested in

$$Q = R\,(K - id) \tag{22}$$

where *id* denotes the six-dimensional unit matrix and $R \in \mathbb{R}^{6\times6}$ the diagonal matrix of rate facors (Kijima (1997); Weber (2007)). Q is well-known from the first order rate equation

$$\frac{\mathrm{d}x\,(t)}{\mathrm{d}t} = Q^{\top}x\,(t) \tag{23}$$

describing changes of the concentration vector $x \in \mathbb{R}^6$ over time t using the (transposed) rate matrix Q. In case of equilibrium concentrations $x\,(t) = \pi\,(t)$ at the systems steady-state, Equation 23 becomes

$$\frac{\mathrm{d}\pi\,(t)}{\mathrm{d}t} = Q^{\top}\pi\,(t) = 0 \iff \pi^{\top}Q = 0. \tag{24}$$

This information is necessary for the computation of the matrix R of rate factors which is the last unknown quantity in Equation 22. For this purpose, the right-hand side of equation 22 was inserted into Q of the second part of Equation 24 resulting in

$$\pi^{\top}R\,(K - id) = 0. \tag{25}$$

Little manipulations of Equation 25 lead us to the eigenproblem

$$r^{\top}\Pi\,(K - id) = 0 \cdot r^{\top} \tag{26}$$

where the diagonal elements of the diagonal matrix R have been transferred into an ordinary vector r and vice versa in case of the steady-state distribution vector π which was transformed into a diagonal matrix Π. This is a sophisticated way to solve rate factors r (and hence, R and Q), handling them as an eigenvector of the eigenvalue zero. A simulation of these theoretical interconversion kinetics can be performed by solving the differential Equation 23 such that

$$x\,(\tau) = x\,(0)\exp\left(\tau Q\right) \tag{27}$$

starting at an initial distribution $x\,(0)$ and iterating over a time span $t = \tau$. All calculations have been performed with the software *Matlab*.

6. Results and discussion

6.1 HMC-sampling of HBCD diastereomers

Global minima of the six major HBCD diastereomers' potential energies are listed in Table 5. Expectedly, the optimal energies are identical for each pair of enantiomers, affirming a sufficient convergence as indicated by the Gelman and Rubin criterion. In contrast to 100.000 HMC steps, a first run with 10.000 steps had turned out to be insufficient to achieve convergence in spite of the high simulation temperature of 1500° C.

Already the simple results from energy minimized samplings considerably support observations of a predominating α-HBCD diastereomer in the environment Becher (2005); Janak et al. (2005); Tomy et al. (2004), in spite of the technical mix mainly being composed of $(+)$-γ-HBCD Peled et al. (1995). A comparison of experimentally determined diastereomeric fractions after a thermal rearrangement ($78\%\ \alpha, 14\%\ \beta, 8\%\ \gamma$) from Table 3 with global potential energy minima (α: 238.7 kJ/mol, β: 249.5 kJ/mol, γ: 256.7 kJ/mol) from Table 6 shows a clear correlation and justifies the predominance of α-HBCD at the thermodynamic equilibrium.

Diastereomer	Global minimum $\left[\frac{kJ}{mol}\right]$	Diastereomer	Global minimum $\left[\frac{kJ}{mol}\right]$
$(+)$-α-HBCD	238.7	$(-)$-α-HBCD	238.7
$(+)$-β-HBCD	249.5	$(-)$-β-HBCD	249.5
$(+)$-γ-HBCD	256.7	$(-)$-γ-HBCD	256.7

Table 5. Global minima of the six main HBCD diateromers' potential energies at 1500 K.

In addition, global potential energy minima have been determined for both conformational subsets (*anti* and *gauche*) of each CBr–CBr-moiety (Table 6). As expected, symmetries were found in the global minima of enantiomeric counterparts of HBCD (same optimum values for $(+)$- and $(-)$-enantiomer) as well as in identical optima for potential energy differences (V^0) associated with C_5Br–C_6Br- and C_9Br–$C_{10}Br$-moieties of α- and γ-HBCD as a result of their configurational C_2-symmetry. Additionally, all energy differences concerning these two moieties are pretty different from those of the C_1Br–C_2Br-moiety which is by reason the fact that an *anti* conformation of bromine atoms is energetically much more favorable on an (*R*,*R*) or (*S*,*S*) configurated moiety such as the latter mentioned one than on an (*S*,*R*) or (*R*,*S*) configuration given in case of the two other moieties.

The results in Table 6 allow a qualitative estimation of the disposition to undergo the interconversion mechanism. The higher the Boltzmann prpbability ratio between the minimum of the *anti* conformation and the corresponding *gauche* conformation's minimum is, the more likely this molecule will interconvert at the respective CBr–CBr-moiety. After these results, for example the interconversion from $(+)$-γ-HBCD to $(+)$-α-HBCD (and analogously for their enantiomeric counterparts) with a Boltzmann ratio of 1 is by far the fastest reaction or rather the most probable one. In contrast, the probability of the opposite reaction, i. e. from $(+)$-α-HBCD to $(+)$-γ-HBCD, is much lower with $2.6 \cdot 10^{-3}$. Again, these results clearly confirm experimental observations concerning the increase of α-HBCD and the decrease of γ-HBCD Peled et al. (1995). The reverse interconversion seems to be quite rare due to the unlikeliness of an *anti* conformation at the C_1Br–C_2Br-moiety of α-HBCD, presenting this stereoisomer as a thermodynamical sink of HBCD.

HBCD diastereomer	Dihedral	Global minimum $\left[\frac{kJ}{mol}\right]$ anti	gauche	Boltzmann ratio	Target HBCD
$(+)$-α	C_1C_2	253.7	238.7	$2.6 \cdot 10^{-3}$	$(+)$-γ
	C_5C_6	272.6	238.7	$1.3 \cdot 10^{-6}$	$(+)$-β
	C_9C_{10}	272.6	238.7	$1.3 \cdot 10^{-6}$	$(+)$-β
$(+)$-β	C_1C_2	263.6	249.5	$3.6 \cdot 10^{-3}$	$(-)$-β
	C_5C_6	285.3	249.5	$6.1 \cdot 10^{-7}$	$(-)$-γ
	C_9C_{10}	278.4	249.5	$9.5 \cdot 10^{-6}$	$(+)$-α
$(+)$-γ	C_1C_2	256.7	256.7	1	$(+)$-α
	C_5C_6	275.1	256.7	$6.2 \cdot 10^{-4}$	$(-)$-β
	C_9C_{10}	289.5	256.7	$2.0 \cdot 10^{-6}$	$(-)$-β
$(-)$-α	C_1C_2	253.7	238.7	$2.6 \cdot 10^{-3}$	$(-)$-γ
	C_5C_6	272.6	238.7	$1.3 \cdot 10^{-6}$	$(-)$-β
	C_9C_{10}	272.6	238.7	$1.3 \cdot 10^{-6}$	$(-)$-β
$(-)$-β	C_1C_2	263.6	249.5	$3.6 \cdot 10^{-3}$	$(+)$-β
	C_5C_6	285.3	249.5	$6.1 \cdot 10^{-7}$	$(+)$-γ
	C_9C_{10}	278.4	249.5	$9.5 \cdot 10^{-6}$	$(-)$-α
$(-)$-γ	C_1C_2	256.7	256.7	1	$(-)$-α
	C_5C_6	275.1	256.7	$6.2 \cdot 10^{-4}$	$(+)$-β
	C_9C_{10}	289.5	256.7	$2.0 \cdot 10^{-6}$	$(+)$-β

Table 6. Global potential energy minima of both conformational subspaces, *anti* and *gauche* of each C_iBr–$C_{i+1}Br$-moiety of each HBCD diastereomer and respective Boltzmann ratios. The higher this value, the more likely the *anti* conformation and thus, the more likely the diastereomer to interconvert at the concerning moiety to the target diastereomer shown in the last column.

6.2 Thermodynamical energy reweighting

An estimation of interconversion rates of the main six HBCD diastereomers for the desired temperature 433 K, i. e. with $\beta_1 = 0.2778\,\text{mol/kJ}$, required the computation of several thermodynamical quantities at the initial simulation temperature 1500 K ($\beta_0 = 0.0802\,\text{mol/kJ}$). These were mean potential energies $\langle V \rangle (\beta_0)$ of each HBCD stereoisomer and differences of the mean potential energy $\Delta_{ga} \langle V \rangle (\beta_0)$, of the globally minimal potential energies $\Delta_{ga} V^0$ and of free energies $\Delta_{ga} A\,(\beta_0)$ associated with the dihedral angle of each C_iBr–$C_{i+1}Br$-moiety. Afterwards, all of these energies but the global minima at absolute zero were reweighted to the desired temperature.

Mean potential energies $\langle V \rangle (\beta)$ of the complete conformational space were easily derived from the high-temperature simulation data for each HBCD diastereomer in the order $(+)$-α, $(+)$-β, $(+)$-γ, $(-)$-α, $(-)$-β and $(-)$-γ: 920.6, 930.9, 926.3, 922.0, 931.2 and 925.9 kJ/mol, respectively. The correponding mean potential energies associated with 433 K were obtained by applying the linear model of the reweighting formula (Equation 15) to the original mean potential energies resulting in 435.6, 446.2, 450.0, 436.0, 446.3 and 449.9 kJ/mol, respectively.

Free $(\Delta_{ga} A)$ and mean potential $(\Delta_{ga} \langle V \rangle)$ energy differences associated with *anti* and *gauche* subspaces of each C_iBr–$C_{i+1}Br$-moiety and for both temperatures are presented in Table 7. Potential energy differences at absolute zero $(\Delta_{ga} V^0)$ in the table were obtained by the difference of global potential energy minima of *anti* and *gauche* conformations at simulation temperature, since these are the conformations, towards which the molecular system moves with decreasing temperature.

Diastereomer	Dihedral	Energies at $T = 1500\,\mathrm{K}$ $\left[\frac{\mathrm{kJ}}{\mathrm{mol}}\right]$			At $T = 433\,\mathrm{K}$ $\left[\frac{\mathrm{kJ}}{\mathrm{mol}}\right]$		Target
		$\Delta_{ga}\langle V\rangle$	$\Delta_{ga}V^0$	$\Delta_{ga}A$	$\Delta_{ga}\langle V\rangle$	$\Delta_{ga}A$	
(+)-α	C_1C_2	−7.8	−14.9	−16.7	−10.4	−12.9	(+)-γ
	C_5C_6	−26.0	−33.9	−40.4	−30.2	−32.9	(+)-β
	C_9C_{10}	−25.6	−33.9	−39.7	−29.7	−32.6	(+)-β
(+)-β	C_1C_2	−0.3	−14.0	−14.3	−4.3	−9.2	(−)-β
	C_5C_6	−19.9	−35.8	−35.5	−24.4	−30.0	(−)-γ
	C_9C_{10}	−17.5	−26.7	−34.0	−22.2	−25.5	(+)-α
(+)-γ	C_1C_2	4.8	0.0	−9.7	0.6	−1.1	(+)-α
	C_5C_6	−28.3	−18.5	−41.3	−32.0	−28.6	(−)-β
	C_9C_{10}	−27.1	−18.5	−41.0	−31.1	−28.1	(−)-β
(−)-α	C_1C_2	−6.9	−14.9	−16.7	−9.8	−12.6	(−)-γ
	C_5C_6	−24.4	−33.9	−38.0	−28.3	−31.7	(−)-β
	C_9C_{10}	−21.9	−33.9	−38.1	−26.6	−30.8	(−)-β
(−)-β	C_1C_2	−1.7	−14.0	−13.5	−5.1	−9.5	(+)-β
	C_5C_6	−19.1	−35.8	−35.3	−23.7	−29.6	(+)-γ
	C_9C_{10}	−15.0	−26.7	−35.9	−21.1	−25.2	(−)-α
(−)-γ	C_1C_2	3.1	0.0	−11.0	−1.0	−2.1	(−)-α
	C_5C_6	−31.3	−18.5	−42.5	−34.5	−30.0	(+)-β
	C_9C_{10}	−30.9	−18.5	−42.2	−34.1	−29.8	(+)-β

Table 7. Mean potential $(\Delta_{ga}\langle V\rangle)$ and free $(\Delta_{ga}A)$ energies of both conformational subspaces (*anti* and *gauche*) of each C_iBr–C_{i+1}Br-moiety of each HBCD diastereomer at the simulation temperature $T = 1500\,\mathrm{K}$ and reweighted to the desired temperature at $T = 433\,\mathrm{K}$, respectively as well as potential energy differences at $T = 0\,\mathrm{K}$, i. e. potential energy differences of the concerning global minima $(\Delta_{ga}V^0)$ gained by sampling at $T = 1500\,\mathrm{K}$ and minimizing.

The estimated equilibrium distribution for 433 K presented in section 6.3 is similar to the experimentally determined distribution after thermal rearrangement Peled et al. (1995). Both methods provide a by far highest fraction of (+)-α-HBCD and decreasing fractions in the order (+)-β-HBCD and (+)-γ-HBCD. If the mean potential energies had been chosen to be interpolated to 630 K instead, the estimated equilibrium distribution would have resulted in equal values with a relative error of only 10 %, which is not presented among these results.

6.3 HBCD interconversion rates and kinetics

By inserting the negated free energy differences from the last but one column of Table 7 into the modified *Arrhenius* Equation 21, the embedded Markov chain was calculated first:

$$K = \begin{pmatrix} 0 & 0.0080 & 0.9920 & 0 & 0 & 0 \\ 0.0107 & 0 & 0 & 0 & 0.9863 & 0.0031 \\ 0.9990 & 0 & 0 & 0 & 0.0010 & 0 \\ 0 & 0 & 0 & 0 & 0.0112 & 0.9888 \\ 0 & 0.9838 & 0.0037 & 0.0126 & 0 & 0 \\ 0 & 0.0009 & 0 & 0.9991 & 0 & 0 \end{pmatrix}.$$

This matrix contains a 0 whenever a interconversion is not possible. Only the 14 interconversions as depicted in Fig. 5 lead to values greater than 0 in matrix K. Row sums were scaled to 1.

The steady-state distribution π of HBCD at 433 K was determined by inserting the corresponding mean potential energy values, interpolated to this temperature as shown above, into the potential energy part of the *Boltzmann* expression, neglecting the partion function but scaling the sum to 1:

$$\pi^{\top} = (0.4912\ 0.0258\ 0.0090\ 0.4396\ 0.0251\ 0.0092)$$

This vector gives evidence about a theoretical distribution of HBCD diastereomers. Summing up the first and forth value of π, i. e. the molar fractions of (+)- and (−)-α-HBCD yields 93.1 % for α-HBCD and analogously, in case of β- and γ-HBCD 5.1 % and 1.8 %, respectively.
After having solved the eigenproblem of Equation 26, the theoretical rate matrix Q was determined

$$Q = \mu \cdot \begin{pmatrix} -0.0184 & 0.0001 & 0.0183 & 0 & 0 & 0 \\ 0.0023 & -0.2200 & 0 & 0 & 0.2170 & 0.0007 \\ 0.9990 & 0 & -1.0000 & 0 & 0.0010 & 0 \\ 0 & 0 & 0 & -0.0167 & 0.0002 & 0.0166 \\ 0 & 0.2231 & 0.0008 & 0.0028 & -0.2267 & 0 \\ 0 & 0.0007 & 0 & 0.7879 & 0 & -0.7886 \end{pmatrix}$$

up to an unknown scaling factor μ which is due to the unknown velocity of the interconversion process. Consequently, simulation of the interconversion kinetics was performed now by applying Equation 27 to an initial distribution $x(0)$

$$x^{\top}(0) = (0\ 0\ 1\ 0\ 0\ 0)$$

with a discretized time step $\Delta\tau = 1$ over a time span of $\tau = 4000$ "seconds" and an arbitrary scaling factor $\mu = 0.007$ resulting in interconversion kinetics as shown in Fig. 10. The initial distribution with 100 % (+)-γ-HBCD was chosen in accordance with the experimental setup which had led to the experimental kinetics depicted in Fig. 6. After these completely theoretical results of HBCD interconversion kinetics starting at 100 % (+)-γ-HBCD (Fig. 10) as also done in the laboratory, the concentration of this stereoisomer rapidly decreases with the highest rate reaching its equilibrium value already after 1000 "seconds", while the concentration of (+)-α-HBCD increases with nearly the same velocity far above its equilibrium value. A longer simulation that is not presented here shows an subsequent decrease towards its equilibrium. The β diastereomers are the next ones to increase towards their steady-state concentration with (−)-β-HBCD starting slightly faster due to its creation from (+)-γ-HBCD. But with increasing (+)-α-HBCD, (+)-β-HBCD, which evolves from (+)-α-HBCD, accumulates faster and overtakes (−)-β-HBCD. The by far slowest growth is in the case of (−)-γ-HBCD.
From a qualitative point of view, all these observations on the kinetics correspond exactly with experimental results (Köppen et al. (2008)) as presented in Fig. 6 and Table 4. The highest and second highest rate was confirmed to be $k_{\gamma\rightarrow\alpha}$ and $k_{\beta\rightarrow\beta}$, respectively, whereas $k_{\alpha\rightarrow\beta}$ ($Q\,(1,2)$ and $Q\,(4,5)$) yielded the lowest value with both approaches. Many assumptions were necessary in order to estimate interconversion rates for the six main HBCD isomers, started off with the vacuum approximation, neglecting any intermolecular interactions in the liquid phase and by the way, reducing the computational effort. Due to sterical reasons and the fact of poor solubility in a polar medium such as water (Janak et al. (2005)), we claim a negligible affect of intermolecular interactions on the interconversion process.
Describing the quantum-chemically motivated inversion process in terms of classical mechanics was a second bold approximation. However, if we consider its rate as a combination of the probability of being activated (*anti* conformation) and the transition itself and under the assumption of an identical velocity of the latter part for all diastereomers, we

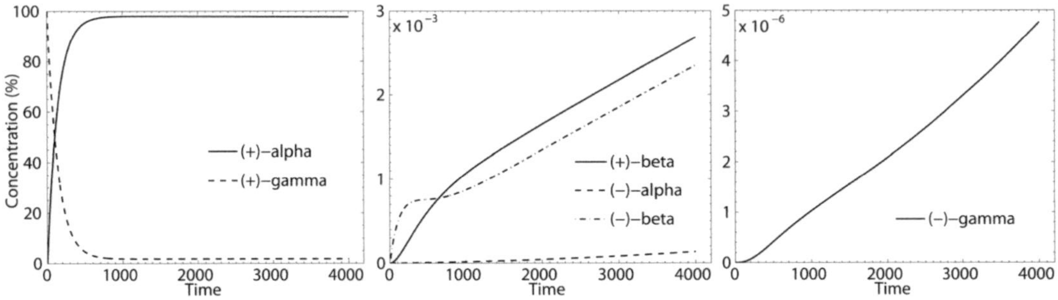

Fig. 10. theoretical determinantion of the HBCD isomerization at 160 C starting at 100 % $(+)$-γ-HBCD and with a scale factor $\mu = 0.007$. Free and potential energy values had been reweighted after a high-temperature HMC simulation at 1500 K.

are able to reduce the interconversion to a classical manner with its rate characterized by differences of energies/probabilities between *anti* and *gauche* subspaces, i. e. the difference in free energies expressing the likeliness of a molecular system to adopt the one or the other conformation. What we lose by this simplification is the knowledge about the absolute velocities of the interconversion and thus, the opportunity to describe rates quantitatively. But what we gain is the ability to calculate this quantum-chemical process (in reasonable time).
Also the application of the *Arrhenius* equation to these free energy differences might seem a little far-fetched, but again, there is an obvious correlation between the free energy difference and the ordinary activation energy. Both describe the delay of energies from an arbitrarily fixed value, differing in accordance with the direction of the reaction. In other words, if the activation energy is low for the forward direction, then the free energy difference is low as well. From the reverse perspective, the free energy difference increases, too, if the activation energy increases. Similar to the free energy difference, the activation energy may be considered in this context as the energy necessary to lead the molecules to the active *anti* conformation. Still, we are able to gain qualitative or even semi-quantitative results.
As we were interested in the kinetics of the HBCD system at 433 K, a reweighting of energy values became unavoidable. Instead of a point-wise scheme that weights up a probably small number of values from the overlap region of high- and low-temperature distributions, we decided to apply a thermodynamical approach assuming a linear temperature-dependency of the mean potential energy (Equation 15). If the potential energy V was a quadratic function in the onformational space Ω, this assumption would be true. However, the potential energy function is not an exact quadratic one but is locally approximable by parabolic functions due to its *Gaussian*-like distributions in a accordingly decomposed conformational space.
In spite of all these approximations, the results well reflect the HBCD interconversion process as determined by experimental methods, and in particular, no experimental data was used for the estimation at all.

7. References

Akhmatskaya, E. & Reich, S. (2004). The targeted shadowing hybrid Monte-Carlo (tshmc) method, *Technical report*, Institut für Mathematik, Uni Potsdam.

Allen, M. P. & Tildesley, D. J. (1987). *Computer Simulations of Liquids*, Clarendon, Oxford.

Andersen, H. C. (1980). Molecular dynamics simulations at constant pressure and/or temperature, *J.Chem.Phys.* 72: 2384–2393.

Barda, H. J., Sanders, D. C. & Benya, T. J. (1985). Bromine compounds, *in* S. Hawkins & G. Schultz (eds), *Ullmann's Encyclopedia of Industrial Chemistry*, Wiley-VCH, Weinheim, Germany, pp. 405–429.

Barontini, F., Cozzani, V. & Petarca, L. (2003). Thermal stability and decomposition products of hexabromocyclododecane, *Ind. Eng. Chem. Res.* 40: 3270–3280.

Becher, G. (2005). The stereochemistry of 1,2,5,6,9,10-hexabromocyclododecane and its graphic representation, *Chemosphere* 58: 989–991.

Binder, K. & Landau, D. (2000). *A Guide to Monte Carlo Simulations in Statistical Physics*, Cambirdge University Press, Cambirdge.

Clamp, M. E., Baker, P. G., Stirling, C. J. & Brass, A. (1994). Hybrid Monte Carlo: An efficient algorithm for condensed matter simulation, *J.Comput.Chem.* 15(8): 838–846.

Covaci, A., Gerecke, A. S. C., Voorspoels, R. J. L. S., Kohler, M., Heeb, N. V., Leslie, H., Allchin, C. R. & DeBoer, J. (2006). Hexabromocyclododecanes (HBCDs) in the environment and humans: a review, *Environ. Sci. Techno.* 40: 3680–3688.

de Wit, C. A., Alaee, M. & Muir, D. C. G. (2006). Levels and trends of brominated flame retardants in the arctic, *Chemosphere* 64: 209–233.

de Witt, C. A. (2002). An overview of brominated flame retardants in the environment, *Chemosphere* 46: 583–624.

Deuflhard, P. (1983). Order and stepsize control in extrapolation methods, *Numer. Math.* pp. 399–422.

Deuflhard, P. (1985). Recent progress in extrapolation methods for ordinary differential equations, *SIAM Review* 27: 505–535.

Deuflhard, P., Dellnitz, M., Junge, O. & Schütte, C. (1999). Computation of essential molecular dynamics by subdivision techniques, *in* P. D. et al (ed.), *Computational Molecular Dynamics: Challenges, Methods, Ideas*, Springer, Berlin, pp. 98–115.

Duane, S., Kennedy, A. D., Pendleton, B. J. & Roweth, D. (1987). Hybrid Monte Carlo, *Phys. Lett. B* 195(2): 216–222.

Fischer, A. (1997). Die Hybride Monte–Carlo Methode in der Molekülphysik. Diploma thesis, Department of Mathematics and Computer Science, Free University Berlin, (in German).

Fischer, A., Cordes, F. & Schütte, C. (1998). Hybrid Monte Carlo with adaptive temperature in a mixed–canonical ensemble: Efficient conformational analysis of RNA, *J. Comput. Chem.* 19: 1689–1697.

Forrest, B. M. & Suter, U. W. (1994). Hybrid Monte Carlo simulations of dense polymer systems, *J.Chem.Phys.* 101.

Frenkel, D. & Smit, B. (1996). *Understanding molecular simulation. From algorithms to applications*, Academic Press, San Diego.

Frenkel, D. & Smit, B. (2002). *Understanding Molecular Simulation – From Algorithms to Applications*, Vol. 1 of *Computational Science Series*, 2nd edn, Academic Press, A Division of Harcourt, Inc., www.academicpress.com/computationalscience.

Gelman, A. & Rubin, D. (1992). Inference from Iterative Simulation using Multiple Sequences, *Statist. Sci.* 7: 457–511.

Göpel, W. & Wiemdörfer, H. D. (2000). *Statistische Thermodynamik*, Spektrum Akademischer Verlag.

Griebel, M., Zumbusch, G. & Knapek, S. (2007). *Numerical Simulation in Molecular Dynamics*, Vol. 5 of *Texts in Computational Science and Engineering*, Springer, Berlin.

Gromov, D. G. & de Pablo, J. J. (1995). Structure of binary polymer blends - multiple time step hybrid Monte Carlo simulations and self-consistend intergal-equation theory, *J.Chem.Phys.* 103(18): 8247–8256.

Gupta, S., Irbäck, A., Karsch, F. & Petersson, B. (1990). The acceptance probability in the hybrid Monte Carlo method, *Phys. Lett. B* 242: 437–443.

Hairer, E., Lubich, C. & Wanner, G. (2004). *Geometric Numerical Integration – Structure-Preserving Algorithms for Ordinary Differential Equations*, Vol. 31 of *Springer Series in Computational Mathematics*, corr. 2nd edn, Springer.

Hairer, E., Nørsett, S. P. & Wanner, G. (1993). *Solving Ordinary Differential Equations I, Nonstiff Problems*, 2nd edn, Springer-Verlag, Berlin, Heidelberg.

Hale, R. C., La Guardia, M. J., Harvey, E., Gaylor, M. O., Matt, T. & Mainor, T. M. (2006). Brominated flame retardant concentrations and trends in abiotic media, *Chemosphere* 64: 181–186.

Halgren, T. A. (1996). Merck Molecular Force Field: I-V, *J. Comp. Chem.* 17(5-6): 490–641.

Hamers, T., Kamstra, J. H., Sonneveld, E., Murk, A. J., Kester, M. H. A., Andersson, P. L., Legler, J. & Brouwer, A. (2006). In Vitro Profiling of the Endocrine-Disrupting Potency of Brominated Flame Retardants, *Toxicol. Sci.* 92: 157–173.

Hammersley, J. & Handscomb, D. (1964). *Monte Carlo Methods*, J. Wiley, New York.

Hansmann, U. H. E., Okamoto, Y. & Eisenmenger, F. (1996). Molecular dynamics, Langevin and hybrid Monte Carlo simulations in a multicanonical ensemble, *Chem.Phys.Lett.* 259: 321–330.

Heeb, N. V., Schweizer, W. B., Kohler, M. & Gerecke, A. C. (2004). 1,2,5,6,9,10-hexabromocyclododecane - a class of compounds with a complex stereochemistry, Book of abstracts, Toronto, Canada, pp. 337–340. The Third International Workshop on Brominated Flame Retardants.

Heeb, N. V., Schweizer, W. B., Mattrel, P., Haag, R., Kohler, M., Schmid, P., Zennegg, M. & Wolfensberger, M. (2008). Regio- and stereoselective isomerization of hexabromocyclododecanes (HBCDs): Kinetics and mechanism of β-HBCD racemization, *Chemosphere* 71: 1547–1556.

Hestenes, M. R. & Stiefel, E. (1952). Methods of Conjugate Gradients for Solving Linear Systems, *J. Res. Nat. Inst. Stand. Technol.* 49: 409–436.

Hockney, R. W. (1970). The potential calculations and some applications, *Methods Comput. Phys.* 9: 136–211.

Hunziker, R. W., Gonsior, S., MacGregor, J. A., Desjardins, D., Ariano, J. & Friederich, U. (2004). Fate and effect of hexabromocyclododecane in the environment, *Organohalogen Compd* 66: 2300–2305.

Irbäck, A. (1994). Hybrid Monte Carlo simulation of polymer chains, *J.Chem.Phys.* 101(2): 1661–1667.

Izaguirre, J. A. & Hampton, S. S. (2004). Shadow hybrid Monte Carlo: An efficient propagator in phase space of macromolecules, *J. Comput. Phys.* 200: 581–604.

Janak, K., Covaci, A., Voorspoels, S. & Becher, G. (2005). Hexabromocyclododecane in marine species from the western Scheldt estuary: diastereoisomer- and enantiomer-specific accumulation, *Environ. Sci. Technol.* 39: 1987–1994.

Johnson-Restrepo, B., Adams, D. H. & Kannan, K. (2008). Tetrabromobisphenol A (TBBPA) and hexabromocyclododecanes (HBCDs) in tissues of humans, dolphins, and sharks from the United States, *Chemosphere* 70(11): 935–1944.

Kennedy, A. D. & Pendleton, B. (1991). Acceptances and autocorrelation in hybrid Monte Carlo, *Nuclear Physics B Proceedings Supplements* 20: 118–121.

Kijima, M. (1997). *Markov Processes for Stochastic Modeling*, Stochastic Modeling Series, Chapman and Hall.

Köppen, R., Becker, R., Jung, C. & Nehls, I. (2008). On the thermally induced isomerisation of hexabromocyclododecane stereoisomers, *Chemosphere* 71: 656–662.

Law, K., Palace, V. P., Halldorson, T., Danell, R., Wautier, K., Evans, B., Alaee, M., Marvin, C. & Tomy, G. T. (2006a). Dietary accumulation of hexabromocyclododecane diastereoisomers in juvenile rainbow trout (Oncorhynchus mykiss) I: Bioaccumulation parameters and evidence of bioisomerization, *Environ. Toxicol. Chem.* 25: 1757–1761.

Leach, A. (2001). *Molecular Modelling - Principles and Applications*, Pearson Educations Ltd., Essex.

Leimkuhler, B. & Reich, S. (2004). *Simulating Hamiltonian Dynamics*, Cambridge.

Lew, A., Marsden, J. E., Ortiz, M. & West, M. (2004). An overview of variational integrators, *in* L. P. Franca, T. E. Tezduyar & A. Masud (eds), *Finite Element Methods: 1970's and Beyond*, CIMNE, ISBN 84-95999-49-8, pp. 98–115.

Manousiouthakis, V. I. & Deem, M. W. (1999). Strict detailed balance is unnecessary in Monte Carlo simulation, *J. Chem. Phys.* 110: 2753–2756.

Meerts, I. A. T. M., van Zanden, J. J., Luijks, E. A. C., van Leeuwen-Bol, I., Marsh, G., Jakobsson, E., Bergman, A. & Brouwer, A. (2000). Potent Competitive Interactions of Some Brominated Flame Retardants and Related Compounds with Human Transthyretin *in Vitro*, *Toxicol. Sci.* 56: 95–104.

Mehlig, B., Heermann, D. W. & Forrest, B. M. (1992). Hybrid Monte Carlo method for condensed-matter systems, *Phys.Rev. B* 45(2): 679–685.

Metropolis, N., Rosenbluth, A. W., Rosenbluth, M. N., Teller, A. N. & Teller, E. (1953). Equation of state calculations by fast computing machines, *J.Chem.Phys.* 21: 1087–1092.

Peled, M., Scharia, R. & Sondack, D. (1995). Thermal rearrangement of hexabromocyclododecane (HBCD), *in* J. R. Desmurs, B. Gérard & M. J. Goldstein (eds), *Advances in Organobromine Chemistry II*, Elsevier, Amsterdam, The Netherlands, pp. 92–99.

Peskun, P. (1973). Optimum Monte Carlo sampling using Marcov chains, *Biometrika* 60: 607–612.

Robert, C. P. & Casella, G. (1999). *Monte Carlo Statistical Methods*, Springer New York, Berlin, Heidelberg.

Schäfer, K. (1960). *Statistische Theorie der Materie*, Vol. 1, Vandenhoeck & Ruprecht in Göttingen. In German.

Schlick, T. (2002). *Molecular Modelling and Simulation*, Springer, New York.

Schriks, M., Zvinavashe, E., Furlow, J. D. & Murk, A. J. (2006). Disruption of thyroid hormone-mediated *Xenopus laevis* tadpole tail tip regression by hexabromocyclododecane (HBCD) and 2,2′,3,3′,4,4′,5,5′,6-nona brominated diphenyl ether (BDE206), *Chemosphere* 65: 1904–1908.

Skeel, R. D. & Hardy, D. J. (2002). Practical construction of modified Hamiltonians, *SIAM Journal on Scienti□c Computing* 23(4): 1172–1188.

Tomy, G. T., Budakowski, W., Halldorson, T., Whittle, D. M., Keir, M. J., Marvin, C., Macinnis, G. & Alaee, M. (2004). Biomagnification of α- and γ-hexabromocyclododecane isomers in a Lake Ontario food web, *Environ. Sci. Technol.* 38: 2298–2303.

Verlet, L. (1967). Computer "experiments" on classical fluids i. thermodynamical properties of lennard jones molecules, *Phys. Rev.* Vol. 159(No. 1): 98–103.

Vos, J. G., Becher, G., van den Berg, M., de Boer, J. & Leonards, P. E. G. (2003). Brominated flame retardants and endocrine disruption, *Pure Appl. Chem.* 75: 2039–2046.

Weber, M. (2007). Conformation-Based Transition State Theory, *Technical Report 07–14*, Konrad-Zuse-Zentrum für Informationstechnik Berlin.

Wendlandt, J. M. & Marsden, J. E. (1997). Mechanical integrators derived from a discrete variational principle, *Physica D* 106: 223–246.

Zhang, H. (1999). A new hybrid Monte Carlo algorithm for protein potential function test and structure refinement, *Proteins* 34: 464–471.